HEALTH ECONOMICS

FIRST EDITION

Jeremiah E. Hurley
McMaster University

The McGraw·Hill Companies

McGraw-Hill
Ryerson
Connect. Learn. Succeed.

Health Economics
First Edition

Copyright © 2010 by McGraw-Hill Ryerson Limited, a Subsidiary of The McGraw-Hill Companies. All rights reserved. No part of this publication may be reproduced or transmitted in any form or by any means, or stored in a data base or retrieval system, without the prior written permission of McGraw-Hill Ryerson Limited, or in the case of photocopying or other reprographic copying, a license from The Canadian Copyright Licensing Agency (Access Copyright). For an Access Copyright license, visit www.accesscopyright.ca or call toll free to 1-800-893-5777.

Statistics Canada information is used with the permission of Statistics Canada. Users are forbidden to copy the data and redisseminate them, in an original or modified form, for commercial purposes, without permission from Statistics Canada. Information on the availability of the wide range of data from Statistics Canada can be obtained from Statistics Canada's Regional Offices, its World Wide Web site at www.statcan.gc.ca, and its toll-free access number 1-800-263-1136.

ISBN-13: 978-0-07-091648-7
ISBN-10: 0-07-091648-9

3 4 5 6 7 8 9 WEB 1 9 8 7 6 5 4 3 2

Printed in Canada

Care has been taken to trace ownership of copyright material contained in this text; however, the publisher will welcome any information that enables them to rectify any reference or credit for subsequent editions.

Vice-President and Editor-in-Chief: *Joanna Cotton*
Executive Sponsoring Editor: *Leanna MacLean*
Sponsoring Editor: *James Booty*
Executive Marketing Manager: *Joy Armitage Taylor*
Developmental Editor: *Andria Fogarty*
Senior Editorial Associate: *Stephanie Hess*
Supervising Editor: *Jessica Barnoski*
Photo/Permissions Research: *Tracy Leonard and Amy Rydzanicz*
Copy Editor: *Judy Sturrup*
Proofreader: *Elspeth McFadden*
Production Coordinator: *Sharon Stefanowicz*
Cover Design: *Liz Harasymczuk*
Cover Image: *Cleo Photography*
Page Layout: *Laserwords Private Limited*
Printer: *Webcom*

Library and Archives Canada Cataloguing in Publication
Hurley, Jeremiah E.
      Health economics / Jeremiah E. Hurley.
Includes index.
ISBN 978-0-07-091648-7
      1. Medical economics—Textbooks. I. Title.
RA410.H87 2010   338.4'73621   C2010-900467-1

About the Author

Jeremiah E. Hurley

Professor Hurley received his undergraduate degree from John Carroll University in Cleveland, Ohio, and his Ph.D. from the University of Wisconsin–Madison. He has been a faculty member at McMaster University since 1988. Throughout his time at McMaster, he has been jointly appointed between the Departments of Economics and Clinical Epidemiology and Biostatistics, and he has been a member of the Centre for Health Economics and Policy Analysis, for which he served as Coordinator. He has conducted research on topics such as physician behaviour, resource allocation and funding in health care, equity in health care, and health care financing, with a particular interest in public and private roles. He has published widely in health economics and health policy journals and has acted as a consultant to regional, provincial, national, and international agencies.

Brief Contents

About the Author   iii

Preface   x

1   Health and Health Care Systems:
An Introduction   1

PART ONE
Essential Economic Concepts   29

2   Efficiency and Equity   32

3   The Basics of Markets   62

4   Methods of Economic Evaluation   98

PART TWO
Economics of Health   125

5   Individual-Level Demand for and
Production of Health   132

6   The Determinants of Population
Health   164

PART THREE
Health Care as an Economic Commodity   183

7   The Nature of Health Care as an
Economic Commodity   184

PART FOUR
Demand for Health Care and Health Care Insurance   205

8   The Demand for Health Care   206

9   The Demand for Health Care
Insurance   232

10   Private Insurance Markets   247

PART FIVE
The Flow of Funds Within a Health Care System   273

11   Systems of Health Care Finance   275

12   Health Care Funding   303

PART SIX
The Supply Side of Health Care Provision   325

13   Physicians, Their Practices, and
the Market for Physician
Services   328

14   Health Care Institutions: Hospitals   355

15   Pharmaceuticals   380

PART SEVEN
Looking Ahead: Aging, Technology, and the Health Care System   403

16   Aging and Technology: Do They Threaten
the Sustainability of the Health Care
System?   405

GLOSSARY   418

PHOTO CREDITS   426

INDEX   427

Table of Contents

About the Author   iii

Preface   x

Chapter 1

Health and Health Care Systems:
An Introduction   1

Learning Objectives   1

1.1   The Health System   1
    1.1.1   Individual-Level Determinants of Health   4
    1.1.2   Community-Level Determinants   4
    1.1.3   Interactions Between Individual-Level and
        Community-Level Determinants   5
1.2   Health Care Systems   5
    1.2.1   Governance   6
    1.2.2   Health Care Financing   9
    1.2.3   Delivering Health Care   16
    1.2.4   Regulating Health Care   22
1.3   Economics and Variation in the Design of
    Health Systems   24
    Chapter Summary   25
    Key Terms   26
    End-of-Chapter Questions   26
    References   26

PART ONE
ESSENTIAL ECONOMIC
CONCEPTS   29

Chapter 2
Efficiency and Equity   32

Learning Objectives   32

2.1   Efficiency   34
    2.1.1   Efficiency in Production   34
    2.1.2   Efficiency in Allocation   36
    2.1.3   Principles Shared by All Three Efficiency
        Concepts   39
2.2   Equity   41
    2.2.1   Distributional Equity   42
    2.2.2   Procedural Equity   43
2.3   Equity and Efficiency   45
    Chapter Summary   46
    Key Terms   47

    End-of-Chapter Questions   47
    References   48
Appendix 2   49
Efficiency   49
    Efficiency in Production   49
    Efficiency in Allocation   53
Equity   57
    Distributional Equity   57
Equity and Efficiency   59

Chapter 3
The Basics of Markets   62

Learning Objectives   62

3.1   Conditions for a Well-Functioning Market   63
    3.1.1   Market Power   63
    3.1.2   Information   65
    3.1.3   No Externalities   66
    3.1.4   Rationales for Government Intervention:
        Market Failure and Equity   66
3.2   The Mechanics of the Market   67
    3.2.1   Individual Behaviour and the Demand for
        Goods and Services   68
    3.2.2   Firm Behaviour and the Supply of Goods and
        Services   76
    3.2.3   Putting Demand and Supply Together:
        A Market   80
    Chapter Summary   91
    Key Terms   92
    End-of-Chapter Questions   92
    Reference   93
Appendix 3   94
Mechanics of the Market   94
    Individual Behaviour and the Demand for
       Goods and Services   94
    Putting Demand and Supply Together:
       A Market   95

Chapter 4
Methods of Economic Evaluation   98

Learning Objectives   98

4.1   What is an Economic Evaluation?   100
    4.1.1   Representation of an Economic
        Evaluation   101

4.1.2   Stages of an Economic Evaluation   102

4.2   Three Methods of Economic Evaluation: Cost-Effectiveness Analysis, Cost-Utility Analysis, and Cost-Benefit Analysis   104
   4.2.1   Cost-Effectiveness Analysis   104
   4.2.2   Cost-Utility Analysis   105
   4.2.3   Cost-Benefit Analysis   108
   4.2.4   Economic Evaluation Methods and Efficiency   109
   4.2.5   The Differing Origins of the Methods   110
   4.2.6   Application of the Three Methods in the Health Sector   110
   4.2.7   Can Society Avoid Placing a Dollar Value on Life-Years Gained?   111

4.3   Some Common Analytic Challenges to Conducting an Economic Evaluation   112
   4.3.1   Shadow Pricing and the Valuation of Resources Used   112
   4.3.2   Double-Counting Costs or Benefits   113
   4.3.3   Discounting: Valuing Costs and Benefits that Occur at Different Times   113
   4.3.4   Aggregating Costs and Consequences: Distributional and Other Issues   116
   Chapter Summary   117
   Key Terms   117
   End-of-Chapter Questions   117
   References   118

Appendix 4   120
Three Methods of Economic Evaluation   120
   Cost-Benefit Analysis   120
   The Differing Origins of the Methods   121
Some Common Analytic Challenges to Conducting an Economic Evaluation   122
   Shadow Pricing and the Valuation of Resources Used   122
References   124

PART TWO
ECONOMICS OF HEALTH   125
   References   131

Chapter 5
Individual-Level Demand for and Production of Health   132

Learning Objectives   132

5.1   The Health Capital Model   132
   5.1.1   The Grossman Health Capital Model   133

5.2   Empirical Evidence on Individual-Level Demand for and Production of Health   142
   5.2.1   The Relationship between Education and Health   142

5.3   Health-Related Behaviours   146
   5.3.1   Economics of Obesity   146
   5.3.2   Economics of Smoking   150
   Chapter Summary   153
   Key Terms   153
   End-of-Chapter Questions   154
   References   154

Appendix 5   155
   The Grossman Health Capital Model   155
   An Alternative Graphical Exposition of the Health Capital Framework   158
References   163

Chapter 6
The Determinants of Population Health   164

Learning Objectives   164

6.1   Determinants of the Level of Health in a Population   165
   6.1.1   Thomas McKeown and the Rise of Populations   166
   6.1.2   Rise of Public Health   168
   6.1.3   Era of Modern Medicine   170
   6.1.4   Lessons for Improving Population Health Today   170

6.2   Health Inequalities   173
   6.2.1   The Social Determinants of Health   176
   Chapter Summary   179
   Key Term   179
   End-of-Chapter Questions   179
   References   180

PART THREE
HEALTH CARE AS AN ECONOMIC COMMODITY   183

Chapter 7
The Nature of Health Care as an Economic Commodity   184

Learning Objectives   184

7.1   What is Health Care?   185

7.2   Characteristics of Health Care as an Economic Commodity   186
   7.2.1   Demand for Health Care Is a Derived Demand   187
   7.2.2   Externalities   190
   7.2.3   Informational Asymmetry Between Providers and Patients   191

7.2.4   Uncertainty   196
7.2.5   Vulnerability to the Integrity of a
          Person   196
7.3   Is Health Care Different?   197
        7.3.1   Economic Analysis in a Second-Best
                  World   197
        7.3.2   Not All Health Care is Alike   198
        Chapter Summary   199
        Key Terms   200
        End-of-Chapter Questions   200
        References   200

Appendix 7   201
Health Care as an Economic Commodity   201
        Demand for Health Care Is a Derived
          Demand   201
        Externalities   202
        Informational Asymmetry Between Providers
          and Patients   203

PART FOUR
DEMAND FOR HEALTH CARE AND
HEALTH CARE INSURANCE   205

Chapter 8
The Demand for Health Care   206

Learning Objectives   206

8.1   Need, Demand, and Utilization   207
        8.1.1   Categorizing Services by Need, Demand, and
                  Utilization   207
8.2   Demand for Health Care Within the Standard
        Economic Framework   208
        8.2.1   Health Status   210
        8.2.2   Preferences   210
        8.2.3   Price of Health Care   210
        8.2.4   Prices of Substitutes and Complements   212
        8.2.5   Income/Wealth   213
        8.2.6   Strengths and Limitations of the Standard
                  Model of Demand   214
8.3   Informational Asymmetry and the Demand for
        Health Care   214
        8.3.1   Measuring Supplier-Induced Demand   216
        8.3.2   Implications of Supplier-Induced
                  Demand   221
        8.3.3   Summing Up: Demand, Supplier-
                  Induced Demand, and Asymmetry of
                  Information   223
        Chapter Summary   223
        Key Terms   224
        End-of-Chapter Questions   224
        References   225

Appendix 8   227
Need, Demand, and Utilization   227
        Measuring Supplier-Induced Demand   230
References   231

Chapter 9
The Demand for Health Care
Insurance   232

Learning Objectives   232

9.1   Risk Pooling and Insurance   232
        9.1.1   Risk   232
        9.1.2   Risk Pooling   233
9.2   Demand for Insurance   234
        9.2.1   The Benefits of Insurance   238
        9.2.2   Some Limitations of the Standard Insurance
                  Model   239
9.3   The Nature of Insurance Contracts   241
        Chapter Summary   242
        Key Terms   242
        End-of-Chapter Questions   242
        References   243

Appendix 9   244
Risk Pooling and Insurance   244
        Risk Pooling   244
Demand for Insurance   244
References   246

Chapter 10
Private Insurance Markets   247

Learning Objectives   247

10.1   Moral Hazard   247
         10.1.1   The Standard Analysis of Moral Hazard in
                   the Health Care Market   248
         10.1.2   Critiques of the Standard Analysis of Moral
                   Hazard   250
         10.1.3   Combatting Moral Hazard from the Supply
                   Side   256
10.2   Risk Selection   257
         10.2.1   Adverse Selection   258
         10.2.2   Favourable Risk Selection
                   (Cream-Skimming)   262
         10.2.3   Risk Selection and Universal Public
                   Insurance   263
10.3   Economies of Scale   263
10.4   A Missing Market for Insurance Against
         Premium Increases   263
         Chapter Summary   264
         Key Terms   265
         End-of-Chapter Questions   265
         References   266

Appendix 10   267
Moral Hazard   267
  Adverse Selection   268

PART FIVE
THE FLOW OF FUNDS WITHIN A HEALTH CARE SYSTEM   273

Chapter 11
Systems of Health Care Finance   275

Learning Objectives   275

11.1 Efficiency and Equity in Pure Private and Pure Public Systems of Finance   275
  11.1.1 Efficiency of Public and Private Systems of Finance   276
  11.1.2 Equity and Alternative Approaches to Health Care Finance   282
  11.1.3 Net Incidence   284
  11.1.4 Summary of Efficiency and Equity Effects   286
11.2 Public and Private Roles in Mixed Systems of Finance   286
  11.2.1 Some Fundamental Configurations of Public and Private Roles   287
  11.2.2 Systems of Health Care Finance: Rube Goldberg or Patchwork Quilt?   293
  Chapter Summary   294
  Key Terms   295
  End-of-Chapter Questions   295
  References   296
Appendix 11   297
  Systems of Health Care Finance: Equity and Alternative Approaches   297
References   302

Chapter 12
Health Care Funding   303

Learning Objectives   303

12.1 The Principal–Agent Framework and Funding Systems   304
12.2 Participants in a Funding Scheme   308
12.3 Funding Mechanisms   309
  12.3.1 Types of Payment Mechanisms   310
  12.3.2 Retrospective Payment, Prospective Payment, Risk, and Efficiency   312
12.4 Designing Funding Schemes   316
  12.4.1 Administrative Feasibility and Efficiency   316

  12.4.2 Distributing Risk   318
  12.4.3 Minimizing the Scope for Self-Interested Strategic Responses by Funded Organizations   318
  12.4.4 Matching the Payment Mechanism to the Context   319
  Chapter Summary   319
  Key Terms   320
  End-of-Chapter Questions   320
  References   320
Appendix 12   321
The Principal–Agent Framework and Funding Systems   321
References   324

PART SIX
THE SUPPLY SIDE OF HEALTH CARE PROVISION   325
  Reference   327

Chapter 13
Physicians, Their Practices, and the Market for Physician Services   328

Learning Objectives   328

13.1 The Physician Services Sector   328
  13.1.1 Regulation of Physicians and Their Practices   331
  13.1.2 The Market for Physician Services   333
13.2 Modelling the Physician Practice and Physician Behaviour   334
  13.2.1 Alternative Assumptions Regarding Physician Objectives   336
  13.2.2 Physician Labour Supply and the Production of Physician Services   340
13.3 Planning Physician Supply: An Economic Perspective   343
  Chapter Summary   347
  Key Terms   347
  End-of-Chapter Questions   347
  References   348
Appendix 13   349
  Alternative Assumptions Regarding Physician Objectives   349
References   354

Chapter 14
Health Care Institutions: Hospitals   355

Learning Objectives   355

14.1 Models of Hospitals as Organizations   358
   14.1.1 Newhouse's Model of Quantity–Quality Trade-off   359
   14.1.2 Hospitals as Doctors' Workshops   361
   14.1.3 The Transactions Costs Model of Hospitals   361
14.2 Hospital Markets and Hospital Competition   363
14.3 Assessing Hospital Efficiency   367
14.4 Not-for-Profit Versus. For-Profit: Does Ownership Matter?   369
   Chapter Summary   374
   Key Terms   374
   End-of-Chapter Questions   374
   References   375

Appendix 14   377
Hospital Markets and Hospital Competition   377
References   379

Chapter 15
Pharmaceuticals   380

Learning Objectives   380

15.1 The Pharmaceutical Industry   381
15.2 Government Regulation of the Pharmaceutical Industry   383
   15.2.1 Patent Regulation   383
   15.2.2 Drug Safety and the Drug Approval Process   386
   15.2.3 Competition in the Pharmaceutical Industry   388
15.3 Design of Pharmaceutical Benefits Programs   393
   15.3.1 Targeting the Type and Quantity of Drugs Consumed   393
   15.3.2 Policies that Attempt to Ensure that the Lowest-Cost Product is Purchased   395
   Chapter Summary   397
   Key Terms   397

   End-of-Chapter Questions   397
   References   398
Appendix 15   399
   Patent Regulation   399
References   401

PART SEVEN
LOOKING AHEAD: AGING, TECHNOLOGY, AND THE HEALTH CARE SYSTEM   403
   Reference   404

Chapter 16
Aging and Technology: Do They Threaten the Sustainability of the Health Care System?   405

Learning Objectives   405

16.1 Health Care and the Aging of the Canadian Population   405
   16.1.1 Fiscal Implications of an Aging Population   406
   16.1.2 Aging and Chronic Disease   410
16.2 Technological Innovation in Medicine   412
16.3 Projections and Policy   414
   Chapter Summary   416
   Key Terms   416
   End-of-Chapter Questions   416
   References   417

Glossary   418

Photo Credits   426

Index   427

Preface

Few sectors garner as much attention and debate in modern societies as health care. Health care constitutes the largest single component of government spending. It is impossible to open a newspaper, magazine, or news site and not be confronted by stories about the latest advance in treatment, strategies for staying healthy, initiatives to improve the health care system, or ads by health professional associations, disease groups, or other health organizations advocating for change to the system. And sitting in the waiting room of your family physician or the hospital out-patient clinic, it is hard not to wonder why the system is organized the way it is and whether there is a better way.

Health Economics will help students make sense of the health sector, by becoming able to analyze critically, from an *economic* perspective, commonly debated health issues in modern societies. The strong policy orientation emphasizes the application of economic concepts and methods to analyze policy problems in the health sector. Because health economics is an applied field, one must have some understanding of how the health system works. Consequently, although this text draws examples from countries around the world, it emphasizes the design and institutional features of the Canadian health system. In this respect, it fills an important gap in the resources available to Canadian students and teachers.

Health Economics reflects many years of teaching health economics at both the undergraduate and graduate levels. It is designed to be used both at the introductory level with students who have no prior economics training and with students with prior training in introductory or intermediate microeconomics. In the author's experience, whether teaching an introductory course for non-economists or a graduate seminar, the focus is on the same core set of ideas and concepts; what differs is the way they are presented and the answers expected from students.

To meet the needs of students with differing academic backgrounds, the book is structured as follows:

- **Chapter 1** lays a foundation of basic information regarding the Canadian health system, placed in the context of selected other comparator countries. Although necessarily brief, it summarizes essential elements of the health system and some of the policy challenges the system faces.

- **Chapters 2, 3, and 4** present a concise summary of essential microeconomic concepts including supply, demand, and the operation of markets. This Part One is designed for those with no prior economics training.

- Most subsequent chapters then have two components: the main body of text and an appendix:

  Main Body of Text   The main body of text presents all the essential ideas related to the topic under consideration at a level that never goes beyond that covered in Part One.

  Appendices   The appendices develop a subset of ideas in each chapter at a level suitable for a student who already has a foundation in microeconomics. The appendices serve two purposes in this respect: they treat material at a more advanced technical level or explore an economic concept or idea in more depth than is appropriate for the main body of the chapter. As such, the appendices are meant for those with a stronger background in economics: an introductory reader need not review any of the material in the appendices to understand all the central ideas presented in the text (and need not be intimidated by the equations and graphs they don't recognize!).

Key Terms and Glossary   Terms are defined in the text as they are introduced and the definitions are collated in a glossary at the end. The glossary contains two types of terms: health sector terms and economic terms. For students who have had little exposure to the health system beyond visits to their doctor, simple, commonly used health system terms—primary care, formulary, fee-for-service—can be stumbling blocks to learning. Analogously, for those with no economics background, commonly used economic terms—elasticity, substitute good, monopoly—can be stumbling blocks. The glossary provides easy access to the meaning of many essential concepts and terms.

Boxes   Each chapter contains a number of "boxes" set off from the text that present examples of concepts under discussion, highlight studies that provide evidence, or generally fill out in a more concrete way material in the body of the text.

Summary of Key Points   The end of each chapter includes a summary of key points, a collection of new terms introduced in the chapter, and set of questions related to chapter material.

Supplemental Chapter   The book also includes online resources, such as a supplemental chapter on basic statistical concepts that can help students read and interpret empirical studies and links to sites with relevant information for health economic analysis.

The material on health economics is organized around the "circular flow diagram" for the health sector, illustrated here, which depicts the flow of money and goods associated with health and health care:

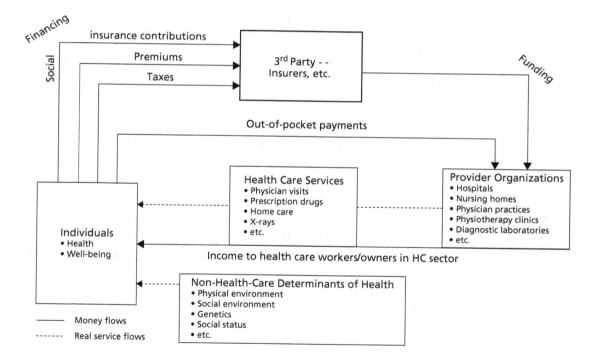

This analysis begins in Part Two with the economics of health, covering both an individual's demand for and production of health (Chapter 5) and an analysis of the determinants of population health (Chapter 6). This sets a broad context for the subsequent focus on health care systems. Chapter 7 analyzes the nature of health care as an economic commodity, introducing a number of themes that are explored in greater depth in subsequent chapters. Chapter 8 considers an individual's demand for health care, which gives rise to the demand for insurance, discussed in Chapter 9. Chapter 10 presents an analysis of insurance markets, which is followed in Chapter 11 by an analysis of health care financing more generally, with a particular focus on public and private roles in financing. Chapter 12 on health care funding examines the next logical problem: having collected revenue through premiums, taxes, or social insurance contributions, a health care insurer (public or private) must decide how to disburse those funds to providers and provider organization that deliver health care services. This necessitates an examination of the behaviour of providers and the markets in which they operate, including physicians (Chapter 13), institutions (Chapter 14), and those in the pharmaceutical sector (Chapter 15). Finally, Chapter 16 examines two commonly discussed phenomena with system-wide implications in the coming years: the aging of the population and continued innovation in health care technology.

Health Economics tackles all of these issues in a logical sequence, and it highlights fundamental policy questions that society confronts with respect to health and health care: how to finance care, how to fund providers, how the behaviour of individuals and the structure of markets affect policy choices, and so forth. This has two corollary benefits: it better enables instructors to demonstrate how economic analysis can inform policy choices, and it reinforces the vital importance of institutions when analyzing the health sector.

As is usual for economics texts, questions of efficiency dominate the analysis. But given the importance of equity in the health sector, the analysis also emphasizes equity as an evaluation criterion. The section on basic economic concepts presents both efficiency and equity as the fundamental criteria economists use to assess policies, and throughout the text where appropriate the analysis discusses the impact of policies on both efficiency and distributional equity.

The field of health economics includes a number of hotly debated issues, including supplier-induced demand and the most appropriate normative framework for evaluating health policies. Throughout, *Health Economics* has tried to present competing ideas and frameworks in a balanced way that highlights the differing assumptions and concepts motivating each perspective and the differing implications of the perspectives. In the author's experience, it is important to present differing perspectives—even those with which one disagrees—so that students can understand the debate and formulate their own judgments on the issues in dispute.

SUPPLEMENTS FOR INSTRUCTORS

Online Learning Centre

The Online Learning Centre, located at www.mcgrawhill.ca/olc/hurley, contains downloadable instructor resources:

Instructor's Manual and Solutions

This manual, prepared by author Jeremiah E. Hurley, McMaster University, includes chapter overviews and suggested lecture outlines. It also addresses concepts students often find difficult, including suggestions for alleviating confusion. Solutions to the problems are given at the end of each chapter.

Test Bank

The test bank, prepared by Lori J. Curtis, University of Waterloo, includes multiple-choice and short-answer and essay questions.

WebCT and Blackboard

Content cartridges are available for the course management systems **WebCT** and **Blackboard**. These platforms provide instructors with user-friendly, flexible teaching tools. Please contact your local McGraw-Hill Ryerson *i*Learning Sales Specialist for details.

E-STAT

E-STAT is an educational resource designed by Statistics Canada and made available to Canadian educational institutions. Using 450,000 current CANSIM (Canadian Socio-economic Information Management System) Time Series and the most recent—as well as historical—census data, E-STAT lets you bring data to life in colourful graphs and maps. Access to E-STAT is made available to purchasers of this book by special agreement between McGraw-Hill Ryerson and Statistics Canada.

CourseSmart

CourseSmart brings together thousands of textbooks across hundreds of courses in an e-textbook format providing unique benefits to students and faculty. By purchasing an e-textbook, students can save up to 50 percent off the cost of a print textbook, reduce their impact on the environment, and gain access to powerful Web tools for learning, including full-text search, notes and highlighting, and e-mail tools for sharing notes between classmates. For faculty, CourseSmart provides instant access to review and compare textbooks and course materials in their discipline area without the time, cost, and environmental impact of mailing print copies. For further details, contact your *i*Learning Sales Specialist or go to www.coursesmart.com.

Create Online

McGraw-Hill's **Create Online** gives you access to the most abundant resource at your fingertips—literally. With a few mouse clicks, you can create customized learning tools simply and affordably. McGraw-Hill Ryerson has included many of our market-leading textbooks within Create Online for e-book and print customization as well as many licensed readings and cases. For more information, go to www.mcgrawhillcreate.ca.

ACKNOWLEDGEMENTS

Over twenty years ago, less than a week after arriving in Canada, I had to teach a course on the economics of the Canadian health care system. It was baptism by fire, as they say, and I relied heavily on Bob Evans's then relatively new (but now out of print) text, *Strained Mercy: The Economics of Canadian Health Care*. I have used it many times over the years, uncovering new layers of meaning each time I re-read it. In my view, large sections of it remain the best economic analysis of health care ever written. It has shaped how I think about health economics in innumerable ways, some of which I am not even conscious of. So, although I am sure that Bob may bristle at some of the passages in this text, I want to acknowledge my intellectual debt to his work. I also want to thank my colleagues in The Centre for Health Economics and Policy Analysis, and especially Greg Stoddart, for lively discussions of wide-ranging issues in health economics and health policy over the years, discussions that have also shaped the perspectives presented in this book.

A book like this is a large undertaking (perhaps not surprisingly, larger than I had anticipated!); and I have had much help and support from many people. I would like to thank those who have provided comments and feedback on various draft chapters: anonymous reviewers, members of McMaster's health polinomics seminar, Neil Buckley, Aleksandra Gajic, and Greg Stoddart. I thank all those who have assisted in some way—gathering data, tracking down references, preparing tables and figures, and performing sundry other tasks—Mitch Bates, Gioia Buckley, Emmanuel Guindon, Gillian Hanley, Taha Jamal, Matthew Kirk, Donna Wilcockson, and Hai Zhong. I apologize to those whom I may inadvertently have failed to mention. Finally, I thank my wife, Mita Giacomini, and my daughter, Shaela, for their patience, forbearance, and good cheer while I was preoccupied with this project, especially during the home stretch.

Jeremiah E. Hurley
McMaster University

REVIEWERS

I am most grateful to the following reviewers for their valuable comments and input:

Catherine Deri Armstrong,
University of Ottawa

Neil J. Buckley,
York University

Lori Curtis,
University of Waterloo

Michael Denny,
University of Toronto

Livio Di Matteo,
Lakehead University

John Dorland,
Queen's University

David Feeny,
University of Alberta

Hugh Grant,
University of Winnipeg

Ehsan Latif,
Thompson Rivers University

Douglas McCready,
Wilfrid Laurier University

Jane Ruseski,
University of Alberta

Anindya Sen,
University of Waterloo

Jennifer Stewart,
Carlton University

Health and Health Care Systems: An Introduction

Learning Objectives

After studying this chapter, you will understand

LO1 Important elements of health systems

LO2 Prominent institutional characteristics of the Canadian health care system

LO3 Variation in the design of health care systems internationally

LO4 Some fundamental health economics questions regarding health and health care systems

Before delving into the economics of health and health care, it is useful to have a basic understanding of the health sector and the design of health care systems. This largely descriptive chapter provides a brief introduction to health systems and some of their essential features and activities; we will focus on the Canadian system, but place it in an international context among selected other developed countries. The aim is to provide the institutional knowledge of health systems you need in order to understand and apply the economic concepts encountered throughout the book.

The chapter is divided into three parts: a discussion of the health system, which focuses on health and its determinants; a discussion of the health care system, which is but one part of the broader health system; and a consideration of some of the economic and policy questions that emerge from the short review of health and health care systems.

1.1 THE HEALTH SYSTEM

The term "health system" refers generally to those aspects of our society that have an important bearing on the health of individuals and the population as a whole. The health system—and correspondingly, health policy—is very broad because a tremendous variety of individual characteristics and behaviours, community factors, and government policies affect health. The health system includes goods, services, and activities (such as health care) primarily intended to improve or maintain health. It also includes a wide variety of other activities (such as transportation) that people pursue for reasons unrelated to health but which nonetheless have important health effects. Accordingly, initiatives to improve the health of the population must consider an array of policies across many sectors, including health care, education, housing, income support, the environment, transportation, and agriculture.

By many measures, Canadians are amongst the healthiest people in the world. Two common measures of population health for which good international data exist are life expectancy at birth (how many years a person born today can expect to live), and infant mortality (the rate of deaths before age 1 per 1000 live births). Canadians can expect to live longer than residents of all but a few countries: life expectancy at birth for Canadians was 80.7 years in 2006. This puts Canada near the top of other countries in the Organization of Economic Cooperation and Development (OECD), and on par with Norway, France, and Sweden, but that is still two years less than life expectancy in Japan (Figure 1.1). Canada, however, does not rank quite as well in terms of infant mortality—Canada's infant mortality rate falls in the bottom half of this set of OECD countries, with a rate almost twice that of Japan (Figure 1.2).

In Canada, as in other countries, health varies systematically with demographic and socio-economic characteristics. Women live longer on average than men: in 2006, life expectancy at birth was 78.4 years for males and 83.0 years for females (Statistics Canada 2009b). Those of higher income live longer on average than do those of lower income: in 2001, life expectancy at birth for males was 78.4 years for those in the top third of the income distribution and 75.2 years for those in the bottom third (Statistics Canada 2009a). And on average, aboriginals do not live as long as non-aboriginals: in 2000, life expectancy at birth was 68.9 years for male aboriginals and 76.7 for males across the entire population (Government of Canada 2009).

The average health of Canadians has been improving steadily over time. Canadian mortality rates today are just a fraction of what they were 100 years ago. Even in the period

FIGURE 1.1

Life Expectancy at Birth, Canada and Selected Countries, 2006

A person born in Canada can expect to live over 2.5 years longer than a person born in the U.S., but over 1.5 years less than a person in Japan.

Source: OECD (2009), OECD Health Data 2009: Statistics and Indicators for 30 Countries, www.oecd.org/health/healthdata.

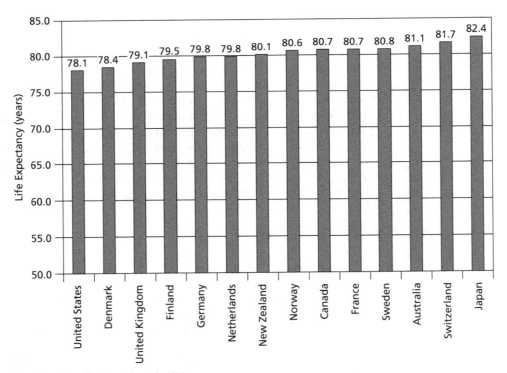

Note: Figure for the United Kingdom is for 2005.

FIGURE 1.2

Infant Mortality Rate, Canada and Selected Countries, 2006

Infant mortality in Canada is near the high end of the range among these OECD countries. Although Canada's rate is notably lower than that of the U.S. (to which it is often compared), it is nearly twice that of the best performer, Japan.

Source: OECD (2009), OECD Health Data 2009: Statistics and Indicators for 30 Countries, www.oecd.org/health/healthdata.

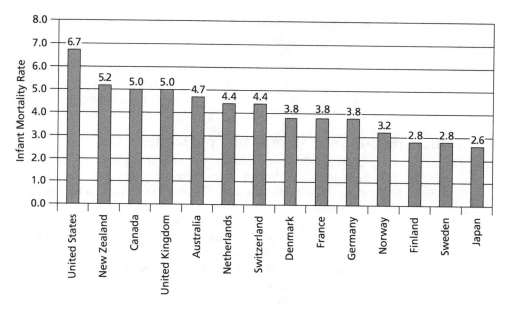

since 1960, life expectancy at birth has risen from 71.3 to 80.7 years; and infant mortality has fallen by more than 80 percent (Figure 1.3). In addition, more of those years are spent in good health, living a full active life. Many elderly Canadians today undertake activities once associated with those years younger, a phenomenon captured in popular culture by expressions such as "70 today is yesterday's 60."

These and other data documenting variations in health over time and populations prompt a number of questions. Why has the health of Canadians risen steadily over time? Why is the average Japanese healthier than the average Canadian; the average high-income person healthier than the average low-income person? For many people, the immediate answer is health care: we live longer today because we have much better health care than did our ancestors, and those with higher income are healthier because they have better access to health care. But this answer is (largely) wrong. Over time, comparisons both within countries and across countries show that the most important determinants of population health

FIGURE 1.3

Life Expectancy at Birth and Infant Mortality Rate, Canada, 1960–2006

Canada's infant mortality fell steadily between 1960 and the late 1990s, from a rate of over 27 deaths per 1000 live births to fewer than 6 deaths per 1000 live births. It has remained stable for the last 10 years. Life expectancy at birth over the same period rose from just over 70 years to more than 80, and continues to rise.

Source: OECD (2009), OECD Health Data 2009: Statistics and Indicators for 30 Countries, www.oecd.org/health/healthdata.

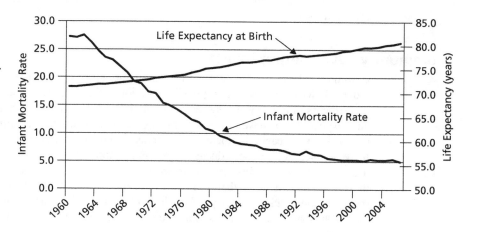

lie outside the health care system. Health care can often help a person who is sick, but more important for the overall health of the population are the forces that cause people to get sick in the first place.

Understanding the causes, or determinants, of health is a major part of health economics and health research generally. These determinants can be usefully divided into two broad categories: individual-level determinants and community-level determinants.

1.1.1 Individual-Level Determinants of Health

Individual-level determinants are of two types: individual characteristics and individual behaviours. An important individual characteristic, for example, is a person's genetic make-up. In rare cases (e.g., Huntington's disease), a specific genetic mutation will determine with certainty if a person will contract a disease. But more generally, genetic research has demonstrated that people's genetic make-up can predispose them to certain types of diseases, a predisposition that may be triggered only by exposure to physical or emotional stresses during their lifetimes.

But while people cannot control their genetic make-up, individuals can (mostly) control their behaviours, and these can expose them to a wide variety of health risks. Economic analyses of individual-level determinants of health focus on individual-level choices and actions. Every day, we make many decisions that have potential health effects, decisions such as what to eat for breakfast, how fast to drive to school, and whether to take the elevator or the stairs.

Economics provides a framework for analyzing the determinants of such choices, and therefore for understanding the underlying causes of certain health trends (Chapter 5 will examine this in detail). As an example, consider the recent increases in the rates of obesity in Canada and other countries, which pose enormous health threats to future generations, possibly even reversing the historical pattern of continual increases in longevity. Between 1978 and 2004, for instance, the percentage of Canadians classified as obese nearly doubled from 13.8 percent to 23.1 percent (Tjepkema 2005). This increase arises from a complex interplay of many social and economic forces, but economic analysis suggests part of the story lies in people's responses to changed prices over the last few decades for calorie-dense foods (e.g., cheeseburgers) relative to low-calorie foods such as fruits and vegetables, and to the falling total cost of obtaining a meal, including both the financial cost and the time cost of preparing a meal (which has fallen, for instance, due to microwave ovens and ready availability of prepared foods). Today Canadians ingest more calories on average, in part because in dozens of small daily choices they have responded to changing prices for food and meals.

1.1.2 Community-Level Determinants

Community-level determinants of health operate at a higher aggregate level beyond individual choices with respect to specific behaviours. Such determinants include public health investments in urban water systems, which deliver clean water to households and remove and dispose of waste water in a safe manner; broad forces such as climate change; or even, as evidence increasingly documents, simply being low in the social hierarchy (measured, for example, by income, education, or occupation) of a modern society and experiencing the stresses that this creates. In these cases, it is difficult for individuals to modify their behaviour in a way that will reduce the risks associated with these determinants. The source of the problem lies beyond the individual. Effectively addressing such determinants of health requires collective action because the forces are largely driven by factors other than individual choices.

1.1.3 Interactions Between Individual-Level and Community-Level Determinants

Although individual- and community-level determinants are distinct, they interact in ways that can reinforce or counteract each other. Evidence suggests that such interaction exerts some of the most powerful effects on health. For example, a genetic predisposition toward disease may only be triggered by exposure to an environmental hazard; although both the genetic predisposition and the environmental hazard each independently represent a risk to health, the combination poses a particularly high risk.

Individual choices are also conditioned by the broader social, economic, and physical environment in which people live. Whether to smoke is an individual decision, but one strongly influenced by social attitudes toward smoking. Smoking was once seen as socially desirable; but in recent years, it has become highly socially undesirable, subject to strong social sanction. This changed social perception of smoking has been an important force behind the decrease in smoking rates since the 1960s. It is also the case that collective, public action is one of the most effective ways to influence individual choice. In the case of smoking, for instance, policy responses such as smoking restrictions in public settings and tobacco excise taxes are collective actions that affect individual choices.

Because these individual determinants interact with the collective action to influence individual choices, the distinction between individual-level determinants and community determinants can, at times, be confusing. Still, the distinction is useful: the two types of determinants invite different analytic methods and consideration of different ranges of policy responses, and can highlight the complex interplay of forces that determine health.

Working with epidemiologists and other health scientists, economists bring their own unique perspective to the study of the determinants of health. As we will see in Chapters 5 and 6, economic models emphasize how people's choices and behaviours are shaped by both the perceived benefits and the perceived costs of an action, where economists interpret these costs and benefits broadly to include any positive or negative effect on the individual. These effects include many things beyond possible health effects; economic modelling is also central to the design of policies to address the determinants of health at both the individual and community levels.

1.2 HEALTH CARE SYSTEMS

The term "health care system" refers to the more narrow set of goods, services, and activities intended to improve or maintain health. Although the health care system is but one part of the broader health system, it is a particularly prominent one that commands enormous policy attention in nearly all modern countries.

One reason it commands such attention is that health care is one of the largest sectors in modern economies. In 2006, health care constituted 10.5 percent of the value of all goods and services produced in Canada (Canada's **gross domestic product** (GDP)) (Canadian Institute for Health Information 2008). In absolute terms, this translates into $4633 per person in Canada (Canadian Institute for Health Information 2008). By international standards, Canada devotes a relatively large share of its national income to health care—well below that of the U.S., but among the upper tier of spenders in the Organization of Economic Cooperation and Development (OECD) along with France, Germany, and Switzerland (Figure 1.4). This share has been rising in Canada as it has been in virtually all countries: in 1975 in Canada, just shortly after Medicare was fully implemented, health care constituted 7.0 percent of GDP; it hit 10.0 percent for the first time in 1992. It fell in response to fiscal cutbacks in the mid-1990s but has been rising since 2000 (Canadian Institute for Health Information 2008). It will likely take a big jump for 2008 and 2009 because the severe recession reduced GDP growth. (See Box 1.1 for more discussion of the rising costs of health care.)

gross domestic product (GDP)
The total value of all goods and services produced within a country.

FIGURE 1.4

Health Care as a Share of Gross Domestic Product, Canada and Selected Countries, 2006

Health care spending in Canada as a percentage of total economic activity (gross domestic product, or GDP) was 10.0 in 2006, which places Canada among the high spenders among comparator OECD countries.

Source: OECD (2009), OECD Health Data 2009: Statistics and Indicators for 30 Countries, www.oecd.org/health/healthdata.

Note: The discrepancy in the estimate of health spending as a proportion of GDP between the Canadian Institute for Health Information and the OECD arises because of slight differences in accounting methods used by the two organizations.

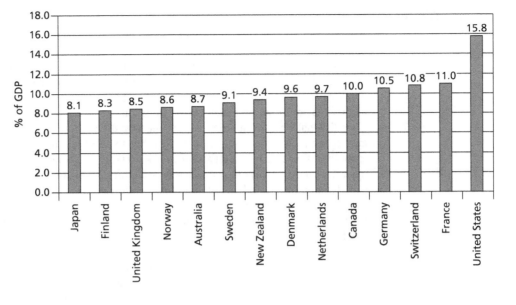

This brief review focuses on four aspects of health care systems: governance, financing, delivery, and regulation. Before undertaking the review, however, one caveat is in order.

The review does not include the public health system in Canada. Public health focuses on promoting health and preventing disease for the population as a whole rather than for individual patients. Public health in Canada carries out six major functions: population health assessment, health promotion, disease and injury control and prevention, health protection, surveillance, and emergency preparedness and response. (Marchildon (2005) provides a relatively recent comprehensive description of the Canadian health care system.)

Public health in Canada is a shared responsibility of the federal government, provincial and territorial governments, and regional/municipal governments. Federal public health initiatives are overseen by the Public Health Agency of Canada; each provincial ministry of health has a branch devoted to public health; and depending on the province, many regional/municipal governments have public health departments. Each level appoints a public/medical officer of health to head public health efforts within its jurisdiction. Although public health has historically garnered less public and policy attention than has the health care system, Canada's recent experiences with the SARS outbreak, the avian flu, the H1N1 virus, and illnesses caused by tainted water and meat have thrust public health into the policy spotlight and reminded Canadians of the importance of public health.

1.2.1 Governance

Governance refers to the set of institutions that oversee the health care system: governance concerns who makes what decisions through what processes. An explicit consideration of governance reflects the prominent role of government in health care—few contemplate the governance of the paper clip industry—and the fact that in most countries the design of the health care system reflects a series of explicit political choices, not simply the outcome of the interplay of market forces (though such forces do exert influence).

In many respects it is a misnomer to speak of Canada's "health care system." Canada does not have a single health care system. Rather, it has a collection of 13 provincial/territorial health care systems, an arrangement dictated by the 1867 British North American Act that established Canada, and the 1982 Constitution, which designate health care as a

Controlling health care costs seems to be a perennial concern for governments in all countries; at times, it seems to be the primary policy objective. From an economic perspective, are rising health care costs always bad? No, they are not. But there is also good reason why governments are concerned about rising costs.

The problem of focusing on costs alone is that such a policy considers only half of the equation. Economics is about costs and benefits. From an economic perspective, any judgment about costs depends on what benefits were generated by the additional spending. If, for instance, costs rose because a newly available treatment doubled the chances of surviving a heart attack, then the increased costs may be judged to have produced important benefits, benefits that exceed the costs themselves. At least two forces in modern economies create tendencies for ever-rising health care costs.

1. Technological advances in treatment. These create an ever-expanding array of interventions that can be offered to people.
2. Growth in income over time. In general, as people's incomes rise, they are willing to spend more on health care to maintain or improve their health. Hence, it is not surprising that we spend more on health care now (as a proportion of GDP or in absolute dollars) than we did 25 years ago.

So why are governments and other health care payers so concerned about rising health care costs?

The most immediate reason is the pressure it puts on their budgets, which require governments to either raise taxes or take money from some other components of government spending. But there is a deeper reason: considerable evidence documents wasteful health care spending. Some new technologies offer genuine improvements in health outcomes, but many others offer small benefits, at best, over existing technologies and come at a substantially higher cost.

Extensive insurance coverage for health care, as we will discuss below, lowers the cost of care to a patient, encouraging the use of services that offer only small benefits but impose large costs. And in some settings, providers have incentive to deliver services that offer small benefit to the patient but which further the interests, financial or otherwise, of the provider.

Although estimates vary somewhat across studies and countries, it has been estimated that 20–25 percent of all hospital procedures performed are unnecessary or inappropriate. In many countries, spending per capita varies substantially across regions with little evidence that it is associated with underlying need or better health outcomes. (The Health Council of Canada (2009) offers a thoughtful discussion of these and other phenomena in its report on getting better value for money in health care.) Governments and other payers hope that, by exerting pressure to control costs, they can selectively squeeze out inefficient, wasteful spending. Still, even in such a context, an over-exclusive focus on cost control as an end in itself is bad economics.

provincial responsibility.[1] Each provincial system, however, adheres to national principles for Canadian "Medicare" that are set out in the 1984 Canada Health Act: universality, comprehensiveness, accessibility, portability, and public administration (Table 1.1).

The primary objective of the Canada Health Act, which these principles are meant to further, is "to protect, promote and restore the physical and mental well-being of residents of Canada and to facilitate reasonable access to health services without financial or other barriers" (Government of Canada 1984). These principles are enforced by the federal government through its health funding arrangement with the provinces, the Canada Health Transfer. Through the Canada Health Transfer, the federal government transfers funds to each province to support the provision of health care. If a province violates one or more of the Canada Health Act principles, the federal government can penalize the province by reducing the amount of funding it provides to the province through the Canada Health Transfer.

Each provincial health care system is overseen by its respective provincial ministry of health, which is responsible for the overall operation of the health care system. The provincial public plans share many basic features; however, the precise set of services that are

[1]The federal government is responsible for health care on aboriginal reserves and for selected other groups such as the armed forces. Throughout this book, I will use the term "provincial" to refer to "provincial and territorial" unless specifically noted otherwise.

TABLE 1.1
The 1984 Canada Health Act, National Principles

Source: Health Canada (2009).

Comprehensiveness	The comprehensiveness criterion requires that the health care insurance plan of a province cover all insured health services provided by hospitals, physicians or dentists (i.e., surgical-dental services which require a hospital setting) and, where the law of the province so permits, similar or additional services rendered by other health care practitioners.
Universality	The universality criterion requires that all insured residents of a province be entitled to the insured health services provided by the provincial or territorial health care insurance plan on uniform terms and conditions. Newcomers to Canada, such as landed immigrants or Canadians returning from other countries to live in Canada, may be subject to a waiting period by a province or territory, not to exceed three months, before they are entitled to receive insured health services.
Accessibility	The accessibility criterion requires that insured persons in a province or territory have reasonable access to insured hospital, medical, and surgical-dental services on uniform terms and conditions, unprecluded or unimpeded, either directly or indirectly, by charges (user charges or extra billing) or other means (e.g., discrimination on the basis of age, health status, or financial circumstances). In addition, the health care insurance plans of the province or territory must provide: (a) reasonable compensation to physicians and dentists for all the insured health services they provide, and (b) payment to hospitals to cover the cost of insured health services.
	Reasonable access in terms of physical availability of medically necessary services has been interpreted under the Act using the "where and as available" rule. Thus, residents of a province are entitled to have access on uniform terms and conditions to insured health services at the setting "where" the services are provided and "as" the services are available in that setting.
Portability	The portability criterion requires that residents moving from one province or territory to another continue to be covered for insured health services by the "home" jurisdiction during any waiting period imposed by the new province or territory of residence. After the waiting period, the new province or territory of residence assumes responsibility for health care coverage.
	Residents who are temporarily absent from their home province or territory or from Canada must continue to be covered for insured health services during the absence.
	The portability criterion does not entitle a person to seek services in another province, territory or country, but is intended to permit a person to receive necessary services in relation to an urgent or emergent need when absent on a temporary basis, such as on business or vacation.
	If insured persons are temporarily absent in another province or territory, the portability criterion requires that insured services be paid at the host province's rate. If insured persons are temporarily out of the country, insured services are to be paid at the home province's rate.
Public Administration	The public administration criterion requires that the provincial health care insurance plan be administered and operated on a non-profit basis by a public authority, which is accountable to the provincial or territorial government for decision making on benefit levels and services, and whose records and accounts are publicly audited.

publicly insured, the way providers are funded for delivering care, the nature of the settings in which care is provided, and many other features vary across provinces.

The most important governance initiative of recent decades was a movement during the 1990s by a number of provinces to decentralize governance to regional health authorities. Each regional health authority within a province was given responsibility for allocating funding among local health care institutions and for designing the delivery arrangements for a broad basket of institutional and public health services. (The regional authorities have never controlled the budgets for physician services or drugs.) This decentralization of governance has been controversial and is perceived to have been a mixed success. At least two provinces (Alberta and Prince Edward Island) that decentralized in the 1990s have since re-centralized; others, such as British Columbia and Saskatchewan, have retained the regionalized system of governance but have changed the number of regional health authorities. Ontario, the lone province to resist decentralization in the 1990s, began decentralizing governance to regional health authorities in 2006.

By international standards, governance in Canada's public system is relatively decentralized, reflecting Canada's federalist structure of government. On the one hand, it can be contrasted with the highly centralized governance in England, which since 1948 has had a single National Health Service (NHS) that covers health services in all of England. The NHS has over the years given varying amounts of authority to its regional or local NHS health authorities, but at all times ultimate responsibility remained with the central Department of Health. On the other hand, governance in Canada is relatively centralized compared to that in some Scandinavian countries, where each county oversees its own health care system within a national policy framework.

From an economic perspective, a number of factors influence the desired level of decentralization of governance. One is the variation across regions in both the nature of the population's health needs and in the best ways to meet those needs. Other things equal, the greater such variation, the stronger the case for more decentralized governance. A second factor is the nature and distribution of the information required to plan effectively. If the information required for good planning is widely distributed among local regions and is difficult to summarize and communicate for use by a central authority, then decentralized governance with local decision-making that can exploit local information may function best.

Variation in needs and in how best to meet those needs, as well as the perception that essential planning information was held locally were major justifications for decentralizing governance in Canada in the 1990s: local communities and regions, it was argued, had much better information on local health needs and how best to meet them, and so were in a better position than the central ministry of health to respond to those needs and meet them efficiently. But the potential gains from decentralization must be weighed against possible negative effects, such as greater duplication of effort, problems of coordination across regions, growing inequities across regions as the regional systems diverge, and the inability to exploit economies of scale (either in planning or delivery) (Hurley et al. 1995).

1.2.2 Health Care Financing

financing health care
The activity of raising the revenue required to support the provision of health care.

One of the fundamental tasks in any health care system is to raise the revenue needed to pay for care, an activity commonly referred to as **financing health care**. There are myriad ways to finance care, and the different approaches have important implications for who bears what financial burdens, for who has access to care, and for the feasible methods of designing delivery systems. Public-sector financing in Canada (a combination of federal, provincial, and municipal or local government revenues) constitutes approximately 70 percent of all health care spending. The remaining 30 percent derives from private

FIGURE 1.5

Public Health Care Spending as a Percentage of Total Health Care Spending, Canada and Selected OECD Countries, 2006

In 2006, public health care spending in Canada accounted for 69.8 percent of all health care spending. While this is higher than in the United States, it is lower than in many other comparator countries and substantially lower than countries such as the United Kingdom, Norway, and Denmark.

Source: OECD (2009), OECD Health Data 2009: Statistics and Indicators for 30 Countries, www.oecd.org/ health/healthdata.

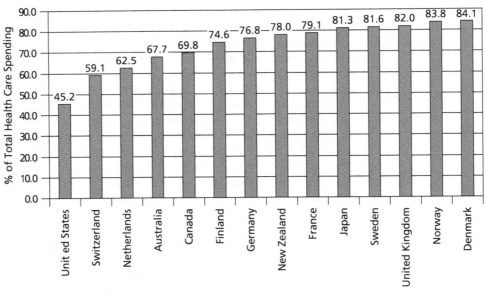

Note: Figure for Netherlands is for 2002.

insurance payments; direct, out-of-pocket spending by individuals for care; and a mixture of private spending on health research, hospital non-patient revenue, and miscellaneous other non-care sources (Canadian Institute for Health Information 2009a).

Public Financing

The public share of total health care spending in Canada peaked in 1976 at 77 percent and fell gradually until 1997, after which it has held steady at 70 percent (Canadian Institute for Health Information 2008). Although many Canadians perceive Canada as having a "publicly financed" health care system, Canada's share of public spending is relatively low by international standards, well below countries such as the United Kingdom, Denmark, and Norway, for which public spending accounts for nearly 85 percent of all health care spending (Figure 1.5).

Canadians' somewhat exaggerated perception of the role of public financing in Canada likely derives in part from the frequent comparison of Canada with the U.S. (one of the few countries with less public financing) and in part from Canada's pattern of public financing. Because the Canada Health Act applies only to medically necessary physician and hospital services, public expenditure is concentrated in those two sectors, for which care is provided free of charge. Hence, Canadians pay nothing for some of the most commonly used services. But outside those two sectors—e.g., drugs, dentistry, physiotherapy—private financing plays a substantial role. Canada's pattern of concentrated public spending in the physician and hospital sectors is distinctive internationally: although physician and hospital services tend to attract the most generous public coverage in all countries, the differences between these and other health services are more pronounced in Canada than elsewhere. Both France and Germany, for instance, provide substantially more public finance outside physician and hospital services than does Canada (Table 1.2).

Tax Financing versus Social Insurance The public component of finance generally takes one of two forms. One, exemplified by Canada and the U.K., finances health care using tax revenue: personal income taxes, corporate taxes, sales taxes, and other sources of government revenue. Public health care spending constitutes government spending.

TABLE 1.2

Share of Spending that is Public, by Type of Health Care Service: Canada, Germany, and France, 2003

Public health care spending in Canada is concentrated on physician and hospital services, with relatively low levels of public financing in other sectors. In contrast, public spending in Germany and France is spread more evenly across health services.

Source: Canadian Institute for Health Information (2005a). Note: Public expenditure figures as a proportion of total health expenditure for Canada and France are estimates.

	Canada (%)	Germany (%)	France (%)
Total expenditure on health	70	78	76
Physician services	98	85	74
Curative and rehabilitative inpatient care	93	84	92
Pharmaceuticals and other medical non-durable goods	38	75	67
Long-term nursing care	78	75	100
Dental services	5	68	36

social health insurance

A system of insurance through social insurance organizations (normally quasi-public, non-profit sickness funds) in which contribution rates, membership, benefit packages, and other aspects are heavily regulated by government.

A second, exemplified by France and Germany, is based on **social health insurance**. Social insurance organizations are legally private, non-profit organizations to which individuals make contributions (which are often mandatory and deducted, for instance, from earnings). Even though the money never flows through government accounts, these social insurance systems are considered public because of the high degree of government regulation of the system, including required contributions, the design of benefit plans, and the social insurers themselves. These regulations ensure virtually 100 percent coverage of the population on terms largely dictated by the government. Depending on the design of the system, individuals may or may not have a choice as to which sickness fund to join. The distinction between tax-financed systems and social insurance systems is important because, as we will see in Chapter 11, each creates distinct policy challenges.[2]

Private Financing

Of the 30 percent of health care in Canada that is privately financed, about 40 percent is financed through private insurance, about 49 percent is direct, out-of-pocket payments by individuals for services they obtain, and about 11 percent is the miscellaneous non-care-related private payments noted above (Canadian Institute for Health Information 2008).

Private Insurance The majority of Canadians have some form of private health insurance coverage; in most cases, it is obtained as a fringe benefit of employment. Private insurance covers selected services not included in the public insurance plan such as prescription drugs, dental care, physiotherapy, certain types of psychological counselling, and so forth. By far the two biggest categories of expenditure are prescription drugs and dental care: more than two-thirds of private insurance spending is concentrated on these two services (Hurley and Guindon 2009). Although private insurance covers only services not included in the public plan, it can influence use of public services. For instance, other things equal, those with private drug insurance are more likely to visit a physician because they are better able to afford drugs the physician may prescribe as part of the visit (Allin and Hurley 2008; Stabile 2001).

Both for-profit and not-for-profit organizations sell private health insurance in Canada (Hurley and Guindon 2009). Slightly more than 100 private, for-profit organizations sell health insurance; the number of not-for-profit organizations is not well documented, but this

---

[2]Two components of the Canadian system outside of Medicare—the Workers' Compensation Board system and the Quebec Pharmacare Program—are social insurance systems.

Debate about the role of private insurance in Canada is vigorous, has grown even more prominent since the 2005 Supreme Court decision that struck down a Quebec law prohibiting private insurance for publicly insured services, and often invokes comparisons with private insurance in Europe. It is important to recognize, however, that while each of Canada, the United Kingdom, France, and Germany have active private insurance industries, the role of private insurance differs in each system.

- *Canada:* As we have seen, the majority of Canadians have private insurance, and such insurance acts exclusively to provide coverage for services not included within the public insurance system. In a sense, it acts to complement public coverage, filling gaps in public coverage.
- *France:* Private insurance in France, which is held by virtually all members of the population, provides coverage for the cost-sharing required by the social insurance system, which can be substantial. When a French resident obtains a health care service, part of it is paid for by the social insurer and part is paid for by the private insurer; private insurance complements the social insurance coverage, filling in gaps in social insurance coverage. But unlike Canada, where the gap is between different types of services, in France the gap is caused by the cost-sharing associated with insured services.
- *United Kingdom:* Private insurance in the U.K., which is held by about 11 percent of the population, functions primarily to provide private insurance for services already included within the public system. A resident with private insurance has two types of insurance for the same service, and if the service is needed, can choose whether to obtain it for free from the National Health Service or to "go private." This decision can be made on a service-by-service basis. The insurance functions primarily to enable individuals to avoid NHS wait times or to purchase what they perceive as higher quality care than that provided by the NHS. Such insurance is sometimes called "parallel" private insurance because it operates in parallel to the public plan.
- *Germany:* Private insurance in Germany is held by a relatively small proportion of the population, almost all of whom are relatively wealthy. Those with high incomes (e.g., above €48,600 per year in 2009) are not included in the mandatory social insurance system. Rather, they can choose to join the social insurance system or to purchase private insurance. Those who opt out of the social insurance system make no contributions and obtain all care privately. Once a person opts out, they cannot re-enroll in the social insurance system. Private insurance in Germany, therefore, acts as a substitute for social insurance for the wealthy, and a person must choose to be wholly in one system or the other.

These different relationships between the public and private insurance sectors create quite different interactions between the two sectors, and have different impacts on efficiency, equity, and costs in the health care system. These distinctions are too often ignored in debates about health care financing. For instance, France's and Germany's experiences with private insurance are not relevant to Canada's debate about whether to allow parallel private insurance alongside Medicare; private insurance in those systems serves a totally different purpose.

segment of the market is dominated by Blue Cross organizations. The for-profit firms dominate the market overall, with a national market share (by revenue) in 2005 of approximately 60 percent; but the relative shares vary considerably across provinces. Although many insurers operate nationally, there are strong regional aspects to the market, with a number of insurers offering products in only a subset of provinces (Hurley and Guindon 2009). (See Box 1.2 for a comparison of Canada's use of private insurance and that of some other OECD countries.)

out-of-pocket spending
Direct payments by individuals for the receipt of a health care service.

cost-sharing
An insurance provision that requires an individual to pay part of the cost of an insured health care service.

Out-of-Pocket Spending Direct, **out-of-pocket spending** derives from two sources. Many Canadians have no private insurance for services not covered by the public insurance system and must pay the full cost of such care. In addition, even those with insurance (public or private) are often required to pay part of the cost of health care that they obtain, an arrangement referred to as **cost-sharing**. Cost-sharing normally takes one of three basic

deductible

A form of cost-sharing that requires an individual to pay the full cost of any services received until the individual's spending has reached a specified limit (the deductible).

forms. **Deductibles** require that the individual pay the full cost of care up to the amount of the deductible; **co-insurance** requires that the individual pay a specified proportion (e.g., 20 percent) of the cost of care; and a **co-payment** requires that the individual pay a fixed dollar amount per unit of the service received (e.g., $5.00 per prescription, regardless of the costs of the prescription). Many policies also specify a **maximum expenditure limit** such that once the policy-holder's out-of-pocket expenses reach the limit, further care is fully insured. As illustrated by Table 1.3, which summarizes the cost-sharing provisions

TABLE 1.3 **Cost-Sharing Policies for Senior Beneficiaries of Provincial Public Drug Programs, December 2008**

Source: Canadian Institute for Health Information (2009a, Table 8).

Province	Beneficiary	Deductible	Cost-Sharing	Maximum Expenditure Limit
NL	Low-income seniors age ≥ 65	None	Mark-up and professional dispensing fee for identified benefits	None
PEI	Seniors age ≥ 65 and eligible for PEI Medicare	None	Up to $11 of medication cost plus the professional dispensing fee	
NS	Non-low-income seniors age ≥ 65	None	33% of prescription cost	$382 per year
NB	Senior with annual inc ≤ $17,198	None	$15 per prescription	None
QC	Non-low-income senior age ≥ 65	$14.30 per month	31% of prescription cost	$77.21 per month
ON	Non-low-income senior age ≥ 65	$100	Up to $6.11 per prescription once deductible is reached	None
MN	All eligible provincial residents	Deductible is a percentage of adjusted family income: 2.69%: inc ≤ $15k 4.02%: $15k < inc ≤ 40k 4.63%: $40k < inc ≤ 75k 5.79%: inc > 75k	None	None
SK	Non-low-income seniors age ≥ 65	None	Up to $15 per prescription	None
AB	Non-low-income seniors age ≥ 65,	None	30% of prescription cost to a maximum of $25 per prescription	None
BC	Born in 1939 or earlier	Depends on family net income (inc): $0: inc ≤ $33k 1%: $33k < inc ≤ $50k 2%: inc > $50k	25% of total prescription cost	Depends on family income (inc): 1.25%: inc ≤ $33k 2.0%: $33k < inc ≤ 50k 3.0%: > 50k

Notes: Income cut-offs differ across provinces; seniors in Quebec and Nova Scotia also pay an annual premium to join the public drug program. See the source for full details regarding the provincial plans.

co-insurance
A form of cost-sharing that requires an individual to pay a specified proportion of the cost of health care services received.

co-payment
A form of cost-sharing that requires an individual to pay a specified, fixed-dollar amount of the cost of a health care service received.

maximum expenditure limit
A specified dollar limit such that once an individual's out-of-pocket expenditures reach this limit, services become fully insured with no cost-sharing required.

within provincial public drug insurance programs, insurance programs often combine one or more types of cost-sharing.

For many, such cost-sharing represents a barrier to care. A recent survey of individuals in seven counties found that residents of the U.S. were most likely to have forgone a prescription medicine or a physician visit because of cost, and were much more likely to have reported difficulty paying a health care bill (Table 1.4). Similarly, a higher proportion of Canadians—who face greater out-of-pocket costs across a range of service than do those in the U.K.—report such a cost barrier than do U.K. residents.

Insurance-Based Financing and Markets for Health Care Services

The dominant role of insurance financing in the health care sector has important implications for the operation of markets for health care services. Figure 1.6(i) depicts a market transaction for most goods and services, which are not covered by insurance, and Figure 1.6(ii) depicts a transaction for an insured good. An uninsured transaction involves only two parties: the purchaser and the seller. The person who pays for the good is by definition the person who gets the good, and the seller obtains its revenue from those individuals to whom the good or service is provided.

But for an insured transaction, the individual first contributes to the insurer (via taxes or premiums); and when the individual receives the good or service (e.g., physician visit), the insurer—not the individual—pays the provider. This creates two distinct money flows: from the individual to the insurer and from the insurer to the provider. This separation allows each to be treated as a distinct policy problem. The way society finances care (i.e., raises the monies from individuals) can differ from the way it funds care (transfers money

TABLE 1.4 Cost-Related Access Problems Among Adults, Canada and Selected OECD Countries, 2007
Variation in insurance coverage and cost sharing across countries can lead to large differences in the extent to which citizens of those countries experience difficulties accessing care.

Source: "State Health System Performance and State Health Reform," Karen Davis and Cathy Schoen (2007).

Percentage who in the past year due to cost:	Australia	Canada	Germany	Netherlands	New Zealand	United Kingdom	United States
- did not fill a prescription or skipped doses	13	8	11	2	10	5	23
- had a medical problem but did not visit a doctor	13	4	12	1	19	2	25
- skipped a test, treatment, or follow-up	17	5	8	2	13	3	23
Percentage who said yes to at least one of the above	26	12	21	5	25	8	37

FIGURE 1.6

Uninsured vs. Insured Transactions

Unlike transactions for goods that are not insured, which constitute the vast majority of daily transactions, insured transactions separate the money flow of payments from individuals (top left of (ii)) and payments to sellers (top right of (ii)).

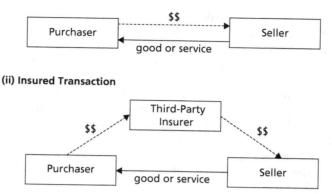

(i) Uninsured Transaction

(ii) Insured Transaction

to providers and provider organizations to support the delivery of care). This enables policy makers to separately craft incentives specific to each flow of funds to pursue efficiency and equity objectives. The separation also means that the receipt of care need not be linked to one's contribution to financing care.

Insurance also modifies incentives: those who seek care do not pay for it directly, and those who provide care know that the recipient will not bear the full cost. In many situations, the incentives of individuals seeking care and those of the providers coincide to increase the likelihood that a service is provided, regardless of the underlying cost. The individuals benefit because they obtain a service that provides benefit (however small); the providers benefit because they earn the associated income. Such incentives can contribute to problems of cost control and inappropriate utilization. In response, insurers try to ensure that only needed services are provided. This requires that it change from a passive financial intermediary that simply collects money and pays bills to an active manager and regulator in the equation of exchange.

When initially created in the 1960s and early 1970s, for example, Canada's provincial public insurance agencies were envisioned purely as bill-payers who were not to "interfere in the practice of medicine" (a deal made in part to get political support for Medicare from the medical associations). But as the provinces have confronted the difficult policy challenges of running modern, evolving health care systems, they have gradually transformed into active policy-makers and system managers. In real-world health care systems, both public and private third-party insurers actively shape the constraints and opportunities that individuals face when seeking care and that providers face when providing health care.

As we will see in subsequent chapters, a surprising number of the policy challenges faced in the health sector can be traced back one way or another to the dominance of insurance in health care. When insured transactions constitute only a small proportion of the output of an industry, such dynamics exert little influence on the industry as a whole. But when the vast majority of transactions in an industry are insured, such as the case for health care services, they become dominant forces in the sector. The issue is not the proportion of people with insurance coverage; the issue is the proportion of industry output sold through insured transactions. For example, in housing, even though all homeowners have house insurance, only a very small proportion of renovations are covered by insurance; similarly for automobiles, although all automobile owners purchase insurance, only a small proportion of all automobile repairs are covered by insurance.

1.2.3 Delivering Health Care

primary care physicians
Physicians, especially general practitioners and family physicians, who are the first point of contact into the health care system. Primary care physicians are one type of provider within the primary care system.

specialist physicians
Physicians who specialize in a particular area of medicine and whose practice is often made up mainly of patients referred by primary care physicians.

self-regulation
When the government delegates regulatory authority with respect to members of a profession to the profession itself.

fee-for-service
A method of physician payment in which physicians receive a fee each time they provide a reimbursable service.

salary
A method of paying physicians in which a physician receives a specified annual amount of income, independent of the number of patients seen or services provided.

capitation
A method of paying physicians in which a physician (or the practice of which the physician is a part) receives a pre-specified amount of money each period (month or year) for each person enrolled in the physician's practice, in return for a commitment by the physician to meet defined health care needs of the individual.

While Canada has a predominantly public system of health care finance, it has a predominantly private system of health care delivery. The vast majority of physicians work in private practices that they own themselves or in partnership with a small number of other physicians. Most hospitals are private, not-for-profit organizations overseen by a religious or community board, though in some provinces publicly owned hospitals play a large role. Nursing homes tend to be a mixture of private not-for-profit organizations, private for-profit organizations, and public institutions. And those sectors with predominantly private finance, such as dentistry and physiotherapy, are dominated by private providers. However, when private providers and organizations receive most of their funding from government, their activities and operations are subject to substantial government influence. This subsection focuses on delivery of those services that constitute Medicare—physician and hospital services.

Physician Services

Physicians are a critical element in the delivery system, both because of the services they provide and because they control access to a wide variety of other health care services. Physicians are grouped into two broad categories: **primary care physicians**, such as family physicians, who are the first point of contact for care and, in many respects, the entry point into the health care system; and **specialist physicians**, who have specialized expertise in particular areas of medicine (e.g., cardiology, ophthalmology, neurosurgery), who can be seen only on referral from a family physician. Nearly all primary care physicians are community-based, with independent practices that are not part of a larger institution. Although it varies from specialty to specialty, most specialists in Canada also have community-based practices, though they provide much of their care in hospitals and larger clinics. This arrangement, which is also found in the U.S., differs from many European countries where specialists are based in hospitals and are salaried employees of hospitals.

Physicians are a **self-regulating profession**, as is common in many countries. Because governments lack the expertise necessary to evaluate the quality and appropriateness of clinical practice, provincial governments have delegated regulatory power with respect to many aspects of quality, conduct, and performance to physician professional colleges such as the College of Family Physicians and the College of Physicians and Surgeons.

Both primary care and specialist physicians in Canada have traditionally been paid by a method called **fee-for-service**: each time a physician provides a service to a patient, the physician sends a bill to the provincial insurance agency, which then pays the physician the designated fee for the service (the fee was negotiated between the provincial medical association and the government). Because physicians are paid each time they provide a service, and only then, fee-for-service payment in the presence of full insurance coverage for patients may encourage physicians to over-provide services—that is, provide services that generate only small benefits to patients compared to the cost of provision. Fee-for-service can also inhibit physicians from integrating other health professionals such as nurse practitioners into their practices because only services provided by physicians are eligible for payment.

Because of these undesirable incentives of fee-for-service, in recent years provinces have attempted to increase the use of other payment methods, including **salary** and **capitation** payment, especially among primary care physicians. Under salary, a physician is paid a fixed amount per year to provide care, an amount that does not vary explicitly with the number of patients seen or the amount and type of services provided. Under capitation, a physician's practice receives a fixed amount of money each month per person enrolled in the physician's practice, and the amount varies with the needs of a patient (i.e., the amount received for caring for a 85-year-old is more than for a 25-year-old). The practice is free to use whatever means it judges best to meet those needs (including, for example, nurse practitioners, counsellors, and other health professionals). Although capitation is still relatively little used in Canada, it has been used for decades in other countries such as the U.K. Capitation also has some undesirable financing incentives, such as incentive to under-provide, or skimp on care. For this reason, provinces are increasingly experimenting with payment methods that blend components of fee-for-service, capitation, and even other methods in an attempt to provide incentives for good quality care.

These changes in payment methods are only one part of a larger initiative to reform primary care in Canada. A central task of a primary care physician is to coordinate care for patients. As the range and sophistication of health care services increases, the mix of potential providers expands, and the needs of aging patients with multiple chronic diseases grow in complexity, good primary care practice requires a number of features that are difficult to integrate into a traditional solo physician practice in which a family physician works alone managing the practice and providing all services. Primary care reform, which is being pursued by all provinces with support from the federal government, is an attempt to create a more coherent primary care system that will place family physicians at the centre of larger, multi-disciplinary practices that can better provide a full range of primary care services, and which themselves are embedded within a better-integrated system. Although evidence indicates that most Canadians receive high-quality primary care (Canadian Institute for Health Information 2009b), comparisons internationally show that the typical primary care practice in Canada currently lacks some features that can improve performance and that will likely grow more important over time for an effective primary care system. (See Box 1.3.)

A second prominent Canadian policy concern in the physician sector has been the supply of physicians. Rural and remote areas of Canada (and other countries) have often suffered limited access to physicians, but beginning in the late 1990s, even some residents of small cities have found it difficult to secure a regular family physician and certain types of specialist care (Chan 2002). After more than thirty years of continuous growth, the supply of physicians per capita in Canada stabilized in the early 1990s, and even dipped slightly in the late 1990s, before beginning to increase again in the early 2000s as a result of expanded medical school enrolment (Figure 1.7). Canada's overall physician supply is relatively low by the norms of other OECD countries (Figure 1.8). Changes in the number of physicians, per se, cannot explain the access problems that developed in Canada in the 1990s; rather, physicians appear to have changed practice behaviour substantially, including providing fewer hours of patient care on average than was the case 25 years ago. The reasons for this are not well understood (Crossley et al. 2009). Chapter 13 will examine these issues in more detail.

Hospitals

Canada had about 740 hospitals in 2004. The vast majority of these were acute-care general hospitals that treat short-term illnesses. In addition, there are specialty hospitals for children, psychiatric care, rehabilitation, and chronic care. As noted, most hospitals in Canada are not-for-profit institutions, either privately owned with community or religious boards, or publicly owned. Most are relatively small: over half have fewer than 100 beds. Care, however, especially specialized care, is concentrated in larger, urban hospitals with hundreds of beds. The 6 percent of hospitals with over 400 beds account for over 25 percent of all in-patient hospital beds in Canada.

Although the number of hospitals has been falling over time (mostly as small, inefficient rural hospitals are closed), the most important source of contraction in the hospital sector has been the reduction in the number of in-patient beds within existing facilities (Figure 1.9).

The Commonwealth Foundation in the United States has conducted a series of international surveys of the general public, patients, and providers as part of an initiative to promote good system design in the U.S. and elsewhere. One survey focused on primary care physicians in seven countries: Australia, Canada, Germany, Netherlands, New Zealand, the U.K., and the U.S.

What it found speaks to the important work to be achieved by primary care reform in Canada. Among the seven countries, Canada has the lowest percentage of primary care physicians who used electronic medical records for any purpose (Table B1.3.1). In all but one case, it had the smallest percentage that used electronic medical records for specific tasks, such as sharing records with other clinicians, accessing records from outside

the office, and ordering tests and receiving test results. Although not the lowest, Canada had among the lowest percentage of primary care physicians who routinely used multi-disciplinary teams in their clinical practice. Lastly, Canada was second lowest, above only the U.S. in terms of the percentage of primary care physicians who had a formal arrangement for after-hours care. Does this mean that Canadians receive poor primary care? No. A recent study indicates that the majority of Canadians receive good primary care. But it does suggest that primary care practices in Canada lag behind in these important dimensions of what are seen as highly effective primary care practices of the future. This is an area in which primary care practices in the Netherlands, New Zealand, and the U.K. stand out.

TABLE B1.3.1 Prevalence of Selected Aspects of Primary Care Practices, Canada and Selected OECD Countries, 2007

	Australia	Canada	Germany	Netherlands	New Zealand	United Kingdom	United States
Percentage of primary care physicians who use electronic medical records:	79	23	42	98	92	89	28
- to share records with other clinicians	10	6	9	45	17	15	12
- to access records from outside the office	19	11	16	32	36	22	22
- to order tests	65	8	27	5	62	20	22
- to prescribe drugs	81	11	59	85	78	55	20
- to access test results	76	27	34	78	90	84	48
Practice uses multi-disciplinary teams	32	32	49	50	30	81	29
Practice has arrangement for after-hours care	81	47	76	95	90	87	40

Source: "State Health System Performance and State Health Reform," Karen Davis and Cathy Schoen (2007).

Canada's current bed supply places it in a large group of OECD countries whose bed supplies range between 2.5 and 3.0 acute beds per 1000 population (Figure 1.10).

But perhaps surprisingly, even though the number of beds has fallen, the numbers of procedures provided through hospitals has steadily increased. The reason is a shift from in-patient stays to day procedures and out-patient care (Canadian Institute for Health Information 2005b).

FIGURE 1.7   **Physicians (Including Interns and Residents) per 100,000 Population, Canada, 1961–2008**
The supply of physicians in Canada, adjusted for population, grew steadily from 1960 through the late 1980s. It remained stable until the mid-1990s, at which point it fell slightly before beginning to rise again in about 2003.

Source: Canadian Institute for Health Information (2007, Table D.2).

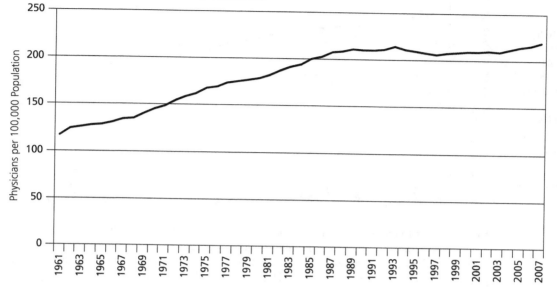

Waiting for Care

Few health care issues in Canada generate as much concern or as much debate as wait-times for care. There is general agreement that wait-times for a number of services are too long. Reliable, high-quality, comparable data on wait-times are difficult to find, either over time within a province or across provinces; but since the 2004 commitment by Canada's

FIGURE 1.8

Physicians per 1000 Population, Selected OECD Countries, 2006

The supply of practising physicians in Canada is at the lower end of OECD comparator countries.

Source: OECD (2009), OECD Health Data 2009: Statistics and Indicators for 30 Countries, www.oecd.org/health/healthdata.

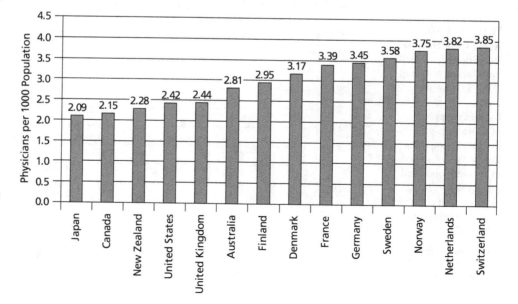

FIGURE 1.9

Hospital Beds per 1000 Population, Canada, 1976–2002

With the exception of a brief period of stabilization in the early 1990s, the number of acute hospital beds per thousand Canadians has been falling steadily since the mid-1970s.

Source: OECD (2009), OECD Health Data 2009: Statistics and Indicators for 30 Countries, www.oecd.org/health/healthdata.

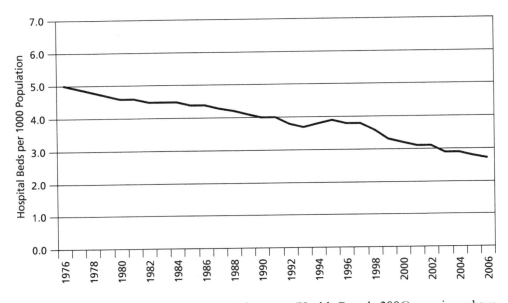

first ministers to reduce wait-times in priority areas (Health Canada 2006), provinces have substantially improved their documentation of wait-times.

The most recent Canadian data indicate that (1) rates of surgery have increased in the priority areas (Canadian Institute for Health Information 2009c); (2) in most provinces for most of the priority areas, more than 75 percent of patients receive their care within the clinically recommended time, though problems persist for hip and knee replacements (Table 1.5); (3) wait-times appear to be falling for joint replacement and cataract surgery, but the evidence is mixed across provinces in other areas (Table 1.6). Again, data comparability is a major problem, but international comparisons suggest that wait-times in Canada for many services are longer than in many other countries (Figure 1.11).

On the surface it would appear that fixing wait-times should be easy. A common analogy is to a water faucet—all that one has to do is open the tap to increase the rate of flow through the system. But reducing wait-times turns out to be a remarkably difficult

FIGURE 1.10

Acute Care Hospital Bed Supply per 1000 Population, Selected OECD Countries, 2006

Canada's supply of acute beds per thousand population falls at the lower end of the rates observed among these OECD countries, on par with that of Sweden, the U.S., and the U.K.

Source: OECD (2009), OECD Health Data 2009: Statistics and Indicators for 30 Countries, www.oecd.org/health/healthdata.

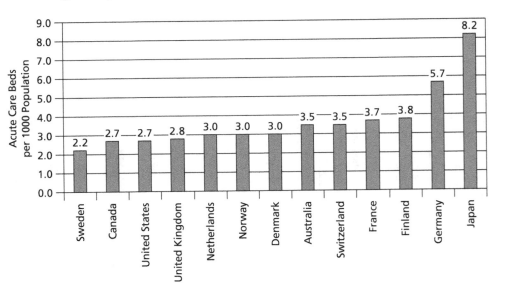

TABLE 1.5

Do at Least 75 Percent of Patients Receive Treatment Within the Clinically Recommended Benchmark Wait-Time? By Province and Procedure

For all provinces for which data are available, more than 75 percent of patients receive cancer radiation treatment and coronary artery bypass within the clinically recommended benchmark time; performance against the benchmarks varies across provinces for the other three designated priority areas.

Source: Canadian Institute for Health Information (2009d).

	Cancer Radiation Treatment	Coronary Artery Bypass Surgery	Hip Replacement	Knee Replacement	Cataract Surgery
NL	Yes	Yes	Yes	No	No
PEI	Yes	NA	No	Yes	No
NS	NA	NA	No	No	Yes
NB	Yes	Yes	No	No	No
QC	Yes	NA	Yes	Yes	NA
ON	Yes	Yes	Yes	Yes	Yes
MN	Yes	Yes	Yes	No	Yes
SK	Yes	Yes	No	No	Yes
AB	NA	Yes	Yes	No	No
BC	Yes	Yes	Yes	No	Yes

Note: NA indicates that benchmark data are not available

problem. The waits in different areas arise for different reasons at different stages in the process from diagnosis to treatment, and not all are amenable to simply providing more resources. Further, the health care system is not a mechanical system like plumbing; rather, it is a complex system populated by humans who respond to changes they observe. For instance, if an influx of resources begins to reduce wait times for a service, providers

TABLE 1.6   **Provincial Wait-Time Trends**

Information on trends in wait-times over the period 2005–2008 for these priority areas are incomplete and reveal mixed progress across provinces and services.

Source: Canadian Institute for Health Information (2009d).

	Cancer Radiation Treatment	Coronary Artery Bypass Surgery	Hip Replacement	Knee Replacement	Cataract Surgery	Diagnostic Imaging	
						CT	MRI
NL		—			NA	NA	NA
PEI	NA	NA	NA	NA	NA	NA	NA
NS	—	↓	NA	NA	NA	↑	NA
NB	NA	NA	NA	NA	NA	NA	NA
QC	NA	NA	NA	NA	NA	NA	NA
ON	NA	NA	↓	↓	↓	↓	↓
MN	—	NA	↓	↓	NA	↓	↑
SK	NA	—	—	↓	↓	NA	NA
AB	↑	↓	↓	↓	↓	↓	↓
BC	—	NA	↓	↓	—	NA	NA

Notes: ↑ means that wait times increased by 10 percent over most recent three years
↓ means that wait times decreased by 10 percent over most recent three years
— means change of less than 10 percent in either direction over most recent three years
NA means trend data not available

FIGURE 1.11   **Wait-Times for Elective or Non-Emergency Surgery, Canada and Selected OECD Countries, 2007**

Wait times for certain types of care appear to be relatively high in Canada. Canada has the smallest percentage of respondents who received their elective, non-emergency surgery within 1 month, and the highest percentage of respondents who waited more than 6 months.

Source: "State Health System Performance and State Health Reform," Karen Davis and Cathy Schoen (2007).

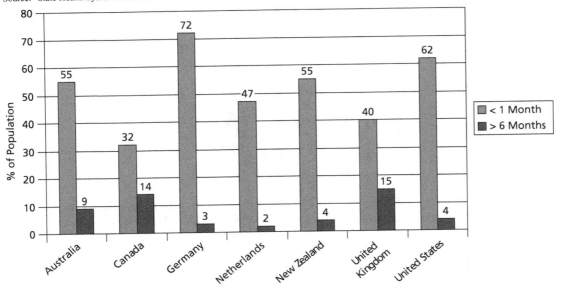

sometimes respond by reducing their threshold for patient referral, increasing the number of patients referred and causing wait-times to creep back up. Overall, more patients are treated, which is good (assuming they all need it), but wait-times do not change (or sometimes even increase). Fixing wait-times requires carefully modelling the processes of care and the behaviour of both suppliers and demanders of the service in question.

1.2.4   Regulating Health Care

regulation
The use of authority to guide or direct the behaviour of individuals, providers, and organizations.

Governments and private funders (and, as we saw above, providers themselves) in all modern health care systems heavily regulate the financing, funding, and delivery of health care. **Regulation** refers to the use of authority to guide or direct the behaviour of individuals, providers, and organizations in the health care sector. Although it is common to debate whether there is "too much" or "too little" regulation, a more useful framing of the issue is to focus on the nature and intent of the regulatory approach adopted. The health care system in the U.S. probably has more regulation than does Canada's, but the public sector in Canada has more extensive regulatory control of health care. More importantly, however, the goals of regulation, especially public-sector regulation, differ between the two countries.

market-led regulatory approach
An approach to health sector regulation that attempts to harness competitive markets to achieve social objectives in the health care sector.

Public-sector regulation in the U.S. exemplifies what can be termed a **market-led regulatory approach**. A market-led approach seeks to harness private markets to achieve social objectives. The approach is individualistic in orientation, emphasizing, for example, the role of consumer choice; it tries to foster competition in relevant markets (e.g., among insurers or among providers); and it attempts to achieve policy goals by guiding choices and behaviour through price signals and competition. Such an approach is built around market competition. Accordingly, market-led regulatory schemes strive to employ the minimum amount of regulation consistent with achieving stated objectives. Market-led approaches can be used even when financing is through public sources.

Canada's Regulatory Approach to
Inhibiting the Development of Privately
Financed Delivery of Physician Services
Included in the Public Insurance System   Box 1.4

As we have noted, over 98.5 percent of physician services in Canada are publicly financed, and the few services that are privately financed are non-medically necessary services that are not covered by the public insurance system. How has Canada prevented the development of privately financed physician services? Many falsely believe that private delivery and payment is illegal in Canada, but it is not. Rather, the lack of privately financed physician services is the result of a web of regulations aimed at private insurers and physicians.

Insurance Regulation

Five provinces (British Columbia, Alberta, Manitoba, Ontario, and Prince Edward Island) prohibit private insurers from covering physician and hospital services that are publicly insured under the principles of the Canada Health Act. Quebec allows such insurance only for a specified set of services.

Regulation of Physicians and Their Fees

A physician's ability and incentive to provide privately financed services is also highly regulated in Canada. For publicly insured physician services, most provinces require that a physician either fully opt into the provincial public plan—meaning that the physician will only accept public payment for services covered by the public plan; or fully opt out—meaning that the physician will not accept any public payment. With a few exceptions across provinces, a physician cannot choose to charge privately for some patients but publicly for others (see Boychuk 2006 for a detailed discussion of the regulations). To provide privately financed, medically necessary services, therefore, a physician would have to support an entire practice through private, out-of-pocket payment by patients, which is not feasible for most physicians.

Many provinces also regulate the fees that can be charged by physicians who opt out of the public plan (Flood and Archibald 2001). Manitoba, Ontario, and Nova Scotia prohibit opted-out physicians from charging private fees greater than the fees paid by the public plan. Other provinces permit opted-out physicians to charge fees higher than those in the public plan; however, all but Newfoundland and Prince Edward Island prohibit such patients from receiving any public subsidy.

The combination of insurance regulations, participation regulations, and fee regulations makes delivery of privately financed services that are covered by the public plan economically unattractive. Consequently, few physicians opt out of the public plan: recent estimates are that no physicians are opted out in 7 of the 10 provinces—Alberta, Saskatchewan, Manitoba, New Brunswick, Nova Scotia, Prince Edward Island, and Newfoundland—while 6 are opted out in British Columbia, 129 in Ontario, and 97 in Quebec (Health Canada 2007).

The logic and rationality of the U.S. system, for example, is premised on the efficacy of market competition and market dynamics. Even within its public insurance programs, government agencies have attempted to create competition among private insurers who provide the actual coverage while the government pays the premium on behalf of the beneficiary. Among European countries, Netherlands has a market-led social insurance system in which insurers compete for patients and receive risk-adjusted contributions (Exter et al. 2004).

non-market-led regulatory approach
An approach to health sector regulation that de-emphasizes the role of competitive market forces by tightly controlling markets, or supplanting markets, to achieve social objectives in the health care sector.

In contrast, public-sector regulation in Canada represents a **non-market-led regulatory approach**, which seeks to supplant the market. Such approaches emphasize the collective population (rather than individuals) and cooperation among organizations over competition. Non-market approaches predominate in Canada and most European social insurance systems. In Canada, this non-market approach is exemplified by the set of regulations respecting private insurance, physician practices, and physician payment, which have been used to inhibit the growth of privately financed services alongside the public system (see Box 1.4)

1.3 ECONOMICS AND VARIATION IN THE DESIGN OF HEALTH SYSTEMS

From an economic perspective, every society faces the same fundamental challenge with respect to health and health care: how to marshal society's resources to improve the health of the population and respond to the health-related needs of its citizens. Yet, when we look around the world, we see a wide variety of approaches to meeting this challenge. Even this brief survey has highlighted the different ways in which countries finance health care, fund the delivery of health services and programs, and deliver those services. The relationship between the public and private sectors in each of these basic health system tasks differs remarkably, even among countries with a shared commitment to universal access to high-quality care met through collective action.

This variation prompts a number of questions. Is there a best way to design a health care system? If not, how can we assess which of the variety of approaches is a harmless response to local tradition, which is a poor design that has important negative consequences, and which is an exceptionally good design that should be adopted more widely? To answer such questions, one must have criteria by which to assess better and worse approaches, and the analytic tools by which to conduct such assessments.

Economics uses two basic criteria to evaluate alternative ways to organize health systems and the myriad policies associated with each of the systems' basic activities: efficiency and equity.

Every society has only a limited amount of resources—human resources, natural resources, machinery, and equipment—available to produce goods and services, including health care. Efficiency emphasizes getting the most out of available resources: in essence, generate as much benefit to members of society as is possible with society's limited resources. It dictates both that society not waste resources in the production of goods and services, and that society use its resources to produce the goods and services most

valued by members of society. Equity emphasizes using society's resources in a way that distributes costs and benefits fairly among members of society. Chapter 2 will explore each of these economic criteria in greater depth.

Economic analysis that assesses the efficiency and equity of alternative health policies demonstrates that some policies are worse than others: some are both less efficient and less equitable. Financing health care through a system of unregulated private insurance markets is one example (and likely explains why we do not see such a system anywhere in the world). Not all variation in design is good: careful attention to economic principles can improve the performance of health systems, making them both more efficient and more equitable.

At the same time, there is no single best way to design a health care system that all countries should rush to imitate. Although most countries share a common set of goals for their systems (e.g., improved health, access to care), countries place different weight on the various goals, so efficiency calls for different designs. Countries also have distinct resources and face distinct constraints, so that the most efficient and equitable designs will differ across settings. It should not be surprising, for example, that the designs of delivery systems differ between a small, densely populated country such as Belgium, and a large, sparsely populated country such as Canada. Further, the design of health systems is not just a technical, economic task; it is also a political task. Designs that may work well in one setting may not be politically feasible in another.

Chapter Summary

This largely descriptive chapter introduced important elements of health and health care systems, with a focus on Canada.

- The health of Canadians has been improving over time, though substantial disparities exist among different groups in society.
- The "health system" refers to all goods, services, and activities with health consequences. It is useful to divide the determinants of health into individual-level determinants and community-level determinants. These two types of determinants can act separately or in combination to affect health.
- The "health care system" refers to that more narrow set of goods, services, and activities whose primary purpose is to maintain or improve health.
- Four important aspects of the design of health care systems are governance, financing, delivery, and regulation:
  - Canada has a relatively decentralized system of governance in which each province oversees its own public health care system within a national framework for health policy.
  - Although a majority of health care in Canada is financed publicly, Canada's share of public financing is relatively low in comparison to other OECD countries.
  - Canada's delivery system is made up predominantly of private providers (e.g., physicians, physiotherapists) and provider organizations (e.g., hospitals, nursing homes).
  - Canada's regulatory system de-emphasizes the use of market competition in the allocation of health care resources.
- Though there is no single best way to design a health care system, economic analysis can provide important principles for efficient and equitable designs, given the goals, resources, and constraints a country faces.

Key Terms

capitation, *16*
co-insurance, *14*
co-payment, *14*
cost-sharing, *12*
deductible, *13*
fee-for-service, *16*
financing health
     care, *9*

gross domestic product
     (GDP), *5*
market-led regulatory
     approach, *22*
maximum expenditure
     limit, *14*
non-market-led regulatory
     approach, *23*

out-of-pocket spending, *12*
primary care physicians, *16*
regulation, *22*
salary, *16*
self-regulation, *16*
social health insurance, *11*
specialist physicians, *16*

End-of-Chapter Questions

For each statement below, indicate whether it is true or false and discuss why it is true or false.

1. Insurance coverage likely has little impact on people's use of needed health care services.
2. Reducing inequalities in health within the population should focus primarily on the distribution of health care.
3. Because it increases GDP, increased health care spending is a sign of a robust economy.
4. The variation in the design of health care systems is a sure sign of inefficiency.
5. The evolution of health care technologies causes the efficient design of a health care system to change over time.

References

Allin, S., and J. Hurley. 2008. Inequity in publicly funded physician care: What is the role of private prescription drug insurance? *Health Economics.* 18(10):1218–32.

Canadian Institute for Health Information. 2005a. *Exploring the 70/30 split: How Canada's health care system is financed.* Ottawa: Canadian Institute for Health Information.

———. 2005b. *Hospital trends in Canada.* Ottawa: Canadian Institute for Health Information.

———. 2007. *Supply, distribution and migration of Canadian physicians, 2007.* Ottawa: Canadian Institute for Health Information.

———. 2008. *National health expenditure trends, 1975–2008.* Ottawa: Canadian Institute for Health Information.

———. 2009a. *Drug expenditure in Canada, 1985–2008.* Ottawa: Canadian Institute for Health Information.

———. 2009b. *Experiences with primary care in Canada.* Ottawa: Canadian Institute for Health Information.

———. 2009c. *Surgical volume trends: Within and beyond wait time priority areas.* Ottawa: Canadian Institute for Health Information.

———. 2009d. *Wait times tables—A comparison by province, 2009.* Ottawa: Canadian Institute for Health Information.

Chan, B. 2002. *From perceived surplus to perceived shortage: What happened to Canada's physician workforce in the 1990s?* Ottawa: Canadian Institute for Health Information.

Crossley, T., J. Hurley, and S.-H. Jeon. 2009. Physician labour supply in Canada: A cohort analysis. *Health Economics* 18(4):437–56.

Exter, A., R. Hermans, M. Dosljak, and R. Busse. 2004. *Health care systems in transition: Netherlands.* Copenhagen: WHO Regional Office for Europe on behalf of the European Observatory on Health Systems and Policies.

Flood C., and T. Archibald. 2001. The illegality of private health care in Canada. *Canadian Medical Association Journal* 164(6):825–30.

Government of Canada. 1984. *Canada Health Act.*

Government of Canada IaNAC. 2009. *Life expectancy at birth, basic departmental data, 2001.* Ottawa: Government of Canada. Available at: http://www.hc-sc.gc.ca/fniah-spnia/diseases-maladies/2005-01_health-sante_indicat-eng.php#life_expect. Accessed September 25, 2009.

Health Canada. 2006. *10-year plan to strengthen health care.* Available at: http://www.hc-sc.gc.ca/hcs-sss/delivery-prestation/fptcollab/2004-fmm-rpm/index-eng.php. Accessed September 27, 2009.

———. 2007. *Canada Health Act—annual report for 2006–2007.* Ottawa: Health Canada.

———. 2009. Canada's health system (Medicare): The Canada Health Act (CHA). http://www.hc-sc.gc.ca/hcs-sss/medi-assur/cha-lcs/index-eng.php. Accessed September 21, 2009.

Health Council of Canada. 2009. *Value for money: Making Canadian health care stronger.* Toronto: Health Council of Canada.

Hurley, J., S. Birch, and J. Eyles. 1995. Geographically-decentralized planning and management in health care: Some information issues and their implications for efficiency. *Social Science and Medicine* 41(1):3–11.

Hurley, J., and G. E. Guindon. 2010 (forthcoming). Private insurance in Canada. In *Private health insurance and medical savings accounts: History, politics and performance,* S. Thomson, E. Mossialos, and R. G. Evans (eds.). Cambridge: Cambridge University Press.

Marchildon, G. 2005. *Health system in transition: Canada.* Copenhagen: WHO on behalf of the European Observatory on Health Systems and Policies.

OECD. 2009. *OECD health data 2009.* Paris: OECD.

Schoen, C., et al. 2007. Toward higher-performance health systems: Adults' health care experiences in seven countries, 2007. *Health Affairs.* Web Exclusive (October 31, 2007).

Stabile, M. 2001. Private insurance subsidies and public health care markets: Evidence from Canada. *Canadian Journal of Economics,* 34(4):921–42.

Statistics Canada. 2009a. *Comparable health indicators—Canada, provinces and territories.* Catalogue 82–401, Table 36b-HLT, accessed at http://www.statcan.gc.ca/pub/82–401-x/2002000/t/pdf/4227729-eng.pdf. September 26, 2009.

———. 2009b. *Life expectancy, abridged life table, at birth and at age 65, by sex, Canada, provinces and territories, annual (years).* Cansim Table 102–0511.

Tjepkema, M. 2005. *Adult obesity in Canada: Measured height and weight.* Ottawa: Statistics Canada, No 82–620-MWE2005001.

Essential Economic Concepts

INTRODUCTION

For an economist, life is but a series of decisions about how to allocate resources. The essential features of your decision about whether to read this book or watch TV are very similar to a hospital's decision whether to expand operating room time or the hours of its out-patient clinic, or a government's decision whether to invest additional resources in highways or in health care. Each decision involves a choice about how to allocate scarce real resources—your time, energy, and abilities; the hospital's nurses, physicians, and equipment; society's workers, materials, and machines.

People are assumed to be purposeful when making such decisions—they have a goal and they systematically try to achieve that goal through the choices they make. In any situation, a person's choice options are restricted by the limited resources available. If we all had an infinite amount of time, energy, and ability, and the earth had infinite resources, there would be no economic problem: we could all literally do and have everything. But resources are scarce, and we face tradeoffs on how to use those limited resources.

Economics is simply a formal way to analyze choices—from the most mundane, such as what cereal to eat for breakfast, to some of the most important choices that shape society, such as how to organize and finance the health care system. Economics is the study of how individuals and societies allocate scarce productive resources among competing uses and distribute the products for these uses among members of society. Every society must answer three fundamental, inter-related economic questions about how it uses its resources:

- How much of each possible good and service should society produce?
- How should it produce those goods and services?
- How should those goods and services be distributed among members of society?

Answering these three questions raises two immediate issues. First, *how can society know which allocation of its resources is best?* Economics emphasizes two criteria for this judgment: efficiency and equity. One allocation is preferred to another if, other things equal, it uses resources more efficiently or is judged to be more equitable. Deciding which allocation is preferred is more complicated when more efficiency can be gained only with a sacrifice of equity (or vice versa); but still, equity and efficiency remain the two principal criteria. Because they play such a central role in economic analysis, we examine them in detail in Chapter 2.

Second, *what allocation policies, processes, and mechanisms will enable society to achieve its most desired allocation?* Throughout history, societies have chosen very different ways of allocating resources. The former communist countries of the Soviet Union used central planning, in which government officials decided how much of each good was to be produced, how it would be produced, and, to a large extent, who got what in society. Other societies, especially those from antiquity, have relied heavily on religious principles and tradition.

Most societies today use market systems. A market is an institutional setting in which individuals and organizations voluntarily exchange goods and services at prices determined by market forces. Although some form of exchange exists in all societies, a market system is distinctive in the extent to which market forces determine resource allocation. In a market system, market forces determine what is produced, how it is produced, who works in what jobs, who gets what goods and services, the prices of goods and services, and so forth. Market-based allocation commands a central place in present-day economics. Markets, however, are only one way to allocate resources. In principle, market-based mechanisms are no more privileged than are central planning, religious-based principles, or tradition. Each must be assessed against the criteria of efficiency and equity. When markets don't work well, society often uses these other methods.[1]

Resolving these fundamental economic questions requires two distinct types of economic analysis. Policy-makers must be able to predict accurately what will happen when society implements different policies and programs. A health policy-maker designing a policy to increase the proportion of adults in the population tested regularly for colon cancer, for example, must predict how many new people will obtain a colonoscopy when the government subsidizes its price. Economic analysis that predicts the response to such a price subsidy is called **positive economics**: it uses economic models to describe and predict observable outcomes. It answers questions about what is or what will be. But simply knowing what will happen is not enough. The policy-maker needs to know if the well-being of members of society is better with the subsidy policy than without the policy.

Economic analysis that assesses the goodness or desirability of the policy outcomes is called **normative economics**. Normative economic analysis tries to answer the question, what should we do? For example, should we use our resources to subsidize the cost of a colonoscopy to increase the detection and treatment of colon cancer or to subsidize the cost of flu shots among elderly? Doing this requires criteria by which to judge what is to be preferred; and as noted, normative economics applies the criteria of efficiency and equity. Normative economics inherently and unavoidably rests on ethical assumptions regarding, for instance, what constitutes well-being or how society should value increases in the overall amount of well-being versus a more equal distribution of well-being among members of society. Indeed, normative economics is simply a form of social ethics.

positive economics
Analysis that attempts to describe and predict accurately economic phenomenon. It attempts to determine what is, or what will be.

normative economics
Analysis that attempts to identify what policies, actions, or outcomes are desirable from an economic perspective. It attempts to determine what society should do.

---

[1] Even in market economies, much allocation (e.g., within households and within most firms) is accomplished through non-market mechanisms.

As we will see, the ethical underpinnings of the standard way economists conduct normative economics are a source of considerable controversy in the health sector. The controversy arises because the ethical assumptions economists use to judge the appropriate distribution of automobiles, CD players, and other consumer goods may be quite different from the ethical assumptions people view as appropriate for judging allocations of health care resources.

The three chapters in Part One focus on concepts central to the economic analysis of policies, practices, and resource allocations. Chapter 2 examines the twin criteria of efficiency and equity, which apply in all societies regardless of the mechanisms used to allocate resources. Chapter 3 examines the operation of markets and the characteristics of market-based allocations, since markets play such a central role in modern economies and the role of markets in health care is hotly debated. Chapter 4 presents the methods economists use to evaluate potential programs and policies governments can undertake when markets do not function well.

By the end of Part One, you should have the foundation necessary to understand economic concepts essential for analyzing the health sector. Although health examples are used in these chapters, many non-health examples are used as well, especially in Chapter 3. This is done for two reasons. Many of the economic concepts can be conveyed most easily with non-health examples. Furthermore, a recurring question in health economics is how well the standard economic model applies to the health sector. It is, therefore, helpful to first introduce the concepts with non-health applications and then, when we subsequently analyze specific health economic questions, identify any wrinkles and caveats necessary to use the concepts in the health sector.

Efficiency and Equity

Learning Objectives

After studying this chapter, you will understand

LO1   The three concepts of efficiency in economics: technical efficiency, cost-effectiveness efficiency, and allocative efficiency

LO2   The two types of equity analysis: distributional equity and procedural equity

LO3   Fundamental aspects of the relationship between efficiency and equity in economics

---

resources
Raw materials such as minerals, wood, oil, and other natural resources; physical capital such as machines; human labour; and intellectual capital in the form of knowledge.

The essential economic question is this: how should society allocate its scarce resources? **Resources** include *raw materials* such as minerals, wood, oil, and other natural resources; *physical capital* such as machines; *human labour*; and *intellectual capital* in the form of knowledge. The phrase "resource allocation" is economic shorthand for a particular way in which society as a whole, or households and organizations within it, use available resources.

Society, for example, could conduct childhood immunizations many different ways, some of which rely primarily on nurse practitioners and others which rely primarily on physicians. Each represents a different allocation of resources to produce immunizations. A society that views health care as a commodity no different from cars, books, TVs, and other consumer goods will allocate and distribute health care resources differently from a society which views access to health care as a right and which publicly subsidizes its use by low-income individuals. Each resulting pattern of health care consumption represents a different "resource allocation."

"Resources" does not include money: money itself is not a resource. Money, however, does provide command over resources—it allows the purchase of real resources—and, under certain conditions, it provides a convenient metric by which to measure an amount of resources. The pivotal consideration in the relation between money and real resources is price. The expenditure required to obtain a given amount of resources is equal to the product of the price of each resource (P) and the quantity of each resource purchased (Q) (i.e., Expenditures = P × Q). If prices increase, a given monetary budget will command fewer real resources. A budget of $100 million will allow a ministry of health to purchase 4 million physician visits when the price is $25.00 per visit but only 2 million when the price is $50.00. If, after the price increase, the ministry wanted to devote the same amount of real physician resources to improving health, it would have to increase its budget to $200 million.

The distinction between money and real resources can be important, for instance, when comparing health systems across countries whose prices differ. Suppose we wanted

TABLE 2.1

A Comparison of Health Care Spending and Health Care Utilization in Selected OECD Countries, 2006
Comparing differences across countries in health care spending and health care utilization highlights the distinction between monetary measures of activity and real levels of activity and resources. The U.S. and Switzerland are the highest-spending countries, but their citizens receive fewer physician and hospital services than do citizens of other countries. The reason for this discrepancy is prices, which are higher in the U.S. and Switzerland. Although they spend more, they do not necessarily get more.

Source: OECD Health Data (2008); [a]Data from 2005; [b]Data from 2004.

	Total Health Care Spending (per capita, $U.S.)	Total Health Care Spending (% of GDP)	Physician Visits (per capita)	Acute Care Hospital Days (per capita)
Australia	3,336	8.7	6.1	1.0[a]
Canada	3,920	10.0	5.9[a]	0.9[a]
France	3,937	11.0	6.4	1.0
Germany	3,718	10.6	7.0[b]	1.7
Switzerland	5,877	11.3	3.4	1.1
United Kingdom	3,332	8.4	5.1	0.9
United States	6,714	15.3	4.0[a]	0.7

to understand international differences in the resources countries devote to health care. Table 2.1 lists spending on health care (converted into a common dollar measure) and real resource commitments as measured by actual use of services for selected OECD countries. U.S. and Swiss citizens spend more on health care than citizens of other countries but receive fewer real services. The U.S., for example, spent $6714 per person while Canada spent $3920 per person. Yet U.S. residents received fewer physician and hospital services: U.S. citizens averaged 4.0 physician visits per year while Canadians averaged of 5.9, and U.S. citizens averaged 0.7 days in hospital per year while Canadians averaged 0.9. These comparisons, though admittedly incomplete—they include only two types of services and do not adjust for possible quality differences or the amount of care delivered during a visit—suggest that, although non-Americans spend less on average than Americans, these countries devote more real resources to health care than does the U.S., and the citizens of those countries may have better access to care. The discrepancy between spending comparisons and actual utilization arises because of differences in prices: input prices such as physician fees and the prices of drugs and medical equipment are all higher in the U.S., leading Americans to spend more while committing fewer resources and receiving fewer real services (Anderson et al. 2003).

Because resources are limited, choosing to use a resource for one purpose precludes using it for another. So the true cost of using a resource for one purpose is the benefits given up by not using it for another possible purpose. The true cost of a movie is not the ticket price, but the lost opportunity to see a basketball game or to study to improve grades. The true cost of expanding in-patient hospital capacity is the increase in health and well-being that could have been achieved had those same resources been used to create a community clinic or to build a school.

opportunity cost
The cost of using a resource for one purpose is the benefits forgone from the highest-valued alternative use.

Economists call this the **opportunity cost**: the opportunity cost of using a resource for one purpose is the benefits forgone from the highest-valued alternative use. Opportunity cost is one of the most fundamental of economic concepts, essential for understanding the economic way of thinking. It emphasizes that the true social cost of an action or a policy is not the associated financial expenditures; rather, the social cost is the benefits which society gives up by not using those resources in an alternative way. Many activities that incur no financial cost still, in fact, impose a substantial economic cost.

2.1   EFFICIENCY

efficiency
Getting as much as is possible from scarce resources.

To make the best use of its limited resources, society should use resources for an activity only if the benefits generated by the activity are larger than the opportunity cost. This insight leads directly to the concept of **efficiency**, one of the two key criteria by which economists judge the desirability of alternative resource allocations. Efficiency in its essence is about getting as much as possible from scarce resources.

Economists distinguish three types of efficiency. The first two pertain to the production of goods and services and can be stated informally this way: (1) do not waste resources when producing a good (technical efficiency); and (2) produce each good using the lowest-cost mix of resources (cost-effectiveness efficiency). The third calls for society to produce the goods and services that people value the most, and to distribute them among members of society in accord with the value that individuals place on them (allocative efficiency).

2.1.1   Efficiency in Production

production
The process whereby an individual or organization transforms inputs into outputs.

production function
The relationship that describes the maximum amount of output that can be produced from a given set of inputs using currently available technologies.

Production is the process whereby an individual or organization transforms inputs—raw materials, labour, intermediate goods such as steel—into outputs—cars, DVDs, haircuts, physician visits, university courses. The amount of output produced depends on the technology available and the quantity and quality of the inputs. This relationship between inputs and outputs is summarized by the **production function**. The production function indicates the maximum amount of output that can be produced from a given set of inputs using currently available technologies. In general, there are many ways to produce a good. A construction company, for example, can produce houses using many workers with hand tools, a small number of workers with power tools, or any combination in between. A physician can treat a depressed individual using primarily drugs (pharmacotherapy) supplemented with small amounts of cognitive-behavioural therapy, or using an intensive regime of cognitive-behavioural therapy supplemented with some drug therapy.

Technical Efficiency

technical efficiency
Producing the maximum possible amount of output from the inputs used, given the chosen production method.

Technical efficiency requires that, whatever method is chosen, the producer waste no resources during production. All the inputs must be used to their maximum potential productivity. In the case of houses, as long as the number of workers matches the number of tools (so that no tools are unused and no workers are idle), the low-tech way of building a house can be just as technically efficient as the high-tech, capital-intensive method.

A technically efficient process maximizes output for the given inputs, conditional on the chosen production technology. Because there are many alternative ways to produce a good without wasting resources, however, the criterion of technical efficiency does not identify a single efficient production method. The easiest way to assess if a production method is

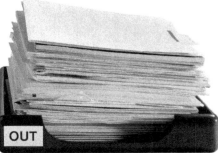

TABLE 2.2

Technical Efficiency and Input Use Among Programs to Treat 100 Depressed Individuals

To be technically efficient, a production process must not waste resources. Among these four programs to treat clinical depression, Program C is not technically efficient because Program B can produce the same output (100 successfully treated individuals) with the same number of hours of cognitive therapy but fewer doses of drugs (250 vs. 300). Hence, Program C wastes drugs, making it technically inefficient.

	Hours of Cognitive-Behavioural Therapy	Daily Doses of Drug Therapy
Program A	2500	200
Program B	1500	250
Program C	1500	300
Program D	500	600

Note: All data are hypothetical. Assumes all programs are equally effective.

technically efficient is to ask: Is it possible to get more output with the same inputs? Or, its converse: Is it possible to get the same output with fewer inputs? If the answer to either is yes, then production is not technically efficient.

Table 2.2 illustrates this in reference to alternative programs for treating one hundred individuals suffering from depression. Programs A, B, and D are all technically efficient. Program C is technically inefficient because Program B achieves the same outcome using less drug therapy and the same amount of cognitive-behavioural therapy. In real-world efficiency analyses, it is usually easier to identify technically inefficient production methods—all that is required is that we observe another method that uses less of one input and no more of other inputs. It is more difficult to identify definitively those methods that are technically efficient (after all, it is possible that even most efficient producers observed are still inefficient relative to an as-yet-unattained ideal).

Cost-Effectiveness Efficiency

cost-effectiveness efficiency

Producing a good using the least-cost method of production from among all technically efficient methods.

Is there any reason for choosing one of the technically efficient methods over all others? Yes. **Cost-effectiveness efficiency** requires that, among all technically efficient methods, the lowest-cost production method is chosen. Cost-effectiveness efficiency takes account of the relative prices of the various inputs. Differences in relative prices are one reason why, even though they have access to the same technology, it is more efficient for developing countries (where labour is cheap and machinery is expensive) to produce houses, health care, and other goods using labour-intensive production methods, while it is more efficient for industrialized countries (where labour is expensive and machinery relatively cheap) to use capital-intensive production methods. In any given setting, cost-effectiveness efficiency identifies the single least-cost method of production from among the set of technically efficient methods.

Table 2.3 adds prices to the previous example of alternative programs to treat depression. Given the relative prices of therapist time ($120 per hour) and the drugs ($20 per daily dose), Program D is the cost-effective method for treating depression. Note that although only a single method is cost-effective in any given setting, the cost-effective method can differ across settings when prices differ.

The Production Possibilities Frontier

production possibilities frontier

A graph that represents the maximum combinations of two goods that society can produce given its available resources and production technologies.

What amounts of alternative goods can a society produce, given its available resources? The essential ideas required to answer this can be illustrated with an example based on a simple society that produces only two goods: health care and houses.[1] The **production possibilities frontier** (PPF) identifies those combinations of health care and houses that

---

[1] This is, of course, a highly unrealistic society. The concepts illustrated with this simple example, however, translate into settings with millions of goods and services. Keeping it simple allows us to use diagrams to illustrate important aspects of the analysis.

TABLE 2.3
Cost-Effectiveness Among Programs to Treat 100 Depressed Individuals
Cost-effectiveness requires that a good or service be produced in the least-cost manner. Given the relative prices of an hour of cognitive therapy and a dose of anti-depressant medication, Program D, which relies most heavily on relatively inexpensive drug therapy, is the cost-effective treatment program.

		Hours of Cognitive-Behavioural Therapy	Daily Doses of Drug Therapy	Total Cost of Program
Cost of hour CBT	$120			
Cost of Daily Dose	$20			
Program A		2500	200	$304,000
Program B		1500	250	$185,000
Program C		1500	300	$186,000
Program D		500	600	$72,000

Note: All data are hypothetical. Assumes all programs are equally effective.

the society can produce if it uses its resources in a technically and cost-effectively efficient manner (Figure 2.1). All points on the production possibilities frontier (e.g., A, B, C, D, E) represent technically efficient production. Points inside the curve (e.g., point F) represent technically inefficient production: it is possible to have more of one output without giving up any of the other by moving to point B, or to have more of both by moving to a point on the curve between B and C. A country might be inside the production possibilities frontier either because some of its resources are idle (e.g., if there is unemployment) or there is a misallocation of resources so that they are not being put to their most productive use (e.g., carpenters have too many screwdrivers and not enough hammers while electricians have too many hammers and not enough screwdrivers). Points outside the production possibilities frontier, such as point G, are not feasible given current technology.

Figure 2.1 also illustrates the concept of opportunity cost. To produce more physician visits, a country would have to reduce its production of houses. At point A, increasing physician visits by 1000 costs 50 houses (taking society to point B). At point D, however, the opportunity cost of 1000 physician visits is 150 houses (taking society to point E).

Why does the opportunity cost increase? At point A, society produces mostly houses, and some of those involved in home construction are not very good at it; however, they would make quite good doctors. To produce additional physician visits, such individuals would be the first shifted from house construction to health care. Because these workers are poor construction workers but good doctors, the opportunity cost of the health care is low. At point D, the opposite is true. Now to produce additional physician visits society must shift workers who are good at house construction and poor at producing health care. So the opportunity costs of additional health care rises as society moves down the frontier from left to right, just as the opportunity cost of houses rises as society moves up the frontier from right to left.

2.1.2 Efficiency in Allocation

allocative efficiency
Using limited resources to produce and distribute goods and services in accord with the value individuals place on those goods and services.

Producing goods in an efficient manner is not sufficient to attain overall efficiency in an economy. Even if a good is produced efficiently, the resources used to produce it are wasted if the good is not valued by anyone. The third economic notion of efficiency—**allocative efficiency**—requires that society produce and distribute goods and services in accord with the value that individuals place on those goods and services.

Identifying an allocatively efficient resource distribution requires that one define what constitutes a source of value, or benefit. Economics generally defines benefit in terms of people's own preferences. People are assumed to have preferences for everything from the trivial (do you prefer vanilla or chocolate ice cream?) to the profound (if you have cancer, do

FIGURE 2.1

Production Possibilities Frontier for Health Care and Houses

The production possibilities frontier (PPF) represents the maximum amount of goods and services a society can produce given its limited resources. In this simple example, a society produces only houses and health care. If it devotes all of its resources to housing production, it can make 1000 houses; if it devotes all of its resources to health care, it can produce 11,000 physician visits. The PPF that connects these two points represents different possible combinations of houses and health care if all resources are used efficiently. Points inside the PPF (e.g., point F) imply that some resources are not being used efficiently; points outside (e.g., point G) are not possible given the society's technology and resources.

utility

The subjective satisfaction an individual derives from consuming a good or undertaking an activity.

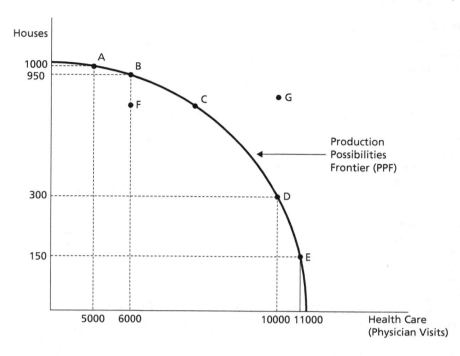

you prefer to live 6 more months free from the negative side effects of treatment or 12 more months with negative side effects?). A person's preferences regarding goods and services are summarized by his or her utility function.[2] **Utility** is, for practical purposes, shorthand for "what people care about." Think of it as the subjective satisfaction an individual derives from consuming a good or undertaking an activity. The level of utility, therefore, is a measure of the benefit derived from a particular resource allocation. Economists sometimes also call a person's level of utility their level of "welfare." The utility, or welfare, of people who prefer chocolate ice cream is higher under an allocation in which they get a lot of chocolate ice cream and a little vanilla than it is under an allocation in which they get a lot of vanilla but little chocolate.

Illustrating allocative efficiency requires that we extend our simple two-good society to include two individuals, Alpha (α) and Beta (β), each of whom has preferences regarding health care and housing. For each feasible combination of houses and health care in this society (i.e., each point on the production possibilities frontier in Figure 2.1), we can determine how much utility each person would obtain under all possible ways to divide the amounts of the two goods between the two individuals.

Starting at point B in Figure 2.1, for example, determine all the ways that 950 units of housing and 6000 physician visits could be divided between Alpha and Beta, and the corresponding levels of utility attained by each individual under each division. Now draw the line that represents the combination of Alpha's and Beta's utilities associated with each division of the housing and physician visits between them (see Figure 2.2). This line is the utility possibilities frontier associated with the production of 950 units of housing and 6000 physician visits. Continue to do this for all other points on the production possibilities frontier, drawing each utility possibility frontier on the same graph. Once this is done,

---

[2] Most of the discussion will emphasize preferences with respect to common goods and services. But the utility function can include things besides goods and services, such as a walk in the woods, a friendly conversation, or intellectual stimulation.

FIGURE 2.2

The Grand Utility Possibilities Frontier Between Alpha and Beta

The Grand Utility Possibilities Frontier (GUPF) represents different levels of utility members of society can attain given the different combinations of goods that can be produced and the preferences members of society have for those goods. In this simple society with only two individuals (α, β), point G represents an allocation in which society produces only those goods most preferred by β and distributes those goods to β, leaving α with the lowest level of utility. Point I represents a situation in which society produces and distributes goods in a way that the two individuals are equally well off (as measured by the level of utility each attains). Point K represents a situation in which either production is inefficient or the distribution of the goods between the two individuals could be changed to make both individuals better off.

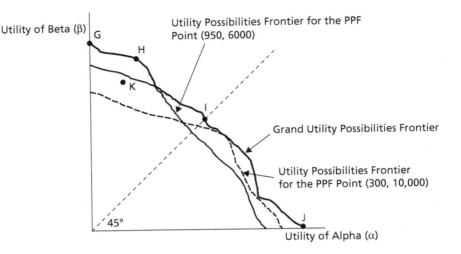

Pareto Criterion

Defines an allocation of resources as allocatively efficient if it is impossible to reallocate the resources so as to make at least one person better off without making someone else worse off.

among the full set of utility possibility frontiers, find all the points that are furthest from the origin (i.e., trace the outer envelope of all the utility possibility frontiers). The resulting line is called the grand utility possibilities frontier for Alpha and Beta as in Figure 2.2. This grand utility possibilities frontier tells us all the combinations of utility that the two individuals can attain given all feasible combinations of goods that can be produced and all the feasible ways to divide those goods between the two individuals.

The Pareto Criterion

We have defined utility as our measure of benefit, and identified all possible combinations of utility among members of society given the available resources, technology, and preferences. Now, how do we decide which allocations are allocatively efficient? The criterion that dominates conceptual economics is the **Pareto Criterion**. The Pareto Criterion declares an allocation to be allocatively efficient if it is impossible to reallocate resources in a way that makes at least one person better off without making someone else worse off. The Pareto Criterion is motivated by the view that society should reallocate resources if it is possible to improve one person's well-being without lowering anyone else's. By the Pareto Criterion, all points on the grand utility possibilities frontier are allocatively efficient. Points inside the grand utility possibilities frontier, such as point K in Figure 2.2, are not allocatively efficient because it is possible to make both individuals better off by moving to the frontier, such as point H. Society should stop reallocating resources at the point where it is no longer possible to make at least one person better off without harming another.

Though the Pareto Criterion is widely used in conceptual economic modelling, it suffers from two severe limitations in applied economics. First, the Pareto Criterion does not identify a single allocation as best—an infinite number of allocations are allocatively efficient—so a preferred allocation still must be chosen from among all those that satisfy the Pareto Criterion. Second, almost no public policies that reallocate resources pass the Pareto test because such policies inevitably hurt at least one group in society while benefiting another (e.g., new housing benefits those in substandard housing but harms those who value open space; expanding home health care may reduce resources to support in-patient care). Strictly applied, the Pareto Criterion would lead to policy paralysis.

potential Pareto Criterion
Defines a reallocation of resources as allocatively efficient if the gains to the winners are sufficiently large that the winners could compensate the losers and still be better off. The criterion does not require that the winners actually compensate the losers; for this reason, it is sometimes called the hypothetical compensation criterion.

In response to these shortcomings, economists developed the **potential Pareto Criterion**. The potential Pareto Criterion holds that if the gains to the winners under a reallocation are sufficiently large that the winners could compensate the losers and still be better off, then even if no compensation is actually paid, the policy is deemed allocatively efficient. The potential Pareto Criterion seeks to allocate resources to maximize net benefit to society, where net benefit is defined as total benefits minus total costs, and costs include both production costs and the welfare losses to those who are harmed by a policy. By this criterion, only a single point on the utility possibilities frontier is allocatively efficient—point H in this case, which maximizes the sum of Alpha and Beta's utility. Point H is the single point on the utility possibilities frontier that satisfies both the Pareto Criterion and the potential Pareto Criterion.

Which point on the utility possibilities frontier is optimal for society? If society cares about more than just efficiency, it is not possible to make such judgments with the tools we have developed thus far. Even though point H is efficient by all the criteria we have discussed, some might judge the allocation inequitable since Beta's utility is considerably higher than Alpha's. Such judgments therefore require integration of equity criteria, which we discuss below. Before discussing equity, however, it would be useful to summarize key principles shared by these three efficiency concepts.

2.1.3 Principles Shared by All Three Efficiency Concepts

Each efficiency concept applies to a different aspect of society's challenge in allocating its resources, but all three reflect common underlying principles.

Efficiency is a purely instrumental concept: it concerns the means by which a stated objective is attained. Efficiency is meaningful only when the desired objective is explicit. The objective for technical efficiency and cost-effectiveness efficiency is the production of a good, so these efficiency criteria apply purely to the methods, or the means, by which the good is produced. The objective of allocative efficiency is social benefit. The concept of allocative efficiency itself, however, says nothing about what benefits should count or how those benefits should be measured. Whenever someone claims that a particular policy or activity is efficient, it is good practice to ask, "Efficient for obtaining what objective?"

All three concepts of efficiency rest on the concept of optimizing behaviour: get the most out of society's resources. Technical and cost-effectiveness efficiency demand that we maximize the output obtained from a given set of inputs. Allocative efficiency demands that we maximize benefits to society under the Pareto Criterion—in the sense that we can't reallocate to make someone better off without hurting someone else—or under the potential Pareto Criterion—in the literal sense that net benefits have been maximized.

marginal analysis
A method of analysis that focuses on the effects of doing just a little bit more or a little bit less than the baseline level of an activity.

Maximizing behaviour depends on marginal analysis. **Marginal analysis** identifies the optimal level of a good or activity by continually asking the following question: what happens if we do something just a little bit more or just a little bit less? On a daily basis, for example, you usually do not ask whether you should study at all, but whether you should study for an extra hour; within your study time, you ask whether you should study health economics for another hour or switch to biology. You think incrementally or, in economic language, at the margin.

The same holds true for health and public policy problems. A health care planner must assess the effects of adding to or removing from the existing number of hospital beds in a region; the Minister of Finance must decide whether, at the margin, to provide additional resources to health care or to education. In each case, we try to determine the additional benefit produced by the one use (additional hour of studying health economics, the

The importance of marginal analysis is well illustrated by a famous example regarding screening for colon cancer (Neuhauser and Lewicki 1975). Colon cancer is asymptomatic in its early stages, but early detection can dramatically improve outcomes. A test called the Guaiac Test can detect colon cancer in its pre-symptomatic stage, but the test is not perfect. In some cases, the test result is negative even though the cancer is present (a false negative result); in others, it is positive even though there is no cancer (a false positive result). In an effort to maximize the chance of detecting cancer, in the early 1970s, the American Cancer Society recommended that, when screening for colon cancer, doctors should carry out six Guaiac tests on a person. From an economic perspective, a key question is whether this recommendation represents a good investment of scarce health care resources to improve population health. Is six the optimal number of tests?

To investigate this, Newhauser and Lewicki simulated the effects of a screening program in a population of 10,000 individuals, 72 of whom had colon cancer (which reflected the known rate of cancer at the time).

Each time the test is performed, it correctly identifies 91.67 percent of the cancer cases. Therefore, if we screened all 10,000 people once, we would expect to detect 65.9469 of the 72 cases (Table B2.1). The cost of performing all the necessary testing is $77,511 for the first round. If a second round of tests is conducted on all those whose first test was negative, the total number of cases detected will increase to 71.4424. Total costs rise to $107,690. Table B2.1(a) lists the results for each round of testing up to the sixth. Six tests will detect effectively all the cases of cancer (71.9420) at a still reasonable cost of $2451 cost per case detected.

This analysis, however, is based on the average cost per case, not the marginal cost per case. Table B2.1(b) re-analyzes the same data in terms of the marginal cost per case detected by each additional round of testing. Compared to no testing, the first round of tests would detect 65.9469 previously undetected cases at a marginal cost of $1175 per case (i.e., $77,511/65.9469 = $1175).

The second round of testing detects only an additional 5.496 cases, for a marginal cost of $5492 per additional case (i.e., $30,179/5.4955). After only two rounds, we have detected 71 of the 72 cases of cancer in the population. The marginal benefits of additional rounds of testing, therefore, become increasingly small though the additional costs of each round do not fall nearly as rapidly.

By the sixth round, we would expect the marginal cost per case detected to have risen to over $47 million. Unquestionably, by using $47 million dollars in another way, we could produce greater health benefit than the detection of a single case of cancer. Marginal analysis makes clear that the optimal number of tests is less than six, and is more likely two or three.

(Continued)

additional hospital beds, and the additional health care) against the associated opportunity cost (lower grades in biology, less primary care, reduced resources for education). Marginal analysis is central to economic analysis because the total amount of benefit associated with an activity is maximized when the activity is undertaken to the point at which the marginal benefit just equals the marginal cost.

Lastly, although economic discussions of efficiency tend to emphasize the technical conditions associated with efficiency criteria, it is important to remember that efficiency as used in economics is an ethical criterion. Economists use efficiency normatively to judge the desirability of an allocation of resources.[3] Efficiency as conventionally defined, for

[3] Assessing efficiency requires the use of highly technical methods, including purely positive economic analysis, to establish the consequences of alternative resource allocations, but such methods are distinct from the principles by which an efficient allocation is defined.

TABLE B2.1 MARGINAL ANALYSIS AND SCREENING FOR COLON CANCER

(a) Analysis of Screening Program Based on Average Costs

Number of Tests	Total Number of Cases Detected	Total Costs Associated with Tests ($)	Average Cost per Case Detected ($)
1	65.9469	77,511	1,175
2	71.4424	107,690	1,507
3	71.9003	130,199	1,810
4	71.9385	148,116	2,059
5	71.9417	163,141	2,268
6	71.9420	176,331	2,451

(b) Analysis of Screening Program Based on Marginal Costs

Number of Tests	Total Number of Cases Detected	Marginal Number of Cases Detected	Total Costs Associated with Tests ($)	Marginal Cost of Testing Round ($)	Average Cost per Case Detected ($)	Marginal Cost per Case Detected ($)
1	65.9469	65.9469	77,511	77,511	1,175	1,175
2	71.4424	5.4955	107,690	30,179	1,507	5,492
3	71.9003	0.4579	130,199	22,509	1,810	49,150
4	71.9385	0.0382	148,116	17,917	2,059	469,534
5	71.9417	0.0032	163,141	15,025	2,268	4,724,695
6	71.9420	0.0003	176,331	13,190	2,451	47,107,214

Source for Box and Table B2.1 (a) and (b): Data are taken from the publication Neuhauser D., Lewicki, A. M. 1975. What Do We Gain From The Sixth Stool GUAIAC. *The New England Journal of Medicine*. 293(5):226–28.

instance, rests on the ethical principle that satisfying preferences is the relevant measure of value to society. The vast majority of economists accept this principle as non-controversial, especially when used to judge the allocation of consumer goods and services. But even among economists, the strength of this consensus breaks down in other contexts, such as when analyzing health care. This book therefore highlights the ethical principles associated with the criterion of efficiency.

2.2   EQUITY

equity
A concern for fairness.

The second key criterion economists use to judge the desirability of alternative allocations of resources is equity. **Equity** concerns fairness. Equity analysis assesses whether a particular allocation of resources is fair. Two key types of equity are distributional equity and procedural equity.

distributional equity
A situation in which the distribution of a good (e.g., income, health care) or a burden (e.g., tax payments) among members of society is judged to be fair.

Distributional equity asks if the distribution of the good in question is fair. An analysis of distributional equity must define the good of concern (what is the thing we want to allocate fairly?), define what constitutes a fair distribution of the good (e.g., should it be an equal distribution?), and compare the amount of the good each member of society has with the characteristics of each individual to see if the actual distribution matches the fair distribution. For example, distributional equity in the health care sector is commonly defined as allocation according to need. Assessing distributional equity in the use of health care, therefore, requires comparing the extent to which variation in health care utilization among members of society corresponds to variation in need for health care among members of society.

procedural equity
A situation in which the process of distributing a good (e.g., income, health care) or a burden (e.g., tax payments) among members of society is judged to be fair.

Procedural equity, in contrast, shifts focus from the actual distribution of a good to the process by which a good is allocated. It asks if the process is fair. A number of individuals might benefit from an organ that has become available for transplantation. The organ, however, can't be divided among them, so procedural equity concerns the fairness of the process by which it is decided who gets the organ.

Equity judgments are often contentious because different individuals have different ideas as to what constitutes a fair distribution or process, and these ideas differ across goods and settings. A fair distribution of health care differs from a fair distribution of ice cream cones. Amid this diversity, however, widely accepted theories of equity share many common elements. This section does not advocate for any single definition of equity, but focuses on key elements in economic approaches to equity, and to distributional equity in particular.

2.2.1 Distributional Equity

Assessing distributional equity requires three types of information: agreement regarding the thing (or "good") whose distribution is of equity concern; the characteristic of individuals (e.g., income, health status) judged relevant to assessing a fair distribution of the good; and a definition of how the distribution of that characteristic among individuals corresponds to a fair distribution of the good among individuals (who should get more and who less?).

The notion of a "good" in equity analysis is very broad, going well beyond physical goods that can be exchanged. The "good" of concern for distributional equity in the health care sector might be health care itself, access to health care, health, or the burden of paying for health care. Many equity debates arise from differing judgments regarding the good that society should distribute fairly. An analysis of distributional equity must state explicitly the good that is of concern.

The characteristic relevant to a fair distribution is the feature that determines how much of the good a person (or household or organization) should get under a fair distribution. Under the equity principle of "allocation according to need," for example, the relevant individual characteristic for assessing distributional equity in health care utilization would be a person's need for care. Under the equity principle of "payment according to ability to pay," the individual characteristic relevant for assessing distributional equity in health care finance would be a person's income or wealth. The specific characteristic of interest will differ depending on the good whose distribution is being analyzed.

horizontal equity
A type of distributional equity whereby those who are equal with respect to an equity-relevant characteristic (e.g., income, need) are treated equally.

The last element in an analysis of distributional equity assesses how the distribution of the good in the population should correspond to the distribution of the individual characteristic in the population. Two widely used criteria are horizontal equity and vertical equity. **Horizontal equity** requires that individuals who are equal with respect to their equity-relevant characteristic receive equal amounts of the good: treat equals equally. Under the principle of "allocation according to need," horizontal equity demands that those in equal need utilize equal amounts of health care; if the relevant health care financing principle is "payment according to ability-to-pay," horizontal equity demands that two individuals with equal ability-to-pay contribute equally to finance health care.

vertical equity
A type of distributional equity whereby those who are unequal with respect to an equity-relevant characteristic (e.g., income, need) are treated in an appropriately unequal manner.

Vertical equity, in contrast, requires that those who are unequal with respect to their equity-relevant characteristic receive appropriately unequal amounts of the good: treat unequals unequally. If two individual have differing needs, they should use differing amounts of health care; if two individuals have differing abilities-to-pay, they should contribute different amounts. A central challenge for vertical equity is to define how much differently unequals should be treated. Should a person with 10 percent greater need receive 10 percent more health care? What about 20 percent? The most commonly invoked notion of vertical equity is proportionality: the differences in the distribution should be in proportion to the differences in the characteristic.[4]

These concepts can be illustrated by comparing the actual distribution of public health care expenditures across districts in Ontario, against an estimate of what the distribution would be if it were based on need (Table 2.4). Hutchison and co-authors (Hutchison et al. 2003) used individual-level information on health status and health care utilization from a population health survey, supplemented with data on provincial expenditures for a range of health care services, to estimate the needs-based allocation of the 1996 provincial health care budget to the province's 16 health districts. The "needs-based allocation" figures in Table 2.4 indicate the per capita allocation of funds that each of the 16 health districts would receive if its share of the budget were based on the health care needs of its residents.

The table indicates substantial variation both in needs and actual expenditure across Ontario's regions. The mean spending across the whole province for the services included in the study was $829 per capita. The needs-based allocations vary from $728 per capita in District 7 to $954 per capita in District 15, while actual spending ranges from $682 per capita in District 7 to $959 in District 11. The correlation between the estimated needs-based allocations and the actual allocation is 0.79, indicating a strong relationship between the two. There is evidence, however, of both horizontal and vertical inequity. The estimated needs for Districts 9 and 13, for example, are essentially equal ($824 and $828 per capita respectively), yet their actual funding differs by more than 10 percent ($781 vs $865 per capita). This represents horizontal inequity: two districts with equal needs receive differing amounts of funding. A comparison of Districts 12 and 4 exemplifies vertical inequity. The needs of District 4 are estimated to be 15 percent greater than the needs of District 12, yet its actual funding is only 0.4 percent higher. The two districts have unequal needs but do not receive correspondingly differing amounts of funding.

2.2.2 Procedural Equity

Procedural equity concerns the fairness of the process by which resources are allocated. Procedural equity is most commonly used in situations where the analysis of distributional equity is not possible. In some situations, we cannot observe one or both of the good and the equity-relevant characteristic of individuals, making it impossible to compare how the two distributions correspond. In our justice system, for example, equity demands that the distribution of punishment correspond to the distribution of guilt: convict those who committed

[4] Students often intuitively invoke the concepts of horizontal and vertical equity in relation to their grades. The two most common complaints after an exam are as follows: "It is not fair. I wrote the same thing as person X but got a different mark" (perceived horizontal inequity); and "It is not fair. My answer is better than that of person X, but we got the same mark" (perceived vertical inequity).

TABLE 2.4

Comparison of the Needs-Based and Actual Allocation of Health Care Funds, Ontario

Comparing actual health care funding allocations to health districts in Ontario against estimated funding needs based on the health status of the populations in each district illustrates the principles of horizontal and vertical equity. The estimated needs for Districts 9 and 13 are essentially identical ($824 and $828 per capita respectively), yet their actual funding differs by more than 10 percent ($781 vs. $865 per capita). This represents horizontal inequity. A comparison of Districts 4 and 12 exemplifies vertical inequity. The needs of District 4 are estimated to be 15 percent greater than the needs of District 12, yet its actual funding is only 0.4 percent higher.

Source: J. Hurley, S. Birch, J. Eyles, S. D. Walter. Equity in Health Care Funding: Comparison of Expenditures in Ontario to Allocations Based on Population Need. McMaster University Centre for Health Economics and Policy Analysis.

	Health District	Needs-Based Allocation (dollars per capita)	Actual Allocation (dollars per capita)
1	Essex-Kent-Lambton	848	890
2	Thames Valley	816	788
3	Grey-Bruce-Huron-Perth	844	856
4	Niagara	903	819
5	Hamilton-Wentworth	861	954
6	Grand River	838	817
7	Halton-Peel	728	682
8	Waterloo-Wellington	793	702
9	Durham-Haliburton	824	781
10	Simcoe-York	743	685
11	Metro Toronto	898	959
12	Champlain	786	816
13	Quinte-Kingston-Rideau-Algoma-Cochrane	828	865
14	Manitoulin	891	911
15	Muskoka-Nipissing	954	895
16	Northwestern	852	818
	Province	829	829

Note: Table refers to public expenditures by the Province of Ontario on physician services, physiotherapists, chiropractors, and acute hospital services. See the original paper for details.

the crime, acquit those who did not. For many crimes, however, we never know for certain who is truly guilty; we can't observe the true distribution of guilt. To reduce the chance of errors, the judicial system has developed elaborate procedures, protocols, and processes to ensure fair trials in the hope that such procedures will minimize the chance that an innocent person will be unfairly convicted.

In other situations, the good of concern can't be divided among those who have a legitimate claim to it. In the case of transplantable organs, as noted, society cannot divide organs to be shared. When the number of people exceeds the available organs, society must devise a process to allocate them fairly. Many societies have developed formal systems for allocating such organs that take into account such factors as the quality of the match between the donated organ and the potential recipients, the potential recipients' health conditions, and how long the potential recipients have been waiting (Elster 1992).

The design of a fair process will vary according to the situation. Fair processes generally ignore aspects of the problem that are not equity-related, treating equally those who would be judged equivalent from the perspective of the problem at hand. A fair process need not be complex. Parents, for example, frequently invoke simple processes to ensure equity among their children. Flipping a coin to decide who gets to go first is one example; "you cut, I choose" is another that is especially useful for dividing a candy bar or piece of cake among children to avoid interminable complaints about unfair division. In each case, the process is designed to achieve fairness.

2.3   EQUITY AND EFFICIENCY

The relationship between efficiency and equity is a complex, often confusing aspect of economics. Efficiency and equity can, *but do not always,* conflict with each other: to achieve greater efficiency, society may have to sacrifice some equity and vice versa. While much economic writing emphasizes this trade-off (e.g., Okun 1974), the trade-off is neither inherent nor inevitable. In fact, at a purely conceptual level, no conflict needs to exist. Recall the grand utility possibilities frontier in Figure 2.2 on page 38. Every point on the frontier is efficient according to the Pareto Criterion, including the point at which the two individuals have equal levels of utility. An efficient allocation exists that is consistent with just about any conceivable criterion of distributional equity between the two individuals. Hence, there is no inherent conflict between efficiency and equity.

Conflict between the two can (and often does) arise under the potential Pareto Criterion for efficiency, which dictates that the single efficient allocation is the one that maximizes the sum of utilities, i.e., point I. If the allocation that maximizes utility is one that is highly unequal, then the efficient allocation by the potential Pareto Criterion may be quite different from the allocation judged to be equitable. But even under the potential Pareto Criterion, such a conflict is not inherent. If those in society who are most in need of health care, for example, are also those who benefit most from health care, then allocation according to need can simultaneously improve both the total benefit and equity in the health care sector. Hence, the empirical relationship between efficiency and equity must be examined on a case-by-case basis for each policy considered.

Evidence shows that people are willing to trade off greater amounts of a good against a fairer distribution of the good. The extent to which individuals are willing to make this trade-off depends on the nature of the good being distributed; but in health care, people seem to place considerable weight on equity and are willing to tolerate quite substantial reductions in total health produced to generate a more equal distribution of health (e.g., see Box 2.2 as well as Dolan and Cookson 2000, Nord et al. 1995, and Yaari and Bar-Hillel 1983).

social welfare function

Depicts how the overall welfare in society depends on the amount and distribution of welfare among individual members of society.

Economics captures such attitudes through the concept of a **social welfare function**. A social welfare function represents society's preferences and attitudes toward the amount and distribution of welfare in society. Conceptually, it can be used to identify the most preferred allocation on the grand utility possibilities frontier. The extent to which members of society stress the importance of the total amount of welfare versus a more equal distribution of welfare determines the nature of the social welfare function. If society cares only about maximizing benefit then, as we saw earlier, point H in Figure 2.2 is the optimal resource allocation for society. In contrast, if society cares only about equality of welfare among its members, the optimal resource allocation is point I. If society cares about both, and is willing to trade off efficiency and equity within certain bounds (as the evidence suggests), the optimal point lies somewhere between point H and point I. The greater the emphasis on the total amount of utility, the closer the optimal point will be to the maximizing point (H); the greater the emphasis on equity, the closer it will be to the egalitarian outcome (I).

It is tremendously challenging to estimate social welfare functions empirically. They therefore do not play a prominent role in empirical economic research. They are, however, a vitally important conceptual tool when analyzing policy choices. Furthermore, members of society do express such preferences, even if imperfectly, through voting in elections and referenda, and we can sometimes gain further insight into social preferences through polls and related techniques.

Kahneman and Varey (1991) explored people's attitudes regarding distributional equity in health care by presenting the following simple scenario to a sample of individuals and asking how they would allocate the pills.

A doctor has two patients, A and B, who both suffer from a rare and debilitating disease. Medication can provide total relief from the symptoms of the disease. Unfortunately, the drug is in very short supply—the doctor's supply is exactly 48 pills per day. She must decide how to allocate the 48 pills to her patients. The following information is known to the doctor and to her two patients:

Patient A's metabolism is such that it takes three pills to give him one hour of relief. Patient B's metabolism is such that it takes one pill to give him one hour of relief.

If you were the doctor, how would you divide the 48 pills between A and B? (No trades can be made after the division takes place.)

The allocation that maximizes the total amount of pain relief is an equal division of the pills: 24 each to patients A and B, providing total relief to patient B and 8 hours of relief to patient A. The allocation that equalizes pain relief between the two individuals is 36 pills to patient A and 12 pills to patient B. Although this equalizes pain relief, it reduces the total amount of pain relief produced by the pills from 32 hours to 24 hours. Nearly 80 percent of the respondents chose the allocation that equalized pain relief.

Source: Kahneman, D., and Varey, C. (1991). Notes on the psychology of utility. In J. E. Roemer and J. E. Elster (eds.). *Interpersonal comparisons of well-being* (pp. 127–163). New York: Cambridge University Press.

Chapter Summary

This chapter has emphasized the centrality of resource allocation to economics and the criteria economists use to judge alternative allocations of resources: efficiency and equity. The discussion has emphasized the following:

- Economics concerns the allocation of scarce resources available to society.
- Economics defines cost using the notion of opportunity cost: the opportunity cost of using a resource for one purpose is the benefits given up by not using the resource for the next most valued activity.
- Economics employs three notions of efficiency:
  1. Technical efficiency: produce goods in ways that do not waste resources.
  2. Cost-effectiveness efficiency: produce goods using the least-cost combination of resources.
  3. Allocative efficiency: produce those goods and services most valued by members of society and distribute them in accord with people's preferences. The two primary criteria for assessing allocative efficiency are the Pareto Criterion and the potential Pareto Criterion.
- Equity concerns the fairness of the distribution of resources. Two principal notions of equity are these:
  1. Distributional equity: is the observed distribution of the good consistent with the chosen principle of fairness (e.g., allocation of health care according to need)?
  2. Procedural equity: is the process by which a good is allocated fair?
- The relationship between efficiency and equity is complex. The two criteria can, but do not necessarily conflict with one another.

Key Terms

allocative efficiency, *36*
cost-effectiveness
   efficiency, *35*
distributional equity, *42*
efficiency, *34*
equity, *41*
horizontal equity, *42*
marginal analysis, *39*

normative economics, *30*
opportunity cost, *33*
Pareto Criterion, *38*
positive economics, *30*
potential Pareto Criterion, *39*
procedural equity, *42*
production, *34*
production function, *34*

production possibilities
   frontier, *35*
resources, *32*
social welfare function, *45*
technical efficiency, *34*
utility, *37*
vertical equity, *43*

End-of-Chapter Questions

A. For each of the statements below, indicate whether the statement is true or false and explain why it is true or false.

1. All production points on the production possibilities frontier are allocatively efficient.
2. Scarcity of resources results from inefficiency.
3. There is no opportunity cost for applications of resources that are technologically efficient, cost-effective, and allocatively efficient.
4. An equitable distribution of a good often implies an unequal distribution of the good among members of society.
5. A cost-effective allocation of productive resources must also be technologically efficient.
6. Pareto-efficient allocations always maximize welfare in society.
7. Achieving an efficient allocation simultaneously ensures that society attains an equitable allocation of resources.
8. Efficiency is a value-laden concept.

B. Consider the following information on production of health care in a nursing home.

		Hours of Nurse Services	Hours of Physician Services	Total cost of Program
Nurse hourly wage	$20			
Physician hourly wage	$100			
Program A		10,000	15,000	$1,700,000
Program B		20,000	7,500	$1,150,000
Program C		15,000	7,500	$1,050,000
Program D		25,000	2,500	$ 750,000

Assume that all methods produce the same level of quantity and quality of output (i.e., health among residents of the nursing home).

a) Identify the technically efficient production method(s).
b) Identify the cost-effectively efficient production method.

C. Based on the (hypothetical) information in the chart on page 48 relating to rates of surgery in Canada:

a) Is there horizontal equity in the utilization of health care in Canada between Toronto and Vancouver?
b) Is there vertical equity in the utilization of health care in Canada between Toronto and Vancouver?

Discuss.

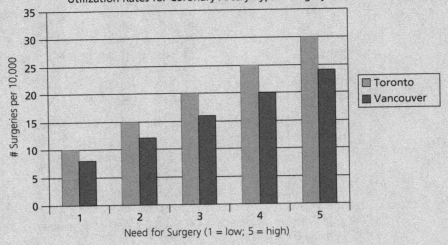

Utilization Rates for Coronary Artery Bypass Surgery

References

Anderson, G., U. Reinhardt, P. Hussey, and V. Petrosyan. 2003. It's the prices stupid: Why the United States is so different from other countries. *Health Affairs* 22(3):89–105.

Dolan, P., and R. Cookson. 2000. A qualitative study of the extent to which health gains matter when choosing between groups of patients. *Health Policy* 51:19–30.

Elster, J. 1992. *Local justice.* New York: Russell Sage Foundation.

Hutchison, B., V. Torrance-Rynard, J. Hurley, S. Birch, J. Eyles, and S. Walter. 2003. *Equity in health care funding: Comparison of expenditures in Ontario Canada to allocations based on population need.* Hamilton, ON: McMaster University Centre for Health Economics and Policy Analysis, Working Paper 03-03.

Kahneman, D., and C. Varey. 1991. Notes on the psychology of utility. In *Interpersonal comparisons of well-being,* J. Elster, and J. Roemer (eds.). Cambridge: Cambridge University Press. 127–163.

Neuhauser, D., and A. M. Lewicki. 1975. What do we gain from the sixth stool GUAIAC. *The New England Journal of Medicine* 293(5):226–28.

Nord, E., et al. 1995. Maximizing health benefits vs. egalitarianism: An Australian survey of health issues. *Social Science and Medicine* 41(10):1429–37.

OECD. 2008. *OECD health data 2008.* Paris: OECD.

Yaari, M. E., and M. Bar-Hillel. 1983. On dividing justly. *Social Choice and Welfare* (1):1–24.

Appendix 2

Chapter 2: Efficiency and Equity

2.1 EFFICIENCY

The three concepts of efficiency can be derived and illustrated graphically.

2.1.1 Efficiency in Production

Technical Efficiency

Consider first the production of a single good—housing. Let the horizontal axis in Figure 2A.1 represent the amount of machines and equipment (i.e., capital) used in production, and the vertical axis represent the quantity of worker hours (i.e., labour). Suppose we wanted to produce 100 houses. We can do this many ways. Point B in the figure represents a labour-intensive method that employs many workers using traditional hand tools; point C represents a capital-intensive method employing few workers using modern power tools, hydraulic equipment, and so forth. Both of these methods are technically efficient as long as no resources are idle or wasted. Indeed, many technically efficient ways to use labour and capital to produce 100 houses are possible, as depicted by the curved line connecting B and C—an isoquant.

An isoquant represents all technically efficient input combinations that produce the same quantity of output, in this case 100 houses. Point D represents a technically inefficient input combination to produce 100 houses because it uses more workers and machinery than is necessary—it is possible to reduce capital and still produce 100 houses by moving to point A. Analogously, point E is an infeasible way to produce 100 houses with existing technology: given the number of workers, more equipment is required to produce 100 houses, such as at point C on the isoquant. The figure also includes a second isoquant, in this case for the production of 200 houses.

FIGURE 2A.1

Technical Efficiency in the Production of Houses

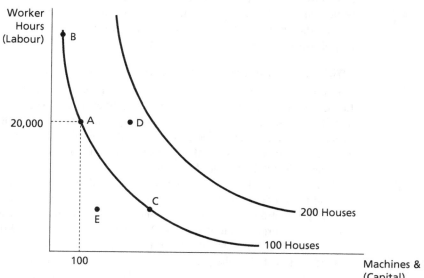

Two isoquants never intersect. The slope of an isoquant represents the rate at which capital must be substituted for labour so as to maintain the same level of output as the amount of labour is reduced. This slope is equal to the ratio of the marginal product of capital to the marginal product of labour and is called the marginal rate of technical substitution. The marginal rate of technical substitution is negative and falls in absolute value as one substitutes capital for labour: when much labour and little capital are employed, the marginal product of capital is large and that of labour is small, so only a small amount of capital is required to compensate for reduced labour. But as more and more capital is employed, the marginal product of capital falls while that of labour increases. Hence, when production already uses much capital and few workers, it takes a large amount of capital to compensate for reducing workers even further.

Cost-Effectiveness Efficiency

By adding the prices of labour and capital to the analysis, it is possible to derive the cost-effectively efficiency production method. Suppose that the hourly wage rate of workers is $10.00 per hour and that the price of a unit of equipment is $500.00. Let isocost lines represent different combinations of inputs with the same total cost. IC_1 in Figure 2A.2(i) represents all those combinations of labour and capital for which the total cost is $250,000, and IC_2 represents all those combinations for which the total cost is $300,000. The slope of the isocost line is the ratio of the prices of the two inputs, $\dfrac{P_{Capital}}{P_{Labour}}$, which represents the rate at which you can substitute capital for labour while holding total cost constant. The least-cost combination of labour and capital that can produce 100 houses is the isocost line closest to the origin that also touches the isoquant. This occurs at point A, the point of tangency between the isocost line and the isoquant.

Given the prices, among all the technically efficient ways to produce 100 houses, point A is the least-cost combination of workers and equipment. Points B and C represent technically efficient but not cost-effective combinations because they produce the same number of houses but cost more ($300,000). If the price of labour or capital were to change, the cost-effective combination would change. If workers cost $20.00 per hour and machines cost only $250.00 (Figure 2A.2(ii)), the least-cost method would be point F, the point of tangency with the isocost lines associated with the new ratio of prices. As one would expect, the least-cost method employs more of the now relatively cheaper equipment and less of the now more expensive labour.

Efficiency in Production with Two Goods: Derivation of the PPF

Now consider a slightly more complex situation with two inputs and two goods to produce. Let society have available 50,000 units of labour, L, and 1000 units of capital, K, to produce two goods, housing and food. To analyze how society should allocate its labour and capital to produce the two goods, we need a device called an Edgeworth Box (Figure 2A.3). The vertical axis represents the total amount of labour in society and the horizontal axis represents the total amount of capital.

The total amount of each input can be allocated to two purposes, the production of housing and the production of food. Let the bottom left (southeast) origin represent the origin for the production of housing (O_H) and the upper right (northeast) corner represent the origin for the production of food (O_F). Hence, any point in the Edgeworth Box represents six quantities: the amount of labour allocated to production of housing (L_H), the amount of labour allocated to the production of food (L_F), the amount of capital allocated to the production of housing (K_H), the amount of capital allocated to the production of food (K_F),

FIGURE 2A.2
**Cost-Effectiveness
Efficiency in the
Production of Houses**

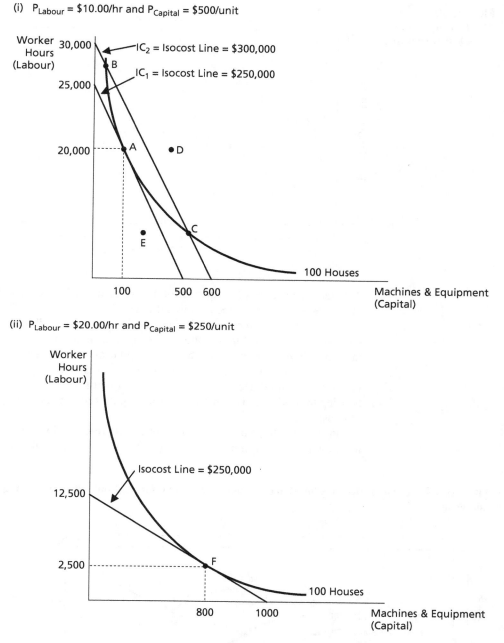

(i) $P_{Labour} = \$10.00/hr$ and $P_{Capital} = \$500/unit$

Worker
Hours
(Labour)

30,000 — IC$_2$ = Isocost Line = $300,000

B

IC$_1$ = Isocost Line = $250,000

25,000

20,000 — A   • D

• C
• E

100 Houses

100   500   600

Machines & Equipment
(Capital)

(ii) $P_{Labour} = \$20.00/hr$ and $P_{Capital} = \$250/unit$

Worker
Hours
(Labour)

Isocost Line = $250,000

12,500

2,500 — F

100 Houses

800   1000

Machines & Equipment
(Capital)

the quantity of housing produced (H), and the amount of food produced (F). At point A, for instance, the respective quantities are 20,000, 30,000, 250, 750, 700, and 600.

To determine whether point A represents a technically efficient allocation of labour and capital, we need to introduce isoquants. Because the southwest corner is the origin for production of housing, isoquants for the production of houses curve toward the origin, increasing in value as they move to the northeast in the box; analogously, isoquants for the production of food curve toward the origin for food production (the upper right corner) and increase in value as they move toward the southwest corner of the box (Figure 2A.4). As

FIGURE 2A.3
The Two-Input, Two-Good Edgeworth Box

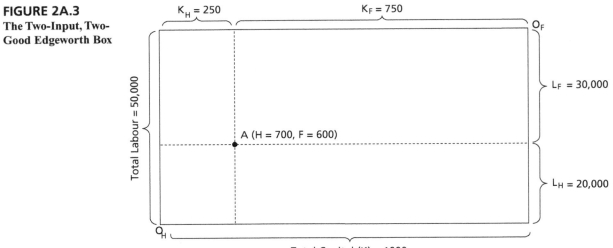

depicted, point A lies on isoquants for the production of 700 units of housing and 600 units of food, and is therefore technically efficient.

Is point A cost-effectively efficient? No. Society can reallocate labour and capital and move to point D to get more food without giving up any housing. At point A, the marginal rates of technical substitution between capital and labour are not equal across the two goods. Capital is relatively more productive than labour for producing housing than it is for producing food. Hence, by reallocating capital from food to housing, and labour from housing to food, society can increase the output of food without decreasing the production of housing.

"Prices" in this simple environment are represented by the opportunity cost of reallocating a unit of an input from one good to the other (i.e., the price of shifting a unit of

FIGURE 2A.4   **The Efficient Allocation of Labour and Capital for the Production of Housing and Food**

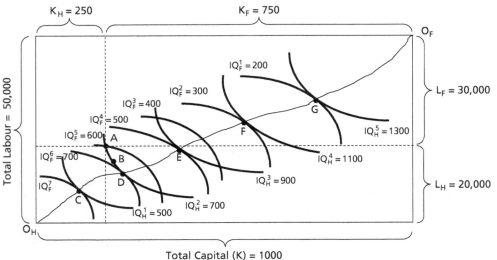

FIGURE 2A.5
Production
Possibilities Frontier,
Housing and Food

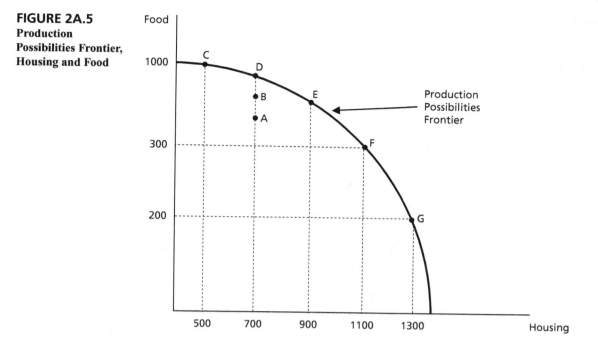

labour from houses to food is the reduced production of houses). The point of tangency between the isoquants for the two goods represents a cost-effectively efficient production combination for producing those two quantities because at that point the marginal rates of technical substitution are equal across goods: it is not possible to increase the production of one good without decreasing production of the other. The whole set of such tangencies, represented by the curved line running from O_H to O_F (and including points C, D, E, F, and G) form the production possibilities frontier (Figure 2A.5). The production possibilities frontier represents all feasible combinations of housing and food when the two goods are produced efficiently.

2.1.2 Efficiency in Allocation

To identify which combination of food and housing society should produce and how that combination should be distributed among members of society requires information on people's preferences over food and housing.

Preferences

Preferences are represented by utility: individuals derive utility from each good that they consume, in this case, housing and food. In Figure 2A.6, the horizontal axis represents the amount of housing a person consumes and the vertical axis represents the amount of food they consume. Point R represents a combination with a lot of food but relatively little housing, which gives them utility of 75. This person may be equally satisfied with a combination that includes less food but more housing—point S. The curved line that connects R and S—an indifference curve—represents combinations of food and housing that provide the same level of utility; in this case, 75. The individual would be indifferent between them because they both provide the same level of utility.

Point T represents a combination that would be preferred to R and S because it provides a higher level of utility (85). The slope of the indifference curve represents the rate at which the person would be willing to trade housing for food, and is called the marginal rate of substitution. It decreases in absolute value as consumption of food falls and consumption of

FIGURE 2A.6
Choosing the
Optimal Mix of
Goods: Houses and
Food

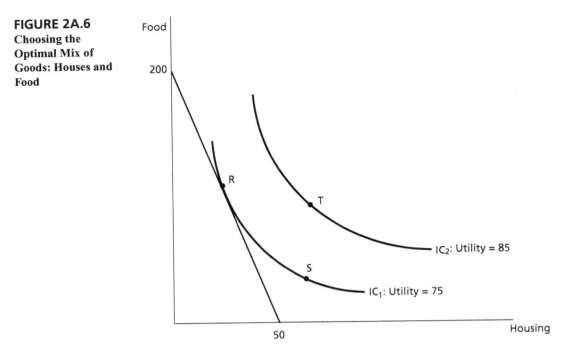

housing rises. Intuitively, when one has little housing and much food, it takes little housing to compensate for reducing food consumption; when one has much housing and little food, it takes a lot of housing to make up for even a small reduction in food.

What combination would this individual choose? We assume that the individual wants to maximize their utility; the major constraint is limited income. The individual's income, or budget constraint, can be represented by a straight line indicating all combinations of food and housing that they can purchase, given the prices of each and their income. If we assume that the price of a unit of food is $25, the price of a unit of housing is $100, and the person's income is $5000, the budget constraint intersects the food axis at 200, the housing axis at 50, and has slope −4.0 (equal to the ratio of prices $\frac{P_H}{P_F}$) which represents the rate at which a person can substitute housing for health care given their relative prices.

The utility-maximizing bundle is the combination that puts the individual on the highest indifference curve possible subject to their budget constraint. This occurs at the point of tangency between the budget constraint and indifference curve: point R in this case, associated with utility of 75. At the point of tangency, the rate at which the individual is willing to trade the two goods just equals the rate at which they can trade the goods given their prices.

Allocative Efficiency

This tells us what any single person would want. How can we determine the allocatively efficient combination of food and housing to produce, and the associated distribution of the two goods among members of society? We once again need to use an Edgeworth Box. To begin, pick any point on the PPF in Figure 2A.5—let's say point F. This gives us a productively efficient combination of food and housing (300 units of food and 1100 units of housing) to be divided between the two members of society, Alpha and Beta.

In Figure 2A.7, the horizontal axis represents the total amount of housing available, and the vertical axis represents the total amount of food available. Into this box, we can draw indifference curves, where the southwest origin is for Alpha (O_α) and the northeast origin is for Beta (O_β). Hence, the indifference curves for Alpha increase in utility as one moves from southwest to northeast while those for Beta increase as one moves from northeast to southwest. Any point in the box represents six quantities, in this case, H_α, H_β, F_α, F_β, U_α and U_β.

Is point X allocatively efficient? Not according to the Pareto Criterion. Starting at point X, it is possible to reallocate housing and food to reach point Y, thereby increasing Beta's utility without decreasing Alpha's. Once point Y is reached, it is impossible to reallocate housing and food in a way that increases one person's utility without decreasing the other's. Hence, point Y is allocatively efficient by the Pareto Criterion. All points of tangency between Alpha's and Beta's indifference curves represent Pareto-efficient allocations. The set of all such Pareto-efficient allocations can be converted into the utility-possibilities frontier (UPF) associated with the amounts of food and housing produced at point F on the production possibilities frontier (Figure 2A.8(i)).

Given the level of utility of one person, the UPF tells the maximum level of utility the other person can attain given society's resources and production technology and the preferences of members of society. Is there any reason to prefer one point on the UPF over another? There is one point on the UPF for which the slope of the tangency between the individuals' indifference curves equals the slope of the PPF. The equality of these two slopes for this point means that the rate at which the individuals want to trade off food and housing, given their preferences, exactly equals the rate at which society can trade off production of the two goods, given the available technology. We have efficiency in production, in exchange, and between the two elements of the economy.

We can repeat the previous exercise for every point on the production possibilities frontier—in each case, there is a resulting UPF. Then trace out the envelope of the most outward points on all the UPFs. Call this the grand utility possibilities frontier (GUPF), as

FIGURE 2A.7
Exchange Efficiency, Food and Housing

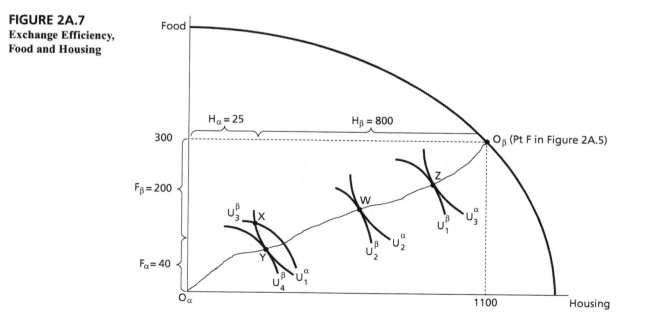

depicted in Figure 2A.8(ii). The GUPF tells us, among all possible combinations of food and housing that society can produce and among all the possible ways the goods can be divided among members of society, these are the maximal combinations of utility that can be attained. All points on the GUPF are Pareto-efficient. How can we choose the optimal combination? To answer this, we need to know something about the views of members of society regarding distributional equity, since the different points on the GUPF distribute well-being differently among members of society.

FIGURE 2A.8

The Utility Possibilities Frontier and the Grand Utility Possibilities Frontier

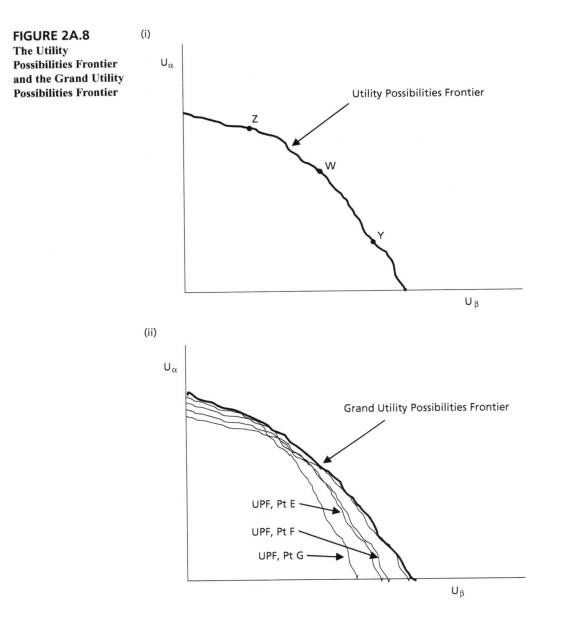

(i)

U_α

Utility Possibilities Frontier

Z

W

Y

U_β

(ii)

U_α

Grand Utility Possibilities Frontier

UPF, Pt E

UPF, Pt F

UPF, Pt G

U_β

2.2   EQUITY

2.2.1   Distributional Equity

Measuring distributional equity presents considerable challenges. Horizontal equity demands that equals be treated equally. But while there is only one way for something to be distributed equally in a population, there are an infinite number of ways for it to be distributed unequally; and it is not always easy to determine whether one unequal distribution is more unequal than another. Economists have devised a number of measures of inequality that try to solve this problem, and much current work on assessing distributional equity in health care rests on one such measure, the concentration index. The concentration index is designed to measure in particular income-related horizontal inequities in the utilization of health care: the extent to which utilization by those with low incomes differs from utilization by those with high incomes.

The concentration index can best be understood by first considering a concentration curve, which depicts income-related inequality in the distribution of a good; in our case, health care. In the graph of a concentration curve for health care utilization, the horizontal axis represents the cumulative proportion of the population ranked by income, beginning with those of lowest income on the left; the vertical axis represents the cumulative proportion of health care utilization in the population. Suppose first that the distribution of health care utilization is perfectly equal: everyone consumes exactly the same amount of health care. In this case, the concentration curve is simply the diagonal line as in Figure 2A.9: the lowest 10 percent of people in the income distribution utilize 10 percent of all health care; the lowest 20 percent of people in the income distribution consume 20 percent of all health care, and so forth.

Now suppose that high-income people consume more health care on average than low-income individuals. In this case, the lowest 10 percent of people in the income distribution consume less than 10 percent of all health care, and so on—the concentration curve lies

FIGURE 2A.9
The Concentration Curve

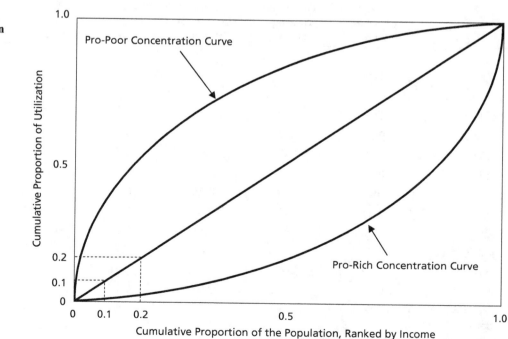

below the 45° line, as depicted in Figure 2A.9. If the opposite were true, if the poor consumed more health care on average than the rich, the curve would lie above the 45° line, as depicted in Figure 2A.9. The stronger the relationship between income and utilization—that is, the greater the income-related inequality in utilization—the greater the curvature in the concentration curve and the associated area between the concentration curve and the diagonal. This provides a basis for quantifying the amount of income-related inequality.

The concentration index is defined as twice the area between the concentration curve and the diagonal. Because the total area of the graph is 1.0 (each side is 1.0), the maximum possible value of the concentration index is 1.0 (2 × 0.5). By convention, the index takes on positive values for pro-rich distributions and negative values for pro-poor distributions, so it takes on values in the interval [-1.0, 1.0], where −1.0 corresponds to a completely pro-poor distribution (the poorest household consumes all health care) and 1.0 corresponds to a completely pro-rich distribution (the richest household consumes all health care).

Table 2A.1 presents some information on the relationship between income and general/family practitioner (GP/FP) visits in Canada. Each row in the table pertains to each of 10 income deciles, going from individuals in the lowest 10 percent of the income distribution ("Lowest") to individuals in the highest 10 percent ("Highest"). Part (a) of the table presents information on the raw, unadjusted number of visits to GP/FPs for three measures of utilization in 2007: the probability that a person had any visits to GP/FP, the number of visits among those who had at least one visit, and the total number of visits (among both users and non-users).

TABLE 2A.1 **Inequality in the Income-Related Distribution of General/Family Physician Visits, Canada, 2007.**

Source: This analysis is based on Statistics Canada publication Canadian Community Healthy Survey: Public Use Microdata File 2005 (Cycle 3.1), released August 31, 2006. Catalogue 82M0013XCB, http://www.statcan.gc.ca/bsolc/olc-cel/olc-cel?catno=82M0013X&lang=eng. All computations, use, and interpretation of these data are entirely that of the author(s).

	(a) Unadjusted Visits			(b) Needs-Standardized Visits		
	Probability of a GP Visit	Number of GP Visits Among Users	Total Number of GP Visits	Probability of a GP Visit	Number of GP Visits Among Users	Total Number of GP Visits
Income Decile	Mean	Mean	Mean	Mean	Mean	Mean
Lowest	0.77	5.14	3.95	0.71	3.96	2.83
Decile 2	0.79	4.54	3.61	0.73	3.83	2.79
Decile 3	0.79	4.17	3.29	0.74	3.74	2.78
Decile 4	0.78	3.93	3.05	0.75	3.69	2.77
Decile 5	0.78	3.73	2.91	0.76	3.63	2.75
Decile 6	0.78	3.53	2.75	0.77	3.54	2.72
Decile 7	0.77	3.46	2.68	0.77	3.54	2.73
Decile 8	0.78	3.31	2.58	0.78	3.50	2.73
Decile 9	0.78	3.22	2.50	0.78	3.47	2.71
Highest	0.78	3.09	2.40	0.78	3.48	2.73
Total	0.78	3.83	2.98	0.76	3.64	2.76
Concentration Index	−0.000	−0.081	−0.081	0.018	−0.023	−0.006

The table indicates, for example, that individuals in the lowest income decile had, on average, a 0.77 probability of seeing a GP/FP during 2007; those who went to a GP/FP at least once had an average of 5.14 visits during the year; and across all individuals in the lowest income decile, the average number of visits during the year was 3.95. A comparison among income deciles reveals the following:

- No relationship between income and the probability of a visit (the probability is nearly constant across income deciles); this is confirmed by the associated concentration index value of -0.000, which is effectively zero.

- A strong pro-poor relationship between income and the number of visits among users (5.15 visits on average among those in the lowest income decile dropping to 3.09 among those in the highest income decile); this is confirmed in the negative concentration index value of -0.081.

- A similar pro-poor relationship between income and the number of visits overall (3.95 dropping to 2.40 as income rises); this is confirmed in the negative concentration index value of -0.081.

These data tell us about inequality in utilization, but not about inequity. To gain insight into inequity, the visits must be adjusted for the differing levels of need across individuals. Part (b) of the table presents the analogous information for the needs-adjusted number of visits, where the needs adjustment used information on each person's self-assessed health status, number of chronic health conditions, activity restrictions, and smoking status. On average, those of lower income have a higher need for health care. This adjustment reveals a different picture:

- A modest pro-rich relationship between income and the needs-adjusted probability of a visit to a GP/FP (adjusted probability rising from 0.71 among those in the lowest income decile to 0.78 among those in the highest); this is confirmed in the concentration index value of 0.018.

- A modest pro-poor relationship between income and the needs-adjusted number of visits among users (adjusted mean number falling from 3.96 among those in the lowest income decile to 3.48 among those in the highest); this is confirmed in the concentration index value of -0.023.

- Effectively no relationship between income and the number of GP/FP visits overall (the mean is flat between 2.73 and 2.83 across income deciles); this is confirmed in the concentration index value of -0.006, which is effectively no different from zero.

Although the evidence indicates no income-related inequity in the overall number of GP/FP visit rates in Canada, this overall rate is composed of two off-setting patterns of inequity: the rich are more likely to see a GP/FP, but among those who make at least one visit, the poor have a higher average number of visits. Additional analysis is required to understand the reasons for the patterns. For more information on methods for measuring inequity using concentration indices, see O'Donnell et al. (2008).

2.3 EQUITY AND EFFICIENCY

The socially optimal point depends on the social welfare function. Consider three commonly invoked social welfare functions. The first (which corresponds to the Potential Pareto Criterion) seeks to maximize the total amount of utility in society. In this case, society does not care at all about the distribution, and the social indifference curve is a straight line of slope -1. The optimal point is the tangency between the GUPF and the social indifference curve, as depicted in Figure 2A.10(i).

FIGURE 2A.10
Socially Optimal
Points Under
Alternative Social
Welfare Functions

(i) Socially Optimal Point: Utilitarian Social Welfare Function

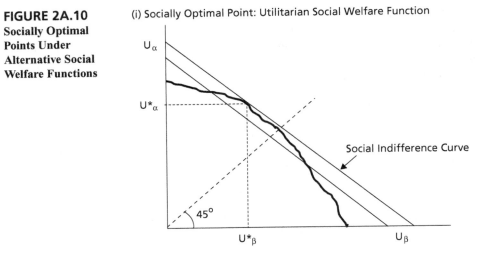

(ii) Socially Optimal Point: Pure Egalitarian Social Welfare Function

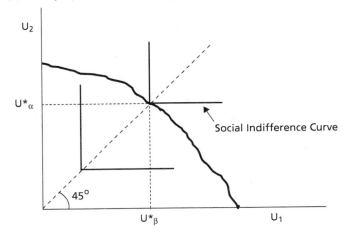

(iii) Socially Optimal Point: Inequality Averse Social Welfare Function

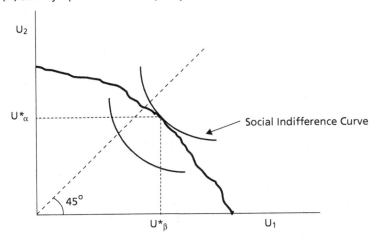

The second notion stresses complete equality: any deviations from equality do not enhance social welfare. In this case, indifference curves are L-shaped emanating from the origin along the 45° line. These rigidly egalitarian social preferences lead to choosing the point at the intersection of the 45° line and the GUPF (Figure 2A.10(ii)).

In between these two extremes are social preferences that give weight to both the overall amount of welfare and its distribution. Such indifference curves are smoothly curved and exhibit inequality aversion. The greater the degree of curvature, the stronger is the inequality aversion, or the weight given to distributional concerns; the smaller the extent of curvature, the greater the weight put on maximizing the total amount of welfare. The optimal point is again at the tangency of the social indifference curve and the GUPF (Figure 2A.10(iii)).

The Basics of Markets

Learning Objectives

After studying this chapter, you will understand

LO1 The consumer decision framework that underlies demand analysis

LO2 The supplier decision framework that underlies supply analysis

LO3 The interactions between demand and supply in a market

LO4 The use of the demand and supply framework in positive economic analysis

LO5 The use of the demand and supply framework in normative economic analysis

---

In a well-functioning market, competition ensures that resources are allocated efficiently. If a producer uses a technically inefficient production method or opts for an input mix that is not cost-minimizing, an efficient competitor will charge a lower price, attract customers, and put the inefficient producer out of business. If a producer makes goods that people do not value, it will be unable to sell them and will likewise soon go out of business. In a market, the goods go to those who value them the most, as measured by their willingness to pay. Well-functioning markets force producers to produce efficiently, produce only goods of value to individuals, and distribute those goods in accord with people's willingness to pay for them.

This power of the market has been a huge force shaping modern societies and modern economics. This power is the reason society so often chooses to allocate resources through markets. But this power of the market is more fragile than is often intimated in popular discussions of the virtues of markets. Markets allocate resources efficiently only *under certain conditions*. In the absence of all the requisite conditions, markets lead to inefficient (often grossly inefficient) allocations.

This chapter focuses on the market as an allocation mechanism and on the economic analysis of markets. Understanding the basic properties of markets, the conditions required for them to function well, and the economic analysis of markets is essential in health economics. Much health care policy debate is about the appropriate role of markets in the health care sector. It is impossible to assess these debates critically without an understanding of markets. Further, because much economic analysis is based on market analogies, even when markets are not the primary allocation mechanism, understanding economic analysis requires a solid grasp of the economics of markets.

3.1 CONDITIONS FOR A WELL-FUNCTIONING MARKET

Three kinds of conditions are necessary for market allocation to be efficient: (1) conditions in the broader environment in which a market operates; (2) ethical principles consistent with the judgment that a person's willingness to pay represents the social value of a good or service; and (3) technical conditions within the market itself.

Markets function well only when surrounded by external institutions that support market exchange. Markets require a well-functioning legal system that can define, adjudicate, and enforce property rights. In the absence of such a system, ownership is meaningless and people have little incentive to invest or produce. Markets also depend upon norms of behaviour and attitudes toward exchange and trade. In the absence of any trust, or an expectation that other parties to a business deal will honour their commitments, exchange and trade break down. Individuals in industrialized market economies often take these general institutions for granted, but in many parts of the world the absence of such institutions impedes economic growth (Zack and Knack 1999).

Markets allocate resources on the basis of willingness to pay. That is, those who are willing to pay the most obtain a given good or service. A person's willingness to pay for a good or service depends in part on their ability to pay, which in turn depends on their income or wealth. Consequently, the specific allocation generated by a market depends on the initial distribution of income and wealth in society. Different initial distributions of income will generate different final allocations of goods, each of which is potentially technically, cost-effectively, and allocatively efficient. The optimality of market allocation—defined in terms of efficiency and equity—depends on the ethical judgment that willingness to pay is the appropriate measure of the value to society of the good in question, and that the initial distribution of income and wealth in society is acceptable. These judgments are generally accepted for most consumer goods.

Provided that the general environment is conducive to market exchange, and willingness to pay is accepted as an appropriate measure of value, three basic conditions internal to the market itself must hold if the market allocation is to be efficient:

1. an absence of market power on both the demand and supply sides
2. adequate information for both purchasers and producers to make good decisions
3. an absence of externalities

3.1.1 Market Power

In a competitive market, the market price is determined by impersonal market forces beyond the influence of any single individual or organization. Each consumer or producer must take market conditions as given; they have no control over them. A competitive market requires that on the demand side no single purchaser account for a large proportion of demand, and on the supply side that multiple producers compete, have access to the same technology and inputs, and can freely enter and exit the market in response to profit opportunities. A market can perform well only if no single individual or organization has market power, where **market power** implies an ability to influence the market price.[1]

market power
An ability to influence the market price.

[1] Sellers are, of course, free to set the price for their own product at any level they choose. But in a competitive market, if the seller sets its price above the market price, the seller will quickly go out of business when people purchase from lower-priced competitors.

Concentration of market power in a small number of either consumers or producers thwarts the discipline imposed by competition, leading to inefficiencies.

Supply-Side Market Power

Supply-side market power can arise when firms cannot freely flow into or out of a market in response to profit opportunities, or when a market cannot sustain a large number of producers. In the limit, a market may have only a single producer, a situation referred to

monopoly
A market with only one producer (seller) of a good or service.

as a **monopoly**. Barriers to entry in a market may arise naturally because of the nature of a good and its production, or they may arise artificially as a consequence of government regulation.

In the market for crude oil, for instance, producers are limited to the relatively small number of countries that have oil deposits within their borders. This has granted considerable market power to a small number of countries that hold the bulk of the world's oil reserves. In the manufacturing sector, natural barriers commonly arise because a potential entrant to an industry must incur large costs just to begin production. Such large fixed costs, incurred simply to initiate production, inhibit competition in two ways. The large fixed costs make it difficult for new firms to enter the market; large fixed costs also mean the efficient level of production is high, so that a market can sustain only a small number of efficiently sized producers. Such natural monopolies arise in a number of industries, including communications, power generation and transmission, and natural gas transportation. Such industries are commonly subject to public regulation to prevent producers from exploiting their market power.[2] When assessing market power, it is essential to consider the size of the relevant market. For instance, although Canada has hundreds of hospitals,

[2] A number of such industries have been deregulated in recent years in many countries. In a number of cases, such deregulation generally applies only to the good itself (e.g., natural gas, electricity), not the infrastructure over which it is transported (pipelines, electrical generation facilities and the associated power grid), which is the source of large fixed costs and which remains regulated.

considerations of efficiency and quality dictate that hospitals be of a certain minimum size, so many communities and regions have access to only one local hospital. Hence, although there is a large number of hospitals overall, within each market the local hospital enjoys a monopoly.

Government regulation is also a source of market power when it inhibits market competition. The government patent awarded to a drug company for a new drug, for instance, grants the company the exclusive right to produce and sell the drug for a defined number of years. The patent creates a monopolist with respect to that specific drug. Why would a government deliberately grant monopoly power? Because it hopes that the incentives created by the patent will spur a sufficiently higher level of research and development to justify granting temporary monopoly power.

Demand-Side Market Power

monopsony
A market with a single purchaser of a good or service.

Analogously, demand-side market power arises when there are a small number of purchasers. In the limit, when a market has only a single purchaser, it is called a **monopsony**. The classic example of monopsony power is a one-company town, where a single organization is the dominant employer (demander of labour), which gives it power to set low wages when people have few options. Monopsony purchasing power plays an important role in many health systems. In public systems such as the system in Canada or the U.K., the government is the primary funder of physician services and can use its monopsony power when negotiating physician fees. In private systems such as the U.S. system, large private health plans that enrol hundreds of thousands or even millions of beneficiaries use their size to negotiate discounts from physicians, drug companies, and other suppliers of health care goods and services.

3.1.2   Information

A well-functioning market requires that both producers and consumers have sufficient information to enable them to make good decisions. On the supply side, all producers must have access to information on production methods for the good and on the prices of production inputs. A producer that has a technological advantage, or that can purchase inputs at lower cost than others, can produce the good at lower cost than can other producers, charge a lower price, and expand market share, thereby gaining market power over time.

On the demand side, consumers can discipline sellers in a market only if they can judge the quality of the good in question, assess accurately the value of the good to themselves, and know the prices charged for the good by alternative producers. Consumers are sometimes not fully informed about the price or quality of different sellers' goods, and they often make the mistake of assuming that a higher price means higher quality.

asymmetry of information
Participants on one side of a market (e.g., sellers) have more information relevant to a transaction than do those on the other side (e.g., purchasers). Depending on the situation, either sellers or purchasers may have an informational advantage.

Gathering information is costly, requiring time and energy, so full information is not necessarily optimal. Nor does the lack of full information necessarily cause a problem. For instance, even if they do not have full information, if all participants in the market have the same information, no one has an advantage. Of particular concern, however, is **asymmetry of information** between buyers and sellers. For goods such as automobile repair services, financial investment advice, and health care, the expertise required to make good decisions is frequently beyond that held by most consumers: an asymmetry of information exists between the seller and the buyer. The sellers (auto mechanic, financial adviser, physician) often have considerably more information than do consumers regarding the quality and appropriateness of the services they offer. Asymmetry of information is a source of market power because sellers have considerable scope to exploit their informational advantage to influence the demand for their own services (via their advice to customers) for their own economic gain.

3.1.3 No Externalities

Markets allocate efficiently only if both consumers and producers consider all the effects of their actions. Producers, if they are to produce at the socially optimal level, must consider *all* costs of production, including the use of *any* valuable, finite resource. Valuable, finite resources include not only purchased labour, capital, and raw materials, but also "free" goods, such as clean air and water. A producer uses up clean water when it dumps raw waste into a river making the water unsuitable for swimming or drinking. The full social cost of using this water, however, does not show up on the producer's private financial statements. In such cases, the private cost to the firm is lower than the social cost.

Analogously, the social benefit of consumption can differ from the private benefit. A person who gets a flu shot obtains private benefit from the reduced chance of getting the flu. But everyone else with whom the person comes into contact also benefits, because the shot reduces the chance that the person will pass the flu on to them. The social benefits of the flu shot exceed the private benefits that accrue to the person who gets the shot in the first place.

externality
Costs imposed or benefits gained by individuals other than the individual or organization that undertakes an action and which are not captured by a relevant market.

Whenever the private costs (benefits) of an activity differ from the social costs (benefits), an **externality** arises. Externalities cause markets to allocate resources inefficiently because people engaged in market exchange base their decisions only on private benefits and costs, ignoring broader social costs and benefits. The market level of production and consumption based on private costs and benefits differs from the socially optimal level. If a steel producer pollutes during the production process, the market price of steel will be too low and too much steel will be produced and consumed. Analogously, a private market for flu shots in which everyone has to pay the full cost will result in an inefficiently low number of people getting the shot because each person's private decision will not take into account the full social benefits of a flu shot.

3.1.4 Rationales for Government Intervention: Market Failure and Equity

Market Failure

These conditions for a well-functioning market seldom hold strictly in the real world. Minor or temporary deviations are common but generally pose few serious problems. Large, persistent deviations arise in certain sectors, however, which if left unaddressed can generate substantial inefficiencies. When one or more of the necessary conditions is violated, an unregulated market fails to generate an efficient allocation of resources: **market failure** occurs.

market failure
A situation in which an unregulated market generates an inefficient allocation of resources.

Market failure is one of the most important concepts in economic policy analysis, lying at the heart of such analysis. Much economic policy analysis rests on the following logic: a principal economic goal is the efficient allocation of society's resources; under the conditions discussed above, freely operating markets produce efficient allocations. Hence, society should use markets to allocate resources *unless there is evidence of market failure.* Market failure—or inefficient market allocation—provides the principal economic rationale for government "intervention" in markets through regulation, price subsidy, tax policy, or other mechanisms. The market is taken as the default optimal allocation mechanism unless economic analysis demonstrates important market failure.

But demonstrating market failure alone is not sufficient to justify government intervention on efficiency grounds. The proposed government policy intervention must also produce an outcome more efficient than the imperfect market outcome. An inefficient market outcome may still be preferred to what can be achieved through feasible policy interventions.[3]

Equity Rationale

Although dominant in most areas of economics, market failure is not the only economic rationale for government intervention into the operation of a market. Equity concerns can also justify government intervention. Equity arguments are distinct from market failure arguments. A market outcome may be efficient, but judged inequitable.

Distinguishing equity arguments from efficiency arguments is important for three reasons. As a practical matter, within most areas of economics, efficiency-based arguments based on market failure carry more weight. This is partly because equity is a more contested notion than efficiency: while economists agree on the meaning of efficiency, even many people who share a concern for equity disagree on what constitutes an equitable allocation. Even when contested, however, in some sectors equity concerns weigh as heavily as efficiency concerns. Health is one such sector.

The greater weight accorded to efficiency-based arguments also arises because of a bias in economic theory. The fundamental theorems of welfare economics demonstrate that when markets function well, *any* allocation (i.e., any point on the grand utility possibilities frontier) can be achieved through a market system given the right initial distribution of income. Hence, if the current allocation is inequitable, the policy solution is not to intervene in the operation of the market but to redistribute income so that market processes (efficiently) generate the equitable allocation. In this view, equity is a question of the appropriate distribution of income in society, which is a political rather than an economic problem. Economic analysis, the reasoning goes, should focus on how to ensure markets operate efficiently, leaving questions of redistribution (and, as a consequence, equity) to the political realm.

Although all of this holds true in theory, the resulting near-exclusive emphasis on inefficiency as the rationale for government intervention fails in the real world of policy-making. It is impossible for governments to redistribute income in the manner assumed by economic theory. Governments do not have all the policy instruments assumed in the theory, and uneven power relationships in society can block redistributive efforts. Society cannot neatly cleave policies into those that only address equity and those that only address efficiency. The two concerns are empirically intertwined.

Finally, even if in reality most government policies create both efficiency and equity effects, distinguishing equity- and efficiency-based arguments can be important because the policies aimed at each often differ. For instance, if a market functions well in all respects except that society would like all individuals (rather than only those who can afford the market price) to have access to the good in question, government intervention can be limited to a system of targeted price subsidies while otherwise leaving the operation of the market alone. In contrast, government policy to correct market failure often requires more interventionist regulatory and related approaches.

3.2 THE MECHANICS OF THE MARKET

This section examines the economics of how markets function. We begin with the demand side of a market, then consider the supply side, and then bring the two together.

---

[3] In economic language, we are in a "second-best" world. The first-best world of fully efficient allocation is not possible, so we must choose among second-best alternatives, all of which include some inefficiency. Sometimes the optimal second-best policy will rely on government policy intervention; sometimes it will be the imperfect market.

3.2.1 Individual Behaviour and the Demand for Goods and Services

A bit of introspection about your own behaviour likely reveals the factors that affect demand for a good. Your tastes, or in economic jargon, "preferences," are of primary importance: do you derive pleasure or satisfaction from consuming the good? Income and wealth also play an important role, particularly in combination with the price of the good. We all might prefer to drive a Rolls Royce, but few of us can afford one. And, the price of the good itself is not the only price that matters: the prices of related goods also matter. The demand for automobiles is affected by the price of gasoline and the price of automobile insurance, which are used jointly with an automobile, and by the price and availability of mass transit, which can be used instead of a car.

The economic model of consumer choice and demand provides a formal framework within which to analyze how these and other factors affect demand for goods and services. It emphasizes three factors:

1. what people care about
2. the goal they are trying to achieve through their choices
3. the constraints they face when making a choice

As discussed in Chapter 2, economics assumes that people have preferences summarized by their utility function. The utility function of a person who cares, among other things, about hamburgers, pizza, and books, can be written as follows:

$$\text{Utility} = U(\text{hamburgers, pizza, books, movies, health, etc.}) \qquad \textbf{(3.1)}$$

People are assumed to make choices among various goods and services so as to maximize their utility (i.e., to best satisfy their preferences). People, of course, face a financial constraint—they only have so much income with which to purchase goods and services.[4] The budget constraint depends on a person's income, or wealth, and the prices of the goods.

The consumer's choice problem can be stated as follows: given the market prices for goods and a person's preferences and income, how should a person allocate their income so as to maximize utility? In real life, people choose among many thousands of goods, services, and activities, but the essential choice principles can be illustrated using a simple example with only two goods, hamburgers and pizza.

Economists make the following crucial assumption about preferences: as a person consumes more and more of a good, the additional amount of utility obtained from each additional unit of a good falls. When we are hungry, the first hamburger tastes very good and satisfies our most urgent hunger; the second may still taste good, but it does not provide as much satisfaction as the first; by the third hamburger, many of us are beginning to wonder if we really want any more. This assumption is called **diminishing marginal utility**: consuming more of a good increases utility, but at a diminishing rate. Table 3.1 lists hypothetical utility values for hamburgers and pizza that reflect the assumption of diminishing marginal utility (utility even becomes negative for this person after seven slices of pizza each week).

Assume that an individual has a food budget of $16.00 per week, the price of hamburgers (P_h) is $2.00, and the price of a slice of pizza (P_p) is $1.00. From this information, we can derive the person's budget constraint in terms of hamburgers and pizza. The individual can purchase any combination of hamburgers and pizza such that the total expenditures are less than or equal to $16.00:

diminishing marginal utility
A property of a utility whereby consuming more of a good increases utility, but at a diminishing rate.

---

[4] People also have a time constraint, which can be very important in the analysis of certain activities. We ignore the time constraint for the moment.

TABLE 3.1 **Total and Marginal Utilities of Hamburgers and Pizza**

The marginal utility of a good or service equals the change in total utility associated with a one-unit increase in consumption of the good. Hence, the marginal utility of the first hamburger is 50 (a change from 0 to 50), while the marginal utility of the second is 40 (90 − 50). Note that both hamburgers and pizza display diminishing marginal utility: as you consume more and more, the increase in utility associated with each extra unit consumed falls.

Hamburgers			Pizza		
Hamburgers per Week	Total Utility	Marginal Utility	Pizza Slices per Week	Total Utility	Marginal Utility
0	0	—	0	0	—
1	50	50	1	40	40
2	90	40	2	56	16
3	120	30	3	70	14
4	144	24	4	80	10
5	166	22	5	88	8
6	186	20	6	90	2
7	204	18	7	90	0
8	220	16	8	88	−2
9	228	8			
10	230	2			

$$[\text{Expenditures on hamburgers}] + [\text{Expenditures on pizza}] \le \$16.00$$

$$Q_h{}^*P_h + Q_p{}^*P_p \le \$16.00$$

$$Q_h{}^*(\$2.00) + Q_p{}^*(\$1.00) \le \$16.00$$

Letting (8, 0) denote the consumption bundle of 8 hamburgers and 0 slices of pizza, at these prices and income, the feasible quantities that exhaust the budget are (8, 0), (7, 2), (6, 4), (5, 6), (4, 8), (3, 10), (2, 12), (1, 14), and (0, 16).

Identifying the utility-maximizing combination is best understood by proceeding incrementally, using marginal analysis. Because individuals want to get as much utility as is possible given their budget, they are particularly interested in the **marginal utility** obtained per dollar spent on each good (Table 3.2). The first hamburger provides 25 utils per dollar while the first slice of pizza provides 40 utils per dollar. The person would first purchase a slice of pizza. After this first purchase, the choice is between the first hamburger (25 utils per dollar) and a second slice of pizza (16 utils per dollar). The second purchase would be a hamburger, and the total amount spent is $3.00 out of the $16.00 budget. Following this logic until the person has spent the entire budget, the utility-maximizing combination of hamburgers and pizza is 6 hamburgers and 4 slices of pizza each week (6, 4). Total utility obtained is 266 utils: 186 from hamburgers and 80 from pizza. (To verify that this is the highest utility possible given the income, prices, and utilities, check the total utility obtained by all other feasible combinations.)[5]

marginal utility
The increase in total utility associated with consuming one more unit of a good.

Income and Substitution Effects

income effect
The change in the demand for a good caused by the change in real (price-adjusted) income.

It is also possible to explore how the utility-maximizing combination of hamburgers and pizza changes when features of the choice problem change. Suppose that the person's income increases by $5.00 to $21.00. Using the same logic as before, the new utility-maximizing bundle is 8 hamburgers and 5 slices of pizza, (8, 5). The change from (6, 4) to (8, 5) is called an **income effect**. Higher income in this case causes the person to

[5] Readers who have studied micro-economics before will recall that utility-maximization requires that the marginal utility per last dollar spent on each good must be equal. This holds for (6,4): marginal utility per dollar is 10 for both hamburgers and pizza.

TABLE 3.2   **Choosing the Utility-Maximizing Combination of Hamburgers and Pizza**

To choose the combination of hamburgers and pizza that maximizes utility given limited income, a person will spend each dollar so as to get the most utility per dollar. In this case, they would first choose a slice of pizza (40 utils per dollar), second they would choose a hamburger (25 utils per dollar), and proceed in this manner until they have spent the budget ($16). The utility-maximizing combination of hamburgers and pizza for this person is 6 hamburgers and 4 slices of pizza.

Budget = $16.00

	Hamburgers Price of Hamburger = $2.00				Pizza Price of Pizza Slice = $1.00		
Hamburg-ers per Week	Total Utility	Marginal Utility	Marginal Utility per Dollar	Pizza Slices per Week	Total Utility	Marginal Utility	Marginal Utility per Dollar
0	0	—	—	0	0	—	—
1	50	50	25	1	40	40	40
2	90	40	20	2	56	16	16
3	120	30	15	3	70	14	14
4	144	24	12	4	80	10	10
5	166	22	11	5	88	8	8
6	186	20	10	6	90	2	2
7	204	18	9	7	90	0	0
8	220	16	8	8	88	−2	−2
9	228	8	4				
10	230	2	1				

increase consumption of both. Higher income does not necessarily increase consumption of all goods—as income rises, many of us consume less macaroni and cheese and more lasagna, or fewer hamburgers and more steak.

When the price of hamburgers falls from $2.00 to $1.00, the utility-maximizing bundle becomes 10 hamburgers and 6 pieces of pizza, (10, 6). (Again, you can verify this.) The increase in hamburger consumption following its price decrease is perhaps not surprising, but why did pizza consumption also increase? Because a change in the price of hamburgers creates two effects: a **substitution (or pure-price) effect** and an income effect. The decrease in the price of hamburgers changes the relative prices of hamburgers to pizza from a ratio of 2:1 to 1:1, creating incentive to substitute hamburgers for pizza. It also increases real income, creating an income effect. The change from (6, 4) to (10, 6) reflects both of these effects.

substitution effect
A change in the demand for a good caused by a change in the relative price of the good, when real income is constant.

We can identify the separate influence of each through the following thought experiment. To identify the substitution effect, determine the bundle that would provide someone with the same level of utility they attained before the price change, but now purchasing the goods at the new prices. This person attained utility of 266 with the original bundle; the second bundle (9, 1) provides 268 utils, which is effectively equal. The substitution effect causes hamburger consumption to increase by 3 and pizza consumption to fall by 3, i.e., from (6, 4) to (9, 1). The change from this hypothetical bundle of (9, 1) to the observed bundle of (10, 6) reflects the income effect: the lower price of hamburgers increases real income and leads the individual to consume more of both.

A price change always creates both substitution and income effects. If the price of hamburgers increases from $2.00 to $3.00, the utility-maximizing bundle changes from (6, 4) to (4, 4). The substitution, or pure-price, effect causes this person to substitute pizza for hamburger, but the fall in real income caused by the price increase reduces consumption

FIGURE 3.1

The Individual Demand Curve for Hamburgers

At any given price, the demand curve tells us how much of the good will be demanded; e.g., at price of $3.00, four hamburgers are demanded per week. Analogously, for any given quantity, the demand curve tells us the maximum amount a person is willing to pay for each unit; e.g., the maximum willingness to pay for the sixth hamburger is $2.00.

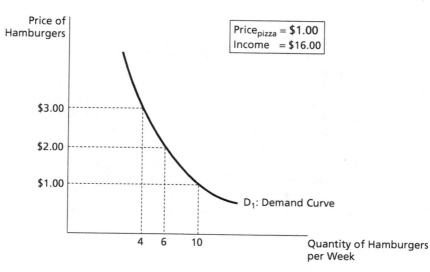

demand curve

A graph depicting the relationship between the price of a good and the quantity of the good demanded, holding all other determinants of demand (e.g., income, price of other goods) constant.

substitute good

A good that can satisfy a similar want, so that an increase in the price of one causes an increase in the demand for the other, and a decrease in the price of one causes a decrease in the demand for the other (e.g., hamburgers and pizza).

complementary goods

Goods that are normally consumed together, so that an increase in the price of one causes a decrease in the demand for the other, and a decrease in the price of one causes an increase in the demand for the other (e.g., hamburgers and hamburger buns).

of both.[6] Analogously, an increase in the price of pizza from $1.00 to $2.00 causes the optimal bundle to change to (7, 1).[7]

The Demand Curve

This basic choice framework enables us to construct the individual's demand curve for hamburgers. The **demand curve** shows how the quantity of hamburgers demanded varies with prices, tastes, and income. Figure 3.1 depicts this person's demand curve for hamburgers. The vertical axis represents the price of hamburgers, the horizontal axis represents the quantity of hamburgers per week, and the demand curve denotes how the quantity demanded per week varies with price. You can read the demand curve from either of two perspectives: (1) at any given price level, the horizontal distance from the y-axis to the curve tells you the quantity demanded at that price (e.g., at $3.00, 4 hamburgers are demanded; at $2.00, 6 hamburgers are demanded); (2) at any given quantity, the vertical distance from the x-axis to the curve tells you the maximum amount a person is willing to pay for that unit of the good (e.g., this person is willing to pay $3.00 for the fourth hamburger and $1.00 for the tenth). The demand curve is negatively sloped because of diminishing marginal utility—the maximum amount that a person is willing to pay decreases as quantity consumed increases; the quantity demanded increases as price falls.

The position of the demand curve relative to the x- and y-axes tells us how the prices of other goods, tastes, and income affect demand. Changes in any of these factors cause the whole demand curve to shift. The curve in Figure 3.1 is drawn for a pizza price of $1.00 and income of $16.00. When the price of pizza increases, we saw above that the quantity of hamburgers demanded increased. The increase in the price of pizza (a **substitute good** for hamburgers) causes the whole curve to shift out (Figure 3.2). Analogously, an increase in the price of a **complementary good**, such as hamburger buns, would cause the demand curve for hamburgers to shift inward.

---

[6] An income of $22.00 would allow the consumer to purchase the original bundle (6, 4) at the new prices. The optimal bundle with this income, and prices of $3.00 and $1.00 for hamburgers and pizza respectively, would be 5.67 hamburgers and 5 slices of pizza (if it were possible to buy a partial hamburger); the income effect then reduces both to the (4, 4) bundle.

[7] An income of $20.00 would allow the consumer to purchase the original bundle at the new prices. The optimal bundle with this income and prices of $2.00 each would be (8, 2), and the income effect reduces both to the (7, 1) bundle.

Changes in tastes also shift the demand curve. The outbreak of bovine spongiform encephalopathy (BSE, or mad-cow disease) in the U.K. in the 1990s, for instance, caused the demand curve for hamburgers to shift inward because people's desire for hamburgers changed (Figure 3.3). At any given price, people wanted fewer hamburgers.

Changes in income also shift the demand curve, though the impact depends on the nature of the good. In this particular case, the demand for hamburgers increases as income increases; analogously, demand for hamburger increases as income falls (Figure 3.4).

The trick in demand analysis is to remember how different factors affect the demand curve. Although the only variables explicitly depicted in the diagram are price and quantity demanded, every demand curve is drawn using some assumed levels for all other factors that affect demand. A change in the price of the good itself causes movement along the good's demand curve. A change in the price of a substitute or complementary good, or in tastes, or in income causes the whole demand curve to shift inward or outward.

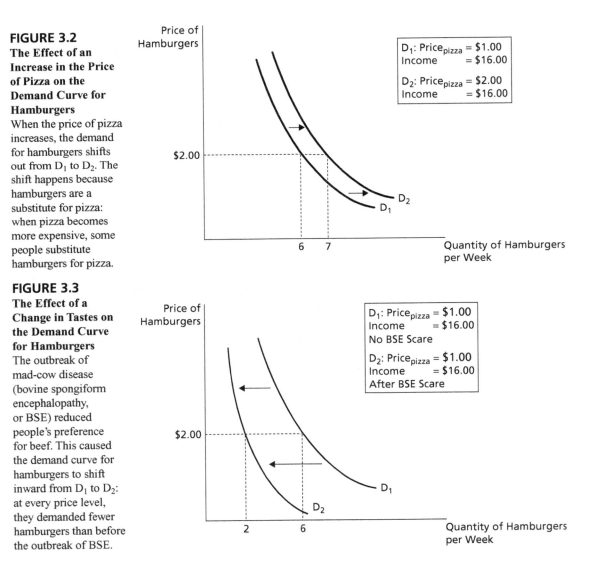

FIGURE 3.2
The Effect of an Increase in the Price of Pizza on the Demand Curve for Hamburgers
When the price of pizza increases, the demand for hamburgers shifts out from D_1 to D_2. The shift happens because hamburgers are a substitute for pizza: when pizza becomes more expensive, some people substitute hamburgers for pizza.

FIGURE 3.3
The Effect of a Change in Tastes on the Demand Curve for Hamburgers
The outbreak of mad-cow disease (bovine spongiform encephalopathy, or BSE) reduced people's preference for beef. This caused the demand curve for hamburgers to shift inward from D_1 to D_2: at every price level, they demanded fewer hamburgers than before the outbreak of BSE.

FIGURE 3.4
The Effect of Changes in Income on the Demand Curve for Hamburgers
An increase in this person's income from $16.00 to $21.00 causes the demand curve for hamburgers of shift outward from D_1 to D_2: at every price level, they demand fewer hamburgers than before their increase in income. Analogously, a fall in income shifts the demand curve outward from D_1 to D_3.

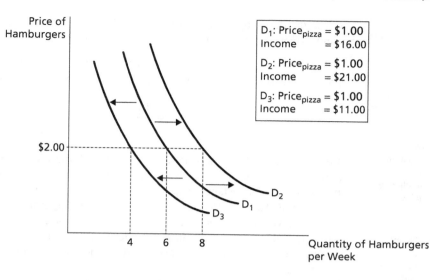

elasticity
A measure of the responsiveness of one variable to a change in the value of another variable; defined as the ratio of the percentage change in the former to the percentage change in the latter.

own-price-elasticity
A measure of the responsiveness of the demand for a good to a change in its price; defined as (percentage change in the quantity of a good demanded)/(percentage change in its price).

income-elasticity of demand
A measure of the responsiveness of the demand for a good to changes in income; defined as (percentage change in demand for a good/(percentage change in income).

Elasticity of Demand

Policy development often requires knowledge of how sensitive demand is to its determinants. Governments and private insurance companies, for instance, need to know how much a change in the price an individual pays for a physician visit will change the demand for visits. Economists use the concept of **elasticity** to measure the quantitative relationship between two variables, one of which wholly or partly determines the other. An elasticity measure is defined as the ratio of the percentage change in the determined variable to the percentage change in the determining variable, other things held constant. The two most commonly used elasticity measures in demand analysis are **own-price-elasticity**, which measures the responsiveness of the quantity demanded for a good to changes in its own price, and **income-elasticity of demand**, which measures the responsiveness of the demand for a good to changes in income.

These elasticities are calculated as follows. Let E_A^P denote the own-price-elasticity of good A to changes in its price.[8]

$$E_A^P = \frac{\text{percentage change in the quantity demanded}}{\text{percentage change in price}}$$

$$= \frac{\dfrac{(Q_2 - Q_1)}{\left[\dfrac{(Q_1+Q_2)}{2}\right]}}{\dfrac{(P_2 - P_1)}{\left[\dfrac{(P_1+P_2)}{2}\right]}} = \frac{\left[\dfrac{(Q_2 - Q_1)}{(Q_1+Q_2)}\right]}{\left[\dfrac{(P_2 - P_1)}{(P_1+P_2)}\right]} \qquad (3.2)$$

[8] The formula is for the "arc elasticity of demand." A percentage change is normally calculated as the change divided by the initial level. But if that formula is used, the estimated elasticity of the price change is from $2.00 to $1.00 is different than a price change from $1.00 to $2.00. To avoid such problems, when calculating the percentage change, the arc elasticity formula is divided by the mean of the initial and post-change values so that the elasticity measure is the same for a given segment on the demand curve whether one is assessing the impact of a price increase or a price decrease. Note that equation (3.2) can also be expressed as: $E_A^P = \dfrac{1}{\text{slope}} \times \left[\dfrac{P_1 + P_2}{Q_1 + Q_2}\right]$, where slope refers to the slope of the demand curve.

Given the demand curve for hamburgers depicted in Figure 3.1, the price-elasticity of demand associated with a change in price from $2.00 to $1.00 is as follows:

Initial price: $P_1 = \$2.00$; Initial quantity demanded: $Q_1 = 6$

Post-change price: $P_2 = \$1.00$; Post-change quantity demanded: $Q_2 = 10$

$$E_H^P = \frac{\left[\frac{4}{16}\right]}{\left[\frac{-1}{3}\right]} = -0.75$$

inelastic
Elasticity of less than 1.0, indicating that one variable is relatively unresponsive to changes in another variable of interest.

Because the demand curve is negatively sloped, the own-price elasticity is negative. The more responsive the quantity demanded is to price, the larger is the absolute value of the elasticity. For instance, when the absolute value is greater than 1.0, it means that the percentage change in the quantity demanded was larger than the percentage change in price. By convention, economists refer to demand as **inelastic** (price insensitive) when the absolute value of the price-elasticity is less than 1, **unitary elastic** when the absolute value of price-elasticity equals 1, and **elastic** (price sensitive) when the absolute value of the price-elasticity is greater than 1.

unitary elasticity
Elasticity of 1.0, indicating that a percentage change in one variable will cause an equal percentage change in a second variable.

The income elasticity of demand measures the responsiveness of demand to changes in income. Again, for hamburgers:

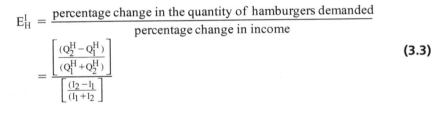

$$E_H^I = \frac{\text{percentage change in the quantity of hamburgers demanded}}{\text{percentage change in income}}$$

$$= \frac{\left[\frac{(Q_2^H - Q_1^H)}{(Q_1^H + Q_2^H)}\right]}{\left[\frac{(I_2 - I_1)}{(I_1 + I_2)}\right]} \qquad (3.3)$$

elastic
Elasticity of greater than 1.0, indicating that one variable is relatively responsive to changes in another variable of interest.

For the increase in income from $16.00 to $21.00, we have:

Initial income: $I_1 = \$16.00$; Initial quantity demanded: $Q_1 = 6$

Post-change income: $I_2 = \$21.00$; Post-change quantity demanded: $Q_2 = 8$

$$E_H^I = \frac{\left[\frac{2}{14}\right]}{\left[\frac{5}{37}\right]} = 1.32$$

inferior good
A good for which the quantity demanded decreases as income rises; a good with a negative income-elasticity of demand.

Economists refer to goods whose quantity demanded falls as income rises as **inferior goods** ($E^I < 0$) and goods whose quantity demand grows as income rises as **normal goods** ($E^I > 0$). Table 3.3 summarizes elasticities of demand.

The elasticity of demand for a good depends on the time period under consideration. The elasticity of demand for gasoline in the very short run—say over the next week—is quite inelastic as people have relatively few opportunities to adjust to a price increase. But over a longer period—say, the next two years—demand is far more elastic because people have more scope to adjust. They can buy a new, fuel-efficient car, they can join a carpool, they can move closer to work and school to reduce the need to drive, and so forth. It is essential to specify the time period of the analysis when assessing the effects that changes in prices, income, or tastes will have on demand.

normal good
A good for which the quantity demanded increases as income rises; a good with a positive income-elasticity of demand.

From Individual to Market Demand

Thus far the analysis has focused on the demand curve for a single individual. Markets, however, are made up of many individuals. Market demand is simply the sum of the individual

TABLE 3.3   Measures of Elasticity of Demand

Three demand-side measures of elasticity are commonly employed in economic analysis. Own-price elasticity measures how sensitive the demand for a good is to changes in its own price; income elasticity of demand measures how sensitive demand for a good is to changes in income.

Elasticity Measure	Definition	Formula	Interpretation
Own-Price Elasticity of Demand	Percentage change in the quantity of good A demanded divided by the percentage change in price of good A	$E_A^P = \left[\dfrac{\frac{(Q_2^A - Q_1^A)}{(Q_1^A + Q_2^A)}}{\frac{(P_2^A - P_1^A)}{(P_1^A + P_2^A)}} \right]$	$\left| E_A^P \right| > 1$ elastic demand $\left| E_A^P \right| = 1$ unitary elasticity $\left| E_A^P \right| < 1$ inelastic demand
Income Elasticity of Demand	Percentage change in the quantity of good A demanded divided by the percentage change in income	$E_A^I = \left[\dfrac{\frac{(Q_2^A - Q_1^A)}{(Q_1^A + Q_2^A)}}{\frac{(I_2 - I_1)}{(I_1 + I_2)}} \right]$	$E_A^I < 1$ inferior good $E_A^I = 1$ normal good $E_A^I > 1$ superior good

FIGURE 3.5   Aggregation of Individual Demand Curves to Construct the Total Market Demand

The market demand curve is the horizontal summation of the individual-level demand curves. In this simple market with two people, when price is P_1, Person 1 demands 5 units, Person 2 demands none, so total market demand is 5. When price is P_3, Person 1 demands 30 units and Person 2 demands 30 units, so market demand is 60 units.

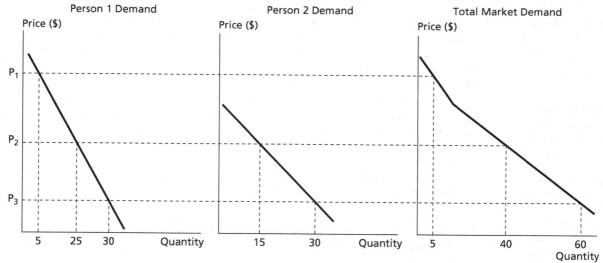

demands of all those participating in the market. Figure 3.5 illustrates this principle for a market with only 2 people. The kink occurs in the market demand curve because at high prices only Person 1 has a positive demand (so the market demand curve is just Person 1's demand curve in this price range). Both Person 1 and Person 2 have positive demand only after price has fallen to the kink point. Note that at the market level, market demand is influenced by both the mean level of income and the distribution of income in society.

With this basic set of concepts and tools, a wide range of economic analyses of the demand side of markets is possible.

3.2.2 Firm Behaviour and the Supply of Goods and Services

The economic analysis of supply considers the choice problem faced by producers. The analysis emphasizes the producers' behavioural objectives and the constraints they face when pursuing those objectives. A producer's principal choices pertain to the method of production and the amount of output to produce.

profits
Total revenue minus total costs.

Producers seek to maximize profits, where **profits** are defined as total revenue from sales less total production costs. A producer's total revenue is equal to the price of the good multiplied by the number of units the producer sells. In a competitive, well-functioning market, a single producer has no influence over the price it receives for the good it produces. Price is determined by the market and is taken as a given by an individual producer. Production costs are determined by the prices of inputs used in production (wages for workers, etc.) and the productivity of those inputs, which is determined by the production function. As we saw in Chapter 2, the production function defines the maximum amount of a good that can be produced with various combinations of inputs using existing technology; it defines the rate at which a producer can transform inputs into outputs. Production is assumed to be subject to **diminishing marginal returns**: as additional units of one input (e.g., labour) are added while holding constant the amounts of all other inputs, beyond a point the marginal output of each additional unit of the input (e.g., workers) falls.

diminishing marginal returns
Successive incremental additions of one input are associated with successively smaller increases in total output, holding the amounts of all other inputs constant.

The Supply Curve

marginal product
The increase in total output associated with a one unit increase in an input.

These basic concepts and their implications for a producer's decision about how much of a good to supply to the market can be illustrated with our hamburger example. Suppose a restaurant has a kitchen with a grill, counter space for food preparation, and the usual kitchen equipment (the capital input), and it gradually adds kitchen workers to produce hamburgers. The marginal product of workers initially rises as each worker specializes on a small number of tasks, but eventually the marginal product of each additional worker begins to fall as the kitchen becomes overcrowded and coordination problems increase so that some workers are temporarily idle while waiting for other workers to complete a task (Table 3.4). **Marginal product** in this example begins to fall after the second worker is hired; marginal product remains positive but falls at least through the ninth worker.

marginal cost
The increase in total cost associated with producing one more unit of a good.

To determine how this production translates into the restaurant's costs, we need to consider the cost of workers (for simplicity we ignore capital costs which are constant when capital inputs are fixed). Assume that the cost of hiring a worker is $90 per day (including wages and benefits).

TABLE 3.4

Production of Hamburgers per Day
This table illustrates how the production of hamburgers in a restaurant changes as the number of workers increases, holding capital inputs (e.g., grills, meat grinders, etc.) fixed. The marginal product is the change in total production associated with adding one worker. Marginal product initially rises, but then falls as the kitchen gets too crowded and it becomes harder to coordinate the activities of a larger number of workers.

The **marginal cost** is the additional cost of producing one more hamburger. The marginal cost of producing a hamburger initially falls as workers are hired, but begins to rise after the

Number of Workers	Total Hamburger Output	Average Output per Worker	Marginal Output per Worker
0	0	—	—
1	50	50.0	50
2	110	55.0	60
3	166	55.3	56
4	217	54.3	51
5	263	52.6	46
6	302	50.3	39
7	333	47.6	31
8	356	44.5	23
9	374	41.6	18

Note: Assumes fixed capital inputs.

TABLE 3.5

Marginal Costs of Hamburger Production

The marginal cost of a hamburger is the change in total costs associated with producing one more hamburger. Assuming workers are paid a constant wage, the decreasing marginal product of workers causes the marginal costs of hamburgers to increase as production rises.

Number of Workers	Total Hamburger Output	Average Output per Worker	Marginal Output per Worker	Total Cost of Labour	Marginal Cost per Hamburger
(a)	(b)	(c)	(d)	(e)	(f)
0	0	—	—	0	—
1	50	50.0	50	$ 90.00	$1.80
2	110	55.0	60	$180.00	$1.50
3	166	55.3	56	$270.00	$1.61
4	217	54.3	51	$360.00	$1.76
5	263	52.6	46	$450.00	$1.96
6	302	50.3	39	$540.00	$2.31
7	333	47.6	31	$630.00	$2.90
8	356	44.5	23	$720.00	$3.91
9	374	41.6	18	$810.00	$5.00

Assumes fixed cost of capital equal to 0 and constant daily wage rate of $90.00 per worker.

FIGURE 3.6

The Marginal Cost Curve for Hamburger Production

This graph depicts the marginal cost curve associated with the production of hamburgers, and is derived from the information in Table 3.5. Marginal cost first decreases, and then begins to increase after 110 hamburgers.

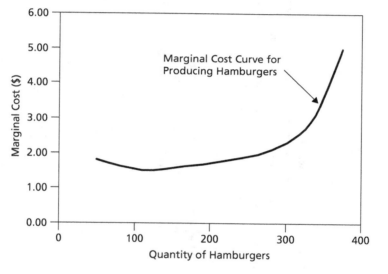

marginal revenue
The increase in total revenue associated with a one-unit increase in sales of a good.

second worker (Table 3.5; Figure 3.6). **Marginal revenue** equals the change in revenue from selling one more hamburger. The profit maximizing rule for a firm is to operate where marginal revenue equals marginal cost. In a competitive market, marginal revenue equals price. Increasing the production of hamburgers will increase profits only if the price received for selling an additional hamburger exceeds the marginal cost of producing an additional hamburger. Table 3.6 presents information on the profit earned by the restaurant at various levels of output under alternative prices it might charge for hamburgers. For any give price level, profits are highest when output is at the level just before marginal costs exceed the price.

Because of this relationship between marginal costs and profit, a firm's supply curve, which depicts how much of a good a producer will produce at each price of the good, is the firm's marginal cost curve (Figure 3.7).[9] The supply curve's position and shape is determined by the price of inputs, the production technology available, and for some goods, natural

[9] Economists call this the short-run supply curve because we have assumed capital is fixed. In the long run, a restaurant could change the size of the kitchen and the amount of kitchen equipment.

TABLE 3.6 Productivity, Costs, and Profits of Hamburger Production

Profit equals revenues minus costs, where revenue equals the price received per hamburger times the quantity sold. Profits are highest when production is set to the level at which price equals marginal cost. At a price of $1.50, it is not profitable to produce any hamburgers. At a price of $2.00, profit-maximizing production occurs at 263 hamburgers. At this price, if the restaurant hires one more worker, the marginal cost of the additional hamburgers produced is $2.31 compared to a price received of $2.00, which causes profits to fall to $64 from $76. Using the same reasoning, at a price of $3.00, the profit-maximizing production is 333 hamburgers, and so forth.

# of Workers (a)	Total Hamburger Output (b)	Average Output per Worker (c)	Marginal Output per Worker (d)	Total Cost of Labour (e)	Marginal Cost per Hamburger (f)	Profits at Different Levels of Output under Various Prices for Hamburgers			
						$1.50 (g)	$2.00 (h)	$3.00 (i)	$4.00 (j)
0	0	—	—	0	—				
1	50	50.0	50	$90.00	$1.80	-$15.00	$10.00	$60.00	$110.00
2	110	55.0	60	$180.00	$1.50	-$15.00	$40.00	$150.00	$260.00
3	166	55.3	56	$270.00	$1.61	-$21.00	$62.00	$228.00	$394.00
4	217	54.3	51	$360.00	$1.76	-$34.50	$74.00	$291.00	$508.00
5	263	52.6	46	$450.00	$1.96	-$55.50	$76.00	$339.00	$602.00
6	302	50.3	39	$540.00	$2.31	-$87.00	$64.00	$366.00	$668.00
7	333	47.6	31	$630.00	$2.90	-$130.50	$36.00	$369.00	$702.00
8	356	44.5	23	$720.00	$3.91	-$186.00	-$8.00	$348.00	$704.00
9	374	41.6	18	$810.00	$5.00	-$249.00	-$62.00	$312.00	$686.00

Assumes fixed cost of capital equal to 0 and constant daily wage rate of $90.00 per worker.

Profits = Revenue − Costs. E.g., at a price of $2.00 per hamburger, profits = [$2.00*(b)] − (e).

FIGURE 3.7   **The Individual-Firm (Short-Run) Supply Curve for Hamburgers**

A firm's supply curve depicts how the quantity of the good that it is willing to supply changes with the price of the good, holding prices of inputs and production technology constant. In this example, at a price of $2.00, the firm will produce 263 hamburgers; analogously, the supply curve indicates the minimum amount a firm must be paid to produce a given unit. To produce the 356th hamburger, this firm would need to be paid $4.00 for that hamburger.

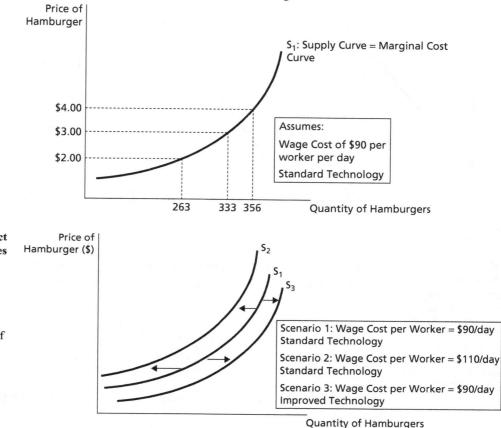

FIGURE 3.8   Effect on Supply of Changes in Wages and Technology

A change in any supply-determining factor other than the price of the good itself causes the supply curve to shift. An increase in the price of an input causes the supply curve to shift inward from S_1 to S_2; improvements in technology cause the supply curve to shift outward from S_1 to S_3.

factors such as weather. As was the case with the demand curve, the effect of a change in the price of the good on the quantity supplied is determined by moving along the supply curve. When the price of a hamburger rises from $2.00 to $3.00, for instance, the producer in Figure 3.7 increases the quantity supplied from 263 to 333 per week. A change in any determinant of supply other than price (e.g., price of inputs, technology) causes the whole supply curve to shift. An increase in worker wages, for example, would cause the entire supply curve to shift to the left, so that at each price a producer is willing to supply less than previously (Figure 3.8). A change in production technology that allows a good to be produced with fewer resources causes the supply curve to shift outward. As with the demand curve, the key to using a supply curve to analyze market dynamics is to remember that changes in the price of the good itself result in movements along the supply curve, while changes in any other factor that influences supply will result in a shift in the supply curve.

The slope of the supply curve indicates the sensitivity of the quantity supplied to the price of the good. As with demand, we can use an elasticity to measure the degree of

FIGURE 3.9 **Aggregation of Individual-Firm Supply Curves to Construct Market Supply Curve**
The market supply curve is the horizontal summation of the firm-level supply curves. In this simple market with two firms, when price is P_3, Firm 1 is willing to supply 5 units and Firm 2 supplies none, so total market supply is 5. When price is P_1, Firm 1 supplies 125 units and Firm 2 supplies 90 units, so market supply is 215 units.

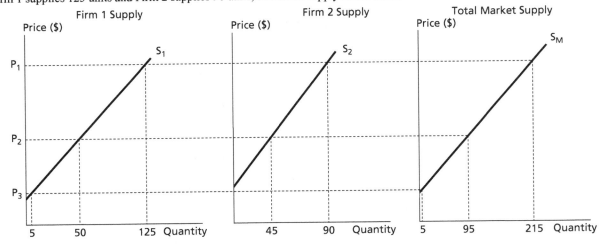

price-elasticity of supply

A measure of the responsiveness of the supply of a good to a change in its price, defined as (percentage change in the quantity of a good supplied)/(percentage change in its price).

responsiveness to price. The **price-elasticity of supply** is defined as the ratio of the percentage change in the quantity supplied to the percentage change in price:

$$E_H^S = \frac{\frac{(Q_2-Q_1)}{\left[\frac{Q_1+Q_2}{2}\right]}}{\frac{(P_2-P_1)}{\left[\frac{P_1+P_2}{2}\right]}} = \frac{\left[\frac{(Q_2-Q_1)}{(Q1+Q_2)}\right]}{\left[\frac{(P_2-P_1)}{(P_1+P_2)}\right]} \qquad (3.4)$$

For the price-elasticity of hamburger supply between prices of $2.00 and $3.00, we have:

$$E_H^S = \frac{\frac{70}{596}}{\frac{1}{5}} = 0.59$$

Price-elasticity of supply is positive, reflecting the positive slope of the supply curve. As with price-elasticity of demand, by convention, $E^S < 1$ is inelastic, $E^S = 1$ is unitary, and $E^S > 1$ is elastic.

As was the case for the demand curve, the elasticity of the supply curve depends on the time period of the analysis. In the short run, it can be very difficult to increase the supply of a good substantially because production capacity is fixed. In the long run, however, producers can expand their production capacity by building additional production facilities.

Finally, the market supply curve is a simple summation of the supply curves of all producers, as depicted in Figure 3.9.

3.2.3 Putting Demand and Supply Together: A Market

A market comprises demand and supply. The interaction between demand and supply in a market determines the price at which a good is exchanged and the quantity of the good exchanged. Because demand and supply for a good are determined by different sets of

FIGURE 3.10

A Market: Demand and Supply Curves
This figure depicts a supply and demand curve for a single market. In this market, the equilibrium price and quantity—the price and quantity to which the market will settle and at which there is no tendency for change—are P* and Q*. If price is below P*, such as P1, there will be excess demand (i.e., the quantity demanded, Q_1^d, exceeds the quantity supplied, Q_1^s), which will bid the price up to P*, at which point the quantity demanded equals the quantity supplied so there will be no more pressure for price to rise. By analogous reasoning, if price were above P*, market forces would push it down to P*, where it would settle.

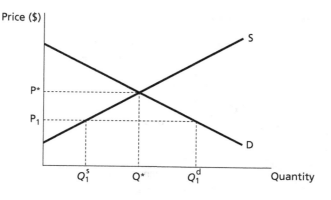

market equilibrium
The price–quantity combination in a market at which there is no tendency for price or output to change unless one of the determinants of demand or supply changes.

factors, demand and supply are assumed to be independent of each other. That is, a change in demand does not cause a change in supply, and vice versa. The supply and demand framework can be used to conduct both positive economic analysis of markets (i.e., what happens to price and quantity when various factors change?) and normative analysis (i.e., do the changes in the market outcomes increase or decrease welfare?).

Positive Economic Analysis of Markets

Figure 3.10 depicts market supply and demand curves for a good. The price at which the quantity demanded just equals the quantity supplied, P*, is called the market-clearing, or equilibrium price, and Q* is the market-clearing, or equilibrium, quantity. At this price, all consumer demand for hamburgers will be satisfied by producers, and producers will sell all the hamburgers they make. This price-quantity combination (P*,Q*) is called the **market equilibrium** because once the market reaches this price–quantity combination, there will be no tendency for price or output to change unless one of the determinants of demand or supply changes.

A well-functioning market will automatically converge to an equilibrium price–quantity combination. To see this, imagine that price is P_1. At this price, the quantity demanded is Q_1^d and the quantity supplied is Q_1^s. The quantity demanded by consumers exceeds the quantity supplied by producers: there is a shortage. Because consumers are willing to pay more than P_1 at the available supply of Q_1^s, some individuals who are unable to obtain the good will bid up the price. As the price is bid upwards, producers will increase output. This will happen until the market reaches (P*, Q*). The analogous process would occur if for some reason price were above P*.

This supply and demand framework allows us to trace the impact of any market-affecting event through its influence on supply or demand. An outbreak of BSE, for instance, will have a number of effects on the market for hamburgers and pizzas (Figure 3.11). Suppose that before the outbreak of BSE, the hamburger and pizza markets were in equilibrium at (P_1^H, Q_1^H) and (P_1^P, Q_1^P) respectively (Figures 3.11(i) and (ii)). BSE will cause some people to switch from hamburgers to pizza, simultaneously shifting the demand for hamburgers inward and the demand for pizza outward. This shift causes the price and quantity of hamburgers to change to (P_2^H, Q_2^H). BSE, however, has a further impact in the hamburger market. Ranchers now have to purchase different, more expensive feed, and cattle must be tested at the slaughterhouse, increasing the cost of producing beef. This causes the supply curve to shift inward to a new equilibrium of (P_3^H, Q_3^H). In the pizza market, the inward shift in both the demand for and supply of hamburgers shifts the

FIGURE 3.11

The Effects of BSE on the Markets for Hamburgers and Pizza

Starting from the initial equilibrium, the outbreak of BSE causes the demand curve for hamburgers to shift inward (Figure 3.11(i)). It also causes the supply curve to shift inward as the cost of raising cattle and bringing beef to market rises (ranchers must use more expensive feed; meatpackers must do more testing and inspection). These changes in the market for hamburgers cause the demand for pizza to shift outward (Figure 3.11(ii)). In the new equilibriums, the equilibrium quantity of hamburgers will definitely be lower than before the BSE outbreak, but the price of hamburgers could be higher or lower depending on the relative sizes of the shifts in the demand and supply curves for hamburgers (in the figure, the new equilibrium price is lower). Both the equilibrium price and quantity of pizza will be higher.

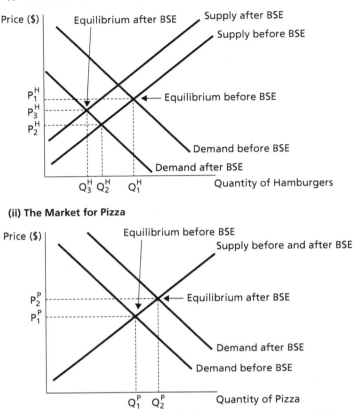

(i) The Market for Hamburgers

(ii) The Market for Pizza

demand for pizza outward, to a new equilibrium of (P_2^P, Q_2^P) (Figure 3.11(ii)). At this new equilibrium, the quantity of hamburgers sold will definitely be less than before BSE (Q_3^H vs Q_1^H), and the price and quantity of pizza will be higher than before. Because both demand and supply of hamburger shifted inward, in principle, the new equilibrium price in the hamburger market could be higher or lower depending on the relative amounts by which each shifts. As shown in Figure 3.11, the inward shift of demand dominates the inward shift in supply, so the new equilibrium price is lower (P_3^H vs P_1^H). However, if the inward shift in supply (caused by rising costs) dominated the reduction in demand, the new equilibrium price would be higher.

This supply and demand framework is essential for analyzing the impact of a wide range of events in society, and many public policies in particular. As an example, consider a perennial policy question in many large cities: access to affordable housing. One policy response is rent control: regulate the price of some apartments so as to make them more affordable. Figure 3.12(i) depicts the impact of rent control on the market for apartments. Suppose that before rent control the monthly rent for an apartment was P* and Q* apartments were rented, but many individuals were priced out of the market. Rent control then set the maximum allowable price to P_{RC}. At price P_{RC}, the quantity of apartments demanded equals Q_{RC}^D and the quantity supplied equals Q_{RC}^S. Because price is held artificially below the market equilibrium, a shortage develops. The rent control policy creates (or at least exacerbates) the shortage of apartments. Nor is it clear that rent control increases access for those who previously could not afford an apartment. We know that Q_{RC}^S units are rented,

FIGURE 3.12 **Analysing the Impact of Alternative Policies to Increase Access to Housing**
Let the equilibrium rent and quantity of apartments before rent control be (P*, Q*). Rent control
set at P_{RC} will cause the quantity of apartments demanded to increase to Q_{RC}^D while the quantity
supplied falls to Q_{RC}^S, generating a shortage equal to $(Q_{RC}^D - Q_{RC}^S)$. Fewer apartments are available,
and it is not possible to know whether those that are available go to those most in need. A policy
of rent subsidy equal to AB paid to renters would lead to an equilibrium quantity of Q_{sub}^*, at which
the market price received by landlords would be P_{sub}^S, the amount renters would pay out-of-pocket
would be P_{sub}^R, and the government subsidy makes up the difference.

(i) Rent Control

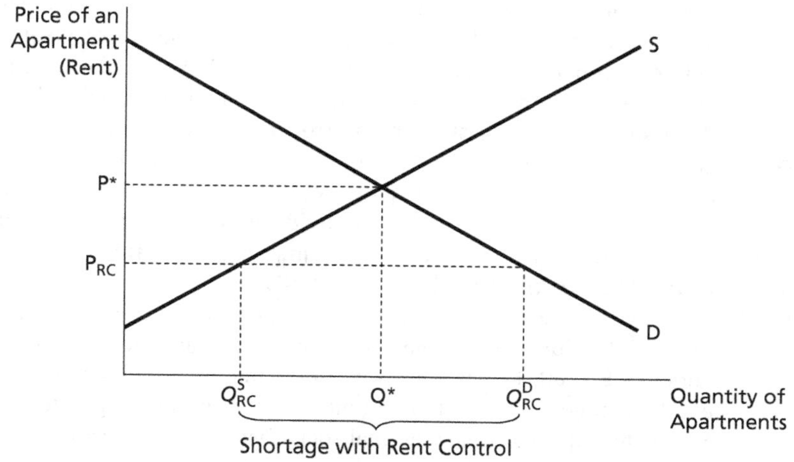

(ii) Rent Subsidy

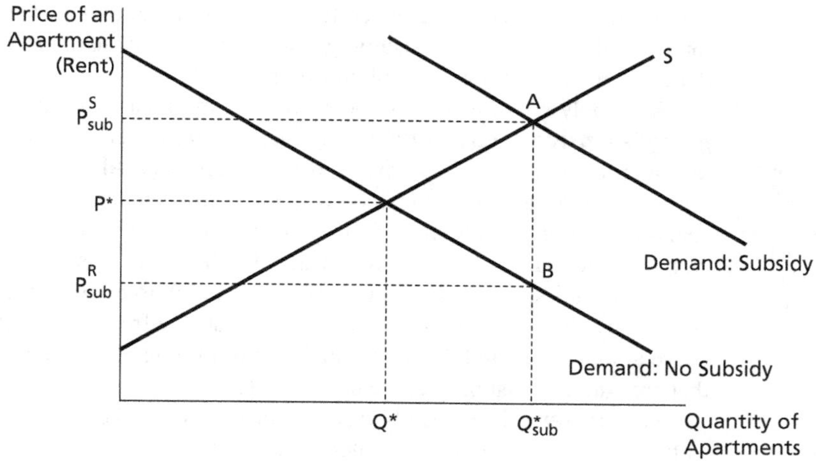

but we don't know who among all those willing to pay P_{RC} gets an apartment. The largest
beneficiaries are those who already rented before rent control was imposed, who still have
their apartment but now face smaller rent increases.

An alternative policy approach would be to provide a housing subsidy to either builders
or low-income renters. The effects of such a policy are depicted in Figure 3.12(ii). If a subsidy of size AB is provided directly to renters, in the new equilibrium their out-of-pocket
cost would be P_{sub}^R while they pay a market rate of P_{sub}^S to suppliers (the difference is the

consumer sovereignty
The assumption that consumers are the best judges of their own welfare, and that their decisions should determine the amount and distribution of goods in society.

marginal private benefit (MPB)
The marginal benefit obtained by the individual who consumes a good.

marginal social benefit (MSB)
The marginal benefit obtained by both the individual who consumes a good and others in society who obtain external benefits.

marginal private cost (MPC)
The marginal cost incurred by the organization that produces a good.

marginal social cost (MSC)
The marginal costs incurred by both the organization that produces a good and others in society who are affected by external costs.

net benefit
Total social benefit associated with the consumption of a good minus the total social cost of its production.

subsidy they receive from government).[10] This increases both the quantity supplied and the quantity demanded to Q^*_{sub}. Access to housing increases, and there is no shortage. An important difference between this policy and rent control, of course, is that a subsidy policy requires government expenditure (equal to the rectangle $P^S_{sub}ABP^R_{sub}$) while rent control does not (though it can be costly to administer). Although this is an incomplete analysis of rent control and housing subsidy policies, it illustrates how the supply and demand framework can be used as part of an overall analysis of such policies.

Normative Economic Analysis of Markets

The supply and demand framework is also a key part of much normative economic analysis. Converting the framework from one suitable for positive analysis to one suitable for normative analysis requires that we add normative, or ethical, assumptions. Two critical assumptions are that consumers are the best judges of their own welfare (called the assumption of **consumer sovereignty**) and that willingness to pay is an appropriate measure of benefit. Under these assumptions, the demand curve, which indicates the amount a person is willing to pay to obtain each unit of a good, provides a measure of the marginal private benefit (MPB) individuals derive from each unit of a good consumed. If there are no externalities in consumption, then **marginal private benefit** equals **marginal social benefit** (MPB = MSB).

The total social benefit from hamburger consumption can be calculated as shown in Figure 3.13. Suppose that the maximum amount anyone is willing to pay for the first hamburger is $10.00. This is a measure of the marginal social benefit to society of consuming one hamburger. If the maximum anyone was willing to pay for the second hamburger is $9.50, this represents the marginal social benefit of the second hamburger. The total social benefit from consuming two hamburgers is $19.50 (the sum of the marginal benefits of the first and second hamburgers). From this, we can see that the marginal benefit of any single hamburger is the vertical distance from the horizontal axis to the demand curve, and the total social benefit from consuming a given number of hamburgers is the area under the demand curve up to that level of consumption.

The supply curve is simply the producer's marginal cost curve. It is a measure of the **marginal private cost** (MPC) of producing hamburgers. Again, if there are no externalities in production, marginal private cost equals **marginal social cost** (MPC = MSC). By reasoning in an analogous fashion as we did for demand, we can calculate the marginal social cost of any single unit of the good and the total social cost of producing any given amount. The marginal social cost of the first hamburger is $2.00, of the second is $2.25 (giving a total social cost of producing two hamburgers of $4.25). The marginal social cost of any single hamburger is the vertical distance from the horizontal axis to the supply curve at that point, and the total social cost of producing a given number of hamburgers is that area under the supply curve up to that level of output.

The **net benefit** to society from the production and consumption of a good is defined as the total social benefit generated by the consumption minus the total social cost of its production. Let us further assume that allocative efficiency is defined as maximizing net benefit (as per the potential Pareto Criterion). Under the normative assumptions identified above, a well-functioning market will be allocatively efficient in the sense of maximizing net benefit to society.

---

[10] If the same per-unit subsidy were provided to housing suppliers, the supply curve would shift out, intersecting the demand curve at point B on the demand curve. The new quantity of housing would be the same as when the subsidy is provided to renters, but the observed market price paid by renters would be P^R_{sub}. The two approaches are therefore formally equivalent though the observed market prices would differ (P^S_{sub} vs. P^R_{sub}).

FIGURE 3.13 **Measuring the Benefits and Costs Using the Demand and Supply Framework**

Under the assumptions that individuals are well-informed, that they are the best judges of their own welfare, that a person's willingness to pay for a good is the appropriate measure of social value, and that there are no externalities, the vertical distance from the horizontal axis to the demand curve represents the marginal benefit of consuming that unit of a good, and the area under the demand curve up to that point measures the social benefit of consuming all those units. The marginal social benefit of the first unit is $10.00, of the third unit is $9.00; the total social benefit of consuming three units is $28.50. Analogously, the supply curve measures the social cost of a good. The marginal social cost of the first unit is $2.00, of the third unit $2.50; and the total social cost of three units is $6.75. Net benefit, the difference between total benefit and total cost is maximized when MSB = MSC, the intersection of supply and demand (Q = 375).

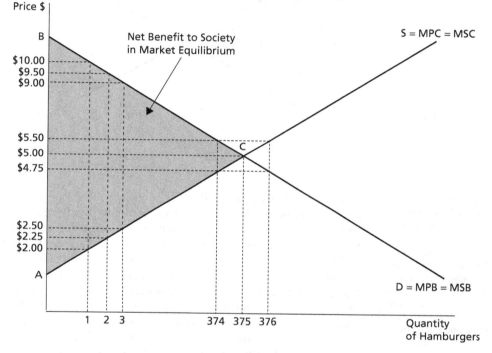

In the supply and demand framework, the measure of net benefit is the area below the demand curve and above the supply curve. The net benefit of the first hamburger is $8.00 ($10.00 − $2.00), of the second is $7.25 ($9.50 − $2.25). The net benefit of two hamburgers is therefore $15.25. For every hamburger up to the 375th, the marginal benefit exceeds the marginal cost, so net benefit to society increases by producing and consuming hamburgers up to that point. But if we produce and consume the 376st hamburger, net benefit falls because the marginal social cost of the hamburger is $5.50, but the marginal benefit is only $4.75. Net benefit to society in a well-functioning market is maximized at the market equilibrium price and quantity.

Consumers' and Producers' Surplus

The supply and demand framework also reveals how society's net benefit is split between consumers and producers. The equilibrium price in the hamburger market is $5.00. Every purchaser has to pay $5.00. But the first individual would be willing to pay $10.00 (Figure 3.14). This difference between the maximum the person would be willing to pay and the amount they actually have to pay represents a benefit to the consumer. Analogously, the

FIGURE 3.14 **Consumers' and Producers' Surplus**
The demand curve represents the maximum consumers are willing to pay for each hamburger. But in equilibrium, each consumer has to pay only P*. Therefore, the area above the price line and below the demand curve represents the net benefit to consumers (consumers' surplus). The supply curve represents the minimum payment a producer would require to produce each hamburger, but producers receive P* for all hamburgers sold. Therefore, the area above the supply curve and below the price line represents net benefit to producers (producers' surplus). Overall, the net benefit to society is the sum of consumers' and producers' surplus.

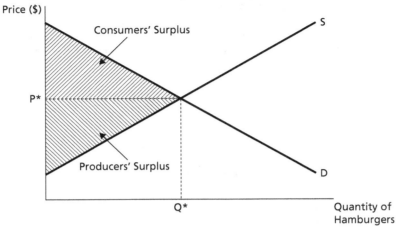

consumers' surplus
The difference between the maximum amount a person is willing to pay for a good minus the amount they actually have to pay. For a well-functioning market in equilibrium, the area above the equilibrium price line and below the demand curve.

producers' surplus
The difference between the amount a firm actually receives for selling a unit of a good, less the minimum amount a firm would accept to sell it. For a well-functioning market in equilibrium, the area above the supply curve and below the price line.

producer would have to be willing to produce the first hamburger for as little as $2.00, but actually receives $5.00. The difference represents benefit accruing to the producer. Hence, of the $8.00 in net benefit generated by producing and consuming the first hamburger, $5.00 of benefit accrues to the consumer and $3.00 accrues to the producer.

Reasoning in the same way for all hamburgers consumed in the market, we see that the area above the equilibrium price line and below the demand curve is a measure of benefit that accrues to consumers (called **consumers' surplus**), and the area below the equilibrium price line but above the supply curve is a measure of the benefit that accrues to producers (called **producers' surplus**). The sum of the two equals the net benefit to society.

More generally, when allocative efficiency is defined in terms of the potential Pareto Criterion, an allocation is efficient only if, for the last unit produced and consumed, marginal social benefit equals marginal social cost:

$$MSB = MSC \qquad \text{(3.5)}$$

In equilibrium in a market with well-informed consumers, no externalities, and no consumers or producers with sufficient market power to manipulate price, the following holds true:

$$MSB = MPB = P^* = MPC = MSC \qquad \text{(3.6)}$$

Equation (3.6) highlights the pivotal role played by prices in a market system. In a market system, to obtain a given resource an individual or organization must bid it away from any other potential user of the resource. They must pay a price just above the price anyone else is willing to pay. If a restaurant wants to hire a cook, it must pay a sufficient amount to attract a person away from other work options, which means paying more than what other sectors are willing to pay a worker. Given that the value, or benefit, of a resource is measured by willingness to pay, this ensures that a resource is always allocated to its highest-valued use, thereby minimizing opportunity cost (which, you will recall from Chapter 2, is defined as the benefit forgone by using a resource in one way rather than another). Price links the demand and supply sides of a market together and embodies the crucial information both demanders and suppliers need to make decisions that will result in an efficient allocation of resources when the necessary conditions hold.

Markets with Imperfect Competition

Up to this point, this analysis of the operation of markets has focused on markets with many buyers, many sellers selling an identical product—what economists call "perfect" competition. Under perfect competition, because the different sellers' products are identical (perfect substitutes), if a producer tries to raise its price above the market equilibrium, it will lose all of its sales to competitors. But as we noted above, markets can be characterized by "imperfect" competition if some producers hold market power, such as the case of a monopoly (a market with only one producer on the supply side). Two other types of market structures with imperfect competition should be noted: monopolistic competition and oligopoly.

monopolistic competition
A market with imperfect competition with many producers selling slightly differentiated products; this product differentiation gives each producer a small amount of market power.

Monopolistic competition refers to a market with many producers, each selling a slightly differentiated version of a good or service, so that the different versions are close, but not perfect substitutes. The market for toothpaste, for example, includes dozens of specific brands that are highly similar, but the slight differences among them create brand loyalty among customers. This brand loyalty gives the producer a modest amount of market power. They can, for example, raise the price without losing all their customers (though they will lose some; demand for an individual firm is highly elastic, even if demand for the whole industry is not). For this reason, producers in such markets actively try to cultivate brand loyalty. So, instead of a single market price, the market is characterized by a set of prices within a relatively narrow band, all above that which would occur in a market with perfect competition. In health care, markets for primary care physicians in large cities can sometimes be usefully characterized as monopolistic competition: different family physicians are close substitutes for each other and produce slightly differentiated services (differentiated, for example, by distance, style of practice, hours of operation, and so forth). These differences are a source of market power.

oligopolistic competition
A market with imperfect competition characterized by a small number of producers, each of which constitutes a large share of the market.

Oligopolistic competition refers to a market with a small number of large producers, each of which holds a substantial proportion of the market. Once again, each firm's market power allows it to raise its price above that which would exist in a perfectly competitive market. But the small number of identifiable competitors creates a highly strategic decision-making environment: one firm's actions are determined in part by how it thinks its competitors will react. The automobile industry in North America is one example of an oligopolistic market; the market for smartphones (e.g., Blackberries, iPhones) is another. In health care, many pharmaceutical markets are best characterized as oligopolistic: a small number of large, international firms engage in highly strategic competition.

The fundamental concern with imperfectly competitive markets is that suppliers exploit their market power for their own advantage, resulting in an inefficient market outcome. The distinctive structure of each type of imperfectly competitive market requires that they be analyzed using models specific to each market type, an issue we will return to in subsequent chapters when we examine specific health care markets.

Markets and Market Failure

Market failure occurs when one or more of the conditions set out in equation (3.6) do not hold. Externalities, poorly informed consumers, or, as noted, market powers cause one of the links in the chain of equalities in equation (3.6) to be broken, so that the market outcome occurs at a point at which MSB ≠ MSC. Let's consider each condition in turn.

FIGURE 3.15

Market Failure and Externalities: The Market for Flu Shots

When a good generates positive consumption externalities, as does a flu shot, the marginal social benefit (MSB) exceeds the marginal private benefit (MPB). Consumption decisions in a private market are based on assessments of private benefits and costs. In this case, the market equilibrium will be at (P_1, Q_1), which is below the socially optimal level of flu-shot consumption of Q_2 (where MSB = MSC). When output is at Q_1, society's net benefit is less than the maximum possible by an amount equal to the triangle ABC. This amount is called the welfare loss to society, and it arises because the private-market consumption is less than the socially optimal level. A price subsidy equal to CD will increase consumption to Q_2, the socially optimal number of flu shots.

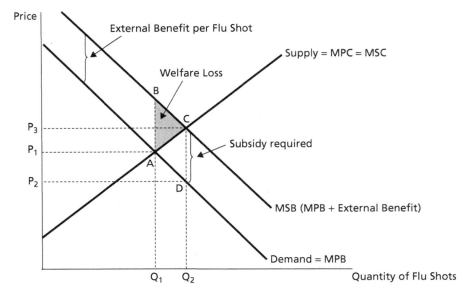

welfare (deadweight) loss

The reduction in welfare due to either market failure or a distortion introduced into a market by policy (e.g., taxes in certain circumstances) compared to the welfare level attained in a well-functioning market.

The Welfare Effects of Externalities Consider a market in which consumption externalities are present. We noted earlier that flu shots generate a positive consumption externality. The flu shot provides private benefit to the person who gets the shot and external benefits to those with whom the person interacts, causing marginal social benefit to exceed marginal private benefit: MSB > MPB (Figure 3.15). As usual, the demand curve represents MPB. The figure, however, also includes a marginal social benefit curve that reflects the sum of the marginal private benefit and the external benefit of flu shots. In a private market, price and output will be determined only by consideration of private costs and benefits (i.e., the intersection of demand and supply), so that equilibrium price and output will be (P_1, Q_1). At this allocation, however, P = MPB = MPC = MSC < MSB. Social welfare could be increased if more people got flu shots. The socially optimal uptake of flu shots occurs where MSB = MSC, at output level Q_2. A precise measure of the loss in social welfare under a private market is the triangular area ABC. ABC is the amount by which social benefits exceed social costs between output levels Q_1 and Q_2. This is called the **welfare loss** (or deadweight loss) associated with the market failure.[11]

How can society achieve the efficient level of flu shots? One option is for the government to subsidize the price of flu shots, thereby increasing uptake. If the per-shot subsidy is equal to the amount of the marginal external benefit, consumption will increase to Q_2, consumers will pay P_2 out-of-pocket, providers will receive P_3, and the subsidy paid by the government will make up the difference $(P_3 - P_2)$.

Using analogous reasoning, a negative externality in consumption or production will cause the market output to be too high, requiring a tax to raise price and reduce consumption to the socially optimal level.

The Welfare Effects of Market Power Market power by either a consumer or a producer also generates a welfare loss to society. Consider a market in which the producer has monopoly power. A monopolist maximizes profit by raising the price above the level that would be charged in a competitive market. This causes consumption and output to be too low. In Figure 3.16, for example, let (P_c, Q_c) be the price and output that would

---

[11] It is sometimes also called the "excess burden" to society.

FIGURE 3.16
Monopoly Power and Market Failure
A profit-maximizing monopolist restricts output to Q_M so as to be able to charge a higher price than would occur in a competitive market (P_M vs. P_C). The inefficiency of a monopolist arises because output is below the socially optimal level (Q_M vs. Q_C), generating a welfare loss equal to the triangle ABC.

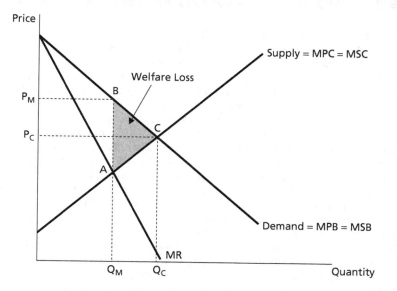

prevail in a competitive market, and (P_M, Q_M) be the price and output that prevails when a monopolist controls the market. (Price will not be bid down to P_C because there is no competition.) At the monopolistic output level, MSB > MSC (or more precisely, P = MPB = MSB > MPC = MSC). The welfare loss, equal to the area ABC, arises because output is below the socially optimal level.

The Welfare Effects of Informational Problems   When consumers are not well-informed, the link equating willingness to pay and marginal benefit is broken. That is, although consumers may be willing to pay a given amount for a good, if the willingness to pay is based on an incorrect belief about the quality of the good or the benefit they will obtain by consuming the good, the demand curve can no longer be interpreted as representing marginal private benefit. Hence, P ≠ MPB = MSB = MPC = MSC. Figure 3.17 depicts a

FIGURE 3.17
Welfare Loss and Informational Problems
Many people with high blood pressure are not aware of the full benefits of regularly taking medication to control their blood pressure. Because of poor information regarding these benefits, consumption of such medication is less than it would be if people fully understood the benefit, causing a welfare loss to society equal to the shaded area.

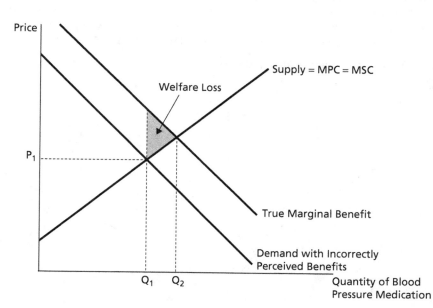

In general, taxes alter the price of goods or activities in the economy. If market failure causes too much of a good to be consumed (e.g., because of a negative externality), a tax may improve efficiency. But in the absence of such market failure, taxes distort prices and generate allocative inefficiency in the market for the taxed goods.

Consider the effect of a 10 percent sales tax on a good for which there is no market failure (Figure B3.1(i)). Let ($50.00, 100) be the equilibrium price and quantity when there is no tax. Under the tax, the full cost of the good to the consumer is the market price plus 10 percent. One way to depict the effect of the sales tax is to shift the effective demand downward by the amount of the tax, since the cost to consumers is the price of the good plus the tax. A consumer willing to pay a maximum of $50.00 for the good can now only be charged $45.45 which, after the 10 percent tax is added, equals their willingness to pay of $50.00. The tax reduces equilibrium consumption of the good from 100 to 75. In the after-tax equilibrium, consumers pay $52.80, producers receive $48.00, and the government collects the difference ($4.80). The tax revenue to the government is equal to $360 (i.e., $4.80*75). The tax, however, also creates a welfare loss equal to ABC, which arises because after the tax is imposed, consumption falls to a level at which MSB > MSC. The price consumers pay equals MSB less the tax.

Different taxes affect different behaviours. An income tax changes the price of leisure relative to working, providing incentive to reduce work hours. A sales or consumption tax changes the price of consumption relative to savings, reducing overall consumption. An inheritance tax changes the price of a person's current consumption and consumption by that person's heirs. In each case, the tax induces changes in behaviour that alter the allocation of society's resources. The size of the welfare loss created by a tax depends on how much behaviour

changes. Hence, the size of the welfare loss depends on the elasticities of demand and supply for the taxed good or activity.

To illustrate the importance of elasticity of demand, consider an identical tax on two goods alike in all respects except for their elasticities of demand (Figure B3.1(i) and Figure B3.1.(ii)). In the first case, the welfare loss is ABC, equal to $60.00. (The area of a triangle is 0.5*height*base, which in this case is 0.5*25*4.80.) In contrast, the welfare loss in the second case with more inelastic demand, DEF, is only $12.38. The welfare loss under the more elastic demand is nearly five times as large. Note that the same tax on the inelastically demanded good also raises more revenue ($470.25 vs. $360.00), making the welfare cost per dollar raised even lower for goods with inelastic demand. Designing a tax system to raise a given amount of government revenue imposing the least cost requires that, other things equal, government should impose higher taxes on those goods, services, and activities whose demand is most inelastic. This optimal tax rule, however, often conflicts with equity considerations: goods whose demand is most inelastic are often goods that people cannot do without, while luxury goods have relatively elastic demands. Tax systems commonly strike a balance between such efficiency and equity concerns.

Elasticity of demand and supply for the taxed good also determine how the burden of the tax is split between consumers and sellers. On the face of it, consumers appear to pay the full cost of a sales tax (because they pay 10 percent above the listed price). But an accurate comparison must take into account how the tax changes the equilibrium price in the market. Comparing the two situations discussed above, the after-tax price to consumers is higher when the demand is inelastic ($54.45 vs. $52.80). When demand is inelastic, sellers

FIGURE B3.1 Welfare Loss Under a 10% Sales Tax

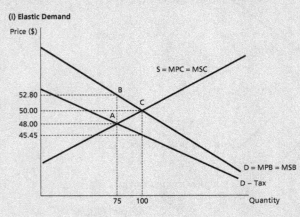

(i) Elastic Demand

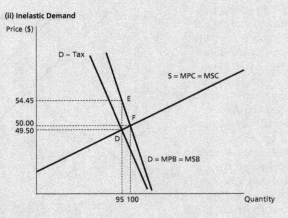

(ii) Inelastic Demand

(Continued)

know that they can pass most of the tax onto consumers with little loss of sales. When demand is elastic, however, competition among the sellers will lead them to absorb more of the tax themselves, passing less on to consumers. In this case, most of the economic incidence (or burden) of the tax falls on sellers. So elasticities of demand and supply play a crucial role in determining the distribution of the true economic burden of a tax among different individuals and organizations in society.

The only taxes that create no welfare loss are head (or poll) taxes. A head tax is a tax of fixed amount per person that must be paid by every person who is alive. The only way to reduce or avoid the tax is to be dead. Hence, short of killing yourself, there is no change in behaviour that can alter the amount of tax you pay. Governments make very limited use of such taxes, however, because they are perceived as highly unfair (the most destitute pay the same as the wealthiest members of society) and politically unpopular. In the 1990s, for instance, the introduction of a head tax (known as the "Community Charge") played an important role in the downfall of Margaret Thatcher as prime minister of England.

situation in which the perceived benefits of blood-pressure medication are lower than the actual benefits. Because of this poor information, consumption of the drug is less than it would be if people understood the full benefits, causing a welfare loss to society. The market still has a downward sloping demand curve; however, the demand curve can no longer be interpreted as measuring marginal benefit for the purposes of normative economic analysis.

The Crucial Role of Prices in Resource Allocation

Within this standard welfare economic framework, allocative inefficiencies arise in markets whenever a wedge is driven between prices, marginal social benefit, and marginal social cost. Because prices play such a crucial role in the efficient allocation of resources in well-functioning market systems, policies that "distort" prices create welfare losses and inefficiencies. This is one reason why economists focus so much analytic energy on taxes and subsidies, both of which "distort" prices and, in the absence of market failure, generate inefficiencies. (See Box 3.1 for a discussion of taxes.)

Chapter Summary

This chapter has provided a brief overview of the operation of markets and the economic analysis of markets. Important elements of the overview include the following:

- A number of conditions are necessary for market-based allocations to be efficient, including these:
  - Conditions in the broader environment that support market exchange.
  - Conditions within the market to ensure competition and sound choices; for example, no concentration of market power, good information on the demand and supply sides, and absence of externalities.
  - Acceptance of the normative principles of consumer sovereignty and willingness to pay as a measure of social value.

- Market failure arises when a market allocation is not allocatively efficient. Rationales for government intervention based on market failure are distinct from those based on equity.

- The demand side of a market can be characterized in this way:
  - Individual-level demand for a good is influenced by preferences, the price of the good, prices of related goods, and income.
  - Individual-level demand curves result from the behaviour of utility-maximizing individuals. Changes in the price of a good cause movement along the demand curve; changes in other factors cause shifts in the demand curve.

- The sensitivity of demand to its determinants is measured using elasticity measures.
- Market demand is determined by the sum of individual-level demand. Market demand is influenced by both the level and distribution of income in society.

- The supply side of a market can be characterized in this way:
  - Firm-level supply of a good is determined by the price of a good, the prices of inputs, and the production technology available.
  - Firm-level supply curves result from the behaviour of profit-maximizing firms. Changes in the price of a good cause movement along a supply curve; changes in other determinants cause shifts in the supply curve. The sensitivity of supply to changes in the price of a good is measured by the elasticity of supply.
  - Market supply is determined by the sum of firm-level supply.

- Together, demand and supply make up a market, for which
  - Market equilibrium occurs at the intersection of the demand and supply curves. Once in equilibrium, there will be no tendency for the equilibrium price and quantity to change unless one of the determinants of demand and supply changes.
  - Under the conditions for a well-functioning market, a freely operating market leads to a price and output combination that maximizes the net benefit to society from the resources used to produce the good—it is allocatively efficient.
  - When the conditions are not met, the inefficiency associated with market allocation can be measured by the welfare loss.

Key Terms

asymmetry of information, *65*
complementary goods, *71*
consumer sovereignty, *84*
consumers' surplus, *86*
demand curve, *71*
diminishing marginal
  returns, *76*
diminishing marginal
  utility, *68*
elastic demand, *74*
elasticity, *73*
externality, *66*
income effect, *69*
income-elasticity
  of demand, *73*
inelastic demand, *74*

inferior good, *74*
marginal cost, *76*
marginal private benefit
  (MPB), *84*
marginal private cost
  (MPC), *84*
marginal product, *76*
marginal revenue, *77*
marginal social
  benefit (MSB), *84*
marginal social cost (MSC), *84*
marginal utility, *69*
market equilibrium, *81*
market failure, *66*
market power, *63*
monopolistic competition, *87*

monopoly, *64*
monopsony, *65*
net benefit, *84*
normal good, *74*
oligopolistic
  competition, *87*
own-price-elasticity, *73*
price-elasticity of
  supply, *80*
producers' surplus, *86*
profits, *76*
substitute good, *71*
substitution (pure-price)
  effect, *70*
unitary elasticity, *74*
welfare (deadweight) loss, *87*

End-of-Chapter Questions

A. For each of the statements below, indicate whether the statement is true or false and explain why it is true or false. Where helpful, use a graph to explain your reasoning.

1. When there is a negative consumption externality for a good, the price that leads to an efficient level of consumption is higher than the price that would result from an unregulated private market.

2. Demand and supply are assumed to be determined independently in a market.

3. If two individuals have identical preferences but differing amounts of goods, it is not possible for both to benefit by trading between themselves.

4. The inability of all individuals to buy DVD players constitutes an important source of market failure.

5. The supply curve for tomatoes is less elastic in the short-run than in the long-run.

6. Other things equal, the welfare loss associated with a negative production externality for a good is larger when the demand for the good is elastic than when it is inelastic.

7. The introduction of Advil likely caused the demand curve for Aspirin to shift inward and become more elastic.

8. In a market with many producers producing similar goods, a firm will be able to create significant profits by setting the price of its product higher than the equilibrium price.

B. Use the information below on output and costs to answer the two questions that follow.

Output	Total Cost	Marginal Cost
1	50	50
2		30
3	120	

a) What is the total cost of production when output equals 2?

b) What is the marginal cost of the third unit of output?

C. The figure below depicts the market for computers.

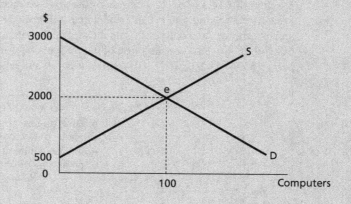

a) What is the total cost to society of producing 100 computers?

b) How will an increase in the price of oil, which is used to make plastic computer components, affect the market?

c) Computer monitors contain a number of highly hazardous substances that can cause environmental damage when disposed of. To achieve the efficient level of production and consumption of computers and the associated monitors, what policies could the government implement?

Reference

Zack, P., and S. Knack. 1999. Trust and growth. *Economics Journal* 111(April): 295–321.

Appendix 3

Chapter 3: The Basics of Markets

3.2.   MECHANICS OF THE MARKET

3.2.1   Individual Behaviour and the Demand for Goods and Services

Price and Income Effects: Pure-price and income effects can be illustrated as follows. Let the initial utility-maximizing bundle of hamburgers and pizza be (H_1, PZ_1) when the prices are $(\$P_{H,1}, \$P_{Z,1})$ respectively (point A in Figure 3A.1). If the price of hamburgers falls to $\$P_{H,2}$, the optimal bundle changes to (H_2, PZ_2) (B). To identify the pure-price (or substitution) effect, draw a new budget line with the slope equal to the new prices so that it is just tangent to the level of utility, as indicated by the indifference curve attained before the price change (C). The pure-price effect is equal to the difference between the optimal bundle at the original prices and the bundle that provides the same level of utility at the new prices $((H', PZ') - (H_1, PZ_1))$. Because the price of hamburgers fell, the pure price effect increases the optimal quantity of hamburgers but decreases the optimal quantity of pizza. The income effect is the difference between the final bundle at the new prices and the bundle that provides the original level of utility at the new prices $((H_2, PZ_2) - (H', PZ'))$. In this case, the income effect was positive for both (Figure 3A.1).

Deriving a Demand Curve: A demand curve is derived by tracing out the path of optimal consumption of a good as the price of the good changes, holding constant income and the price of the second good. This is depicted in Figure 3A.2. In the figure, the price of pizza and income are held constant while the price of hamburgers falls from $3 to $1. As the price of hamburgers falls, consumption of hamburgers rises from 4 to 6 to 10. The price–quantity pairs (($3, 4), ($2, 6), ($1, 10)) represent points on the demand curve for hamburgers.

FIGURE 3A.1
**Income and
Substitution Effects**

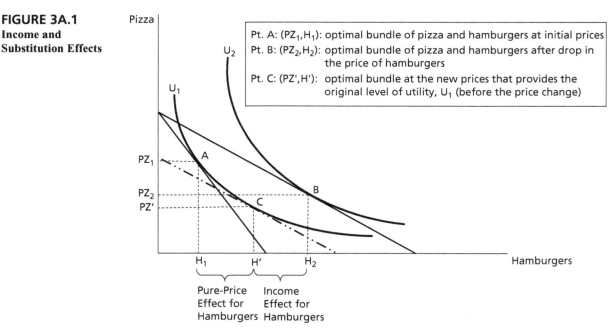

Pt. A: (PZ_1, H_1): optimal bundle of pizza and hamburgers at initial prices
Pt. B: (PZ_2, H_2): optimal bundle of pizza and hamburgers after drop in the price of hamburgers
Pt. C: (PZ', H'): optimal bundle at the new prices that provides the original level of utility, U_1 (before the price change)

FIGURE 3A.2
**Deriving a
Demand Curve for
Hamburgers**

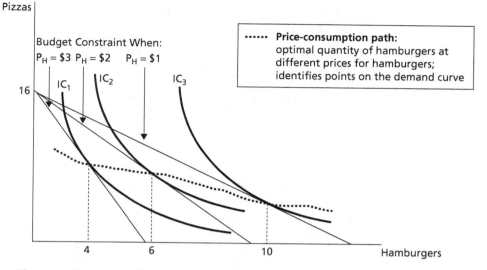

The same diagram can be used to determine whether the second good is a complement or a substitute. In Figure 3A.2, as the price of hamburgers falls (holding the price of pizza and income constant), the consumption of pizza falls, indicating that pizza and hamburgers are substitutes. If they had been complements, the consumption of pizza would have increased as the price of hamburgers fell.

3.2.3   Putting Demand and Supply Together: A Market

The analysis presented in the text focuses on only a single market, and is therefore called partial equilibrium analysis. Analyses that consider the impact across many markets are general equilibrium analyses.

Normative Economic Analysis of Markets

The attractiveness of markets for economists can be summarized by the Two Fundamental Theorems of Welfare Economics. Under the conditions noted in the beginning of this chapter:

1. *All competitive equilibria are Pareto optimal.* This important theorem says that under specified conditions, a system of markets produces an efficient outcome. In many respects, this is a modern-day analogue to Adam Smith's claim about the working of the "invisible hand." Although this is a powerful result, its relevance is limited in three ways: (1) the conditions may not hold—market failure is present; (2) the economist's chosen definition of optimality—Pareto optimality—may not correspond with the views of society more broadly; and (3) there is no guarantee that the market will take us to the most desired outcome among the infinite number of Pareto-optimal outcomes.

2. *Any Pareto-optimal allocation can be reached through a system of competitive markets given the appropriate initial distribution of income and wealth in society.* In other words, any Pareto-optimal allocation can be achieved by markets. Therefore, the role of government can be limited to redistributing income so as to ensure the desired outcome; it does not have to get involved in modifying market processes or the allocation of productive resources. The relevance of this is limited by the fact that government cannot actually undertake the lump-sum taxes and transfers required by this theorem.

Together, the two theorems underpin the predisposition of economists to use markets unless it can be shown that markets do not function well.

Comparison of Outcomes for a Single Producer in Imperfectly Competitive Markets

The long-run equilibria in imperfectly competitive markets are as follows:

Monopoly   A monopolist is the only producer and so faces the full-market demand curve (Figure 3A.3). Because it must decrease price to increase sales, the marginal revenue curve falls faster than the demand curve (i.e., has a steeper slope). The profit maximizing output level is that at which the monopolist's marginal revenue equals marginal cost. This occurs at output level Q_m, at which the monopolist goes up to the demand curve to set price (P_m). In this equilibrium, the monopolist earns positive profits. Price is above and output is below that which would arise in a perfectly competitive market (P_c, Q_c).

Monopolistic Competition   A producer in a monopolistically competitive market faces a downward sloping demand curve (because of product differentiation), but the producer's demand curve is more elastic (less steep) than the full-market demand curve because there are a number of close substitutes for an individual producers' product (Figure 3A.4). A profit-maximizing producer sets output where marginal revenue equals marginal cost and goes up to the demand curve to set price. In this case, however, because there is free entry and exit (many producers), producers compete away profits in long-run equilibrium: in essence, the producers' demand curve is pushed down to a tangency with its average cost curve. In the equilibrium, price is higher than that which would prevail in a perfectly competitive market.

Oligopoly   Behaviour in an oligopoly depends on what is assumed about the strategic beliefs of the firms in the market. Consequently, there is no single model of oligopoly; rather, a set of models corresponds to different assumptions about the strategic behaviour of firms. Some commonly encountered models include the following:

- In the Cournot model, firms make output decisions simultaneously. Each firm chooses its optimal output level based on an expected level of output by the other firms (which may, for example, be their most recent output levels). Market equilibrium arises when no firm has any incentive to change its output given the output levels of all the other firms.

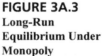

FIGURE 3A.3
Long-Run Equilibrium Under Monopoly

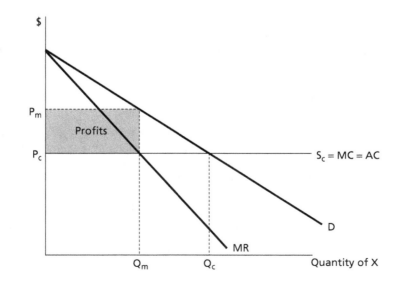

- The Stakelberg model assumes one dominant, or leader, firm and a number of "followers." The followers behave as in the Cournot model, and make output decisions assuming expected levels of output by other firms. The dominant firm, however, recognizes that the other firms will react; in fact, it makes assumptions about how the other firms will react and uses this information in choosing its output level. Again, equilibrium occurs when no firm has incentive to change output given the output levels of all the other firms.

- A second type of dominant firm model assumes that the group of smaller, follower firms behave as competitive firms when setting output levels. The dominant firm sets price and the other firms accept this price and behave as competitive firms, choosing the output level at which price equals marginal cost; the output of the dominant firm is the residual between total market demand at that price and the combined output of the follower firms. The challenge for the dominant firm is to choose the price that will maximize profits in this environment.

In all of these models, price and output fall *between* those that would arise in a perfectly competitive market and those that would arise in a monopolistic market. Exactly where they fall in this range depends on the specific assumptions made by the model.

FIGURE 3A.4
Long-Run Equilibrium for a Firm in a Monopolistically Competitive Market

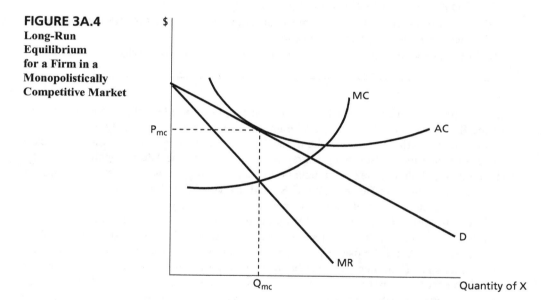

Methods of Economic Evaluation

Learning Objectives

After studying this chapter, you will understand:

LO1 The elements and purposes of an economic evaluation

LO2 The principal types of economic evaluation methods

LO3 Key components of an economic evaluation and some of the main challenges faced in conducting an evaluation

LO4 Challenges in using the results of such analyses to inform policy

---

Should the government fund a flu vaccination program to reduce the annual health toll of the flu? If so, should the program be universal or should it target only high-risk populations such as the elderly, children, and health care workers? Should the health care system replace its existing mammography machines with the latest machines that take digital images? Should the government build additional highways or invest in mass transit to reduce mounting traffic congestion? Should it invest in nuclear power, coal power, or energy conservation to meet the future energy needs of society?

These are just a sampling of the difficult questions government policy-makers face on a daily basis. Each question challenges government to identify how best to invest public resources or to direct the use of private resources to achieve society's goals. Resources are scarce, so difficult choices must be made as to how they are used. As we saw in the last chapter, when a market allocation works well, government policy can focus on sustaining the market, which through the interaction of buyers and sellers, effectively does its own cost-benefit analysis. But when a market fails, policy-makers must identify the best policy to either regulate the market or replace the market altogether with a non-market allocation process. Governments must continually ask if each service, procedure, or program is worth doing, especially compared to other services, procedures, or programs. That is, do the benefits gained from using the resources in this way exceed the opportunity cost?

This chapter provides an overview of the basic frameworks and methods economists use to evaluate empirically the efficiency of alternative policy options. Such economic evaluation explicitly measures and values the resources used by a policy as well as the associated consequences (good and bad). The use of economic evaluation methods has expanded greatly in the health sector in recent years as governments (and private insurers) have striven to get better value for the money they devote to health.

As the number of potential health care services and goods expands, governments around the world increasingly strive to ensure that they fund only services of proven effectiveness and demonstrated efficiency. This is commonly done in two ways: (1) governments mandate that the maker of a new product submit evidence regarding the product's effectiveness and efficiency when seeking approval for public insurance coverage; and/or (2) governments establish publicly funded advisory health technology assessment agencies that assess technologies by rigorously synthesizing available evidence, by commissioning new economic evaluations, or by conducting economic evaluations in-house.

Mandating evidence of economic efficiency is most commonly done for new drugs. This approach was pioneered in Australia within its national public pharmacare insurance program; since 1993, its Pharmaceutical Benefits Advisory Committee has required that drug companies provide evidence of efficiency (derived using the methods described in this chapter) to be considered for coverage (Birkett et al. 2001). The Ontario Provincial Formulary Committee, which decides which drugs will be covered by the Ontario Drug Benefit Program (the province's publicly financed drug insurance program for seniors and low-income citizens) was the first agency in Canada to adopt this approach. The national Canadian Common Drug Review program, which standardizes and streamlines the process of drug approval for Canadian provincial formularies, now also requires evidence of efficiency as part of the evaluation process. (More information on the Common Drug Review can be found at: http://www.cadth.ca/index.php/en/cdr.)

Public health technology assessment agencies focus on the evaluation of a wide variety of services, procedures, products, and even ways of organizing and delivering health care services. Nearly every developed country now has at least one health technology assessment agency. In Canada, a number of provinces have technology assessment organizations to advise them on the value of new health services. At the national level, the Canadian Agency for Drugs and Technologies in Health (CADTH) plays an important role in producing evidence the federal and provincial governments need to ensure coverage decisions align with evidence on effectiveness and efficiency (see http://cadth.ca/). Perhaps the most prominent such organization internationally is the United Kingdom's National Institute for Health and Clinical Excellence (NICE; see http://www.nice.org.uk/), which makes recommendations to the U.K. Department of Health regarding the public coverage and optimal use of a health care service or technology.

One of the most important uses of economic evaluation methods in the health sector is to assess new technologies and medical services to determine if they are more efficient than existing treatments and therefore should be covered by public insurance systems. Many governments now require the makers of a new product to submit evidence of efficiency before approving public coverage of new drugs and medical procedures in their health care systems (see Box 4.1).

Economic evaluation in the health sector is one part of a broader evaluation strategy called health technology assessment (Feeny et al. 1986). "Technology" in this context is defined broadly to include "the set of techniques, drugs, equipment and procedures used by health care professionals in delivering medical care to individuals and the systems within which such care is delivered."[1] "Technologies" include not only new drugs, tests, and devices, but also new ways of organizing the delivery of services, such as a multidisciplinary primary health care practice that includes family physicians, nurse practitioners, psychologists, and nutritionists; and day surgery versus in-patient surgery. Health technology assessment examines a broad array of clinical, economic, ethical, and social issues associated with new health technologies.

---

[1] This definition was developed by the U.S. Congress Office of Technology Assessment. The quotation is taken from Feeny et al. (1986; p. 5).

The most basic question about any technology is this: does it work? Does day surgery, for example, produce health outcomes at least as good as in-patient delivery? Does a premium subsidy increase insurance coverage? Do multi-disciplinary primary care practices improve continuity of care? This is called an effectiveness evaluation. Determining the effectiveness of a new technology logically precedes an economic evaluation of efficiency. A program that is not effective, that does not achieve its objective, cannot be efficient no matter how small its cost.

The primary methodology used to evaluate effectiveness, especially of clinical interventions, is the randomized controlled trial. Randomized controlled trials, however, are often not feasible when assessing the effectiveness of policies and programs regarding the financing, funding, and delivery of services. A wide array of other evaluation methodologies have been developed to assess effectiveness in such situations (for examples, see Cook and Campbell 1979, and Haynes et al. 2005). Economic evaluation goes one step further than effectiveness analysis: among effective services, it assesses whether or not the benefits generated are sufficiently large to justify the resources required to produce the services.

The methods of economic evaluation are designed to assess the relative efficiency of policy options. But two types of equity concerns also arise when conducting economic evaluations. First, assessing efficiency using economic evaluation methods unavoidably requires a variety of equity judgments. An evaluation of efficiency, for instance, must weigh benefits and costs that accrue now against those that will accrue to future generations, raising issues of intergenerational equity. Second, the information gathered during the efficiency analysis can be summarized in ways that also provide insight into the impact of alternative policies on distributional equity. So, while most of the discussion in this chapter is framed in terms of assessing efficiency, in a number of places it also touches on issues of distributional equity.

4.1 WHAT IS AN ECONOMIC EVALUATION?

economic evaluation
A systematic, comparative analysis of two (or more) courses of action in terms of both their costs and their consequences.

An **economic evaluation** is the systematic, comparative analysis of two (or more) courses of action (such as the delivery of health care services or programs, or the implementation of specified policies) in terms of both their costs and their consequences (Drummond et al. 2005).

- *Systematic* means that the analysis is done within a unified framework that articulates the relevant components of the analysis, how they relate to each other, and how the analysis should be conducted.
- *Course of action* means a particular way to use resources. The basic evaluation methods can be applied to very broad economic policies, ranging from the North American Free Trade Agreement or a policy to deregulate the communications industry, to specific programs such as a policy to regulate the diffusion of high technology in the health sector or a municipal program to reduce traffic congestion in the city core. It can also include individual projects or interventions, such as a specific mass transit line or a specific health care procedure, drug, or device. The basic framework of economic evaluation guides the assessments that many government projects must undergo prior to approval (Treasury Board of Canada Secretariat 1998; HM Treasury 2007). This chapter focuses in particular on these methods as they are applied to evaluate health care policies, programs, and interventions (terms that will be used interchangeably to refer to alternatives being evaluated).
- *Comparative* means that at least two alternatives are compared against each other *and* that costs are compared against consequences. Comparison between at least two

alternatives is essential because the goal of an economic evaluation is to identify which among a set of options is most efficient, so there must be more than one alternative in the analysis. Sometimes, the alternative may not be a formal program or policy—it could be "whatever happens currently" in the absence of a formal program. For example, an economic evaluation of specialized coronary care units in hospitals could compare such units against a current practice in which cardiac patients receive care in regular hospital wards. Comparing costs and consequences is essential because, by definition, efficiency requires getting the most output from a given set of inputs.

4.1.1 Representation of an Economic Evaluation

Policy Objective

An economic evaluation begins with a desired policy objective (Figure 4.1). The ultimate objective of most health sector programs and policies is to produce health or health-related welfare. However, an intermediate objective can sometimes be specified more precisely for particular types of programs or interventions. The objective of a cancer-screening program, for example, is to detect cases of cancer; the objective of a program to improve health care for infants is to increase the proportion of infants who "thrive."

Policy Alternatives

The policy objective determines the most relevant alternatives that should be compared in an evaluation. Suppose, for instance, health policy-makers wanted to address the growing burden associated with kidney disease (renal failure). If the defined policy objective is to reduce the burden among those who suffer from kidney disease, this limits the relevant treatments to options such as home dialysis, in-patient dialysis, or kidney transplantation. But a broader definition of the policy objective—such as reducing the social and economic burden of end-stage renal disease—expands relevant policy options to include measures to prevent renal disease (such as reducing or better controlling diabetes, a leading cause of renal disease). Because the stated objective is pivotal in guiding the analysis, a sound evaluation must start with a carefully articulated objective that effectively explains why the

FIGURE 4.1

A Schematic Representation of an Economic Evaluation
This figure presents a schematic diagram of an economic evaluation. A decision-maker has a defined objective to be achieved and must determine which of the alternative ways to achieve the objective is efficient. To determine which alternative is efficient, the analysis must assess and compare all of the resources used by each program and all of the effects, or consequences, generated by each program.

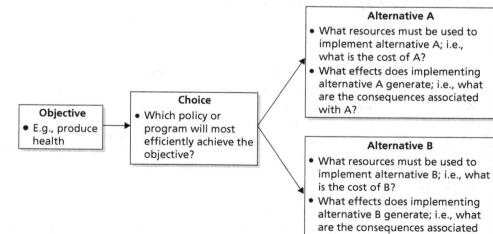

objective is sensible and ensures that the most policy-relevant alternatives are chosen for evaluation.

Viewpoint

viewpoint
The perspective adopted for an economic evaluation; the set of people and organizations whose costs and benefits are included in the evaluation.

Once the objective has been set and the alternatives chosen, the analysis weighs the costs and consequences of each alternative. Exactly which costs and consequences are assessed depends on the viewpoint adopted. The **viewpoint** refers to the perspective taken when assessing costs and consequences. If the analytic viewpoint is that of all society, then all costs and consequences would count in the analysis, regardless of where or to whom in society they accrue. In contrast, if the analytic viewpoint is narrower, say that of the Ministry of Health, only costs incurred or consequences felt by the Ministry of Health would be included.

To understand the difference, imagine an evaluation of a publicly funded rehabilitation program for those who suffer a brain injury. Such a program would use physiotherapists, equipment, and the time of patients and their families. An evaluation conducted from the societal perspective would include the value of all these resources; an evaluation done from the perspective of the Ministry would include only the physiotherapist time and the equipment funded by the Ministry, excluding the value of time for the patient and the patient's family because that time does not accrue in any way to the Ministry.

Economists recommend that evaluations adopt the societal perspective because the goal is the efficient allocation of society's resources. At times, however, it is useful to consider a more narrow perspective, especially if we wish to gain insight into the barriers that might affect program implementation or if we want to examine distributional issues. Evidence indicates, for instance, that from a societal perspective, a program of universal vaccination for chicken pox is more efficient than no program of vaccination (Getsios et al. 2002; Brisson and Edmunds 2002), and that a large source of benefit is fewer days of lost work for parents who otherwise have to stay home with the sick child. But when evaluated from the perspective of a Ministry of Health, the costs of such vaccination programs generally exceed the health care treatment costs saved by averting cases of chicken pox, which leads to an increase in overall Ministry costs. This distribution of the costs and benefits explains in part why universal vaccination has not been rapidly adopted in an era of fiscal restraint, even though it is efficient from the societal perspective.

4.1.2 Stages of an Economic Evaluation

An economic evaluation generally proceeds in three stages: identification, measurement, and valuation (see Figure 4.2).

Identification of Costs and Consequences

identification of costs and consequences
The enumeration (as part of an economic evaluation) of all the resources used, and all the effects generated by, each alternative being compared.

The **identification of costs and consequences** is a process that enumerates all the resources used, and all the effects generated by, each alternative. It is often useful to separate the resources (costs) used by a program into those drawn from the health care sector (e.g., physician visits, hospital care), those of patients and their families (e.g., time spent providing informal care, transportation costs to receive treatment), and those that are drawn from other sectors (e.g., social services, the educational system). The major consequences of a program include changes in health status, non-health effects (e.g., changes in work time), and changes in the use of resources (e.g., reduced use of health care, changed use of other public services).

The enumeration of the resources used by a universal vaccination program for chicken pox, for example, would include health sector resources, such as the vaccine and physician

FIGURE 4.2 Principal Stages of an Economic Evaluation: Identification, Measurement, and Valuation

Three principal stages in an economic evaluation are the identification, measurement, and valuation of the costs and consequences of each alternative included in the analysis. In this figure, these are illustrated by a program to vaccinate children against chicken pox.

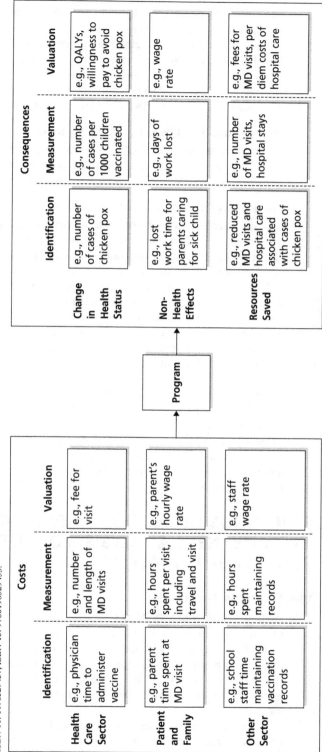

Source: "Methods for the Economic Evaluation of Health Care Programmes," Michael F. Drummond, Mark J. Sculpher, George W. Torrance, Bernie J. O'Brien, and Greg L. Stoddart. F2.1, p. 19. ISBN-10: 0198529457, ISBN-13: 9780198529453.

time to administer the vaccine; patient and family resources, which include the time spent at the clinic by the child and parent; and other-sector resources, such as those used by the school system to verify and maintain vaccination records when a child first enters school. The consequences of a vaccination program would include averted cases of chicken pox (health effect), a reduction in lost work-time for parents (non-health effect), and a reduction in physician visits and the use of related health care resources needed to treat chicken pox (resources saved). The enumeration of costs and consequences should be comprehensive, including even those that ultimately may not be able to be measured or valued.

Measurement of Costs and Consequences

measurement of costs and consequences
The quantification (as part of an economic evaluation) of the amount of each resource used and the effect generated by each alternative being compared.

The **measurement of costs and consequences** is the process of quantifying the amount of each resource used, the magnitude of any effects generated, and for multi-year assessments, the year during which any resources are used or effects generated.

Valuation of Costs and Consequences

valuation of costs and consequences
The process of assigning (as part of an economic evaluation) the social value of the resources used and the effects generated by each alternative being compared.

Lastly, the **valuation of costs and consequences** is the process of assigning social value to the resources used and the effects generated by a program. Valuation raises some of the most challenging and controversial issues in economic evaluation, especially in health-related evaluations for which many of the most important effects are health gains.

Valuation of the resources (costs) used is generally straightforward—in principle, if not always in practice. With the exception of situations we will discuss in section 4.3, resources used are valued at market prices. In a well-functioning market, price equals the marginal social opportunity cost of a resource.

Valuation of consequences is more complicated, both conceptually and empirically. Because people hold differing views on the appropriate way to assign social value to a health gain, analysts have developed many different methods for valuing health outcomes. In fact, the three principal types of economic evaluation in the health sector—cost-effectiveness analysis, cost-utility analysis, and cost-benefit analysis—are distinguished solely by their approach to valuation. All three employ the same methods for identifying, measuring, and valuing costs and for identifying and measuring the consequences; they differ, however, with respect to how the health-related consequences are valued. This single difference has important implications for the kinds of questions each analysis can answer, the methods required to conduct the analyses, and how the analysis can be used to guide policy development.

4.2 THREE METHODS OF ECONOMIC EVALUATION: COST-EFFECTIVENESS ANALYSIS, COST-UTILITY ANALYSIS, AND COST-BENEFIT ANALYSIS

4.2.1 Cost-Effectiveness Analysis

cost-effectiveness analysis
Measures consequences in the natural units in which they occur (e.g., life-years gained, cases prevented); does not assign a social value to the consequences as part of the evaluation.

Cost-effectiveness analysis forgoes explicit valuation of the consequences. A cost-effectiveness analysis comparing screening programs for breast cancer, for example, might measure the outcome in terms of the number of cancer cases detected; a cost-effectiveness analysis of programs to improve the control of hypertension (high blood pressure) might measure the outcome as the average reduction in blood pressure; a cost-effectiveness analysis comparing treatments for heart attacks might measure the outcome as life-years gained.

Because costs are valued in dollars and consequences are measured in natural units, cost-effectiveness analysis assesses efficiency in terms of costs per unit effect achieved. Evaluating the relative efficiency of two programs requires that we compare the incremental effects gained by one program over the other against the incremental resources used by the one program over the other, to reveal, at the margin, the extra effects we gain by expending extra resources. Accordingly, results are expressed using an incremental cost-effectiveness ratio (ICER). For a comparison of two programs, A and B, the **incremental cost-effectiveness ratio** is:

incremental cost-effectiveness ratio
Expresses the results of a cost-effectiveness analysis as the ratio of the difference in costs between two alternatives to the difference in the effects between the two alternatives.

$$ICER = \frac{(Cost_A - Cost_B)}{(Effect_A - Effect_B)}$$

This ratio tells us the additional cost incurred per additional unit of effect achieved when we use alternative A compared to alternative B.

A review of cost-effectiveness studies that analyzed prevention programs (Goldsmith et al. 2004), for instance, found that, compared to no formal vaccination program, the estimated incremental cost-effectiveness of a universal chicken pox vaccination program ranged from $50,000 per life-year gained (Brisson and Edmunds 2002) to $94,000 per life-year gained (Getsios et al. 2002). Estimates of the cost per case of chicken pox averted ranged from $68 (Scuffham et al. 1999) to $81 (Scuffham et al. 2000) (figures in 2003 Canadian dollars).

Incremental cost-effectiveness ratios from evaluations that compared formal programs of colorectal cancer screening with the usual care (which may include people who initiate their own screening) ranged from $12,000 per life-year gained (Whynes et al. 1998; Flanagan et al. 2002) to $26,000 (Salkeld et al. 1996) (figures in 2003 Canadian dollars).

A cost-effectiveness study generates one of nine possible outcomes (Table 4.1). Cells 2, 3, and 6 in Table 4.1 represent cases in which A is definitely more efficient than B, either because it is less costly and at least as effective, or because it is equally costly but more effective. Cells 4, 7, and 8 of the table represent cases in which A is definitely less efficient than B, either because it is more costly and no more effective, or because it is equally costly and less effective. Cells 1 and 9 represent indeterminate cases in which one alternative does not clearly dominate the other: A is more effective than B (or vice versa) but also more costly. In these cases, any judgment as to the economic desirability of one program over the other depends on the relative magnitude of incremental costs and effects: Are the extra effects worth the extra costs?

cost-utility analysis
Values health outcomes in terms of quality-adjusted life-years.

4.2.2 Cost-Utility Analysis

quality-adjusted life-year (QALY)
A measure that evaluates the effect of a health intervention on both the quantity (length) of life and the quality of life (as indicated by people's subjective rating of the health state).

Cost-utility analysis (CUA) uses the same structure as cost-effectiveness analysis, but outcomes are valued in terms of **quality-adjusted life-years** (QALYs).[2] A QALY is a health outcome measure that incorporates the effect of an intervention on both the quantity (length) of life and quality of life (as indicated by people's subjective rating of the health state).[3] The subjective health state rating, or valuation, is a number between 0 and 1, where 0 is immediate death and 1 is full health (see Box 4.2). The number of QALYs is equal to

[2] Some writers do not distinguish cost-utility analysis from cost-effectiveness analysis (e.g., Gold et al. 1996, Garber and Phelps 1997). I retain the distinction because assessing outcomes in terms of QALYs incorporates people's subjective valuation of health states. This adds an important new dimension to the analysis of efficiency.

[3] The QALY is just one way to do this. A large number of measures exist that integrate quantity and quality of life in different ways (see discussion in Drummond et al. 2005). I couch this discussion in terms of QALYs because the QALY measure has the longest history and is the most widely used.

TABLE 4.1 **Possible Results from Cost-Effectiveness and Cost-Utility Evaluations**
When the relative efficiency of two programs is assessed using cost-effectiveness or cost-utility analysis, nine outcomes are possible, depending on the relative effectiveness and the relative costliness of the two programs. Cells 2, 3, and 6 represent cases in which A is definitely more efficient than B, because it is either less costly but no less effective or more effective but equally costly. Cells 4, 7, and 8 represent cases in which A is definitely less efficient than B, because it is either more costly and no more effective or less effective but equally costly. Cell 5 implies that they are equally efficient and there is no economic reason to prefer one over the other. Cells 1 and 9 represent the most difficult choice outcomes. In cell 1, A is less costly but also less effective; in cell 9, it is more costly but also more effective. The choice between A and B depends on an assessment of whether the extra effects generated are worth the extra cost. Note that for cost-effectiveness analysis, the effects (E_A, E_B) are measured in natural units for the intervention; for cost-utility analysis, effects are measured using quality-adjusted life-years (QALYs).

		Incremental Effectiveness of Program A Compared to Program B ($E_A - E_B$)		
		Less Effective	**Equally Effective**	**More Effective**
Incremental Cost of Program A Compared to Program B ($C_A - C_B$)	Less Costly	(1) Indeterminate	(2) A definitely more efficient than B	(3) A definitely more efficient than B
	Equally Costly	(4) A definitely less efficient B	(5) A and B equally efficient	(6) A definitely more efficient than B
	More Costly	(7) A definitely less efficient than B	(8) A definitely less efficient than B	(9) Indeterminate

the number of years spent in a particular health state multiplied by the subjective valuation of the health state compared to full health.

Imagine two programs, each of which produces 10 additional life-years for each person treated. For one program, individuals spend the 10 years in full health; for the second program, individuals spend those 10 years confined to a wheelchair and suffering from chronic pain. If individuals rate their quality of life when confined in pain to a wheelchair as only half that of their quality of life in full health, its valuation would be 0.5 on the 0–1 scale. The first program, which restores individuals to full health, produces 10 QALYs. The second program produces only 5 QALYs (10 years spent in a health state with a quality of life half that of being in full health equals 5 QALYs). Hence, although a cost-effectiveness analysis would judge the consequences of the two programs as equal (10 additional life-years for each), a cost-utility analysis would judge the consequences of the first program as better than the second (10 QALYs versus 5 QALYs).

Like cost-effectiveness analysis, the results of a cost-utility analysis are summarized in a ratio of incremental costs to incremental effects:

$$\text{Incremental Cost-Utility Ratio}: \frac{(\text{Cost}_A - \text{Cost}_B)}{(\text{QALY}_A - \text{QALY}_B)}$$

Cost-utility analyses of a colorectal screening program examined as part of the review of prevention programs found, for instance, that the incremental cost for every QALY gained ranged from about $5000 (U.K. CRC Screening Pilot Evaluation Team 2003) to $11,000 (Whynes et al. 1998). Like cost-effectiveness analysis, nine outcomes for the incremental cost-utility ratio are possible (Table 4.1).

Imagine that you suffer from chronic lung disease. The disease causes you to cough, wheeze, and have difficulty breathing, especially when exerting yourself physically. When severe, it can limit your ability to undertake normal daily activities. How would you rate your quality of life in this health state compared to being in full health? How much would you be willing to pay for a medication that restored full lung function with no side effects?

O'Brien and Viramontes (1994) explored these issues among a sample of individuals suffering from chronic lung disease who attended a respiratory clinic. Here is what they found.

Utility-Based Quality Weight for Living with Chronic Lung Disease

Utility scores used as quality weights for constructing QALYs were estimated using the standard gamble method. The utility scale defined the utility of immediate death as 0 and the utility of full health for the rest of one's life as 1.0. Living with chronic lung disease will have a utility score between 0 and 1.0. The standard gamble method assumes that, when faced with uncertainty, people choose the option that provides the highest expected utility. The expected utility is the sum of utility of each possible outcome multiplied by the probability that the outcome will occur. If, for example, a treatment has a 75% chance of returning you to full health (whose utility is 1.0) and a 25% chance of creating a complication that leaves you in a disabled health state with utility of 0.60, the expected utility of the treatment is this: $(0.75)(1.0) + (0.25)(0.60) = 0.90$. The standard gamble exploits this property to estimate the utility of a health state as follows. In the study of chronic lung disease, the respondents were given the following choice problem:

Option 1: Live the rest of their lives in current health state with chronic lung disease.

Option 2: "Gamble" on a treatment that will return them to full health for the rest of their lives with probability p or cause them to die immediately with probability $(1-p)$.

An initial value of p is chosen and the individual is asked whether they prefer option 1 or option 2. If they prefer option 1 (option 2), the value of p is increased (decreased) and they are asked to express their preference with this new value of p. This process continues until the value of p is such that the person has no preference

TABLE B4.2.1 Mean Utility and Willingness-to-Pay Values for Chronic Lung Disease Severity

Total	Sample	Mild	Moderate	Severe
Utility Scores	0.83	0.91	0.87	0.78
WTP per month	$113	$56	$63	$150

Source: O'Brien, B. and J. L. Viramontes. 1994. "Willingness to Pay: A Valid and Reliable Measure of Health State Preference?" *Medical Decision Making*. Vol. 14(3):289–97. Table 2, p. 293.

between the two options. Call this value p*. At this point, we know that:

$$U(\text{Option 1}) = U(\text{Option 2})$$
$$U(\text{chronic lung disease}) = (p*)U(\text{Full Health})$$
$$+ (1-p*)U(\text{Immediate Death}) = (p*)(1.0)$$
$$+ (1-p*)(0.0) = p*$$

Hence, on a scale in which the utility of immediate death is 0 and full health is 1.0, the utility of living with chronic lung disease is p* (which we know will be between 0 and 1). Table B4.2.1 lists the results. Over the full sample, the mean utility score was 0.83. As expected, those whose condition was more severe rated their quality of life lower: mean utility of 0.78 for those with severe disease compared to 0.91 for those with mild disease. Based on these estimates, a treatment that restored full lung function for someone who suffered from severe chronic lung disease would produce 7.8 QALYs.

Willingness to Pay as a Measure of Value

The study also assessed value using a willingness-to-pay approach called contingent valuation. The respondents were asked the following question:

Assume that choice Y offers a 99 percent chance of restoring you to healthy lung functioning, and there is a 1 percent chance of immediate death. That is, of 100 people who take the medicine in choice Y, 99 will have healthy lung functioning restored and one person will die. Now assume that the medication in choice Y is expensive and not fully covered by your health insurance, so you are required to pay some amount out-of-pocket, each month and for the rest of your life, for this medication. Thinking about the value of the medication to you and how much you could, realistically afford to pay each month, would the maximum amount you be willing to pay be X?

(Continued)

The interviewer begins with an amount X. If the person is willing to pay more (less) than X, in a second round of the interview they would increase (decrease) this amount, continuing until they have identified the maximum amount the respondent is willing to pay. Table B4.2.1 lists the willingness to pay for the drug. On average, people were willing to pay $113 per month for this medication which has a 99 percent chance of restoring full lung function. Again, as expected, those with a more severe disease were willing to pay more: on average, $150 compared to $56 for those with severe and mild disease respectively.

The study findings also exhibited a pattern which underlies a major objection to this method of valuing health states: the direct relationship between a person's ability to pay and their willingness to pay. The authors note that, while there was "... no obvious difference or trend [in the values] with respect to any of the health measures ... there appeared to be a marked and significant gradient, in the predicted direction, between income and unadjusted mean willingness-to-pay." (O'Brien and Viramontes 1994; p. 294) That is, while the utility-based quality of life scores did not systematically vary with a person's income, the mean willingness to pay did: for those with an income over $60,000, for example, the mean willingness to pay was $343, while for those with an income less than $20,000, it was $34. This predictable but, for many, troubling relationship between income and willingness to pay has prompted efforts to develop willingness-to-pay approaches that purge the income effect (see Drummond et al. (2005) for a discussion of such efforts).

Source: O'Brien, B. and J. L. Viramontes. 1994. "Willingness to Pay: A Valid and Reliable Measure of Health State Preference?" *Medical Decision Making.* August 1994. Vol. 14(3):289–97. Table 2, p. 293.

4.2.3 Cost-Benefit Analysis

cost-benefit analysis
Values health outcomes in monetary terms.

human capital approach
Values a health gain in terms of the accompanying increase in a person's market productivity, as measured by their wage rate.

willingness to pay
Values a health gain in terms of the amount a person is willing to pay to obtain the health gain.

contingent valuation
A hypothetical scenario in which individuals assess a health risk and their willingness to pay to mitigate that risk.

Finally, **cost-benefit analysis** (CBA) values health outcomes in monetary terms. The monetary value of health effects is most commonly estimated using one of two basic approaches. Early cost-benefit studies used the **human capital approach**. The human capital approach values the health gain in terms of the increase in a person's productivity, as measured by their wage rate. If an intervention improves health so that work-time lost to illness falls by half, and on average a person is able to continue working for an additional five years, then the human capital method values this health gain in terms of the additional earnings made possible by the increased work-time. Although the human capital approach is still used on occasion to assign a monetary value to health effects, it is no longer the preferred method: it is not consistent with welfare economic theory, and it is judged by many to be inequitable since, for example, it assigns a value of zero to health gains among the retired and stay-at-home parents.

The economically preferred method for assigning monetary values to health is to value the consequences of a program in terms of people's **willingness to pay** for them. People's willingness to pay for health gains can be estimated a number of different ways. One approach uses people's actual choices in situations where there is risk of injury or even death (Viscusi 1992; 1993). For instance, examining the wage increment an employer must pay workers to accept a job that has greater risks to health, or the amount people are willing to pay to have a particular safety feature installed on their car, provides some insight into the monetary value people place on their health. But because such choices are influenced by many things besides health risks, in recent years the dominant methodology for estimating people's willingness to pay is "contingent valuation." **Contingent valuation** presents individuals with hypothetical scenarios that include health risks and elicits their willingness to pay to mitigate that health risk (see Box 4.2).

Because cost-benefit analysis values both the costs and the benefits in monetary terms, it is possible to calculate the net benefit:

$$\text{Net Benefit} = (\text{Benefit}_A - \text{Benefit}_B) - (\text{Cost}_A - \text{Cost}_B)^4$$

If the net benefit is positive, implementing program A would increase welfare for society; if it is negative, implementing it would lead to a welfare loss.

A number of the prevention programs discussed above also include cost-benefit analyses. In many cases, a crucial factor in assessing the net benefit is the viewpoint taken. Evidence indicates that both chicken pox vaccination programs and colorectal screening programs generate a positive net benefit

from the societal perspective (Huse et al. 1994; Scuffham et al. 1999; Getsios et al. 2002; Brisson and Edmunds 2002), but a negative net benefit from the perspective of public payers (Lieu et al. 1994; Huse et al. 1994; Diez et al. 1999; Scuffham et al. 1999). That is, unlike some claims for prevention programs, they do not reduce costs for the funder. But the benefits that accrue to everyone in society, including gains in work-time and other aspects of the health benefits themselves, exceed program costs. Some preventive programs, such as needle-exchange programs and water fluoridation, are cost-saving even from the narrow perspective of payers ((Niesson and Douglass 1984; Gold et al. 1997; Holtgrave et al. 1998; Griffin et al. 2001; Health Outcomes International Pty Ltd et al. 2002).

Table 4.2 summarizes important differences among the three methods of economic evaluation.

4.2.4   Economic Evaluation Methods and Efficiency

Cost-effectiveness analysis, cost-utility analysis, and cost-benefit analysis answer different efficiency questions. Both cost-effectiveness analysis and cost-utility analysis can only identify the least-cost way to achieve the stated objective. The objective in cost-effectiveness is a specific health-related outcome (such as detecting cases of colon cancer); the objective for cost-utility analysis is more general (producing QALYs). Still, neither can provide insight into whether or not pursuing the objective itself is worthwhile.

Cost-effectiveness analysis and cost-utility analysis implicitly assume that the objective is worth pursuing; the analysis informs the question of efficient strategies for attaining the objective. In contrast, cost-benefit analysis can, in principle, indicate whether a program is worthwhile at all. Cost-benefit analysis addresses questions of allocative efficiency under the potential Pareto Criterion. If net benefit is positive, implementing the program represents a potential Pareto improvement (because winners could, in principle, compensate the losers and still be better off) and it should be considered for investment. If the net benefit is negative, then from an efficiency perspective the program should not be undertaken because it would lead to a decrease in net benefit to society (i.e., impose a welfare loss).

---

[4] Sometimes results of cost-benefit studies are reported as a ratio of benefits to costs. This should be avoided because it can lead to different conclusions depending on whether certain aspects of the analysis (e.g., cost savings) are classified as costs or benefits. The net benefit measure, however, is not affected by such classification conventions.

TABLE 4.2
A Comparison of the Three Methods of Economic Evaluation

Type of Analysis	Costs	Consequences	Outcome Measure
Cost-Effectiveness	Costs valued in monetary terms	• Consequences measured in natural units (e.g., cases of cancer detected); no value explicitly placed on them	Incremental Cost-Effectiveness Ratio
Cost-Utility	Costs valued in monetary terms	• Consequences valued in terms of quality-adjusted life-years (QALYs), which incorporate utility-based assessments of health-related quality of life	Incremental Cost-Utility Ratio
Cost-Benefit	Costs valued in monetary terms	• Consequences valued in monetary terms based on individual willingness to pay	Net Monetary Benefit

4.2.5   The Differing Origins of the Methods

These differences reflect the differing origins of the methods. Cost-benefit analysis formally derives from the welfare economic framework discussed in Chapters 2 and 3. It was developed by economists to guide government policies to correct market failure. In contexts in which markets fail, cost-benefit analysis is designed to identify policies that mimic the allocations that would result from a well-functioning market. Cost-benefit analysis derived from welfare economic principles takes the allocation that would result from a well-functioning market as the social ideal.

In contrast, cost-effectiveness and cost-utility analyses were developed by decision analysts, whose overall analytic framework assumes that an objective has been specified by a decision-maker. The analysis is designed to identify how best to achieve the objective. Cost-effectiveness and cost-utility analyses are consistent with what has been called the "decision-maker" approach to economic evaluation (Sugden and Williams 1978). Cost-benefit analysis values all consequences in terms of each individual's willingness to pay, following directly from the welfare economic principle of respecting preferences and assessing the strength of preferences in the metric of each person's willingness to pay. Cost-effectiveness and cost-utility analyses are consistent with the extra-welfarist view that preferences are not the only relevant factor in judging policies, and that evaluation should be guided by articulated social objectives rather than solely by a conception of the social good defined by a particular scientific framework.

4.2.6   Application of the Three Methods in the Health Sector

Although cost-benefit analysis is the dominant approach used in economics outside the health sector, cost-effectiveness analysis and cost-utility analysis predominate in the health sector because many health analysts reject the ethical assumptions that underlie the optimality of market-based allocation (see Chapter 3). Some (mostly non-economists) reject the validity of ever explicitly assigning a dollar value to an extra life-year; others (including many health economists), who accept the validity of doing this in principle, reject the willingness to pay principle for health sector analyses because it conflicts with the view that a person's wealth should not influence the allocation of health care resources. A person's willingness to pay for an expected health gain is a direct function of the person's income and wealth (see Box 4.2). Interventions targeted at wealthier groups would, other things equal, systematically be judged to produce more benefit.

Cost-effectiveness analysis is the most commonly used method of economic evaluation in health. This partly reflects the ethical concerns noted above, but it also partly reflects the fact that, because health gains are not valued, cost-effectiveness analysis is the easiest of the three to conduct. In addition, non-economist health professional users of economic evaluation evidence find it easier to interpret results expressed in terms of the natural units associated with the interventions under evaluation.

These advantages, however, come at a price. Cost-effectiveness analysis is best suited to situations in which there is a single, dominant outcome of concern. If a program generates multiple distinct outcomes, cost-effectiveness analysis cannot integrate all of them into a single summary measure for the analysis. For example, needle exchange programs generate multiple types of benefits, including reduced cases of HIV and Hepatitis C, as well as other social benefits. Cost-effectiveness also provides decision-makers with a relatively limited ability to compare the efficiency of investments in programs across areas within health care. If the cost-effectiveness of a cancer screening program assesses effects in terms of cost per case of cancer detected, an evaluation of a needle exchange program for drug addicts does so in terms of cost per overdose avoided, and an evaluation of a new anti-depressant medication does so in terms of the cost per day free from depression, it is not possible to compare the relative efficiency of investing in each of these different areas of care because outcomes are measured in different units. The relative efficiency of investments in different areas of care can only be assessed directly when outcomes are measured in the same units.

Cost-utility analysis, and the QALY measure on which it is based, was developed to overcome these limitations of cost-effectiveness analysis while still avoiding the need to value outcomes in monetary units. Because the QALY integrates diverse health effects into a single summary measure, cost-utility analysis is well suited to situations with multiple health effects, where interventions increase life expectancy at the expense of negative side effects (e.g., many chemotherapy treatments), or where interventions have important effects on quality but not on length of life (e.g., treatments for arthritis). Because the QALY can be used to value outcomes for a wide variety of health interventions, the results of cost-utility analysis can be used to compare the relative efficiency of a wide range of health interventions. For example, if the cancer screening programs, the needle exchange programs, and the anti-depressant medications all noted above are evaluated in terms of their efficiency in producing QALYs, then the results can be used to guide investment decisions among these alternative health interventions. Cost-utility analysis, however, is not well suited for situations in which important outcomes are not directly health related (because such outcomes cannot be integrated into a QALY calculation).

Cost-benefit analysis can, in principle, integrate the most comprehensive set of outcomes, providing the widest scope for assessing the efficiency of different types of programs and interventions. As a practical matter, however, this theoretical ability can be severely circumscribed by the practical challenges of estimating the monetary value of many outcomes. Methodological advances in recent decades in measuring willingness to pay, however, have considerably expanded the range of effects than can be explicitly and quantitatively incorporated into a cost-benefit analysis. Related methodological advances have also tried to reduce the bias associated with the respondents' wealth, though the extent to which such influence can be purged from estimates continues to be debated.

4.2.7 Can Society Avoid Placing a Dollar Value on Life-Years Gained?

Even cost-effectiveness analysis and cost-utility analysis do not avoid the need for society to place a dollar value on a life-year gained (or any other health effect). Both methods avoid the need to explicitly value a health gain in monetary terms as part of the economic evaluation itself. But if the evaluations guide resource allocation, ultimately society must make a judgment regarding the monetary value of health improvements. For instance, a drug formulary committee deciding whether a public drug program should cover a new drug with an incremental cost-utility ratio of $70,000 per QALY has to decide if a QALY is worth $70,000. Such judgments are unavoidable.

When, where, and how such judgments are made, however, differ in important ways between cost-effectiveness analysis and cost-utility analysis on one hand, and cost-benefit analysis on the other. Cost-benefit analysis asserts that policy should be guided by individual-level monetary valuations (as happens in markets). The value of a particular health outcome varies across individuals depending on their willingness to pay. These differences across individuals in monetary valuations are integral to the cost-benefit analysis underlying conception of social benefit.

Cost-effectiveness and cost-utility analyses, in contrast, are premised on the principle that, when deciding how to allocate health care resources, the dollar value of a health gain should be the same for all members of society. Hence, the methods do not incorporate variation across individuals in the monetary value of health gains; indeed, the analysis itself does not incorporate monetary valuations of benefits. Only at the decision stage do we confront the necessity to assess the monetary value of benefits. Once made, this judgment in principle can be applied to all programs and interventions, regardless of the economic and social status of the individuals who benefit. Therefore, although cost-effectiveness and cost-utility analyses cannot avoid placing a social monetary value on health gains, the approach to doing so differs in important ways from that used in cost-benefit analysis.

4.3   SOME COMMON ANALYTIC CHALLENGES TO CONDUCTING AN ECONOMIC EVALUATION

Thus far, this chapter has emphasized the principal elements of an economic evaluation and the three basic approaches to evaluation. We now turn to some key challenges encountered when conducting an economic evaluation.

4.3.1   Shadow Pricing and the Valuation of Resources Used

As noted in section 4.2, valuing resources used by a program is normally straightforward: the social value of a resource is indicated by its market price. If a health care program requires office space, the space should be valued at the prevailing rental rate; if a home care program requires transportation for its providers, the vehicles, gas, and other transportation resources should be valued at market prices. The principle of valuing resources at market prices follows directly from our observation in Chapter 3 that the equilibrium price in a well-functioning market equals the marginal social opportunity cost of a good or resource. Hence, in most instances valuation is straightforward: when a resource is obtained through a well-functioning market, the resource is valued using the price paid.

In some circumstances, however, it is either impossible or inappropriate to value resources using a market price. Volunteer labour and informal care provided by family members, for instance, are not purchased in a market, so no prices exist. Still, both inputs constitute real resources that must be factored into the evaluation. Other resources may be purchased from markets known to be monopolistic. Such prices do not reflect true social cost because monopolists set price above the socially optimal level.

shadow price
Imputed value of a resource; assigned by an analyst when a market price does not exist or does not reflect the true social cost of the resource.

When market prices for a resource do not exist, or the market price does not reflect true social cost, the analyst must impute a value. The imputed value is called the **shadow price**. The shadow price for volunteer time, for instance, might be set at the average wage in the community; the shadow price for a resource purchased in a monopolistic market would be the market price adjusted downward to remove the monopolistic distortion. Shadow pricing always seeks to identify the value that best approximates the true marginal social cost of the resource. While the principle of shadow pricing is clear, the practice of imputing a shadow price often is not, because the correct approach varies by context and requires considerable judgment by the analyst (Mishan 1988; Boardman et al. 2006).

4.3.2 Double-Counting Costs or Benefits

Double-counting occurs when the value of a cost or benefit inadvertently gets counted twice in an economic evaluation. For example, suppose that when responding to a willingness-to-pay survey about the health effects of a treatment, in addition to considering the value of the health gain itself, respondents take into account the impact on their ability to earn income and the changed health care costs they would expect to incur.

If the analyst, thinking that the responses represent only the value of the health gain, separately includes changed worker productivity and health care costs averted in the analysis, these latter costs and benefits would get counted twice (once in the respondent's willingness-to-pay response and once by the analyst), making the benefits appear larger than they really are. Double-counting can be avoided only by careful design and execution of a study.

4.3.3 Discounting: Valuing Costs and Benefits that Occur at Different Times

Consider programs A and B depicted in Table 4.3. Which program is more efficient? Most would say program B: B produces the same number of QALYs each year as does A, yet program B defers most costs into future years while A incurs all the costs in the first year. Even though the total costs of the two programs are equal, the time streams of the costs differ.

We can quantify the value of this different time stream of costs by asking how much we would have to set aside today to pay $10,000 every year as required by program B. If the interest rate earned on savings were 5 percent per year, for example, we would only need to set aside $8227 today to have $10,000 in year five ($8227 invested today at 5 percent annual interest will grow to be $10,000 in five years) (Table 4.4).

present discounted value

The value, in today's dollars, of a future, multi-year stream of costs or benefits.

Doing this same calculation for each year and adding them up, we find that we need only set aside $45,459 today to pay all the costs of program B over its five-year life. This figure—$45,579—is the **present discounted value** of the five-year stream of costs associated with program B. The present discounted value is directly comparable with the costs of program A, all of which arise in the first year. This comparison reveals why program B is more efficient: both programs generate identical consequences but the present discounted cost of program B is $45,579 while the present discounted value of program A is $50,000.

rate of time preference

Measures the extent to which individuals value benefits and costs that arise in the future differently (usually less) than if they arise today.

What about consequences? Should we also discount the health effects produced in future years? Consider programs C and D depicted in Table 4.3. The timing of the stream of costs is identical but the timing of the health benefits is different: in C, all benefits accrue in the first year while in D the benefits don't accrue until year five. Which would you prefer? Most individuals would choose program C—it costs the same but generates health effects sooner. This reflects a general economic phenomenon known as the **rate of time preference**: other things equal, people generally prefer to obtain things sooner rather than later. If the rate of time preference is 5 percent, the present discounted value of 75 QALYs in five years is 68.2 QALYs. Hence, program C is more efficient than program D: the present discounted value of the costs of both is $50,000, but program C generates a discounted stream of health benefits of 75 QALYs while program D generates a discounted stream of only 68.2 QALYs.

↳ *why do we do this?*

discounting
The process of converting a multi-year stream of costs or consequences into its present-discounted value.

The process of converting a multi-year stream of costs or consequences into its present-discounted value is called **discounting**. The mechanics of doing this can be illustrated using the stream of costs associated with program B from Table 4.3. Let the rate of interest be 5 percent and assume we have $10,000 today. One year into the future that $10,000 will have grown to ($10,000)(1 + 0.05) = $10,500. Two years into the future it will have grown into ($10,000)(1.05)(1.05) = ($10,500)(1.05) = $11,025. In general,

$$\text{Future Value}_t = (\text{Present Value})(1 + r)^{(t-1)} \qquad \textbf{(4.1)}$$

and

$$\text{Present Value} = \frac{\text{Future Value}_t}{(1 + r)^{(t-1)}} \qquad \textbf{(4.2)}$$

where t is the year under consideration ($t = 1, 2, 3, \ldots T$), r is the discount rate, and future value refers to the dollar value in future year t. The present discounted value of a multi-year stream of future costs is simply the sum of the present discounted costs each year:

$$\text{Discounted present value of a stream of costs} = \sum_{t=1}^{T} \frac{1}{(1 + r)^{(t-1)}} (\text{cost}_t) \qquad \textbf{(4.3)}$$

TABLE 4.3   The Rationale for Discounting
These hypothetical programs illustrate why discounting makes sense. If we compare programs A and B, both have identical time streams of lives saved, and both cost the same amount. But for program A, all those costs are incurred in the first year, while for program B the costs are spread evenly across the five years. If we compared the total costs and total life-years gained, the programs would be judged equal. From a financial point of view, however, it is preferable to push costs into the future since we could set aside less than $50,000 today and let it grow through interest to pay the future cost. Hence, program B would be preferred to program A. Discounting the costs would reflect this. Analogously, programs C and D both cost $50,000 in the first year and both generate the same total number of life-years gained. But for program C, those life-years accrue in the first year, while for program D we have to wait five years. Given society's rate of time preference, it would prefer program C, which yields the immediate benefit. Again, discounting the outcomes would lead to this conclusion.

	Yr 1	Yr 2	Yr 3	Yr 4	Yr 5	Total
PROGRAM A						
Costs	$50,000	$0	$0	$0	$0	$50,000
Life-Years	15	15	15	15	15	75
PROGRAM B						
Costs	$10,000	$10,000	$10,000	$10,000	$10,000	$50,000
Life-Years	15	15	15	15	15	75
PROGRAM C						
Costs	$50,000	$0	$0	$0	$0	$50,000
Life-Years	75	0	0	0	0	75
PROGRAM D						
Costs	$50,000	$0	$0	$0	$0	$50,000
Life-Years	0	0	0	0	75	75

TABLE 4.4 Calculating Discounted Present Values (Discount rate = 0.05)

The discounted present value of a stream of costs or consequences is calculated by first calculating the discounted present value in each year using equation 4.2 and then summing across all the years. This table lists the undiscounted values each year, the discounted present value, and the formula used to calculate the present discounted value. In year 5, for instance, the undiscounted cost is \$10,000 but the discounted present value of this is \$8227; the undiscounted number of life-years gained is 15, and the discounted present value of life-years is 12.34.

	Yr 1	Yr 2	Yr 3	Yr 4	Yr 5	Total
PROGRAM B						
Costs (C_t)						
Undiscounted	\$10,000	\$10,000	\$10,000	\$10,000	\$10,000	\$50,000
Discounted Present Value	\$10,000	\$9524	\$9070	\$8638	\$8227	\$45,459
Formula	$\dfrac{C_1}{(1.05)^0}$	$\dfrac{C_2}{(1.05)^1}$	$\dfrac{C_3}{(1.05)^2}$	$\dfrac{C_4}{(1.05)^3}$	$\dfrac{C_5}{(1.05)^4}$	$\displaystyle\sum_{t=1}^{5}\dfrac{C_t}{(1+0.05)^{(t-1)}}$
Life-Years Gained (LY_t)						
Undiscounted	15	15	15	15	15	75
Discounted Present Value	15	14.29	13.61	12.96	12.34	68.19
Formula	$\dfrac{LY_1}{(1.05)^0}$	$\dfrac{LY_2}{(1.05)^1}$	$\dfrac{LY_3}{(1.05)^2}$	$\dfrac{LY_4}{(1.05)^3}$	$\dfrac{LY_5}{(1.05)^4}$	$\displaystyle\sum_{t=1}^{5}\dfrac{LY_t}{(1+0.05)^{(t-1)}}$

By analogous reasoning, the discounted present value of a multi-year stream of health effects is:

$$\text{Discounted present value of a stream of effects} = \sum_{t=1}^{T}\frac{1}{(1+r)^{t-1}}(\text{effect}_t) \qquad \textbf{(4.4)}$$

Choosing the Discount Rate

discount rate
The rate of discount applied to convert a multi-year stream of costs or benefits to its present value.

How do we determine the appropriate **discount rate** (r)? This question has been debated extensively within economics, and there is no purely objective answer. The market rate of interest for private funds is not appropriate because it reflects both risk attitudes and time preference. Some economists argue that the interest paid on government treasury bonds, which carry almost no risk, is a good approximation. As a practical matter, governments and technology assessment agencies in some countries recommend a specific rate for use in evaluating public projects; by convention, rates in the range of 3–5 percent are most commonly used (Gold et al. 1996; Canadian Coordinating Office for Health Technology Assessment 1999; Drummond et al. 2005). The rate can vary from society to society, since different societies may have different rates of time preference.

Discounting Is Not an Adjustment for Inflation

Discounting is *not* an adjustment for inflation. Discounting is done even when there is no inflation; it bears no conceptual relationship to inflation or to adjustments for inflation.

Some Implications of Discounting

As with any valuation exercise, discounting has important ethical and distributional consequences. Choosing a high discount rate is equivalent to saying that society places much greater value on costs incurred and benefits generated today than it does on costs incurred and benefits generated in the future. Hence, discounting has important implications for intergenerational equity.

Discounting also affects the likelihood that various types of health interventions will be judged efficient. Other things equal, high discount rates make it less likely that programs of health protection or disease prevention, which require the outlay of funds today to generate benefits in future years, will be judged efficient compared to a treatment program that generates benefits in the near future.

The rate of discount, for instance, turns out to be a crucial parameter, when determining the relative efficiency of alternative approaches to deal with antibiotic resistance. Antibiotic-resistant strains of bacteria make it increasingly difficult to treat diseases once thought to be conquered by the introduction of antibiotics. Evaluations of strategies to reduce the impact of resistant bacteria find that, when a high rate of discount is used, programs that inhibit the transmission of already antibiotic-resistant strains of bacteria (which provide immediate benefit) appear more efficient than programs that reduce the emergence of resistant bacteria in the first place (for which benefits occur into the future and continue indefinitely) (Wilton et al. 2002; Coast et al. 2002).

4.3.4 Aggregating Costs and Consequences: Distributional and Other Issues

Once the disparate costs and consequences have been measured and valued, they must be aggregated in some way to assess the efficient alternative. The conventional approach is to simply add up all the costs (expressed in dollars), add up all the consequences, and then calculate the relevant efficiency measure as discussed in section 4.2 above. The results can guide the selection of programs to achieve the largest health for a given budget (in the case of CEA and CUA) or to maximize net benefit (in the case of CBA).

Simply adding up costs and benefits, however, ignores distributional issues such as who bears the costs of a program and who enjoys the benefits. It implicitly assumes that society has no concern for these distributional questions. A program that generates 1000 additional QALYs, for instance, is judged the same whether it produces 25 extra QALYs for each of 40 people or 1 extra QALY for each of 1000 people. Evidence indicates, however, that the distribution of outcomes does matter (Dolan and Olsen 2002). Increasingly, decision-makers want results to be presented in ways that facilitate examination of distributional issues.

Distributional concerns are typically incorporated into an analysis in one of two ways. One approach presents the results in a disaggregated manner that allows a user to see how the various benefits and costs are distributed among relevant sub-groups in society. Because *any* aggregation process unavoidably embeds distributional assumptions, presenting the data in a less aggregated format gives the user the greatest flexibility to base judgments on their own equity criteria. A disadvantage of this approach is that highly disaggregated data can be difficult to process.

distributional weights
Used to help evaluate the costs and consequences of a program, policy, or service. The weights differ depending on the characteristics of the person or organization to whom the costs and benefits accrue.

As an alternative, some recommend the use of **distributional weights**. If, as appears to be true, people value differently health gains produced among sub-groups of society, then these differential valuations can formally be incorporated into the aggregation process through the use of distributional weights (Weisbrod 1968). A system of distributional weights, for example, might assign a higher value to producing QALYs among parents raising young children than it does to producing a QALY among elderly persons. Hence, if two programs are identical, except that one produces 500 QALYs among those over age 85 but the other produces 500 QALYs among young parents, and the relative weight for the elderly compared to young parents is 0.80, then the second program would be preferred on the grounds that it produces 500 QALYs while the former produces only 400 (500*0.80). Such a system of age-related weights was used by the World Health Organization, for instance, in estimating the global burden of disease using disability-adjusted life-years (DALYs) (Murray and Lopez 1996).

Chapter Summary

This chapter has provided a brief introduction to the methods of economic evaluation, with an emphasis on applications in the health sector.

- The various methods of economic evaluation are used primarily to assess the efficiency of alternative public policies, programs, and interventions. Economic evaluations can also provide insight into the equity effects of alternative public policies, programs, and interventions.

- An economic evaluation is the systematic comparison of the costs and consequences of at least two policy alternatives that could be used to achieve a policy objective.

- Crucial stages in an economic evaluation include a clear articulation of the policy objective; choice of the policy alternatives to be evaluated; choice of viewpoint for the analysis; the identification, measurement, and valuation of relevant costs and consequences; and the aggregation and formal comparison of costs across the policy alternatives.

- Three types of economic evaluation predominate in the health sector: cost-effectiveness analysis, cost-utility analysis, and cost-benefit analysis. The methods are identical except with respect to how consequences are valued within the evaluation, and as a result, how costs and consequences are aggregated to assess efficiency.

- The methods derive from distinct conceptual foundations, and address different dimensions of efficiency.

- The conduct of an economic evaluation raises a number of conceptual and practical challenges. Some of the prominent challenges include shadow pricing, discounting, and incorporating distributional concerns.

Key Terms

contingent valuation, *108*
cost-benefit analysis, *108*
cost-effectiveness analysis, *104*
cost-utility analysis, *105*
discounting, *114*
discount rate, *115*
distributional weight, *116*

economic evaluation, *100*
human capital approach, *108*
identification of costs and consequences, *102*
incremental cost-effectiveness ratio, *105*
measurement of costs and consequences, *104*

present discounted value, *113*
quality-adjusted life-year, *105*
rate of time preference, *113*
shadow price, *112*
valuation of costs and consequences, *104*
viewpoint, *102*
willingness to pay, *108*

End-of-Chapter Questions

A. For each of the statements below, indicate whether the statement is true or false and explain why it is true or false.

1. Cost-effectiveness analysis is poorly suited for programs with multiple types of health outcomes.

2. A recent study by Health Canada which calculated the economic costs of leading diseases in Canada constitutes an economic evaluation.

3. An economic evaluation of the relative efficiency of two government program options does not require any equity-related judgments.

4. Economists generally recommend that economic evaluations be conducted from the viewpoint of all members of society.

5. Because it incorporates a subjective utility weight into the calculation of quality-adjusted life-years, cost-utility analysis can address questions of allocative efficiency.

6. As an incentive to induce physicians to locate in under-served rural and remote areas, some Canadian provinces pay physicians who locate in such regions a special fee premium (e.g., the fee they receive for each service provided is 10% higher than the fee received by a physician practising in an urban area). Because a physician visit is the same whether provided by a physician in an under-served area or by a physician practising in a city, an analyst was correct to assign the same cost to all physician visits made by individuals enrolled in a treatment program being evaluated.

7. Other things equal, the higher the rate of time preference, the more attractive investments in prevention programs will be from an economic point of view.

8. The use of the net-benefit measure to summarize the results of a cost-benefit study follows directly from the Pareto efficiency principle.

9. By not discounting when aggregating benefits that occur at different points in time, it is possible to avoid making intergenerational equity judgments.

B. The table below presents data on costs and effects for two programs with 15-year time horizons. Calculate the discounted costs and effects, and their associated ICERs, assuming discount rates of 3 percent and 7 percent.

	Program A: Prevention		Program B: Treatment	
	Cost ($)	Effect (QALYs)	Cost ($)	Effect (QALYs)
Year 1	2500	0	1000	1 QALY
Year 2	2500	0	1000	1 QALY
Year 3	2500	0	1000	1 QALY
Year 4	2500	0	1000	1 QALY
Year 5	2500	0	1000	1 QALY
Year 6	0	0	1000	1 QALY
Year 7	0	0	1000	1 QALY
Year 8	0	0	1000	1 QALY
Year 9	0	0	1000	1 QALY
Year 10	0	1.0 QALY	1000	1 QALY
Year 11	0	2.5 QALY	1000	1 QALY
Year 12	0	2.5 QALY	1000	1 QALY
Year 13	0	5.0 QALY	1000	1 QALY
Year 14	0	5.0 QALY	1000	1 QALY
Year 15	0	5.0 QALY	1000	1 QALY

References

Birkett, D. J., A. S. Mitchell, and P. McManus. 2001. A cost-effectiveness approach to drug subsidy and pricing in Australia. *Health Affairs* 20(3):104–15.

Boardman, A., D. Greenberg, A. Vining, and D. Weimer. 2006. *Cost-benefit analysis: Concepts and practice.* Upper Saddle River, NJ: Pearson Education Ltd.

Brisson, M., and W. J. Edmunds. 2002. The cost-effectiveness of varicella vaccination in Canada. *Vaccine* Vol. 20:1113–25.

Canadian Coordinating Office for Health Technology Assessment. 1999. *The revised Canadian guidelines for the economic evaluation of pharmaceuticals.* Ottawa: Canadian Coordinating Office for Health Technology Assessment.

Coast, J., R. D. Smith, A. M. Karcher, P. Wilton, and M. Millar. 2002. Superbugs II: How should economic evaluation be conducted for interventions aimed to reduce antimicrobial resistance? *Health Economics* 11(7):637–47.

Cook, T. D., and D. T. Campbell. 1979. *Quasi-experimentation: Design and analysis issues for field settings.* Chicago: Rand McNally.

Diez, D., M. Ridao, J. Latour, A. Ballester, and A. Morant. 1999. A cost-benefit analysis of routine varicella vaccination in Spain. *Vaccine* 17:1306–11.

Dolan, P., and J. A. Olsen. 2002. *Distributing health care.* Oxford: Oxford University Press.

Drummond, M., M. Sculpher, G. Torrance, B. O'Brien, and G. Stoddart. 2005. *Methods for the economic evaluation of health care programmes.* Oxford: Oxford University Press.

Feeny, D., G. Guyatt, and P. Tugwell. 1986. *Health care technology: Effectiveness, efficiency and public policy.* Montreal: Institute for Research on Public Policy.

Flanagan, W., C. Le Petit, J.-M. Berthoelot, K. While, A. Coombs, and E. Jones-McLean. 2002. Modelling colorectal screening in POHEM. In *Technical report for the National Committee on Colorectal Cancer Screening,* A. Coombs, E. Jones-McLean, C. Le-Petit and others (eds.). Ottawa: Health Canada.

Garber, A. M., and C. E. Phelps. 1997. Economic foundations of cost-effectiveness analysis. *Journal of Health Economics* 16:1–31.

Getsios, D., J. J. Caro, G. Caro, P. De Wals, B. J. Law, Y. Robert, and J. M. Lance. 2002. Instituting a routine varicella vaccination program in Canada: An economic evaluation. *Pediatric Infectious Disease Journal* 21:542–47.

Gold, M., A. Gafni, P. Nelligean, and P. Millson. 1997. Needle exchange programs: An economic evaluation of a local experience. *Canadian Medical Association Journal* 157:255–62.

Gold, M. R., J. E. Russell, L. B. Siegel, and M. C. Weinstein, eds. 1996. *Cost-effectiveness in health and medicine.* New York: Oxford University Press.

Goldsmith, L., B. Hutchison, and J. Hurley. 2004. *Putting health back into health care: Economic evaluation across the four faces of prevention: A Canadian perspective.* Ottawa: Canadian Medical Association.

Griffin, S. O., K. Jones, and S. L. Tomar. 2001. An economic evaluation of community water fluoridation. *Journal of Public Health Dentistry* 61:78–86.

Haynes, R. B., D. Sackett, G. Guyatt, and P. Tugwell. 2005. *Clinical epidemiology: How to do clinical practice research.* Philadelphia: Lippincott, Williams, Wilkins.

Health Outcomes International Pty Ltd, National Centre for HIV Epidemiology and Clinical Research, and M. Drummond. 2002. *Return on investment in needle and syringe programs in Australia. Summary report.* Canberra, Australia: Commonwealth Department of Health and Ageing.

HM Treasury 2007. *The green book: Appraisal and evaluation in central government.* London: TSO.

Holtgrave, D. R., S. D. Pinkerton, T. S. Jones, P. Lurie, and D. Vlahov. 1998. Cost and cost-effectiveness of increasing access to sterile syringes and needles as an HIV prevention intervention in the United States. *Journal of Acquired Immune Deficiency Syndrome and Humane Retrovirology* 18 (Suppl 1):S133–A138.

Huse, D. M., H. C. Meissner, M. J. Lacey, and G. Oster. 1994. Childhood vaccination against chicken pox: An Analysis of the benefits and costs. *Journal of Pediatrics* 124:869–74.

Lieu, T. A., S. L. Cochi, S. B. Black, M. E. Halloran, H. R. Shinefield, S. J. Holmes, M. Wharton, and A. E. Washington. 1994. Cost-effectiveness of routine varicella vaccination program for U.S. children. *Journal of the American Medical Association* 271:375–81.

Mishan, E. 1988. *Cost-benefit analysis.* London: Undwin Hyman.

Murray, C., and A. Lopez. 1996. *The global burden of disease.* Cambridge, MA: Harvard School of Public Health. On behalf of World Health Organization.

Niesson, L. C., and C. W. Douglass. 1984. Theoretical considerations in applying benefit-cost and cost-effectiveness analysis to preventive dental programs. *Journal of Public Health Dentistry* 44:156–68.

O'Brien, B., and J. L. Viramontes. 1994. Willingness to pay: A valid and reliable measure of health state preference? *Medical Decision Making* 14(3):289–97.

Salkeld, G., G. Young, L. Irwig, M. Haas, and P. Glasziou. 1996. Cost-effectiveness analysis of screening by faecal occult blood testing for colorectal cancer in Australia. *Australian and New Zealand Journal of Public Health* 20:138–43.

Scuffham, P., N. Devlin, J. Eberhart-Phillips, and R. Wilson-Salt. 1999. The cost-effectiveness of introducing a varicella vaccine to the New Zealand immunisation schedule. *Social Science and Medicine* 49:763–79.

Scuffham, P. A., A. V. Lowin, and M. A. Burgess. 2000. The cost-effectiveness of varicella vaccine programs for Australia. *Vaccine* 18:407–15.

Sugden, R., and A. Williams. 1978. *The principles of practical cost-benefit analysis.* Oxford: Oxford University Press.

Treasury Board of Canada Secretariat. 1998. *Benefit-cost analysis guide.* Ottawa: Treasury Board Secretariat.

U.K. CRC Screening Pilot Evaluation Team. 2003. *Evaluation of the U.K. colorectal cancer screening pilot—Final report.* Sheffield: NHS Cancer Screening Programmes.

Viscusi, W. K. 1992. *Fatal trade-offs.* Oxford: Oxford University Press.

Viscusi, W. K. 1993. The value of risks to life and health. *Journal of Economic Literature* 31:1912–46.

Weisbrod, B. 1968. Income redistribution effects and benefit-cost analyses. In *Problems vs. public expenditure analyses,* S.B. Chase (ed.). Washington: Brookings Institute., 395–428.

Whynes, D. K., A. R. Neilson, M. H. E. Robinson, and J. D. Hardcastle. 1998. Faecal occult blood screening for colorectal cancer: Is it cost-effective? *Health Economics* 7:21–29.

Wilton, P., R. D. Smith, J. Coast, and M. Millar. 2002. Strategies to contain the emergence of anti-microbial resistance: A systematic review of effectiveness and cost-effectiveness. *Journal of Health Services Research and Policy* 7(2):111–17.

Appendix 4

Chapter 4: Methods of Economic Evaluation

4.2 THREE METHODS OF ECONOMIC EVALUATION

4.2.3 Cost-Benefit Analysis

Willingness to Pay as a Measure of Benefit

Cost-benefit analysis requires that the analyst assign a monetary value to the change in utility associated with a change in resource allocation (such as the receipt of a health care service). One such measure asks the following question: before the change is implemented, how much would the individual be willing to pay to ensure that the change occurs? Economists call this the compensating variation. It is a monetary measure of the distance between two indifference curves.

Compensating variation can be illustrated as follows. Let there be two goods, x_1 and x_2, where the initial price of x_1 is p^*_1, and the price of x_2 is 1. The individual has income Y. The optimal consumption of x_1 and x_2 is initially point A in Figure 4A.1. Now assume the price of x_1 decreases to $\hat{P}_1$, for which the optimal consumption bundle is at point B. What

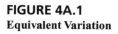

FIGURE 4A.1
Equivalent Variation

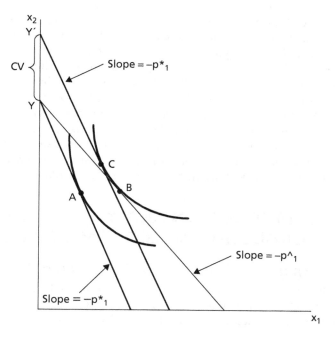

is the compensating variation measure of the change in the person's welfare caused by this price change? To derive this, draw the budget line with slope of $-p^*_1$ (the original price) that is just tangent to the post-change indifference curve. This point of tangency is point C. The compensating variation is the vertical difference between the original budget line and the budget line of the same slope tangent to the after-change indifference curve $(Y - Y')$, which in this case is negative. This is the maximum amount of money the individual would be willing to pay rather than forego the price decrease.

A second, directly analogous measure can be derived by asking this: after the change has occurred, how much would the individual have to be paid to reverse the change and return to the original situation? This is called the equivalent variation. It is directly analogous to the compensating variation but uses a post-change reference point rather than a pre-change reference point.

The Invariance of Net Benefit to the Classification of Costs and Benefits

The problem we encounter with measures other than net benefit can be illustrated as follows. Suppose that $\geqq$a program uses resources valued at C, and produces health benefits valued at B, but also results in costs savings (i.e., averted resources used) equal to D. If these averted costs are classified as negative costs, the benefit-cost ratio is $B/(C - D)$; if these averted costs are classified as benefits of the program, the benefit-cost ratio is $(B + D)/C$. The first ratio is greater than the second, which could lead to a different program recommendation, depending on how the averted costs are classified. Under the net benefit approach, the answer is invariant to whether one calculates the net benefit as $[(B + D) - C]$ or $[B - (C - D)]$.

4.2.5 The Differing Origins of the Methods

Because both cost-utility and cost-benefit analyses place a value on health benefits achieved (albeit using different methods), a series of papers has explored whether cost-utility analysis can be given a formal basis in welfare-economic theory (Garber and Phelps 1997; Garber 2000; Phelps and Mushlin 1991). The short answer is yes, but only under restrictive conditions on the nature of people's utility function (so that a QALY is actually an indicator of utility) and only if the threshold cost-per-QALY value that determines if an intervention is acceptable is allowed to vary across individuals. In particular, the threshold must be allowed to be higher for the wealthy, who are more willing to sacrifice a larger absolute amount of material wealth (though not necessarily utility) to achieve a given health improvement than are the poor. This is equivalent to using individual-level willingness to pay in order to value a program, an approach explicitly rejected by many practitioners of cost-utility analysis. Hence, although both methods base valuation of health states on individual preferences, the different ways in which this is done and the different ways the information is incorporated into the analysis generate distinct answers that reflect the different conceptual foundations of the methods (see also Hurley 2000).

4.3 SOME COMMON ANALYTIC CHALLENGES TO CONDUCTING AN ECONOMIC EVALUATION

4.3.1 Shadow Pricing and the Valuation of Resources Used

The debate regarding the conceptual basis for choosing a discount rate and the precise rate to use in evaluating public policies has been long and contentious.[1] The conceptual basis for choosing a discount rate is generally one of two types.

1. One derives from the notion of opportunity cost: the discount rate should equal the rate of return to private investments because public investments draw resources away from private investment; if the public project does not generate positive net benefit using this rate, the resources are better left in the private sector.
2. The other derives from the notion of time preference: the discount rate should equal the rate at which individuals in society are willing to trade current consumption for future consumption.

In a world of perfect capital markets for borrowing and lending, these two rationales lead to the same discount rate: the market rate of interest. To see this, consider a simple two-period model in which a person is able to borrow freely to shift consumption between the two periods so as to maximize utility. Let C_1 denote consumption in the first period and C_2 consumption in the second period (Figure 4A.2). Indifference curves representing preferences over consumption in the two periods are downward sloping with the usual curvature. The slope equals the rate at which a person trades current and future consumption—the rate of time preference—which changes along the indifference curve: at point A, the person has much more consumption in period 2 than in period 1, so it takes only a little additional consumption in period 1 to compensate for a reduction in consumption in period 2. At point B, the opposite is true.

The budget constraint can be derived as follows. Let T be the present value of income earned over the two periods. If the individual receives all of this income in the first period and spends it all in the first year, they attain point T ($C_1 = T$, $C_2 = 0$). If, instead, they invest it all for consumption in period 2, they would have $T(1 + r)$, where r is the market rate of interest, attaining consumption point $T(1 + r)$ ($C_1 = 0$, $C_2 = T(1 + r)$). So the slope of the budget constraint is $- (1 + r)$. The optimal consumption combination occurs at the tangency of an indifference curve with the budget constraint, point D in this example. At this

---

[1] This discussion draws heavily on Boardman et al. (2006).

FIGURE 4A.2

The Social Discount Rate with Perfect Capital Markets

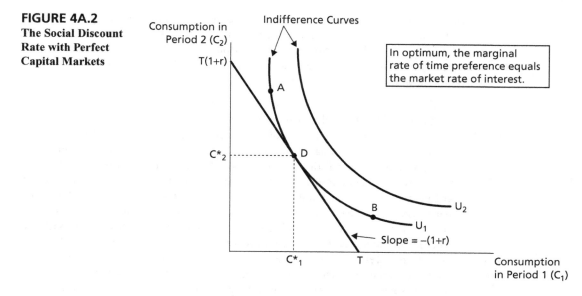

point, the individual's marginal rate of time preference (denote this by p) equals the market rate of interest. Further, because everyone in society faces the same market rate of interest, everyone's marginal rate of time preference will be identical (r = p). Both the opportunity cost argument and the time preference argument point to using the market rate of interest as the social discount rate.

Ramsey (1928) extended this analysis to a setting with economic growth. In an economy that grows over time, those in the future will enjoy higher per-capita consumption than the current generation. If the marginal utility of consumption falls as consumption rises, as is commonly assumed, the additional consumption enjoyed in the future produces smaller increments to welfare than does current consumption. In such a world, the marginal rate of time preference, p, comprises two components: p = d + ge. The first component, d, reflects pure time preference as discussed above (the preference for current consumption over future consumption, other things equal). The second component, ge, reflects economic growth and the associated decrease in the marginal utility of consumption as future real income increases: g is the rate of growth in the economy and e is the elasticity of social marginal utility of consumption (how quickly marginal utility falls as consumption rises). Ramsey further showed that on the optimal growth path for the economy, the marginal rate of return on investment equals the marginal social rate of time preference:

$$r = p = d + ge$$

But this equivalency breaks down in the real world with taxes and imperfect capital markets. Taxes, for instance, mean that the rate of return on investments exceeds the marginal rate of time preference. If a person saves by investing money, the pre-tax return (which corresponds to the opportunity cost of investment) exceeds the after-tax return (which equals their marginal rate of time preference). This divergence necessitates a choice between them for the discount rate.

- Proponents of the opportunity cost argument advocate for a discount rate based on the private sector rate of return, as approximated, for instance, by the before-tax rate of return on corporate bonds.

- Proponents of the time preference argument advocate for a discount rate based on the marginal rate of time preference (denote this p), as approximated, for instance, by the yield on government treasury bonds.

- A hybrid approach advocates for a discount rate that is a weighted average of the two, where the weights reflect how the project is financed. If w is the proportion of the project that is financed by borrowing (which displaces private investment) and $(1 - w)$ is the proportion financed by taxes (which primarily displaces consumption), then the discount rate would be $rw + p(1 - w)$.

Some analysts go further and ask whether the individual preferences of current members of society should be the basis for the social discount rate. A long line of economists have argued that individual private rates of time preference are myopic and unreflective, and that public policy should be based on a longer view. Ramsey, for instance, argued that d should be 0, so that the social discount rate should simply be proportional to the rate of economic growth. Others cite the lack of correspondence between the assumptions of the standard intertemporal model and actual behaviour. For instance, although the model predicts that a person will be either a borrower or lender, many individuals simultaneously borrow and lend. Recent evidence from behavioural economics indicates that individuals' intertemporal choices are time inconsistent (rather than a constant rate of time preference, rates of time of time preference decline as the time horizon for the choice increases) and are sensitive to how an intertemporal choice problem is framed (Frederick et al. 2002).

In the face of such a lack of consensus among economists regarding the appropriate discount rate, and recognizing the advantages of standardization of methods that enhances comparability across projects, governments have prescribed rates to be used in evaluating government programs. Early on, such prescribed rates were influenced more heavily by opportunity cost arguments, and tended to be in the range of 10 percent (e.g., the rate set in the 1980s by the U.S. Office of Management and Budget and in 1976 by the Canadian Federal Treasury Board Secretariat); more recently, rates have been more heavily influenced by time preference arguments and have been revised downward (e.g., the U.S. Office of Management and Budget lowered its required rate to 7 percent; recent rates recommended by the U.K. government are 3.5 percent).

For a more detailed discussion of both the conceptual foundations of the social discount rate and the practical choices used in policy, see Boardman et al. (2006); Moore et al. (2004).

References

Boardman, A., D. Greenberg, A. Vining, and D. Weimer. 2006. *Cost-benefit analysis: Concepts and practice.* Upper Saddle River, NJ: Pearson Education Ltd.

Frederick, S., G. Loewenstein, and T. O'Donoghue. 2002. Time discounting and time preference: A critical review. *Journal of Economic Literature* 40(2):351–401.

Garber, A. 2000. Advances in cost-effectiveness analysis of health interventions. In *Handbook of health economics*, A. J. Culyer, and J. P. Newhouse (eds.). Amsterdam: Elsevier Science B.V., 181–221.

Garber, A. M., and C. E. Phelps. 1997. Economic foundations of cost-effectiveness analysis. *Journal of Health Economics* 16:1–31.

Hurley, J. 2000. An overview of the normative economics of the health sector. In *Handbook of health economics*, A. J. Culyer , and J. P. Newhouse (eds.). Amsterdam: Elsevier Science B.V., 55–118.

Moore, M., A. Boardman, A. Vining, D. Weimer, and D. Greenberg. 2004. "Just give me a number!" Practical values for the social discount rate. *Journal of Policy Analysis and Management* 23(4):789–812.

Phelps, C. E., and A. I. Mushlin. 1991. On the (near) equivalence of cost-effectiveness and cost-benefit analysis. *International Journal of Technology Assessment in Health Care* 7(1):12–21.

Economics of Health

INTRODUCTION

Health is priceless, right? Nothing is more important. People don't trade off their health just to gain a few dollars here or a bit of pleasure there. Or do they? Have you ever sped in your car—probably just a little faster than was really safe—to get to a movie on time? Or stepped on the top rung of a ladder because it wasn't worth the effort to get the taller one from the garage? Or done any one of the thousands of things people do every day that increase the risk of illness or injury in order to avoid some tangible cost (monetary or otherwise)? If so, you risked your health for something else you desired.

We base our economic analysis of health on the premise that we can gain important insights into a wide range of health issues by analyzing health as an economic good, one that is subject to many of the same fundamental forces as other goods. Good health provides an individual with invaluable benefits, but staying in good health can be costly and sometimes conflicts with other things we care about. Good health has a price. As such, we might expect people's decisions about health to reflect the time, money, and psychic costs and benefits of health. The economic analysis of health proceeds from this expectation.

People care about health for many reasons. The first and most obvious has already been noted: good health is a source of intrinsic benefit. Feeling good is better than feeling lousy. Because health is one of the most important sources of well-being, it is a vital concern for public policy. This intrinsic value of health makes it of interest in its own right, but health is also highly valued as a determinant of a person's ability to live a "normal" life and achieve other things of value. Health influences other socially important outcomes such as educational attainment, labour market participation, and workplace productivity.

Health also presents interesting analytic and research puzzles. Although health is subject to many of the same fundamental economic forces as standard goods and services, it also has distinctive features. Individuals, for example, both demand health and play a pivotal role in producing their own health. This means we require a unified framework for analyzing both the individual-level demand for health and the production of health.

In addition, the link between many behaviours and health is subject to substantial time delays: eating that extra piece of pie today gives immediate pleasure but won't affect the eater's health for many years to come. So, understanding health-related behaviours and their health impacts also requires an understanding of people's preferences over time.

As we noted in Chapter 1, health is determined by more than individual choices. The health of individuals and populations is also shaped by broad social and economic forces. Social forces influence many of our individual choices: the strong relationship between smoking and income, for instance, suggests that context and conditioning have an important effect on smoking behaviour. Social policies can also affect the consequences of our individual actions: an individual driver may decide to speed, but transportation policy and highway safety also play a role in determining if that speeding causes a crash and if the crash leads to death.

Finally, the ubiquitous socio-economic gradient in health—people of higher socio-economic status are healthier, on average, than those of lower socio-economic status—suggests that social context influences health quite apart from specific behaviours or health problems.

The difference between an individualistic focus and a focus on the broader determinants of health of populations is nicely illustrated by Michael Marmot (2000) (also discussed in Evans 2002). Figure II.1 depicts age- and sex-specific homicide rates for two regions, Chicago and England/Wales. The curves for the two regions display remarkable similarity. In both regions, homicide rates for males are many times the rates for females; and both display a similar age structure, with male rates peaking at age 20–24 and then gradually decreasing. An analysis of the determinants of homicide in Chicago or England/Wales would rightly highlight the important roles of age and sex. But notice the scales of the vertical axes: the rates of homicide in Chicago are 25–30 times those of England and Wales. Even though the individual patterns of variation are similar in both regions, something in the social and economic context of Chicago causes males to kill at much higher rates. The factors that drive variation within a population (e.g., age and sex) can be quite different from the factors that drive variation across populations (e.g., gun regulations, culture).

Accordingly, the two chapters in this section take different points of view. Chapter 5 focuses on models of individual-level demand for and production of health. Although modifications are necessary to integrate distinctive features of

FIGURE II.1
Crime Rates in Chicago and England/Wales

Source: Cronin H. 1991. *The Ant and The Peacock.* New York: Cambridge University Press, p. 332. ISBN: 052132937X.

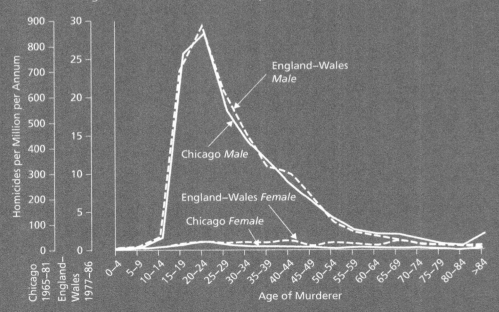

health, the analysis proceeds very much in the spirit of familiar microeconomic models. Health is one of many things that an individual cares about; an individual faces different ways to produce health and must also choose the level of health so as to maximize utility subject to constraints.

In contrast, Chapter 6 focuses on broader determinants of health in populations, including a historical look at the factors responsible for the dramatic improvement in health over the last 300 years and an examination of factors responsible for inequality in the distribution of health in populations.

These distinct determinants do not act separately, but rather interact in ways that can reinforce or counteract the effects of each (see discussion in Chapter 1).

The Health Production Function

The unifying economic framework for much of this section is that of the health production function, which defines how much health is produced by differing combinations of health inputs, or determinants of health (see Chapter 2 regarding production functions). The health production function can notionally be written as follows:

$$H = F(\underbrace{\text{genetics, exercise, health care, income, etc.}}_{\text{(a) Individual-level determinants}}; \underbrace{\text{pollution, social status, social support, etc.}}_{\text{(b) Community-level determinants}}; \underbrace{\text{interactions}}_{\text{(c)}})$$

where H represents the level of health. The first set of determinants listed (a) are all individual-level characteristics or behaviours that will be the focus of Chapter 5; the second set of determinants (b) are community-level attributes of the physical and social environment that will be the focus of Chapter 6; and the third set represents the effects of interactions among the various determinants (e.g., smoking is a risk factor and air pollution is a risk factor, but the combination of smoking and living in a community with high levels of air pollution harms health more than the sum of each; recall the discussion from Chapter 1).

If scientists could ever estimate such a health production function, it would tell us the contribution each determinant makes to health, it would provide insight into the distribution of health in society, and perhaps most importantly for policy, it would tell us at the margin which determinants to invest in so as to achieve the most improvement in health with our limited resources. For this reason, this production function is sometimes called the "dream equation" by population health researchers.

Unfortunately, a number of conceptual and practical reasons prevent us from estimating such a dream equation. At a conceptual level, we don't know all the factors that determine health. In addition, there is complex web of relationships among them that is difficult to disentangle: in some cases, a strong relationship among determinants merely represents a high **correlation** (e.g., smoking and alcohol consumption); in others, it represents a **causal relationship** (e.g., levels of stress can influence drinking and smoking behaviours); and the scope for interactions among the different variables is almost beyond imagination. At a practical level, data are available on only a small number of determinants.

Still, economists and others have tried to estimate such models (see Auster et al. (1970) and Rosenzweig and Shultz (1983) for examples of seminal attempts by economists). But the more common strategy is to hive off part of the overall

correlation
A measure of the strength of the (linear) relationship between two variables. The correlation can be positive when two variables increase or decrease together (e.g., rain and use of umbrellas) or negative when two variables move in opposite directions (e.g., amount of sunshine and use of umbrellas).

causal relationship
A situation in which one variable determines (in whole or in part) the value of a second variable. Causation is one possible source of a correlation between two variables.

process and examine particular aspects of that relationship for a particular subset of determinants. This is more manageable and it allows deeper investigation of specific aspects of the production of health.

Before delving into the economic analysis of health, however, it will be useful to briefly review what we mean by health and some ways in which health is measured.

Defining and Measuring Health

No single definition can serve all the varied analyses that require a meaningful concept of health. Probably the most widely cited definition of health is that developed by the World Health Organization in its constitution (World Health Organization 1947):

> Health is a state of complete physical, mental and social well-being, and not merely the absence of disease or injury.

This definition emphasizes that health is a positive construct, not just the absence of disease, and stresses the different dimensions of health—physical, mental, and social. But because it is so all encompassing, it effectively equates health with "well-being" and risks obscuring the important point that health is but one contributor to our overall well-being.

One useful taxonomy of definitions of health distinguishes two dimensions: objective versus subjective definitions, and "within-the-skin" versus "beyond-the-skin" definitions. Objective definitions define health relative to an objective standard, where the assessment is normally done by a third party (or device). Subjective definitions, in contrast, define health from the perspective of how it is experienced by the individual.

"Within-the-skin" definitions consider only the physiological function of an individual's body; "beyond-the-skin" definitions emphasize how physiological function translates into a person's ability to function normally in everyday life.

The interaction of these two dimensions leads to four types of definitions (Table II.1). Consider someone who suffers from arthritis. An *objective, within-the-skin* definition would focus on counting the number of inflamed joints and their degree of inflammation. A *subjective, within-the-skin* definition would focus on the amount of pain as experienced by the individual. An *objective, beyond-the-skin* definition would assess health in terms of a standardized test of grip strength. A *subjective, beyond-the-skin* definition would assess health in terms of the person's ability to carry out the activities of daily living, such as dressing and preparing meals.

The usefulness of these alternative conceptions of health varies with context. The diagnosis of a health problem emphasizes within-the-skin definitions—what is physiologically wrong? But deciding what, if anything, must be done should integrate beyond-the-skin considerations of the individual's experience. Many physiological abnormalities never manifest as illness for an individual. The goal is not to correct every physiological abnormality, it is to improve people's well-being as they live their lives.

Health scientists and researchers have devised thousands of measures of health. The measures can be usefully classified along two dimensions: individual versus population measures, and mortality versus morbidity measures. Individual measures of health indicate the presence or absence of a condition, such as diabetes, in an

TABLE II.1   Definitions of Health

	"Within-the-skin": physiological function	"Beyond-the-skin": functional abilities in normal activities

Objective: assessed by a third party against a defined standard	Health is the absence of abnormal physiological function.
	• Sample Measures:
	  • Mortality (dead/alive)
	  • Blood sugar levels
	  • Blood Pressure
	  • Vision score
	  • Degree of swelling in arthritic joints
		Health is the ability to function normally relative to a defined standard
		• Sample measures:
		  • Functional Status Scores
		  • Grip strength

Subjective: as experienced by the individual	Health is the absence of physical symptoms of underlying disease
	• Sample Measures
	  • Self-rated pain
		Health as experienced and rated by the individual
		• Sample Measures
		  • Self-assessed health status
		  • Ability to carry out activities of daily living

incidence rate
Measures the number of new cases of a given condition that arise in a given population during a given time period.

prevalence rate
Measures the proportion of people in a population who have a given condition at a given point in time.

individual. Population measures, because they are defined over many individuals, generally indicate the rate of some aspect of health or illness in a population.

There are two prominent types of rates: incidence rates and prevalence rates. **Incidence rates** measure the number of new cases that arise in a given population during a given time period. The annual incidence of diabetes in Canada, for example, has been estimated to be 6.0 cases per 1000 people (Public Health Agency of Canada 2008). **Prevalence rates**, in contrast, measure the proportion of people in a population who have a specific condition at a point in time. The prevalence of diabetes among Canadians in 2004/05 was estimated to be 55 cases per 1000 people, or 5.5 percent of the population (Public Health Agency of Canada 2008).[1] Population-based measures of health are often aggregate analogues of individual-level measures, such as the diabetes example just given. But some measures can only be defined at the population level. Measures of inequality in the distribution of health, for example, can only be defined over populations.

Mortality-based measures derive from vital statistics: is a person dead or alive? Morbidity-based measures derive from measures of illness or injury among the living (Table II.2). At the individual level, mortality is often too crude a measure to be useful in many contexts, but mortality-based measures are widely used to measure population health, in part because nearly all countries collect vital-statistics data. A number of alternative measures can be derived from mortality data, including mortality rates, life expectancy, and potential life-years lost (the gap between the expected and actual age of death).

Table II.3 provides information on some commonly used measures of population health for selected OECD countries. No one country ranks highest in all these dimensions of health.

[1] The prevalence exceeds the incidence because people live for many years with diabetes, so the prevalent cases at any point in time include those just diagnosed plus all those diagnosed in previous years who are still living.

TABLE II.2   Measures of Population Health

	Mortality-based	Morbidity-based
Individual-level	*Mortality:* dead or alive	*Presence/absence of a health condition:* heart disease, diabetes, etc. *Body-Mass Index (BMI):* weight in kilograms divided by the square of height in meters (kg/m^2) *Self-Assessed Health Status:* In general, would you rate your health as excellent, very good, good, fair, poor?
Population-level	*Crude Mortality Rate:* number of deaths per year per 1000 people in a population *Infant Mortality Rate:* number of deaths in children less than 1 year of age per 1000 live births *Life Expectancy at Birth:* number of years a person born today can expect to live *Potential Life-Years Lost:* number of years of life lost due to premature mortality [deaths*(life expectancy – age at death)] *Standardized Mortality Rate:* ratio of the actual number of deaths observed in a population to the expected number. The expected number is derived from the mortality experience in a relevant reference population.	*Prevalence or Incidence of a specific health condition in a population:* prevalence/incidence of heart disease, diabetes, etc. *Mean value of a measure:* e.g., mean value for BMI in a population

TABLE II.3   Alternative Health Indicators, Selected OECD Countries, 2006

Source: OECD (2009), OECD Health Data 2009: Statistics and Indicators for 30 Countries, www.oecd.org/health/healthdata.

	Mortality Rate (per 100,000)	Life Expectancy at Birth Male	Female	Potential Years of Life Lost	Self-Assessed Health Status > Good	2002 Cancer Incidence (per 100,000)
Australia	497.2[b]	78.7	83.5	3122[b]	84.1%	312.0
Canada	534.3[b]	78.4	83.0	3365[b]	88.4%	299.9
Finland	568.7	75.9	83.1	3627	67.6%	
France	500.0	77.2	84.1	3448	75.7%	289.5
Germany	562.2	77.2	82.4	3134	—	283.3
Japan	442.7	79.0	85.8	2683	—	
Netherlands	564.8	77.6	81.9	2894	77.7%	
New Zealand	530.1[c]	78.0	82.2	3635[c]	89.7%[d]	
Norway	529.2	78.2	82.9	2925	81.0%[c]	
Sweden	517.2	78.7	82.9	2610	73.2%	
Switzerland	467.5	79.2	84.2	2796	86.7%[d]	
United Kingdom	597.1	77.1[c]	81.1[c]	3461	76.0%	273.6
United States	631.2[c]	75.4	80.7	4965	88.5%	357.7

Note: See Table II.2 for definitions of the alternative measures.

References

Auster, R. D., I. Leveson, and D. Sarachek. 1970. The production of health, an exploratory study. *The Journal of Human Resources* 4(4):412–35.

Cronin, H. 1991. *The ant and the peacock.* New York: Cambridge University Press.

Evans, R. G. 2002. *Interpreting and addressing inequalities in health: From Black to Acheson to Blair to . . .?* London: Office of Health Economics.

Marmot, M. 2000. Multilevel approaches to understanding social determinants. In *Social Epidemiology.* L. Berkman, and I. Kawachi (eds.). New York: Oxford University Press. 15:349–367.

OECD. 2009. *OECD health data 2009.* Paris: OECD.

Public Health Agency of Canada. 2008. *Diabetes in Canada: Highlights from the National Diabetes Surveillance System 2004–2005.* Ottawa: Public Health Agency of Canada.

Rosenzweig, M. R., and T. P. Schultz. 1983. Estimating a household production function: Heterogeneity, the demand for health inputs, and their effects on birth weight. *Journal of Political Economy* 91(5):723–46.

World Health Organization. 1947. The constitution of the World Health Organization. *WHO Chronicles* 1:29.

Individual-Level Demand for and Production of Health

Learning Objectives

After studying this chapter, you will understand

LO1 The health capital framework that economists use to analyze individual-level demand for and production of health

LO2 Predictions from the human capital framework regarding the impact of factors such as age, income, and education on the demand for health

LO3 Principal elements of the economic analysis of health-related behaviours

LO4 The impact of selected health-related behaviours

Though you probably don't think of it in terms of economic demand, almost everyone wants to be healthy; furthermore, people attempt to achieve their desired level of health through diet, exercise, medication, and other personal choices. That is, they are both demanders of health and producers of health.

An economic analysis of this demand and production seeks to understand the factors that determine the demand for health and how individuals choose to achieve health. Grossman (1972) presented the first formal economic model of individual-level demand for and production of health. His model has spawned much literature analyzing health-related decisions, using what has come to be called the health capital framework.

Although the framework is highly technical, this chapter provides a non-technical introduction that describes essential ideas from the model. It then examines in detail a relationship of particular interest within the health capital framework—that between education and health—followed by an economic analysis of health-related behaviours, focusing on obesity and smoking.

5.1   THE HEALTH CAPITAL MODEL

The **health capital model** is one example of the human capital framework used by economists to analyze people's investments in themselves and the effects of those investments on important economic outcomes. Just as a firm can invest in machinery and

health capital model

An economic model of the individual-level demand for and production of health over a lifetime, based on the assumption that health can be analyzed as a durable capital good.

equipment to increase its productivity, the human capital framework posits that people can invest in their capital stock of knowledge and skills—for example, through education—to increase their productivity both inside and outside the work place. Similarly, the health capital framework emphasizes investments in health and analyzes both an individual's demand for health and individual decisions regarding how to produce the desired level of health. The health capital model developed by Grossman (1972) has been highly influential within health economics and provides insight into a wide range of health-related phenomena. (Grossman's health capital model is a specific example of a household production model; see Box 5.1.)

5.1.1   The Grossman Health Capital Model

Grossman sought to understand the individual's life-long demand for health and to gain insight into how factors such as education, income, and age affect both the demand for health and ways to achieve a desired level of health. Grossman assumes that health is just one of many goods that provide utility and that, within bounds, people are willing to trade off health against other things that also provide utility. People desire health for three basic reasons:

1. Good health provides direct benefits and enables them to undertake activities that provide utility.
2. Good health enables them to work more days in the labour market and earn a higher income, which allows them to purchase more goods and services.
3. Good health enables them to live longer, enjoying the benefits of their activities and consumption for more years.

Given preferences, income-earning potential, the cost of maintaining health, and other factors discussed below, the model implies that each person has an optimal level of health at each point in life. To keep the problem manageable, Grossman made a number of simplifying assumptions; but before we discuss them, let's consider the central ideas of his approach and some implications of his work.

We assume people care about two things: their level of health and the acquisition of "final consumption goods." Health is modelled as a type of human capital, that is durable and lasts over a number of periods; that naturally depreciates (or is used up) over time; and that a person can, by investing in it, maintain at a desired level (within bounds).

People produce health by using their own time, skills, and health care, and they produce final consumption goods using their own time, skills, and goods purchased in the market. People don't care intrinsically for either health care or other market goods; they value them only to the extent that such goods contribute to the production of health and final consumption goods.

For instance, if entertainment is what is ultimately desired, a TV plus time produces the final consumption good: entertainment. A car, gas, and time produce travel; groceries, kitchen utensils, appliances, and time produce a meal; and health care plus time produces health. This provides one of the first important insights of the model: the demand for health care is a **derived demand**, derived from the demand for health itself. To understand the demand for health care, we must first understand the demand for health.

derived demand for health care

The demand for health care derives from the demand for health.

Individuals face a number of constraints in deciding the optimal levels of health and final consumption goods. They face a *time constraint* (24 hours per day, 365 days per year). They can spend this time four different ways: in working (which generates the income used to purchase market goods); in producing health; in producing final consumption goods; and in illness (during which they can do nothing else).

Grossman's health capital model is a specific example of a household production model. Household production models are commonly used to study human capital investments. Although individuals are assumed to be utility maximizers, their choice problem is distinct from that of standard demand theory as described in Chapter 3. In standard demand theory, people maximize utility by purchasing market commodities.

In a household production model, however, people don't care about market goods per se. For instance, neither a TV nor a car is valued in and of itself. Rather, people care about final consumption goods, such as entertainment and transportation. They cannot buy these goods on a market; instead they have to produce them. They do this by combining their own time with market goods: entertainment is produced by using a TV and time; transportation is produced using a car and time.

Maximizing utility therefore requires solving two problems: a production problem (how to produce the final consumption goods) and a consumption problem (what mix of final consumption goods is most desired). The individual must do this facing multiple constraints: a money constraint—the amount of money available to purchase market goods depends on the income available; production constraints—final consumption goods can be produced subject to the technology available; and a time constraint—only 24 hours are available each day to be allocated between work and producing the final consumption goods (which may include leisure). The model is particularly useful in contexts where non-market production is important. For this reason, it has been widely applied to understand household behaviour in developing countries where many essential goods are produced at home rather than purchased on the market.

It is similarly valuable for investment decisions that require commitments of individual time, such as investments in health. Although health can sometimes be purchased using primarily market goods and little time (e.g., certain medicines), many aspects of investing in health, such as regular exercise, preparing healthy meals, and even staying informed about health matters, take time. We will encounter the household production model in other contexts in subsequent chapters.

They also face an *income constraint:* the total amount of money that they spend on health care and other market goods cannot exceed their income. And people face two *production constraints.* The first is the amount of health that can be produced by different combinations of health care and the time spent producing health. The second is the amount of final consumption goods that can be produced using market goods and time.[1] Grossman assumes that education makes people more efficient at producing both health and final consumption goods. Consequently, someone with more education can produce more health with a given amount of time and health care than can someone with less education.

depreciation rate of health capital

The amount by which health diminishes each period if an individual does not invest in maintaining health.

The last critical piece of his model is the **depreciation rate of health capital**: the depreciation rate is the amount by which health diminishes each period if an individual does not invest in maintaining health. Grossman assumes that the depreciation rate increases with age, so that over time it takes larger and larger investments to maintain health.

People demand health for two reasons. Health provides a direct, "consumption" benefit: other things equal, we all prefer to be healthy. Illness is unpleasant and prevents us from doing things we care about. Health also provides an "investment" benefit: good health increases the time available to work and generate income. Furthermore, because a person's stock of health capital depreciates slowly, investing in health this year creates effects that persist many years into the future. Consequently, when deciding the optimal level of health in each year, individuals must take into account the effect of health on lifetime utility.

The optimal investment in health in any given year is that level at which the marginal benefit of an additional unit of health just equals the marginal cost of an additional unit

---

[1] Although Grossman does consider the possibility that final consumption goods can affect health (e.g., smoking, drinking, exercise), for simplicity this analysis assumes that final consumption goods have no impact on health.

of health. Because the benefits of additional health this year accrue over many years into the future, the relevant quantity is the discounted stream of current and future benefits of health (discounting is discussed in Chapter 4).

To summarize, people care about their levels of health and the consumption of other goods and services each year they are alive. They produce health and other goods using their own time plus goods purchased in the market. They must choose the optimal level of health and consumption each year, subject to the time available, the income available, and the production relationships that determine how much health and other goods they can produce using their time and purchased market goods. Each person then allocates time among health production, production of final consumption goods, work, and time spent ill. Individuals also decide how to allocate available income between health care and market goods.

Of particular interest is how factors such as age, wage level, and education influence the optimal level of health and the optimal way to produce health. To analyze these relationships, Grossman distinguishes between the investment demand for health and the consumption demand for health.

Investment Demand for Health

investment demand for health
An individual's demand for health capital that derives from the monetary benefits (due to increased time available for work) associated with improved health.

For simplicity, the **investment demand for health** makes the assumption that the direct benefit of health is zero: people demand health only for its impact on their ability to work and earn income (which they can use to purchase both health care and market goods). If this is the case, we can draw demand and supply curves for health capital for a given period (Figure 5.1).

The demand curve depicts how the marginal benefit of health capital depends on an individual's level of health capital. For investment demand, the marginal benefit of health capital derives from the increased earnings made possible when people have more healthy days available to work. The curve is downward sloping on the assumption that producing healthy days from health capital is subject to diminishing returns: a one-unit increase in health capital produces more healthy days when health capital is low than it does when health capital is high. Hence, when health capital is high, the marginal benefit from an additional unit of health capital is lower, and the demand curve is downward sloping.

FIGURE 5.1

The Optimal Level of Health Capital
The optimal level of health capital in period t (H_t^*) is that level at which the marginal benefit of a unit of health capital (as indicated by the downward-sloping demand curve) equals the marginal cost of health capital (as indicated by the supply curve, which is assumed to be constant with respect to health capital).

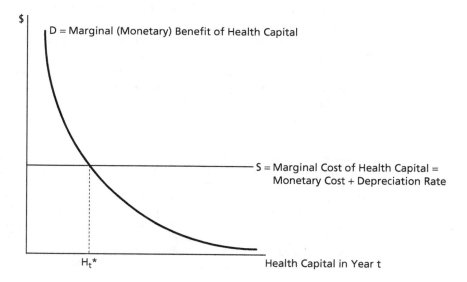

The supply curve for health capital equals the marginal cost of supplying a unit of health capital for a given period. This marginal cost includes two components: the money cost and the depreciation rate of health capital. The money cost depends on the cost of investing in health[2] and the rate of interest (because the opportunity cost of spending money on health is the interest that could have been earned on that money during the period in question). The depreciation rate affects the marginal cost because, during that period, any health capital supplied to an individual will depreciate; this is a cost of holding a unit of health capital. We assume this marginal cost does not vary with the level of health capital (i.e., marginal cost is constant). Hence, the supply curve is a horizontal line.

The intersection of the demand and supply curves denotes the optimal level of health, H_t^*, the level at which the marginal benefit of more health just equals the marginal cost. With this diagram, we can identify how a variety of factors affect the optimal level of health.

Aging and the Optimal Level of Health Consider first the effect of aging on the optimal level of health. As people age, the depreciation rate of health increases; for each year of aging, health declines by an increasing amount in the absence of investment. An increase in the depreciation rate causes the cost of supplying a unit of health to go up. As a result, to maintain the same level of health, an older person must invest more time and health care than a younger person does (Figure 5.2(i)). This causes the supply curve to shift upward. As people age, the optimal level of health falls. Eventually individuals become unwilling to invest the necessary time and health care, and the result is death.[3]

Although the optimal level of health falls with age, the demand for health care may increase or decrease, depending on the elasticity of the demand curve for health. Figure 5.3 illustrates this. Panels (i) and (ii) show the impact of aging on a young person whose depreciation rate is relatively small. As expected, aging causes a smaller drop in the optimal level of health capital when the demand curve is inelastic (i) than when it is elastic (ii).

Panels (iii) and (iv) show the impact of aging on an older person whose depreciation rate is higher. As expected, the increase in age causes a larger decrease in health capital. But note that, in the case of inelastic demand, the decrease is still relatively small. The only way such people can maintain their health capital is to invest heavily in health through, for example, health care. Hence, although aging causes the optimal health capital to fall, for those with inelastic demand for health the consumption of health care increases as they fight the effects of aging.

In contrast, someone with elastic demand can achieve a decrease in the optimal level of health capital only by investing little in health. For such a person, both health and health care consumption fall with age. Grossman showed that if the elasticity of demand for health capital is less than 1, health care consumption will rise with age; if it is greater than 1, health care consumption will fall with age.

---

[2] More precisely, it depends on the change in the cost of investing in health. Suppose a person invests in health at a given cost at the beginning of the relevant period, and that during that period the cost of health care increases. Because the person invested in health before the price increase, the cost of achieving future levels of health is lower than if they had delayed the investment for a period. This is directly analogous to capital gains associated with holding capital assets, such as a house.

[3] In real life, of course, death is normally not a choice: today most people die when no technology exists to prevent death. But individuals in a similar condition often display quite different survival experiences, depending on whether or not they are "fighters." And at a certain point, many people choose to forgo further medical intervention designed to forestall death—they choose to die.

FIGURE 5.2

The Impact of Aging, Wages, and Education on the Optimal Level of Health Capital Under the Investment Demand Model

As a person ages, the depreciation rate of health capital increases, raising the marginal cost of health capital and decreasing the optimal level of health. As wage rate increases, the marginal benefit of health capital increases (because working time is now more valuable), causing the optimal level of health to rise. Finally, an increase in education makes a person more productive, increasing the marginal benefit of health capital and the optimal level of health.

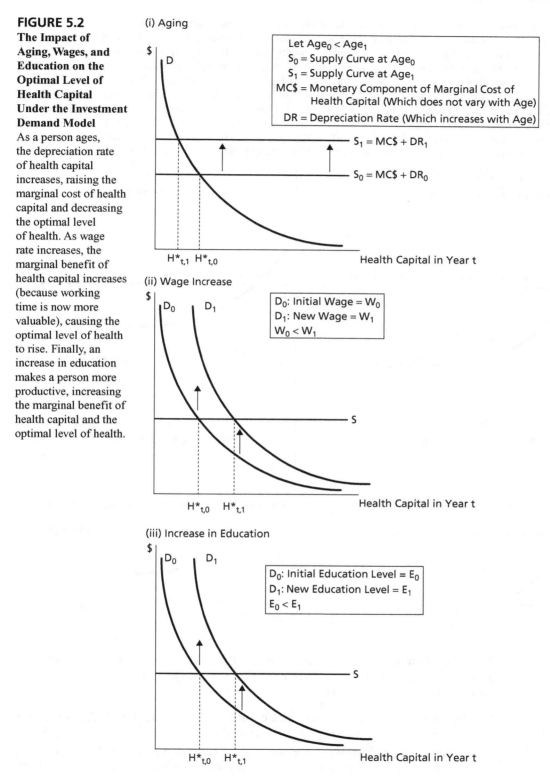

(i) Aging

Let $Age_0 < Age_1$
S_0 = Supply Curve at Age_0
S_1 = Supply Curve at Age_1
MC\$ = Monetary Component of Marginal Cost of Health Capital (Which does not vary with Age)
DR = Depreciation Rate (Which increases with Age)

$S_1 = MC\$ + DR_1$
$S_0 = MC\$ + DR_0$

$H^*_{t,1}$ $H^*_{t,0}$

Health Capital in Year t

(ii) Wage Increase

D_0: Initial Wage = W_0
D_1: New Wage = W_1
$W_0 < W_1$

S

$H^*_{t,0}$ $H^*_{t,1}$

Health Capital in Year t

(iii) Increase in Education

D_0: Initial Education Level = E_0
D_1: New Education Level = E_1
$E_0 < E_1$

S

$H^*_{t,0}$ $H^*_{t,1}$

Health Capital in Year t

FIGURE 5.3 The Impact of Aging Under Different Elasticities of Demand for Health Capital

This figure illustrates the importance of the elasticity of the health demand curve for the optimal level of health capital and for investment in health via health care spending. Comparing graphs (i) and (ii) or (iii) and (iv) reveals that the more elastic the demand curve, the greater will be the decrease in optimal health capital for a given increase in the depreciation rate. Comparison of (i) and (iii) shows that when the demand curve for health is very inelastic, even large increases in the depreciation rate cause the optimal health level to fall only slightly. This necessitates large investments in health to maintain the optimal level of health capital. Hence, even though optimal health falls as one ages, consumption of health care rises with age. In contrast, comparison of (ii) and (iv) shows that when the demand curve is highly elastic, large increases in the depreciation rate cause large decreases in the optimal level of health. Such an individual invests little in maintaining health. If the demand curve is sufficiently elastic, both the optimal level of health and health care spending fall as one ages.

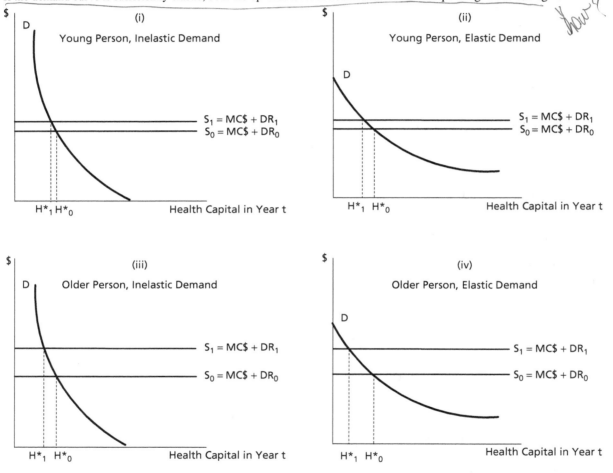

The Wage Rate and the Optimal Level of Health Next, consider the impact of an increase in wage rate on the demand for health. The change in the wage rate affects the optimal level of health in two ways:

1. A higher wage rate increases the value of time spent working, shifting the demand for health capital upward and increasing the optimal level of health capital (Figure 5.2(ii)).

2. A higher wage increases the opportunity cost of time spent producing health, inducing a person to substitute health care for their own time to achieve a given level of health (e.g., to take a cholesterol-lowering medication rather than exercise regularly).

As a result, an increase in income is predicted to increase both the demand for health and the demand for health care.[4]

Education and the Optimal Level of Health Finally, consider the impact of an increase in education level. A higher level of education raises productivity in generating both health and final consumption goods. The higher productivity raises the return on a given investment in producing health capital, shifting the demand curve for health capital up and increasing the optimal level of health (Figure 5.2(iii)). The magnitude of the increase in productivity determines the amount of the upward shift.

If we assume for simplicity that education increases productivity in the use of both time and market goods (so that the additional education does not create any tendency to substitute one input for another), then the impact of an increase in education on the demand for health care depends on the elasticity of the health capital demand curve. A given increase in productivity causes a smaller increase in the optimal level of health capital when the demand curve is inelastic than when it is elastic (Figure 5.4). The education-induced increase in productivity may allow someone with inelastic demand to achieve the new optimal level of health while actually decreasing consumption of health care.

In contrast, when demand is elastic, achieving the new higher optimal level of health requires an increase in health care consumption. Grossman showed that, once again, the critical value of the elasticity of demand is 1: if the elasticity is less than 1, education and health care consumption are negatively correlated; if the elasticity is greater than 1, education and health care consumption are positively correlated.

The Consumption Demand for Health

consumption demand for health
An individual's demand for health capital that derives from the non-monetary, direct utility benefits associated with improved health.

The **consumption demand for health** refers to the demand for health that derives solely from the direct utility effects of health. To analyze this demand, consider a situation in which better health provides no monetary reward through an effect on earnings. Because benefits derive purely from utility effects, the consumption demand introduces a range of new considerations, such as an individual's **rate of time preference** (see Chapter 4). The predictions of the consumption model differ in important ways from the investment model, and overall they are more ambiguous.

rate of time preference
How much an individual values health today compared to the future.

Aging and the Optimal Level of Health If someone has a positive rate of time preference, then aging and the associated increase in the rate of depreciation of health cause the optimal level of health to fall over the life cycle. The rate of time preference, or more formally, the elasticity of substitution between present and future consumption, plays a role analogous to the elasticity demand in the investment model. People with a high rate of time preference strongly prefer current health to future health, so the optimal level of health capital will fall more rapidly as they age.

The Wage Rate and the Optimal Level of Health The impact of an increase in the wage rate on the optimal level of health is ambiguous. The effect depends in part on whether the production of health is more time intensive (e.g., relies on exercising) or more health-care intensive (e.g., relies on drugs). If health production is time intensive, then an increase in the wage rate raises the relative price of health compared with final consumption goods and reduces the optimal level of health. The opposite is true if production of health

---

[4] This analysis assumes that the individual has to purchase health care. Grossman has explored these issues when health care is fully covered by insurance, and the primary cost of obtaining health care is time. The predicted impact of a wage increase on health care demand becomes indeterminate (Grossman 2000).

FIGURE 5.4

The Impact of Education on Demand for Health Capital
An increase in education causes a person's productivity to improve, shifting the demand curve for health capital upward. A given change in productivity will cause a smaller increase in the optimal health capital for a person with inelastic demand (H_t^* to $H_t^{\wedge}$) than for a person with elastic demand (H_t^* to $H_t^{\sim}$). Given their increase in productivity, a person with inelastic demand may be able to achieve the new, only slightly higher, optimal level of health while reducing health care consumption, while the person with elastic demand must increase health care consumption to achieve the new, substantially higher optimal level of health.

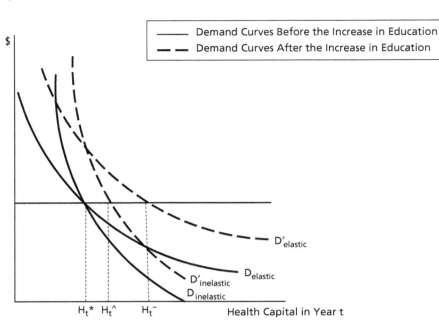

is health-care intensive, because this increases both the optimal level of health and health care consumption.

Education and the Optimal Level of Health   Education increases productivity in the production of both health and final consumption goods. This increase in productivity reduces the real cost of both health and non-market goods, increasing real wealth. If the productivity effects differ across goods, it can also induce substitution effects among them.

Consider three alternatives. If the productivity effects are neutral across goods, then only the real-wealth effect occurs. If the demand for health increases with wealth, then the optimal level of health rises. If the productivity effects are larger with respect to the production of health than with the production of final consumption goods, both the real-wealth effect and the substitution effect occur, reinforcing each other to increase the optimal level of health.

If, however, the productivity effects favour production of final consumption goods, the real-wealth effect and substitution effect work in opposite directions, and their relative size determines the ultimate impact on the optimal level of health. The impact of education on health care consumption is not clear, and depends on the values of a number of parameters.

Table 5.1 summarizes the predictions of the human capital framework.

Assessment of the Human Capital Model

The formal human capital model makes a number of obviously unrealistic assumptions. An individual does not have full and perfect information regarding the impact of different activities on health, or the impact of health on both income and utility over the course of a lifetime. Unlike the model, which assumes that there is no uncertainty regarding individuals' health status and the effectiveness of health care, a great deal of illness and injury is random and the effectiveness of many medical treatments is uncertain.

TABLE 5.1   **Predictions from the Grossman Human Capital Model Regarding the Impact of Aging, Wage Rates, and Education**

	Aging	Increase in Wage Rate	Increase in Education
Investment Demand			
Demand for Health	Decreases demand for health	Increases demand for health	Increases demand for health
Demand for Health Care	Demand for health care can increase or decrease Increases if demand for health is inelastic	Increases demand for health care	Demand for health care can increase or decrease Decreases if demand for health is inelastic
Consumption Demand			
Demand for Health	Decreases demand for health	Ambiguous effect on demand for health Depends on time-intensity of health production	Ambiguous
Demand for Health Care	Depends on a person's rate of time preference	Ambiguous	Ambiguous

Note: See text and Grossman (1972) for additional details.

Since its original publication in 1972, people have tried to enrich the human capital model in a variety of ways (Grossman 2000). The most common extension has been to integrate uncertainty regarding future levels of health. The main conclusions remain consistent with the original model, although, not surprisingly, people demand higher levels of health than are called for in a model with no uncertainty.

The strong assumptions of the Grossman health capital framework, especially those regarding full information and foresight over a lifetime, have led some people—especially non-economists—to dismiss the framework. But a model, by definition, abstracts from reality; and the central issue is not abstraction versus reality, but whether the model abstracts in useful ways. Does it provide insight into the relationships of interest? On this score, most economists would judge the health capital framework a success.[5]

By analyzing health in a human capital framework over the human life cycle, Grossman provided a new, structured way for economists to think about individual-level demand for and production of health. The household production framework (see Box 5.1 on page 134) emphasizes aspects of these questions that had previously been neglected—such as the role of time costs in determining behaviour—and that we still mine for new insights (e.g., see the discussion below about the role of time costs in recent analyses of obesity).

Its central point, that the demand for health care must be seen as a derived demand for health, plays a crucial role in the analysis of many health care issues (see the discussion in Chapter 7 in particular). Its analysis of how the demand for health and health care inputs responds to aspects of each person's circumstances, such as income and education, offers insight into a number of phenomena, such as why people with higher income use more health care than those with lower income even in health systems that strive to provide equal

---

[5] This is with respect to its application in positive economics to provide insight into behaviour and the relationship between health and other variables of interest. See the discussion of models of smoking in section 5.3.2 (pages 150–153) for distinct issues that arise when assessing a model's value for normative analysis.

access. (The human capital model suggests that, other things equal, those with higher incomes demand higher levels of health and greater amounts of health care.)

Quite apart from the specific assumptions and predictions of the Grossman model, the human capital model is influential because it provides a structured way to think about a number of factors that affect the individual-level demand for and production of health. Even acknowledging its limitations, Grossman's health capital framework has spurred, directly or indirectly, a tremendous amount of valuable health economic research.

5.2   EMPIRICAL EVIDENCE ON INDIVIDUAL-LEVEL DEMAND FOR AND PRODUCTION OF HEALTH

The health capital framework offers a number of specific predictions about how the demand for health will relate to factors such as wage rate, education level, time constraints, and the money prices of inputs. A small number of studies have tried to formally test the Grossman model (Grossman 2000). The results of such tests are mixed, and the findings must be judged as tentative because a number of data and statistical challenges preclude definitive empirical tests.

More important are a large number of studies that draw on the Grossman framework to examine the demand for health and related phenomena. This literature is diverse, investigating issues such as the impact of income and income inequality on health, the relationship between education and health, health-related behaviours such as addictions (tobacco, alcohol), the impact of health information on health behaviours, epidemics of communicable diseases, and safety regulations (e.g., see Cawley and Kenkel 2008). One of the most important strands in this literature is the one investigating the education–health relationship.

5.2.1   The Relationship Between Education and Health

A positive correlation between education and health has been documented for many measures of health, over many decades, among countries that vary widely in levels of development (Cutler and Lleras-Muney 2008; Grossman 2006). Between 1991 and 2001 in Canada, for instance, for men aged 25 or older, the age-adjusted risk of dying among those who did not graduate from high school was 55 percent higher than among those with a university degree. For women, it was 42 percent higher (Wilkins et al. 2008).

gradient
An increase (decrease) in one variable is associated with an increase (decrease) in another variable throughout the relevant range of the variables.

This **gradient** is also present for morbidity measures. Table 5.2 presents information on the education–health gradient in Canada for two health measures: self-assessed health status and number of chronic conditions. The upper half of the table lists, for each of three levels of education, the proportion of Canadians who rate their health as excellent, very good, good, fair, or poor. Nearly twice as many of those with a university degree rate their health as excellent than do those with less than high school education (29.8 percent versus 16.8 percent) while only about one-quarter as many rate their health as poor (1.2 percent versus 4.4 percent).

The lower half of the table lists the proportion of people in each level of education who suffer from chronic conditions (none, one, two to three, and more than three). This gradient is less pronounced than the one for self-assessed health status, but is clearly present: 34.1 percent of people with university degrees have no chronic disease versus 30.7 percent of people with less than secondary education, and only 10.5 percent of people with university degrees have three or more chronic conditions compared to 17.8 percent of people with less than secondary education.

TABLE 5.2
Education–Health Gradient, Canada, 2005
The average health status of individuals, in this case measured by their self-assessed health status and their number of chronic health conditions, increases the greater is their level of education.

Source: Author's calculation, Canadian Community Health Survey, 3.1 (Statistics Canada 2009).

	Less than High School Diploma (%)	High School Graduate (%)	University Graduate (%)
Self-Assessed Health Status			
Excellent	16.8	21.5	29.8
Very Good	33.4	39.5	42.2
Good	32.2	29.0	22.5
Fair	13.2	7.6	4.3
Poor	4.4	2.4	1.2
Total	100.0	100.0	100.0
Number of Chronic Conditions			
0	30.7	30.3	34.1
1	23.7	26.2	28.7
2–3	27.8	28.3	26.7
More than 3	17.8	15.2	10.5
Total	100.0	100.0	100.0

Although the education–health gradient is well documented, the underlying causes are not. From a policy perspective, three questions are paramount:

spurious correlation
Two variables are correlated, but neither is causally related to the other. Ice cream consumption and swimming are positively correlated, but they do not cause each other. Both are caused by hot weather.

1. Does the positive gradient represent a causal relationship or is it a **spurious correlation?**
2. If the relationship is causal, to what extent does the causation run from education to health or from health to education?
3. If education contributes importantly to health, what is the mechanism by which education does this?

If the positive gradient merely reflects a spurious correlation, or the causation runs from health to education, public investments in education will have no impact on health. But if education causes improved health, then overall benefits of education have historically been underestimated and education policy is a potential way to achieve health goals. Whether education is the best way to achieve health goals, however, depends in part on how education acts to improve health—there may be more direct approaches than working through education policy.

Consider in turn each of these three (not necessarily mutually exclusive) bases for the education–health gradient.

Education and Health: Sources of Spurious Correlation

The positive correlation between education and heath would be spurious if it was caused by a third factor (or set of factors) that influenced both educational achievement and health status. The list of potential "third factors" is quite large, including genetic endowment, family life, and household wealth; but economists have focused particularly on the rate of time preference.

Someone with a low rate of time preference is more willing to sacrifice immediate or short-term benefits for a larger future amount of benefits. Such individuals tend to be savers and investors. Because both education and health represent investments in human capital, someone with a low rate of time preference is more likely to invest in both education and health. Hence, the positive correlation between educational attainment and health may simply reflect variation across individuals in rates of time preference: those with low rates of time preference invest a lot to achieve both high education and high health levels; those with high rates of time preference invest relatively little and achieve both low education and low health levels.

The empirical evidence regarding the presence or strength of the relationship between rates of time preference, education, and health is inconclusive, in part because it is very difficult to measure the rate of time preference (and very few data sets have information on all three variables). But recent reviews of evidence conclude that, at most, this spurious correlation accounts for a small proportion of the observed education–health gradient (Cutler and Lleras-Muney 2008).

Education and Health: The Impact of Health on Education

Two conditions are necessary for the education–health gradient to be caused by the impact of health on education: (1) health in childhood and adolescence must affect educational attainment, and (2) health in childhood and adolescence must affect adult health. Poor health in childhood can affect educational attainment in a number of ways. A child in poor health is more likely to miss school, to learn less when in school, and to complete fewer years of education (Case et al. 2002; Case et al. 2005). Children born with low or very low birth weight (a marker for poor health) obtain less schooling on average than those born with normal weight (Cutler and Lleras-Muney 2008). So the evidence supports the first condition.

Evidence further indicates that poor health in childhood is associated with poor health in adulthood (Case et al. 2005). The empirical evidence suggests, therefore, that part of the positive gradient between education and health originates in the effect of childhood health on educational attainment. The quantitative importance of this explanation is unknown, but it appears that this can explain, at most, a small proportion of the observed gradient (Cutler and Lleras-Muney 2008).

Education and Health: The Impact of Education on Health

Education could contribute to improved health in a number of ways. Indeed, as we will see, research on this question suffers from an embarrassment of riches—many hypothesized pathways, but limited ability to distinguish among them. Isolating the potential causal impact of educational attainment on health is exceedingly difficult, in part because individuals can influence both outcomes, making it hard for the analyst to control for unobserved individual characteristics that affect both. On balance, the evidence indicates that education has a positive causal effect on health status (Cutler and Lleras-Muney 2008; Grossman 2006), but findings vary among studies (Mazumder 2008) and we still have a poor understanding of the pathways along which any causal effects of education operate.

A number of hypotheses have been put forth regarding the causal pathways.

Hypothesis 1: Education Affects Health Through the Income Effect   Higher education leads to higher income in the labour market, and higher income could affect health status in two ways: it could increase demand for health as per Grossman's human capital investment model, and it could increase demand for (and access to) health care. The evidence, however, suggests that such effects are small. The education–health gradient

persists even after controlling for income, and we do not consistently observe a "diploma" effect in the education–health gradient.[6]

Hypothesis 2: Education Improves Efficiency in Producing Health   Education could increase efficiency in health production in two ways. Grossman (1972) theorized that education could increase productive efficiency so that, given the same set of health inputs, a more-educated individual is able to produce more health than is a less-educated individual. In this case, more education is analogous to technological progress in a normal production context: it allows an individual to produce more health given the same amount of resources. (We presently have little or no evidence as to whether the more educated are more productively efficient in this way.)

Education might also improve a person's efficiency in production: by enabling them to choose a better, more efficient mix of health inputs. This would happen, for instance, if the more educated were better able to access and use information on the health impact of different inputs.

The evidence is consistent with such effects. A dramatic example is the differential response (by educational status) to information about the negative health effects of smoking. Following the release of evidence on the link between smoking and cancer, smoking rates fell faster and further among the well educated than they did among those with less education (Sander 1995a; Sander 1995b). Studies also indicate that the better educated are more likely to understand and comply with treatment regimes, especially for complex, chronic diseases (Goldman and Smith 2002). And although the evidence is mixed, the more educated also appear more likely to seek out and use health-related information (Grossman 2006).

Hypothesis 3: Education Changes Preferences   Education has the potential to change preferences in ways that lead individuals to invest in better health. Education and its associated impact on future possibilities (career options, income, etc.) could induce someone to become more future-oriented, lowering their rate of time preference and leading them to invest more in health.

Hypothesis 4: Education Improves Rank in the Social Hierarchy   Evidence increasingly indicates that health status is strongly linked to rank in the social hierarchy: the higher a person's rank, the better their health. The exact mechanisms responsible for this are not well understood, though hypotheses focus on the effects of reduced stress that are associated with a higher position in the social hierarchy. Because education level is one determinant of position in the social hierarchy, the education–health gradient may operate in part through this effect (we will consider this evidence in more detail in the next chapter).

The Implications for Policy

The different causal mechanisms suggest different policy actions. To the extent that education works through income effects, it might be more efficient to redistribute income directly. To the extent that education affects the use of health-related information, more targeted informational policies might accomplish the same end. To the extent that education operates through its effect on social rank, policies that raise educational attainment

---

[6] The "diploma" effect refers to the fact that completing the 12th year of education and obtaining a high school diploma has a much larger marginal impact on wages than does completing the 11th year or 13th year. If the effect of education on health operates through its impact on earnings, completing the 12th year of education and obtaining a diploma should also have a larger marginal impact on health than completing the 11th or 13th years.

among those with currently low levels may be self-defeating because they equalize the distribution of education in society: if such policies were successful, education would no longer be a marker of social rank. At the moment, it appears that the education–health gradient likely results from the combined operation of multiple channels, raising the prospect that education policy itself may be the best lever.

5.3   HEALTH-RELATED BEHAVIOURS

Many everyday activities that people undertake primarily for pleasure or satisfaction have unavoidable health consequences. Understanding these health-related behaviours, such as smoking, alcohol consumption, overeating, and risky sexual practices, has long been of interest to health researchers and health policy makers. Their health effects are large, direct (even if not deterministic), and often understood by the individuals who pursue them. Approximately one-third of morbidity and mortality in high-income countries around the world, for example, can be attributed to obesity, smoking, unsafe sex, use of alcohol and illicit drugs, lack of exercise, and poor diet (Ezzati et al. 2006).

Modelling such behaviours poses unique challenges. Many health-related behaviours have elements of addiction, either physiological as in the case of smoking and alcohol consumption, or psychological as in the case of food consumption. Deciding whether to engage in these behaviours often requires weighing benefits and consequences that are widely separated in time: in the case of "bads" such as overeating, the pleasures are immediate but the negative health consequences are probabilistic and arise in the distant future. In the case of "goods" such as exercise, the cost (including displeasure) is immediate but the health benefits are probabilistic and accrue in the distant future. Consequently, individuals' propensity to engage in "bads" and to avoid "goods" is strongly affected by their time preferences. Many people exhibit imperfectly rational time preferences that predispose them to poor health-related behaviours (see Box 5.2).

Economic models emphasize how people's responses to changes in the economic environment in which they live—such as changes in relative money and time prices, changing patterns of income and the economic returns of certain behaviours, and complementarity and substitute relationships among goods—can influence their health-related behaviours.

To illustrate the economic approach and contribution to understanding the behaviours described above, we now examine two specific health behaviours that have been the focus of much recent economic research and policy interest, obesity and smoking.

5.3.1   Economics of Obesity

The Rise in Obesity

Obesity refers to the proportion of body weight that is composed of fat. Obesity is most commonly measured using the **Body Mass Index** (BMI), which is a person's weight in kilograms divided by the square of their height in metres (BMI = kg/m^2). Conventions vary slightly across countries, but values are generally classified as follows:

Body Mass Index
A person's weight in kilograms divided by the square of their height in metres (BMI = kg/m^2).

BMI < 20:	underweight
$20 \leq$ BMI ≤ 24.9:	normal
$25 \leq$ BMI ≤ 29.9:	overweight
$30 \leq$ BMI ≤ 34.9:	moderately obese
$35 \leq$ BMI ≤ 39.9:	severely obese
BMI ≥ 40:	extremely obese

Which would you rather receive: (a) $50 now or (b) $75 in two years? How about: (c) $50 in 10 years or (d) $75 in 12 years?

For a person whose preferences are time consistent, the ranking of the options is the same regardless of whether the payments happen now or in 10 years. If you are like many people, however, you chose (a) in the first instance but (d) in the second. Your preferences are time inconsistent. Many people display time inconsistency in daily choices, especially health-related behaviours. Do you regularly decide that you are going to begin exercising . . . next week? Or that you are going to begin a diet . . . next month? It is as if you have two people vying for attention in your brain: your better self, the rational planner who knows what is best in the long run and plans dispassionately from a distance, and your weaker self, who gives in to the immediate pleasure at the decisive moment.

Economists and psychologists increasingly appreciate the role that time inconsistency plays in people's health-related decisions. Many such choices require a person to weight the benefits and costs of an action when they accrue at widely separated times. Exercising today imposes substantial costs now but returns health benefits only in the distant future; eating dessert tonight provides immediate pleasure but imposes health costs only in the distant future.

A central determinant of such choices is how a person discounts future costs and benefits. Standard economic models assume that individuals have a single discount rate that is constant over time. This rate varies across individuals but is constant for a given individual. Such people are always time consistent: if in year 1, they decide that it will be optimal for them to undertake a certain action in year 3, when year three arrives, they will still judge it optimal to undertake that action (assuming nothing else changed). The smoker who started at age 17 planning to quit at age 21 actually quits at age 21. The person who in September decides to start a diet on January 1 actually starts the diet and sticks with it.

Economists and psychologists have developed models that incorporate time inconsistency (Frederick et al. 2002). For instance, time-inconsistent choices can be generated if, instead of assuming that a person's discount rate is constant, we assume that it decreases the further one gets from the present. Such models not only help predict behaviour better, they may suggest strategies people can use to overcome such inconsistencies that foil the best-laid plans.

While some people are unaware of their inconsistencies, others are acutely aware of their tendencies and develop strategies to overcome them. Such strategies need not be elaborate: they can be as simple as making public your plan to quit smoking so as to raise the costs (in the form of public shame) of breaking your promise.

As noted in Chapter 1, obesity rates in Canada and internationally have been increasing in recent decades, in some countries doubling or even tripling since the late 1970s. OECD data for selected countries during the period from 1978 to 2006, for example, reveal notably different rates across countries but a distinct upward trend in all countries (Table 5.3).

Canada's rates fall in the middle among OECD countries, Japan consistently has the lowest obesity rate, and the United States the highest. But even in Japan the rate of obesity nearly doubled between 1978 and 2005 from 2.1 percent of the population to 3.9 percent. The absolute increase was greatest in the United States, rising from 15.0 percent of the population to 34.3 percent; but the percentage increase was greatest in the United Kingdom, where the rate of obesity more than tripled from 7.0 percent to 24.3 percent.

Causes of the Obesity Epidemic

A person gains weight when the number of calories ingested exceeds the number of calories expended. The central challenge for understanding the obesity epidemic is to identify why, beginning in the late 1970s and early 1980s, the balance between caloric in-take and expenditure changed. Evidence indicates that the primary explanation is increased caloric intake rather than reduced energy expenditure (Finkelstein et al. 2005). Increases in per capita calorie consumption coincide with rising obesity rates; the caloric increase is related to increased consumption of carbohydrates and changed eating habits that include more snacking.

Evidence also indicates that energy expenditure has not fallen appreciably. On average, leisure time activities have become more active, with greater emphasis on exercise. And although television is an often-cited culprit (by making us couch potatoes), the largest growth in television viewing occurred before obesity rates began rising. Total screen time (television, computer games, web-surfing, etc.) has increased since 1980, and may be a contributing factor for children; but the increases in obesity across age groups, sexes, and socio-economic groups suggest that this is not a primary cause.

Commentators offer a variety of hypotheses for the increased consumption of calories, ranging from evolutionary tastes to working mothers to conspiracies by the fast-food industry. But careful analysis and close examination of the data reveal that many of these popular explanations cannot be true, while some basic economic forces might account for a large portion of the change (Cutler et al. 2003; Finkelstein et al. 2005).

Hypothesis 1: Primal Tastes Evolutionary biologists emphasize the potential role played by evolution in our food tastes. Our food preferences were developed over many millennia in times of highly uncertain food supplies. Consequently, we have deep-seated drives to accumulate surplus calories in times of plentiful food supplies, which are then available to be drawn on in times of scarcity. These tastes were adaptively beneficial in times of scarce and uncertain food supplies, but they are maladaptive in times of constant plenty, possibly leading to obesity.

While such primal drives undoubtedly influence our eating habits, and may interact with some changes in the food industry to exacerbate dietary trends, they cannot alone explain the obesity epidemic: food was plentiful in many OECD countries well before obesity rates began rising in the 1980s.

TABLE 5.3
Percentage of the Population Obese, Selected OECD Countries and Years
The proportion of the population that is obese varies considerably across countries but has been increasing since the late 1970s in all of the countries listed.

Source: OECD (2009), OECD Health Data 2009: Statistics and Indicators for 30 Countries, www.oecd.org/health/healthdata.

Note: exact year of data differs across countries within the ranges indicated.

	1978–1980	1989–1991	1999–2001	2005–2007
Australia	8.3	10.8	21.7	
Canada			13.9	15.4
Finland	6.6	8.4	11.2	14.3
France		5.8	9.0	10.5
Germany			11.5	13.6
Japan	2.1	2.3	2.9	3.9
Netherlands		6.1	9.4	11.3
New Zealand		12.7		26.5
Norway				9.0
Sweden		5.5	9.2	10.2
Switzerland				8.1
United Kingdom	7.0	14.0	21.0	24.0
United States	15.0	23.3	30.5	34.3

Hypothesis 2: Increased Labour Force Participation by Women The increased rate of women's participation in the labour force reduces the time they have available for home food preparation (women continue to spend more time preparing food than do men), and increases demand for ready-prepared foods, restaurant meals, and fast food. Rates of female participation in the labour force have increased in recent decades, making this at least a plausible contributing factor.

On the other hand, rates of female participation in the labour force began rising before the 1980s, and formal tests of the hypothesis based on individual-level data that include both working mothers and non-working mothers have produced a mixture of findings, suggesting that this is not a primary cause (Cutler et al. 2003; Finkelstein et al. 2005).

Hypothesis 3: The Role of Changing Prices Economic explanations focus on the role of changing food prices. Food prices rose faster than general prices between 1960 and 1980; but since 1980, food prices have risen more slowly than general inflation, so food has gradually become relatively less expensive. Furthermore, among food types, prices of energy-dense, high-calorie foods (e.g., cheeseburgers, chocolate) have risen more slowly than have prices of less energy-dense foods such as fruits and vegetables.

Consequently, the fall in the relative money price of a calorie has been even larger than the general decrease in real food prices, and this change in relative prices among food types has shifted consumption toward energy-dense foods.

The Effects of Technology on Cost Cutler (2003) has argued that changes in the technology of food production and processing not only have contributed to reducing the real money price of food, but also, even more importantly, have lowered the time cost of preparing a meal. These technological changes have replaced highly decentralized, labour-intensive methods of food preparation within households with highly centralized processes located in large food-processing plants that exploit economies of scale.

Processing changes include machinery that can automatically slice, dice, and peel foods, new chemicals and additives that preserve freshness and extend the shelf life of prepared foods, new modes of packaging and distributing food, and new equipment for home kitchens such as microwave ovens. The result is that more and more of the typical diet consists of food that is largely processed before delivery to the supermarket and simply heated up in the microwave before serving. This has reduced both the money costs and the time costs of preparing a meal. This has induced greater consumption of food.

Cutler et al. (2003) find empirical support in American data for specific implications of such technological change:

• Compared to the 1970s, American households today consume both a wider range of foods and eat more times per day. Consumption of snack foods has increased most markedly. These trends are consistent with reduced fixed costs in the preparation of a "meal" rather than just lower money costs of food.

• The changes in consumption have been largest for foods—such as snacks—that are most affected by such technological change.

• The increase in obesity in the U.S. has been largest amongst those most affected by such reduced costs, particularly women, who spend more time than men preparing meals. The impact of technological change is also consistent with changes in obesity among both children and adults, and with particularly high rates of growth in obesity among those at the high end of the obesity scale. Such individuals may be particularly subject to self-control problems that lead to overeating and be particularly responsive to reduced time costs.

Some have argued that taxing junk food is a promising way to reduce the obesity epidemic. The effectiveness of such a tax policy depends on how responsive junk-food consumption is to its money price. A study by Auld and Powell (2008) that investigated the impact of prices for energy-dense foods and less energy-dense foods on obesity among adolescents in the United States suggests that such a tax would have modest effects. The prices of energy-dense foods and less energy-dense foods did affect obesity as expected: lower prices for energy-dense food increased the risk of obesity while lower prices for less energy-dense foods lowered the risk of obesity. Furthermore, those who were already overweight exhibited greater sensitivity to food prices.

Based on these estimates, a $1.00 tax on a typical fast food meal is predicted to reduce the number of overweight adolescents by approximately 19% while a policy of cutting the price of a basket of fruits and vegetables in half is predicted to reduce the number of overweight adolescents by approximately 8%. These taxes/subsidies are quite high (e.g., $1.00 is more than 30% of the price of a typical fast-food meal as defined in the study); tax rates closer to the levels commonly discussed would have commensurately smaller effects. Overall, these results suggest that such a tax would likely have a modest impact on obesity rates.

The social desirability of a junk-food tax depends on a full analysis of the costs of such a tax and a range of other issues, including distributional effects (such a tax would likely be regressive given the differences by income in the share of income spent on food and in food consumption patterns). Cash and Lacanilao (2007a) provide a review of evidence and arguments related to taxing junk food.

The causes of the rising rates of obesity are complex and we still have much to learn; but economic analyses focusing on relative prices within a household production framework (in which meal preparation and food consumption are undertaken subject to a number of time, money, and production constraints) provide useful insights that complement the insights from nutritionists, clinicians, and other health professionals. (See Box 5.3 to read about the possibility of taxing lunch food in order to fight obesity.)

5.3.2   Economics of Smoking

The addictive nature of tobacco poses challenges for modelling smoking behaviour, and smoking-related externalities pose challenges for policy. Models of smoking behaviour divide into three broad types: smoking as irrational behaviour, smoking as fully rational behaviour, and smoking as quasi-rational behaviour.

Smoking as Irrational Behaviour

Some argue that smoking is essentially an irrational behaviour (Elster and Skog 1999), not governed in any rational way by assessments of risk, costs, or benefits. In this view, smoking, like other addictive activities, is ruled by emotional responses, circumstances, and the immediate effects of consumption: a person tries smoking in a moment of "weakness," responding to peer pressure, stress, or any number of internal emotions and external triggers. Once addicted, the individual finds it difficult or impossible to quit, and consumption defies normal economic laws such as responsiveness to price. This view of smoking as governed by fundamentally irrational forces is very influential, especially outside economics. Taken literally, it counsels that no policy will be effective in curtailing smoking short of banning tobacco (and somehow preventing black market trade).

rational addiction model
An economic model of the consumption of addictive substances that assumes people make fully rational choices.

Rational Addiction Model

Economists, in contrast, argue that smoking can be usefully analyzed within a framework of rational decision-making, albeit with some adjustments to account for the addictive nature of tobacco. This view is represented most forcefully in the **rational addiction model** (Becker and Murphy 1988; Chaloupka and Warner 2000), which is now the dominant model used by economists to study the consumption of addictive substances, including tobacco.

The rational addiction model incorporates three salient features of addiction: tolerance, reinforcement, and withdrawal. The model incorporates a person's growing tolerance for an addictive good by assuming that the higher the past rate of consumption, the lower the utility derived from a specific level of current consumption. The model incorporates reinforcement by assuming that those who consume larger amounts of the good derive greater utility from the consumption of an additional unit of the good than do those who consume smaller amounts. Finally, the model incorporates withdrawal by assuming that overall utility falls when the individual stops consuming the good.

time-consistent preferences
Rates of time preference in which judgments of what will be optimal at a future time remain optimal when the time arrives, assuming no other change but the passage of time. Such preferences can be characterized by a single, constant rate of discount.

The rational addiction model analyzes the lifetime profile of consumption of an addictive good by a fully rational, fully informed individual with **time-consistent preferences** who understands that consumption leads to addiction and possible negative health consequences. It makes a number of predictions regarding consumption behaviour that are supported by empirical evidence.

As is standard, the model predicts that current consumption of cigarettes depends in part on current prices for cigarettes. But it also makes the novel prediction that current consumption depends on past prices of cigarettes and expected future prices of cigarettes. The dependence of current consumption on past and future prices arises from the link between past smoking and current utility of smoking, and between current smoking and the future utility of smoking. If I think prices will increase in the future, and I know that current consumption will cause me to smoke more in the future (because of addiction), then I will reduce current consumption in response to the expected higher future prices.

Smoking unquestionably responds to current period price, with elasticity estimated to be in the range of -0.25 to -0.50 (Chaloupka and Warner 2000). And although it is very difficult to test formally, most tests find that current consumption is negatively related to future prices. The most convincing evidence on this point comes from an analysis of how legislation to raise cigarette taxes in the future affects current tobacco consumption (Gruber and Koszegi 2001).

As expected, the model predicts that an individual's rate of time preference exerts an important influence, both on whether or not an individual smokes and the amount. It further predicts that the rate of time preference will influence an individual's responsiveness to the money price of cigarettes and to information on the effects of smoking. Specifically, the model predicts that younger individuals and those with higher rates of time discounting, lower education, and lower income will be more responsive to the money price of cigarettes. Older individuals and those with lower rates of time discounting, higher education, and higher income are predicted to be less responsive.

The model predicts the converse for responses to information on the negative health consequences of smoking. Again, empirical estimates generally support these predictions: much (though not all) evidence indicates higher price-elasticities of demand for youth, the less-educated, and lower-income individuals. The fact that smoking has fallen most among highly educated and high-income individuals since the negative health effects of smoking have become widely understood is also consistent with the model's predictions.

Finally, the model also predicts that the most effective way to quit smoking will be to go "cold turkey." Gradual quitting does not work because an addicted smoker always derives a great deal of utility from smoking a cigarette (recall that addiction raises the marginal utility of the next cigarette). The key to quitting is to break the addiction, reducing the marginal utility from smoking the next cigarette. Indeed, many who quit smoking do it by going cold turkey.

imperfectly (or quasi) rational addiction model
Economic models of the consumption of addictive substances that assume people strive to be rational but suffer from biases in decision-making.

But the rational addiction model is contradicted by other types of evidence. Specifically, the model predicts only "happy" smokers who do not regret having started smoking (the decision to smoke, after all, was based on a rational, fully informed assessment that smoking, even with its addictive properties, would lead to higher lifetime utility than not smoking). Yet, the majority of those who smoke say that they regret starting and would like to quit if they could.

Quasi-Rational Addiction

This type of evidence has led to the development of **imperfectly (or quasi) rational addiction model** (Chaloupka and Warner 2000). Imperfectly rational models begin with the rational addiction model but integrate insights from behavioural economics about the ways in which individual decision-making—and especially inter-temporal decision-making—systematically fail to be fully rational.

Individuals are rational in the sense that they take into account the future consequences of current decisions; but they fail to be fully rational because they may, for instance,

- have preferences that are time-inconsistent
- underestimate the probability that they will become addicted
- misperceive the nature and size of the negative effects of smoking

time-inconsistent preferences
Rates of time preference in which judgments of what will be optimal at a future time are no longer judged to be optimal when the time arrives, even though nothing has changed but the passage of time. Such preferences can be characterized by rates of discount which are not constant but which decrease the further is an event in the future.

In some cases, this may reflect a simple lack of information; but in others, it is caused by underlying biases in decision-making. Experiments consistently find, for instance, that people fail to understand probabilities and that they focus on salient, dramatic types of information (the grandfather who lived to 90 smoking every day) that confirm their predispositions over disconfirming scientific evidence.

Several variants of the quasi-rational decision-making model focus on **time-inconsistent preferences**. Time inconsistency can result from a number of biases in decision-making, but of particular importance are rates of time discounting that decline over time. For a time-inconsistent individual, it will always be optimal to quit "tomorrow." Time inconsistency creates a type of intra-personal conflict whereby individuals always foil their best-laid plans. Sophisticated individuals who know that they are time inconsistent anticipate this and use self-control or **commitment devices** to help counter this. (See Box 5.2 on page 147.)

commitment devices
Strategies that people with time-inconsistent preferences develop to help ensure that they honour commitments they make to themselves regarding aspects of their behaviour, such as quitting smoking or losing weight.

Models of imperfect rationality that incorporate time-inconsistent preferences make many of the same predictions as the perfectly rational addiction model. This includes the prediction that current consumption depends on past and future prices—individuals are still forward looking, are still subject to addiction, and still attempt to optimize. But it also makes predictions regarding patterns of smoking behaviour that the rational addiction model fails to predict, including regret over a previous decision to start smoking, unfulfilled promises to try to quit smoking, failed attempts to quit smoking, and the use of commitment devices when attempting to quit.

The rational addiction and quasi-rational addiction models have very different policy implications. Within the rational addiction framework, the only policy concern associated with smoking is the externalities smokers impose on non-smokers via second-hand smoke, increased risk of fires in multiple-dwelling buildings, and so forth. Estimates of the monetary value of such externalities are highly variable, but generally fall in the range of $0.90–$1.50 per pack of cigarettes.

If individuals are time-inconsistent, however, an additional policy concern arises: a person's inability to reduce smoking levels as desired due to time inconsistency. That is, individuals continue to smoke, imposing considerable costs on themselves in the form of increased risk of adverse health consequences, long after they judge it optimal to quit.

Over a lifetime, such a person's observed level of smoking exceeds the optimal level as judged by the smoker's own preferences. Gruber and Koszegi (2001) estimated that such costs to smokers far exceed the external costs of smoking to non-smokers. As noted above, the former has been estimated to be up to $1.50 per pack, but the latter was estimated to be approximately $30 per pack.

Chapter Summary

This chapter examined individual-level demand for and production of health. It focused on Grossman's health capital model, which is used by many economists to understand people's demand for and production of health.

- The health capital model assumes that health provides individuals with two types of benefits, direct utility benefits and increased capacity to earn income.
- In deciding the optimal level of health, an individual takes into account these benefits and the time and money costs of producing health.
- The model makes a number of predictions relating to the relationship between aging and health, wage rates and health, and education levels and health.

The chapter then examined both conceptual issues and empirical evidence regarding three specific aspects of health and health-related behaviours: education and health, obesity, and smoking.

- Although not definitive, empirical evidence suggests that education has a causal impact on health status, but we do not have a good understanding of the pathways through which this effect operates.
- Economic analyses document that the reaction of consumers to changing food prices and to the changed costs of preparing meals is one factor underlying the growth in obesity rates in recent decades.
- Economic analyses document that many aspects of smoking behaviour are consistent with models based on rational decision-making, but that "quasi-rational" models, which integrate insights on decision-making bias, can account for a wider range of behaviours.

The discussion highlighted how an economic approach emphasizing people's responses to costs and benefits can provide considerable insight into health phenomena, insight that complements the perspectives offered by other disciplines.

Key Terms

Body Mass Index *146*
causal relationship *127*
commitment device *152*
consumption demand
   for health *139*
correlation *127*
depreciation rate of health
   capital *134*
derived demand for
   health care *133*

gradient *142*
health capital model *133*
imperfectly- (quasi-) rational
   addiction model *152*
incidence rate *129*
investment demand
   for health *135*
prevalence rate *129*
rate of time preference *139*
rational addiction model *150*

spurious correlation *143*
time-consistent preferences
   151
time-inconsistent
   preferences *152*

End-of-Chapter Questions

For each of the statements below, indicate whether the statement is true or false and explain why it is true or false.

1. Variation across individuals in rates of time preference is one possible explanation for the observed correlations between smoking, education levels, and health levels.

2. An increase in the demand for health always causes the demand for health care to increase.

3. A recent study found that an expansion in MRI capacity in Canada (where MRIs are fully insured by the public insurance system) was associated with an increase in the income gradient in the use of MRIs. This increase in the income gradient in the use of MRIs is inconsistent with predictions from the Grossman model.

4. The unrealistic assumptions of the Grossman model invalidate its use as a tool for policy-oriented economic analysis.

5. People with a low rate of time preference will make only small sacrifices to current consumption to achieve higher levels of consumption in the future.

6. More-educated people tend to demand more health capital.

7. Externality arguments are more compelling for government intervention to reduce obesity levels than they are for policies to reduce smoking levels.

8. Evidence that Canadians over age 65 make up 25–30 percent more physician visits each year than those under age 35 is inconsistent with the predictions of the Grossman model that demand for health decreases with age.

9. Within the Grossman health capital framework, an increase in unearned income (e.g., a pension for a retired person) would be expected to increase the demand for health.

10. Unlike the rational addiction framework, within a quasi-rational addiction framework a reduction in tobacco taxes is not expected to increase tobacco consumption.

References

Auld, C., and L. Powell. 2008. Economics of food energy density and adolescent body weight. *Economica* 76(374):719–40.

Becker, G. S., and K. Murphy. 1988. A theory of rational addiction. *Journal of Political Economy* 96(4):675–700.

Case, A., A. Fertig, and C. Paxson. 2005. The lasting impact of childhood health and circumstance. *Journal of Health Economics* 24(2):365–89.

Case, A., D. Lubotsky, and C. Paxson. 2002. Economic status and health in childhood: The origins of the gradient. *American Economic Review* 92(5):1308–34.

Cash, S. B., and R. D. Lacanilao. 2007. Taxing food to improve health: Economic evidence and arguments. *Agricultural and Resource Economics Review* 36(2):174–82.

Cawley, J., and D. Kenkel. 2008. *The economics of health behaviours.* Northampton, MA: Edward Elgar Publishing Ltd.

Chaloupka, F., and K. Warner. 2000. The economics of smoking. In *Handbook of Health Economics,* A. J. Culyer, and J. P. Newhouse (eds.). Amsterdam: Elsevier Science B. V. 29:1539–627.

Cutler, D., E. L. Glaeser, and J. M. Shapiro. 2003. Why have Americans become more obese? *Journal of Economic Perspectives* 17(3):93–118.

Cutler, D., and A. Lleras-Muney. 2008. Education and health: Evaluating theories and evidence. In *Making Americans healthier: Social and economic policy as health policy,* J. House, R. Schoeni, G. Kaplan, and H. Pollack (eds.). New York: Russell Sage Foundation.

Elster, J., and O.-J. Skog. 1999. *Getting hooked: Rationality and addiction.* Cambridge: Cambridge University Press.

Ezzati, M., S. van der Hoorn, A. Lopez, G. Danaei, A. Rodgers, C. Mathers, and C. Murray. 2006. Comparative quantification of mortality and burden of disease attributable to selected risk factors. In *Global burden of disease and risk factors,* C. Murray (ed.). New York: Oxford University Press. 241–68.

Finkelstein, E., C. Ruhm, and K. Kosa. 2005. Economic causes and consequences of obesity. *Annual Review of Public Health* 26:239–57.

Frederick, S., G. Loewenstein, and T. O'Donoghue. 2002. Time discounting and time preference: A critical review. *Journal of Economic Literature* 40(2):351–401.

Goldman, D., and J. Smith. 2002. Can patient self-management help explain the SES health gradient? *Proceedings of the National Academy of Sciences* 99(16):10929–34.

Grossman, M. 1972. On the concept of health capital and the demand for health. *Journal of Political Economy* 80(2):223–55.

———. 2000. The human capital model. In *Handbook of Health Economics,* A. Culyer, and J. Newhouse (eds.). Amsterdam: Elsevier Science B.V. 7:347–408.

———. 2006. Education and non-market outcomes. In *Handbook of the Economics of Education,* E. Hanushek, and F. Welch (eds.). Amsterdam: Elsevier.

Gruber, J., and B. Koszegi. 2001. Is addiction "rational"? Theory and evidence. *Quarterly Journal of Economics* 116(4):1261–303.

Mazumder, B. 2008. Does education improve health? A re-examination of the evidence from compulsory schooling laws. *Economic Perspectives* 32(2):2–16.

OECD. 2009. *OECD health data 2009.* Paris: OECD.

Sander, W. 1995a. Schooling and quitting smoking. *Review of Economics and Statistics* 77:191–99.

Sander, W. 1995b. Schooling and smoking. *Economics of Education Review* 14:23–33.

Statistics Canada. 2009. *Canadian community health survey, cycle 3.1.*

Wilkins, R., M. Tjepkma, C. Mustard, and R. Choinere. 2008. The Canadian census mortality follow-up study, 1991 through 2001. *Health Reports* 19(3):25–43.

Appendix 5

Chapter 5: Individual-Level Demand for and Production of Health

5.1.1   The Grossman Health Capital Model

Although deriving the results of Grossman's model requires technical skills beyond the scope of this text, the formal structure of the model can be summarized succinctly.

Preferences   Utility can be written as

$$U = U(\varphi_0 H_0, \ldots, \varphi_n H_n, Z_0, \ldots, Z_n) \qquad \textbf{(5A.1)}$$

where

H_0 = an individual's inherited stock of health capital (e.g., a person's genetic endowment)

H_t = an individual's health stock in period t (a person lives for n periods)

φ_t = the rate of service flow of health per unit of health capital; e.g., the number of healthy days each unit of health capital produces

$\varphi_t H_t = h_t$ = the amount of health consumed in the period, measured in the number of healthy days ($\varphi > 0$)

Z_t = composite final consumption good

So utility is obtained from two goods: the service flow of healthy days and a final consumption good. The stock of health capital is not consumed directly; rather, there are three sources of benefit that flow from health capital:

1. *consumption benefit:* h_t, the number of healthy days
2. *investment benefit:* a person is only productive on healthy days
3. *life expectancy:* an individual controls life expectancy (n), by increasing their stock of health

Household Production Functions Individuals produce both health and the final consumption good by using their own time and market goods purchased with income earned by working. Gross health investment can be written as follows:

$$I_t = I_t(M_t, TH_t; E_t) \qquad \textbf{(5A.2a)}$$

Production of a consumption good can be written as

$$Z_t = Z_t(X_t, T_t; E_t) \qquad \textbf{(5A.2b)}$$

where

M_t = quantity of medical care
TH_t = time spent producing health
X_t = market inputs into production of Z_t
T_t = time spent producing Z_t
E_t = stock of human capital (measured by level of education)

Education increases productivity in producing both health and consumption goods.

Net Investment An individual's net investment, which equals the change in health capital from period to period, equals gross investment less the depreciation of health capital:

$$H_{t+1} - H_t = I_t - \delta_t H_t \qquad \textbf{(5A.3)}$$

where

I_t = gross investment in health (assumed always to be positive)
δ_t = rate of depreciation of health capital; this is assumed to grow as a person ages

Time Constraint The total amount of time available (Ω) is fixed (e.g., 365 days per year). A person's time can be spent in four possible ways: (1) producing health; (2) producing a consumption good (Z); (3) working to earn income (at wage rate (W_t); and (4) being sick, during which time a person can do nothing productive.

$$TW_t + TL_t + TH_t + T_t = \Omega \qquad \textbf{(5A.4)}$$

where

TW_t = time spent working in market
TL_t = time lost to illness
T_t and TH_t are as above

Income/Wealth Constraint The present discounted value of goods purchased in the market cannot exceed the present discounted value of wealth available (income earned plus initial unearned wealth), so

$$\sum_{t=0}^{n} \frac{P_t M_t + V_t X_t}{(1 + r)^t} = \sum_t \frac{W_t TW_t}{(1 + r)^t} + A_0 \qquad \text{(5A.5)}$$

where

P_t = price of medical care
V_i = price of X_i
W_t = wage rate
A_0 = initial wealth

The Individual's Choice Problem The individual's choice problem is to choose $H_0, \ldots, H_n$ and $Z_0, \ldots, Z_n$ to maximize utility (equation (1)), subject to equations (2a), (2b), (3), (4), and (5).

As in all consumer optimization problems, in the optimum, the marginal cost must equal the marginal benefit. In this case, the marginal cost of health capital must equal the marginal benefit (measured in dollars) of health capital:

$$\underset{\text{(a)}}{W_t G_t} + \underset{\text{(b)}}{\left(\frac{Uh_t}{\lambda}(1 + r)^i G_t \right)} = (\underset{\text{(c)}}{r} - \underset{\text{(d)}}{\tilde{\pi}_{t-1}} + \underset{\text{(e)}}{\delta_t})\pi_{t-1} \qquad \text{(5A.6)}$$

where

G_t = $\varphi \partial h_t / \partial H_t$ = marginal product of health capital in producing healthy days
Uh_t = $\partial U / \partial h_t$ = marginal utility of a healthy day
λ = marginal utility of wealth
π_{t-1} = marginal cost of gross investment (depends on input prices, P_{t-1} and W_{t-1})
$\tilde{\pi}_{t-1}$ = change in the marginal cost of gross investment between $t-1$ and t
r = real rate of interest

- (a) and (b) are the marginal benefits of a unit of health capital
  - (a) is the investment effect of increased time available for market and non-market production, valued at the wage rate. With additional healthy days, individuals can spend more time investing in health capital, producing the consumption good, and working.
  - (b) is the direct consumption (utility) effect, valued in monetary terms
- (c), (d) and (e) are the costs of holding a unit of health capital for one period (the marginal supply price of health capital)
  - (c) is the interest payment forgone by investing in health rather than another asset
  - (d) is the "capital gain" associated with holding capital for one period (implicitly, any change in the marginal cost of investing in health capital between this and the next period)
  - (e) is the depreciation cost of holding a unit of health capital for one period

This condition is the basis for analyzing the impact of aging, wage rates, and education on the optimal level of health capital and health care. The analysis of investment demand assumes that (b) equals zero; the analysis of consumption demand assumes that (a) equals zero.

An Alternative Graphical Exposition of the Health Capital Framework

Goodman, Stano, and Tilford (1999) present a graphical adaptation of the Grossman model that is more accessible than Grossman (1972; 2000). Although the adaptation is a single-period model (there is no inter-temporal aspect to decision-making), it retains the household production framework and therefore highlights the role of market versus non-market goods, time costs, and production and income constraints.

Assume an individual cares about health (H) and entertainment (E): U(H, E). The model focuses exclusively on the consumption benefits of health investment: health has no impact on time available for other activities, on wage rates, or any other aspect of the decision environment. As in Grossman, the individual seeks to maximize utility subject to three kinds of constraints: a *time constraint*—the individual can allocate their fixed amount of time between work, health production, and production of leisure; *production constraints* that define how the individual's time and health care can be transformed into health, and how the individual's time and consumer goods can be transformed into entertainment; and finally, an *income constraint*—the dollar value of health care and consumer goods purchased cannot exceed income earned through work and unearned income. A utility-maximizing individual must therefore decide:

- how to allocate time between formal work and leisure
- how to produce health and entertainment, with the associated decisions regarding
  - the division of leisure time between health production and entertainment production
  - the division of income between purchasing health care and other consumer goods

In this framework, production of health and entertainment is analytically separable from decisions regarding the optimal combination of health and entertainment. We begin by considering the production and then, having defined the feasible combinations of health and entertainment, we will consider the optimal combination.

Production of Health and Entertainment Figure 5A.1(i) depicts the income constraint, assuming no unearned income: the horizontal axis shows the amount of time spent on leisure (i.e., not in formal work) and the vertical axis shows the corresponding amount of income available. If the individual works all the time, leisure is zero and income Y_{max} is available. If they don't work at all, income is zero and leisure is 365. The slope of the income constraint equals the wage rate.[1]

Consider point S on the constraint: this defines a total amount of time available (TL_s) to be divided between the production of health (T_H) and entertainment (T_E), and the total amount of income available (Y_S) to purchase health care (HC) and consumer goods (C).[2] Draw the Edgeworth Box associated with the production of health and entertainment using the income and time available, where the southwest corner is the origin for health, the northeast corner is the origin for entertainment, and isoquants ($H_1, H_2 \ldots; E_1, E_2, \ldots$) have the usual desirable properties.[3] The efficient set of production combinations is the locus of points of tangency between health isoquants and entertainment isoquants.

[1] If unearned income is positive, the income constraint shifts vertically by the amount of unearned income.
[2] Following Goodman et al. (1999), assume the prices of HC and C are both equal to 1, so quantities equal expenditures.
[3] Assume CRTS production.

FIGURE 5A.1 **Choosing the Optimal Combination of Health and Entertainment**

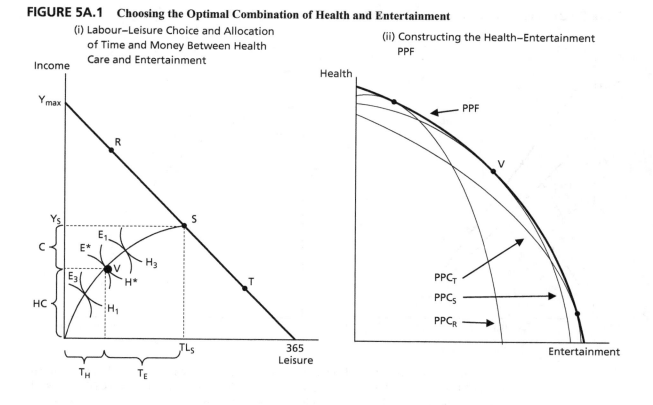

(i) Labour–Leisure Choice and Allocation of Time and Money Between Health Care and Entertainment

(ii) Constructing the Health–Entertainment PPF

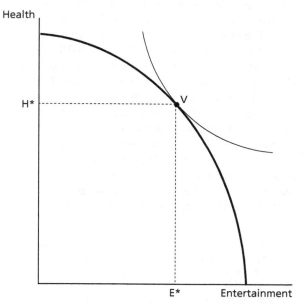

(iii) The Optimal Combination of Health and Entertainment

FIGURE 5A.2   **Impact of an Increase in Wages on the Optimal Level of Health**

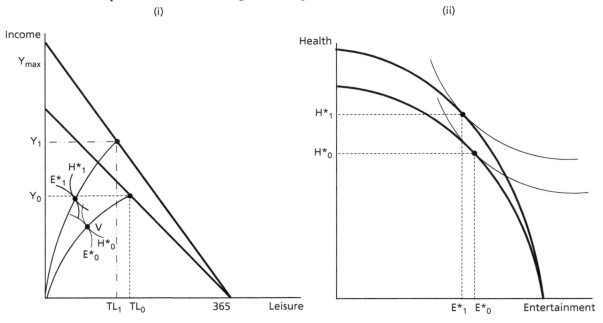

As shown, the production of entertainment is more time-intensive than is the production of health.[4] This locus of the efficiency point is the production possibilities curve (PPC) associated with the labour–leisure combination represented by point S; the PPC is depicted in Figure 5A.1(ii). Each point on the income constraint has a PPC associated with it. It is possible to trace out the production possibilities frontier (PPF), which represents the outer envelope of points on the various PPCs.[5] The PPF represents the maximum combinations of health and entertainment feasible for this individual. The individual has well-defined preferences between health and entertainment, represented by indifference curves in the Health–Entertainment space. The utility-maximizing combination of health and entertainment occurs at point V in Figure 5A.1(iii), the tangency of the PPF and the individual's indifference curve: at this point, the rate at which the individual prefers to trade off health and entertainment equals the rate at which health and entertainment can be traded off in production.

This framework allows us to examine how changes in the environment affect the optimal amount of health demanded by the individual and the inputs combinations used to produce the health and entertainment. Figure 5A.2 shows the impact of an increase in a person's wages. A wage increase rotates the income constraint outward around the intercept with the leisure axis. The opportunity cost of leisure is now higher, which will induce income and substitution effects regarding the optimal split between work and leisure. In the case shown, the substitution effect dominates and the person consumes less leisure after the wage increase (optimal point changes from (TL_0, Y_0) to (TL_1, Y_1)). The wage increase

---

[4] If the production of both had the same factor intensities, the locus of efficient points would be the diagonal. As emphasized by Goodman et al. (1999), their analysis requires that health care and entertainment have differing factor intensities; if they did not, the two goods would be analytically indistinguishable.

[5] This exercise is directly analogous to that done to construct the grand utility possibilities frontier in Chapter 3.

FIGURE 5A.3   **Impact of Education When Education Increases Efficiency in Health Production**

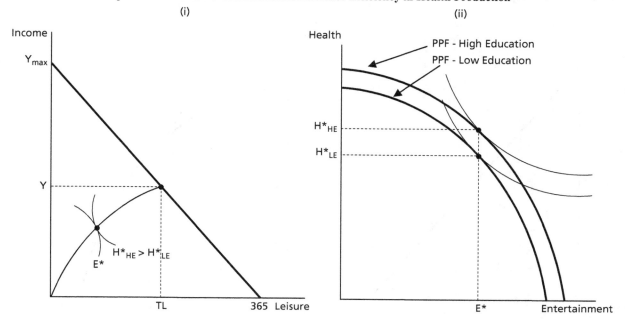

expands the income available to purchase market goods. Because there is now more of this input (and its price is lower), a particular advantage goes to the good that uses the market good more intensively in the production process. In this case, we assume that the production of health uses the market good more intensively than does entertainment, while entertainment uses time more intensively than does health production. (This is reflected in the shape of the contract curve within the Edgeworth production box.) In the new equilibrium (E^*_1, H^*_1), the optimal level of health is higher and the optimal level of entertainment is lower than before the wage increase.[6]

The framework can also provide insight into the relationship between education and health. As discussed in the chapter, the positive association has been hypothesized to derive from both production effects and preference effects.

Education has been hypothesized to affect the production of health in at least two distinct ways. The first is that education changes a person's health production function, making those with greater education more efficient producers of health: for a given combination of inputs, a more highly educated person will produce more health than will a less educated person. This shifts the production possibilities frontier outward for a more highly educated individual as depicted in Figure 5A.3, causing the optimal level of health to be higher than for a less educated individual $(H^*_{HE} > H^*_{LE})$.

The second is that education causes people to choose better, more efficient combinations of inputs. The health production function is identical for those with high and low education levels; but because those with high education are better able to process information, they choose more efficient input mixes. In Figure 5A.4, the more-educated person has

[6] Goodman et al. (1999) note that, according to Rybczynski's Theorem, in this environment a decrease in the relative price of one input will always result in a new equilibrium with a higher level of consumption of the good that uses the input more intensively, and a lower level of consumption of the good that uses the input less intensively. So if the production of entertainment had been more market-good-intensive than health production, its optimal level would have increased and health's would have decreased.

FIGURE 5A.4 **Impact of Education When Education Increases Allocative Efficiency in Choice of Health Inputs**

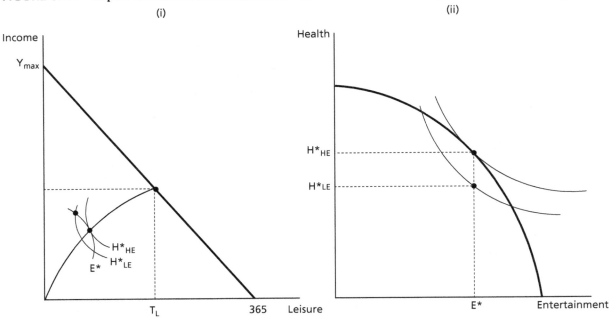

chosen the optimal combination of time and health care, while the less-educated person has chosen a point off the PPF (too high a ratio of health care to time inputs), resulting in less health for the given level of entertainment chosen. In both of these cases, the link between education and health is causal: higher education causes greater health through an effect on health production.

There are also two hypothesized preference-related sources for the education–health association. Both of them manifest themselves in a greater taste for health among those with more education, as depicted by the flatter indifference curves in Figure 5A.5. One

FIGURE 5A.5
Impact of Education When Education Changes Preferences

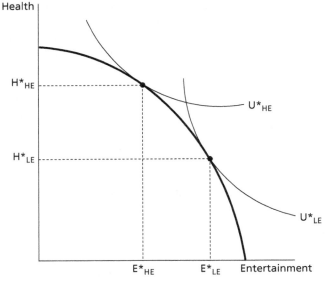

hypothesis is that education induces the greater taste for health. Here again, education and health are causally related. A second hypothesis is that the taste for more education and the taste for higher levels of health are both caused by a third factor, such as a lower rate of time preference that induces greater investment in both. In this case, the relationship between education and health is not causal; it is simply a spurious correlation caused by the third factor that drives both. In either case, the effect is to flatten the indifference curve, reflecting an increased taste for health, increasing the optimal amount of health.

References

Goodman, A., M. Stano, and J. Tilford. 1999. Household production of health investment: Analysis and applications. *Southern Economic Journal* 65(4):791–806.

Grossman, M. 1972. On the concept of health capital and the demand for health. *Journal of Political Economy* 80(2):223–55.

———. 2000. The human capital model. In *Handbook of Health Economics* A. J. Culyer, and J. P. Newhouse (eds.) Amsterdam: Elsevier Science B.V. 7:347–408.

The Determinants of Population Health

Learning Objectives

After studying this chapter, you will understand

LO1 The major causes of increased population health in industrialized countries in recent centuries

LO2 Current understanding of the role of the physical and social environments in begetting the socio-economic gradient in health

This chapter shifts focus from individual-level determinants of health to broader, non-individual determinants of the level and distribution of health in a population. Many features of the physical and social environment influence the level and distribution of health in society: the purity of the air we breathe and the water we drink, the design of the transportation networks by which we travel, the safety of workplaces, the availability of places to meet and play, and myriad other things. The unequal exposure to health risks and unequal access to health-enhancing features of the physical and social environment generate systematic inequalities in the distribution of health among members of society. Policy seeks both to raise the average level of health in society and to reduce inequalities in its distribution.

For well over one hundred years, since the acceptance of germ theory and pioneering work in epidemiology that demonstrated the link between the physical environment and health in over-crowded, squalid cities of the industrial revolution, public health officials and health scientists have appreciated the vital role of the broader environment in determining health. But recent economic and epidemiological evidence attests to a more complex relationship than previously imagined between population health and the larger environment of people's lives.

Simple, deterministic models of disease fail to capture the contingent nature of disease transmission. Exposure to a germ does not necessarily induce disease; whether it does or does not depends on the response and resiliency of the host. Nor do genes deterministically cause disease. Instead, genes create predispositions that, in interaction with an individual's social and physical environment, can manifest in disease.

social gradient in health
A pattern of population health, observed in many countries, in which average health status is directly related to social rank or social status throughout the range of social ranks.

The **social gradient in health**—whereby those of higher socio-economic status are healthier on average—is not eliminated when everyone has access to good housing, clean water, and decent nutrition (though all of these things help reduce the gradient). The social gradient in health persists in all societies and extends throughout the range of social status.

Threshold effects associated with minimum levels of education, income, housing, and other necessities for healthy living do not cause the gradient; it extends even among those comfortably in the middle and upper classes. Further, the gradient has persisted over many decades, even as the dominant causes of death have changed. The causes of the gradient exert their force at a more fundamental level than specific diseases. Observed patterns of ill health derive from a complex interaction of biology, behaviour, and environment.

While economic models—such as those we examined in the last chapter—emphasize autonomous individuals exercising conscious choice, much of the literature on the broader determinants emphasizes external forces acting on individuals, often without their explicit awareness. These forces can directly influence people's health, shaping both the context in which people make choices and people's responses to the broader environment. Indeed, by deliberately manipulating features of the physical and social environments in which people live, policy aspires to give people the resources to respond to the health challenges they confront. As noted earlier, the economic policy problem is to identify the nature of the underlying production function and to identify the factors that produce health, as well as how they act alone and in combination to produce the observed level and distribution of health in society.

We begin Chapter 6 by examining the causes of the remarkable—and to our knowledge, unprecedented—rise in average health status in modern societies. We then consider the social gradient in health which has persisted through the period of this general increase in average health status, and which even shows signs in many countries of having widened in recent decades.

6.1 DETERMINANTS OF THE LEVEL OF HEALTH IN A POPULATION

Figure 6.1 plots the expected age of death for a person living in England and Wales for the period 1751 to 2000. The dramatic increase in life expectancy for the English population is self-evident: life expectancy at birth was approximately 35 years during the second half of the eighteenth century, began inching upward in 1800 only to stagnate at 40 years during the middle of the nineteenth century, and then in about 1865 began a steady, steep rise until the present, with the rate of increase moderating in the years following World War II.

The gradual narrowing of the gap between the expected age of death at birth and at ages 10, 45, and 65 implies that much of this gain is derived from reducing deaths among young children. In 1850, simply surviving infancy and young childhood increased the expected

FIGURE 6.1

Life Expectancy, England and Wales, 1750–2000

These data from England and Wales document the substantial increases in life expectancy in recent centuries. Although only from one setting, they are broadly representative of the experience in North America and Europe.

Source: Wrigley E. and R. Schofield. 1981. *The Population History of England.* Cambridge, MA: Harvard University Press.

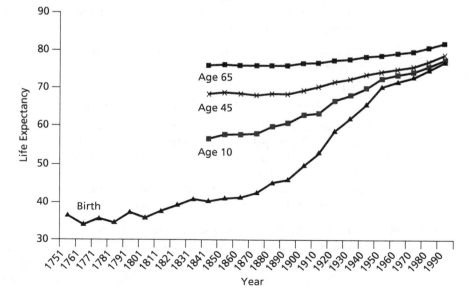

FIGURE 6.2

Male Life Expectancy at Various Ages, Canada, 1921–1974

Life expectancy at birth among Canadian males rose rapidly into the 1950s, after which the rate slowed. Life expectancy at older ages rose very modestly over this period, implying that most of the gains were achieved among younger men.

Source: Adapted from Statistics Canada publication, Historical Statistics of Canada, 1983 Edition, Catalogue 11-516-XWE, Table B65-74, http://www.statcan.gc.ca/pub.11-516-x/index-eng.htm.

Note: The apparent decrease at ages 40 and 60 between 1871 and 1921 likely reflects problems of data quality and measurement.

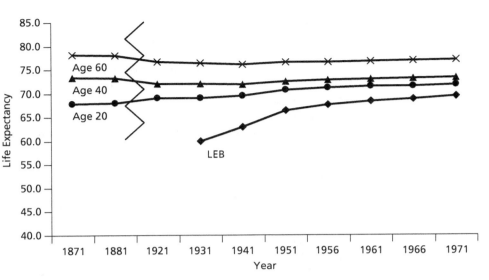

age of death by nearly 20 years; by 1950, the reduction in infant mortality had closed the gap to less than 2 years.

Chapter 1 presented information on Canadian life expectancy at birth for recent years. Although the data for Canada do not extend as far back into history as they do for England, they suggest a similar pattern: rising life expectancy at birth, with a convergence over time in life expectancy at birth with expected age of death, conditional on reaching specified ages (Figure 6.2). Canadian data clearly document the differential gains by age group: death rates among those under age 14 fell by over 80 percent between 1921 and 1974; they fell by just under 25 percent for those ages 55–75 (Statistics Canada 1983).

What caused this dramatic, historically unprecedented improvement in health? Understanding the causes of these health gains is of more than historical interest. Such knowledge may help create policies to improve the health of populations around the world today, especially in developing countries where life expectancy remains at levels that were observed decades ago in more developed countries.

No single dominant cause operated over this entire period, but demographers and historians of both medicine and economics cite three forces that exerted significant influence at different times during this period:

1. economic growth, which raised living standards and improved nutrition, especially early in the period
2. public health and related initiatives, especially in the period from about 1870 to 1940
3. modern medicine in the period from 1940 to the present

Debate continues regarding the relative importance of general economic growth compared to deliberate public health policies and social policies during certain decades, and of the precise contribution of medicine in the modern era; but historians agree unanimously that clinical medicine played only a minor role in these historical gains, exerting a measurable influence beginning only after the middle of the twentieth century, by which time the biggest health gains had already been achieved.

6.1.1 Thomas McKeown and the Rise of Populations

Thomas McKeown (1976; 1979) marshalled detailed death records for England and Wales from 1837 onward to argue two complementary theses that have served as the reference point for subsequent debate and research. His first thesis was the negative claim noted above regarding, the role of medicine: contrary to conventional wisdom at the time, he argued that medicine was not primarily responsible for the historical improvements in health in England and Wales. His second thesis was a positive claim: economic growth, rising living standards, and the accompanying improvement in diet were the primary sources of improvements in health.

To establish his first claim, McKeown presented a series of graphs for death rates from leading causes of death, demonstrating convincingly that clinical medicine could not possibly have been responsible for the historical health improvements. Figure 6.3 presents the graph for respiratory tuberculosis for the period 1838 to the 1960s, noting key dates in our scientific understanding of the disease: approximately 90 percent of the decrease in mortality during this period occurred before any treatment was available; 95 percent had occurred before the BCG vaccination was available. Similar analyses for the other leading causes of death such as whooping cough, diphtheria, and measles led to the same conclusion: the major cause of increased life expectancy during this period must lie outside medicine.

Again, Canadian data do not extend as far back as those available to McKeown for England and Wales, but they tell a similar story: rapidly falling rates of mortality for common diseases, well before effective medical treatments became available (Figure 6.4).

The major cause, McKeown argued, was a general improvement in living standards and diet associated with economic development. Improved health was an unintended by-product of economic development. Better nutrition strengthened people's immune systems, making them more resistant to disease and more likely to survive a disease. McKeown did not provide direct evidence of improved nutrition and its potential impact on health. Rather, he identified and then eliminated other possible explanations—such as a decline in the virulence of micro-organisms, reduced exposure to potentially harmful organisms, and improved treatment—leaving improved nutrition as the likely cause.

McKeown's thesis has received direct empirical support in the work of economic historian and Nobel laureate Robert Fogel (1997; 2004). Fogel demonstrated that average caloric intake increased substantially in the middle of the eighteenth century and that this was associated with increased average heights. Based on this evidence, Fogel attributed most of the reduction in mortality between the eighteenth and late nineteenth centuries, and approximately half of the reduction through the twentieth century, to improved nutrition.

FIGURE 6.3
Annual Mortality Rate from Respiratory Tuberculosis, England and Wales, 1838–1970
These data document that most of the reduction in mortality from tuberculosis occurred before any effective medical interventions became available. The causes of this reduction therefore lie outside medicine.

Source: McKeown T. 1976. *The Modern Rise of Population.* New York: Academic Press. Figure 8.1 on p. 192. The book ISBN is 0124855504.

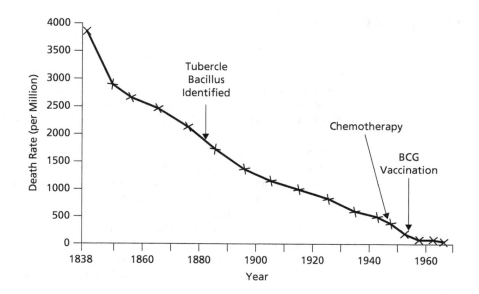

FIGURE 6.4
Annual Death Rates, Selected Diseases, Canada, 1921–1974
Consistent with the longer-term trends noted by McKeown, mortality rates from infectious diseases fell steadily in Canada prior to the advent of effective medical interventions.

Source: Adapted from Statistics Canada publication, Historical Statistics of Canada, 1983 Edition, Catalogue 11-516-XWE, Table B65-74, http://www.statcan.gc.ca/pub.11-516-x/index-eng.htm.

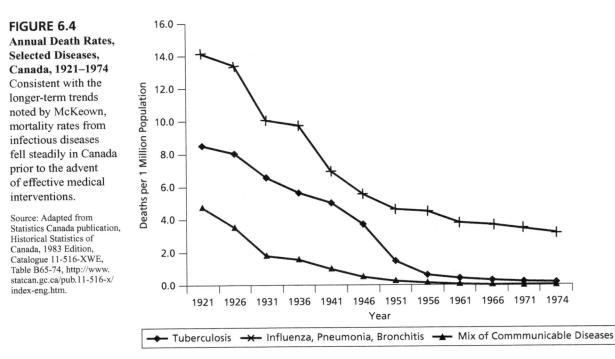

A number of analyses, however, have challenged the thesis that better nutrition caused the fall in mortality rates. Historians argue that mortality rates had fluctuated in the centuries before 1750 and that the change between 1750 and 1820 was a characteristic fluctuation for pre-industrial Europe (Wrigley and Schofield 1981). Others contend that similar rates of mortality between aristocrats (who presumably had better nutrition) and the common folk contradict a nutritional explanation. For the period after 1870, subsequent research has argued that the primary driver was not economic growth and nutrition but deliberate social policy in the form of large-scale public health initiatives (Cutler et al. 2006; Szreter 1988).

6.1.2   Rise of Public Health

The flat mortality profile in Figure 6.1 from the 1820s to the 1860s presents a puzzle. The industrial revolution was in full swing in England by the 1820s; economic growth was vigorous. If rising standards of living and better nutrition were the underlying causes of improved health, why did the rise in life expectancy stall? One explanation is divergent trends in rural and urban areas: mortality continued to fall in rural areas, but rising mortality in the cities offset this. The industrial revolution drew hundreds of thousands of people from the countryside to factory work in booming, densely populated, squalid cities that lacked the basic infrastructure to support the working classes: clean water, clean air, and decent housing.

Large, nineteenth-century cities were ideal settings for the spread of infectious disease. This led to differential rates of mortality between rural and urban areas, and the development of what we can call the "urban penalty" for those living in cities. In Britain, this began in the mid-nineteenth century; in Canada, it occurred in the late nineteenth and early twentieth centuries (Ostry 1994; Ostry 1995). Around 1870, however, overall rates of mortality in Britain began to fall again. What happened?

The squalor of the cities and the greater acceptance of the germ theory to explain the transmission of disease gave birth to the modern public health movement. The public health movement emphasized three types of action: increased regulation to improve housing and workplaces, public investment in large infrastructure projects such as those required to provide clean water and remove waste, and investments in public health education to improve health behaviours and practices. Among other accomplishments, these initiatives created better-ventilated, healthier housing and broke the "water circle" (whereby human waste seeps into the water supply only to re-enter the home) that caused much disease and death. They also improved food processing, distribution, and handling. Cutler and Miller (2005), for instance, estimate that water purification by large-scale water facilities in American cities contributed up to one-half of the total reduction in mortality between 1900 and 1936.

Samuel Preston's multi-country analysis of the relationship between life expectancy and income provides a second, more general type of evidence suggesting that economic development alone does not account for health gains (Preston 2001). Figure 6.5 shows this life-expectancy–income relationship for various years. Four features are prominent:

1. Life expectancy rises with income per capita. Such evidence is consistent with the idea that economic development is associated with health improvement (though we must be cautious about inferring that economic growth, per se, is the direct cause; many things about a society change with development).

2. This relationship is highly curvilinear: in 2005, for instance, increasing income is associated with large health gains up to about $7000, then becomes shallower up to the highest incomes.

FIGURE 6.5

Relationship Between GDP Per Capita and Life Expectancy, Selected Countries, 1975 and 2005

These data document two features of the relationship between GDP-per-capita and life expectancy: the highly non-linear relationship among countries at a given point in time, with rapid gains in life expectancy at low incomes followed by a flattening of the curve, and the gradual shift up in the relationship over time.

Data sources: United Nations Statistics Division 2009; curves based on author's calculations.

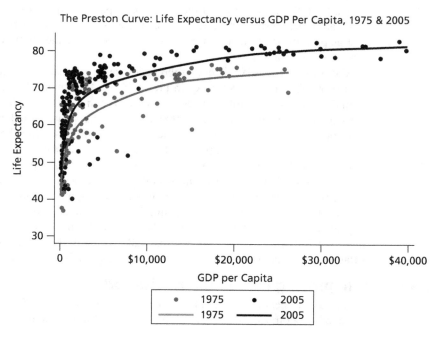

3. The curves have shifted upward over time. This upward shift is inconsistent with explanations based on economic growth: if the primary driver of the relationship were economic development, countries would simply move along a single curve as they developed, but the entire relationship would not shift. Something is causing the health–income relationship to shift over time.

4. The levels of health achieved by low-income countries are highly variable: some low-income countries are able to achieve "first-world" life expectancies while others with moderate incomes seem to substantially underachieve.

Something beyond economic growth alone is at work. Investments in public health and related social infrastructure (including in recent years, health care systems) are obvious explanations for the shift of the curve over time and the substantial variability at low income levels.

6.1.3 Era of Modern Medicine

The start of the era of modern medicine is generally dated from the introduction of antibiotics in the 1930s. This also roughly coincides with a number of other medical advances such as the manufacture of insulin (1923) and the development of vaccines for common diseases including diphtheria (1923), pertussis (1926), tetanus (1927), and yellow fever (1935). For the first time, physicians could actually do something direct and concrete to prevent and cure common illnesses.

While the impact of medicine on health has been small in the historical context, it has been measureable since the middle of the twentieth century. In fact, medical advances were a dominant driver of increased life expectancy in developed countries during this period. Figure 6.3 showing the historical decline in mortality from tuberculosis demonstrates the small role of medicine overall, but it also demonstrates the measurable role of modern medicine since the 1930s. The impact of the TB vaccination is clear: although the absolute declines are small by historical standards, beginning in the 1940s chemotherapy, the vaccine, and antibiotic treatments cut TB mortality rates in half.

Cutler (2004) attempted to quantify the impact of advances in modern medicine on population health since the early 1950s. He focused on two areas that together account for a large proportion of the increase in life expectancy since the 1950s, cardiovascular disease and neonatal mortality.

Cardiovascular disease is one of the major causes of death in modern societies and is an area of notable medical advances in prevention and treatment. Cardiovascular mortality in both Canada and the United States rose steadily from 1900 to 1950, but has fallen steadily since the 1950s; between 1960 and 2000, cardiovascular mortality fell by over 50 percent. This reduction accounts for 70 percent of the increase in life expectancy between 1960 and 2000. Using evidence from clinical trials that document the effectiveness of cardiovascular medical interventions for preventing and treating heart disease (e.g., drugs, coronary artery bypass surgery), he attributes up to two-thirds of the decrease in cardiovascular mortality to medical progress (the balance is due to a variety of other factors, most importantly reduced smoking).

Decreases in infant mortality account for an additional 20 percent of the increase in life expectancy between 1960 and 2000. Using a similar methodology, Cutler estimates that advances in the treatment of newborns, and especially the treatment of low-birth-weight infants, is responsible for the majority of this decrease in infant mortality.

6.1.4 Lessons for Improving Population Health Today

The historical health increase in modern developed countries reflects the gradual development of economies, public institutions, and health knowledge. The steady rise in life expectancy over the last 150 years has an air of inevitability: it is something that we have come to expect.

But the modern record establishes that a continual, uninterrupted increase is not automatic: life expectancy can and has fallen in a number of countries around the world, even in "first-world" countries. Furthermore, in a more hopeful vein, societies today do not have to progress sequentially through each of the stages in the historical record. Rather, modern societies have the full set of policy options available to improve the health of their populations, and strategic use can dramatically improve population health. The experiences of two countries—Russia and Cuba—illustrate these lessons.

The Reversal of Life Expectancy in the Former USSR

Figure 6.6 displays post-war trends in life expectancy at birth, for males and females combined, for two republics of the former USSR (Russia and Ukraine), two countries of eastern Europe (Poland and the Czech Republic), and the average of the countries making up the European Union "15" as defined by the OECD.[1] Three distinct phases are notable during this period.

In the years following World War II, life expectancy in the USSR and the countries of Eastern Europe rose markedly, and by the early 1960s was approaching parity with the countries of Western Europe.

Beginning in about 1965, however, life expectancy stagnated in the USSR and Eastern Europe, causing the gap to again widen as life expectancy continued to rise in Western Europe.

The breakup of the USSR and the turn from communism beginning in 1989 is marked by small, short-lived dips in life expectancy in Poland and the Czech Republic, but steep declines in Russia and Ukraine, while life expectancy continued to rise in western Europe.

Four primary hypotheses have been put forth regarding what happened in Russia and Ukraine and, to a lesser extent, in Poland and the Czech Republic: statistical reporting, famine, alcohol, and stress induced by the economic and social disruption that accompanied the transition from the communist organization of society (Cornia and Paniccia 2000).

[1] Austria, Belgium, Finland, France, Germany, Greece, Ireland, Italy, Luxemburg, Netherlands, Portugal, Spain, Denmark, Sweden, and the United Kingdom.

FIGURE 6.6
Life Expectancy at Birth, Selected Countries of the European Union and Eastern Europe, 1950–1997
After rising rapidly during the 1950s, life expectancy in Russia and Eastern Europe began to stagnate in the 1960s while it continued to grow in Europe; the break-up of the Soviet Union was associated with substantial declines in life expectancy in Russia and Ukraine.

Source: Cornia, G. and R. Paniccia. 2000. "The Transition Mortality Crisis: Evidence, Interpretation, and Policy Responses." In G. Cornia and R. Paniccia, eds. *The Mortality Crisis in Transitional Economies.* Oxford: Oxford University Press, 3–37.

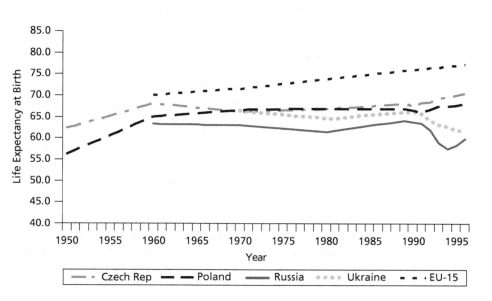

Statistical Reporting   Evidence indicates that the large drop is not just an artifact of changed statistical practices associated with the transition from communism. Apart from direct assessments of data quality, the decrease was much larger for men than for women, and was much larger among the working-age population than among either younger or older individuals. We would not expect to see selective effects in certain population groups if a general change in data procedures were responsible.

Famine   Although food shortages and related economic hardship likely caused a less healthy diet for many caught in the transition, the patterns of mortality (e.g., the groups affected, the seasonal pattern of deaths) are not consistent with famine as an important factor.

Alcohol   Alcohol consumption appears to have been an important contributing factor. Alcohol consumption per capita in Russia increased over 20 percent between 1989 and 1994, and was particularly noteworthy among working age males. In addition, mortality from liver disease, accidents, and other alcohol-related causes rose. Estimates suggest that alcohol consumption accounts for 27 to 40 percent of the rise in male mortality.

Economic and Social Disruption   Finally, some believe that psychosocial stress associated with the transition, amplified by the associated changes to fundamental institutions of society, was perhaps the most important factor. The transition caused substantial displacement, marital dissolution and family instability, unemployment, and heightened insecurity. Such stress can contribute to mortality both directly (e.g., cardiovascular disease, psychosis) and indirectly (e.g., through increased alcohol consumption).

The decrease in life expectancy in Russia and its associated republics is instructive because it was caused neither by the outbreak of a previously unknown communicable disease, such as some countries in Africa have experienced with HIV-AIDS, nor by traditional scourges such as famine or war. It appears to have been induced by the breakdown in the basic social institutions that people had relied upon for decades.

Exceeding Expectations: The Case of Cuba

Cuba has managed to achieve first-world health outcomes with third-world resources (Evans 2008; Spiegel and Yassi 2004). Figure 6.7(i) shows life expectancy at birth plotted against GDP per capita for 139 countries: Cuba is the labelled dot in the upper left hand corner above the cluster of countries with similarly low income. Figure 6.7(ii) shows the same relationship, but now only for its comparator countries in the Americas. Cuba's life-expectancy-at-birth of 78 equals that of the United States, is just below that of Canada, and is anywhere from 5 to 12 years greater than other countries with similar GDP per capita.

The origins of this "Cuban health paradox" are not well understood, but a few explanations stand out. Cuba has invested heavily in education, and has the highest-ranking literacy rate in the world at 99.8 percent of the population. It has invested heavily in primary health care, and has more doctors per capita than any other country in the Americas, and perhaps most significantly, its primary care teams are fully integrated into the broader public health system. Lastly, it has pursued strongly egalitarian social and economic policies. This set of complementary policies has managed to achieve remarkable health levels for the Cuban population.

Implications for Health Policy

This understanding of the determinants of population health has important implications for health policy today. Society must ensure that it does not lose ground against some of the hard-won gains of the last century, and it must ask hard questions about how best to invest new resources. Some argue, for instance, that medicine is currently at the "flat of the curve" in the production function: additional heath care spending on average may achieve only small gains in health.

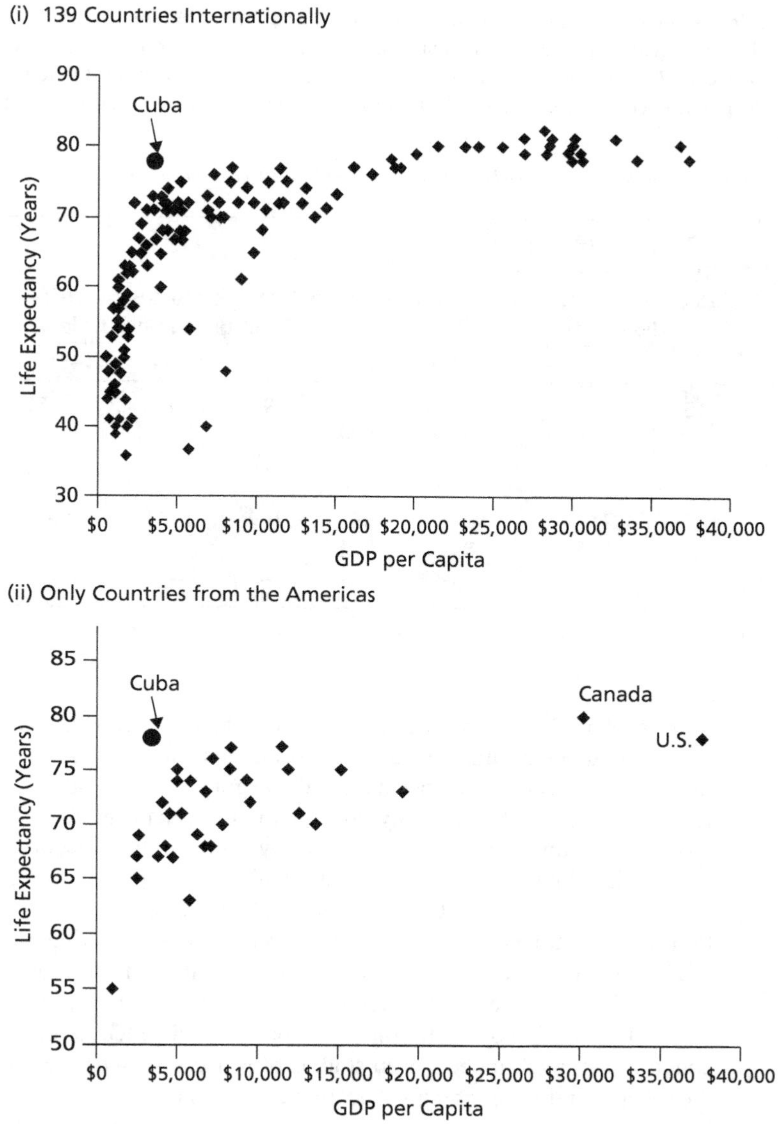

FIGURE 6.7
Life Expectancy at Birth versus Per-Capita GDP: Cuba's Relative Success
Life expectancy at birth in Cuba far exceeds what would be predicted based on its GDP per capita, demonstrating that many factors other than wealth can influence population health.

Source: For (i) and (ii): Evans, R. 2008. "Thomas McKeown, Meet Fidel Castro: Physicians, Population Health, and the Cuban Paradox." *Healthcare Policy.* Vol. 3(4):21–32.

(i) 139 Countries Internationally

(ii) Only Countries from the Americas

One of the first government documents to suggest this was the Canadian government's seminal Lalonde Report (named after the minister of health at the time) (Lalonde 1974). The report articulated a framework that emphasized the broad range of determinants of health. It argued that, at the margin, investments in the physical and social environment may well offer the best investments for improving population health. It called for a re-orientation of health policy away from a heavy emphasis on health care. Ironically, the Lalonde Report appears to have exerted more influence internationally than it did in Canada (Hancock 1986).

6.2   HEALTH INEQUALITIES

Research on the determinants of health emphasizes both the level and distribution of health in the population. An aspect of the unequal distribution of health that is of great concern, and is still relatively poorly understood, is the social gradient in health—the fact that, in

TABLE 6.1 **Mortality by Social Class—Canada, and England and Wales, Various Years**
The social gradient in health is evident in recent Canadian data, which document, for instance, that males over age 25 working in unskilled occupations were 37% more likely to die between 1991 and 2001 than were professionals. The data from England and Wales document the persistence of the social gradient during the 20th century over a period when the causes of death changed substantially.

Source: Evans, R. G. 2002. *Interpreting and Addressing Inequalities in Health: From Black to Acheson to Blair to . . .?* London: Office of Health Economics.

	Relative Risk of Dying, Males Aged 25 or over, Canada, 1991–2001	Standardized Mortality Rates by Social Class, Males (Aged 15–64), England and Wales, 1911–1981						
		1911	1921	1931	1951	1961[a]	1971[a]	1981[b]
Professional	1.0	88	82	90	86	76 (75)	77 (75)	66
Managerial	1.11	94	94	94	92	81	81	76
Skilled Manual and Non-Manual	1.17	96	95	97	101	100	104	103
Semi-Skilled	1.30	93	101	102	104	103	114	116
Unskilled	1.37	142	125	111	118	143 (127)	137 (121)	166
No Occupation	2.20	–	–	–	–	–	–	–

Notes: a. Figures in parentheses have been adjusted to the classification of occupations used in 1951.
b. Men, 20–64 years, Great Britain.

every society that has been examined, individuals of lower status experience worse health than individuals of high status. To illustrate this, Table 6.1 presents mortality rates by one indicator of social class—occupational category—for Canada and for England and Wales for various years. The mortality information for Canada indicates the age-adjusted relative risk of dying for a male aged 25 or over by occupational category.

The data indicate that such a male with no occupation was 2.2 times more likely to die between 1991 and 2001 than was a male professional. A male in an unskilled occupation was 1.37 times more likely to die. Those in lower-ranking occupations were far more likely to die than were professionals, and we see this effect at each step in the occupational grades: Canada has a large socio-economic gradient in mortality.

But Canada is not alone. Mortality data would reflect a similar pattern in nearly any country examined; indeed, even studies of primate societies reveal such a gradient across the social hierarchy of chimps. The gradient exists for different measures of socio-economic status (e.g., income, education) and different measures of health (e.g., self-reported health status, chronic disease, disability).

The mortality information for England and Wales is slightly different: for each year, it lists the standardized mortality ratios for each social class. For each year of data, a value of 100 represents the national average death rate in the population; a value greater than 100 represents a death rate above the national average and a value less than 100 represents a death rate below the national average. In every year between 1911 and 1981, the standardized mortality rate was lowest for those in the professional rank and highest for those in the unskilled rank.[2]

[2] The specific values are not comparable across years. For instance, the change from 96 to 103 for skilled manual and non-manual workers does not imply that death rates increased. Absolute death rates fell in all classes; however, the change does imply that, relative to the national average, the death rate rose in that class.

FIGURE 6.8
Coronary Heart Disease Mortality by Year of Follow-up: Whitehall Study
These data document the social gradient in health among British civil servants, all of whom are relatively well off. Those who work in the highest ranks of the civil service (e.g., Administrative) have substantially lower rates of mortality from heart disease than do those in the lower ranks (e.g., Clerical).

Source: Marmot, M., G. Rose, M. Shipley, and P. Hamilton. 1978. "Employment Grades and Coronary Heart Disease in British Civil Servants." *Journal of Epidemiology and Community Health.* Vol. 32(4):244–49.

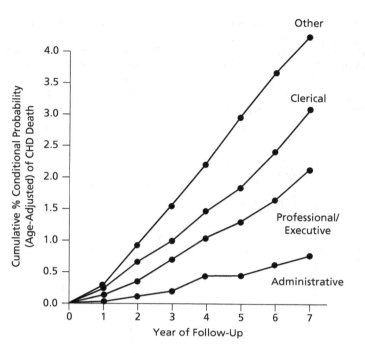

What is remarkable about this persisting gradient is that the underlying causes of death changed dramatically over this period. In 1911, the leading causes of death were infectious diseases; by 1981, they had changed to cancers and chronic diseases such as heart disease. Whatever is responsible for this gradient is not specific to particular disease processes; it is a more fundamental process that manifests itself through the predominant diseases of an era.

Figure 6.8 narrows the focus, allowing us to dig deeper. It is taken from one of the most famous health studies of the post-war era—the Whitehall Study—which has followed the health status of thousands of British civil servants over many years. The figure plots cumulative risk of dying from coronary heart disease in each year of follow-up, revealing once again a clear social gradient: those in the highest rank (the administrative rank) have the lowest probability of dying each year; those in the second highest rank (professional/ executive) have the next lowest; third is the clerical rank; and finally, members of the low-est class of civil servants (other) have the highest probability of dying each year.

The study is important because it rules out two commonly hypothesized causes. Absolute deprivation among those in the lower ranks does not cause the gradient: all of these individuals work in the British civil service earning decent wages. They can afford the basic necessities of life and they are at least minimally engaged in social interaction. Furthermore, as in the earlier examples, the gradient extends across the full spectrum of ranks: those in both the administrative and professional/executive classes are highly educated, highly effective individuals earning well-above-average incomes, yet we still observe a difference. Something both more fundamental and more widespread is at work than deprivation.[3]

---

[3] This does not imply that deprivation does not contribute to the social gradient more generally. Very low incomes and associated impaired access to certain advantages in society and basic health care services can and do exert a negative impact on health status. The larger point is simply that a gradient exists independent of any such effects.

FIGURE 6.9 **Contribution of Risk Factors to Relative Risk of Death from Coronary Heart Disease (Age-Standardized)**

Consistent with Figure 6.8, low-ranking Other workers in the British civil service are 4 times more likely to die of coronary heart disease than the highest-ranking Administrative workers. Clerical workers are 3.2 times more likely to die of CHD, and so forth. Differences in individual risk factors (e.g., smoking, hypertension) explain only a small part of the gradient in cardiovascular mortality; the vast majority of the gradient remains unexplained by traditional medical factors.

Source: Marmot, M., G. Rose, M. Shipley, and P. Hamilton. 1978. "Employment Grades and Coronary Heart Disease in British Civil Servants." *Journal of Epidemiology and Community Health.* Vol. 32(4):244–49.

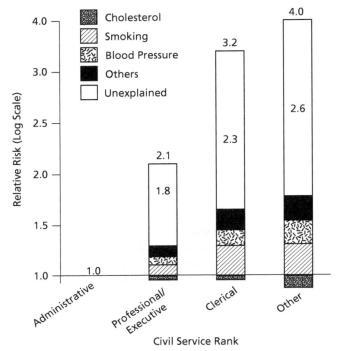

Neither does differential prevalence of high-risk health behaviours across the ranks cause the gradient. Figure 6.9 displays the contribution of common risk factors to the relative risk of dying from cardiovascular disease. As expected, the lowest rank has a higher prevalence of common risk factors, but the contribution of such risk factors to the gradient is small. The explanation lies elsewhere.

Education and income correlate with the civil servant ranks, and as discussed in Chapter 5, are thought to contribute causally to health status. But given our current evidence regarding their impact on health, it is unlikely that they could generate such a large gradient. More likely, education and income in part are simply alternative proxy measures of social status and class.

Finally, it is always possible that the relationship is purely spurious, that some unobserved factor(s) cause both better health and better performance in rising through the ranks of the civil service. While we must admit that this is possible, given the gradient's persistence across diverse settings, diverse measures, and diverse time periods, it seems unlikely.

6.2.1 The Social Determinants of Health

Research on the social determinants of health (e.g., Barer et al. 1994; Berkman and Kawachi 2000; Evans 2002) offers some tentative explanations for the social gradient in health, drawing on research into the social hierarchies, the stresses associated with various positions in a social hierarchy, our bodies' responses to such stresses, and the health consequences associated with these responses. The chains of causation are complex, but we can summarize the essence of the story.

Every society has a social hierarchy. People in different positions in the hierarchy are exposed to different levels of stress (both in the frequency and the severity of the stress). Psychosocial stress can induce physiological reactions within the body that were advantageous from an evolutionary perspective (a threat caused increased adrenalin, primed the muscles, and readied the body either to run or to fight), but that are not advantageous in modern societies that create repeated, low-level exposure to stresses. Over time, these physiological responses can manifest in disease. The rate of exposure to such daily stresses within the social hierarchy varies inversely with rank, generating the socio-economic gradient in health.

The full model is, of course, much more complex. The total amount of stress experienced, for example, is affected by the amount of control each person perceives that they exert over the stress-inducing events. In the workplace, for example, high-level executives face highly stressful demands, but also exert substantial control and have wide latitude in responding to these demands. A worker on an assembly line, in contrast, experiences the stress of having to keep up with production, but has little or no control over the rate of production. The effects of stress are greatest in high-demand, low-control environments in which people are constantly under stress but have no power to manage the source of that stress.

A number of factors affect the ability to cope with stress, including personality, early-life experiences, social support, and the availability of other support resources. In addition, the effects of life's stresses are not simply cumulative: events that individuals can handle one at a time may cause them to break down physically and mentally when the events occur in close proximity.

The body's response to outside stresses is also more complex and subtle than previously appreciated. Earlier models of genetic transmission were largely deterministic: someone with a certain genetic trait would manifest the associated genetic condition with certainty, regardless of social, economic, and physical environment. Current models of genetic transmission, in contrast, emphasize the conditional, contingent nature of the expression of genetic disease: whether a genetic trait manifests as a genetic disease also depends partly on the social, economic, and physical environment, and partly on how it combines with other genes.

Evans and Stoddart (1990) represented many of these ideas schematically as in Figure 6.10. Their framework distinguishes between disease (abnormal physiological function), health

FIGURE 6.10
The Evans and Stoddart Conceptual Framework for Understanding the Determinants of Health

This framework depicts the relationship among different determinants of health, highlighting the various environmental factors and the role of individual response in mediating the impact of these factors.

Source: Evans R. G. and G. L. Stoddart. 1990. "Producing Health, Consuming Health Care," *Social Science and Medicine.* Vol. 31(12): 1347–63.

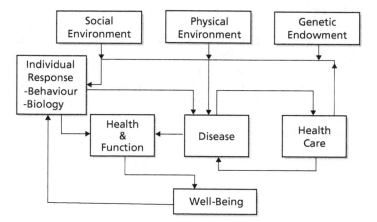

and function (how people experience the disease and how it affects their ability to function), and overall well-being. It acknowledges the role of the health care system in curing and preventing disease—ill health triggers the health care system—but the purpose of the framework is to represent the causes of ill health. The framework includes two environmental factors: the social environment and the physical environment. The social environment includes the network of friends and support, violence, variously defined hierarchies (work, social), norms of behaviour, and other institutions of society. The physical environment includes natural (e.g., weather, sunlight) and manufactured (e.g., toxins, transportation network) features of the physical world we inhabit.

The critical component, especially for integrating emerging evidence regarding the social determinants of health, is individual response—behavioural and physiological—to these environments. People's genetic endowments as well as the physical and social environments in which they live cause direct health effects—but often our biological and behavioural responses mediate these health effects. Behaviourally, for instance, some people respond to stress by smoking, drinking, or seeking other avenues of release that carry health risks. Biologically, stress can compromise immune system function as well as induce diseases such as hypertension, ulcers, and cholestermia. In this vision, a person's sense of well-being determines his or her response to stress and is, in turn, determined by that response. Consequently, host response—which is, in part, socially conditioned and malleable—emerges as a pivotal link in the chain of causation in health from the physical and social environment to the socio-economic gradient.

A number of important ideas about the determinants of health and inequalities in the distribution of health emerge from this line of research:

- the impact of social forces—and the type of society in which people live—on individuals and their health
- a causal understanding of how such social forces "get under the skin" to produce health effects
- the need to significantly redefine notions about public health policy, moving its parameters beyond traditional concerns such as infectious disease

We face a two-fold challenge in developing concrete policy proposals from this approach to the source of health inequalities. Although evidence is accumulating that these forces do generate health inequalities, it not clear what specific policies could eliminate them or reduce their adverse effects on health and its distribution. As well, the social determinants framework shows a complex, organic, interacting network of forces; manipulating any single policy lever may not have much impact.

In the last century, we have seen that targeting diseases that are experienced disproportionately by low socio-economic groups is not effective. Conquering most infectious disease has reduced mortality, but has not reduced the social gradient—the poor now die disproportionately from different causes. Furthermore, in terms of reducing the gradient, a single "fix" may have little impact in the absence of policies that also address the intermediary factors in the path from that factor to health effects.[4] Hence, although health policy discussions increasingly emphasize the impact of these broader social determinants on both the level and distribution of population health, the ideas have yet to be widely translated into policy reforms.

---

[4] This does not imply that taking a certain action is not socially desirable. It may reduce considerable suffering and harm; it just may not reduce the gradient.

Chapter Summary

This chapter examined important determinants of population health and of the social gradient in health. The main points include the following:

- Research emphasizes three dominant sources of the large increase in life expectancy in high-income countries over the last three hundred years:
  - economic growth and the associated improvement in nutrition
  - public health initiatives that followed increasing urbanization as part of the industrial revolution
  - advances in modern medicine in the period since World War II
- The variation in population health across countries in the modern world reveals that public policies, both inside and outside the health sector, can have dramatic effects on population health.
- There is a large and persistent socio-economic gradient in health in all societies.
  - People of lower socio-economic status are in poorer health on average than those of higher socio-economic status.
  - This gradient has persisted over time even as the causes of mortality and ill health have changed.
- Current understanding of the causes of the socio-economic gradient in health emphasizes broad forces in the social and physical environments.
  - These environmental determinants operate through many channels that can affect health, both directly, such as through differential exposure to health risks, and indirectly, by affecting how individuals and populations respond to health risks and the impact of exposure on health.
  - Evidence suggests that these myriad factors affect health in part through their effect on the overall level of stress (physical, psychological) that people experience.

Key Term

social gradient in health, *164*

End-of-Chapter Questions

For each of the statements below, indicate whether the statement is true or false and explain why it is true or false.

1. For many of the most common communicable diseases (e.g., tuberculosis), medical treatment and vaccinations have played a minor role in reducing mortality.
2. The fact that health and income are positively correlated suggests that a policy of transferring income from the wealthy to the poor will increase overall health in society.
3. The fact that the social gradient in health has persisted over many decades implies that factors other than exposure to specific pathogens cause it.
4. The important determinants of population health today are quite different than they were 100 years ago.
5. Even though non-health-care determinants have been responsible for the largest health gains over the last 200 years, additional health care spending is likely the most effective way to improve population health today.
6. Urbanization was one of the largest causes of improved health in the last part of the nineteenth century and the first part of the twentieth century.

7. Evidence documents an important threshold effect in the relationship between a person's socio-economic status and their health status.

8. Common, behaviour-based risk factors for disease primarily explain the social gradient in health.

9. The fact that residents of countries with the same GDP per capita have widely different life expectancies confirms that the fundamental forces cited by McKeown are still dominant forces affecting health today.

10. If people's psychological well-being depends on their relative status (i.e., keeping up with the Joneses), then increasing average incomes may exert only modest impact on population health.

References

Barer, M. L., R. G. Evans, and T. R. Marmor, eds. 1994. *Why are some people healthy and others not? The determinants of the health of populations*. New York: A. de Gruyter.

Berkman, L., and I. Kawachi. 2000. *Social epidemiology*. New York: Oxford University Press.

Cornia, G., and R. Paniccia. 2000. The transition mortality crisis: Evidence, interpretation and policy responses. In *The mortality crisis in transitional economies*, G. Cornia, and R. Paniccia (eds.). Oxford: Oxford University Press. 3–37.

Cutler, D., A. Deaton, and A. Lleras-Muney. 2006. The determinants of mortality. *Journal of Economic Perspectives* 20(3):97–120.

Cutler, D., and G. Miller. 2005. The role of public health improvements in health advances: The 20th century United States. *Demography* 42(1):1–22.

Cutler, D. M. 2004. *Your money or your life*. Cambridge, MA: MIT Press.

Evans, R. 2008. Thomas McKeown, meet Fidel Castro: Physicians, population health and the Cuban paradox. *HealthCare Policy* 3(4):21–32.

Evans, R. G. 2002. *Interpreting and addressing inequalities in health: From Black to Acheson to Blair to . . . ?* London: Office of Health Economics.

Evans, R. G., and G. L. Stoddart. 1990. Producing health, consuming health care. *Social Science and Medicine* 31(12):1347–63.

Fogel, R. 1997. New findings on secular trends in nutrition and mortality: Some implications for population theory. In *Handbook of population and family economics*, M. Rosenzweig, and O. Stark (eds.). Amsterdam: Elsevier Science B. V. 433–81.

———. 2004. *The escape from hunger and premature death, 1700–2100*. Cambridge: Cambridge University Press.

Hancock, T. 1986. Lalonde and beyond: Looking back at "A new perspective on the health of Canadians." *Health Promotion* 1(1):93–100.

Lalonde, M. 1974. *A new perspective on the health of Canadians*. Ottawa: Tri-Graphic Printing Ltd. 5–77.

Marmot, M., G. Rose, M. Shipley, and P. Hamilton. 1978. Employment grades and coronary heart disease in British civil servants. *Journal of Epidemiology and Community Health* 32(4):244–49.

Marmot, M. G. 1986. Social inequalities in mortality: The social environment. In *Class and health: Research and longitudinal data*, R. G. Wilkinson (ed.). London: Tavistock. 21–33.

McKeown, T. 1976. *The modern rise of population*. New York: Academic Press.

———. 1979. *The role of medicine: Dream, mirage, or nemesis?* Oxford: Basil Blackwell.

OECD. 2008. *OECD health data 2008*. Paris: OECD.

Office of Population Censuses and Surveys. 1978. *Occupational mortality: The Registrar-General's decennial supplement for England and Wales*. London: Her Majesty's Stationary Office, Series DS, No. 1.

Ostry, A. S. 1994. Theories of disease causation and their impact on public health in nineteenth century Canada. *Canadian Journal of Public Health* 85(5):368–9.

Ostry, A. S. 1995. Differences in the history of public health in 19th century Canada and Britain. *Canadian Journal of Public Health* 86(1):5–6.

Preston, S. H. 2001. The changing relation between mortality and level economic development. *Population Studies* 29(2):231–48.

Spiegel, J., and A. Yassi. 2004. Lessons from the margins of globalization: Appreciating the Cuban health paradox. *Journal of Public Health Policy* 25(1):96–121.

Statistics Canada. 1983. *Historical statistics of Canada*. Ottawa: Statistics Canada Catalogue No 11-516-XIE, pdf available at http://www.statcan.gc.ca/bsolc/olc-cel/olc-cel? catno=11-516-X& lang=eng.

Szreter, S. 1988. The importance of social intervention in Britain's mortality decline c. 1859–1940. *Social History of Medicine* 1(1):1–37.

United Nations Statistics Division. 2009. *World population prospects: The 2008 revision*. New York: United Nations, available at http://data.un.org/.

Wilkins, R., M. Tjepkma, C. Mustard, and R. Choinere. 2008. The Canadian census mortality follow-up study, 1991 through 2001. *Health Reports* 19(3):25–43.

Wrigley, E., and R. Schofield. 1981. *The population history of England, 1541–1871*. Cambridge, MA: Harvard University Press.

Health Care as an Economic Commodity

We begin our economic analysis of health care and health care systems with a brief consideration of the nature of health care as an economic commodity. Although health care is only one of many determinants of health, it is singled out for detailed analysis for two important reasons:

1. It is one of the few determinants primarily intended, in most applications, to maintain or improve health. For this reason, it is of particular interest for health policy.
2. In addition to representing significant economic activity in modern societies (as documented in Chapter 1), in many countries health care is the single largest component of government spending. As such, it invites scrutiny, and more importantly, generates a demand for evidence that health care policies are effective in creating an efficient, equitable health care system. Governments face increasingly vocal calls for evidence-based health care policies grounded in sound analytic reasoning, empirical evidence, or both. Health economics has a major role to play in furnishing the analytic methods and empirical evidence required by policy-makers.

Whenever government is involved in a sector with substantial public and private activity, such as health care, the relationships between the public and private segments raise a host of efficiency and equity problems. Issues regarding the respective roles of the public and private segments are among the most fiercely debated issues in health care. Once again, health economics is uniquely poised to inform such policy debates.

The Nature of Health Care as an Economic Commodity

Learning Objectives

After studying this chapter, you will understand

LO1   The characteristics of health care that are important for the efficient and equitable allocation of health care resources

LO2   How each of these characteristics affects the efficient and equitable allocation of health care resources

LO3   The policy challenges created by the interaction of these characteristics

Is health care different from the "regular" goods and services we buy every day? The answer for many is obvious: of course, health care is different. Health care involves life and death. Nothing can be more important. Surely society cannot treat health care the same as soft drinks, CDs, pencils, and other goods and services.

Economists have for decades debated whether health care is "different" (Arrow 1963; Culyer 1971; Mushkin 1958; Pauly 1988; Pauly 1992). This economic debate concerns a specific sense of differentness: does health care differ from a standard economic commodity in ways that

- create market failure or equity concerns, implying that health care cannot be optimally allocated through freely operating markets?

- require economists to modify aspects of their standard methodological approach when analyzing the health care sector?

If health care is not different in either of these ways, then society can use freely operating health care markets to achieve efficient, equitable allocations of health care, and economists can analyze the operation of health care markets using the standard toolkit of economic methods without modification. There would be no reason to have a specialized field of "health economics."

Alternatively, health care markets could fail or health care could generate important equity concerns such that freely operating health care markets would not be optimal but would still create no special methodological challenges. In this case, health care would be no different from many goods of policy interest, such as housing.

The situation is more difficult if health care differs from a standard economic commodity in both these ways. In such a situation, the efficient and equitable distribution of health care poses both policy challenges and scientific, methodological challenges.

We now examine health care as an economic commodity, stressing those characteristics of health care that differ from the standard good of microeconomic theory and the implications of these differences.

The analysis focuses on health care itself, not the health care sector. Simple observation reveals that every country organizes its health care sector differently than it does the rest of its economy. The crucial question from an economic perspective is whether or not, given the nature of health care as a commodity, these distinct institutional arrangements make economic sense. This chapter sets the context for the more detailed analysis of later chapters, presaging themes that will occur repeatedly as we examine various aspects of the health care sector. We begin with a brief discussion of the goods and services that constitute "health care" and then examine several characteristics of health care relevant to the economic analysis of health care.

7.1 WHAT IS HEALTH CARE?

Defining health care is surprisingly difficult, given how readily we use the term without apparent confusion. Formally defining health care may seem an overly academic exercise (we all recognize health care when we see it!), but distinguishing health care from other commodities is of considerable practical importance for many policies.

Chapter 1 noted that many people define health care as that subset of goods and services primarily intended to maintain or improve health. This is both too inclusive and too narrow. It is too inclusive because many goods and activities meant to improve health—such as a guardrail along a dangerous highway or a publicity campaign to reduce smoking—do not constitute health care. It is too narrow because many services—such as cosmetic surgery—do constitute health care even though their primary purpose is not to improve health.

Others argue that health care is the set of goods and services provided by health care professionals. While this does solve some problems, it creates others. Quite apart from circularity (how do we define a health care professional?), some health care professionals provide goods and services that no one considers health care; for example, many pharmacists sell greeting cards.

"Health care" seems to lie at the intersection of these and other considerations. The Venn diagram in Figure 7.1 depicts this idea. The largest rectangle, A, represents all goods and services in the economy; B is the subset of all goods and services primarily intended to improve health; C represents the subset of goods and services provided through individual-level exchange; D is the subset of goods and services provided by health care professionals.

To interpret the diagram, consider the example of a radio broadcast—a good that falls in A but not B, C, or D (i.e., its primary purpose is not to produce health, it is not provided to individuals through individual exchange, and it is not provided by health care professionals). The radio itself falls within C but not B or D (it is sold through individual level exchanges but not to improve health and not by a health care professional). A guardrail along a highway falls within B but not C or D (i.e., its primary purpose is to produce health, but it is neither provided through individual exchange nor by a health care professional).

FIGURE 7.1 **The Subset of Goods and Services that Constitutes Health Care**
This figure illustrates how the aspects of goods and services—the purpose of a good, the nature of exchange, and the provider of the good—combine in defining the set of goods and services called health care. Health care includes that subset of all goods and services delivered through individual-level exchanges by health care professionals with the primary purpose of improving health (areas ABC and $ABCD_1$) plus those services (ACD_2) delivered by a health care professional through an individual-level exchange that improves well-being by means other than improved health but that draws on specialized medical expertise (e.g., cosmetic surgery).

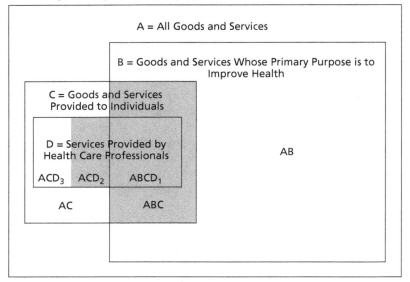

Health care would seem to constitute those goods that fall in the shaded areas labelled *ABC* (their purpose is health improvement and they are sold through individual exchange but not by a health professional—for example, aspirin sold in a grocery store), $ABCD_1$ (their purpose is health improvement and they are provided to an individual by a health professional—for example, appendectomies), and ACD_2 (they are provided to individuals by health professionals utilizing specialized professional expertise, but they are not intended to improve health—for example, cosmetic surgery).

The borders among these categories are often blurry but the principles underlying these distinctions are essential for many aspects of health policy. They guide insurers' health care coverage decisions—public insurance in many countries is intended to cover only services effective in improving health. They define important regulatory categories—drugs are regulated differently than food products. And they are the basis of many pragmatic issues, such as consistently calculating health care expenditures so as to enable meaningful international comparisons of health system performance.

7.2 CHARACTERISTICS OF HEALTH CARE AS AN ECONOMIC COMMODITY

Five characteristics of health care are central to economic analysis: derived demand for health care, externalities, informational asymmetry between providers and patients, uncertainty regarding both the need for and effectiveness of health care, and the vulnerability of individuals at the time they consume health care.

7.2.1   Demand for Health Care Is a Derived Demand

Most of us would be happy never to consume health care. Visiting a doctor or dentist often elicits considerable fear and anxiety. Health care often causes discomfort, pain, and short-term disability. As emphasized in Chapter 5, people demand health care primarily to improve their health and, thereby, their well-being. This demand for health care derives from the demand for health. We can represent this as follows in terms of utility:

$$U = u(H(Z, HC), HC, X) \qquad\qquad (7.1)$$

where

      U   =   utility
      H   =   health status
      H( ) =   the production function for health
      Z   =   non-health-care goods, services, and activities that affect health status
      HC =   health care goods and services
      X   =   the set of all other goods, services, and activities that provide utility

Health care can affect a person's utility in two ways: it can improve health, a relationship captured by the production function for health, H( ); and it can directly affect utility, such as when health care causes discomfort. Most health care probably affects utility in both ways, but the two channels are important to distinguish. For health care consumed to improve health, the direct (often negative) effects on utility are usually short-lived and dominated by the increase in well-being from improved health. Hence, the analysis of such demand can (often) safely ignore the direct effect on utility. But people consume some kinds of health care (e.g., cosmetic surgery) for reasons other than health, and in such cases the negative effects on health are short-lived and dominated by the ultimate direct effects on utility. Unless noted explicitly, the discussion in this chapter focuses on health care that is consumed to improve health.

Derived Demand and Assessing the Efficiency of Health Care Consumption

When a person consumes goods and services (e.g., X in equation (1)) solely for their direct effects on utility, it is difficult to assess allocative efficiency in consumption because it requires us to measure an unobserved quantity: the marginal utility the individual derives from consuming the good. Unless there is a clear source of market failure, or a distortion in the market due to taxes or regulation, economists assume that consumption is efficient because we have no basis for questioning people's decisions.

The situation is quite different in health care, and the difference arises because the demand for health care derives from the demand for health. A person benefits from health care only if it improves his or her health; improved health is a necessary (though not sufficient) condition for a person to benefit from health care consumption. If the health care consumed could not be expected to improve health, then the consumption cannot have been efficient.

Our knowledge of the health production function can tell us if a particular health care service will likely improve health. Does the best medical evidence indicate that the service is effective in treating the patient's health problem? Unlike the direct relationship between consumption and utility, this relationship between consumption and health is observable and measurable. Because this is a production relationship, an analyst can make efficiency judgments about health care consumption using supply-side notions of technical and cost-effectiveness efficiency. If a service cannot be expected to improve health, then consuming it will produce no benefit; providing this service represents a waste of resources, and must be technically inefficient. If someone uses a higher-cost service (a brand-name drug instead of a bio-equivalent generic), the consumption is not cost-effective.

As discussed in Chapter 2, if an allocation is either technically or cost-effectively inefficient, it cannot be allocatively efficient. Consequently, in some circumstances it is possible to make judgments regarding the allocative efficiency of health care consumption without knowing anything about unobservable patient preferences.

This insight underlies two prominent types of health research. One studies **small-area variation** in health care utilization, comparing rates of utilization across geographic areas, such as counties or regions, in order to identify those services for which rates of variation exceed those that would be expected given variation in needs across residents of the regions.

A study of prescription drug consumption among British Columbia's Local Health Areas (LHAs), for instance, found substantial variation in use across LHAs for some of the most widely prescribed medicines, even after controlling for need. The use of cholesterol-lowering medications was more than 30 percent lower than would be expected for a number of regions but 20 percent higher for another set of regions. The use of anti-depressants varied from nearly 50 percent above expected levels to nearly 50 percent below expected levels. The use of anti-acid drugs varied from more than 60 percent above expected levels to 25 percent below expected levels (Morgan et al. 2009). Such research cannot identify definitively when allocatively inefficient use occurs (Diehr et al. 1992; Folland and Stano 1990), but it can identify an area of potential inefficiency that deserves closer examination.

Another type of research studies the **appropriateness** of health care utilization. Researchers first review the clinical research evidence to identify the clinical criteria for the appropriate provision of a service, and then review medical records to identify when the service was provided inappropriately. This research indicates that a substantial proportion of care is inappropriate (Health Council of Canada 2009; Box 7.1.).

The production relationship between health care and health provides a basis for normative efficiency assessments of the utilization of health care that are not possible for other goods, while respecting the fundamental tenet of consumer sovereignty, since production relationships do not depend in any way on preferences. Allocative efficiency—how much people value the resulting health gains—remains important in health care, but it is not the only efficiency concept relevant to assessing consumption patterns.

Need for Health Care

Derived demand, and the associated production relationship between health care and health, help distinguish needs from wants in health care. The notion of need carries with it a normative obligation by others to act to satisfy the need; there is no such normative obligation to satisfy a want. But empirically it is often difficult to distinguish a need from a want. For this reason, economists are generally skeptical of claims of need. Economists often view claims of need as an attempt by some to privilege one set of preferences over others—by claiming that what they prefer is a need rather than a want—and economics holds firm to the principle that society should not judge one type of preference as more or less important than any other (all preferences are equal). The production relationship between health care and health, however, allows a meaningful interpretation of the concept of need in health care that is not possible in other sectors.

A **need** exists only if two conditions hold (Culyer 1995; Williams 1978). First, need is a purely instrumental concept, so to be needed a good or service must be effective in achieving a stated objective; something that is ineffective in achieving the stated aim cannot be needed. Second, the sought-after objective must provide a legitimate basis for drawing on

small-area variation
A health research approach that investigates patterns of variation in health care utilization across small geographic areas.

appropriateness
A health research approach that investigates the appropriateness of health care utilization by examining the clinical records of those who have received care, and assessing that care against established criteria for the appropriate delivery of a service.

need
A good is judged to be needed if it meets two conditions: (1) the good is effective in achieving a stated objective, and (2) the objective has been judged as a legitimate reason for drawing on others' resources to attain the objective.

A team of researchers investigated the appropriateness of six types of elective surgery in British Columbia: cataract replacement, cholecsytectomy, lumbar diskectomy, prostatectomy, and total hip replacement (Wright et al. 2002). The study used a prospective design that gathered two types of information:

1. For each patient booked for surgery in a participating hospital, the surgeon completed a clinical indications sheet that was sent to the research team.

2. The research then surveyed each patient before and after surgery to assess their health-related quality of life.

As would be expected, for each of the six procedures, most patients experienced improvements in health-related quality of life following surgery. The largest improvements were observed for those who received lumbar disk surgery or total hip replacement. Also as would be expected, some patients for each procedure experienced decreases in health-related quality of life following surgery. But the results for cataract replacement were particularly striking.

Fully 26 percent of those who received cataract surgery rated their health-related quality of life as worse after the surgery than it was before (another 1 percent rated it as the same). A review of the clinical information found that 32 percent of those who received the cataract operation had scored higher than 90 on a 100-point test of visual function (0 = blind; 100 = perfect sight); 15 percent scored over 95. It appears that a large proportion of those undergoing surgery had only minor vision problems before the operation. The researchers concluded that threshold indications for surgery were very low.

Given the inherent risk of surgery and the finding that over one-quarter of those who received this routine surgery were worse off for having had it, it is difficult to avoid the conclusion that the thresholds were inefficiently low. This finding is particularly striking given that cataract surgery is a procedure consistently cited for long wait-times and which was included as one of the five priority areas for wait-time reductions in the 2004 First Ministers' Health Accord intended to reduce wait-times.

Source: Yaari, M. E. and M. Bar-Hillel. 1984. "On Dividing Justly." *Social Choice and Welfare*. Vol. 1:1–24.

others' resources to attain it. Satisfying a whim does not constitute such an objective; in most societies, however, health does. Health is a basic prerequisite for living, essential to many normal activities of daily life. Health often fails people randomly, for reasons beyond their control. Hence, the objective of improving health has a social legitimacy, unlike the objective of "making me happy," or more generally, "satisfying my wants."

Other goods, such as food or housing, can also satisfy these two conditions. Health care, however, differs from them in two ways that are important for using need as a basis for policy. First, the limited substitutability among health care services allows for a more precise assessment of health care need. Hundreds of alternative foods can satisfy even severe hunger. If a someone has appendicitis, however, only an appendectomy can address the need. The link between the needed service and the need is often very tight, with no close substitutes. Second, as has been noted, much health care can be unpleasant, even painful. Few would deliberately seek an unnecessary operation just for the pleasure. In contrast, many foods that satisfy hunger also provide considerable pleasure. In the limit, a person could feign hunger to get a nice meal.

None of this is intended to imply that defining and empirically identifying health care needs is straightforward. It is not. But as a practical matter, health care needs can often be distinguished from health care wants (Hurley et al. 1997), and this distinction lies at the heart of all publicly financed health care systems. The Canada Health Act, for example, strives to ensure equitable access to *medically necessary* physician and hospital services. Although policy-makers and analysts debate services that are in the grey zone between health care needs and wants, much of health care is easily classified as necessary or unnecessary.

7.2.2 Externalities

physical (selfish) externality
A health-related externality in which even a purely selfish person cares about others' consumption of health care because such care reduces the chances that a communicable disease is spread.

caring externality
A health-related externality that arises when a person cares about the health status of others and, consequently, their consumption of needed health care.

Health care generates important externalities that cause market failure (Culyer and Simpson 1980; Evans and Wolfson 1980; Hurley 2000). (See Chapter 3 for a discussion of externalities.) **Physical, or selfish, externalities** originate in physical health effects associated with communicable disease. **Caring externalities** originate in concern over others' access to needed health care.

Physical (Selfish) Externalities

The example of flu shots discussed in Chapter 3 exemplifies physical externalities rooted in the transmission of disease. When one person obtains a flu shot, the people around that person benefit because they have a reduced chance of getting the flu. One person's consumption of a flu shot generates a positive external benefit to others with whom they come into contact even if these individuals are selfishly concerned only about their own health and welfare.

Such physical, selfishly based, externalities arise for the prevention or treatment of all communicable diseases. These externalities provide the economic rationale for public provision or subsidy of public health services such as vaccinations, immunizations, and the testing for and treatment of tuberculosis, sexually transmitted diseases, and other communicable diseases.

Public health initiatives were among the first widespread government interventions in the health sector and, as discussed in Chapter 6, have been responsible for dramatic increases in health and well-being. Such efforts have been so successful, in fact, that most people in developed countries today have no experience of how devastating such diseases can be. The international Severe Acute Respiratory Syndrome (SARS), Avian flu, and H1N1 flu crises have reminded us that public health programs to prevent the spread of communicable diseases benefit all citizens.

Caring Externalities

A broken leg is not contagious. Mending a broken leg, therefore, does not generate physical, selfish externalities. Left untreated, however, a broken leg can cause an individual considerable pain, suffering, and long-term impairment. Because of this, in a caring society, others may derive benefit from the knowledge that the injured person has access to effective treatment for the broken leg. The repair of the broken leg generates caring externalities.[1]

More generally, if one person cares about another person's health status, caring externalities would arise whenever the second person obtains an effective, needed health care service. Purely market-based allocation of such care would result in an inefficiently low level of health care consumption, so achieving the optimal level requires some form of public intervention in the health care market. Caring externalities provide an economic rationale for a large public role in the financing, organization, and delivery of needed health care.

The emphasis on *needed* health care is crucial. Caring externalities do not arise for health care, *per se*, only for needed health care (see Box 7.2). This distinction provides the economic rationale for public coverage of only those health care services that are medically necessary. Cosmetic surgery does not usually generate such externalities. Hence, cosmetic surgery and other health care services consumed for direct, non-health benefits are allocated through private markets (subject to quality regulation). An ultrasound to verify the health of a fetus is covered publicly; an ultrasound to generate pictures to show relatives is not.

---

[1] Such externalities are sometimes also referred to as "good-specific" externalities (e.g., see Tobin 1970); Evans and Wolfson (1980) refer to them as "paternalistic" externalities. The main point is that the externality is associated with the consumption of a particular commodity—effective health care—not with another person's general level of consumption or well-being.

The importance of differentiating needed health care from unneeded health care was highlighted by an experiment conducted by B. Yaari and M. Bar-Hillel (1984). In the experiment, they created two scenarios concerning the distribution of the same good. In one scenario, however, the good was desired because it was needed for health reasons; in the second, the good was desired simply to satisfy tastes. Respondents judged the just allocations of the same good quite differently in the two situations.

The first scenario is as follows:

A shipment containing 12 grapefruit and 12 avocados is to be distributed between Jones and Smith. The following information is given, and is known also to the two recipients:

- *Both Jones and Smith are interested in the consumption of grapefruit and/or avocados only insofar as such consumption provides vitamin F—and the more, the better. All other traits for the two fruits (such as taste, calorie content, etc.) are of no consequence to them.*
- *Doctors have determined that Jones's metabolism is such that his body derives 100 milligrams of vitamin F from each grapefruit consumed, while it derives no vitamin F whatsoever from avocado.*
- *Doctors have also determined that Smith's metabolism is such that his body derives 50 milligrams of vitamin F from each grapefruit consumed and also from each avocado consumed.*
- *No trades can be made after the division takes place.*

How should the fruits be divided between Jones and Smith if the division is to be just?

Over 82 percent of respondents chose to allocate the fruit to equalize the amount of vitamin F that each person gets (8 grapefruit for Jones; 4 grapefruit and 12 avocados for Smith).

In the second scenario, the formal structure remained identical but the problem was changed so that it reflected tastes rather than need. It was presented as follows:

A shipment containing 12 grapefruit and 12 avocados is to be distributed between Jones and Smith. The following information is given, and is known also to the two recipients:

- *Jones likes grapefruit very much and is willing to buy a number of them, provided that the price does not exceed $1.00 per pound. He detests avocados, so he never buys them.*
- *Smith likes grapefruit and avocados equally well, and is willing to buy both grapefruit and avocado in any number, provided that the price does not exceed $0.50 per pound.*
- *Jones and Smith are in the same income tax bracket.*
- *No trades can be made after the division takes place.*

How should the fruits be divided between Jones and Smith if the division is to be just?

In this case, only 28 percent of respondents chose the division that had been favoured earlier. The most frequently chosen distribution (by 35 percent of respondents) was allocation through a competitive market (12 grapefruit for Jones and 12 avocados for Smith).

Although selfish and caring externalities constitute an important rationale for the public subsidy of health care, empirical evidence regarding the nature or size of such externalities is limited. The fact that people repeatedly elect politicians who support public funding for health care represents a type of evidence, but such voting is based on many issues besides health care so the evidence that such behaviour provides about health care externalities is ambiguous. A small number of recent studies have tried to measure the size and nature of health-related externalities (Jacobsson et al. 2007; Smith 2007). The evidence from such studies confirms the presence of caring externalities and suggests that their magnitude is non-trivial. (See Box 7.3 for a summary of Jacobsson's study.)

7.2.3 Informational Asymmetry Between Providers and Patients

Why do you go to your physician when ill? If you are like most people, often you seek a diagnosis. You want to know, "What is wrong with me?" Once you get a diagnosis, your next question is likely, "What should I do?"

These two questions epitomize the informational problems individuals face in making health care choices. Individuals often lack the information and knowledge required to

Swedish researchers used a clever experimental approach to assess whether health care generates paternalistic, caring externalities (Jacobsson et al. 2007). The design of the experiment was as follows.

Working with a primary health care clinic, the researchers recruited a pool of diabetes patients who smoked, would like to quit, and indicated that they would be willing to try nicotine patches if they received them for free but that they were not willing to pay the cost of the patches. Hence, these are individuals who would be made better off by receiving money rather than the nicotine patches with the same total value (because they have indicated that they would rather spend money on things other than nicotine patches). The researchers then recruited a sample of individuals who were randomly assigned to two experimental groups. The situation of the diabetic patients was explained to all participants.

Individual members of the first group were then given 20 Swedish kronor (at the time of the experiment, one Swedish krona equalled 1 U.S. dollar) and told to divide the money between themselves and one of the diabetic smokers. Individuals in the second group were given the same amount of money and told that they were to divide the money between themselves and one of the diabetic smokers—and that their donation would be used to purchase nicotine patches to help the patient quit smoking. In all cases, neither the researchers nor other participants would know how much each person in the group chose to donate (eliminating any bias from a desire to appear generous in front of others). The donated money and nicotine patches were actually given to the patients, so subjects knew that their decisions would have real consequences for patients.

If people are pure altruists, interested only in the general well-being of others, the donations for the first group should equal or exceed those of the second group. In contrast, if they are paternalistic altruists who experience good-specific caring externalities for health care, the donations of the second group should exceed the first. The findings were as follows:

- Those in the second (nicotine-patch) group donated, on average, 41 percent of their money, while those in the first (money) group donated 29 percent.
- 13 percent of those in the money group donated more than 80 percent of their money, while 28 percent of those in the nicotine group did so.
- After finishing the experiment, 75 percent of those in the money group said they would have donated more if the money had been converted into nicotine patches; 81 percent of those in the nicotine group said that they would have donated less if the money had not been used to purchase nicotine patches.
- The researchers varied this design in a number of ways to test the robustness of the findings; in each case, the findings were consistent.

These findings support the idea that health care does generate good-specific externalities.

make intelligent health care choices on their own. What they seek most from a physician is information.

The physician's informational advantage over patients has profound implications for the functioning of health care markets. Well-functioning markets require that both buyers and sellers have sufficient information to enforce market discipline, and that, to the extent that informational problems exist, such problems are symmetric between buyers and sellers. When information is asymmetric—when one party has more relevant information than the other—the more knowledgeable party can exploit that informational advantage.

The Information Required for Efficient Decisions

Attaining the efficient level of health care consumption, at which the marginal benefit of care just equals the marginal cost, requires two distinct kinds of information:

1. information regarding the expected impact that a health care service will have on health
2. information regarding the value to the individual of that health improvement

Providers generally have better information regarding the effectiveness of health care services in improving health (i.e., of the health production function); but patients know better the value of a health improvement. Neither provider nor patient has the full set of information required. Yet, in order to make good decisions regarding health care utilization, we must somehow integrate these two types of information. When they are not integrated, a health care market generates inefficient outcomes: individuals may fail to obtain care because they are not well informed about its effectiveness, they may purchase care they would not have purchased if they'd had more information, or they may purchase care of differing quality than expected, and so forth. All of these "errors" represent inefficiency, or market failure.

Informed Patients: The Information Challenge

Why can't patients learn the required health care information, just as people do for many goods and services they buy? When making purchases, people generally inform themselves through one of two routes: through research using consumer report magazines or similar internet sources, and through experience by trying a good or service. A number of features of health care limit the potential for learning through each of these approaches.

Learning by Gathering Information   The technical complexity of the information as well as the impenetrability of much medical and scientific jargon inhibits, at least in part, learning through research. This technical barrier is distinct even from that faced with many modern technological goods. Buying a computer can present a mind-numbing onslaught of detailed technical specifications. In the end, however, if you know what tasks a computer will physically do, you can make a good choice. In health care, even if an individual happens to know how an MRI works, they will likely have difficulty knowing when they should have an MRI. The technical demands in health care are not about how to use a gadget but about *when* to use it. Furthermore, the urgency of many health care choices precludes serious research into alternative treatments.

Learning Through Experience   Learning through experience also presents problems. Even simple, seemingly innocuous health care interventions can create severe side effects, raising the risks and making us cautious about learning by unnecessary trial and error. And learning from experience is difficult even when we do undergo a treatment.

counterfactual problem
The difficulty in knowing what the outcome would have been had an alternative course of action (the counterfactual) been pursued.

One important barrier is called the **counterfactual problem** (Weisbrod 1978). To learn about the value of health care from experience, a person must know what would have happened had they not obtained the health care service, and vice versa. The person must know the counterfactual. It is often difficult, however, to know the counterfactual for health conditions. Many common conditions resolve themselves naturally without treatment. Those who obtain treatment sometimes mistakenly attribute the improvement to a health care service that actually had no effect, such as taking antibiotics to treat a viral respiratory infection.

The fact that the effectiveness of a specific health care service for a specific individual is inherently uncertain further compromises the ability of patients to become informed (Arrow 1963). Clinical research can demonstrate which health care services work on average—precisely the knowledge that physicians possess and that patients often do not. But even services that are highly effective on average, and that are provided in a high-quality manner, fail in some patients. This is an irreducible element of uncertainty faced by patients and providers, rooted in the unique genetic, biochemical, physiological, and psychological makeup of each person. This uncertainty makes it difficult to know whether the outcome occurred because of inappropriate or low-quality care or because of unavoidable, random variation in the effectiveness of services.

These problems are exacerbated by the fact that, except for routine conditions like colds and the flu, or chronic conditions such as arthritis or diabetes, many health care services are utilized infrequently, perhaps only once or twice in a lifetime. Hence, people do not have enough exposure to the service or the provider to learn from experience.

Policies to Address Asymmetry of Information

Problems associated with informational asymmetry between patients and providers are deep and not easily solved. Identifying effective approaches to overcome the problems associated with informational asymmetry is one of the most important areas of health economic and health services research.

licensure
A regulatory policy that requires an individual to pass a qualifying exam before being legally permitted to perform specified medical acts.

Professional Licensure   One regulatory response is professional **licensure.** We permit only individuals who have demonstrated a prescribed level of competence and knowledge to practice medicine. Without a valid license, it is illegal to provide defined medical services. Licensure, whether for physicians, nurses, optometrists, or any other health professionals, tries to ensure a minimum level of quality in the associated health care market.

physician agency
A principle that holds that in making treatment decisions a physician is to act in the interest of patients rather than out of self-interest, providing those services that the patients would want if they had the same medical knowledge as the physician.

Physician Agency   A second policy response is **physician agency.** A physician has the professional obligation to act as an agent for the patient, making recommendations that reflect both the patient's interests and the best evidence of the effectiveness of health care. This agency relationship creates role expectations that differ markedly from what we normally expect for suppliers of services. We assume suppliers in standard markets are wholly self-interested profit-maximizers. Consumers in the marketplace must watch out for their own interest—*caveat emptor.* Physician agency rejects this: the physician ideal is to put aside personal self-interest for the interests of the patient.

Physicians' training socializes them into the professional ethic of agency. In addition, many regulations in the health care market that reduce competitive pressures on physicians, such as limited entry and the prohibition against advertising, create an economic environment that enhances a physician's ability to act as patient agent rather than out of economic self-interest. Even so, physicians can never be perfect agents, because some self-interest is unavoidable and because they can never fully know patient preferences. Still, they are expected to strive for this ideal. The inability of physicians to realize this ideal is one reason many have attempted to provide patients with the requisite technical information, thereby integrating scientific evidence with the patients' values and preferences. Perhaps not surprisingly, this movement is strongest in areas where the direct effects of care on utility are comparatively large, affording a larger role for patient preferences. (See Box 7.4 for a discussion of informed patient decision-making.)

Informational Asymmetry and Market Power

Both informational asymmetry and the policy responses confer considerable market power on providers. A physician often becomes effectively both the demander and supplier of care: the physician both recommends specific services to a patient (which many accept without reservation) and provides the services. Physicians could use this market power to pursue their own self-interest, leading to inefficient market allocations (a phenomenon called supplier-induced demand, which we will examine in more detail in Chapter 8).

The potential abuse of market power to pursue self-interested financial gain underlies concerns that physicians will over-provide services when they are paid a fee-for-service and under-provide services when they are paid by capitation. Such activities need not be blatant or even conscious. If a physician has time available, for example, it is only natural to fill it providing services with positive but small value—services that that might not be performed in a busier practice. Asymmetry of information is an important source of market failure in health care.

In some clinical decision-making contexts, the health considerations are so unequivocal that virtually all patients will make the same choice because the treatment decision is obvious to everyone. For a person who suffers from appendicitis, surgery is the only treatment option, and the health impact is so dramatic (typically a return to normal health versus the likelihood of death) that, except in highly unusual circumstances, otherwise healthy individuals would always choose the appendectomy.

In other contexts, however, patients face multiple treatment options. Various treatments offer different risk and benefit profiles, both in the magnitude of risk and benefit, and in the specific ways that patients' health and lives may be affected by treatment. In addition, there might be uncertainty regarding the estimated risks and benefits. No single treatment is clearly superior.

In such settings, good treatment decisions depend on integrating technical information about treatment alternatives with patient preferences; the best treatment for an individual is closely linked to patient preferences. Rather than rely on the traditional physician-as-agent model, in which the physician must elicit and integrate information on patient preferences in recommending treatment, many advocate the reverse flow of information: they convey detailed information regarding risks and benefits to patients so that patients can integrate the information with their preferences to reach a decision.

Such approaches rely on evidence-based patient decision aids to convey relevant information in a manner that patients can understand and that is meaningful for the patient. The decision aids range from print materials, to specially designed "decision boards," to interactive videos, and increasingly, interactive Internet-based tools.

All of them draw on psychology, economics, sociology, decision theory, and other disciplines to convey information in an understandable, unbiased manner that helps patients assess it for their own situation and that helps them clarify their preferences.

Randomized control trials (in which some individuals are randomly assigned to use the aids while a control group of individuals does not) measure the effects of decision aids on treatment decisions and reveal that such aids increase patient knowledge, increase the proportion of patients with realistic perceptions of the risks and benefits, lower the decision conflict scores, and increase agreement between patient values and treatment decisions without negative effects on patient satisfaction or anxiety (O'Connor et al. 2004). The studies also reveal that patients who use decision aids systematically make different choices than those who do not use such aids. Studies of major elective surgery, for instance, indicate that in six of seven cases, a higher proportion of patients who use the decision aids opt for a less aggressive "watchful waiting" approach to care rather than immediate surgery (O'Connor et al. 2004). Though not a universal finding, physician-led treatment decisions tend to be more aggressive than those of well-informed patients.

Patient decision aids are being developed for an increasing range of medical conditions. Inventories of such aids that have been verified to be of high quality (both in terms of the quality of evidence presented and a balanced presentation of the information) can be found on the Web sites for the Ottawa Health Research Institute (http://decisionaid.ohri.ca/AZinvent.php), the U.S. National Cancer Institute, and the U.S. Centers for Disease Control and Prevention.

Asymmetry of Information and Economic Analysis

Asymmetry of information also has potentially important implications for positive and normative economic analysis in the health care sector.

Asymmetry of Information and Positive Economic Analysis

As we saw in Chapter 3, the standard methods of positive economic analysis assume that the supply and demand sides of a market are independent; the factors that determine demand are distinct from those that determine supply. If physicians influence both demand and supply, however, this assumption of independence is no longer valid. Models based on this assumption will make misleading predictions.

Health economists do not agree on the extent to which physician market power derived from asymmetry of information compromises the predictive ability of the standard economic model, and this lack of agreement fuels both scientific and policy debate. Those who view this market power as important argue that we must base health policies on models that explicitly take account of such power. Those who believe that the standard independence assumption sufficiently approximates the real world, however, argue that we should base policies on the predictions of the standard model. These differing views underlie much policy debate including questions of physician supply and physician payment policies.

Asymmetry of Information and Normative Economic Analysis Asymmetry of information also has important implications for normative economic analyses. The assumption that consumers are well informed is crucial for normatively interpreting the area under a demand curve as a measure of social benefit. If observed health care demand reflects poorly informed choices by an individual, or the preferences of the provider rather than the individual, the normative interpretation of the demand curve ascribed by welfare economics evaporates: the area under the demand curve no longer represents a valid measure of benefit.

Once again, health economists differ in their beliefs about the extent to which asymmetry of information compromises the standard normative model. In Chapters 9 and 10, we will see that debates about the normative interpretation of the demand curve play a central role in many policy debates surrounding the design of health care insurance.

7.2.4 Uncertainty

Illness and injury—the primary reasons for demanding health care—are largely random events. At the individual level, this uncertainty makes the demand for health care and the associated health care expenditures highly uncertain, thereby creating demand for health care insurance. As we will see in Chapter 9, health care insurance has the potential to make people better off by reducing the financial risks associated with obtaining health care and by expanding access to care.

The high prevalence of health care insurance (whether private or public) complicates the operation of health care markets in a number of ways. Most health care insurance lowers the price of care for patients, often making care free. The prices consumers face when making health care choices no longer reflect the cost to society of providing the service.

This creates the classic kind of distortion (whereby price does not reflect marginal cost) that leads to inefficiencies in resource allocation in standard markets. Assessing the efficiency effects of insurance-induced price reductions is a central concern of health economics. Furthermore, unlike normal market transactions that involve only a purchaser and seller, as discussed in Chapter 1, health care insurers often become active players in health care transactions, pursuing their own interests by shaping the behaviour of both patients and providers. "Managed care" in the United States and similar initiatives in other countries represent an attempt by insurers to influence the choices of patients and providers.

Because health care insurance exerts such a strong influence on the health care market, analysis of the health care sector must include insurance markets. Health care insurance markets are themselves subject to market failure. The analysis of such market failures will be the focus of Chapter 10.

7.2.5 Vulnerability to the Integrity of a Person

Many goods and services carry risks to our health and welfare. Health care, however, is unusual in its concentrated focus on our very being. People must often make health care decisions in highly stressful contexts. Their ability to function is compromised and they feel vulnerable; their sense of self may be under assault from disease, injury, or the health care itself. While this may not have direct economic implications, it affects the ability of individuals to make the thoughtful, reasoned choices assumed by economics; it affects the ethical, equitable allocation of health care; and it affects the mechanisms by which society governs access to and the allocation of health care resources.

7.3   IS HEALTH CARE DIFFERENT?

These characteristics of health care imply that health care markets are subject to many sources of market failure and that health care is of particular equity concern. Does this make health care unique? Not necessarily. Markets for many commodities fail. Further, many other goods and services share features with health care. We can view the demand for schooling, for example, as a derived demand—derived from the demand for knowledge. Externalities are pervasive and arise in many settings. Even caring externalities arise, in social policy and the justice system. Similar kinds of informational asymmetry exist for automobile repair and financial services. The widespread use of insurance for many goods (housing, automobiles, life, etc.) reflects uncertainty in many aspects of our lives. These issues are not unique to health care.

While many goods and services share at least one of these characteristics with health care, however, no other good or service appears to share all of them. The demand for education may be a derived demand, but it is subject to neither the uncertainty nor the informational problems associated with health care. Automobile repair is subject to considerable asymmetry of information, but it does not generate externalities as does health care.

The uniqueness of health care derives from the simultaneous presence of these features (see Table 7.1), and so do some of the most difficult economic challenges associated with health care. Economics has sophisticated models and frameworks by which to analyze each of these deviations from the idealized commodity of perfectly competitive markets. Well-developed economic literatures and models analyze externalities, insurance, and asymmetric information in detail.[2] Such models, however, nearly always consider only one or perhaps two features at a time. But they do not simultaneously integrate, for example, externalities, uncertainty, and asymmetric information. Dealing with all of these concurrently is one of the challenges facing sound economic analysis and sound policy formulation in the health care sector.

7.3.1   Economic Analysis in a Second-Best World

second-best
A situation in which it is not possible to correct all sources of market failure and in which correcting a single source may make matters worse.

In the health care sector, we often find ourselves in a **second-best** world with multiple sources of market failure. In such situations, fixing a single source of market failure while leaving the other(s) unaddressed does not necessarily improve things; indeed, fixing only part of the problem can sometimes actually make matters worse (the problem of the "second-best"). Policy mechanisms developed to address a problem when it occurs in isolation may either be ineffective or create unintended adverse effects when used in the presence of multiple sources of market failure.

Challenges in the insurance market illustrate these issues. The standard economic model of insurance assumes that the good being insured is sold in a perfectly competitive market with perfectly informed consumers and no externalities. In such a setting, the optimal response to insurance-induced over-consumption of the insured good (the price of which has been lowered by insurance) is to impose consumer cost-sharing. Cost-sharing requires an individual to pay a portion of the cost of insured goods and services they obtain. Automobile insurance, for example, normally requires that you pay a portion of the repair costs

---

[2] See, for example, texts on public economics, such as Leach (2004), Boadway and Bruce (1984), and Ng (1979).

TABLE 7.1 **A Comparison of Health Care with Selected Other Commodities**

	Education	Auto Repair	Financial Services
Derived Demand	Yes • derived demand for knowledge • reasonable understanding of the production function • substitution possibilities in many cases	Yes • derived from demand for transportation • often a "bad" that we would prefer to avoid • production function usually well-understood • substitution possibilities vary (e.g., alternative transportation options)	Yes • derived from demand for income/consumption • poor knowledge regarding production function (i.e., link between advice and financial success) • many substitution possibilities in many contexts
Externalities	Generally accepted • Good-specific	Minimal • Perhaps some selfish, safety-related externalities (e.g., "I hope your brakes work as I approach the intersection")	No
Uncertainty Demand	No	Yes • accident, breakdown	No
Effectiveness	Yes	Yes • probably more limited than in health care	Yes
Asymmetry of Information	Minimal if present	Yes—substantial • fewer learning problems than in health care	Yes—substantial
Vulnerability	No	No	Generally no, but perhaps in certain contexts, such as with the elderly

for a car following an accident. Cost-sharing aims to reduce unnecessary and frivolous use of insured services.

The desirability of such cost-sharing in the health care market is less obvious, however, given the asymmetry of information, market power by providers, and externalities associated with needed health care. Imposing cost-sharing reduces access to health care, and because of informational problems does not systematically reduce only frivolous use (Rice and Morrison 1994; Stoddart et al. 1993; Tamblyn et al. 2001). Hence, the standard policy response when uncertainty is the only problem does not carry over in a straightforward manner when uncertainty is only one of multiple sources of market failure.

7.3.2 Not All Health Care is Alike

We must temper the conclusion that health care is different from other goods with the recognition that health care is not a single, homogenous commodity. The health care sector includes a wide range of goods and services that vary considerably in the extent to which one or more of these features are present.

The demand for Botox injections does not derive from a demand for health. Such injections are not subject to physical or caring externalities, or uncertainty of demand.

The informational asymmetry faced in deciding whether or not to take a cold medicine is substantially less than in deciding whether or not to undergo brain surgery. The uncertainty regarding the effectiveness of repairing a broken bone is substantially less than uncertainty regarding the effectiveness of many types of cancer chemotherapy. The uncertainty in the coming year regarding the need for and expenditures on insulin for a diabetic is substantially less than the uncertainty regarding the need for antibiotics. In analyses of specific health care services, therefore, one or more of these characteristics may be particularly salient. In any given analysis it is important to assess the extent to which each characteristic may bear on the problem at hand.

Amid this heterogeneity, however, the basic truth remains that, as a set of goods and services whose primary purpose is to improve health, health care shares the five features discussed in this chapter; and good economic analysis of the health care sector must take them into account.

Chapter Summary

This chapter analyzed the nature of health care as an economic commodity. Important points include the following:

- The importance of the nature of health care as an economic commodity lies in its implications for
  - the efficient and equitable allocation of health care resources
  - the most appropriate models and methods for analyzing the health care sector
- From an economic perspective, the five most important characteristics of health care are that
  - demand for health care derives from the demand for health
  - externalities are generated by health care
  - informational asymmetries exist between providers and patients
  - there is uncertainty regarding both the need for and the effectiveness of health care
  - individuals are vulnerable at the time health care is consumed
- The derived nature of health care demand expands the scope for normative assessment of health care consumption and provides a basis for a meaningful concept of "need" in the health care sector.
- Externalities cause market failure and provide an economic rationale for governments to subsidize access to health care.
- Asymmetry of information causes market failure, motivates the notion of physician as patient agent, and undermines the assumption of independence between supply and demand in economic models of markets.
- Uncertainty regarding the need for health care generates a demand for health care insurance.
- The vulnerability of individuals in many health care encounters creates special ethical concerns and can compromise the ability of individuals to make decisions.
- None of these five characteristics is unique to health care, but a combination of all five in a single commodity is unique and creates special challenges both to the efficient and equitable allocation of health care and to the economic analysis of the health care sector.

Key Terms

appropriateness, *188*
caring externality, *190*
counterfactual problem, *193*
licensure, *194*

need, *188*
physical (selfish)
 externality, *190*
physician agency, *194*

second-best, *197*
small-area variation, *188*

End-of-Chapter Questions

For each of the statements below, indicate whether the statement is true or false and explain why it is true or false.

1. Uncertainty regarding the effectiveness of a specific health service for a particular individual is an important reason why patients have difficulty assessing quality of care.

2. A finding that Canadian hospitals are technically inefficient in producing operations is a good example of the kinds of efficiency analysis possible in health care that are not possible in other sectors.

3. The problem of informational asymmetry in health care markets can undermine the normative interpretation of the demand curve as representing marginal benefit.

4. Regulations that prohibit people from obtaining certain medications except by physician prescription are most likely a response to informational asymmetry.

5. Doctors who act as perfect agents for their patients will always provide care that is expected to improve patients' health.

6. The Internet has eliminated problems of informational asymmetry in health care.

7. A physician's ability to influence the consumption of health care services arises from externalities.

8. Uncertainty regarding the effectiveness of a car repair is less than that associated with health care treatment.

9. If we define a health care service as "needed" when the expected health effect for a person is positive, then society should ensure that all health care needs are met.

10. The concept of "need" in health care derives from the presence of externalities in health care markets.

References

Arrow, K. J. 1963. Uncertainty and the welfare economics of medical care. *American Economic Review* 53(5):941–73.

Boadway, R., and N. Bruce. 1984. *Welfare economics*. Oxford: Basil Blackwell.

Culyer, A. J. 1971. The nature of the commodity 'health care' and its efficient allocation. *Oxford Economic Papers* 23:189–211.

———. 1995. Need: The idea won't do—but we still need it. *Social Science and Medicine* 40(6):727–30.

Culyer, A. J., and H. Simpson. 1980. Externality models and health: A rückblick over the last twenty years. *Economic Record* 56:222–30.

Diehr, P., K. C. Cain, W. Kreuter, and S. Rosenkranz. 1992. Can small-area analysis detect variation in surgery rates? The power of small-area variation analysis. *Medical Care* 30(6):484–502.

Evans, R. G., and A. D. Wolfson. 1980. Faith, hope and charity: Health care in the utility function. Vancouver, BC: University of British Columbia, Discussion Paper 80–46.

Folland, S., and M. Stano. 1990. Small area variations: A critical review of propositions, methods, and evidence. *Medical Care Review* 47(4):419–65.

Health Council of Canada. 2009. *Value for money: Making Canadian health care stronger*. Toronto: Health Council of Canada.

Hurley, J. 2000. The normative economics of heath and health care. In *Handbook of health economics*, A. J. Culyer, and J. P. Newhouse (eds.). Amsterdam: Elsevier Science B. V. 56–118.

Hurley, J., S. Birch, G. Stoddart, and G. Torrance. 1997. Medical necessity, benefit and resource allocation in health care. *Journal of Health Services Research and Policy* 2(4):223–30.

Jacobsson, F., M. Johannesson, and L. Borgquist. 2007. Is altruism paternalistic? *Economic Journal* 117(520):761–81.

Leach, J. 2004. *A course in public economics*. Cambridge, UK: Cambridge University Press.

Morgan, S., C. Cunningham, G. Hanley, and D. Mooney. 2009. *The British Columbia Rx atlas, 2nd edition*. Vancouver, B.C.: Centre for Health Services and Policy Research, University of British Columbia.

Mushkin, S. J. 1958. Toward a definition of health economics. *Public Health Reports* 73(9):785–93.

Ng, Y. 1979. *Welfare economics: Introduction and development of basic concepts*. London: MacMillan.

O'Connor, A., H. Llewellyn-Thomas, and A. B. Flood. 2004. Modifying unwarranted variation in health care: Shared decision making using patient decision aids. *Health Affairs* Web Exclusive (October 7, 2004):VAR-63-VAR-72.

Pauly, M. 1988. Is medical care different? Old question, new answers. *Journal of Health Politics, Policy and Law* 13:227–37.

Pauly, M. V. 1992. Is medical care different? In *Issues in Health Economics*, R. D. Luke (ed.). Rockville: Aspen Systems. 3–24.

Rice, T. H., and K. R. Morrison. 1994. Patient cost sharing for medical services: A review of the literature and implications for health care reform. *Medical Care* 51(3):235–87.

Smith, R. 2007. Use, option and externality values: Are contingent valuation studies in health care mis-specified? *Health Economics* 16(8):861–9.

Stoddart, G. L., M. L. Barer, and R. G. Evans. 1993. *Why not user charges? The real issues*. The Premier's Council on Health, Well-being and Social Justice.

Tamblyn, R., R. Laprise, J. Hanley, M. Abrahamowicz, S. Scott, N. Mayo, J. Hurley, R. Grad, E. Latimer, R. Perreault, P. McLeod, A. Huang, P. Larochelle, and L. Mallet. 2001. Adverse events associated with prescription drug cost-sharing among poor and elderly persons. *Journal of American Medical Association* 285(4):421–29.

Tobin, J. 1970. On limiting the domain of inequality. *Journal of Law and Economics* 13(1):263–77.

Weisbrod, B. 1978. Comment on paper by Mark Pauly. In *Competition in the health sector: Past, present and future*, W. Greenberg (ed.). Washington: Bureau of Economics, Federal Trade Commission. 49–56.

Williams, A. 1978. Need—An economic exegeisis. In *Economic aspects of health services*, A. Culyer, and K. Wright (eds.). London: Martin Robertson. 32–45.

Wright, C., G. K. Chambers, and Y. Robens-Paradise. 2002. Evaluation of indications for and outcomes of elective surgery. *Canadian Medical Association Journal* 167(5):461–6.

Yaari, M. E., and M. Bar-Hillel. 1984. On dividing justly. *Social Choice and Welfare* 1:1–24.

Appendix 7

Chapter 7: The Nature of Health Care as an Economic Commodity

7.2   HEALTH CARE AS AN ECONOMIC COMMODITY

7.2.1   Demand for Health Care Is a Derived Demand

The concept and some implications of derived demand for health care can easily be derived from

$$U = u(HS(Z, HC), HC, X) \qquad \text{(7A.1)}$$

The impact of health care consumption on utility is

$$\frac{\partial U}{\partial HC} = \underbrace{\frac{\partial U}{\partial HS}\frac{\partial HS}{\partial HC}}_{a} + \underbrace{\frac{\partial U}{\partial HC}}_{b} \tag{7A.2}$$

The two-part term on the right side (a) of equation (2) is the indirect effect of health care on utility that operates through health care's effect on health status. This captures the sense in which the demand for health care is derived from the demand for health. If someone cares little about maintaining or improving their health, that is, if $\frac{\partial U}{\partial HS}$ is very small, then this source of demand for health care will be correspondingly small, no matter how productive health care may be in producing health. The second term (b) is the direct effect of health care on utility. This is usually, but not always, temporary or small relative to (a). Most public policy concern—and most of the analysis of this book—focuses on health care that has (or is expected to have) an impact on health status.

Need

A necessary condition for health care to be needed is that health care be effective. The effectiveness of health care in producing health is represented by the term $\frac{\partial HS}{\partial HC}$. Health care can be needed only if $\frac{\partial HS}{\partial HC} > 0$. If this marginal product is not positive, health care cannot improve health and well-being.

7.2.2   Externalities

Consider two people, A and B. If they are only self-interested—if they care only about their own health status and their own consumption of goods and services—then selfish, physical externalities can be represented as follows for person A:

$$U_A = u(X_A, HS_A(Z_A, HC_A, HS_B(Z_B, HC_B)), HC_A) \tag{7A.3}$$

The utility of person A depends, as is usual, on that person's consumption of other goods and services (X_A), as well as his or her health status (HS_A) and consumption of health care (HC_A). But A's health status also depends in part on B's health status (HS_B), which depends on B's consumption of health care (e.g., a flu shot).[1] The externality arises because A selfishly has no concern for B, per se; the only component of B's health care consumption that affects A's utility is that part that affects A's health.

Caring externalities, on the other hand, can be incorporated as follows. If we assume that A cares about B's health status, then

$$U_A = u(X_A, HS_A(Z_A, HC_A, HS_B(Z_B, HC_B)), HC_A, HS_B(Z_B, HC_B)) \tag{7A.4}$$

B's health care consumption now affects A's utility both indirectly (through A's health status, as before), and directly, as captured by the last term. Note that A does not care about B's consumption of health care, per se; what A cares about is B's health status. Hence,

---

[1] For the purpose of this illustration, ignore the fact that B's health status also depends on A's health status. We do this for two reasons. First, the impact of A's health status on B's health status operates through a communicable disease. If B catches the disease from A, then often A will already have been immunized and B's status as no impact on A (e.g., measles, mumps, and other conditions that you can get only once; it does not hold for some infections, such as many sexually transmitted diseases). Second, the point is intended as an illustration, not a complete analysis.

A cares only about B's consumption of health care such that it improves B's health (i.e., needed, effective health care).

7.2.3.   Informational Asymmetry Between Providers and Patients

From equation (2), other things equal, we see that the optimal consumption of health care depends on three factors: the impact of health care on health $\left(\dfrac{\partial HS}{\partial HC}\right)$; the utility of the health improvement induced by health care $\left(\dfrac{\partial U}{\partial HS}\right)$; and the direct effect of health care on utility $\left(\dfrac{\partial U}{\partial HC}\right)$. The physician has better knowledge of the first of these, $\left(\dfrac{\partial HS}{\partial HC}\right)$; but the patient has better knowledge of the impact of both health improvements, $\left(\dfrac{\partial U}{\partial HS}\right)$, and health care directly $\left(\dfrac{\partial U}{\partial HC}\right)$, on the patient's utility. The informational asymmetry regarding effectiveness gives physicians market power.

Optimal utilization requires that these three distinct pieces of information be integrated in decision-making. The model of physician agency attempts to do this by giving the physician responsibility for learning about patients' preferences—how they value health improvements as well as the direct impact of care on their utility—and for combining this with the physician's clinical knowledge to make a treatment recommendation. The patient decision-making model attempts to give patients the information they need about effectiveness so that they can integrate it with their preferences and make an informed choice.

Demand for Health Care and Health Care Insurance

This section begins with an analysis of the demand for health care, which draws heavily on the analysis of markets presented in Chapter 3. First, we use conventional demand concepts to examine various determinants of health care demand. Then we consider in detail the consequences of informational asymmetry between patients and providers for both the positive and normative analyses of health care demand. Of particular importance is the controversial concept of supplier-induced demand; Chapter 8 provides a detailed conceptual analysis of supplier-induced demand as well as a view of empirical attempts to measure it.

Chapter 9 expands on observations that the demand for health care is a derived demand for health, that health is subject to large random shocks, and that demand for health care in any given period is highly uncertain. This uncertainty in the demand for health care creates a demand for health care insurance. Chapter 9 provides a detailed economic analysis of the benefits people derive from health care insurance and the conditions under which they demand insurance.

Chapter 10 then asks how well private insurance markets can meet this demand for health care insurance. A full analysis of the welfare effects of insurance must consider both the effects that arise in insurance markets (by reducing the financial risk people face with respect to health care expenditures) and the effects that arise in the market for health care services (because insurance changes people's utilization of health care services). Market failures in markets for health care insurance are an important economic justification for the large public role in health care financing.

The Demand
for Health Care

Learning Objectives

After studying this chapter, you will understand

LO1 The determinants of an individual's demand for health care

LO2 Challenges to empirically estimating the demand for health care

LO3 Empirical evidence associated with the importance and role of the various determinants of demand for health care

LO4 The importance and implications of informational asymmetry for demand analysis

LO5 Supplier-induced demand, including its meaning, empirical analysis, and implications for policy

---

The analysis of health care demand informs a wide range of health care policies, such as the design of insurance systems for health care services, health human resource planning and policies to ensure the optimal number and distribution of health professionals, and policies designed to improve distributional equity in the use of health care.

The analysis of health care demand is one of the most debated areas of health economics. The debate arises from differing views regarding the extent to which informational asymmetry between patients and providers compromises the validity of standard demand analysis (discussed in Chapter 3). The vigour of the debate reflects the pivotal role of health care demand analysis in the design of many health care policies.

This chapter begins by distinguishing among three often confused concepts—need, demand, and utilization. The distinctions are essential for sound policy development. It then examines the determinants of health care demand as well as demand relationships among various health care services and providers, using the standard demand framework and highlighting the ways in which this framework can provide insight into the demand for health care and demand-side dynamics of health care markets. The chapter goes on to explore the implications of informational asymmetry for both positive and normative demand analysis in the health sector, with a particular focus on the concept of supplier-induced demand.

Health care markets in most societies are highly regulated, and health care insurance pays most if not all of the costs of care. Often in this chapter, you will have to imagine a world without such regulation, with little or no health insurance, and where health care prices are set by the interaction of supply and demand. Only by understanding the outcomes that would occur in such situations can we assess whether the current regulatory and insurance arrangements make economic sense.

8.1   NEED, DEMAND, AND UTILIZATION

utilization
The amount of health care that is consumed.

Much analysis and policy debate in health care fails to distinguish properly between need, demand, and **utilization**.

- Health care *need,* as we saw in Chapter 7, does not depend on individuals' preferences; rather, it depends on their health status, the availability of an effective service that can improve health, and social judgment as to what constitutes a need as opposed to a want.

- In contrast, health care *demand*—the expression of a desire to obtain a health care good or service given its price—does depend on individual preferences and resources.

- Health care *utilization* is simply the amount of health care actually consumed.

Need, demand, and utilization are causally related (Figure 8.1). Need is one determinant of demand; and demand, in interaction with supply-side factors, determines utilization, which is often the only one of the three that is directly observable.

Failure to distinguish among need, demand, and utilization can lead to poor policy analysis. At times, for instance, health human resources planning uncritically accepts observed patterns of utilization as representing need, rather than appreciating the fact that need is only one determinant of observed utilization. Also, analyses of income-related inequity of health care utilization that find a pro-rich bias even when care is free (controlling for need, the rich utilize more health care than the poor) assume that the cause lies with system barriers; they do not recognize that some of the bias may arise from differences in demand for care by those of differing incomes (as predicted by the health capital model of Chapter 5).

8.1.1   Categorizing Services by Need, Demand, and Utilization

The goal of most systems is to ensure that need for care gets expressed as a demand, resulting in utilization of care. But this does not always happen. Among the universe of possible health care exchanges (both realized and unrealized), we can distinguish those in which the care would be judged to be needed, those in which the care is demanded by an individual, and those in which the care is actually utilized (Figure 8.2).

The set of all services can be divided into seven categories according to whether they are needed, demanded, or utilized, where each category raises distinct policy problems.

Category 1 represents the health care bulls-eye—services that are needed, demanded, and utilized. A need is recognized, expressed through demand, and met by the delivery of care.

FIGURE 8.1
Causal Relationship Among Need, Demand, and Utilization
This figure depicts the causal relationship among need, demand, and utilization. Need is a determinant of demand; utilization arises from the interplay of demand and supply-side forces in the health care market.

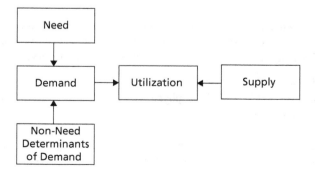

FIGURE 8.2

Need, Demand, and Utilization

This figure schematically represents the relationship among services that are needed, demanded, and actually utilized. It emphasizes that a given service can sometimes reflect all three (i.e., those that fall into (1)), but that this is not always the case. Services that fall into each of categories 1–7 present distinct policy problems and challenges. Distinguishing among the three phenomena is essential for economic analysis in the health sector.

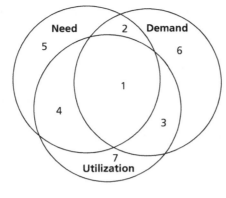

Category 2 includes services that bedevil many public health care systems today: services that are needed and demanded but not utilized due to a supply or other constraint. All those who wait unreasonably for care fall into this category—they have demanded a needed service but not yet received it.[1]

Category 3 includes services that are demanded and utilized but not needed. As noted in the last chapter, such unnecessary, inappropriate utilization constitutes a disturbing amount of inefficiency in health systems (Bentley et al. 2008).

Category 4 includes needed utilization that is not demanded. Although this seems impossible, it occurs in rare circumstances, such as when a Jehovah's Witness is ordered to have a blood transfusion against his or her wishes. Such care raises thorny ethical issues, but does not pose a major policy problem.

Category 5 includes needed care that is neither demanded nor utilized. Such unmet need normally is not registered by the system since there is no expressed demand. It arises for many reasons: individuals may not recognize their need and therefore not demand the service; they may recognize their need and desire care, but do not express a demand because of an inability to pay or another barrier to access; or they may recognize the need and have access to care, but prefer not to meet the need. The first and second represent important policy problems; the third, if fully informed, is an individual choice.

Category 6 includes services that are demanded but neither needed nor utilized. This represents an increasingly prevalent category of services due, for instance, to direct-to-consumer drug advertising that spurs people to request specific drugs from their physicians.

Category 7 includes services that are utilized but neither needed nor demanded. This is possible only if the demand is limited to that initiated by an individual. Under these circumstances, this category could represent unnecessary services provided by a physician in the absence of demand by a patient—a form of supplier-induced demand that we will analyze in detail below.

Because utilization is the only one of the three issues that is directly observable, it is often the starting point for gaining insight into both need and demand. To identify demand, the focus of this chapter, observed utilization must be purged of the influence of supply-side factors.

8.2   DEMAND FOR HEALTH CARE WITHIN THE STANDARD ECONOMIC FRAMEWORK

The standard demand framework provides a natural starting point for analyzing the demand for health care, though aspects of it must be modified to accommodate features of health care. We can analyze the demand for many different sets of services:

- all health care
- broad sets of services such as physician services, hospital services, dental services, drugs, or long-term care

---

[1] The qualifier "unreasonable" is important. A positive wait-time, even if short, is normally optimal. "Unreasonable" captures the notion of a wait beyond that which is appropriate given a person's clinical condition.

- specific subsets of goods or services within sectors, such as family practitioner services versus specialist services, prescription versus non-prescription drugs, or specific classes of drugs such as cholesterol-lowering drugs
- specific products or services such as MRI scans, a particular brand of cholesterol-lowering drug, and so forth

The scope and nature of services included in the analysis affects the relative importance of different demand determinants. The chapter focuses on the demand for health care as a whole, but it highlights differences across subsets of services where that is important.

When deciding whether to demand health care, people are assumed to pursue their own well-being in light of their health status; their preferences regarding health, health care, and other goods; the prices of goods and services; and their financial and other constraints. An individual's demand for health care can be represented as follows:

$$\text{Demand}_{HC} = F(\text{preferences, price}_{HC}, \text{price}_{sub}, \text{price}_{compl}, \text{income; health status; provider})$$

(8.1)

where

Demand_{HC}	=	demand for health care
Preferences	=	preferences over health, health care, and other goods and services
price_{HC}	=	price of health care
price_{sub}	=	prices of substitutes
price_{compl}	=	prices of complements
income	=	individual or household income
health status	=	health status of the individual
provider	=	the individual's provider

Note that, at this stage, we allow for possible provider influence on demand due to informational asymmetry but defer discussion of it until Section 8.3. We will consider each of these demand determinants in turn.

8.2.1 Health Status

Health status is, in general, the single most important determinant of an individual's demand for health care. Health status also plays a role distinct from other determinants: it affects the relationship between other determinants and health care demand. That is, the responsiveness of demand to the price of health care, prices of other goods, or income differs depending on the individual's health status.

8.2.2 Preferences

A number of distinct preferences influence demand for health care.

- Preferences over health: how much a person values good health
- Preferences over health care itself: some people dislike being poked and prodded by a health care professional, staying in a hospital, and other aspects of health care consumption. Other things equal, such people demand less health care.

risk attitude
The extent to which a person likes or dislikes risk. A person who likes to take risks is risk loving; a person who does not like to take risks is risk averse; a person who is indifferent is risk neutral.

- Preference regarding risk (**risk attitude**): health care outcomes, both positive and negative, are inherently uncertain. Deciding whether or not to obtain care often requires weighing positive and negative risks. Some individuals are more willing to risk a negative outcome for the chance to improve their health; others are less willing to take a risk, and in the same situation prefer a more conservative, watchful-waiting approach.

Preferences regarding health care and risk play an important role in determining the demand for a specific service, especially when a number of alternative treatments are available that offer similar effectiveness but different risk profiles (e.g., for side-effects).

8.2.3 Price of Health Care

The price of health care includes the money price and the non-money price. The money price is the financial cost of obtaining a health care service. The non-money price is primarily the time required to obtain a health care service. The time price can be important because much health care can be consumed only by being present for receipt of the service.

Money Price

The impact of money price on the quantity of health care demanded is measured by the own-price elasticity of demand (see Chapter 3 regarding elasticities). Estimating the price-elasticity of demand can be difficult in the best of circumstances, but it is even more difficult for health care than for standard commodities.

In health care, the money price often depends on the patient's insurance coverage, and the level of insurance coverage can be the result of personal choice. When an individual can choose how much insurance coverage to buy, the money price of care is (within bounds) under the individual's control. Other things equal, individuals who expect to need a lot of health care in the coming year are more likely to purchase health care insurance that provides generous coverage, both in terms of the scope of services covered and the proportion of the cost covered by the insurance company.

If we estimated a demand curve using data on the prices individuals pay out-of-pocket and the amount of health care they purchase, we get an incorrect answer that overestimates the price-elasticity of demand. To see this, suppose the following:

- There are only two types of people in a population, low-need and high-need.
- The money price paid for health care exerts no influence on the quantity of health care demanded; but high-need individuals, on average, purchase twice as much health care as low-need individuals.

- High-need individuals deliberately purchase more generous insurance coverage that, on average, lowers the money price more than does the insurance purchased by low-need individuals.

Statistical analysis would identify a negative correlation between the money price paid and the amount of care purchased (high-need individuals face a lower price and use more care); but this would be a spurious correlation, incorrectly suggesting that the lower price caused the increase in the quantity of care purchased. In fact, price exerted no influence: it is just that people who were more likely to get sick and use services purchased insurance that lowered the price.

RAND Health Insurance Experiment   Recognizing these problems, but wanting an estimate of the price-elasticity of demand for health care to guide the development of insurance policies, the United States government sponsored the RAND Health Insurance Experiment (Newhouse 1993). In the experiment, people were randomly assigned to different levels of health insurance coverage: 100 percent coverage (free care); 75 percent coverage (25 percent co-insurance); 5 percent coverage (95 percent co-insurance). By randomly assigning people to different levels of insurance coverage (and thereby to different money prices), the experiment ensured that the price people paid was unrelated to their expected health care utilization.

As demand theory predicts, health care utilization fell as the money price individuals paid increased (Table 8.1). Those in the free plan, for instance, saw a health professional an average of 4.55 times per year while those who paid 95 percent of the cost (up to a $1000 annual maximum expenditure limit) saw a health professional an average of 2.73 times per year. Expenditures on such out-patient care show a similar gradient. Those in the free plan had higher rates of admission to hospital than those who had to pay some of the cost, but the rates of admission did not differ notably among the 25 percent, 50 percent, and 95 percent plans.

As expected, overall the demand for health care is price inelastic, with demand for hospital care less elastic than is demand for out-patient care. The estimated price-elasticity of demand for out-patient care between free care and 25 percent co-insurance was estimated to be -0.13 (i.e., a 10 percent increase in price would cause the quantity demanded to fall by 1.3 percent); between the 25 percent plan and the 95 percent plan, it was estimated to be -0.21. The elasticities for all care (out-patient and in-patient) over these ranges were estimated to be -0.10 and -0.14 respectively (Manning et al. 1988).

While the randomized design of the experiment substantially increased the validity of the estimate of the influence of money price for those participating in the experiment, the

TABLE 8.1   **The Impact of Price on Health Care Use: Results from the RAND Health Insurance Experiment**

Insurance Plan	Out-Patient Care		In-Patient Hospital Care		Total
	Visits	Expenditures (1984 $U.S.)	Admissions	Expenditures (1984 $U.S.)	Expenditures (1984 $U.S.)
Free Care	4.55	340	0.128	409	750
25% Co-Insurance	3.33	260	0.105	373	617
50% Co-Insurance	3.03	224	0.092	450	573
95% Co-Insurance	2.73	203	0.099	315	540

Note: Visits are face-to-face contacts with physicians or other covered health professionals. Total expenditures do not exactly equal the sum of out-patient and in-patient expenditures because the total expenditures have been adjusted for the imbalance of the different plans across the sites of the experiment. See Manning et al. (1988) for further details.

Source: Manning, W. G., J. P. Newhouse, N. Duan, E. B. Keeler, A. Leibowitz, and M. S. Marquis. 1987. "Health Insurance and the Demand for Medical Care: Evidence from a Randomized Experiment." *The American Economic Review.* Vol. 77(3):251–277. Adapted from Manning et al. (1988), table 4.1, p. 19.

artificial nature of the study context has led many to question the external validity of the estimates as a guide for health systems policy. We will discuss this point in more detail in section 8.3.

Non-Monetary Costs of Care

Consuming health care normally takes time and resources (patients must travel to a clinic, wait for an appointment, and receive the care itself; and depending on the nature of the intervention, they may experience activity restrictions during the recovery period). When health care insurance pays for much of the money cost of care, non-money time costs can exert considerable influence on demand. And because the value of time varies directly with work status, wage rate, and other responsibilities, non-money costs vary among individuals, even when the amount of time associated with obtaining care is identical.

Hence, someone who works full-time at a high-paying job may exhibit relatively low money-price elasticity but very high time-price elasticity (since they have a lot of money but time is scarce), while a retired person living on a pension may exhibit high money-price elasticity but low time-price elasticity (since money is scarce but time is relatively plentiful).

The limited amount of empirical investigation into the effect of time costs confirms that such costs matter, especially when money prices are low. Acton (1975) examined demand for medical care in New York City, and estimated the elasticity of demand with respect to distance from the clinic (a proxy for time cost) to be -0.14. Coffey (1983) found that time price reduced the probability that a woman would use ambulatory medical services, and estimated the time–price elasticity to be -0.09. As is the case for the relationship between money price and demand, these elasticities are relatively low; but they indicate that a full understanding of demand must take these types of costs into account. Differences in non-money costs can play a particularly important role in the choice among alternative providers or services once a person has decided to seek care.

8.2.4 Prices of Substitutes and Complements

The lower the price for a substitute service, the smaller will be the demand for a particular health care service. Psychotherapy of comparable quality, for instance, can be provided by a psychiatrist or a clinical psychologist. Because the services of a psychiatrist (who is an MD) are often insured more generously than those of a psychologist, people demand more psychiatry services than would be the case if insurance coverage was equivalent for the two providers. Similarly, services are sometimes covered when received as a hospital in-patient but not when received as an out-patient or in the community. Such differential coverage skews utilization to in-patient settings. People who do not really need to be hospitalized may be admitted to obtain free access to services not covered on an out-patient basis.

Analagously, a drop in the price of a complementary good increases the demand for the good of interest. Prescription drugs and physician visits are complementary health care goods: an individual can obtain a prescription drug only by visiting a physician and obtaining a prescription. Consequently, the price people pay for drugs influences the rate of physician visits, just as the price of a physician visit influences the demand for drugs (see Box 8.1). Analagously, the costs of immunosuppressant drugs that a transplant recipient must take for their lifetime can exceed the cost of the transplant itself, causing the price of such drugs to influence demand for transplants.

Understanding patterns of health care utilization, therefore, requires that we consider all relevant prices, not just the prices of the specific services of interest. This is particularly

Physician services and prescription drugs are complements, which suggests that policies that affect the demand for one will affect the demand for another. In Canada, physician services are available free of charge as part of government policy to ensure equitable access to medically necessary physician services. Prescription drugs, however, are primarily privately financed. The government provides a tax subsidy to those who obtain private, supplemental drug insurance as an employment benefit: the government does not include value of the drug insurance benefit (provided by an employer to workers) when calculating a worker's income from employment.

Stabile (2001) investigated both the effect of the tax subsidy on demand for drug insurance and the impact of drug insurance coverage on the demand for physician visits. He found that the tax subsidy does increase the demand for private supplemental drug insurance: the elasticity of demand is approximately −0.3. He found that holding private drug insurance increased the demand for

publicly financed physician care by 10 percent. To verify that this was, in fact, due to the complementary nature of drugs and physician care, he also tested whether holding private dental insurance influenced the demand for physician care. Dental care and physician care are not complements so one would not expect to find a relationship, which is what Stabile found. Holding private dental insurance had no impact of utilization of physician services.

This analysis illustrates the complex nature of the relationship between the private and public elements in a health care system. Although the government fully subsidizes physician care so as to provide equal access for all citizens, because drugs are still predominantly privately financed—with the wealthy both more likely to hold private drug insurance and better able to afford drugs even in the absence of insurance—this skews actual uptake of physician services toward the wealthy.

important because insurance coverage varies across different providers and services in health care.

8.2.5 Income/Wealth

Income exerts influence on the demand for health care in three ways:

1. Individual (or household) income or wealth is a primary determinant of the ability to pay for health care, except where people can obtain care free of charge.
2. The investment demand for health care is positively related to an individual's earning ability. Following from the Grossman model discussed in Chapter 5, other things equal, the higher an individual's earning capacity, the more value they place on good health status (because the value of lost work time is higher).
3. The time cost of obtaining care increases with an individual's income.[2]

The income-elasticity of demand for health care is positive but small. The estimates fall in the range of 0.2 to 0.6 (Manning et al. 1987; Wagstaff 1986). Health care is, therefore, a "normal" good, but relatively income inelastic. This is consistent with the notion that health care is a necessity for which demand is determined primarily (though not exclusively)

[2] This relationship is somewhat muddied by the fact that higher-income earners are often paid by salary and have more flexible work arrangements than lower-income earners who are paid a wage and have fixed hours of work. In such cases, the real time cost to a higher-income earner can be less than that for a low-income earner.

by health status.[3] The low income-elasticity of demand at the individual level also likely derives in part from the fact that in most developed countries health care consumption is heavily subsidized by insurance, so that ability to pay is not a strong determinant of demand.

In contrast, aggregate cross-national studies find that a country's per capita income is the single most important determinant of a country's health care spending per capita. Such studies consistently find high income-elasticities: current estimates for the aggregate income-elasticity of demand are about 1.0 (Gerdtham and Jonsson 2000). Low individual-level income-elasticities and high aggregate elasticities are not necessarily incompatible findings. Health care consumption for most individuals is heavily subsidized by insurance, so the individual-level budget constraint is substantially relaxed. At the national level, however, the budget constraint always binds. Countries with higher incomes are able to better meet the health needs of their populations by devoting higher proportions of their economic resources to health care.

8.2.6 Strengths and Limitations of the Standard Model of Demand

The previous section emphasized the usefulness of the standard model of demand for thinking about demand for health care in a systematic, structured way. But as useful as it can be in many circumstances, the standard framework suffers from a serious limitation that can undermine its usefulness for both positive and normative economic analysis of health care markets: it assumes no informational problems.

As discussed in Chapter 7, health care is often characterized by high levels of informational asymmetry between patients and providers. Once this information asymmetry is integrated into the analysis, some principal conclusions of the standard framework no longer necessarily hold. Therefore, while the standard model of demand is useful for understanding aspects of health care demand, the model must be used carefully, with a full understanding of its limitations in health care. At times, it must be modified to accommodate special aspects of health care markets.

8.3 INFORMATIONAL ASYMMETRY AND THE DEMAND FOR HEALTH CARE

supplier-induced demand

At its most general, an individual's demand for care that arises at least in part from the influence of the individual's care provider.

Asymmetry of information gives providers market power. Providers can use their market power to influence the demand for their services, a phenomenon referred to as **supplier-induced demand**; hence the inclusion of "provider" as a demand influence in equation (8.1). There is much confusion in the literature as to what constitutes supplier-induced demand and the welfare implications of induced demand. The different definitions fall roughly into two categories (Labelle et al. 1994): positive definitions and normative definitions. Positive definitions stress simply the ability of physicians to shift the demand curve (for better or for worse). Normative definitions, in contrast, stress the financial self-interest of physicians in providing unnecessary services. Perhaps the most commonly cited definition of supplier-induced demand is very much in this spirit: services that are provided

---

[3] Controlling for health status is essential to obtaining valid income-elasticity estimates. On average, those with higher income are healthier (Chapter 6). A simple comparison of health care utilization by people with different income levels (unadjusted for health status) often reveals that total health care utilization is lower among those with higher incomes. But, controlling for health status, those with higher income consume more health care.

in response to a provider's economic self-interest, but that a patient with the same knowledge as the provider would not demand. In this view, all supplier-induced demand is bad.

Labelle et al. (1994) instead stress the heterogeneous nature of supplier-induced demand and the need for a more nuanced understanding of the phenomenon. Much supplier-induced demand is efficient and desirable: the provider, acting as agent, recommends needed care that a poorly informed patient would not otherwise have demanded. The physician motive does not matter in this case: the delivery of good-quality, effective care may or may not be motivated by self-interest. Labelle et al. recommend that investigations of supplier-induced demand ask two questions:

1. Would the patient have demanded the service if he or she had the same information as the physician?
2. Did the service contribute positively to the patient's health status?

The first question pertains to the effectiveness of the agency relationship, the second to the effectiveness of the services provided. These questions lead to four possible outcomes (Figure 8.3), each of which may call for a different policy response.

i. If the answer to both questions is yes, the physician acted in the patient's interest and the patient's health was improved; this is a good outcome. Note that even this case does not ensure that the utilization is efficient: the benefit could be small relative to the cost of the services.

ii. If the answer to the first is no but the second is yes, the physician and patient disagree. The services do improve health, but the patient does not value those health gains. Such care may commonly arise near the end of life.

iii. If the answer to the first is yes but the second no, the outcome reflects poor information on the part of the provider, the patient, or both.

iv. If the answer to both is no, this approaches the pejorative type of supplier-induced demand that has been the focus of much debate: the provider is not acting as agent, and is recommending services that are ineffective or even harmful.

The consequences of inducement differ, therefore, depending on the type of inducement.

Most health economists acknowledge that physicians have the power to shift demand (Feldman and Morrissey 1990). There would seem to be two crucial issues. Where does such inducement fall in Figure 8.3? And can physicians systematically exploit this power for their own economic advantage (and potentially to the detriment of patients), especially in response to health care policies? The empirical literature on supplier-induced demand focuses on the latter question.

FIGURE 8.3 **A Framework for Supplier-Induced Demand**
This figure presents a framework for thinking about and examining supplier-induced demand that goes beyond the traditional focus on self-interested physician responses to financial incentives. It emphasizes the importance of the concepts of agency and effectiveness for the analysis of supplier-induced demand. The Roman numerals in each cell relate to the different types of inducement listed in the text.

Source: Adapted from Labelle et al. (1994), Figure 1, p. 354

	Effectiveness: Did the service contribute positively to the patient's health status?	
	Yes	No
Agency: Would the patient have demanded the service if the patient had the same information as the physician? — Yes	(i)	(iii)
No	(ii)	(iv)

8.3.1 Measuring Supplier-Induced Demand

Roemer's Law
"A bed built is a bed filled." An adage that reflects the fact that in the presence of full insurance, capacity often defines the level of facility utilization.

The extent and policy importance of supplier-induced demand has been one of the most debated issues in health economics. The notion was born during the 1960s and early 1970s when health care analysts noted a number of phenomena that suggested providers exerted considerable control over the utilization process. These phenomena included a tendency for new facilities to be used seemingly without regard to the baseline supply already in place. (This tendency is immortalized in **Roemer's Law**: "A bed built is a bed filled" (Roemer 1961); a positive correlation between physicians per capita and utilization per capita (Evans 1974); and the surprising capacity of urban areas to absorb ever-increasing numbers of physicians without adversely affecting physician incomes in those areas.)

The concept of supplier-induced demand, even interpreted in the purely positive sense of the power to shift demand, is controversial for a number of reasons. The phenomena that first led to the hypothesis are consistent with alternative explanations; and, as we will see below, unambiguously identifying supplier-induced demand is difficult if not impossible. Further, supplier-induced demand undermines the standard model of demand: if supplier-induced demand is important, demand and supply are not independent, and both positive and normative economic analyses based on the standard model are misleading.

Although the conceptual debate about supplier-induced demand tends to be framed normatively, in terms of physicians providing unnecessary services in response to self-interested economic motives, empirical tests for supplier-induced demand have been limited almost exclusively to testing whether or not physicians have the power to shift demand. Dozens and dozens of studies since the 1970s have attempted to identify utilization patterns that are consistent with supplier-induced demand but inconsistent with the standard economic model. Achieving even this modest goal is difficult because, even at the conceptual level, a model with supplier-induced demand predicts very few outcomes that the standard model could not generate once we account for all the factors that can affect demand and supply (McGuire and Pauly 1991; Reinhardt 1978). Even when such outcomes can be identified, data limitations often preclude a definitive test. Nonetheless, economists have displayed remarkable creativity in devising tests for induced demand.

Testing for inducement requires a variation (across physicians or time) in some aspect of the physicians' practice environment that creates an incentive to induce demand. The most common sources of such variation are with respect to physician supply or payment policies. Table 8.2 lists some conditions conducive to testing for inducement. Below, we discuss a selected number of studies that represent different basic approaches used by economists to test for inducement.

Exploiting Variation in Physicians' Incentive to Induce Demand

Most early attempts to identify supplier-induced demand used aggregate data on physician utilization and physician supply across regions to test if greater physician supply (which would exert downward pressure on individual physician incomes) was associated with greater use per capita. This is perhaps the most difficult way to identify supplier-induced demand, but it was all that the data allowed at the time. To understand the challenges, imagine an analyst has data, by county, on the annual rate of utilization of physician services and the supply of physicians. The analysis reveals that counties with more physicians per capita also have higher per capita rates of utilization of physician services. Does this prove supplier-induced demand? No. To see why, suppose that

- Physicians in the three counties practise medicine in exactly the same way; i.e., they treat identically all patients with the same need.

TABLE 8.2
Conditions
Conducive to Testing
for Inducement

Some conditions conclucive to testing inducement include the following:

- The source of the variation in the incentive to induce should be beyond the control of physicians and should not be correlated with other changes in the practice environment that could also lead physicians to change behaviour. Otherwise, it is not possible to establish which factor caused observed changes in behaviour.
- The forces that generate the variation in incentive to induce should not affect patients' demand for care. Otherwise, it is impossible to know if changes in utilization derive from physician behaviour or from patient behaviour.
- An ability to examine a variety of contexts of care for which the likelihood of inducement differs even when physicians face the same financial pressure to do so, such as:

Across types of service

- Services that require a lot of physician time and effort (e.g., psychotherapy) versus those that require little time and effort (e.g., ordering and interpreting diagnostic tests)
- Services for which the clinical indications for appropriate provision are well-established (e.g., carotid endarterectomy among those with severe blockage of the carotid artery) versus those for which there is considerable scope for physician judgment (e.g., hysterectomy, MRI)
- Services for which the volume of cases is beyond the control of physicians (e.g., childbirth, setting broken bones) versus those for which physicians can influence level of use (number of visits)
- Services that pose high risks to patients (e.g., complex surgery) versus services that pose few, small risks (e.g., extra follow-up visits)

Across types of people:

- Those for whom informational problems are likely to be minor (e.g., family members of physicians) versus those for whom they are large (general public)
- An ability to examine variety of ways that physicians might induce demand, such as:
  - See more patients
  - See patients more often
  - Provide more services during a visit
  - Substitute more-profitable services for less-profitable services

- Populations in the three counties are identical in all respects except for health status. Those in County 1 have better health status than those in County 2, who have better health status than those in County 3.

The differing levels of health status cause demand for health care to differ across the three counties (D_1, D_2, and D_3 in Figure 8.4(i)), generating the observed positive correlation between utilization per capita and physician supply (points A, B, C). The underlying differences in health status cause both the increase in demand per capita and the increase in the quantity supplied per capita. The positive correlation between the two is fully consistent with the standard theory of demand.

But even if the analyst was able to control perfectly for differences in health status, there is still a problem: differences in physician supply can affect the non-money costs of obtaining care. Other things equal, residents of regions with higher physician density may face smaller time costs due to the increased availability of physicians. This "availability effect" would shift the demand curve outward, resulting in a positive correlation between physician supply and utilization per capita through a mechanism other than supplier-induced demand (Figure 8.4(ii)).

To identify supplier-induced demand, the analysis must control for all determinants of demand and supply that could influence utilization through channels other than

FIGURE 8.4

Does a Correlation Between Utilization and Physician Supply Imply Self-Interested Supplier-Induced Demand?

(i) If three regions are identical in all respects except for health status, a simple analysis of the relationship between the supply of providers per capita and utilization per capita would find a positive relationship. But this relationship is rooted in the differing needs for care (and hence, demand) across the regions, not supplier-induced demand. (ii) Even where underlying health status is the same, reduced time costs would shift the demand curve outward in regions with greater physician supply, again resulting in a positive correlation between utilization per capita and physician supply.

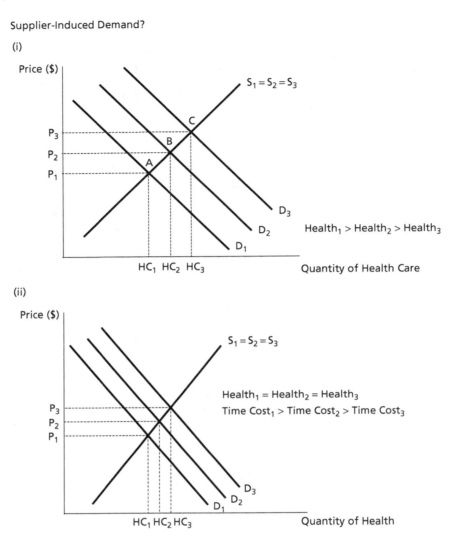

Supplier-Induced Demand?

(i)

(ii)

cross-sectional design
Research studies that use variation across units (people, jurisdictions, etc.) at a single point in time to investigate the phenomenon under study.

supplier-induced demand. If an analysis cannot do this, then it is impossible to know if variation in utilization is driven by self-interested supplier-induced demand or some other factor—such as variation in health status, or variation in the non-money cost of obtaining care—that could generate the same pattern within the standard model for demand.

Fuchs (1978) and Cromwell and Mitchell (1986) are two seminal studies that used this aggregate, **cross-sectional design** to test for inducement of surgeries, which are not likely to be strongly influenced by time costs. Using sophisticated statistical techniques in an attempt to overcome other potential problems associated with the approach, the studies found evidence of supplier-induced demand. Even after controlling as well as possible for alternative explanations, rates of surgery were higher in regions with more surgeons per capita. However, a subsequent a test of the validity of the statistical methods they employed concluded that the methods might not be reliable (Dranove and Wehner 1994). The test applied the statistical methods to a context in which supplier inducement is not possible: number of childbirths. And even though physicians have little or no influence over the number of women who become pregnant,[4] the results of the statistical analysis suggested that physicians induced demand for childbirths.

This and other related methodological critiques have led many to conclude that tests of supplier-induced demand are not reliable when they are based on regional variation in aggregate utilization per capita and physicians per capita.

More recent cross-sectional studies have exploited variation among individual physicians, commonly among physicians whose practices differ in size and therefore the ability to generate income (Grytten and Sorensen 2007; Grytten and Sorensen 2008; Iversen 2004; Iversen and Luras 2000). In some cases, researchers even had information on whether a physician's practice was larger or smaller (in terms of number of enrolled patients) than desired by the physician. The researchers hypothesized that physicians with practices smaller than desired would provide more services per patient in an attempt to maintain their income. Although the results were somewhat mixed, overall they were not supportive of supplier inducement: the analyses that control best for possible determinants of utilization do not find the expected negative relationship between practice size and service per patient.

One of the best cross-sectional study designs in the inducement literature is that of Hickson et al. (1987), who used a prospective experimental design that randomly assigned pediatric resident physicians to receive fee-for-service or salary payment. Compared to salary payment, fee-for-service payment creates incentive to provide more services to patients. This study found that those paid a fee for service scheduled more visits per patient and saw their patients more often. Most of the additional visits were to well patients (in this case babies), some of which were in excess of the number of visits recommended by the American Academy of Pediatrics.

Exploiting Variation Across Time in the Incentive to Induce Demand

An alternative approach, **time-series design**, exploits variation across time to identify inducement. Such an approach can be used to examine situations where the supply of physicians changed in a region during a period in which there is no reason to believe that the underlying needs of the population had changed. As before, we must control for underlying need: physician supply may have increased in response to previously unmet need. Once again, it is important to consider the availability effect.

A classic Canadian study of physician services in Manitoba used such an approach and found evidence of substantial physician responses to increased supply (see Box 8.2). More recently, a **panel design** study in France tested for inducement among a sample of French physicians over a 14-year period during which physician supply increased dramatically (Delattre and Dormont 2003). By following a panel of individual physicians over a relatively long period of time, the study was able to control for physician-specific attributes in a way not possible using cross-sectional data. The study found evidence for inducement: increases in supply were associated with a decreased number of consultations but an increase in the number of services provided per encounter.

Rice and Labelle (1989) argue that **natural experiments or quasi-experiments** caused by abrupt changes in payment policies provide the cleanest, most direct test of supplier-induced demand possible with observation data. A quasi-experiment occurs when there is an important change in policy (ideally both unanticipated and not linked to other

time-series design
Research that uses variation within the units under study (people, jurisdictions) over time to investigate a phenomenon.

panel design
Research that follows a number of units (people, jurisdictions) over time, and that can exploit both cross-sectional variation at each point in time and time-series variation over a number of periods to investigate the phenomenon under study.

natural experiment or quasi-experiment
Research that exploits a discrete, measurable change in an environment, often the result of policy reform, that can be used to identify the effect of the change on an outcome of interest.

---

[4] The development of in-vitro fertilization and other fertility treatments imply that this is no longer strictly true, but such effects are quantitatively trivial, and were especially so during the period analyzed by the study. Note also that although the number of births is beyond physicians' control, the type of birth (vaginal versus Caesarean section) is not. In fact, a supplier-inducement study found that the relative proportion of vaginal and Caesarean births is responsive to their relative medical fees (Gruber and Owings 1996).

A study of how physicians responded to steady growth in physician supply in Winnipeg, Manitoba, illustrates how utilization patterns can change in response to large changes in supply over a relatively short period.

In the ten-year period 1971–1981, the number of physicians per capita in the province of Manitoba increased by 26.8 percent, while the number of general practitioners per capita in its principal city, Winnipeg, increased by 56 percent. There is no reason to believe that the underlying need in the population changed during the period. Remarkably, however, real gross income per physician remained virtually unchanged even though physician density increased by more than 50 percent.

How did physicians do this? Solo general practitioners tended to do this by "sharing" their patients more. On average, each patient saw more physicians in 1981 than in 1971 so that, based on the number of visits, the average patient load of solo general practitioners increased over the period (with the same patient appearing in more than one physician's practice). In contrast, group practice general practitioners simply increased the number of contacts with existing patients—so much so that their average revenue actually increased. In each case, general practitioners appear to have adjusted their practice patterns to compensate financially for their increasing density (Roch et al. 1985).

The study did not control for all possible influences, such as previous unmet need or reduced non-monetary costs, so the findings are not definitive; but most analysts have attributed a large part of the change to physician behaviour.

system changes) imposed on some physicians but not others. The impact of a policy can then be identified by comparing changes in behaviour between those who experienced the policy change and those who did not.

A change in physician fees (which are beyond the control of physicians) exerts unambiguous economic impact on a medical practice. Further, unlike changes in physician supply, fee changes do not affect non-money costs to patients and, if services are fully insured, also does not change patients' money costs. A series of studies of fee changes in the U.S. (Medicare) and in Canada have used this approach to identify physician responses consistent with supplier-induced demand.

Rice (1983; 1984) examined the effect of a change in fees paid to physicians by the U.S. Medicare program in the state of Colorado in 1977 in which fees paid to non-urban physicians increased substantially while fees to urban physicians remained virtually unchanged. Rice found that in response the urban physicians increased their provision of surgical services and laboratory tests, and provided a more complex bundle of medical and surgical services.

A series of studies also examined physician responses to a change in U.S. Medicare policy in the late 1980s that increased fees for a number of services that had previously been under-valued, and decreased fees for a number of services that had previously been over-valued. Overall, the results are mixed. Escarce (1993a; 1993b; 1993c) found little evidence of strategic response to the reductions in payment rates for selected over-valued services, but Yip (1998) found evidence that surgeons whose incomes were most reduced by the reduction in Medicare fees increased the number of surgeries performed on both Medicare patients and private-sector patients.

Periods of overall fee freezes or substantial restraint in the rate of growth in fees in both Canada and the U.S. indicate that physicians can respond to such attempts at cost control by increasing the number of services they provide (thereby thwarting the goals of the policies) (Barer et al. 1988; Hadley et al. 1979; Holahan et al. 1979; Mitchell et al. 1989).

Finally, changes in physician payment policies in Quebec during the 1980s, which alternately imposed and relaxed limitations on the total amount Quebec physicians were allowed to bill the province, provide an excellent natural experiment for studying physician behaviour. Two studies that examined the effect in detail (Nassiri and Rochaix 2006; Rochaix 1993) showed that physicians responded to downward pressure on their income by adjusting both the number and mix of services they provided.

The Supplier-Induced Demand Debate Today

After 40 years of extensive testing, many researchers have concluded that irrefutable evidence of supplier-induced demand will likely never emerge (Fuchs 1986). It is difficult to create a test that definitively separates supplier-induced demand from a standard market outcome, and limitations of the available data always leave room for debate. Even those who believe that self-interested supplier-induced demand exists and can be large enough to be of policy importance recognize that such behaviour is neither automatic nor mechanical. Both providers and the markets for provider services are complex, responding to many facets of their environments. In the end, no clear-cut picture emerges. It is not correct to argue that self-interested supplier-induced demand does not (or cannot) exist and, therefore, that the standard model of demand and market behaviour can be used with complete confidence. It is also incorrect to say that self-interested, supplier-induced demand is ever-present and will foil any and all policies that rely on market signals. The challenge is to identify those contexts in which it will manifest as an important problem.

8.3.2 Implications of Supplier-Induced Demand

The debate over supplier-induced demand is vigorous, in part because of its implications for positive and normative economic analysis of health care markets.

Supplier-Induced Demand and Positive Economic Analysis

Predictions regarding the effect of physician supply policies, physician payment policies, and user charge policies have important differences, depending on whether or not we believe self-interested supplier-induced demand is empirically important.

Physician Supply Policies   For decades, rural and remote areas of all countries have experienced persistent shortages of physicians. Within the standard market model, a logical policy response to this shortage is to increase the supply of physicians. As the supply increases, markets already reasonably well served will become saturated, physician incomes in those markets will fall, and more physicians will migrate to rural and remote areas where income opportunities are better. The natural dynamics of the market will alleviate shortages. If, however, physicians can engage in self-interested supplier-induced demand, this standard market dynamic breaks down. Supplier-induced demand makes it feasible for physicians to maintain practices in well-served urban areas even while physician density increases, blunting the policy's effect on shortage areas. As a result, even when the supply of physicians increases, the gains in under-served markets will be small and will come at a disproportionately high cost, making this policy economically unattractive.

Physician Payment Policies   When physicians are paid a fee for each visit, procedure, or service they provide (fee-for-service) and patients are fully insured for the cost of care, a standard economic model predicts that restraining fee increases will control overall physician expenditures. If physicians can induce demand, however, controlling fees may be insufficient to control expenditures because physicians can increase demand to offset fee constraints. Even though fees are controlled, overall expenditures are not. While physicians' power to induce demand is not unlimited, evidence cited earlier indicates that physicians can respond to fee controls by increasing utilization (Barer et al. 1988; Hadley et al. 1979).

The persistent rise in expenditures even in the face of fee controls prompted most Canadian provincial governments in the 1990s to impose fixed budgets in the physician sector. If utilization grew so that expenditures at current fee levels exceeded this budget, fees were reduced proportionately so that expenditures did not exceed the budget (Hurley et al. 1996; Hurley and Card 1996).

The Design of Insurance   A major policy concern associated with health care insurance, which reduces the price of care to individuals, is over-utilization of health care (Chapter 9 will provide a detailed analysis of this issue). A policy recommendation based on standard market analysis would be demand-side cost-sharing, whereby patients pay more money out-of-pocket to obtain care, reducing the amount of care utilized.

The primary purpose of the RAND Health Insurance Experiment was to estimate how responsive the quantity demanded is to increases in cost-sharing, so as to guide the development of insurance policy in the United States. But if supplier-induced demand is important, the impact of system-wide user charges may be quite different than suggested by the results of the RAND Health Insurance Experiment. If system-wide user charges cause all individuals to reduce their demand for physician visits, this will cause a corresponding decrease in physician incomes. Where possible, physicians may respond to this fall in income by inducing demand. The net effect of the user charge policy on utilization, therefore, may be substantially less than predicted by standard demand analysis. The RAND Health Insurance Experiment could not identify any such potential response because experiment participants constituted only a small fraction of any single physician's practice. As a result, the reduction in visits by participants who faced increased cost-sharing did not exert any economic pressure on physicians.

Asymmetry of Information and the Normative Interpretation of Demand

In the standard demand framework, two ethical assumptions cause the demand curve to represent the social benefit of consumption: (1) consumer sovereignty—individuals are the best judges of their own welfare and have the information required to judge the impact of a good or service on their welfare; and (2) an individual's willingness to pay for a service is the appropriate measure of social value.

Informational asymmetry invalidates the assumption of consumer sovereignty. There is no guarantee that observed utilization accurately reflects well-informed choices based on individual preferences. If made by an individual, observed choices may be poorly informed; if informed by a provider, observed choices may reflect a mixture of both provider and patient preferences rather than patient preferences alone. Hence, even if we accept willingness to pay as a measure of social value in health care, informational asymmetry can invalidate the normative interpretation of the demand curve as a measure of social benefit.

This undermines the standard economic approach to assessing the efficiency of insurance-induced health care consumption. Insurance that lowers the price of care may cause individuals to over-consume care—consume care for which the marginal cost of production exceeds the marginal benefit. With fully informed individuals, cost-sharing selectively reduces the use of low-benefit, "frivolous" care. With poorly informed individuals, however, cost-sharing does not reduce the use of frivolous care only. Patient cost-sharing decreases both necessary and unnecessary health care utilization.

The RAND Health Insurance Experiment, for example, revealed that cost-sharing reduced both effective care and ineffective care (or care of marginal effectiveness), leading the researchers to conclude, " . . . cost-sharing did not seem to have a selective effect in prompting people to forgo care only or mainly in circumstances when such care probably would be of little value" (Lohr et al. 1986). We will return to this issue in more detail when examining insurance markets (Chapter 10).

8.3.3   Summing Up: Demand, Supplier-Induced Demand, and Asymmetry of Information

The debate surrounding supplier-induced demand has consumed more of health economists' energy than perhaps any other issue in the field. After reaching a feverish pitch in the 1980s, the debate has subsided—possibly because it is unresolvable. The challenges of unequivocally proving its existence, or lack thereof, are daunting; and interpretation of the results is heavily influenced by the preconceived attitudes of the opposing sides (Reinhardt 1985).

Rigid views on either side are unwarranted. Too much evidence is consistent with self-interested supplier-induced demand to dismiss the notion as irrelevant to health care policy; but too much evidence also demonstrates that providers do not easily and automatically exert their market power to counter policy initiatives or more general market conditions.

Chapter Summary

This chapter has examined a range of issues associated with the demand for health care. The major points are as follows:

- It is crucial to distinguish among the related concepts of need, demand, and utilization. This is especially so in empirical analysis, for which only utilization is directly observable.
- Demand analysis can be conducted for health care as a whole, for specific sectors in health care, or for specific services or providers. The importance of different determinants on demand varies depending on the level of analysis and the specific services being examined.
- The standard economic demand framework, which rests on a model in which people make choices to maximize their well-being, posits that the demand for health care will depend on individual preferences regarding health, health care and other goods, the price of health care, the prices of substitutes and complements, income, and health status.
  - Health status is the most important determinant of demand for health care.
  - The own-money price-elasticity is negative and demand is inelastic. The elasticity is generally higher for specific health care goods and services than for health care as a whole.
  - Elasticity with respect to time price is also negative and inelastic.
  - Individual level income-elasticities are small; aggregate income-elasticities are in the range of 1.0.
- While the standard model of demand can often provide useful insight, it must be used with care because asymmetry of information can invalidate both positive and normative analyses based on the standard model.
- Asymmetry of information can invalidate standard assumptions about well-informed consumers.
- Asymmetry of information and the associated agency relationship give providers considerable market power, leading to a dependence between the supply and demand sides of a market.
- The demand curve may not accurately represent social benefit, invalidating standard normative analysis.
- Asymmetry of information can generate supplier-induced demand for health care.
  - Much induced demand is efficient if it reflects well-functioning agency relationships.
  - Economic analyses have particularly emphasized self-interested supplier-induced demand in which providers exploit their market power for their own advantage.

- Empirically identifying supplier-induced demand is extremely difficult. A large number of studies find evidence of supplier-induced demand while a similarly large number find no evidence.
- The empirical evidence demonstrates that providers can induce demand for care for economic reasons; that they sometimes do so in response to policy reforms, but that such responses are neither automatic nor mechanical; and that we do not have a good understanding of the conditions under which providers will respond in such ways.

Key Terms

cross-sectional design, *218*
natural experiment or
   quasi-experiment *219*
panel design, *219*

risk attitude, *210*
Roemer's Law, *216*
supplier-induced
   demand, *214*

time-series design, *219*
utilization, *207*

End-of-Chapter Questions

For each of the statements below, indicate whether the statement is true or false and explain why it is true or false.

1. Even when care is free at the point of service, we expect low- and high-income individuals with the same level of need to demand different quantities of health care.
2. Emergency rooms and walk-in clinics are close substitutes.
3. The demand curve for health care provides a good measure of the benefits of health care to a consumer.
4. Suppose the following is true: physicians choose their practice size based on the style of medicine they prefer to practise, with those who prefer longer consultations with patients opting for smaller practices. Patients choose their physician based in part on the physician's practice style, with patients who prefer longer consultations joining the practices of physicians who offer such care.

   If a researcher testing for supplier-induced demand by comparing the types of services provided by physicians with different practice sizes fails to adjust for these selection processes, the analysis will overestimate the extent of supplier-induced demand.
5. We would expect the demand curve for physician visits to be more price elastic than the demand curve for in-patient hospital care.
6. In a setting where physicians are allowed to set their own fees, a study that finds a positive correlation between physician supply per capita and physician prices represents clear evidence of supplier-induced demand.
7. Supplier-induced demand is the most plausible explanation for the findings from small-area-variation studies that variation across regions in age- and sex-adjusted per-capita utilization is positively associated with physician supply.
8. A decision by the provincial governments to include counselling by psychologists within the public insurance plan would decrease the demand for physician services.
9. A decision to restructure the delivery of fully insured orthopedic services from a large number of local clinics to a small number of regional referral centres would reduce demand for orthopedic treatment.
10. The uncertain nature of need for health care is one of the primary reasons some health economists argue that we should not interpret the area under the demand curve for health care as representing the value of health care to an individual.

References

Acton, J. P. 1975. Nonmonetary factors in the demand for medical services: Some empirical evidence. *Journal of Political Economy* 83(3):595–614.

Barer, M. L., R. G. Evans, and R. J. Labelle. 1988. Fee controls as cost control: Tales from the frozen north. *Milbank Quarterly* 66(1):1–64.

Bentley, T., R. Effros, K. Palar, and E. Keeler. 2008. Waste in the U.S. health care system: A conceptual framework. *Milbank Quarterly* 86(4):629–59.

Coffey, R. M. 1983. The effects of time price on the demand for medical services. *Journal of Human Resources* 18(3):407–24.

Cromwell, J., and J. B. Mitchell. 1986. Physician-induced demand for surgery. *Journal of Health Economics* 5:293–313.

Delattre, E., and B. Dormont. 2003. Fixed fees and physician-induced demand: A panel data study of French physicians. *Health Economics* 12(9):741–54.

Dranove, D., and P. Wehner. 1994. Physician-induced demand for childbirth. *Journal of Health Economics* 13(1):60–73.

Escarce, J. J. 1993a. Effects of lower surgical fees on the use of physician services under Medicare. *Journal of the American Medical Association* 269(19):2513–18.

———. 1993b. Effects of the relative fee structure on the use of surgical operations. *Health Services Research* 28(4):479–502.

———. 1993c. Medicare patients' use of overpriced procedures before and after the Omnibus Reconciliation Act of 1987. *American Journal of Public Health* 83(3):349–55.

Evans, R. G. 1974. Supplier-induced demand: Some empirical evidence and implications. In *The economics of health and medical care*, M. Perlman (ed.). New York: John Wiley. 162–173.

Feldman, R., and M. Morrissey. 1990. Health economics: a report from the field. *Journal of Health Politics, Policy and Law* 15(3):627–46.

Fuchs, V. R. 1978. The supply of surgeons and the demand for operations. *The Journal of Human Resources* 13:35–56.

———. 1986. Physician-induced demands: A parable. *Journal of Health Economics* 5:367.

Gerdtham, U.-G., and B. Jonsson. 2000. International comparisons of health care expenditures. In *Handbook of health economics,* A. J. Culyer, and J. Newhouse (eds.). Amsterdam: Elsevier Science B. V. 11–54.

Gruber, J., M. Owings. 1996. Physician Financial Incentives and Cesarean Section Delivery. *RAND Journal of Economics* 27(1):99–123.

Grytten, J., and R. Sorensen. 2007. Primary physician services—List size and primary physicians' service production. *Journal of Health Economics* 26(4):721–41.

———. 2008. Busy physicians. *Journal of Health Economics* 27(2):510–8.

Hadley, J., J. Holahan, and W. Scanlon. 1979. Can fee-for-service reimbursement coexist with demand creation? *Inquiry* 16:247–58.

Hickson, G. B, W. A. Altemeier, and J. M. Perrin. 1987. Physician reimbursement by salary or fee-for-service: Effect on physician practice behaviour in a randomized prospective study. *Pediatrics* 80(3):344–50.

Holahan, J., J. Hadley, W. Scanlon, R. Lee, and J. Bluck. 1979. Paying for physician services under Medicare and Medicaid. *The Milbank Memorial Fund Quarterly* 57(2):183–211.

Hurley, J., and R. Card. 1996. Global physician budgets as common-property resources: Some implications for physicians and medical associations. *Canadian Medical Association Journal* 154(8):1161–68.

Hurley, J., J. Lomas, and L. Goldsmith. 1997. Physician responses to global physician expenditure caps in Canada: A common property perspective. *Milbank Quarterly* 75(3): 343–64.

Iversen, T. 2004. The effects of a patient shortage on general practitioners' future income and list of patients. *Journal of Health Economics* 23(4):673–94.

Iversen, T., and H. Luras. 2000. Economic motives and professional norms: The case of general medical practice. *Journal of Economic Behaviour and Organization* 43(4):447–70.

Labelle, R., G. L. Stoddart, and T. H. Rice. 1994. A re-examination of the meaning and importance of supplier-induced demand. *Journal of Health Economics* 13(3):347–68.

Lohr, K., R. Brook, and C. Kamberg. 1986. Effect of cost-sharing on use of medically effective and less-effective care. *Medical Care* 24:S31–S38.

Manning, W., J. Newhouse, N. Duan, E. Keeler, B. Benjamin, A. Leibowitz, M. S. Marquis, and J. Zwanziger. 1988. *Health insurance and the demand for medical care: Evidence from a randomized experiment.* Santa Monica, CA: The RAND Corp, Report R-3476-HHS.

Manning, W. G., J. P. Newhouse, N. Duan, E. B. Keeler, A. Leibowitz, and M. S. Marquis. 1987. Health insurance and the demand for medical care: Evidence from a randomized experiment. *The American Economic Review* 77(3):251–77.

McGuire, A., and M. V. Pauly. 1991. Physician response to fee changes with multiple payers. *Journal of Health Economics* 10(4):385–420.

Mitchell, J. B., G. Wedig, and J. Cromwell. 1989. The Medicare physician fee freeze: What really happened? *Health Affairs* 8(1):21–33.

Nassiri, N., and L. Rochaix. 2006. Revisiting physicians' financial incentives in Quebec: A panel system approach. *Health Economics* 15(1):49–64.

Newhouse, J. 1993. *Free for all? Lessons from the RAND health insurance experiment.* Cambridge, MA: Harvard University Press.

Reinhardt, U. E. 1978. Comment on paper by Sloan and Feldman. In *Competition in the health care sector: Past, present and future,* W. Greenberg (ed.). Washington: U.S. Federal Trade Commission. 156–90.

———. 1985. Editorial: The theory of physician-induced demand. Reflection after a decade. *Journal of Health Economics* 4:187–93.

Rice, T. 1984. Physician-induced demand for medical care: New evidence from the Medicare program. *Advances in Health Economics and Health Services Research* 5:129–60.

Rice, T. H. 1983. The impact of changing Medicare reimbursement rates on physician-induced demand. *Medical Care* 21(8):803–15.

Rice, T. H., and R. Labelle. 1989. Do physicians induce demand for medical services? *Journal of Health Politics Policy and Law* 14(3):587–600.

Roch, D. J., R. G. Evans, and D. W. Pascoe. 1985. *Manitoba and Medicare: 1971 to the present.* Winnipeg: Manitoba Health.

Rochaix, L. 1993. Financial incentives for physicians: The Quebec experience. *Health Economics* 2(2):163–76.

Roemer, M. I. 1961. Bed supply and hospital utilization: A national experiment. *Hospitals, J. A. H. A.* 35:988–63.

Stabile, M. 2001. Private insurance subsidies and public health care markets: Evidence from Canada. *Canadian Journal of Economics* 34(4):921–42.

Wagstaff, A. 1986. The demand for health: Some new empirical evidence. *Journal of Health Economics* 5:195–233.

Yip, W. 1998. Physician response to Medicare fee reductions: Changes in the volume of coronary artery bypass graft (CABG) surgeries in Medicare and the private sectors. *Journal of Health Economics* 17(6):675–99.

Chapter 8: The Demand for Health Care

8.1 NEED, DEMAND, AND UTILIZATION

As noted, utilization is the only variable we can actually observe. How, then, do we empirically distinguish need and demand from utilization?

Need versus Utilization

In economic analysis, need is usually distinguished from observed utilization using a two-step need-adjustment procedure:

Step 1: Estimate a full model of utilization including all need and non-need variables thought to affect utilization.

Step 2: Use the estimated coefficients from Step 1 to predict need-related utilization in this way: set the values of need variables equal to their actual value for each individual, but set the values of all non-need variables equal to their means. This ensures that variation in need-predicted utilization across individuals arises only from differences in need variables.

The resulting need-predicted utilization represents what each individual would have been expected to utilize given their need and the average relationship between need and utilization in the sample. In other words, the result is not an estimate of absolute need based only on clinical criteria and a general standard of best practice. It is an estimate of what individuals would have been expected to utilize given their need and how the system they use responds to needs. Hence, three individuals with identical values of need variables might have quite different need-predicted utilization if one resides in Canada, one in the U.S., and one in the U.K., because of the different ways the three systems respond, on average, to health care need.

Demand versus Utilization

As a point of reference, first consider how we estimate demand for a good in a well-functioning market that is in equilibrium. In this situation, the market determines the price (over which no individual exerts any control) and individuals can purchase as much as they want at that market price. For every individual, the observed level of consumption represents a point on their demand curve (Figure 8A.1). With data on enough individuals from markets (e.g., defined by cities) with different prices, we can estimate individual demand using the following regression:

$$Q = \beta_0 + \beta_1 \text{Price} + \beta_2 \text{Income} + \ldots + \beta_n \text{Price}_{\text{substitute}} + e$$

The estimate of β_1 provides information on the slope of the demand curve, and the other coefficients provide information on how the demand curve shifts as values of these other determinants change.

Estimating demand for health care is more difficult:

- Often there is no variation in price (it is zero or a fixed positive value for everybody).
- Where prices do vary across individuals, price is often endogenous, depending in part on the individuals' chosen insurance coverage and their level of health care utilization.
- Markets are often not in equilibrium and care is rationed on the basis of criteria that affect demand (e.g., health status).

FIGURE 8A.1
Estimating Demand Curves in a Standard Market

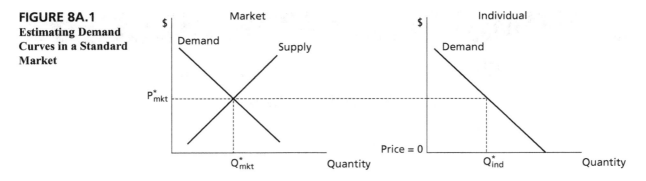

Endogenous Price Contoyannis et al.'s (2005) analysis of the demand for prescription drugs in Quebec illustrates both the problem of endogenous price and one approach to resolving the problem statistically. Endogenous pricing can create a problem even in settings where people have no choice of insurance, such as in Canada's public drug insurance programs. The problem arises because the out-of-pocket price a person must pay per drug drops as the person's total prescription drug expenditures rise.

In Quebec's public drug insurance program, for instance, senior beneficiaries not classified as having low income must pay the full cost of their prescription drugs each month up to $14.30. They then pay 31 percent of the cost up to $77.21, after which they get all prescribed drugs free. This design results in a kinked budget constraint rather than the usual straight budget constraint (Figure 8A.2). A naïve approach to estimating the responsiveness of drug consumption to price would overestimate the responsiveness; by design, those with high expenditures pay a lower price.

The problem is that the amount consumed in the current period determines price to the consumer in the current period and vice versa. The problem can be corrected by finding a variable that is highly correlated with price in a specific period, but not determined by that period's level of consumption. This variable can then be used as an instrument for current period price. In the analysis, the instrument Contoyannis et al. used was the price consumers paid at the margin in the previous month: because drug consumption is highly correlated over time, last month's price is highly correlated with the current month's price, but last month's

FIGURE 8A.2
Monthly Piecewise Linear Budget Constraint Under the Quebec Public Pharmacare Program, 2008

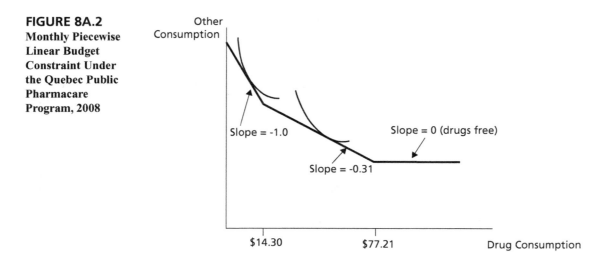

FIGURE 8A.3
A Market for
Physician Services
with Non-Price
Rationing

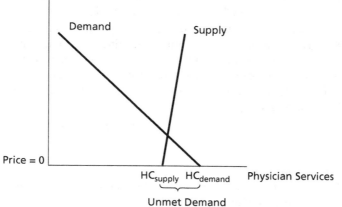

price cannot be determined by this month's consumption. Price-elasticity estimates, without correction for endogeneity, were in the range of -0.45 to -0.50; estimates after correcting for endogeneity of price, using the previous month's price as explained above, ranged from -0.12 to -0.16, approximately one-fourth as large. In this instance, correcting for endogeneity of price made a big difference to the estimated price-elasticity of demand for drugs.

No Price Variation It is not possible to estimate a demand curve if there is no variation in price, although in principle it is possible to estimate the impact of other determinants on demand. The presence of non-price rationing, however, complicates this enormously. To see why, consider Figure 8A.3, which depicts a market for visits to a family physician. The quantity demanded at price zero (HC_{demand}) exceeds the amount supplied (HC_{supply}). Note that this does not necessarily signal a poorly performing system; the supply may be accurately set equal to needs, and the demand above the supply indicates inefficient low-benefit care.

Of those who demand care, what determines whose demand is met by the system? In a well-functioning system, it is the need for care. This has two consequences:

1. Observed utilization no longer represents points on a demand curve. Additionally, the process that determines whose demand is registered is not random; indeed, factors that affect demand are part of what determines who gets care—not as perceived by the individual but as processed by the system. Consequently, unlike the case in a well-functioning market, estimating a model of utilization only imperfectly registers demand: the estimated coefficients on the demand variables represent a mixture of patient preferences and the criteria of the system.

2. Including measures of supply may help identify demand parameters by purging the coefficient estimates of supply-side influences. Hence, utilization models that include both need and non-need factors, including supply-side measures, represent perhaps the best hope for recovering demand parameters.

Demand as a Two-Part Process The distinctive role of providers in influencing demand for care has led to the development of two-part models of demand for health care (Manning et al. 1981; Pohlmeier and Ulrich 1995; Stoddart and Barer 1981). The first part models patient-initiated visits to providers, which are determined predominantly by patient factors. The second part models demand among those with at least one visit, and is determined by a mixture of patient and provider influences. This two-part model is also frequently well-suited for examining the nature of utilization data. Some health services (such as in-patient hospital care) are used by only a small proportion of people each year, so the amount of utilization is zero for most of the sample. The two-part model has desirable statistical properties in such cases.

Perhaps more importantly, the processes that determine utilization often differ across these two components. The probability of making any visit is influenced more strongly by the individuals themselves; once a person sees a provider, however, utilization results from the joint influence of the provider and the individual. Separating the model into two parts allows the role of determinants to differ across these distinct aspects of utilization.

For an analysis of physician visits, for instance,

$$\text{Visits} = \text{Prob}(Y = 1|X) \cdot E(V|X, Y = 1) + e$$

where

Prob = probability
Y = 1 if the individual made at least one visit during the period under study
V = the number of visits
X = the set of independent variables that determine utilization
E() = the expected value
e = the random error term

The model is estimated in two parts. For the first part, the dependent variable is a 0 (no visit) or a 1 (at least one visit) and is estimated using a logistic or probit model. For the second part, which is estimated only using those individuals who made at least one visit, the dependent variable is the actual number of visits. This model allows the influence of various determinants on the likelihood of a visit to differ from their influence on the number of visits.

8.3.1 Measuring Supplier-Induced Demand

The challenges of estimating demand using aggregate market data are quite different from those encountered using individual-level data as described above. Because we observe points at the intersection of the market demand and supply curves, the challenge is to identify the demand curve. If we have data from different markets with differently positioned supply curves, we can trace out the demand curve. That is the essence of the strategy. Let the market be characterized as follows:

$Q_d = Q(\text{Price}, X_d)$ Demand Curve (X_d = non-price determinants of demand)

$Q_s = Q(\text{Price}, Z_s)$ Supply curve (Z_s = non-price determinants of supply)

$Q_d = Q_s = Q_e$ Equilibrium Condition (demand equals supply)

In this situation, as long as X_d contains variables that are not included in Z_s, and vice versa, then it is possible to identify the demand curves and supply curves separately (because changing an element of Z_s that is not in X_d causes supply to shift without affecting demand, allowing us to trace out the demand curve).

However, if we allow for inducement,

$$Q_d = Q(\text{Price}, X_d, Q_s) \rightarrow Q_d = Q(\text{Price}, X_d, Z_s)$$

and it is impossible to separately identify the demand curve and the supply curve. Now, when there is a change in the factors that affect supply, both supply and demand shift. This is the essence of the problem that has bedevilled attempts to identify supplier-induced demand using aggregate market data. Auster and Oaxaca (1981) and Ramsey and Wasow (1986) provide a detailed treatment of the issues.

The use of micro-data resolves these problems but introduces others. A common problem is that of selection on unobservable characteristics of physicians, patients, or both. Suppose, for instance, that physicians base decisions about where to locate, the type of setting in which to practise, the type of payment to receive, the size of their practice, and so forth, in part on the style of medicine they prefer to practise, and that these preferences are not observable to the researcher. In that case, studies that use variation in one or more of these aspects of practice as a way to identify supplier-induced demand may falsely attribute to inducement what is in reality an underlying difference in physician practice styles.

Similarly, if patients with unobservable differences in need and demand for care sort themselves according to physician practise styles (e.g., high-need patients disproportionately sign up with physicians who practise more intensively), then a failure to fully account for difference across physicians in the characteristics of their patient populations can lead to biased estimates of supplier-induced demand. Good research designs are those which allow researchers to control for, or eliminate, the influence of such unobservable factors.

References

Auster, R. D., and R. L. Oaxaca. 1981. Identification of supplier induced demand in the health care sector. *The Journal of Human Resources* 16(3):327–42.

Contoyannis, P., J. Hurley, P. Grootendorst, S.-H. Jeon, and R. Tamblyn. 2005. Estimating the price elasticity of expenditure for prescription drugs in the presence of non-linear price schedules: An illustration from Quebec, Canada. *Health Economics* 14(9):90–923.

Manning, W. et al. 1981. A two-part model of the demand for medical care: Preliminary results from the health insurance study. In *Health, economics, and health economics*, J. van der Gaag, and M. Perlman (eds.). New York: North-Holland. 103–123.

Pohlmeier, W., and V. Ulrich. 1995. An econometric model of the two-part decision making process in the demand for health care. *Journal of Human Resources* 30(2):339–61.

Ramsey, J. B., and B. Wasow. 1986. Supplier induced demand for physician services: Theoretical anomaly or statistical artifact? *Advances in Econometrics* 5:49–77.

Stoddart, G. L., and M. L. Barer. 1981. Analyses of demand and utilization through episodes of medical service. In *Health, economics, and health economics*, J. van der Gaag, and M. Perlman (eds.). New York: North-Holland Publishing Company. 149–176

The Demand for Health Care Insurance

Learning Objectives

After studying this chapter, you will understand

LO1 The nature of the risks people face with respect to health and health care

LO2 How and why pooling risk through insurance can improve people's welfare

LO3 The essential elements of the basic economic model of insurance

---

risk

Risk is present when it is not certain whether an event will occur. The amount of risk depends on the size of the potential gains or losses associated with the event, and the probability that the event will occur.

Most illness and injury is unpredictable. This unpredictability makes it impossible for individuals to budget for health care expenditures the way they can for food, clothing, housing, entertainment, and other goods. Health care expenditures can also be very large—sometimes many times larger than a person's annual income—so paying for unexpected health care can place considerable strain on household budgets. In fact, in the United States, medical bills are one of the most common reasons for bankruptcy (Himmelstein et al. 2005). Insurance that reduces the uncertainty of health expenditures and helps pay for large expenditures, therefore, has the potential to increase well-being.

This chapter examines the nature of the risks associated with health and health care expenditures, how risk can be pooled through insurance, the economic model of the demand for insurance, and the conditions under which insurance can improve welfare. The analysis focuses on insurance and the benefits associated with insurance, regardless of whether it is privately or publicly provided. Understanding why people demand insurance and the nature of the benefits they derive from insurance can help us devise better approaches to health care financing.

9.1 RISK POOLING AND INSURANCE

9.1.1 Risk

Risk is present when we are uncertain whether a particular event will happen.[1] Two factors determine the degree of risk: the probability that the event will occur, and the size of the potential loss or gain associated with the event.

[1] Economists sometimes distinguish between risk and uncertainty. A situation is said to be *risky* when we know all the possible outcomes and the probability that each outcome will occur. We face risk when we play the lottery. A situation is said to be *uncertain* when we do not know all possible outcomes, do not know the probabilities associated with the outcomes, or both. We face uncertainty with respect to who will be prime minister in ten years. Risk is quantifiable; uncertainty is not. As is common, we will ignore this technical distinction between risk and uncertainty and use the terms interchangeably.

Consider two simple lotteries: one offers a 95 percent chance of winning $10,000 and a 5 percent chance of winning nothing, the second offers a 50 percent chance of winning $10,000 and a 50 percent chance of winning nothing. Risk is greater in the second lottery. The risk is greater in the second lottery because both have the same possible outcomes (to win $10,000 or nothing), but the uncertainty about the outcome is greater in the second lottery (50-50 odds of winning $10,000 in the second lottery versus the near certainty of winning it in the first lottery).

Analogously, a lottery with 50-50 odds of winning $10,000 or nothing is riskier than one with 50-50 odds of winning $10 or nothing, because the probabilities are the same in both, but the stakes are greater in the first.

9.1.2   Risk Pooling

We all face dozens of small risks every day with no particular concern; but when the risks become large, we often seek ways to reduce the risk. Individuals can reduce risk in a variety of ways; but all of them boil down to altering the probability that an event will occur, or altering the consequences if the event does occur, or both. When it is difficult to alter the probability that an event will happen, our strategies focus on minimizing the adverse consequences of the event. The most common way to do this is through risk pooling.

risk pooling
When each member of a large group contributes a small amount to the "pool" in return for the promise that, if a specified risky event happens to one of the members, money from the pool will be used to compensate the individual for the loss experienced.

The essential principle of **risk pooling** is that individual members of a group (the risk pool) each contribute a small amount to the pool on the understanding that if an uncertain adverse event occurs to an individual, the contributions of the other group members will be used to compensate the individual for the losses experienced. The contributions that members of the risk pool make can be real effort, such as the labour to help rebuild a house or harvest the crops of a neighbour who suffers a disaster, or they can be financial, such as paying premiums to an insurance company for home or crop insurance that will provide money to rebuild after a disaster. In both cases, a large number of people agree to each contribute a little with the knowledge that each will receive a lot if the disaster strikes them. Risk pooling does not just share risks: risk pooling reduces the total risk borne by the group. This reduction in risk is a source of welfare gain to the members of the group.

The following example illustrates how pooling reduces risk. Suppose each member of a group of individuals faces a 20 percent chance of falling seriously ill during the year, requiring them to spend thousands of dollars on medical care. For each individual, the outcome is uncertain. Among a group of 100,000 such individuals, however, we can predict with considerable confidence that very close to 20,000 of them will become ill. We don't know which 20,000 individuals will get sick, but we know that the total number will be close to 20,000.

What is uncertain at the individual level (will a person get sick or not?) is quite predictable in a large group through the statistical law of large numbers (20,000 out of 100,000 will get sick). If the 100,000 individuals get together and pool their risks through a collective insurance agency, the premium each person pays can eliminate their own financial risk. And because the number of people who will get sick can be accurately predicted, the risk to the insurance agency is small. All insurance rests on this principle.

What Kinds of Risks Can Be Pooled?

Unfortunately, not all risks can be pooled. Only risks that can be traded among individuals can be pooled. Individuals cannot eliminate the uncertainty of falling ill. Health cannot be traded among individuals: individuals cannot each contribute a small amount of health at the beginning of the year in return for the assurance that if they fall ill, other members will transfer some of their health to them. Health risks, therefore, cannot be pooled. Nor can many other aspects of illness, injury, and disability.

The financial risks of illness, however, can be traded. A person can pay a small amount (a premium) to an insurer at the start of the year in return for the promise that, should the individual become ill, the insurer will pay a specified proportion of the costs incurred to treat the illness. Most health care insurance does this. Similarly, a person can pay premiums to a disability insurer so that if illness makes the person unable to work for an extended period, disability insurance will pay a specified proportion of the person's lost earnings. Insurance focuses on the financial consequences of adverse events.

The Effectiveness of Risk Pooling

The effectiveness of pooling financial risks depends on three factors: the size of the risk pool, the independence of the risks among members of the risk pool, and independence between the size of loss experienced and the presence of insurance.

The risk pool must be large enough for the law of large numbers to work its magic, increasing the precision with which the total number of adverse events can be predicted. The size of the risk pool is especially important when some of the risks being pooled have a very low probability of a very large loss. A pool of 2000 individuals might be adequate to pool the financial risks for common minor ailments, but it would be inadequate to pool risks associated with rare and expensive events such as organ transplants. Most years, no one in a risk pool of 2000 would require a transplant; but if in one unlucky year two or three members required such care, the costs could bankrupt the entire risk pool. In a risk pool with a million members, however, even such rare events can be smoothed. The optimal size of the risk pool depends on the nature of the underlying risks.

To be effective, the risk pool must comprise sufficiently independent risks. Independence in the health context means that illness or injury for one person in the risk pool does not materially affect the probability of illness or injury for another person in the pool. If the risks are not independent, many members of the risk pool may simultaneously suffer illness, bankrupting the risk pool when they all claim their insurance payout. This is why localized insurance markets cannot sustain home insurance for events like earthquakes or floods. If a big disaster strikes, and many members of a community lose their homes, a local insurer can't pay all the claims. Similarly, a pandemic of a very costly communicable disease could wreak financial havoc for health care insurers. The vast majority of health care expenditures today are associated with health conditions that are reasonably independent across individuals.

moral hazard
A tendency for the expected loss associated with an adverse event to change in the presence of insurance. The expected loss can change because insurance changes the probability that the event will occur (a person takes less care to avoid the loss) or because, conditional on the event happening, the loss is larger (those affected seek more expensive care than if the loss was not insured).

Finally, the effectiveness of pooling requires independence between the expected loss and the presence of insurance. This implies that the expected loss is fixed, and is not affected by the presence or extent of insurance coverage. In health care, this means that the care a person receives when ill is the same whether or not they have insurance. The violation of this assumption, whereby insurance coverage causes the expected loss to change, is called **moral hazard.** Moral hazard is potentially a significant problem in health care insurance markets because insurance coverage tends to cause people to consume more health care than if they had no insurance, a point discussed in detail in Chapter 10.

9.2 DEMAND FOR INSURANCE

An economic model of the demand for insurance formalizes these intuitive ideas about the benefits of risk pooling, providing a framework for analyzing important aspects of insurance and insurance markets. To keep the analysis tractable, and to highlight key elements that influence demand for insurance, the economic model of insurance makes a series

The notion of expectation is central to models of decision-making under risk. Economics commonly assumes that people are *expected* utility maximizers, so that decisions made in risky situations depend in part on variables such as the *expected* value of a risky situation, the *expected* loss, *expected* wealth, and so forth. For any quantity X (utility, money, wealth, etc.) that can take on n possible values, each with probability p_n, the expected value of X is

$$\text{Expected value}(X) = p_1 X_1 + p_2 X_2 + \ldots + p_n X_n$$

But what does this mean and why should it matter for decision-making? Suppose someone whose current wealth is $100,000 faces the following gamble: they have a 40 percent chance of losing $25,000 and a 60 percent chance of winning $25,000. Suppose further that when their wealth is $75,000 their utility is 100, and when their wealth is $125,000 their utility is 120. If they take this gamble once, they will either lose $25,000 (ending up with $75,000 and a utility of 100) or win $25,000 (ending up with $125,000 and a utility of 120).

Now suppose that instead of gambling only once, they take this gamble 1000 times; 40 percent of the time they would lose $25,000 and 60 percent of the time they would win $25,000. After taking this gamble 1000 times, the expected net winnings are $5,000,000 (400 times losing $25,000 and 600 times winning $25,000), for average winnings of $5000 for each gamble. This is the sense in which they can expect to win $5000 on the gamble. Similarly, their average level of wealth over the 1000 repetitions of the gamble is $105,000 (400 times ending up with $75,000 and 600 times with $125,000). Finally, the average utility attained across all the gambles is 112 (400 times they would have had a utility of 100, and 600 times they would have had a utility of 120).

This is what is meant by expected value: facing the risky prospect many, many times, the expected value is the average value across all the repetitions of a risky prospect (i.e., the amount, on average, that the gambler would end up with). Here are the precise values we get for the gamble described above:

$$\text{Expected winnings} = -\$25,000 * 0.4 + \$25,000 * 0.6$$
$$= \$5000$$
$$\text{Expected wealth} = \$75,000 * 0.4 + \$125,000 * 0.6$$
$$= \$105,000$$
$$\text{Expected utility} = 100 * 0.4 + 120 * 0.6 = 112$$

Why is this relevant if a person actually only faces the risky prospect once? Even if we face each particular risky situation only once, we face many slightly different such situations in our life. If we always choose the option with the highest expected utility, then under certain assumptions about our preferences, this will make us as well off as we can be, on average.

monetary equivalent of the loss
The amount of money that can be paid to an individual to exactly balance the negative effects of an event. The result is that the person is just as well off as they would have been if the event had not occurred.

expected utility
In a risky situation, the sum over all possible outcomes of the product of the utility associated with each outcome and the probability that the outcome will occur.

of simplifying assumptions about the nature of the loss being insured and the behaviour of individuals. The model was developed to explain decision-making under risk and the demand for insurance generally; it is not specific to health insurance. After presenting the basic model, we will consider some modifications that have been proposed to better integrate features of health and health care.

The model assumes that people in a risky situation know all the possible outcomes and the probability associated with each, and that the loss (or gain) associated with each possible outcome can be expressed in monetary terms. That is, if a particular event makes an individual worse off, the model assumes that there is an amount of money that can be paid to the individual that would make them just as well off as if the event had not occurred. This amount is called the **monetary equivalent of the loss**.

Individuals care only about their absolute level of wealth: U = U(W), where W is wealth. In making choices, individuals seek to maximize **expected utility**. A person's expected utility in a risky situation is equal to the sum over all possible outcomes of the product of the utility associated with each outcome and the probability that the outcome will occur (See Box 9.1):

$$\text{Expected Utility} = p_1 U_1 + p_2 U_2 + \ldots + p_n U_n \qquad \textbf{(9.1)}$$

where there are n possible outcomes, $p_1 \ldots p_n$ are the probabilities that each outcome will occur, and $U_1 \ldots U_n$ are the utilities associated with each outcome. For instance, if a person enters a lottery and has a 70 percent chance of winning $10,000 and a 30 percent chance of winning $5000, and the utility associated with $10,000 and $5000 is 200 and 120 utils respectively, the expected utility of the lottery is $(0.70)(200) + (0.30)(120)$, or 176 utils.

Risk Aversion

risk averse
A person who prefers a certain (perfectly predictable) level of wealth over a risky alternative that has the same expected value.

Individuals are assumed to be **risk averse**. A risk-averse person dislikes risk. A risk-averse individual prefers a certain (perfectly predictable) level of wealth over a risky alternative that has the same expected value. If offered a choice, for example, between getting $20,000 with certainty or facing a gamble with a 50 percent chance of $10,000 and a 50 percent chance of $30,000, a risk-averse person would prefer $20,000 with certainty. The expected value of both is identical ($20,000), but in the first case there is no risk and in the second there is. A **risk-loving** person would prefer the gamble; they actually get utility from the risk. A **risk-neutral** person would be indifferent between the two options. Only a risk-averse person benefits by reducing or eliminating risk.

risk loving
A person who prefers a risky alternative with a given expected value over a certain (perfectly predictable) level of wealth equal to the expected value of the gamble.

Risk aversion is equivalent to assuming that individuals have diminishing marginal utility of wealth. With diminishing marginal utility of wealth, the utility gain from an additional dollar is smaller when a person has wealth of $1 million than wealth of $1000. The reason diminishing marginal utility of wealth implies risk aversion can be seen in the following example: consider a bet with a 50 percent chance of winning $10,000 and a 50 percent chance of losing $10,000. Diminishing marginal utility of money implies that the increase in utility from winning $10,000 would be less than the decrease in utility from losing $10,000. Most people would refuse the bet, preferring the certain outcome of no change in wealth. A person's degree of risk aversion is measured by how quickly the marginal utility of wealth falls as wealth increases.

risk neutral
A person who is indifferent between a certain (perfectly predictable) level of wealth and a risky alternative that has the same expected value.

Assume that a person is risk averse with the following utility function defined over wealth:

$$U = U(W) = \sqrt{wealth} \tag{9.2}$$

Utility is graphed in Figure 9.1. The horizontal axis represents a person's level of wealth, the vertical axis represents the level of total utility, and the curve U(W) depicts the relationship between wealth and utility given in equation 9.2. Utility increases with wealth at a decreasing rate; i.e., the person exhibits diminishing marginal utility of wealth. Assume that the individual currently has wealth of $50,000. During the coming year, this individual faces a 0.6 probability of becoming ill and incurring $20,000 in health care expenses, and a 0.4 probability of staying completely healthy and incurring no health care expenses. It follows that

- The loss (L) associated with becoming ill is $20,000.
- The expected loss (EL) is
  $$EL = (p)(Loss) + (1 - p)(No\ Loss) = (0.6)(\$20,000) + (0.4)(0) = \$12,000$$

  where p denotes the probability of getting ill.
- The expected wealth level (EW) is
  $$EW = (p)(W_0 - L) + (1 - p)^*(W_0) = (0.6)(\$30,000) + (0.4)(\$50,000) = \$38,000$$
- The level of utility attained by a person who does not fall ill is $\sqrt{\$50,000}$, or 224 utils (point A).

FIGURE 9.1   **The Welfare Gain of Risk Pooling Through Insurance**

This figure shows the welfare gains from insurance for a risk-averse individual. The curved line represents utility defined over wealth. If this individual has $50,000 at the beginning of the year and faces a 60 percent chance of falling ill and incurring $20,000 in health care expenditures, their expected level of wealth is $38,000 and the expected level of utility is 193 utils (point C). If they can buy full insurance at an actuarially fair premium of $12,000, they can attain utility level 195 (point D) with certainty. The change from an expected utility level of 193 without insurance to a certain level of 195 with insurance is a measure of welfare gain from insurance for the risk-averse person.

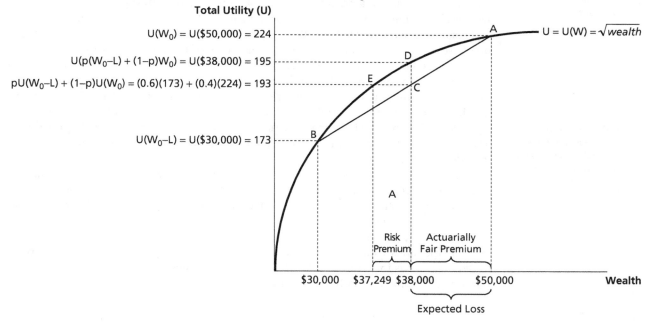

- The level of utility attained by a person who falls ill and incurs the $20,000 loss is $\sqrt{\$30,000}$, or 173 utils (point B).
- The person's expected level of utility is

$$p^*U(W_0 - L) + (1 - p)U(W_0) = (0.6)(173) + (0.4)(224) = 193 \text{ utils(point C)}$$

9.2.1 The Benefits of Insurance

actuarially fair premium
An insurance premium that is equal to the expected value of the insured loss.

Should the person in the above example buy insurance? Because that person is risk averse, insurance has the potential to make the person better off. Whether it would or not depends on the price of insurance. Suppose the price of insurance exactly equals the expected loss of $12,000. This is called the **actuarially fair premium**. If everybody in the insurance pool pays an actuarially fair premium, the revenue of the insurance agency will exactly equal its expected payouts to reimburse the claims of the insured. If the individual buys full insurance paying an actuarially fair premium, the person will be left with a certain wealth of $38,000 ($50,000 less the premium of $12,000), and an associated utility of $\sqrt{\$38,000}$, or 195 utils (point D).[2]

Recall from the calculation above that if the person doesn't buy insurance, the person's expected level of utility is 193 utils. The difference between the utility level if they do buy insurance (195 utils) and the expected level of utility if they do not buy insurance (193 utils) is a measure of the increase in welfare (2 utils in this example) associated with buying insurance at an actuarially fair price. The expected level of wealth is the same ($38,000) both for no insurance and for insurance purchased at an actuarially fair premium, but the level of risk differs; so a risk-averse person is better off with insurance at this price.

loading costs
The administrative costs associated with providing insurance.

Will an insurance agency offer insurance at this price? No. The insurance agency has administrative costs in addition to the cost of paying beneficiary claims. Such administrative costs include those incurred calculating premiums for beneficiaries, advertising, processing claims, and so forth; and they are referred to as **loading costs**. No insurance company can survive unless it charges a premium that covers both the claims costs and the loading costs—that is, a premium greater than the actuarially fair premium. Is a person who wants insurance willing to pay a premium above the actuarially fair premium? Yes.

Presumably, an individual is willing to pay a premium up to the point where the utility of after-premium certain wealth just equals the expected level of utility with no insurance. The expected utility without insurance is 193, so they would be willing to pay a premium up to the point where the utility of their after-premium wealth just equalled 193. Given that $U = \sqrt{wealth}$, the level of wealth that provides 193 utils is $(193)^2$ or $37,249 (point E). Hence, this individual would be willing to pay up to $12,751 for full insurance coverage. The $751 amount above the actuarially fair premium is called the **risk premium**.

risk premium
The amount of money above the actuarially fair premium that a person is willing to pay for insurance.

The size of the risk premium a person is willing to pay depends, other things equal, on their degree of risk aversion.

The greater a person's risk aversion, the larger will be their welfare gain from insurance. Greater risk aversion is represented in Figure 9.1 by greater curvature in the utility function. Greater curvature increases the vertical distance between points C and D, which is the measure of welfare gain.

Similarly, the greater the level of risk, the larger the welfare gain from insurance. The level of risk varies with the size of the loss and the probability of the loss. If you rework the above analysis for a cost of $10,000 for the required medical care, you will see that the welfare gain from actuarially fair insurance falls from 2 utils to 0.32 utils. As we would

---

[2] All figures are rounded to the nearest digit.

expect, based on the relationship between the size of the loss and the risk, health care insurance first emerged for high-cost, low-probability hospital care and then spread to a broader range of health services.

This simple model helps explain why people desire insurance when faced with risky situations; it also explains the nature and source of a welfare gain from insurance. As long as the premium is sufficiently close to an actuarially fair premium, a risk-averse person benefits by reducing risk through the purchase of insurance. For decades, this has been the dominant model used by economists to frame decision-making under uncertainty in general, and economic issues associated with insurance in particular.

9.2.2 Some Limitations of the Standard Insurance Model

While this basic expected utility model remains the mainstay of economic analysis of decision-making under risk, recent research indicates that it does not always accurately reflect how individuals make decisions in risky situations. Neither does it fully represent the gains from insurance, especially health care insurance. Maximizing expected utility has a certain intuitive plausibility—if done consistently over a series of uncertain choices, this ensures that a person will obtain the highest possible outcome, on average—but it does impose strong restrictions. It implies, for instance, that the magnitudes of the gains and losses do not matter (a gamble with a 50-50 chance of winning $10 and losing $10 is equivalent to one with a 50-50 chance of winning $100,000 and losing $100,000). The expected utility hypothesis also implies that individuals view gains and losses symmetrically.

loss aversion
A tendency to prefer to avoid losses over accruing gains, when making decisions under uncertainty.

Research into decision-making under uncertainty and attitudes toward risk, however, demonstrates that, when faced with uncertainty, potential losses weigh more heavily in decision-making than potential gains, a phenomenon referred to as **loss aversion** (Shoemaker 1982; Machina 1987). People's choices are surprisingly sensitive to changes in what should be irrelevant features of how a problem is framed. For example, people's choices differ when two formally identical problems are posed differently (Box 9.2).

Experimental evidence also indicates that risk attitudes are more complex than assumed by the model. In particular, diminishing marginal utility of wealth is not the only source of risk aversion. According to the standard model described above, two individuals who have the same preferences over wealth in a world of certainty (i.e., where there is no risk) by definition have the same risk preferences. This appears too restrictive: people with the same preferences over wealth in a certain world may still exhibit very different attitudes toward risk (see Box 9.2).

Economists and psychologists working together have developed modifications to this model that better predict the choices people make when faced with uncertain outcomes. The most prominent is Prospect Theory (Kahneman and Tversky 1979), for which Daniel Kahneman shared the Nobel Prize in Economics in 2002. Prospect Theory incorporates the fact that people appear to weigh losses more heavily than gains when making choices. Still, no single model has replaced the expected utility model.

Finally, the standard model of insurance posits that risk reduction is the only source of welfare gain to those who buy insurance. Recent work on the demand for insurance, however, argues that people demand health care insurance for other types of benefits as well (Nyman 2003). In particular, insurance acts as a way to increase income when ill. This transfer of income from all those who buy insurance and remain healthy to those who have insurance and get sick has two effects. First, if a person who falls ill could have afforded the treatment without insurance (as is assumed in the standard model described above), the monies obtained through full insurance make it unnecessary to reduce consumption of

Framing Effects

Suppose you were minister of health and had to choose among programs to prevent two potential disease outbreaks in your country. Read the descriptions of the alternative programs below. For each disease, choose which program you would recommend.

Imagine that Canada is preparing for the outbreak of an unusual disease that is expected to kill 600 individuals. Two alternative programs to combat the disease have been proposed. The cost for each program is identical. Assume that the exact scientific estimates of the consequences of the programs are as follows:

If program A is adopted, 200 people will be saved.

If program B is adopted, there is 1/3 probability that 600 people will be saved and a 2/3 probability that no people will be saved.

Would you choose Program A or Program B?

For the very same disease, assume the alternative programs are as follows:

If program C is adopted, 400 people will die.

If program D is adopted, there is 1/3 probability that nobody will die and a 2/3 probability that 600 people will die.

Which would you choose, Program C or Program D?

If you chose a combination of A and C, or a combination of B and D, congratulations—you were not fooled by the changed framing of the question in terms of gains or losses. Note that the problems are identical; the only difference is that the alternatives are first described in terms of how many people are saved (gains), and then in terms of how many people die (losses). Experiments show that when framed in terms of lives saved, most people (72 percent) choose the certain option (A) (i.e., they are risk averse); when framed in terms of lives lost, however, most people (78 percent) choose the program with uncertain effects (D) (i.e., they are risk seeking) (Tversky and Kahneman 1988).

Risk Aversion and the Utility of Money

Consider the following puzzle drawn from Rabin and Thaler (2001), which illustrates why diminishing marginal utility of money does not fully represent risk aversion.

Suppose we know that a person is a risk-averse expected-utility maximizer, and will always refuse a gamble that risks losing $10 or gaining $11. Based on this information, can we say anything about how this person will respond to other bets? In particular, can we conclude anything about the amount of money ($Y) that would make the person willing to accept a gamble with a 50 percent chance of losing $100 and a 50 percent chance of winning $Y?

It turns out that there is no value of $Y for which this person would accept a gamble if the only source of their risk aversion is decreasing marginal utility of money. The fact that this person always turns down the gamble involving $10 and $11, as described above, implies a degree of risk aversion such that a gamble with a risk of a $100 loss would never be accepted, no matter how much the potential winnings. While turning down the initial bet is reasonable, very few people would turn down a bet with a 50 percent chance of winning $1 million and a 50 percent chance of losing only $100. The example illustrates that some other factors beyond diminishing marginal utility of money must play a role in explaining risk attitudes.

other goods and services to finance needed health care. This allows people to reduce variability in well-being across healthy and ill times.

In addition, unlike the assumption in the standard model, the cost of treatment for some conditions (e.g., stroke, heart problems, liver failure) can exceed the amount many households could either save over their lifetimes or borrow.[3] In reality, therefore, the choice

[3] This highlights an important difference between health care insurance markets and insurance markets for automobiles, housing, and other valuable assets. The magnitude of the financial risks associated with these material possessions is directly associated with a person's income or wealth: only those who can afford a large expensive house risk large financial losses if the house is damaged. In health care, however, a person's financial risk is not bounded by their income or wealth. Indeed, given the negative relationship between health and wealth, those with lowest incomes have the highest average financial risks. Furthermore, no bank would lend money to a person for the treatment of a potentially fatal disease knowing that they would be unable to pay it back if the treatment were unsuccessful.

people often face is not simply between insurance and paying the full cost themselves, but between insurance (which creates access to high-cost services they could not otherwise afford if they fell ill) and no access to care. That is, insurance creates access to high-cost medical care. Insurance does this because it transfers income from the healthy to the unhealthy in the insurance pool, allowing those who are sick to purchase services they otherwise could not afford. Nyman (2003) terms this the **access motive** for purchasing insurance. These benefits derived from the income transfers associated with insurance are distinct from and in addition to the benefits of pure risk reduction emphasized by the standard model.

access motive
The benefit of insurance that arises because insurance enables an individual to obtain extremely high-cost care to which they would otherwise not have access.

Although these ideas modify aspects of the standard model, they reinforce the fundamental conclusion that, when faced with uncertainty regarding health care expenditures, insurance to cover the costs of care can substantially improve welfare.

9.3 THE NATURE OF INSURANCE CONTRACTS

The model discussed thus far posits that an individual purchases full insurance to cover all the costs of care. As discussed in Chapter 1, however, in the real world much public health insurance and most private insurance contracts do not cover the full cost of care. Individuals are required to pay some of the cost themselves. Recall that such out-of-pocket costs take a number of forms, including deductibles (which require an individual to pay the full cost of care up to the amount of the deductible), co-insurance (which requires an individual to pay a specified proportion of costs), and fixed co-payments (which require an individual to pay a fixed amount for each unit of care consumed, such as a charge of $5.00 per prescription).

coverage limit
Some insurance contracts specify that once the dollar amount of benefits paid to an individual by the insurer reaches a certain amount, no further coverage is provided.

Some policies include a maximum expenditure limit, so that once an individual's out-of-pocket spending reaches the limit, further services are fully covered. Policies can also include a **coverage limit**, which specifies the maximum amount of coverage an insurer will provide during a defined period. Any expenditure beyond the limit must be paid by the enrollee. The time period can vary, but the period is commonly specified as one year or a person's lifetime.

cost-sharing
An insurance provision that requires an individual to pay part of the cost of an insured health care service. Also called a **user charge**.

Each of these constitutes a way to impose **cost-sharing** or **user charges** on enrollees. They are not mutually exclusive so, for instance, a policy can impose a deductible, co-insurance above the deductible, and a maximum coverage limit. Such cost-sharing arrangements are highly controversial in the health sector. Within the standard analysis of insurance model, such changes can be welfare-improving for enrollees if they reduce administrative and related costs (e.g., by reducing claims processing costs) thereby lowering premiums. While such reasoning may motivate some user charges observed in the real world, most such user charges are primarily intended to reduce utilization by forcing individuals to pay part of the cost of care and to make insurance selectively attractive to certain types of (profitable) individuals. Such motivations for cost-sharing are highly debated, as we will see in the next chapter when we examine the operation of health care insurance markets.

risk adjustment
The process by which insurers adjust premiums to reflect observable characteristics of an individual that are associated with expected health care costs.

community-rated premium
Insurance premiums for which there is no risk adjustment; the premium is the same for everyone.

Informational problems also make it impossible for insurers to calculate each individual's actuarially fair premium. Too many unobservable characteristics of a person determine their expected health care costs in a given period. The process by which insurers adjust premiums to reflect the expected health care costs associated with observable characteristics of an individual is called **risk adjustment**. Risk adjustment remains relatively crude, relying on a small set of characteristics such as age, sex, and certain chronic conditions. Premiums for which no risk adjustment is performed are called **community-rated premiums**—everyone is charged the same premium regardless of their risk status.

Chapter Summary

This chapter has examined the benefits of insurance in the face of uncertainty and the associated demand for insurance by individuals. The main points are as follows:

- Risk pooling through insurance can reduce the amount of risk a group of individuals face.
- Only risks that can be traded can be pooled, so insurance focuses on the financial consequences of illness and injury.
- Economic analysis emphasizes two motives for purchasing health care insurance:
    - risk reduction—the motive for purchasing insurance within the standard economic model of insurance, which is based on the assumption that people are expected utility maximizers and risk averse
    - access—more recent modifications to the standard model also emphasize the access motive for purchasing insurance; the income transfers associated with insurance allow individuals to gain access to very expensive health care services they otherwise could not afford
- Insurance policies often impose cost-sharing requirements in the form of deductibles, co-insurance, fixed charges, and spending limits; such requirements remain highly controversial and a full analysis requires consideration of the operation of health insurance and health care markets.

Key Terms

access motive, *241*
actuarially fair premium, *238*
community-rated premium, *241*
cost-sharing, *241*
coverage limit, *241*
expected utility, *235*
loading costs, *238*

loss aversion, *239*
monetary equivalent of the loss, *235*
moral hazard, *234*
risk, *232*
risk adjustment, *241*
risk averse, *236*

risk loving, *236*
risk neutral, *236*
risk pooling, *233*
risk premium, *238*
user charge, *241*

End-of-Chapter Questions

A. Suppose an individual has the following utility function defined over wealth: $U = U(\sqrt{wealth})$. The individual has an initial wealth level of $20,000.

1. The individual has a 20 percent chance of a heart attack and the loss associated with the attack is $5000.

    a) What is the expected loss from a heart attack?
    b) What is the maximum amount this individual is willing to pay for insurance against a heart attack?
    c) What is the risk premium?

2. A new drug has been developed that is effective in preventing heart attacks. Taking the drug reduces the chance of a heart attack to 10 percent, but the loss associated with the attack increases to $10,000.

    a) Now what is the expected loss?
    b) What is the maximum amount this individual is willing to pay for insurance against a heart attack?
    c) What is the risk premium?

3. Explain why some of the answers change before and after the individual begins taking the drug.

B. For each of the statements below, indicate whether the statement is true or false and explain why it is true or false.

1. Health insurance can cover the full amount of losses associated with becoming ill.

2. The actuarially fair premiums are the same for two individuals who have identical probabilities of being ill and identical monetary losses associated with being ill, but who have differing risk preferences.

3. The effectiveness of pooling financial risk through insurance increases as the number of individuals in the risk pool grows.

4. A risk-averse individual prefers all situations that are a certainty over a risky prospect.

5. The individual whose utility over wealth depicted below is risk loving.

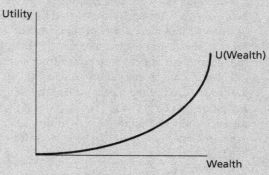

6. If an insurance company charges more than the actuarially fair premium, people will not buy insurance.

7. Insurance always makes a risk-averse person better off.

8. Risk aversion is a necessary condition for insurance to be welfare improving to an individual.

9. A community-rated premium is always less than a risk-adjusted premium.

References

Himmelstein, D., E. Warren, D. Thorne, and S. Woolhandler. 2005. Illness and injury as contributors to bankruptcy. *Health Affairs* Web Exclusive (W5):W63–W73.

Kahneman, D., and A. Tversky. 1979. Prospect theory: An analysis of decision under risk. *Econometrica* 47:263–91.

Machina, M. 1987. Choice under uncertainty: Problems solved and unsolved. *Journal of Economic Perspectives*. 1(1):124–54.

Nyman, J. 2003. *The theory of demand for health insurance.* Stanford, CA: Stanford University Press.

Rabin, M., and R. H. Thaler. 2001. Anomalies: Risk aversion. *Journal of Economic Perspectives* 15(1):219–32.

Shoemaker, P. 1982. The expected utility model: Its variants, purposes, evidence and limitations. *Journal of Economic Literature* 20(2):529–63.

Tversky, A., and D. Kahneman. 1988. Rational choice and the framing of decisions. In *Decision making: Descriptive, normative and prescriptive interactions,* D. Bell, H. Raiffa, and A. Tversky (eds.). Cambridge: Cambridge University Press. 167–92.

Appendix 9

Chapter 9: The Demand for Health Care Insurance

9.1 RISK POOLING AND INSURANCE

9.1.2 Risk Pooling

Risk pooling does not simply transfer risk from individuals to the insurer; it also reduces total risk. This can be illustrated as follows (Phelps 1992).

Assume that there are N people, each of whom faces a risky situation with mean loss X_i with mean μ and variance of σ^2. If each individual pays an actuarially fair premium (μ) to purchase an insurance policy from an insurer, each individual's risk goes to zero and the insurer collects premiums, P, equal to $N\mu$. The average per-person premium (P/N) is a weighted sum of the means, where the weights are $w_i = 1/N$. The variance of this average premium is $\sigma^2_{AP} = \sum^N_{i=1} w_i^2 \sigma_i^2$ if the risks are uncorrelated. When σ_i is the same for each individual, and $w_i = 1/N$, this equals $\sigma^2_{AP} = \sigma^2/N$. Hence, the variance in the expected loss per person for the insurer decreases proportionately as the number of independent risks increases.

9.2 DEMAND FOR INSURANCE

Risk Aversion The more concave the utility function is with respect to wealth (e.g., the more rapidly the marginal utility of wealth falls), the greater is a person's degree of risk aversion. Based on this, a prominent measure of risk aversion is the Arrow-Pratt Measure of (Absolute) Risk Aversion, defined as the ratio of the second and first derivatives of the utility function:

$$(-U''(L)/U'(L))(\sigma^2/2) = R_A(\sigma^2/2), \text{ where } R_A \text{ is the measure of risk aversion}$$

Welfare Gain from Insurance An alternative way to analyze the benefits of insurance, which will have certain advantages for analyzing aspects of insurance markets, is to view the problem an individual faces as one of allocating wealth between two uncertain states, illness and full health. In Figure 9A.1, the horizontal axis represents wealth if healthy, and

FIGURE 9A.1
Contingent Wealth Diagram for an Individual Facing a Probability of Ill Health

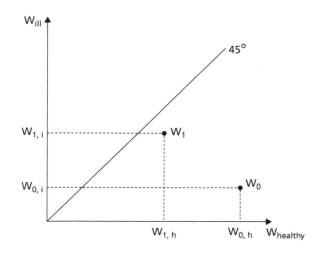

the vertical axis represents wealth if ill. Point W_0 represents the initial situation in which the individual has wealth $W_{0,h}$ if they remain healthy and wealth $W_{0,i}$ if they fall ill.

Wealth is less when ill, because the individual suffers a financial loss due to cost of treatment. Insurance allows individuals to trade wealth across health states: by paying a premium (reducing wealth in healthy state), they can increase wealth if they fall ill. An insurance policy might allow them to move from W_0 to W_1, for instance, where the premium paid is $(W_{0,h} - W_{1,h})$ and the insurance payment if illness strikes is $(W_{1,i} - W_{0,i})$. Whether this would make the individual better off depends on the individual's risk attitudes and the probability of falling ill.

Let p be the probability that the individual falls ill, and assume that the individual's preferences can be represented by a von Neuman-Morgenstern (vNM) utility function[1] and that the individual is risk averse. In the initial state, the individual's expected utility is this:

$$E[u(W_0)] = (1 - p)u(W_{0,h}) + pu(W_{0,i})$$

We can derive all other combinations of wealth levels and probabilities that provide the same level of expected utility, i.e., indifference curves defined over expected utility. Taking the total derivative of utility,

$$dE[u(W_0)] = dW_h[(1 - p)u'(W_h)] + dW_i[pu'(W_i)],$$

Setting this equal to 0 and rearranging, we get

$$dW_i/dW_h = -[(1 - p)u'(W_h)]/pu'(W_i)] < 0$$

The slope of the indifference curve is negative and depends both on p and on the individual's preferences over wealth. When wealth levels in the two states are equal (along the 45° line), the slope of the indifference curve equals the ratio of the probabilities of being healthy versus ill: $[-(1-p)/p]$. Figure 9A.2 shows one such indifference curve. In this case, the individual would prefer W_1 to W_0. But would an insurance company offer a contract that allowed such a move?

The insurance company can only offer contracts for which it can expect, at minimum, to break even. To break even, it must be the case that

$$(1 - p)(W_{0,h} - W_{1,h}) + p(W_{0,i} - W_{1,i}) \geq 0$$

FIGURE 9A.2
Indifference Curve with Respect to Expected Utility

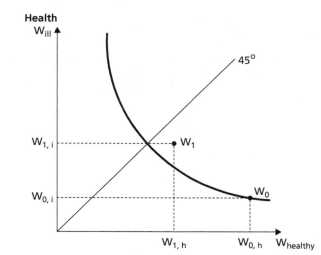

[1] vNM utility is defined over risky states and therefore reflects risk attitudes (e.g., see Luce et al. 1957).

This condition determines the set of feasible contracts an insurance company would offer. When this condition is binding (so the insurer earns a profit of zero), we get the fair-odds line, which passes through W_0 and has slope equal to $(-(1-p)/p)$ (Figure 9A.3). Starting from W_0, all points on or below the fair-odds line are feasible in the sense that the insurance company would at least break even.

W_1 is in the set of feasible contracts, but it is not the most preferred—the individual would prefer a contract that takes them to W^*. For an individual starting at W_0, the optimal feasible contract occurs where the indifference curve is tangent to the set of feasible trades, defined by the fair-odds line. Given the curvature of the indifference curves (which reflects risk aversion), individuals can improve their welfare by purchasing full insurance, moving from W_0 to W^*, and thereby attaining the same wealth whether healthy or ill.

As before, we can see that actuarially fair insurance is welfare improving for a risk-averse individual (the welfare gain is measured by the increase in utility associated with moving to the higher indifference curve), and that the welfare gain is increasing in the riskiness of the situation and in a person's degree of risk aversion.

FIGURE 9A.3
Optimal Insurance Contract

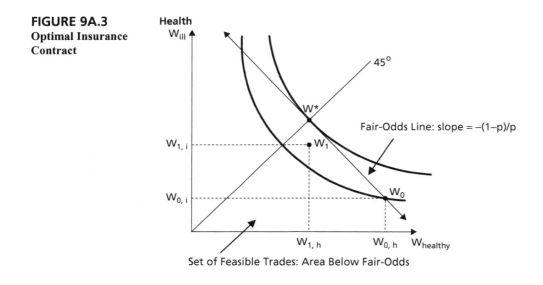

References

Luce, R., D. Raiffa, and H. Raiffa. 1957. Utility theory. In *Games and decisions*. New York: John Wiley and Sons. 12–39.

Phelps, C. 1992. *Health economics*. New York: Harper Collins.

Private Insurance Markets

Learning Objectives

After studying this chapter, you will understand

LO1 Sources of market failure in health care insurance markets
LO2 Economic analysis of moral hazard
LO3 Economic analysis of risk selection
LO4 Implications of insurance market failures for public policy in both insurance and health care service markets

---

Private markets for health care insurance developed in the early part of the twentieth century and expanded greatly in the decades following World War II as medical technologies advanced, treatment possibilities expanded, and the associated costs of health care increased. As the power of medicine to cure illness and injury grew, so did the view that all citizens should have access to necessary health care. This, in turn, spurred the analysis of markets for health care insurance.

This chapter focuses on the operation of private insurance markets. It emphasizes sources of market failure and potential policy responses to correct market failure. Because of the close interactions between health care insurance markets and health care service markets, an assessment of the efficiency of insurance arrangements must also consider the impact of insurance on health care consumption. The analysis examines four sources of market failure: moral hazard, risk selection, economies of scale in insurance provision, and missing (or incomplete) markets for insurance.

This chapter does not explicitly address equitable access to health care insurance. If insurance markets were not subject to market failure, equitable access could be achieved through a well-designed system of subsidies to those who could otherwise not afford insurance. But the joint policy challenges of market failure and strong equity concerns necessitate a broader, coordinated set of policies toward insurance markets and health care financing more generally, which we take up in Chapter 11.

10.1 MORAL HAZARD

The standard insurance model (presented in the previous chapter) assumes that insurance coverage does not influence the size of a person's expected loss. In reality, however, this does not hold. Individuals often have some control over the probability that they will get sick or injured and the associated costs of treatment. This creates the possibility of moral hazard—the tendency of insurance coverage to change behaviour and, thereby, the expected value of the insured loss—in this case, the expected costs of health care.

ex ante moral hazard

Insurance-induced changes in behaviour that alter the probability that an insured event occurs.

ex post moral hazard

Insurance-induced changes in behaviour that alter the insured loss after the insured event occurs.

Insurance-induced changes in behaviour that alter the probability of a loss are called **ex ante moral hazard** (e.g., an individual might be less careful to lock a car that is insured). The *ex ante* moral hazard is a larger concern for insurance that covers material possessions than it is in health insurance, because illness and injury impose substantial pain and suffering not compensated by insurance.

Changed behaviour after the event occurs is called **ex post moral hazard** (e.g., after a car accident, an individual might replace damaged parts with nicer versions than were originally installed or than are really necessary). In health care, it means consuming more care or higher-priced care than you would if you did not have health insurance. *Ex post* moral hazard is a large concern in the health sector. Most health insurance lowers the price that beneficiaries pay for health care. Individuals with insurance often respond to this lower price by lowering their threshold for seeking care or by increasing demand for care once diagnosed: they consume more health care than if they did not have insurance. If the value of such insurance-induced care is less than the social cost of producing the care, the additional consumption is inefficient.

All health economists agree that moral hazard is a potentially important source of inefficiency, but rival schools of thought differ on its magnitude, the appropriate methods to assess its efficiency impacts, and the factors most responsible for over-consumption. Consequently, they disagree on the policies required to correct moral hazard. We begin with the commonly presented "standard" analysis derived from Mark Pauly's influential 1968 paper (Pauly 1968) and then consider critiques of this analysis.

Pauly's analysis of moral hazard treats health care as a standard commodity exchanged in perfectly competitive markets, and uses people's "willingness to pay" (measured by the area under the health care demand curve) to value health care consumption. In this view, health care markets are no different from other markets and the policy solution is demand-side cost-sharing: make people pay part of the cost of the care they obtain. But as our analysis of demand for health care in Chapter 8 emphasized, the applicability of these standard assumptions can be questioned, invalidating welfare analysis based on them. Admitting asymmetry of information, externalities, and other features of health care into the analysis changes the magnitude of the problem and shifts policy attention to supply-side rather than demand-side solutions.

10.1.1 The Standard Analysis of Moral Hazard in the Health Care Market

Arrow (1963) emphasized the pervasive uncertainty that individuals face with respect to health and health care, and the potential welfare gains of expanding access to insurance. Pauly (1968) counter-argued that, because insurance induces inefficient over-consumption of health care, insurance causes large welfare losses in the market for health care services.

Consequently, a full analysis of the welfare effects of insurance must consider both the welfare gains in the insurance market (from risk reduction and increased access to costly care) and the welfare losses in the market for health care services (from moral hazard). With full insurance (i.e., no cost-sharing), at the margin the welfare losses from moral hazard potentially exceed the welfare gains in the insurance market. Indeed, Pauly's analysis led some to conclude that the paramount insurance-related policy problem in modern societies is not inefficiently *low* levels of insurance but inefficiently *high* levels of insurance.

Pauly reasoned as follows.[1] Assume that the health care market is perfectly competitive, that the demand curve is downward sloping and accurately reflects marginal private and social benefit, that the supply curve accurately reflects the marginal private and social

---

[1] If you are unsure how to assess welfare losses and gains in using demand and supply curves, review the relevant section in Chapter 3.

FIGURE 10.1

The Standard Analysis of Moral Hazard

In the standard analysis of moral hazard based on Pauly (1968), health care is assumed to be exchanged in perfectly competitive markets. With no insurance, equilibrium price and quantity are P_{PC} and HC_{NI}^{PC} respectively. Full insurance that lowers the price of care to P_{FI} causes consumption to increase to HC_{FI}. This moral-hazard-induced increase in consumption creates a welfare loss equal to the shaded triangle $abHC_{FI}$. Hence, the full welfare effects of insurance must consider both the welfare gains from risk reduction and the welfare losses from moral hazard in the health care market. The policy response to combat moral hazard is to impose patient cost-sharing, in this case, raising the price to P_{CS}, reducing utilization to HC_{CS}, and reducing the welfare loss from moral hazard from the triangle $abHC_{FI}$ to the triangle ace.

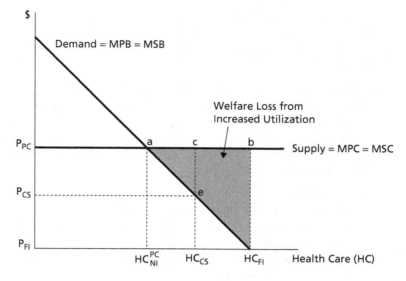

costs of production, and, for simplicity, assume that health care is produced at a constant marginal cost so that the supply curve is a horizontal line (Figure 10.1). In this context

- In the market equilibrium with no insurance, the price of health care will be P_{PC} and individuals will pay the full cost, consuming HC_{NI}^{PC} health care, which is the socially efficient amount (because it is assumed that there are no externalities or other sources of market failure).

- If there is full insurance coverage that lowers the price of health care to zero (P_{FI}), the demand for health care will increase to HC_{FI}. Insurance increases health care consumption by the amount ($HC_{FI} - HC_{NI}^{PC}$).

- Because the demand curve is assumed to accurately reflect the marginal social benefit of care to individuals, the increased benefit derived from additional health care utilization is the triangle below the demand curve between the two levels of consumption ($aHC_{FI}HC_{NI}^{PC}$). The increased cost of producing the additional care is the area under the supply curve, the rectangle $abHC_{FI}HC_{NI}^{PC}$. The insurance-induced increase in utilization generates a welfare loss equal to $abHC_{FI}$.

This welfare cost of the increased utilization in the health care market must be weighed against the welfare gain in the insurance market. The optimal amount of insurance coverage balances these two counteracting welfare effects. The policy solution in this analysis is partial insurance, or cost-sharing: make patients pay part of the cost of care they use. In Figure 10.1, let price P_{CS}, which results in health care consumption HC_{CS}, be optimal (welfare maximizing) when both welfare effects are taken into account. In this analysis, full insurance coverage that provides care free of charge, such as Canada provides for physician and hospital services, can never be optimal.

This analysis and the associated policy recommendations have been extremely influential, in part because they have tremendous intuitive appeal. Free care "obviously" leads to "frivolous" use that provides little benefit. The sensible response is to charge people for at least some of the cost of their care to reduce such utilization. This analysis directly led to the somewhat surprising conclusion (given the number of people in the United States with no or minimal insurance) that the major health policy problem in the U.S. was over-insurance (Feldman and Dowd 1991; Feldstein 1973; Manning et al. 1987). And because the optimal level of cost-sharing depends critically on the price elasticity of demand for health care, the U.S. government invested tens of millions of dollars to conduct the RAND Health Insurance Experiment (discussed in Chapter 8) to estimate this elasticity. This analysis implicitly or explicitly underlies nearly every call for user charges in health care.

10.1.2 Critiques of the Standard Analysis of Moral Hazard

Many health economists challenge this standard analysis and its associated policy recommendations. The analysis, they argue, rests on questionable assumptions regarding the health care market, on faulty economic analysis, and on inappropriate normative assumptions (e.g., see Evans 1984; Nyman 2003; Rice 1992; Rice 1998). The critiques divide into three types:

1. critiques that do not challenge the basic neo-classical economic framework of analysis, but relax certain assumptions to correspond better with actual health care markets
2. critiques arguing that violations of the standard assumptions are sufficiently severe as to nullify the normative status of the demand curve
3. critiques that reject on ethical grounds a normative framework based on willingness to pay as a measure of value

Critique 1: Modifying Assumptions Within the Standard Neo-Classical Framework

Three considerations—the fact that health care markets are not perfectly competitive, the presence of positive externalities, and the positive income-elasticity of demand—imply that even within the standard economic framework, the welfare loss caused by moral hazard will be smaller than implied by Pauly's analysis. The first two of these—imperfect competition and externalities—imply that the equilibrium level of utilization without insurance is below the socially optimal level, so that a portion of the insurance-induced increase in utilization is welfare-improving.

Imperfect Competition and the Welfare Loss from Moral Hazard   Health care markets are, for a number of reasons, not perfectly competitive. Physician entry is restricted by licensure and physicians are prohibited from certain types of advertising, hospitals often enjoy substantial local market power, and so forth. Markets that are not perfectly competitive have higher prices and inefficiently low levels of output and consumption (Chapter 3).

In Figure 10.2, let HC_{NI}^{NPC} be the no-insurance equilibrium in an imperfectly competitive health care market. Introducing insurance increases utilization from HC_{NI}^{NPC} to HC_{FI}. Of this increase, the portion over the range HC_{NI}^{NPC} to HC_{NI}^{PC} is welfare increasing (MSB > MSC). Consequently, the welfare loss associated with the insurance-induced utilization increase is the area of the large triangle (abHC$_{FI}$) minus the area of the small triangle (cad). This is smaller than in Pauly's original analysis, which assumed a perfectly competitive market.

Externalities and the Welfare Loss from Moral Hazard   The impact of integrating externalities into the analysis is illustrated in Figure 10.3. Consumption of needed health care generates positive externalities, so the social benefit curve lies above and to the right of the demand curve. Because the market is assumed to be imperfectly competitive, the no-insurance equilibrium level of utilization is HC_{NI}^{NPC}, but the socially optimal level of utilization is HC_{SO}. When insurance is introduced, utilization again increases to HC_{FI}. A portion ($HC_{SO} - HC_{NI}^{NPC}$) of this increased utilization is welfare-increasing, not welfare-decreasing. The welfare cost associated with moral hazard in the health care market is equal to the triangle fbg minus the triangle def. In this example, the welfare cost is substantially smaller than Pauly's original analysis would suggest.

FIGURE 10.2   Moral Hazard and Welfare Loss with Imperfect Competition

In an imperfectly competitive market, price is higher than in a competitive market (P_{NPC} versus P_{PC}) resulting in a lower level of consumption (HC_{NI}^{NPC} versus HC_{NI}^{PC}) that is below the socially optimal level. The introduction of insurance, therefore, increases utilization from HC_{NI}^{NPC} to HC_{FI}. But because the no-insurance output level is below the socially optimal level, a portion of this increased utilization (that from HC_{NI}^{NPC} to HC_{NI}^{PC}) is welfare improving. The total welfare loss, therefore, is triangle $abHC_{FI}$ less the triangle cad.

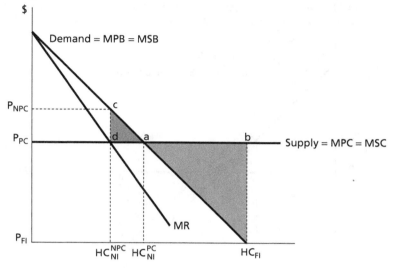

Income Effects and the Welfare Loss from Moral Hazard   Integration of the third consideration—income effects—reduces even further the implied welfare costs of insurance. When insurance lowers the price of health care, it increases the insured person's real income. Pauly's analysis assumes that the income-elasticity of demand for health care is zero, so the observed increase in utilization is attributed fully to the pure price effect, which induces the welfare losses (the artificially low price does not reflect the social costs of producing the care). But in reality the income-elasticity of demand is not zero: it is positive (Chapter 8). And because the income effect represents a response to increased real income (and not to a distorted price), changes in utilization caused by an income effect do not create welfare losses. Consequently, that portion of insurance-induced increase in utilization due to an income effect generates a welfare gain, not a welfare loss.

The Net Effect   The net effect of integrating these three considerations is to reduce—but not eliminate—the welfare loss induced by moral hazard. In the view of this critique, the standard analysis rightly identified moral hazard as a source of welfare loss, and cost-sharing as the correct policy response; but it overstated the magnitude of the welfare loss.

Critique 2: Asymmetry of Information, Moral Hazard, and Welfare Loss

A second set of critiques poses a more fundamental challenge to the standard analysis by questioning the normative status of the demand curve. Recall that the demand curve represents social benefit of consumption only under two assumptions:

1. consumers are able to judge the benefits of consuming a good
2. the appropriate measure of social value is a person's willingness to pay for the good

FIGURE 10.3 **Moral Hazard and Welfare Loss with Imperfect Competition and Externalities**

Incorporating externalities into the analysis further reduces the size of welfare loss associated with moral hazard. Once again, with imperfect competition the no-insurance level of utilization is HC_{NI}^{NPC} and full insurance increases utilization to HC_{FI}. Taking externalities into account, the socially optimal level of utilization (where MSB = MSC) is HC_{SO}. Hence, increases in utilization between HC_{NI}^{NPC} and HC_{SO} are welfare improving; only increases above HC_{SO} create welfare losses, and this welfare loss is measured by the difference between the MSB curve and the supply curve. In this example, the net welfare effect of the insurance-induced increase in utilization is triangle fbg less triangle def.

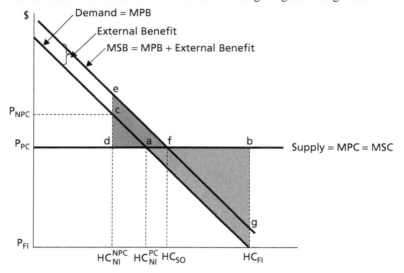

Pauly's analysis of moral hazard assumes that consumers are able to accurately judge the benefits of health care before they purchase it. Informational asymmetry, however, invalidates this assumption. There is no guarantee that observed utilization accurately reflects either individual preferences (it may also reflect physician preferences) or an accurate understanding of the benefits of health care.

Consequently, the demand curve no longer represents a valid measure of social benefit. Nor is demand-side patient cost-sharing necessarily the best policy by which to correct moral hazard. As noted in Chapter 8, in the face of poor information, cost-sharing does not reduce only "frivolous," low-benefit care. Because cost-sharing often forces individuals to make choices without good information, patient cost-sharing decreases both necessary and unnecessary health care utilization.

This has been observed in the RAND Health Insurance Experiment that studied the effects of cost-sharing (Lohr et al. 1986, p. S36; Siu et al. 1986), as well as other studies (Rice and Morrison 1994; Stoddart et al. 1993). Tamblyn et al. (2001) found that increased cost-sharing for prescription drugs in the province of Quebec reduced overall utilization of prescription drugs and reduced utilization of both essential and less-essential drugs. Also, among those who reduced their consumption of essential drugs, it led to increased rates of adverse health events, including hospitalization, admission to long-term care facilities, and even death (Box 10.1).

The Policy Change

In 1996, the government of Quebec reformed its insurance system for prescription drugs. The reform expanded coverage to groups that were previously uninsured, but it also increased cost-sharing among those previously covered: welfare recipients and the elderly. Prior to August 1, 1996, welfare recipients and the low-income elderly received drugs free of charge. Non-low-income elderly paid $2.00 per prescription for the first 50 prescriptions per year, after which all drugs were provided free.

Beginning August 1, 1996, all beneficiaries had to pay 25 percent co-insurance up to a maximum annual expenditure of $200 for welfare recipients and $200, $500, and $750 respectively for low-, middle-, and high-income elderly. Beginning January 1, 1997, all beneficiaries were required to pay a $100 deductible in addition to the 25 percent co-insurance rate, though the maximum expenditure limits were pro-rated quarterly rather than annually (i.e., rather than $200 annually, people paid a maximum of $50 per quarter). On July 1, 1997, the deductible and maximum expenditure limits were both applied on a pro-rated monthly basis. The new policy increased the out-of-pocket costs for the vast majority of beneficiaries.

The Impact

Tamblyn et al. (2001) examined the impact of increased cost-sharing on the use of essential and less-essential medications, and on the rate of adverse health events (hospitalization, admission to long-term care facilities, or death). Figure B10.1 documents the impact on drug utilization. Increased cost-sharing reduced utilization of essential and less-essential medications among both the elderly and welfare recipients. For both groups, reductions in less-essential medications were not associated with an increase in either adverse health events or emergency room visits. Reductions in the use of essential medications, however, were associated with increased adverse effects and emergency room visits. Indeed, the authors found a clear dose–response relationship: the larger the reduction in utilization of essential medications, the greater the probability of an adverse event or an emergency room visit.

FIGURE B10.1   Observed and Predicted Use of Essential and Less-Essential Medication in the Pre- and Post-Policy Period

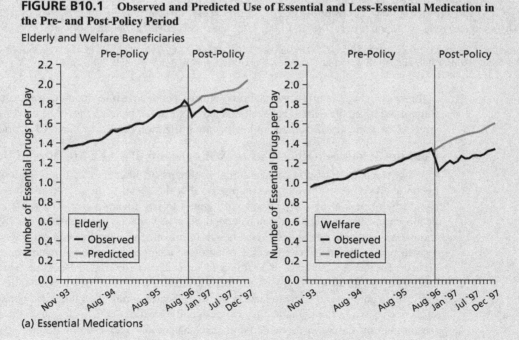

(a) Essential Medications

(Continued)

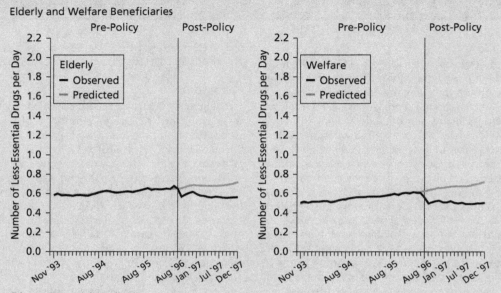

Elderly and Welfare Beneficiaries

(b) Less-Essential Medications

The reduction in the use of essential drugs, and the association of these reductions with adverse health effects, indicates that cost-sharing does not simply reduce frivolous use. For many people, especially those with low incomes, the reductions can have substantial health impacts. Further, once we factor in the greater use of non-drug health care services such as physicians, hospitals, and long-term care, it is not clear if the increased cost-sharing led to a reduction in government spending overall. In other settings, the evidence indicates that increased non-drug expenditures actually exceed the cost savings from user charges in the drug sector (Soumerai et al. 1991).

Source: Soumerai, S. B., D. Ross-Degnan, T. Avorn, T. J. McLaughlin, and I. Chodnovsky. 1991. "Effects of Medicaid Drug-Payment Limits on Admission to Hospitals and Nursing Homes." *The New England Journal of Medicine*. Vol. 325(15):1072–77.

In short, given the informational problems associated with health care, we must be cautious about using the demand curve—indeed, some argue it should never be used—to make welfare assessments of changes in health care utilization caused by changes in price.

Critique 3: Ethical Objections to Willingness to Pay as a Measure of Benefit

Finally, irrespective of any informational problems or other market imperfections, many health analysts reject the ethical assumption that the social value of a health care service should be measured by the person's willingness to pay for a service. The social value of health care, they argue, should not depend on a person's economic resources. Rather, it should be measured by the associated health improvement. Substituting health for willingness to pay as the measure of social value often changes conclusions regarding the efficiency of observed patterns of health care utilization (Box 10.2). Because cost-sharing can cause low-income individuals to forgo effective, necessary treatment, while wealthy individuals continue to consume care with small health benefits, in this view benefit measures derived from the demand curve are ethically invalid. Once again, but for a different reason than the case above, the demand curve has no normative status in judging patterns of health care consumption.

The analytic importance of using health rather than willingness to pay as a measure of social value can be illustrated using an example adapted from Reinhardt (1998, pp. 12–15).

Consider two families, the Chens and the Smiths, with identical preferences. The Chens are wealthy and the Smiths are poor. Each family has just had a baby. Baby Chen is perfectly healthy but Baby Smith is somewhat sickly. Each family currently has full insurance for physician visits. Figure B10.2.1 depicts the two families' demand curves for physician visits. With full insurance, the Smiths demand 9 physician visits during the period and the Chens demand 6. Because of concerns about moral hazard, the insurer imposes a co-payment equal to $15 per visit. Under cost-sharing, both families demand 5 visits per period, for a reduction of 5 visits overall (from 15 to 10). Given the objective of reducing overall visits by 5 (which is implied in this analysis by setting the user charge at $15), within the standard welfare economic analysis the reductions of 4 and 1 respectively for the Smiths and the Chens are the optimal way to do this, in the sense that they impose the lowest welfare loss as measured by willingness to pay.

Figure B10.2.2, however, depicts the marginal health product curves for physician visits for these two families. Because Baby Smith is sickly while Baby Chen is healthy, the marginal health gain associated with physician visits is always greater for the Smiths than for the Chens.

If we measure benefit by the health effects rather than willingness to pay, then to reduce overall visits by 5 in a way that minimizes health effects, the Chens' visits should be reduced from 6 to 2 while the Smiths' are reduced from 9 to 8 (given the initial full-insurance combination of 9 and 6 visits respectively for the Smiths and the Chens).

To see why, imagine a series of incremental decisions to reduce total physician visits by 5 while minimizing the health loss. Starting with the combination of 6 visits for Baby Chen and 9 for Baby Smith, the marginal health losses of reducing the Chens' visits from 6 to 5 and from 5 to 4 are less than reducing the Smiths' visits from 9 to 8. The health losses are the same when going from 4 to 3 visits for the Chens and from 9 to 8 for the Smiths. Finally, reducing the Chens' visits from 3 to 2 causes a smaller reduction in health than reducing the Smiths' from 8 to 7. A single user-charge policy could never accomplish this.

Theoretically, we could have different user charges based on family income or the effectiveness of a service. But such policies are complicated to administer, so the administrative costs can outweigh the gains from reduced utilization. An alternative is to use supply-side policies that encourage providers to reduce utilization of services that generate a small benefit.

The more important point is that a decision about whose utilization should be reduced, and in what manner, depends on the normative framework of the analysis. Hence, even if these analysts agreed on the aggregate amount of moral hazard, they would differ regarding the policy approach to correcting the moral hazard.

FIGURE B10.2.1 Welfare Effects of Cost-Sharing

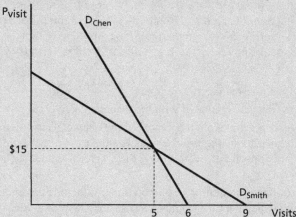

FIGURE B10.2.2 Health Effects of Cost-Sharing

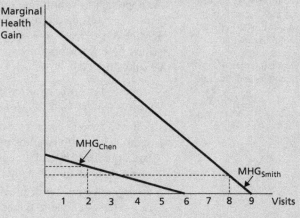

Source: Based on information found in Reinhardt, U. 1998. "Abstracting from distributional effects, this policy is efficient." In M. Barer, T. Getzen, and G. Stoddart, Eds., *Health, Health Care, and Health Economics: Perspectives on Distribution.* Toronto: John Wiley and Sons, 1–53.

The Critics Do Not Reject Moral Hazard as a Policy Problem

It is important to emphasize that although critics reject the standard analysis of moral hazard, as well as the associated estimate of the magnitude of the welfare loss and the demand-side policy prescription for cost-sharing, they acknowledge that insurance can cause moral-hazard-induced, inefficient health care consumption. Moral hazard remains a policy concern. These critics argue for policies that combat moral hazard from the supply side.

10.1.3 Combatting Moral Hazard from the Supply Side

Supply-side approaches to combatting moral hazard target physicians and other care providers with regulations or incentives in an attempt to ensure that only necessary, effective care is provided. Supply-side approaches are motivated by two considerations:

1. Providers possess the knowledge and information required to judge when a service is necessary and to selectively reduce use of low-benefit care.

2. Providers themselves can be a source of moral hazard—for instance, in situations where there is incentive to induce demand (Chapter 8). With patients insulated from the full cost of care, providers may either increase prices where there is scope to do so or provide services of only marginal (but positive) expected benefit. Consequently, supply-side approaches try to limit a provider's ability to engage in moral hazard.

gatekeeper model
A delivery model in which the primary care provider (normally a family physician) regulates access to specialist and diagnostic services, which patients are not permitted to access directly.

Gatekeeper Model   One supply-side approach is the **gatekeeper model** of access. Under the gatekeeper model, the primary care provider (normally a family physician) regulates access to specialist and diagnostic services. Patients cannot go directly to a cardiologist when concerned about a heart problem, to the ophthalmologist about an eye problem, to a neurologist about headaches, and so on. Rather, they must first pass through the "gate" of the primary care provider, who judges whether further diagnostic testing and assessment by a specialist is required.

The gatekeeper model embodies the principle that access to primary care should be broad and as equal as possible, while access to higher levels of care should be based on professional judgments of need. The gatekeeper model is an integral part of many publicly financed systems—including Canada's—and managed care plans in the United States.

managed care
A delivery model that monitors and controls the provision of care in an effort to reduce moral hazard and increase quality by regulating the choices of providers and patients.

Managed Care   More controversial is **managed care**, which rose in prominence in the United States during the 1980s and 1990s, and is perhaps the most publicized supply-side approach to controlling utilization. Managed care arrangements are often motivated by the twin considerations of reducing moral hazard and improving quality through better coordination of care and closer monitoring of care patterns. Managed care cannot be defined by reference to any specific set of policies, but in general, it is characterized by the following:

- lower cost-sharing requirements than non-managed-care plans
- limited patient choice of providers (to those affiliated with the managed care plan)
- limited access to certain services except with explicit approval of the managed care plan (approval usually requires pre-authorization: the provider has to contact the managed care organization to obtain explicit approval before providing the service; without such approval, the plan can deny payment)
- retrospective review of provider utilization patterns (e.g., how long a doctor's patients stay in hospital; the frequency with which certain diagnostics tests are ordered) to identify physicians whose practice styles are not consistent with the standards of the plan

Managed care has been vilified by the medical profession for interfering in clinical practice and by patients for limiting choice, impeding access to what they judge to be necessary services, and for being bureaucratically rigid. For these reasons, a backlash against managed care occurred in the U.S., though a milder version that provides greater flexibility for patients willing to pay extra costs remains a dominant delivery model there.

Capacity Control Supply-side policies in systems that are publicly financed, such as in Canada and the United Kingdom, rely less on micro-management of clinical practice and more on aggregate, system-level capacity constraints. For example, rather than allowing unfettered introduction of MRIs and other expensive diagnostic technology and then struggling to control their use, Canada has limited the overall number and distribution of MRI machines within the system.

capacity constraint approach
Supply-side model to control moral hazard and expenditure growth; relies primarily on aggregate, system-level capacity constraints rather than micro-management of individual decisions of clinicians.

Publicly financed systems can also exert more centralized control over budgets, which can affect the patterns of both investment and utilization. Within this **capacity constraint approach**, the public insurer limits the resources that are available, but delegates considerable authority and autonomy to health professionals to use those resources to meet the health needs of the population. The growing evidence of inappropriate utilization within even tightly constrained health care systems, however, has prompted public funders to play a more active managerial role in the provision of services, though in most cases it falls well short of the managed care strategies widely used in the U.S.

Supply-Side Financial Incentives Finally, supply-side approaches emphasize the importance of aligning the financial incentives for good medical practice through careful design of the funding mechanisms by which insurers pay providers. The trend has been toward funding methods that better balance the incentives for over- and under-use and give greater flexibility to providers in deciding how best to meet the needs of patients. These and related health care funding issues are discussed in Chapter 12.

10.2 RISK SELECTION

risk class
Individuals classified by an insurance agency as having the same risk (based on observable characteristics) and who are, therefore, each charged the same premium.

The model of the demand for insurance presented in Chapter 9 assumes that an insurer charges each individual a premium that exactly reflects the person's true financial risk status, measured in terms of expected health care expenditures during the period of insurance coverage. In reality, risk adjustment is imperfect, based on only a small number of observable characteristics such as age, sex, residential location, and sometimes crude indicators of health status. Insurers then charge all individuals with the same *observable* characteristics the same premium, equal to the average risk status of people with those characteristics.

But some people with the same observable characteristics carry more risk than others. On average, 85-year-olds have higher health care expenditures than 25-year-olds, so age is a useful predictor of risk status. But within each age group, there are still considerable differences in expected expenditures. This inability to perfectly risk adjust premiums causes no problems as long as neither the individuals themselves nor the insurer know which members of the group have a risk status that is below average within a **risk class** and which members have a risk status that is above average.

risk selection
The phenomenon whereby an insurer's risk pool systematically attracts individuals of either below-average or above-average risk status given the premiums charged.

If, however, individuals have better information about their risk status than does an insurer, or if the insurer has better information than the individuals, the informational asymmetry can give rise to risk selection. **Risk selection** refers to the phenomenon whereby an insurer's risk pool systematically attracts individuals of either below-average or above-average risk status given the premiums charged. It can arise whenever the insurer cannot charge each individual an actuarially fair premium, either because of informational asymmetry or because of regulation such as that which requires insurers to charge community-rated premiums. The risk selection can be favourable or unfavourable to the insurer.

adverse risk selection
When an insurance pool systematically attracts individuals of above-average risk status within a risk class.

When the insurance pool systematically attracts individuals of above-average risk status, it is called **adverse risk selection**; when the insurance pool systematically attracts individuals of below-average risk status, this is called **favourable risk selection**, **cream-skimming**, or **cherry picking**. Risk selection can cause market failure by preventing a full set of insurance markets from developing or by inducing insurers to expend valuable resources trying to cream-skim to increase their profits with no attendant increase in social welfare.

10.2.1 Adverse Selection

favourable risk selection
When an insurance pool systematically attracts individuals of below-average risk status within a risk class. Also called **cream-skimming** or **cherry picking**.

Very often an individual has information not available to an insurer regarding their true risk status. Individuals know, for instance, whether they wear seat belts, how much alcohol they drink, their preferences for seeking care when sick, and many other aspects of themselves and their behaviour that influence their expected health care use. Individuals can use this information to judge how their own risk status differs from the average risk of those with the same observable characteristics on which the premium is based. Those members of the group with higher-than-average risk status within the risk class are systematically more likely to purchase insurance than are those members with lower-than-average risk status. Adverse selection arises from the voluntary decisions of the insurance beneficiaries when they have better information than insurers regarding their true risk status.

Figure 10.4 illustrates this using the insurance diagram developed in Chapter 9 (Figure 9.1). Figure 10.4 assumes two individuals, A and B, who are in the same risk class. The two individuals have identical preferences over wealth (U(wealth)) and identical initial wealth (W_0), but have different expected health care costs. The expected health care costs

FIGURE 10.4 **Adverse Selection Occurs with Differing Risks in the Same Risk Class**
Adverse selection can occur when people within a risk class have differing levels of risk. In this example, two people, A and B, have identical preferences over wealth and identical initial levels of wealth (W_0). They differ, however, in their risk: the expected loss for person B is larger than for person A. We can see this because the expected wealth level of B, EW_B, is less than that of A, EW_A. Because they are in the same risk class, the premium each has to pay is the same and is marked in the diagram: if each buys insurance, they will attain certain utility equal to U(W_0−premium). For B, this is a bargain: it gives B much higher utility than if he or she did not purchase insurance (EU_B). But for A, this certain level of utility is less than expected utility (EU_A): the premium exceeds A's maximum willingness to pay for insurance (WTP_A). Hence, only B will purchase insurance. Adverse selection has occurred.

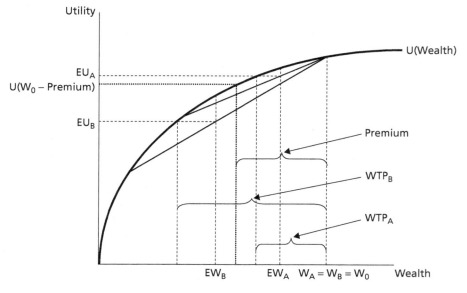

for B are higher than for A; this is represented in the figure by the fact that the expected wealth of B (EW_B) is smaller than the expected wealth of A (EW_A). Because they are in the same risk class, they pay the same premium, as indicated in the figure.

At this premium, B finds insurance a good deal: for B, the certain utility attained after paying the premium (W_0−premium) is well above the expected utility with no insurance (EV_B). Person B will buy insurance. For A, however, the certain utility attained after paying the premium is less than the expected utility without insurance (EV_A). The premium exceeds A's maximum willingness to pay for insurance. Person A declines insurance. Hence, the higher-risk individual purchased insurance while the lower-risk person did not. Adverse selection occurred.

Adverse Selection and Market Failure

Adverse selection can lead to incomplete insurance markets.[2] To see why, consider a simplified risk pool with five members who are observationally equivalent but actually differ in their risk status. Table 10.1 lists, for each individual, their expected costs, risk premium, and maximum willingness to pay for insurance. The mean expected expenditure of all five individuals is $112.

Assume each individual knows his or her true risk status but does not convey it to the insurer.[3] The insurer offers to sell each member of the group an insurance policy for $112. At this price, however, individuals One and Two decline to purchase the policy; only Three, Four, and Five buy insurance. The insurer will lose money because revenue equals $336 (3 x $112), but expected costs across Three, Four, and Five are $500 (sum of $100, $150, and $250). Realizing that the premium was too low, given those who actually bought

[2] This type of market failure, caused by asymmetric information, was first analyzed by George Akerlof in the market for used cars (Akerlof 1970), an analysis for which he shared the 2001 Nobel Prize with Joseph Stiglitz and Michael Spence.

[3] In real insurance markets, there is a good reason people do not signal their true risk status: people have incentive to lie. To get a lower premium, they could claim that they eat healthily, exercise regularly, don't smoke, and so forth, when these claims are not true. Insurers would soon distrust any such virtuous claims. A premium must be based on verifiable information.

TABLE 10.1 **Market Failure Cause by Adverse Selection**

Assume that there are five risk-averse people with differing expected costs in the insurance pool. For each person, note the expected costs, the risk premium the person is willing to pay, and the total amount the person is willing to pay for insurance. The mean expected cost across all five individuals is $112. If this is the premium the insurer charges, only Three, Four, and Five purchase insurance in Period 1. This provides the insurer with revenue of $336 but expenses of $500, leading to negative profits. In response, the insurer raises the premium to $167 in Period 2, which causes Three to decline insurance. This pattern continues until the market disappears and adverse selection causes market failure.

Person	Expected Costs	Risk Premium	Willingness to Pay	Period 1 Premium = $112	Period 2 Premium = $167	Period 3 Premium = $200
One	$ 10	$ 1	$ 11	Decline	Decline	Decline
Two	$ 50	$ 6	$ 56	Decline	Decline	Decline
Three	$100	$15	$115	Buy	Decline	Decline
Four	$150	$25	$175	Buy	Buy	Decline
Five	$250	$50	$300	Buy	Buy	Buy
Total	$560					
Mean	$112					
Insurer Revenue				$336	$334	$200
Insurer Expenses				$500	$400	$250
Profit				($164)	($66)	($50)

insurance, in the next period the insurer raises the premium to $167 to reflect the expected costs of those who actually bought insurance.

At this new, higher price, however, Three now declines the insurance. Once again, the insurer loses money (revenue is $2 \times \$167 = \$334$; expected costs are now $400). When the insurer raises premiums again, Four drops out of the insurance pool, leaving only Five. The insurance pool is not sustainable—it will disappear. Adverse selection caused the market to fail.

Why does the unsustainability of this insurance market constitute market failure while the unsustainability of firms or even industries in other contexts does not represent market failure? The distinction lies in the difference between individuals' maximum willingness to pay and the minimum payment the supplier requires to supply the good. The fact that most cities cannot sustain even a single Rolls-Royce dealership does not constitute market failure. It simply reflects the reality that an insufficient number of people are willing to pay the price for a Rolls-Royce and so the community cannot sustain a dealership. Given the maximum amount a typical person is willing to pay for a Rolls-Royce and the minimum amount a dealer will accept to sell one, there is no scope for a mutually beneficial exchange.

The insurance example, however, is different; each individual is willing to pay a premium sufficiently large to allow an insurer to profit by selling them insurance. There is potential for mutual gain between each individual and the insurer—but informational asymmetry prevents the insurer from charging an individual-specific, risk-adjusted premium. As a consequence, mutually beneficial, welfare-enhancing exchanges cannot take place. The private market outcome is inefficient. Complete disappearance of the insurance market is an extreme example, but adverse selection can also cause incomplete markets where insurance is available only to certain groups of individuals or insurers sell only limited kinds of insurance policies (Box 10.3). Such incomplete insurance markets do not allow individuals to pool all the risks they would prefer to pool.

Adverse Selection Between Private and Public Insurance: The Case of Australia

Australia has a mixed public and private system of health care insurance. During most of the post-war period, private (regulated) insurance dominated, and in 1970, about 80 percent of Australians held private health care insurance. For a brief period in 1974–1975, public insurance was introduced, but was effectively removed after a change in government. A system of universal public insurance was reintroduced in 1984, and has remained in place ever since. Individuals, however, are permitted to purchase private insurance (with community-rated premiums) for services covered by the public plan.

With the introduction of universal public insurance in 1984, private health insurance holdings began to decline; but membership declined in a non-random way, as we would expect under adverse selection. By the mid-1990s, the insurance industry was in crisis and losing money. Large premium increases that were intended to restore profitability only caused relatively healthier people to drop private insurance. Between 1989 and 1995, for instance, private insurance premiums rose by 9.8 percent per year, well above increases in general inflation (2.9 percent per year) and per-capita growth in health spending (5.6 percent per year). Yet the industry continued to lose money as the average age of those holding private insurance rose over time.

Two factors contributed to the adverse selection. First, the industry operated alongside a free, highly regarded public insurance system, leading many to drop or forgo private insurance. This was especially true of young people who saw little reason to purchase private insurance unless they had a specific health care need that could make private insurance advantageous (e.g., they anticipated an elective surgery or a pregnancy). Second, private insurance premiums were community rated, which made such insurance particularly attractive to those who had higher health care needs. In a controversial policy, rather than let the industry wither and die, in 1997 Australia's federal government created a system of subsidies and incentives to encourage the purchase of private health insurance and sustain the industry (see Butler 2001; Donato and Scotton 1998; Hall et al. 1999).

Adverse Selection Within a Private Health Insurance System: The Case of Harvard Employee Benefits

Cutler and Reber (1998) present an example of the adverse selection death spiral within a competitive insurance market. In the early 1990s, Harvard University employees could choose among a number of health plans as part of their package of employee benefits. The plans varied in terms of comprehensiveness, generosity of coverage, and extent of choice of providers. Harvard partially subsidized the cost of the plans, providing larger subsidies to more generous (and more expensive) plans. In 1995, in the face of rising employee benefit costs, Harvard changed its subsidy policy.

Beginning in 1995, each Harvard employee was paid a fixed dollar subsidy equal to the premium for the lowest-cost plan. Employees then paid the difference between this fixed contribution and the full premium for their chosen plan. The out-of-pocket premium costs rose substantially for employees who chose more generous plans. The employee cost of enrolling as an individual in the most generous plan, for example, rose from $555 to $1152, while the cost of a less generous, managed care plan rose from $277 to $421. The changed subsidy policy should induce many people to change their choice of insurance plan, and the theory of adverse selection says that these changes should be non-random: among those who were initially in the comprehensive plan, those who switch to the less generous managed care plan should, on average, be healthier and less costly.

This is precisely what happened. Using age as a proxy for risk status, Cutler and Reber found that the average age of those who chose to stay in the comprehensive plan was 50 while the average age of those who switched from the comprehensive plan to the managed care plan was 46. The average annual health care expenses of those who stayed in the comprehensive plan in 1996 were $2648, while the average costs of those who were originally in the comprehensive plan but switched to the managed care plan were $1893. This adverse selection caused the comprehensive plan to lose money in 1995, so it raised it premiums by 16 percent. This induced another round of adverse selection and the plan lost money again in 1996. In early 1997, the insurance company and the University cancelled the comprehensive plan when they realized that it could not be sustained in the face of adverse selection.

Source: Donato, R. and R. Scotton. 1998. "The Australian Health Care System." In G. Mooney and R. Scotton, Eds., *Economics and Australian Health Policy*. St. Leonards, NSW: Allen and Unwin, 20–39.

Policies to Combat Adverse Selection Policies to combat adverse selection usually entail either better risk adjustment or better definitions of risk pools to prevent adverse selection. Better risk adjustment is of only limited effectiveness because even the most sophisticated current approaches to risk adjustment are crude and leave considerable scope for selection problems (van de Ven and Ellis 2000). Too many risk factors associated with health care expenditures are unobservable, making it impossible for a formal risk adjustment process to eliminate risk selection. Furthermore, fully risk-adjusted premiums raise important equity concerns since, on average, those with higher risk are of lower income and least able to afford high premiums.[4]

Private insurers have generally opted for strategies that define risk pools in ways that minimize the chances of adverse selection. A common strategy is to sell only group insurance policies in which all members of a group are automatically included, such as when private health care insurance is provided as a benefit of employment. The insurer contracts with the employer and all employees are covered, regardless of their risk status. This allows the insurer to charge a premium based on the average risk status of all employees without fear that low-risk employees will exit the insurance pool.

Group policies also enable the insurer to reduce administrative costs compared to selling individual policies through a retail network. In Canada, for instance, over 90 percent of private supplemental insurance policy premium payments are associated with group policies; less than 10 percent derive from policies sold to individuals (Hurley and Guindon 2009).

While this strategy can effectively combat adverse selection, it can have important negative side effects. Insurance effectively becomes available only to those who are employed in positions that offer such benefits. In the United States, which relies heavily on employer-sponsored health insurance, most of the millions of individuals without health insurance either don't work, work part-time, or work in low-wage jobs that do not offer health insurance benefits.

Employment-based insurance can also reduce the efficiency of the labour market by impeding the mobility of workers, who may be less likely to change jobs because of the effect it has on their insurance coverage (a phenomenon call "job lock") (Gruber 2000). We will examine this in more detail in Chapter 11.

10.2.2 Favourable Risk Selection (Cream-Skimming)

Favourable risk selection, referred to hereafter as cream-skimming, occurs when an insurer's risk pool has below-average risks given the premium it charges. Cream-skimming arises from the actions of an insurer and has two causes.

1. **Cream-Skimming by Exploiting an Informational Advantage** An insurer may be able to assess a person's risk status better than the individual. While many individuals know little about their underlying risk factors, an insurer has access to the basic characteristics and utilization histories of millions of beneficiaries. It can use this information to assess actuarial risk and increase profits. If, for example, a group of potential beneficiaries who all perceive themselves as being of the same risk status actually includes both high- and low-risk individuals, and if the insurer can use its informational advantage to distinguish the two risk types, then the insurer can selectively market its policies to low-risk individuals while charging them the average premium for the whole group.

2. **Cream-Skimming Through Strategic Policy Design** Even when the insurer does not have an informational advantage, it can strategically design and market insurance policies that induce individuals to sort themselves according to their risk status. A policy that includes a high deductible and a limited range of service coverage will be more attractive to relatively low-risk individuals than to high-risk individuals;

---

[4] This again highlights the point made in Chapter 9 regarding the magnitudes of financial risk and income. The value of material possessions varies directly with income, so only those who can afford an expensive house pay high premiums to insure it. In health care, however, a person's financial risk is not bounded by a person's income or wealth, and given the negative relationship between health and wealth, those with lowest incomes, on average, would have to pay the highest premiums.

a comprehensive policy with generous coverage is attractive to relatively high-risk individuals. Private insurers can also market policies to selectively attract low-risk individuals. Insurers have developed many strategies to do this; for example, some insurers offer free health club memberships to new members. (Such memberships are most attractive to those who are health conscious and physically active.)

Cream-Skimming and Market Failure Cream-skimming constitutes market failure because the real resources insurers expend to cream-skim constitute social waste. Cream-skimming increases neither coverage nor social welfare; it simply redistributes income toward the insurers. It can also break risk pools in ways that harm social welfare. Cream-skimming is normally combatted through regulation. Many countries, for instance, prohibit insurers from refusing insurance to an applicant on the basis of health status; others restrict the types of insurance policies that an insurer can offer. Switzerland, for example, which provides universal coverage through highly regulated private insurers, requires that all insurance organizations offer the same policy with identical coverage for "core services."

10.2.3 Risk Selection and Universal Public Insurance

Risk selection—both adverse and favourable—can also be eliminated through universal, single-payer insurance systems. Risk selection arises from the voluntary choices of either individuals or insurers. Universal, single-payer insurance systems eliminate such choice. In Canada every resident of a province is covered by the public insurer for medically necessary physician and hospital services, just as all residents of the U.K. are covered by the National Health Service. Individuals cannot opt out of the program and the public insurer cannot refuse coverage to a qualifying resident. Eliminating risk selection is therefore one important economic rationale for universal, single-payer insurance systems.

10.3 ECONOMIES OF SCALE

economies of scale
A situation in which the average cost of production falls as output rises over most of the relevant range of production in the industry.

In production, **economies of scale** arise when the average cost of producing a good or service falls as output increases. Economies of scale can make it impossible to sustain competition in small markets because larger firms with lower average costs drive smaller, higher-cost firms out of business.

The provision of private insurance is subject to large fixed costs that generate economies of scale. Activities such as calculating risk-adjusted premiums must be done regardless of the number of people covered by an insurance agency. The optimal firm size depends on the risk being insured and the regulatory environment, and we have little good empirical evidence regarding the optimal size of an insurance firm. While large markets such as the national market in the U.S. can sustain a competitive market with insurers that exploit scale efficiencies, smaller markets such as provinces within a country or even countries with small populations may have to choose between a large number of smaller, less technically efficient firms, a public utility approach that regulates a small number of large insurers, or public insurance.

10.4 A MISSING MARKET FOR INSURANCE AGAINST PREMIUM INCREASES

Imagine a world in which each person purchases private insurance that is fully risk adjusted (no informational asymmetries). Each year everyone must re-contract, paying the premium that reflects his or her risk status at the time of purchase. To simplify matters, assume that each person must be in one of two health states: fully healthy or suffering from an expensive chronic disease.[5] Over a lifetime, everyone has some probability of acquiring the chronic disease, but there is inherent uncertainty about who will acquire it and when. If a person acquires the disease, all expenditures on health care will be covered, but the individual will have to pay a higher insurance premium to reflect risk status.

Even with full insurance coverage (i.e., all care is free), as long as premiums are risk-adjusted a person faces financial risk. This financial risk derives not from paying the cost of care, but from needing to pay a much higher insurance premium if the uncertain chronic illness strikes. A risk-averse person would potentially benefit by eliminating the risk of a future increase in the insurance premium. The risk could be eliminated by a second type of insurance policy—"premium" insurance—which guarantees that, if a person acquired the chronic illness and faced higher premiums, the premium insurer would pay an amount equal to the difference between the health care insurance premiums when healthy and the premiums when suffering from the chronic disease. If the cost of this insurance was actuarially fair, risk-averse individuals would purchase it.

Although real-world private insurance markets often do require people to re-contract each year (or at least regularly), no such "premium insurance" is available. It is a missing market that could improve welfare but which, for a number of reasons, does not exist.[6] Why not?

Such an insurance contract would have to cover many years rather than a single year. This creates logistical difficulties—the contract must be portable as people move around at different stages of their lives. The insurance would have little value if a person had to re-contract (at a rate that reflected current health status) when they moved in mid-life.

Even more important, however, are the unpredictable changes in the cost of treating specific conditions. The cost of treating heart disease has increased astronomically since 1970. The premium charged for such an insurance contract would have to incorporate the expected costs of care many years into the future. This requires knowledge of how health care technology will develop. Furthermore, insurers themselves cannot pool against the risk of increased costs; the increased costs would affect all those who are insured, violating the independence assumption of risk pooling.

Note that tax-financed public insurance avoids this market failure altogether. In Canada and the U.K., individuals' contributions to support public insurance do not depend on their risk status. Hence, a person does not have to fear increased premium payments from becoming a high health risk.

---

[5] This example is adapted from Cutler and Zeckhauser (2000), which provides a fuller discussion.

[6] Recall the test for efficiency loss if a transaction does not take place: are individuals willing to pay a price at least equal to the minimum amount a supplier requires to produce the good? If the answer is yes, we have an efficiency loss because a chance is lost to make both better off; if the answer is no, there is no efficiency loss.

Chapter Summary

This chapter has analyzed sources of market failure in health care insurance markets.

- Primary sources of market failure include moral hazard, risk selection, economies of scale, and missing markets in insurance.
- Moral hazard—the tendency for health care insurance to change a person's expected health care utilization—causes inefficiently high levels of health care consumption:
  - The analysis of moral hazard based on the standard economic model argues that insurance-induced over-consumption is a major policy problem and that the appropriate policy response is high levels of cost-sharing.

- Critics of this analysis challenge its assumptions and argue that, when more realistic assumptions regarding market structure, externalities, and informational problems are incorporated, the magnitude of moral-hazard-induced welfare loss falls. They argue that the appropriate policy response is not demand-side cost-sharing but supply-side policies.
- Risk selection arises from informational asymmetry between insurers and individuals:
  - Adverse selection, whereby the risk pool attracts individuals with above-average health care risks, arises when individuals have better information regarding their true risk status than do insurers.
  - Cream-skimming, or favourable risk selection, arises when insurers have better information regarding individuals' risk status than do the individuals themselves.
  - Policy responses to risk selection include premium risk adjustment, regulation of insurers, and provision of insurance through group policies rather than individual policies. Universal public insurance systems avoid problems of risk selection.
- Economies of scale arise from fixed costs associated with the provision of insurance. Economies of scale can make it difficult to maintain competitive markets for insurance.
- A key missing private insurance market is insurance against becoming a bad risk in a world in which insurance contracts must be renewed regularly at premiums that reflect a person's risk status at the time of renewal. Publicly provided insurance can correct for such market failure.
- All of these sources of market failure associated with private insurance provide a rationale for large public involvement in health care financing.

Key Terms

adverse risk selection, *257*
capacity constraint
   approach, *257*
cherry picking, *258*
cream-skimming, *258*

economies of scale, *263*
ex ante moral hazard, *248*
ex post moral hazard, *248*
favourable risk selection, *258*
gatekeeper model, *256*

managed care, *256*
risk class, *257*
risk selection, *257*

End-of-Chapter Questions

For each of the statements below, indicate whether the statement is true or false and explain why it is true or false.

1. Adverse selection is likely to be most severe when the government requires private insurance companies to charge all individuals the same premium.
2. *Ex post* moral hazard is more amenable to correction by supply-side policies than is *ex ante* moral hazard.
3. Adverse selection can occur only in insurance markets with individual choice.
4. Adverse selection explains why most private health insurance policies in Canada are group policies linked to employment.
5. Moral hazard arises only in private insurance markets.
6. The greater a person's risk premium, the less likely they are to drop out of an insurance pool that charges a common premium to a group of individuals of differing risks.
7. Moral hazard means insurance necessarily leads to a welfare loss in the market for health care.
8. If the production of health care generated positive externalities, the welfare costs of moral hazard would be smaller than is suggested by M. Pauly's analysis.
9. The fact that some people cannot afford insurance constitutes an important market failure.
10. Risk selection arises only because of differences in expected losses; differences in risk preferences play no role.

References

Akerlof, G. A. 1970. The market for "lemons": Quality uncertainty and the market mechanism. *The Quarterly Journal of Economics* 84(3):488–500.

Arrow, K. J. 1963. Uncertainty and the welfare economics of medical care. *American Economic Review* 53(5):941–73.

Butler, J. 2001. Policy change and private health insurance: Did the cheapest policy do the trick? In *Daring to dream: The future of Australian health care. Essays in honour of John Deeble*, G. Mooney, and A. Plant (eds). Perth: Black Swan Press.

Cutler, D., and R. Zeckhauser. 2000. Anatomy of health insurance. In *Handbook of health economics*, A. J. Culyer, and J. P. Newhouse (eds.). Amsterdam: Elsevier Science B. V. 11:563–644.

Cutler, D. M., and S. J. Reber. 1998. Paying for health insurance: The trade-off between competition and adverse selection. *The Quarterly Journal of Economics* 113(2):432–66.

Donato, R., and R. Scotton. 1998. The Australian health care system. In *Economics and Australian health policy*, G. Mooney, and R. Scotton (eds.). St. Leonards, NSW: Allen and Unwin. 20–39.

Evans, R. G. 1984. *Strained mercy: The economics of Canadian health care*. Toronto: Buttersworth.

Feldman, R., and B. Dowd. 1991. A new estimate of the welfare loss of excess health insurance. *American Economic Review* 81:297–301.

Feldstein, M. S. 1973. The welfare loss of excess health insurance. *Journal of Political Economy* 81(2):251–80.

Gruber, J. 2000. Health insurance and the labour market. In *Handbook of health economics*, A. J. Culyer, and J. P. Newhouse (eds.). Amsterdam: Elsevier Science B. V. 12:645–706.

Hall, J., L. De Abreu, and R. Viney. 1999. Carrots and sticks: The fall and fall of private insurance in Australia. *Health Economics* 8(8):653–60.

Hurley, J., and G. E. Guindon. 2009. Private insurance in Canada. In *Private health insurance and medical savings accounts: Lessons from international experience*, S. Thomson, E. Mossialos, and R. G. Evans (eds.). London: Cambridge University Press. Forthcoming.

Lohr. K., R. Brook, and C. Kamberg. 1986. Effect of cost-sharing on use of medically effective and less-effective care. *Medical Care* 24:S31–S38.

Manning, W. G., J. P. Newhouse, N. Duan, E. B. Keeler, A. Leibowitz, and M. S. Marquis. 1987. Health insurance and the demand for medical care: Evidence from a randomized experiment. *American Economic Review* 77(3):251–77.

Nyman, J. 2003. *The theory of demand for health insurance*. Stanford, CA: Stanford University Press.

Pauly, M. V. 1968. The economics of moral hazard: Comment. *American Economic Review* 49(June):531–37.

Reinhardt, U. 1998. Abstracting from distributional effects, this policy is efficient. In *Health, Health Care and Health Economics: Perspectives on Distribution*, M. Barer, T. Getzen, and G. Stoddart (eds.). Toronto: John Wiley and Sons. 1–53.

Rice, T. 1992. An alternative framework for evaluating welfare losses in the health care market. *Journal of Health Economics* 11(1):85–92.

———. 1998. *The economics of health reconsidered*. Chicago: Health Administration Press.

Rice, T. H., and K. R. Morrison. 1994. Patient cost sharing for medical services: A review of the literature and implications for health care reform. *Medical Care* 51(3):235–87.

Siu, S., F. Sonneberg, W. Manning, G. Goldberg, E. Bloomfield, J. Newhouse, and R. Brook. 1986. Inappropriate use of hospitals in a randomized trial of health insurance plans. *New England Journal of Medicine* 315(20):1259–66.

Soumerai, S. B., D. Ross-Degnan, T. Avorn, T. J. McLaughlin, and I. Chodnovsky. 1991. Effects of Medicaid drug-payment limits on admission to hospitals and nursing homes. *New England Journal of Medicine* 325(15):1072–77.

Stoddart, G. L., M. L. Barer, and R. G. Evans. 1993. *Why not user charges? The real issues.* Toronto: The Premier's Council on Health, Well-Being and Social Justice.

Tamblyn, R., R. Laprise, J. Hanley, M. Abrahamowicz, S. Scott, N. Mayo, J. Hurley, R. Grad, E. Latimer, R. Perreault, P. McLeod, A. Huang, P. Larochelle, and L. Mallet. 2001. Adverse events associated with prescription drug cost-sharing among poor and elderly persons. *Journal of American Medical Association* 285(4):421–29.

van de Ven, W., and R. Ellis. 2000. Risk adjustment in competitive health plan markets. In *Handbook of Health Economics*, A. J. Culyer, and J. P. Newhouse (eds.). Amsterdam: Elsevier Science B.V. 755–846.

Appendix 10

Chapter 10: Private Insurance Markets

10.1 MORAL HAZARD

Welfare Effects of Market Power

The impact of market power on price and the equilibrium level of consumption is most easily seen for the case of a monopolist (Figure 10A.1). The long-run supply curve in a competitive industry is a horizontal line equal to marginal cost; the market equilibrium occurs at the intersection of the market demand curve and supply curve (P_{comp}, Q_{comp}).

A profit-maximizing monopolist restricts output to the point where marginal revenue equals marginal cost, and charges a price based on the demand curve at that level of output (P_{monp}, Q_{monp}). Hence, equilibrium output under a monopolist is less than that for a competitive market, and social welfare is reduced by the area equal to the triangle ABC. Because suppliers in many health care markets hold some market power, equilibrium output in the absence of insurance is below the socially optimal level, implying that some of the insurance-induced increase in health care consumption is welfare-improving.

FIGURE 10A.1
Market Power: Equilibrium Under a Monopolist

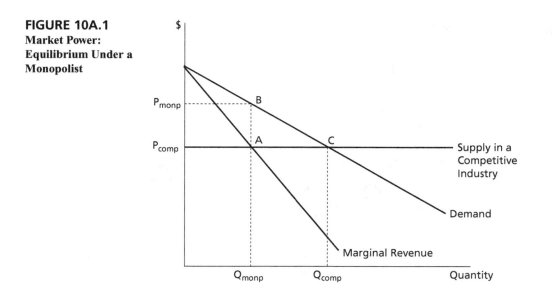

Positive Income Effect It is straightforward to decompose the overall insurance-induced increase in utilization into that caused by pure price effect, which is welfare decreasing, and that caused by the income effect, which is welfare enhancing. Let an individual's utility-maximizing combination of health care and other consumption be (HC_{NI}, C_{NI}) when they have no insurance and face the full price of health care (Figure 10A.2). If the individual purchases full insurance that lowers the price of care by the proportion s, the budget constraint changes as follows: the intercept with the vertical axis falls by the amount of the insurance premium and the slope of the price line is now $-(1-s)P_{HC}$. The optimal consumption bundle becomes (HC_I, C_I). The total change in health care consumption induced by insurance decomposes into the pure-price effect ($HC'-HC_{NI}$) and the income effect (HC_I-HC').

10.2.1 Adverse Selection

We can use the contingent incomes framework (see appendix to Chapter 9) to analyze adverse selection. Consider a situation with two individuals of differing risk profiles starting from the same initial situation. The loss associated with illness is identical for the two individuals, but the higher risk individual faces a higher probability of becoming ill ($P_H > P_L$).

Assume that there are no information asymmetries, so that an insurer can identify each person's risk status and offer each person full insurance at an actuarially fair price (P_H and P_L). The market will be characterized by a separating equilibrium in which both individuals purchase full insurance, ending up at W^*_H and W^*_L respectively for the high-risk and low-risk individual (Figure 10A.3).

Now assume that there is asymmetric information: individuals know their own health status but the insurer knows only the average risk across both individuals and cannot distinguish the high-risk individual from the low-risk individual. The insurer will charge a premium that equals the average risk (AR), represented by the average fair-odds line in Figure A10.4 (call this the "population" fair-odds line). Is a pooled equilibrium sustainable on the population fair-odds line? No. Imagine that an insurer offers the contract on the population fair-odds line that is most preferred by the high-risk types, point W'_H. As drawn in Figure 10A.4, low-risk types would prefer no insurance to this insurance contract and so would not join the pool.

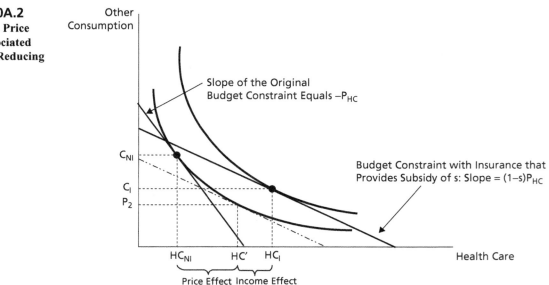

FIGURE 10A.2
Income and Price Effects Associated with Price-Reducing Insurance

Other Consumption

Slope of the Original Budget Constraint Equals $-P_{HC}$

C_{NI}

C_I
P_2

Budget Constraint with Insurance that Provides Subsidy of s: Slope = $(1-s)P_{HC}$

HC_{NI} HC' HC_I

Health Care

Price Effect Income Effect

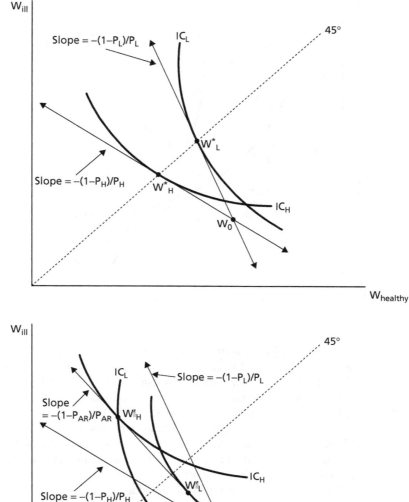

FIGURE 10A.3
Separating Equilibrium with Two Risk Levels and Perfect Information

FIGURE 10A.4
Separating Equilibrium, Population Fair-Odds Line

In a competitive insurance market, a firm would realize that it could offer a contract on the population fair-odds line to the southeast of W'_H and attract only low-risk individuals (high-risk types prefer to stay at W'_H). Through the competitive process, equilibrium would occur with high-risk individuals at W'_H and with low-risk individuals at W'_L—a separating equilibrium. Indeed, no pooling equilibrium is possible.

What separating equilibrium will occur in a competitive market? Imagine that an insurer offered a contract at W^*_H as in Figure 10A.5. Only high-risk types would purchase this contact. In a competitive market, a firm would quickly realize that it could offer a contract

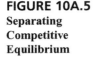

FIGURE 10A.5
Separating
Competitive
Equilibrium

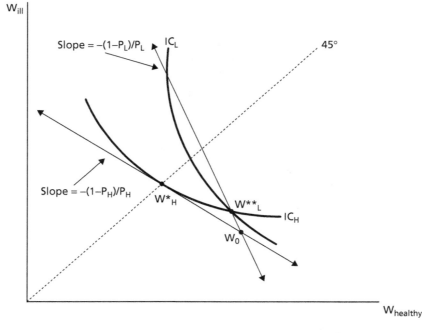

on the low-risk fair-odds line below the point W^{**}_L, attract only low-risk types, and break even (Figure 10A.5). The competitive process would drive the low-risk contract to point W^{**}_L. If a firm offers a contract any higher on the low-risk line, it will attract high-risk types (who would prefer it to W^*_H) and lose money; if it offers a contract below W^{**}_L, another firm will offer a contract closer to W^{**}_L.

In this equilibrium, high-risk individuals purchase full insurance, ending up at (W^*_H), and low-risk individuals purchase partial insurance, ending up at W^{**}_L. The result is a separating equilibrium with incomplete insurance. This is known as the Rothschild-Stiglitz equilibrium under asymmetric information.

The Rothschild-Stiglitz analysis provides considerable insight into the dynamics of insurance markets under asymmetric information, but two aspects of the equilibrium do not accord well with what we observe in real-life insurance markets:

1. We do observe pooling equilibrium in many contexts.
2. Usually the low-risk individuals have little trouble getting insurance but high-risk individuals do have trouble getting insurance.

Newhouse (1996) showed that by introducing a transaction cost into this framework, it is possible to generate such a pooling equilibrium on the population fair-odds line. Consider the best contract on the population fair-odds line for a low-risk individual, W'_L, in Figure 10A.6. In the absence of transaction costs, this is not a stable pooled equilibrium, but if the transaction costs associated with writing separate contracts for high- and low-risk individuals are sufficiently large, this pooling equilibrium is sustainable. This will be true if transaction costs exceed ($W^{\sim} - W'$).

FIGURE 10A.6
Pooling Equilibrium on Population Fair-Odds Line with Transaction Costs

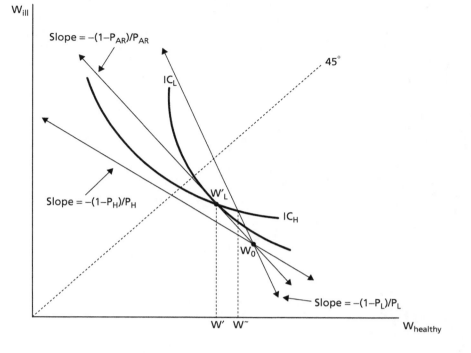

Note that in this situation, we have to worry about cream-skimming by insurance companies: if an insurance company can devise a way to attract a disproportionate share of low-risk individuals from the pool, it will make a profit rather than simply break even.

The Flow of Funds Within a Health Care System

This section, comprising Chapters 11 and 12, analyzes three principal means by which funds flow within a health care system: financing, funding, and remuneration. As noted in Chapter 1, health care financing refers to the activity of raising the monies required to pay for the operation of the health care system from individuals. This is most commonly done through direct out-of-pocket payments, private insurance premiums, social insurance contributions, and taxes.

Health care **funding** refers to the activity of allocating those monies to alternative activities within the health care sector, normally to health care programs and providers who deliver health care services. This is most commonly done through a combination of fee-for-service payments, capitation, and various approaches to setting budgets.

Remuneration refers to compensation for individuals employed in the health care sector in return for their labour. This is most commonly done through salary or wage payments to individuals.

Together, the methods of financing, funding, and remuneration create the financial incentives that individuals, insurers (public and private), and providers face in the health care system.[1] These methods play a crucial role in determining who seeks what care in which settings, how the burden of paying for care is distributed among members of society, and who has incentive to provide what care in what settings.

The financing, funding, and remuneration methods also determine the distribution of financial risk among individuals, insurers, and providers. By financing health care through insurance, individuals transfer risk to the insurer. Insurers, in turn, can transfer some or all of the risk to providers and other funded organizations through the chosen funding method. Consequently, the total amount of risk and its distribution among health care system participants depends on the combination of financing, funding, and remuneration methods used.

funding
The allocation of revenue, raised through financing, to alternative activities within the health care sector—normally the health care programs and providers delivering health care services.

remuneration
Compensation to individuals employed in the health care sector.

---

[1] Economic and policy discussions often use the three terms interchangeably, especially financing and funding. We stress the distinction among them because each constitutes an analytically distinct activity and raises distinct analytic challenges.

The ultimate distribution of risk has a number of important efficiency effects. Other things equal, bearing risk makes risk-averse individuals and organizations worse off. The various health system participants also have differing abilities to pool risk, so a well-designed system matches the distribution of risk to the ability to pool risk.

Bearing financial risk can create strong incentives to produce and use health care services efficiently—but it also creates incentives to engage in inefficient practices such as risk selection.

Financing, funding, and remuneration schemes can be tremendously complex. A full analysis of the effects of financing, funding, and remuneration schemes requires an analysis of both the financial incentives embedded within the schemes and behavioural models of what motivates individuals, insurers, and providers. The two chapters in this section focus on the schemes themselves, providing the basic principles and concepts necessary to understand and analyze them. Subsequent chapters examine behavioural models of providers. Further, the two chapters focus particularly on financing and funding, because many of the key analytic issues associated with remuneration correspond directly to those faced in the design of funding schemes, and because the design of remuneration schemes within organizations is generally of lesser public policy concern than is financing and funding.

Systems of Health Care Finance

Learning Objectives

After studying this chapter, you will understand

LO1 Common efficiency and equity effects of alternative approaches to financing health care

LO2 Basic principles of public finance as they bear on health care finance

LO3 Commonly observed roles and relationships among different financing organizations within systems of health care finance, especially between the public and private sectors

---

Health care in nearly all countries is financed through a complex arrangement of public and private organizations. Market failure in private insurance markets and ensuring equity of access to health care mean that in many countries private insurance plays a relatively minor role in the overall system of finance and is heavily regulated where present. The public sector has a direct, often dominant role in financing health care.

This chapter provides an overview of a range of issues associated with health care finance. It begins with a comparison of the efficiency and equity effects of two polar cases of finance: pure private finance and pure public finance. Though no country's system of finance is either purely private or purely public, comparison of the two cases highlights the general efficiency and equity effects of each. Following this, we consider basic configurations of public and private roles within systems of mixed public and private finance, and the efficiency and equity effects of these mixed systems.

11.1 EFFICIENCY AND EQUITY IN PURE PRIVATE AND PURE PUBLIC SYSTEMS OF FINANCE

Three caveats are in order before beginning the analysis:

1. Pure private and pure public systems of finance can each include a tremendous variety of possible designs. Private systems can differ, for example, in the extent of reliance on private insurance versus out-of-pocket payment, in how premiums are calculated, and in a host of other regulations. Public systems can differ in the relative importance of taxes versus social insurance contributions, in the contributions of different types of taxes,

TABLE 11.1 **Sources of Health Care Finance**
Health care can be financed using a variety of public and private sources.

Source of Finance	Definition	Examples
Public		
Tax Revenue	revenue collected from taxpayers by a government tax agency to support the provision of publicly financed goods and services	personal income tax, corporate income tax, goods and services tax, sales tax, customs tariffs
Tax Expenditure	forgone tax revenue not collected due to preferential treatment of a good, service, or activity within the tax code	tax deductibility of employer-provided health benefits; medical expense tax credit
Social Insurance Contributions	contributions made to a social insurance fund that insures health care for members of the fund	mandatory payroll contributions in France and Germany; worker compensation contributions in Canada
Private		
Private Insurance Premiums	premiums paid to a private insurer for coverage of defined health care events	premiums for private dental insurance, critical care insurance, and private disability insurance
Out-of-Pocket Spending	money paid directly by the recipient of a service at the time the service is received	direct payment by those with no insurance; payments associated with cost-sharing required by insurance policies
Private Donations/Non-Patient Revenue	monies collected by health organizations not related to the delivery of a health good or service	donations to support health research; hospital non-patient revenue (e.g., parking fees)

in the structure of the tax schedules, and in a number of regulatory features. These variations in design within each category can create quite different efficiency and equity effects. The analysis below, therefore, focuses on tendencies associated with each system of finance. Specific systems must be evaluated on a case-by-case basis.

2. Judgments of efficiency and equity on certain aspects of financing depend on the normative framework used in the analysis. As we have learned, judgments about efficiency in utilization depend on whether the analyst subscribes to the standard welfare economic framework that assesses benefit by willingness to pay or to an extra-welfarist framework that emphasizes health benefits. Our discussion will highlight these issues as appropriate.

3. It will be helpful to familiarize yourself with alternative sources of finance. These were discussed in Chapter 1 and are summarized in Table 11.1.

11.1.1 Efficiency of Public and Private Systems of Finance

Analyses of the efficiency of a system of health care finance must assess the efficiency of the health care financing system itself, the impact of the system of finance on efficiency in the health care services market, and the impact on efficiency in the economy more generally.

Efficiency of the System of Health Care Finance Itself

The efficiency of a system of finance is judged in terms of its technical and cost-effectiveness efficiency in collecting revenue and its allocative efficiency in responding to the risk preferences of members of society.

Administrative Efficiency in Raising Revenue   Technical efficiency and cost effectiveness demand that, other things equal, the chosen financing method minimizes the administrative costs per dollar of revenue raised. Public insurance that is financed through the tax system is, in general, more cost effective than is private finance. Cost per dollar raised in tax-financed systems is generally less for these reasons:

- Revenue collection piggybacks on the already established infrastructure for collecting taxes (in principle, all that public health care financing requires is a change to the tax rate).
- Tax finance avoids the cost of calculating premiums and related charges to individuals.
- Single-payer, tax-financed systems can substantially reduce administrative costs incurred by providers. In multi-payer, private insurance systems, each insurer sets its own payment regulations, eligibility rules, set of covered services, and so forth, requiring providers to employ staff whose primary responsibility is simply to submit claims for payment that conform to the myriad rules imposed by different insurers. In contrast, with a single public insurer, providers face only one set of rules, substantially reducing the administrative costs of a practice because claims for reimbursement are easily processed and submitted (see Box 11.1).

Similarly, beneficiaries within multi-payer voluntary systems of private insurance can incur substantial real time costs determining coverage policies and eligibility policies, and submitting claims related to their use of services.

Allocative Efficiency Responding to Risk Preferences   Allocative efficiency requires that consumption of health care insurance conform to people's preferences about risk and the income transfers associated with insurance. Where such preferences vary importantly across individuals, a voluntary, multi-payer private insurance system that offers a variety of insurance policies with varying coverage levels is more allocatively efficient, in principle, than a public insurance system that forces everyone to consume the same amount of health insurance. Such a public system forces risk-lovers to consume more insurance than they prefer and the strongly risk-averse to consume less insurance than they prefer.

But the ability of private, multi-payer insurance systems to respond to variations in risk levels and risk preferences is compromised by the market failures analyzed in Chapter 10. Adverse selection can lead to incomplete and missing markets in health insurance and thus reduced access to insurance for some members of the population. Private insurers' strategic design of insurance policies to combat adverse selection and to cream-skim means that individuals are often not able to buy their preferred policy given their risk status and willingness to pay—and the resources expended by insurers to cream-skim are an inefficient waste that simply redistributes income. In reality, therefore, private systems of finance include many individuals who are not able to purchase their preferred insurance policy even though they would be willing to do so if the market could offer it.

Hence, both public and private systems of finance suffer from allocative inefficiency in risk-pooling. Whether one system is more allocatively efficient is an empirical matter that depends on the distribution of risks and risk preferences in society and the extent of market failure in private insurance markets.

It is well established that administrative costs are higher in the private, voluntary insurance sector than in tax financed systems or social insurance systems. A review of private insurance in Europe, for example, found that administrative costs as a percentage of premium revenue in the voluntary insurance sector were 2–5 times larger than administrative costs as a percentage of expenditures within the statutory insurance sector (Table B11.1.1).

Woolhandler, Campbell, and Himmelstein (2003) provide the most detailed examination of differences in administrative costs between a tax financed system (Canada) and a multi-payer, private insurance-based system of finance (the U.S.). They examine six categories of

administrative costs: insurance overhead (loading costs), employer's costs to manage health care benefits (costs associated with external benefits consultants and internal costs of administration of benefits), hospital administration, administrative costs incurred by health care practitioners (includes the value of provider time as well as staff time), administrative costs in nursing homes, and administrative costs in home care agencies.

As expected, overhead in both countries for private insurance was considerably higher than for public insurance—in the U.S., 11.7 percent of premium income among private insurers versus 3.6 percent and 6.8 percent respectively for Medicare and Medicaid; in Canada, 13.2 percent of premium revenue versus 1.3 percent of expenditures in

TABLE B11.1.1 Administrative Costs Among Voluntary and Statutory Insurers

Source: Mossialos, E., and S. Thomson. 2004. *Voluntary health insurance in the European Union.* Copenhagen: World Health Organization on behalf of the European Observatory on Health Systems and Policies.

Country	Voluntary Insurers (% of Premium Income)	Statutory Insurance System (% Public Health Expenditure)
France	10–15% (mutual funds)	
	15–25% (commercial)	4.8%
Germany	10.2%	5.1%
United Kingdom	15% (approximately)	3.5%
United States	15% (approximately)	4.0%

(Continued)

Efficiency in the Market for Health Care Services

The method chosen to finance health care affects allocative efficiency in the market for health care services by influencing patterns of health care consumption. Financing influences the prices of health care services, the amount individuals must pay for services, and the options providers face concerning when, where, and how to deliver services.

Efficiency of Utilization As we discussed in Chapter 10, judgments regarding efficiency of utilization under the two financing schemes depend on the analyst's views regarding the magnitude of externalities, the degree of imperfect competition in health care markets, and the normative framework of analysis.

If the analyst views health markets as closely approximating perfectly competitive markets, and individual willingness to pay as the appropriate metric for assigning the social value, then private insurance with cost-sharing is more efficient. Full insurance, such as public plans. Because of the much larger role for private insurance in the U.S., this caused per-capita expenditures on insurance overhead to be $212 higher in the U.S. than in Canada. U.S. employers spent almost $50 more per capita administering health benefit plans than employers in Canada. U.S. hospitals spent $315 per capita on administrative costs—24.3 percent of their total spending—while Canadian hospitals spent $108—12.9 percent of their budgets—on administration, leading to a difference of $207 per capita in hospital administration costs.

The analogous costs differentials for nursing homes and home care programs were $33 and $29 per capita. Finally, health care practitioners in the U.S. spent $217 more per capita on administration in their practices than did their counterparts in Canada. (Table B11.1.2). Overall, therefore, Woolhandler et al. estimate that U.S. residents spend $752 more per capita on administration costs within their health care system than do Canadians. To put this in perspective, this constitutes 21 percent of total Canadian per capita spending on health care in 2002.

TABLE B11.1.2 Administrative Costs in the U.S. and Canadian Health Care Systems

Source: Woolhandler, S., T. Campbell, and D. U. Himmelstein. 2003. "Costs of Health Care Administration in the United States and Canada." *The New England Journal of Medicine.* Vol. 349(8):768–75, Table 1, p. 772.

Cost Category	Spending per Capita ($U.S.)		
	U.S.	Canada	Difference
Insurance Overhead	259	47	212
Employer's Cost to Manage Health Benefits	57	8	49
Hospital Administration	315	108	207
Nursing Home Administration	62	29	33
Home Care Administration	42	13	29
Administrative Costs of Practitioners	324	107	217
Total	**1059**	**307**	**752**

that provided in a system with only public finance, generates substantial inefficiencies in the market for health care services.

In contrast, if the analyst views externalities, imperfect competition, and income effects as important, and further believes that health gain is the appropriate metric for assigning the social value to utilization, then pure public finance would be judged more efficient. Evans (1983; 1984) has further argued that a single-payer public approach, such as Canada's, is better able to control moral hazard and to target resources in line with needs in order to improve efficiency in the health care market over that associated with private finance.[1]

---

[1] He also argues that large public payers are also better able to combat the market power of providers when negotiating prices. Such ability does not generate efficiency effects; it simply redistributes income from providers to taxpayers.

Critics of single-payer public approaches highlight the allocative inefficiencies associated with wait-times, which have been a serious policy concern in Canada since the mid-1990s. Allocative inefficiency unquestionably suffers when waits are unreasonable.[2] Even while acknowledging this, two counter points should be noted:

1. Wait-times are not an inherent feature of public systems of finance.
2. A focus on wait-times and wait-lists alone misses the fundamental issue for allocative efficiency in health care consumption. Allocative efficiency depends on the extent to which individuals are able to obtain services for which the benefit exceeds the social cost. While there are no published wait-lists in the U.S., the lack of access to needed services for the uninsured and under-insured constitutes allocative inefficiency (again, the seriousness of this depends in part on judgments of the relevant normative framework). Analyses must consider both those on wait-lists and those who lack access to needed care and, therefore, never show up on a wait-list.

free riding

Some producers or consumers obtain benefit from a good, service, or activity without contributing toward the cost of producing the good, service, or activity.

Challenges to Efficient Levels of Investment in Practice Infrastructure   Multi-payer systems suffer from a type of market failure in the delivery system that can inhibit the adoption of delivery infrastructure subject to **free riding** (Cutler 2004).

Providers in multi-payer systems treat patients covered by many different insurers. Innovations introduced by one payer might be used by providers to improve care or lower the cost of care for patients of other payers; i.e., other payers will "free ride" on the innovation supplied by the innovating health plan. If, for instance, one insurance plan supplies its affiliated providers with an information system that includes automated reminders about preventive care services, it cannot prevent the provider from using the system for patients of other insurance plans. Because of the potential for free riding, insurers refrain from making such infrastructure investments, resulting in lower-than-optimal investment in such elements of provider practices. Single-payer public systems do not suffer from this incentive problem.

Efficiency in the Broader Economy

Finally, the system of finance can affect efficiency in the broader economy. Two commonly cited effects on allocative efficiency outside the health care sector are efficiency in the labour market and general welfare losses associated with taxation.

job lock

Impediment to labour mobility that arises when health care insurance is obtained as a benefit of employment.

Efficiency in the Labour Market   The coupling of health care insurance coverage to employment, as is common in private insurance markets, can influence a number of labour market outcomes, including job mobility among workers, decisions to enter or exit the labour force, wages, and hours worked. When health care insurance is linked to employment, changing jobs can mean changing insurers, loss of coverage for a period of time either in full or for pre-existing conditions,[3] or a change in health care providers.

All of these effects can reduce labour mobility and allocative efficiency in the labour market. In Canada, for instance, the common practice of linking private drug insurance to employment can create such an effect. The problem is far more severe in the United States, where employer-based private insurance is the largest source of health insurance for working-age individuals. Empirical studies from the U.S. find evidence of **job lock** among workers. They also find that health insurance coverage affects retirement decisions,

---

[2] The definition of "unreasonable" is crucial here. The optimal wait-time for most services is not zero. Defining "reasonable" is not simple, but depends on the impact of waiting on a patient's well-being.

[3] In order to counter adverse selection, private insurance policies often do not cover conditions that already exist when the individual's insurance policy takes effect.

FIGURE 11.1 An Illustration of the Welfare Costs of Taxation

This figure depicts a labour market. In this market, firms demand labour to produce goods and services; workers supply labour based on the opportunity cost of their time. Before an income tax is imposed, the market is in the equilibrium ($W_{no\ tax}$, $H_{no\ tax}$). After the 10 percent income tax is imposed, workers reduce their hours of work to H_{tax}, are paid a gross wage of $W_{tax,\ gross}$, but take home a wage of $W_{tax,\ net}$. The difference between the two is the government tax revenue. Because it has distorted the wage, causing hours of work to fall, this imposes a welfare cost on society equal to the shaded triangle. For society, the marginal benefit to employers (measured by the demand curve) of the hours of work between H_{tax} and $H_{no\ tax}$ exceeds the marginal cost (as measured by the worker's no-tax supply curve).

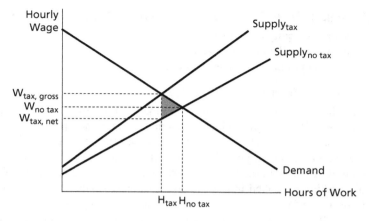

though there is considerable uncertainty regarding the magnitude of these effects (Gruber 2000). The impact of the loss of health care insurance on job uptake by welfare recipients is consistently estimated to be quite large (Gruber 2000).

Welfare Costs of Taxation Recall from Chapter 3 that any price distortions in a well-functioning market (from the price that equates marginal benefit and marginal cost) creates allocative inefficiency—a welfare cost. Nearly all taxes, except those introduced specifically to correct an externality, create allocative inefficiency in the economy because they alter prices from those that would prevail in the market. Consumption taxes create inefficiency by distorting the choice between consumption and saving. Payroll taxes and income taxes create a welfare loss in the labour market.

An income tax, for example, changes the take-home wage rate, altering the relative price of work and leisure. To see the welfare cost of this, suppose there are no sources of market failure in the labour market depicted in Figure 11.1. The no-tax outcome of market wage $W_{no\ tax}$ and hours of work equal to $H_{no\ tax}$ is efficient. Now suppose an income tax is imposed, equal to 10 percent of earnings. This can be represented in the figure by shifting the labour supply curve upward, reflecting the fact that the gross wage paid to workers must increase to induce them to work a given number of hours (the tax equals the vertical distance between Supply$_{tax}$ and Supply$_{no\ tax}$, and equals 10 percent of the gross wage). In the after-tax equilibrium, the gross market wage would be $W_{tax,\ gross}$, the net after-tax wage for workers would be $W_{tax,\ net}$, and hours of work would equal H_{tax}. This creates a welfare loss equal to the shaded triangle. The tax on wages alters the relative price of work and leisure, causing individuals to work less, generating the welfare loss.

Does this imply that all taxes are bad? No. But it implies that government should use tax revenue in ways that generate benefit for society. As long as the benefits associated with the activities funded by the tax revenue outweigh the welfare losses associated with taxation, net benefit for society increases. Taxation and government provision allow society to achieve collective goals that individuals could not accomplish individually. But the costs of such taxation must be recognized.

Lastly, note that the welfare costs arise from the distortionary effect of changing the price of leisure. This implies that some forms of private financing, such as mandatory private premiums linked to employment, can also create similar welfare costs (Mitchell and Phelps 1976; Summers 1989). Hence, in some cases, aspects of private finance can be subject to some of the same welfare considerations as those associated with taxation.

11.1.2 Equity and Alternative Approaches to Health Care Finance

Analyses of equity in financing health care emphasize the impact of alternative approaches on distributional equity with respect to the burden of payment, and on distributional equity with respect to health care utilization.

Equity of Health Care Finance

benefit principle
The amount individuals contribute should be proportional to the benefit they receive from the goods financed.

ability-to-pay principle
The amount individuals contribute should depend on their ability to pay, not their need or their ability to benefit from the goods financed.

Distributional equity of financing normally draws on two general principles of finance: the **benefit principle**, which holds that the amount a person contributes should be proportional to the benefit they receive; and the **ability-to-pay principle**, which holds that the amount a person contributes should depend on their ability to pay, not their need or their ability to benefit. These two principles often conflict. Although the benefit principle is sometimes invoked in health care to support financing through user charges, the ability-to-pay principle overwhelmingly dominates analyses of equity of health care finance, especially with respect to publicly financed services. Accordingly, our discussion emphasizes this equity criterion.

People's ability to pay is normally measured by their income (the amount of money they earn during a specified time period) or their wealth (net financial assets at a given point in time).[4] Income and wealth are generally highly correlated, but the choice between the two can make a difference to assessments of distributional equity because the strength of the relationship between them varies over a lifetime. The ratio of income to wealth, for example, is generally larger among younger and middle-aged households than among older household that have accumulated savings and rely on unearned income from their savings. We assume that income accurately measures ability to pay.

Horizontal equity in finance demands that two individuals with equal ability to pay contribute the same amounts. Vertical equity in finance demands that two individuals with differing abilities to pay contribute appropriately different amounts (recall these equity concepts from Chapter 2). Vertical equity normally demands that those of higher income pay more than those of lower income, though exactly how much more is often disputed.

regressive financing
The proportion of income that a person pays falls as income increases.

proportional financing
The proportion of income that a person pays is constant as income increases.

progressive financing
The proportion of income that a person pays increases as income increases.

Economists describe how payments vary with income in three ways. A system of finance is said to be **regressive** when the proportion of income that a person pays falls as income increases; the system is **proportional** when the proportion of income that a person pays is constant as income increases; and the system is **progressive** when the proportion of income that a person pays increases as income increases. These concepts are illustrated with hypothetical data in Table 11.2, which lists the annual average amount paid to support health care by people of differing incomes in four different countries.

Country One's system of finance is proportional, Country Two's is progressive, and both Country Three's and Country Four's are regressive. Note that for Country Four, although the absolute amount paid increases with income, the system is regressive because the contributions increase more slowly than income, causing them to be a falling proportion of income. Such a regressive system of finance could be consistent with vertical equity (since payments increase with income), though most commonly vertical equity calls for either proportionality or progressivity in finance.

Studies of health care finance generally find the following with respect to progressivity of finance (Wagstaff and van Doorslaer 2000):

---

[4] The relevant measure is household income/wealth adjusted to reflect the composition of the household. Ability to pay differs, for example, between two households with the same total income, when one household includes only one person and the other includes two parents and five children. Economists use "equivalence" scales that adjust household income to reflect the size and composition of households (Atkinson et al. 1995).

TABLE 11.2 **Progressive, Proportional, and Regressive Systems of Finance**
This table presents hypothetical examples to illustrate regressive, progressive, and proportional systems of finance. In Country One, the proportion of income contributed is constant across all income levels. Its tax system is proportional. Country Two's system is progressive because the proportion of income paid in taxes rises with income. Countries Three and Four have regressive systems of finance because the proportions of contributions decrease as income increases.

Income	Country One Contributions	Country One Proportion of Income	Country Two Contributions	Country Two Proportion of Income	Country Three Contributions	Country Three Proportion of Income	Country Four Contributions	Country Four Proportion of Income
$ 20,000	$ 500	0.025	$ 200	0.0100	$2,500	0.1250	$1,100	0.0550
$ 40,000	$1,000	0.025	$ 600	0.0150	$2,000	0.0500	$1,300	0.0325
$ 60,000	$1,500	0.025	$1,200	0.0200	$1,500	0.0250	$1,500	0.0250
$ 80,000	$2,000	0.025	$2,000	0.0250	$1,000	0.0125	$1,700	0.0213
$100,000	$2,500	0.025	$3,500	0.0350	$ 500	0.0050	$1,900	0.0190
Overall	$7,500		$7,500		$7,500		$7,500	

- Personal income taxes are progressive in all countries.
- Consumption taxes are regressive in all countries.
- Tax revenue overall (combining direct and indirect taxes) tends to be either approximately proportional or progressive.
- Social insurance systems exhibit a mixture of progressivity and regressivity depending on their design.
- Private finance is, in general, regressive.
- Direct out-of-pocket payments are the most regressive source of finance.

A country's overall degree of progressivity is determined by the progressivity of each source of finance and the extent to which the country relies on each source. As a general finding, systems of public finance share the burden of payment more equitably than do systems of private finance.

incidence
The ultimate distribution of the burden of a tax or the benefits of a good.

In Canada, public finance for health care appears to be proportional or mildly progressive. The two largest sources of public revenue—income and consumption taxes—have counteracting effects. Income taxes are progressive but consumption taxes are regressive. McGrail (2007) estimated that public financing for physician and hospital services in British Columbia in both 1992 and 2002 was proportional; Hanley et al. (2007) found that public finance for prescription drugs in British Columbia over the period 2000–2005 was proportional; and Mustard et al. (1998) similarly found that public finance in Manitoba in both 1986 and 1994 was essentially proportional. Smythe (2002), however, found public financing in Alberta to be progressive. As a proportion of income, contributions to finance the public system, for example, rose from 4 percent to 8 percent between the lowest and highest income deciles.

Studies of the **incidence** of private insurance financing in Canada are more limited. Because the prevalence of private insurance is strongly positively related to income (Bhatti et al. 2007; Smythe 2001), high-income individuals are more likely to finance health care through private insurance, raising the possibility of proportional or even progressive patterns

FIGURE 11.2
Expected Annual Number of Visits to a General Practitioner and Dentist, Canada, 2001
This figure depicts the expected number of general practitioner and dentist visits per year by Canadians of differing income levels, as measured by income decile. GP visits, which are publicly financed, are negatively associated with income (the wealthy are, on average, healthier); but dental visits, which are privately financed, are strongly positively related to income level.

Source: Author's calculation using the 2001 Canadian Community Health Survey.

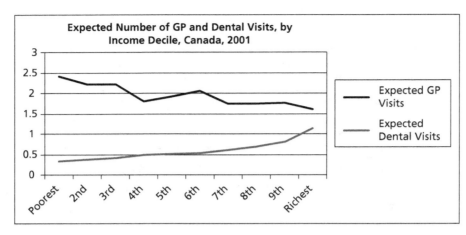

for private insurance. Hanley et al. (2007) estimated that prescription drug financing through private insurance in British Columbia was mildly regressive in both 2000 and 2005. Smythe (2002) estimated that private financing (including both out-of-pocket and private insurance payments) in Alberta was moderately regressive.

Equity of Health Care Utilization

Because the system of finance determines the extent to which individuals face financial barriers when seeking care, it plays an important role in determining equity in the utilization of health care. In general, the greater the breadth and depth of insurance, the more equitable the patterns of utilization. Consequently, full public coverage (sometimes called "first-dollar" coverage because coverage begins with the first dollar of expenditure) results in more equitable patterns of health care utilization than do systems of private financing.

The different patterns of utilization between physician and dental services in Canada illustrate this. Physician services are publicly insured and free to all residents; dental care is predominately privately financed through private insurance (which is frequently linked to employment) and direct out-of-pocket payments.

- Low-income Canadians actually have more visits to general practitioners than do high-income Canadians (Figure 11.2), reflecting the fact that low-income users, in general, have lower health status and greater need for care. Most studies find no meaningful difference between high- and low-income Canadians in the needs-adjusted number of general practitioner visits (Allin 2008).

- In contrast, for dental care, visit rates for high-income Canadians are three times higher than for low-income Canadians (Figure 11.2), and even after adjusting for need there is a substantial pro-rich bias in the use of dental services (Allin 2008; Grignon et al. 2008).

Public financing with first-dollar coverage has led to far more equitable distribution of physician services. Similarly, in a cross-country comparison of utilization of physician services, van Doorslaer and colleagues (van Doorslaer et al. 2005) found that countries that rely more heavily on public finance have higher visit rates than do U.S. residents and more equitable distributions of visit rates across income groups.

11.1.3 Net Incidence

net incidence
The distribution of the difference between tax benefits and burdens.

Economists refer to the ultimate distribution of the burden of a tax or the benefits of a good as its incidence. **Net incidence** analysis examines how society's resources are redistributed through both the system of finance and the patterns of service utilization. That is, the analysis simultaneously compares an individual's financial contributions to health care with the dollar value of the health care services the individual receives. The difference between the two reveals the redistribution of resources among members of society that is induced by the system of health care finance and delivery.

Two Canadian studies (McGrail 2007 and Mustard et al. 1998) conducted net fiscal incidence analyses that considered both tax payments into the system (excluding tax expenditures) and benefits received in the form of publicly financed health care services. Utilization of health care services is highly regressive—the value of services received by low income individuals is a much higher proportion of their income than it is for high-income individuals. As noted above, tax contributions are proportional. Because contributions are roughly proportional to income, but use is highly regressive, the incidence of net benefits is highly regressive: for low income groups in Canada, the value of publicly financed services received far exceeds those groups' contributions, so the health care system redistributes economic resources from high-income groups to low-income groups.

This can be illustrated with two figures from the Manitoba study conducted by Mustard et al. (1998). Figure 11.3(a) shows that the dollar value of the physician and hospital services used by individuals in the lower income deciles was higher than for those in the higher income deciles, while the tax contributions to finance health care made by Manitoba residents rose with income, as would be expected under a proportional/progressive tax system.[5] In absolute dollar terms, the value of services received by those of low income and the institutionalized (Inst) exceeds the value of the tax contributions, so they received a net positive financial transfer through the health care system. The opposite was true for those of high income, for whom the value of tax payments exceeded the value of services received.

FIGURE 11.3(a)
Incidence of Taxation and Incidence of Health Care Benefits by Economic Family Income Decile, Manitoba 1994
The value of health care services used is higher among those who are institutionalized ("Inst") and low-income households (e.g., decile 1) than among high-income households (decile 10). In contrast, tax payment increases with income. The net effect is that those of low income (and especially those who are institutionalized) receive more in benefits than they pay in taxes.

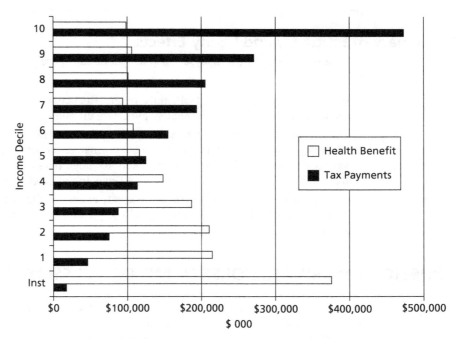

[5] Each decile contains the same number of people. The 1st decile is the 10 percent of the population with the lowest incomes, decile 2 is the 10 percent of the population with the next highest level of income, and the 10th decile is the 10 percent of the population with the highest incomes.

FIGURE 11.3(b)
Net Benefit as a Percent of Household Income by Economic Family Income Decile, Manitoba 1994

The net benefits of the health care system are positive and comprise a large share of household income among low-income households; they are negative, though a smaller share of household income, among high-income households.

Source: For (a) and (b): Mustard C., M. L. Barer, R. G. Evans, et al. 1998. *Paying Taxes and Using Health Care Services: The Distributional Consequences of Tax Financed Universal Health Insurance in a Canadian Province.* Ottawa, Canada.

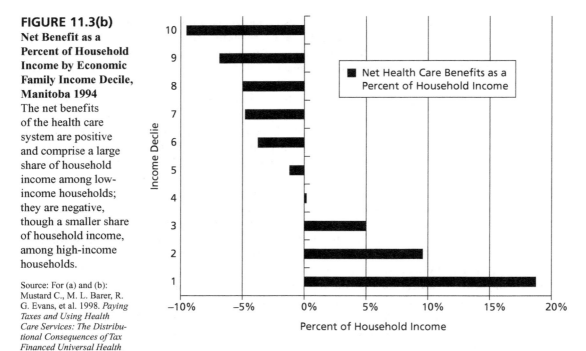

Figure 11.3(b) presents this net transfer for decile groups as a proportion of income. The net gain by those of lower incomes constituted a substantial proportion of income; the net transfer from high-income households constituted a smaller proportion of their income.

11.1.4 Summary of Efficiency and Equity Effects

In summary (Table 11.3), analyses of pure public and pure private finance suggest the following:

- With respect to financing itself, pure public financing is more equitable and more administratively efficient; the relative allocative efficiency is indeterminate.

- With respect to the market for health care services, public finance is more equitable; efficiency judgments depend in part on the normative framework, with extra-welfarists who emphasize health benefits more likely to judge public financing more efficient, and welfarists more likely to judge private financing more efficient.

- In the broader economy, the two systems create counteracting efficiency effects: private systems create inefficiencies such as job lock; public systems create welfare costs from taxation.

11.2 PUBLIC AND PRIVATE ROLES IN MIXED SYSTEMS OF FINANCE

In reality, all systems of health care finance are mixed systems that include elements of both private and public finance. Public and private roles can be configured myriad ways within mixed systems, even among systems with similar shares of public and private spending. These different configurations can have differing effects on efficiency and equity.

TABLE 11.3 **Efficiency and Equity in Pure Private and Pure Public Systems of Finance**

This table summarizes some of the efficiency and equity effects associated with private and public systems of finance. See text for a fuller discussion.

	Pure Private	Pure Public
Efficiency		

Finance	• missing or incomplete markets due to adverse selection
	• cream-skimming
	• in principle, better able to meet heterogeneous risk preferences
	• higher administrative costs
	  • rate setting
	  • advertising
	  • provider offices
	  • beneficiary time/effort
		• avoids all selection problems
		• forces consumption of same amount of insurance
		• lower administrative costs
		  • piggyback on tax collection
		  • streamlined administrative processes for providers
		  • avoids need to calculate premiums

Health Care Markets	• judgment depends partly on normative framework employed
	  • private finance more consistent with judgments that willingness to pay is an appropriate measure of value
	• insurance-induced moral hazard
	• fragmentation of authority that can inhibit adoption of certain technologies due to potential for free riding
	• reduced access for those with low levels of coverage
		• judgment depends partly on normative framework employed
		  • public finance more consistent with extra-welfarist frameworks that focus on health gain as the measure of value
		• greater concern for insurance-induced moral hazard associated with full coverage
		• greater scope for combatting moral hazard through supply-side policies
		• wait-times for some services

Broader Economy	• job lock and related problems	• welfare costs of taxation
Equity		
Finance	• generally regressive, violating the ability-to-pay principle	• generally proportional or progressive (though certain taxes and contribution schemes can be regressive)
Health Care Markets	• less equitable patterns of utilization than under public finance	• more equitable patterns of utilization than under private finance

11.2.1 Some Fundamental Configurations of Public and Private Roles

In addition to the cases of pure public and pure private finance already considered, there are three fundamental configurations of public and private roles:

1. *joint public and private financing,* in which a given service is partly paid for through public sources and partly through private sources (e.g., a user charge within a public system of finance)

2. *public and private financing as alternatives,* in which either public or private financing is chosen (e.g., someone chooses to pay privately for service that is also publicly insured)

3. *complementary public and private financing,* in which the private sector pays for expenses not covered by the public plan

Each configuration creates different incentives for providers and patients, and leads to different kinds of distributional effects with respect to both the burden of finance and the use of services.

Joint Finance

Joint finance means that a portion of the cost of a service is paid publicly and a portion is paid privately. The two sectors do not compete with each other, nor are they seen as alternatives. Public and private expenditures must move lock-step with each other: in order to trigger public expenditure, there must also be private expenditure, and vice versa. The efficiency and equity effects depend, in part, on whether the analysis takes private finance or public finance as its baseline. It is useful to distinguish between these two situations.

Public Finance to Expand Individuals' Private Market Choices In this situation, pure private finance is the baseline and the partial public subsidy is intended to increase access to the health care service while retaining the operation of private markets. The public subsidy is normally the smaller share of finance. Such subsidy is normally motivated by equity concerns, and the increased utilization improves equity in the market for health care services and equity of finance. Although conclusions about efficiency are more tentative, if the increased utilization is of needed services it would also be expected to increase efficiency in the health care market relative to no-subsidy baseline.

Private Finance to Displace Public Expenditure and/or Provide a Steering Effect
This situation takes pure public finance as the baseline and introduces a user charge that is intended to do one or both of two things:

1. To relieve fiscal pressure in the public sector. This is the most common purpose and is exemplified by general user charge policies such as those found in provincial public pharmacare programs (see Chapter 1).
2. To steer people toward a particular type of service or a particular setting in which to receive the service. This is exemplified by a policy that fully covers only generic drugs but allows an individual to pay the difference between the generic and brand-name versions.

A general user charge shifts the burden of finance onto users of care and reduces utilization of health care, including necessary health care. This would be expected to reduce efficiency and equity in both the market for health care services and within the system of finance itself.

A steering charge is different. To the extent that it applies only to services that are not seen as medically necessary (the public system already fully covers an effective substitute), the charge would have neutral or positive effects on efficiency and neutral effects on equity in the market for health care services. Because the charge is for a non-medically-necessary service, it would have a neutral effect on both equity and efficiency in the system of finance.

Private and Public Finance as Alternatives

Configurations in which public and private finance are alternatives can take two primary forms:

supplementary (or parallel) private finance
When a service included within the public health plan can also be obtained (and paid for) privately if desired.

substitutive private finance
When an individual is permitted to opt out of the public plan altogether (making no contributions) and finance health care privately.

1. **Supplementary (or parallel) private finance** exists when a service that is included within the public plan can also be obtained privately if desired—an individual who contributes to the public plan and who is eligible for obtaining the service publicly has the additional option to pay privately and can exercise this choice on a case-by-case basis.
2. **Substitutive private finance** exists when an individual is permitted to opt out of the public plan altogether (making no contributions) and finance care privately.

Supplementary insurance is the more common of the two.

Supplementary Private Finance   Most countries with predominately public systems of finance allow parallel, supplementary private insurance, though its role remains relatively minor in terms of the proportion of finance (e.g., in the U.K., approximately 11 percent of the population holds such supplementary private insurance, largely to avoid queues in parts of the National Health Service). Although it constitutes a relatively small portion of total finance in most countries, such insurance is politically highly contentious. Canada has strongly discouraged such private finance, but debate about expanding the role of parallel private finance is persistent and was re-ignited by a 2005 Supreme Court ruling that struck down Quebec's law prohibiting private insurance for publicly insured services (Box 11.2)

Advocates for such parallel private insurance argue that it can reduce wait-times in the public system, increase access to the public system, increase quality and efficiency (by fostering competition between the public and private sectors), and relieve fiscal pressure on the public system. Detractors argue that it will increase wait-times by drawing resources away from the public system, reduce equity and give privileged access to those who can afford the private insurance, and weaken support for public financing (Hurley et al. 2001; Tuohy et al. 2004).

Again, the specific effects will depend in part on a variety of institutional features of the setting in which it is introduced, including, for example, how providers are paid, the practice options for providers, and the resource allocation processes in the public sector. Nonetheless, it is possible to make some general conclusions based on both analytic reasoning and empirical evidence:

- It is not possible to say *a priori* whether parallel finance will increase or decrease wait-times in the public system compared to a system of public finance only (Box 11.3). The effect depends on a number of factors in the physician labour market, the market for publicly financed services, and the market for privately financed services. Further, the current evidence does not document large effects of such finance on wait-times in either direction.
- There is no evidence that introducing parallel private insurance fosters meaningful competition between the public and private sectors. The private sector tends to focus on a small number of relatively lucrative, non-complex elective procedures; the public sector retains responsibility for the full spectrum of services.
- The presence of a parallel private sector creates wasteful cream-skimming, cost-shifting, and strategic behaviour by providers who can now see patients in both systems.

The June 2005 Supreme Court decision in *Chaoulli vs. Quebec* (Supreme Court of Canada 2005) shook the foundations of the Canadian health care system. The suit was launched by G. Zeliotis, a Quebec businessman needing hip surgery and J. Chaoulli, a Quebec physician wishing to establish a private surgical clinic. They argued that the Quebec law prohibiting the sale of private insurance for services covered by the public insurance plan violated the Quebec Charter of Human Rights and Freedoms and the Canadian Charter of Rights and Freedoms. The Supreme Court ruled that, "in the presence of unreasonable wait times," the law violated the Quebec Charter but it did not violate the Canadian Charter. The ruling therefore stuck down the law within Quebec but had no legal repercussions outside Quebec. The court ruled, in essence, that if the public system cannot provide care in a timely manner, it cannot prohibit private financing for those services.

The government of Quebec responded to the ruling by essentially leaving the law in place, but

- Offering wait-time guarantees for a defined set of procedures for which wait-times had been long, including cancer surgery, heart surgery, hip replacement, cataract surgery, and selected diagnostic tests
- Allowing hospitals to establish contracts with private clinics to deliver a small number of elective procedures in the private clinics but paid for publicly (i.e., "contracting out" the delivery to private clinics)

- Allowing Quebec residents to purchase private insurance for three procedures with long wait-times (hip replacement, knee replacement, cataract surgery)
- Establishing two types of surgical clinics: clinics that could bill the public plan directly, staffed by physicians participating in the public insurance plan; and private clinics that could not bill the plan directly, staffed by physicians who had opted out of the public plan. The importance of this design was that physicians could not choose on a patient-by-patient basis whether to treat a person privately or publicly

This response addressed the immediate concerns of the legal ruling while preserving the existing system for the vast majority of services. Although a number of surgeries had been performed in private clinics under the contracting arrangement (paid for publicly), as of March 2009, not a single private insurance policy had been sold for the three publicly insured services for which it was permitted.

In 2009, however, Quebec passed new legislation that made a number of significant modifications:

- It expanded from 3 to over 50 the number of surgical procedures that can be performed in the private clinics. In fact, only private clinics will be allowed to do certain surgeries.
- The legislation now allows doctors to work in both the public and private clinics, splitting their time between them.

- Parallel private finance exerts upward pressure on the prices of inputs to care (physician time, nurse time, etc.), reducing the real (inflation-adjusted) budget of the public insurer and its corresponding ability to fund services.

Overall, parallel finance would be expected to reduce equity in finance and access to services, since access is now based in part on willingness to pay rather than need. Similarly, it would be expected to reduce efficiency in the sense that less health is produced with the available health care resources (since resources are now used to treat those in lesser need but who are willing to pay privately), but it may increase aspects of allocative efficiency by, for instance, allowing the risk-averse to supplement the public insurance with additional private insurance.

On the whole, parallel private finance is associated neither with the benefits claimed by advocates nor the dire consequences claimed by opponents. With the exception of Ireland, Portugal, and Australia, OECD countries in recent years have generally reduced public subsidy for such insurance, believing that, on net, it does not generate the claimed benefits to the public system (Mossialos and Thomson 2004).

Substitutive Private Finance Substitutive private insurance, although rare, is used in a few European social insurance systems such as in Germany, the Netherlands, Belgium, and Austria. In Germany, approximately 10 percent of the population, mostly individuals with

The supply and demand framework can provide insight into the effects on wait-times of introducing parallel finance alongside the public system. To simplify things assume the following:

- There is a single health care good: physician visits.
- Visits are produced in a particularly simple way: 1 unit of physician labour produces 1 visit.
- Patients can obtain a physician visit free of charge through the public system.
- The public insurer has a fixed budget from which to pay for physician visits.
- The introduction of parallel private finance will shift some demand from the public to the private sector and create new demand in the private sector that was not present with only the public sector.

Analysis of the situation with public insurance requires the analysis of two markets: the market for physician labour and the market for publicly financed health care (Figure B11.3(a)). Demand for physician labour comes only from the public sector; the demand curve is negatively sloped as usual. The physician labour supply curve is upward sloping. Equilibrium physician wage is $W^*_{pubonly}$ and the equilibrium amount of physician labour is $L^*_{pubonly}$. The market for publicly financed care provided by the public insurer is a bit unusual: the supply curve is negatively sloped. This is because the public sector has a fixed budget: as the cost of providing a patient visit goes down, it can afford to provide more visits to patients with its fixed budget. Demand is assumed to be negatively sloped and relatively price inelastic, as usual. When price is zero, the quantity demanded is $HC_D^{pub,pubonly}$. Given the physician wage, the quantity supplied by the public insurer is $HC_S^{pub,pubonly}$. A shortage exists equal to $(HC_D^{pub,pubonly} - HC_S^{pub,pubonly})$. Some patients must wait.

FIGURE B11.3 Using Supply and Demand to Analyze the Impact of Introducing Parallel Private Finance

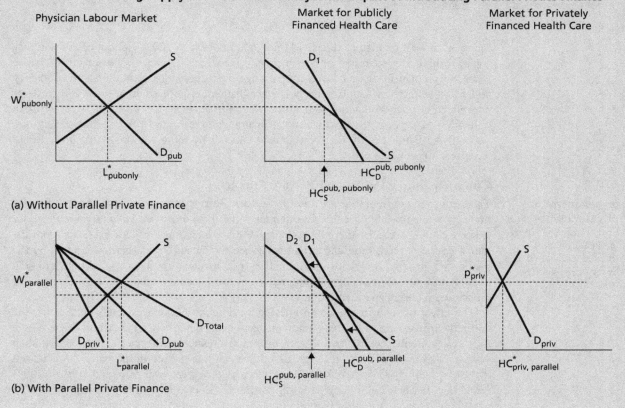

(a) Without Parallel Private Finance

(b) With Parallel Private Finance

Now introduce parallel private finance. The analysis must now consider a third market, that for privately financed visits (Figure B11.3(b)). The total demand for physician labour increases as it is now the sum of demand from the public sector and the demand from the private sector. In the new equilibrium, the wage has increased to $W^*_{parallel}$, and the quantity of labour supply has increased to $L^*_{parallel}$. The physician wage increase reduces the number of visits supplied in the public sector to $HC^{pub,parallel}_S$. The introduction of the private sector shifts public demand inward, so that the quantity demanded is $HC^{pub,parallel}_D$. In the private market equilibrium, the price of a visit is P^*_{priv}, and the number of private visits is $HC^*_{priv,parallel}$.

Although the total number of visits has increased, the effect on wait-times in the public sector is indeterminate: it depends on the relative sizes of the reduced capacity in the public sector and the reduction in demand in the public sector. This in turn depends on these factors:

- the elasticity of physician labour supply: the less elastic the physician labour supply, the less likely that wait-times will fall in the public sector

- the extent to which private demand represents a diversion of public demand or new demand by individuals who did not express demand in the public system

The introduction of parallel finance also changes the basis for who gets a service, from need alone to a mixture of need (in the public sector) and willingness to pay (in the private sector).

This simple analysis made a number of assumptions. However, the same basic framework can be used to examine the impact under alternative assumptions. For instance, what if we did not assume a single labour market and physicians were able to charge higher prices in the private sector than in the public sector? The potential impact of these and other factors on wait-times and overall number of services provided can be traced through a supply and demand model.

---

incomes above a regulatory threshold (€48,600 per year in 2009), opt out of the statutory social insurance system and purchase private insurance. Because a person must choose to be fully opted-in or opted-out, this arrangement does not create the same efficiency and equity effects as supplementary private insurance. Perhaps its most notable effects are related to equity in access to health care and in finance. It relieves the wealthy of an obligation to support the broader social insurance system and because the wealthy are generally in better health, their withdrawal takes away more resources than they would have been expected to use.

Complementary Public and Private Finance

complementary private finance

Private financing (often through insurance) of services not covered by the public insurance plan.

The last mixed configuration we consider is **complementary private finance**—finance that complements public finance. It often takes the form of private voluntary insurance for expenses not covered by the public insurance plan, including services excluded from the public coverage (e.g., drug and dental insurance in Canada), cost-sharing required by the public system (e.g., in France), and ancillary non-medical costs associated with utilizing publicly insured services (e.g., an upgrade from ward accommodation to a semi-private or private room during an in-patient stay).

The effect of such insurance on efficiency and equity effects depends on whether the covered expenses are economic complements to needed publicly financed services. Where they are economic complements, such insurance creates spillover effects into the public system. Stabile (2001), for instance, found that holding private drug insurance increased the use of publicly financed physician services by 5 percent, and Allin and Hurley (2009) found that, because holding private drug insurance is positively correlated with income, it contributes to income-related inequity in the use of publicly financed physician services.

Private insurance creates a number of unavoidable spillover effects on the public insurance system, making it impossible to create a fully independent privately financed system. Glied (2008) provides a useful analysis of such effects, including the following:

- a reduction in public sector monopsony power and the associated competition between the public and private sectors that will bid up prices for health care inputs, resulting in either reduced service delivery by the public sector (if there is no budget increase) or an increase in public sector spending to maintain the same levels of real service delivery

- changed patterns of use in the public system—induced by both complementary private insurance and parallel private insurance because of complementarities between the services purchased privately and the services obtained publicly

- selection effects between the public and private sectors

- negative external effects from increased inequality in, access to, and use of services among members of society

- an impact on public-sector health spending. Models of a political economy with a mixed system of finance (e.g., Epple and Romano 1996) suggest that private spending to supplement the public spending will lead to a reduction in public spending. Tuohy et al.'s (2004) analysis of spending in OECD countries is consistent with this.

Similarly, private insurance to cover cost-sharing reduces the patient price of public services, increasing their utilization among those with such insurance. Studies of Medicare beneficiaries in the U.S. find that, even after controlling for selection effects, those who hold private insurance that covers the co-insurance charges within the public system incur public expenditures that are about 6 percent higher than those without such insurance (Atherly 2002).

Policy Debate and Different Configurations in Mixed Systems

These considerations highlight two points relevant to the policy debate in Canada over the role of private financing, particularly private insurance. First, it is not possible to create an independent system of privately financed services that will have no impact on the public system (Glied 2008; Hurley et al. 2001) (see Box 11.4).

Second, the policy debate often fails to adequately distinguish among these different configurations. For example, participants in the debate over whether Canada should relax restrictions on private parallel insurance sometimes point to France and Germany as examples of systems that use mixed finance successfully. But private finance in France almost wholly takes the form of joint finance through cost-sharing; the primary purpose of private insurance is to cover the high rates of cost-sharing within the social insurance system. In Germany, the primary role of private insurance is substitutive among the wealthy. As described above, the impact of such private insurance differs notably from that being debated in Canada: those countries' experiences are largely irrelevant to the core issues in the Canadian debate.

11.2.2 Systems of Health Care Finance: Rube Goldberg or Patchwork Quilt?

Every county's system of health care finance is an amalgam of subsystems defined by the nature of the service, the characteristics of the recipient, or the cause of the need. Table 11.4 lists some common criteria by which systems divide what people and services are fully publicly insured, partially publicly insured, or not publicly insured, and when a person can opt for private finance rather than use the public system.

The question economic analysis must ask is whether all these distinctions make economic sense. Do they enhance or detract from efficiency and equity? Is there a consistent

TABLE 11.4
Criteria for Determining Public and Private Arrangements
Health care systems use many different criteria to determine which specific configuration of roles will be used for a subset of services or people. The most commonly used criteria distinguish among different types of services, different groups of people, and the source of the injury or illness.

Criteria for Public Coverage	Examples from Canadian Health Care
Dividing the Set of All Services	
Medical Necessity	if medically necessary, public funding; if not, private; e.g., diagnostic ultrasound during pregnancy versus ultrasound for picture of child in utero
Health Care Sector	physician versus dental services
Dividing the Population	
Age	elderly eligible for public drug coverage in many provinces
Income	low-income eligible for public drug coverage
Occupation	RCMP and military insured directly by federal government
Level of Health Care Expenditure	eligibility for certain public insurance programs in the event of catastrophic out-of-pocket expenditures
Disease Type	those suffering from specified diseases, e.g., eligibility for public drug coverage
Dividing on the Basis of the Place of Injury	
Workplace	workplace-related illnesses and injuries are covered by the Workers' Compensation system
Automobile Accident	health care costs for injuries sustained in automobile accidents are covered by automobile insurance

logic, or does the scheme represent simply the accidents of history and policy? And these questions cannot be answered once and for all: what makes the most economic sense changes with the evolution of technology. The development of day surgery, for instance, has made the differential treatment of many types of in-patient and out-patient care archaic. And the expanded role of drugs in prevention and therapy has made them an essential element in providing the full range of medically necessary care.

Finally, quite apart from the question of whether the arrangements ensure that those in need of care are able to access appropriate services, the presence of numerous subsystems creates borders between components with different eligibility criteria. Borders create strategic incentives for patients and providers to expend valuable time and resources engaging in cost-shifting, rent-seeking, and other forms of gaming to exploit the fragmentation to their advantage.

Chapter Summary

This chapter examined a range of issues associated with financing health care. The main points are as follows:

- Equity concerns and market failure in private insurance markets mean public financing dominates in nearly all developed countries; where present, private insurance is often heavily regulated.

- Systems of public finance raise funds through taxes or contributions to publicly regulated social insurance schemes.
- Private sources of finance include out-of-pocket payments, private insurance premiums, and non-consumption contributions (e.g., charitable donations).
- Analyses of the efficiency effects of alternative systems of finance must assess the efficiency of the health care financing system itself, efficiency in the health services market, and efficiency in the broader economy.
- Analyses of the equity effects of alternative systems of finance must assess the distributional effects with respect to the burden of payment and the utilization of health care services.
- A comparison of the efficiency and equity effects of pure private finance and pure public finance concluded that
  - With respect to financing itself, pure public finance is more equitable and more administratively efficient; the relative allocative efficiency is indeterminate.
  - With respect to the market for health care services, public finance is more equitable; efficiency judgments depend in part on the normative framework, with extra-welfarists likely to judge public finance more efficient and welfarists likely to judge private finance more efficient.
  - In the broader economy, the two systems create distinct efficiencies.
- Three additional configurations of public and private roles are found in health care systems around the world, each of which creates distinct incentives for efficiency and equity:
  - joint public and private finance
  - public and private finance as alternative (supplementary and substitutive private insurance)
  - complementary public and private finance
- Overall systems of finance comprise many subsystems with varying configurations of public and private roles:
  - The subsystems are frequently defined by the type of services, population subgroups, or the cause of the injury or illness.
  - It is essential to ask if the variations in financing across the subsystems makes economic sense.

Key Terms

ability-to-pay principle, *282*
benefit principle, *282*
complementary private
  finance, *292*
free riding, *280*
funding, *273*

incidence, *283*
job lock, *280*
net incidence, *284*
progressive financing, *282*
proportional financing, *282*
regressive financing, *282*

remuneration, *273*
substitutive private
  finance, *289*
supplementary (or parallel)
  private finance, *289*

End-of-Chapter Questions

For each of the statements below, indicate whether the statement is true or false and explain why it is true or false.

1. If the poor are, on average, sicker than the wealthy, a fixed user charge (e.g., $25) imposed for each day of in-patient hospital care would likely constitute a regressive form of health care finance.

2. An increase in private health care spending is normally accompanied by a decrease in public health care spending.

3. Time spent by a physician clarifying coverage policies by a private insurer constitutes a source of inefficient waste in a private system of finance, but time spent by a physician negotiating with a hospital administrator for access to a bed for a patient does not constitute inefficient waste because it results in beneficial care.

4. Private complementary health insurance for non-medically necessary services would not be expected to have a negative effect on equity in the public health care system.

5. The growth in the provision of non-medically necessary, privately financed services (e.g., Botox treatments) could be expected to create the same effect on wait-times in the public sector as growth in the parallel private provision of medically necessary, publicly insured services.

6. The presence of parallel financing for the Workers' Compensation System in Canada might be expected to exert upward pressure on the fees within the public health care system.

7. A progressive financing scheme will never violate horizontal equity.

8. The negative welfare effects of an income tax in the market for casual and part-time workers is likely less than in the market for full-time workers.

9. Other things equal, the welfare loss associated with raising money through taxation is smaller the more inelastic is the demand for the good that is taxed.

10. A system of universal public finance is in every way superior to a system of private insurance.

References

Allin, S. 2008. Does equity in health care use vary across the provinces? *HealthCare Policy* 3(4):83–99.

Allin, S., and J. Hurley. 2009. Inequity in publicly funded physician care: What is the role of private prescription drug insurance? *Health Economics* 18(10):1218–32.

Atherly, A. 2002. The effect of Medicare supplemental insurance on Medicare expenditures. *Journal of Health Care Finance and Economics* 2(2):137–62.

Atkinson, A. B., L. Rainwater, and T. M. Smeeding. 1995. *Income distribution in OECD countries.* Paris: OECD Social Policy Studies, No. 18.

Bhatti, T., Z. Rana, and P. Grootendorst. 2007. Dental insurance, income and the use of dental care in Canada. *Journal of the Canadian Dental Association* 73(1):57a–h.

Cutler, D. M. 2004. *Your money or your life.* Cambridge, MA: MIT Press.

Epple D., and R. E. Romano. 1996. Public provision of private goods. *Journal of Political Economy* 104(1):57–84.

Evans, R. G. 1983. The welfare economics of public health insurance: Theory and Canadian practice. In *Arne Ryde symposium on social insurance*, L. Söderström (ed.). Elsevier Science Publishers B.V. 71–103.

———. 1984. *Strained mercy: The economics of Canadian health care.* Toronto: Buttersworth.

Glied, S. 2008. Universal public insurance and private coverage: Externalities in health care consumption. *Canadian Public Policy* 34(3):345–57.

Grignon, M., J. Hurley, L. Wang, and S. Allin. 2008. *Inequity in a market-based health system: Evidence from Canada's dental sector.* Hamilton, ON: McMaster University Centre for Health Economics and Policy Analysis, Working Paper 08-05.

Gruber, J. 2000. Health insurance and the labour market. In *Handbook of health economics*, A. J. Culyer, and J. P. Newhouse (eds.). Amsterdam: Elsevier Science B. V. 12: 645–706.

Hanley, G., S. Morgan, J. Hurley, and E. van Doorslaer. 2007. Distributional consequences of the transition from age-based to income-based prescription drug coverage in British Columbia, Canada. *Health Economics* 17(12):1379–92.

Hurley, J., R. Vaithianathana, T. Crossley, and D. Cobb-Clark. 2001. *Parallel private health insurance in Australia: A cautionary tale and lessons for Canada.* Hamilton, ON.: McMaster University Centre for Health Economics and Policy Analysis, Working Paper 01-12.

McGrail, K. 2007. Medicare financing and redistribution in British Columbia, 1992–2002. *HealthCare Policy* 2(4):123–37.

Mitchell, B., and C. Phelps. 1976. National health insurance: Some costs and effects of mandated employee coverage. *Journal of Political Economy* 84(3):553–71.

Mossialos, E., and S. Thomson. 2004. *Voluntary health insurance in the European Union.* Copenhagen: World Health Organization on behalf of the European Observatory on Health Systems and Policies.

Mustard, C., M. L. Barer, R. G. Evans, J. M. Horne, T. Mayer, and S. Derksen. 1998. *Paying taxes and using health care services: The distributional consequences of tax financed universal health insurance in a Canadian province.* Ottawa, Canada.

Smythe, J. G. 2001. *Tax subsidization of employer-provided health care insurance in Canada: Incidence analysis.* Edmonton, AB: University of Alberta, Department of Economics, Working Paper.

———. 2002. *The redistributive effect of health care finance in Alberta, 1997.* Edmonton: Institute of Health Economics, Working Paper.

Stabile, M. 2001. Private insurance subsidies and public health care markets: Evidence from Canada. *Canadian Journal of Economics* 34(4):921–42.

Summers, L. 1989. Some simple economics of mandated benefits. *American Economic Review* 79(2):177–83.

Supreme Court of Canada. 2005. *Chaoulli vs. Quebec.* Ottawa.

Tuohy, C., C. Flood, and M. Stabile. 2004. How does private finance affect public health care systems. *Journal of Health Politics, Policy and Law* 29(3):359–96.

van Doorslaer, E., C. Masseria, and X. Koolman, OECD Health Equity Research Group. 2005. Inequalities in access to medical care by income in developed countries. *Canadian Medical Association Journal* 174(2):177–83.

Wagstaff, A., and E. van Doorslaer. 2000. Equity in health care finance and delivery. In *Handbook of health economics*, A. J. Culyer, and J. P. Newhouse (eds.). Amsterdam: Elsevier Science B.V. 34:1804–1862.

Woolhandler, S., T. Campbell, and D. Himmelstein. 2003. Costs of health care administration in the United States and Canada. *New England Journal of Medicine* 349(8):768–75.

Appendix 11

Chapter 11: Systems of Health Care Finance

11.2.2   Systems of Health Care Finance: Equity and Alternative Approaches

Incidence Analysis

Incidence analysis distinguishes between statutory incidence and economic incidence. The distinction can be seen most readily in the case of a tax:

- Statutory incidence refers to the individual or organization actually making the payment to the government.
- Economic incidence refers to who actually bears the burden of a tax.

Consider the case of a new per-litre tax on soft drinks. Figure 11A.1 depicts two markets for soft drinks. In the first market, demand is highly inelastic; in the second, demand is highly elastic. The no-tax equilibrium price and quantity sold (P^*_{NT}, S^*_{NT}) are identical in the two markets. The new tax must be paid by the store owner for each litre of product sold.

FIGURE 11A.1

The Incidence of a Per-Litre Tax on Soft Drinks

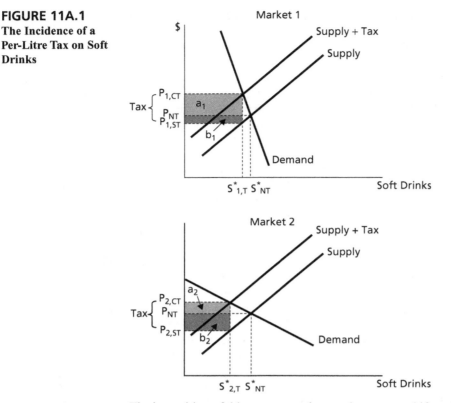

The imposition of this tax causes the supply curve to shift up by the amount of the tax: after the tax, to sell a given litre of soft drinks the store must receive the price indicated by the supply curve plus the amount of the tax, which must be sent on to the government.

In the first market, the post-tax equilibrium amount of soft drinks is $S^*_{1,T}$, the price paid by consumers is $P_{1,CT}$, the price retained by the store is $P_{1,ST}$, and the difference between them is the tax that is collected by the government. Note that although the store owner officially pays the tax to the government, most of the tax is borne by the consumer; the store owner passes on most of the tax in the form of a higher price. The total tax collected by the government is the sum of areas $a_1 + b_1$, where consumers pay a_1 and the store owner pays b_1. The store owner is able to do this because demand is highly inelastic.

But in the second market with highly elastic demand, the store owner has to absorb most of the tax. The price of the soft drinks increases by less than half the amount of the tax: the consumer pays a_2 and the store owner b_2. In each case, the owner "pays" the tax to the government (i.e., the statutory incidence is the same), but the economic incidence differs. Note also that the government collects less tax from the second market because the equilibrium quantity falls by more in the second market than in the first $(a_1 + b_1) > (a_2 + b_2)$.

Measuring the Progressivity of a Tax System

There are a number of ways to measure the progressivity of a tax system. Many of them derive from the concepts of a concentration curve introduced in the Appendix to Chapter 2 (see Figure 2A.9) and a closely related measure called the Lorenz curve. One common measure is the Kakwani index.

To calculate the Kakwani index, establish the degree of pre-tax income inequality in society as a baseline. This is depicted by the Lorenz curve (Figure 11A.2). In a Lorenz curve, the horizontal axis represents the cumulative proportion of the population ranked

FIGURE 11A.2
The Lorenz Curve

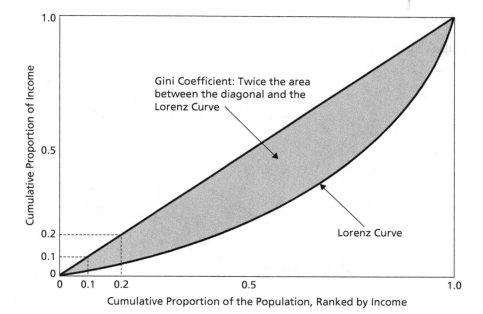

by income, and the vertical axis represents the cumulative proportion of income in society. If income is distributed with perfect equality in society, the Lorenz curve is simply a 45° line: the 10 percent of the population with the lowest income account for 10 percent of the income in society, the lowest 20 percent of the population ranked by income accounts for 20 percent of income in society, and so forth. If there is any income inequality, the Lorenz curve lies below the 45° line.

The area between the Lorenz curve and the 45° line is a measure of the degree of inequality. A commonly used measure of inequality is the Gini coefficient, which is equal to two times the area between the Lorenz curve and the 45° line. The Gini coefficient takes a value in the interval [0,1], where 0 indicates complete equality and 1 indicates complete inequality.

The second piece of information we need in order to assess progressivity is the distribution of tax payments. We can depict this using the concentration curve for tax payments (Figure 11A.3). Once again, let the horizontal axis represent the cumulative proportion of the population ranked by income. This time, let the vertical axis represent the cumulative proportion of tax payments. The tax concentration curve shows the share of income accounted for by the given share of the population with the lowest incomes. The concentration index is equal to twice the area between the concentration curve and the 45° line. It takes on a value in the interval [−1,1], where −1 indicates that the tax burden is borne completely by those with the lowest incomes and 1 indicates that the tax burden is borne completely by those with the highest incomes.

We are now in a position to determine the progressivity of the tax system. Graph the pre-tax income Lorenz curve and the tax concentration curve on the same axis.

- If the concentration curve and the Lorenz curve lie exactly on top of each other, the tax system is proportional: the share of taxes paid by those in the bottom 10 percent of the income distribution is exactly equal to their share of income, the share of taxes paid by those in the bottom 50 percent of the income distribution exactly equals their share of income, and so forth.
- If the tax concentration curve lies below the Lorenz curve, the tax system is progressive: the share of taxes paid by those with low incomes is less than their share of income.

FIGURE 11A.3
The Tax Concentration Curve

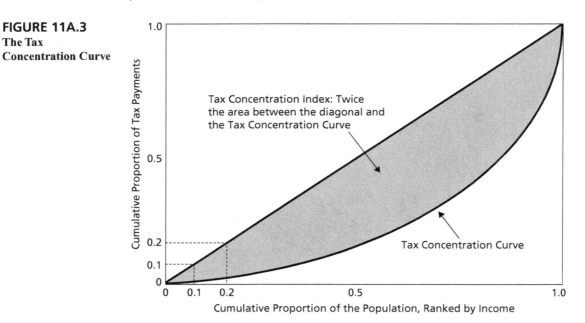

- If the tax concentration curve lies everywhere above the Lorenz curve, the tax system is regressive: the share of taxes paid by those with low incomes exceeds their share of income.

The Kakwani index is defined as twice the area between the tax concentration curve and the Lorenz curve (Figure 11A.4). It can be calculated as

$$\text{Kakwani index} = \text{CI}_{\text{tax}} - \text{Gini}_{\text{pre-tax income}}$$

The Kakwani index takes on values in the range $[-2, 1]$. Where negative values indicate regressivity, zero indicates proportionality, and positive numbers indicate progressivity.

Table 11A.1 lists Kakwani indexes of progressivity for selected countries (no comparable data are available for Canada). Although somewhat dated, the figures are the most recent available internationally, and they illustrate some important principles.[6] Columns 1–3 indicate the progressivity of tax revenues. Direct taxes—primarily personal income taxes—are progressive in all countries, with the United Kingdom showing the greatest progressivity and Sweden the least. In contrast, indirect taxes—primarily consumption taxes—are regressive in all countries.

Tax revenue overall (combining direct and indirect taxes) tends to be either approximately proportional or progressive. Social insurance systems exhibit a mixture of progressivity and regressivity depending on their design. The social insurance systems in Germany and the Netherlands are regressive because those with high income are either required to opt out and purchase private insurance (Netherlands) or can voluntarily do so (Germany). Hence, only low- and middle-income individuals contribute to the social insurance system. In addition, in Germany, even for those in the social insurance system, contribution rates apply only to income below a specified level. Switzerland has the most progressive system of public finance (column 5), France is second, and the U.S. third.

---

[6] A number of countries have reformed their systems of finance since the time of the data on which these estimates are based. Hence, one must be cautious about making inferences to the current systems of finance for specific countries. The table is useful, however, for illustrating certain patterns by type of finance.

TABLE 11A.1   Kakwani Indexes of Progressivity for Selected OECD Countries

Country	(1) Direct Taxes	(2) Indirect Taxes	(3) General Taxes	(4) Social Insurance	(5) Total Public	(6) Private Insurance	(7) Direct Payments	(8) Total Private	(9) Total Payments
France (1989)				0.1112	0.1112	−0.1956	−0.3396	−0.3054	0.0012
Germany (1989)	0.2488	−0.0922	0.1100	−0.0977	−0.0533	0.1219	−0.0963	−0.0067	−0.0452
Netherlands (1992)	0.2003	−0.0885	0.0714	−0.1286	−0.1003	0.0833	−0.0377	0.0434	−0.0703
Sweden (1990)	0.0529	−0.0827	0.0371	0.0100	0.0100		−0.2402	−0.2402	−0.0158
Switzerland (1992)	0.2055	−0.0722	0.1590	0.0551	0.1389	−0.2548	−0.3619	−0.2945	−0.1402
United Kingdom (1993)	0.2843	−0.1522	0.0456	0.1867	0.0792	0.0766	−0.2229	−0.0919	0.0518
United States (1987)	0.2104	−0.0674	0.1487	0.0181	0.1060	−0.2374	−0.3874	−0.3168	−0.1303

Source: Van Doorslaer, E., A. Wagstaff, H. van der Burg, T. Christiansen, D. De Graeve, I. Duchesne, U.-G. Gerdtham, M. Gerfin, J. Geurts, L. Gross, U. Häkkinen, J. John, J. Klavus, R. E. Leu, B. Nolan, O. O'Donnell, C. Propper, F. Puffer, M. Schellhorn, G. Sundberg, and O. Winkelhake. "Equity in the delivery of health care in Europe and the U.S." *Journal of Health Economics* (2000), Table 2, p. 1825.

FIGURE 11A.4
The Kakwani Index of Progressivity

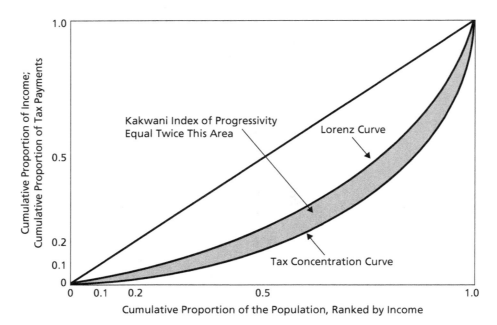

Private finance is, in general, regressive. Direct out-of-pocket payments are most regressive. Private insurance is progressive only in those countries where it is purchased by only high-income members of society who either opt out of the public plan or purchase it in addition to public coverage.

A country's overall degree of progressivity (column 9) is determined by the progressivity of each source of finance and the extent to which a country relies on different sources. For example, although the public sources are strongly progressive in each of Switzerland and the U.S., overall finance in both is regressive because each country relies heavily on regressive private finance. The U.K. exhibits the greatest degree of progressivity in its overall system of finance.

The Canadian studies of incidence have obtained estimates as follows: McGrail (2007) obtained Kakwani indexes of 0.021 and 0.026 for physician and hospital services in 1992 and 2002 respectively. Hanley et al. (2007) found that public finance for prescription drugs in British Columbia over the period 2000–2005 was proportional (annual Kakwani indexes of −0.002 to 0.008 over the period). Smythe (2002) estimated that private financing (including both out-of-pocket and private insurance payments) in Alberta was regressive (K = −0.12).

References

Hanley, G., S. Morgan, J. Hurley, and E. van Doorslaer. 2007. Distributional consequences of the transition from age-based to income-based prescription drug coverage in British Columbia, Canada. *Health Economics* 17(12):1379–92.

McGrail, K. 2007. Medicare financing and redistribution in British Columbia, 1992–2002. *Health-Care Policy* 2(4):123–37.

Smythe, J. G. 2002. The redistributive effect of health care finance in Alberta, 1997. Edmonton: Institute of Health Economics Working Paper.

Wagstaff, A., and E. van Doorslaer. 2000. Equity in health care finance and delivery. In *Handbook of health economics,* A. J. Culyer, and J. P. Newhouse (eds.). Amsterdam: Elsevier Science B.V. 34:1804–62.

Health Care Funding

Learning Objectives

After studying this chapter, you will understand

LO1 The nature of funding as an economic activity in a health care system

LO2 The basic elements of a health care funding system

LO3 The basic features of principal–agent models as they bear on health care funding

LO4 The most common funding mechanisms used in health care

LO5 The role of retrospectiveness and prospectiveness of payment in a funding system

LO6 Key principles and considerations in the design of a health care funding system

---

Funding provides health care organizations with the financial resources required to carry out a defined set of health-related activities. The "funding problem" arises in health care because a third-party insurer must allocate the revenue it has collected through premiums, taxes, or social insurance contributions to providers and programs that deliver health care services to individuals. Funding influences system performance because it creates financial incentives related to who provides services, what services are provided, the quality of the services provided, where services are provided, and to whom services are provided.

Designing funding schemes that encourage efficiency in the production and distribution of health care is consequently a central concern of health economics and health policy. Indeed, some argue that reform of funding policies is perhaps *the* fundamental challenge for improving the performance of health care systems (Cutler 2004; *Economist* 2005).

Funding Schemes

All funding schemes have three basic elements that can be combined in a variety of ways: the participants, the services and activities included, and the funding mechanism.

- *Participants* include the parties to the exchange or transfer of funds. The most common participants include government, health care insurers, providers, health care organizations, and enrollees.

- *Funded services and activities* can range from a narrow subset of health care services (e.g., only mental health services, only drugs) to a broad basket that includes primary care, specialized care, public health services and other health-related activities, and even non-care activities such as risk bearing.

- The *funding mechanism* refers to the method by which funds are transferred between participants in a funding scheme. The funding mechanism answers the question, what actions by which participants trigger a payment?

These basic elements correspond closely to the three questions to ask about any payment arrangement:

1. *Who* is being paid? Is it a health care delivery organization? A health care professional who delivers care? A patient? A financial intermediary such as a regional health board?
2. *What* is being paid for? Risk bearing? The delivery of care?
3. *What* is the unit of funding? Is it an individual health care service? A day of care? An episode of care?

Answers to these questions reveal who has the financial incentive to do what in the health care system. Funding primary care by a fee-for-service payment, whereby physicians receive a payment each time they provide a reimbursable service, discourages the use of non-physician providers (because only physicians can bill the insurer). It also encourages the provision of care as listed in the fee schedule (because only such care is funded) and discourages the provision of care not explicitly defined in the fee schedule.

Changing the scheme so that a primary care organization (rather than a physician directly) is paid a fee-for-service now encourages delivery by both physician and non-physician providers. The incentives change even further if fee-for-service funding is replaced by a system in which the provider organization is paid by capitation, so that it receives a fixed sum of money each period per person enrolled in the practice, with the concomitant responsibility to meet all defined health care needs of the enrollees. The organization still has incentive to use a mix of providers, but it now also has incentive to minimize the provision of unnecessary services (indeed, it has incentive to under-provide care) and to increase the provision of preventive services that will reduce future need for care by enrollees.

Changing who is paid, for what, and on what basis changes the incentives individuals and organizations have to pursue various ends in health care (See Box 12.1).

principal–agent problem

One individual or organization (the principal) wants to accomplish some task or objective but must contract with another individual or organization (the agent) to undertake the work necessary to achieve the desired objective.

The design of a health care funding scheme is one example of a more general problem in economics called the **principal–agent problem**. A principal–agent problem arises whenever one individual or organization (the principal) wants to accomplish some task or objective but must contract with another individual or organization (the agent) to undertake the work necessary to achieve the desired objective. The principal's challenge is to motivate the agent through financial and non-financial incentives to pursue the principal's objective instead of the agent's own objective.

We have already seen one vital principal–agent relationship in health care—that between a patient (principal) and provider (agent). This principal–agent relationship is a bit unusual in that we expend considerable effort through professional training trying to shape physicians' objectives so that they align with those of patients. More generally, the principal–agent literature has analyzed the ability of alternative systems of financial rewards to align the actions of the agent with the principal's goal even when the two have different interests and objectives.

12.1   THE PRINCIPAL–AGENT FRAMEWORK AND FUNDING SYSTEMS

The Principal–Agent Problem

The principal–agent problem would be trivial if the principal and agent had full information—allowing the principal to write and enforce a perfect contract—or if the principal and agent had identical preferences—in which case a fully self-interested agent would do exactly what the principal wanted. The problem becomes economically challenging in the presence of asymmetrical information between the parties, uncertainty regarding

Pharmacists: Pill Counters or Full-Fledged Health Care Professionals?

In most settings, a pharmacist's role is almost exclusively to dispense medicines. The dispensing fee associated with filling a prescription is the primary source of payment for a pharmacist/pharmacy.

At one time, dispensing medicine required not only knowledge of drugs but also skill in formulating the medicine for a patient. But with the advent of mass-manufactured drugs, dispensing medicines in many situations has become little more than "pill counting." How can the health care system better use the expertise of pharmacists?

The Home Medicines Review program of the Government of Australia is one example of new roles for pharmacists linked to innovative funding arrangements (Australia Department of Health and Aging 2005). Under the Home Medicines Review program, pharmacists work collaboratively with general practitioners to ensure appropriate pharmaceutical therapy for individuals living in the community. When the general practitioner has a concern about a patient's current regime of drug therapy, especially when individuals are on multiple medications or have recently undergone changes in drug therapy, the GP can arrange for a home review by an accredited pharmacist. The pharmacist assesses the appropriateness of the current drug regime, issues of compliance, and other factors that may detract from optimal drug therapy. The pharmacist discusses the findings with the patient's GP, who then decides on any changes required. The community-based pharmacy with which the pharmacist is affiliated receives payment for undertaking the review.

Creating Public Markets Through Funding Arrangements

Prior to reforms during the 1990s, funds in the U.K.'s National Health Service flowed from the central department of health to regional health authorities, who owned hospitals, diagnostics labs, and other facilities, and employed the staff within them. It was a classic hierarchical organization.

In the early 1990s, the British government undertook reform to create competition within the publicly financed system through a split of purchasers and providers. A key element of this reform was changing funding arrangements. Under the new model, hospitals and other facilities became independent trusts no longer tied to the regional health authority. The regional health authority received a budget from the Department of Health and used the budget to purchase services from provider organizations to meet the health needs of residents of the region.

The regional authority could purchase the services from any provider organization it desired. Hospitals, labs, and other service providers had to compete to win contracts with regional health authorities. The goal of the revised funding and governance arrangements was to instill competition among providers, reaping efficiency gains for the public health care system while retaining the equity principle of public financing. The ultimate effects of the reform on, for example, price, quality of care, transactions costs, and efficiency are still being debated (Propper et al. 2004).

The contracting approach that underlies the purchaser–provider split has been adapted to many contexts (Ranade 1998; Saltman and von Otter 1995), including Canada.

Funding In-Patient Hospital Care in the U.S. Medicare Program

The U.S. Medicare program provides health care insurance coverage for residents age 65 or over. Prior to 1983, it funded hospital care for enrollees through a system whereby a hospital billed the government for the cost of all goods and services provided to a Medicare enrollee during an in-patient stay.

In 1983, it changed to a "prospective, diagnosis-based" system of funding whereby the hospital was paid a predetermined, fixed amount for each in-patient admission (regardless of the actual cost of services provided). The payment varied according to the patient's diagnosis (e.g., uncomplicated pneumonia versus coronary artery bypass surgery), and was set equal to the expected cost of treating a patient with that diagnosis.

Hospital reactions to the changed incentives were swift. The length of stay per hospital admission fell substantially through earlier discharge (to home or to a skilled nursing facility), hospitals created utilization review committees to reduce the provision of unnecessary services by physicians, and hospitals shifted care from the in-patient setting to day surgery (which was still funded on the older cost-based reimbursement model). Indeed, there was concern that length-of-stay in some instances became too short, that necessary services may have been withheld, and that hospitals may have engaged in efforts to risk-select relatively low-cost patients.

The change in funding methods had profound effects (both positive and negative) on the operation of hospitals and the patterns of care delivery, and such case-based funding has spread to may countries around the world.

how an agent's actions translate into observed outcomes, and differences among agents in their ability to accomplish the objective.

Principal–agent problems arise in many contexts, including every workplace. A firm seeks to maximize profits, yet the firm must hire an employee without knowing for certain the employee's abilities or work ethic. The firm often can't fully monitor an employee's work activities, especially the level of effort expended, and it has trouble assessing performance because an individual employee's output is influenced by many factors (especially when teamwork is involved). The challenge for a firm is to structure compensation to motivate workers properly.

For health care funding, the principal is most commonly a public or private third-party insurer and the agent is a provider, such as a hospital or physician,[1] though it can include other types of organizations in the health care system. The insurer wants the provider to meet the health care needs of the insurer's enrollees efficiently.

Elements of the Principal–Agent Framework

The principal–agent framework includes five key elements (aside from the principal) (Petersen 1994):

1. *Agents* (e.g., providers) who differ in ways relevant to the contracting situation: for example, some are more able, or more hard-working, than others.
2. *Actions* (e.g., delivery of a health care service) undertaken by an agent that affect the achievement of the desired outcome (e.g., improved health). Undertaking an action is costly to an agent.
3. *Random factors* beyond the control of both the principal and the agent that influence the outcome in addition to any actions undertaken by the agent (e.g., the random nature of health and of the effectiveness of a given health care service for an individual).
4. *Outcomes* (e.g., health) that are observable to both the principal and the agent.
5. *Asymmetric information* that exists between the principal and the agent. This may take different forms depending on the context, but may include situations in which
   - only the agent is aware of its own capabilities (e.g., ability, work ethic) and/or actions
   - the principal may observe the action undertaken by the agent (e.g., what service was provided) but not the random factor, so it is not possible to know the extent to which the observed outcome is the result of the agent's action or the result of the random factor.

Two further behavioural assumptions are that agents are rational in the usual economic sense and that agents behave with self interest to maximize their own utility.

A typical health care funder faces most of the challenges associated with this basic framework. Providers differ considerably in the quality of care they provide and in their efficiency, yet the funder cannot easily distinguish good and bad performers at the beginning of a contract. As previously noted, enrollees' health and the effectiveness of health care have irreducible random components that can make it difficult in any individual case to assess whether a bad outcome is due to poor quality care or bad luck. Further, some providers systematically attract patients of differing risk statuses, so that differing outcomes (even averaged over many encounters) could be due not to the quality of care but to unobserved patient characteristics.

---

[1] Unless the distinction is important, in this chapter the term "provider" refers to individual providers such as physicians, dentists, and physiotherapists, as well as to provider organizations such as clinics and hospitals.

Finally, because much of the information required to judge the appropriate care is known only to the patient and provider, a funder faces substantial informational barriers.

Strategies to Solve the Principal–Agent Problem

A funder has three primary strategies in the face of these challenges:

1. reduce its informational deficit and uncertainty
2. create a "culture" with norms that encourage the desired behaviour
3. carefully design the system of financial rewards to align incentives

In an effort to reduce informational problems, for instance, funders have developed "health care scorecards" that attempt to measure the quality and appropriateness of the care provided by a provider organization (Canadian Institute for Health Information 2007). Such efforts, however, can never fully overcome informational problems, making other approaches essential.

Much of the training of physicians and health professionals inculcates a professional ethic for the delivery of high-quality care and instills the notion that providers are to act in the interests of their patients. That is, they try to create a professional culture to better align the preferences of the providers with those of patients. While this usually advances the interests of the funder, at times it can create a divergence, such as when it leads to the provision of care with positive but small benefit to the patient but at high cost to society.

Policy increasingly emphasizes the use of financial incentives. It is not possible to design a system of financial incentives that perfectly aligns the interests of funders and provider organizations (Sappington 1991). Principal–agent analyses, however, offer important guidance. In general, the optimal approach shares financial risk between the funder (principal) and providers (agents). Risk sharing implies that neither the funder nor provider is fully at risk for the cost of providing necessary care. Sharing financial risk also means that the incentives of the agent and the principal are not perfectly aligned. For instance, rather than having a pharmacist receive 100 percent of the gain from the increased efficiency due to dispensing a generic rather than a brand-name drug, having a pharmacist share the gain with the funder (e.g., the pharmacist and government split the savings 50-50) reduces the incentive of the pharmacist to realize all efficiency gains.

Optimal arrangements often rely on "monitoring"—efforts by the principal to review and evaluate the work of the agent. Where actions and effort can be linked to sought-after outcomes, it can be advantageous to link payment to the actions. Such efforts include performance-based pay in health care, whereby providers receive bonuses linked to the regular and consistent delivery of care that is documented to improve patient health.

Finally, real-world contracts differ from theoretically optimal arrangements in two important ways:

1. We observe much simpler contracting arrangements than economic theory recommends, in part because of administrative feasibility.
2. Organizations usually rely on a wider set of rewards to induce good performance than just financial incentives.

The remainder of this chapter focuses on the design of funding schemes that create incentives to produce and deliver high-quality health care in an efficient manner. The power of financial incentives to modify behaviour in desired ways must be considered in the context of other instruments. Financial incentives, however, are unavoidable within systems of funding; and well-designed funding systems can play an important role in achieving the overall objectives of a health care system.

12.2 PARTICIPANTS IN A FUNDING SCHEME

Numerous types of individuals and organizations can participate in a funding scheme; but, aside from the funder, participants are most commonly an enrollee, a provider, and a financial intermediary. Enrollees, of course, are the individuals covered by the insurance scheme. Providers are those health professionals, organizations, and institutions that deliver care to enrollees (including everything from a solo practitioner to a large hospital). A financial intermediary is an organization that raises or receives monies used to fund the provision of health care services.

Financial intermediaries do not normally provide health care services themselves; rather, monies flow through a financial intermediary as part of the overall financing and funding scheme. Within a publicly financed system, a financial intermediary will normally be a governmental agency at the central, regional, or local level. Within private systems, financial intermediaries may include a private insurer or an employer who collects and pays insurance premiums on behalf of employees. A funding scheme can include multiple layers of financial intermediaries.

Figure 12.1 illustrates key participants in typical funding schemes:

- Scheme (i) represents the simplest arrangement—enrollees pay the full cost of care directly to the provider. This is found for some services in all countries' health systems. In Canada, this scheme dominates funding for non-physician providers who fall outside both the public plans and many private insurance plans.
- Scheme (ii) represents a common arrangement whereby an enrollee pays part of the cost of care directly to a provider and also pays a premium/tax to a third party insurer who reimburses the provider for the balance of the cost. In Canada, this scheme applies to the purchase of prescriptions drugs both for people who hold private insurance that requires patient cost-sharing, and for those enrolled in provincial pharmacare programs that require cost-sharing.
- Scheme (iii) represents funding for physician services in Canada. Patients pay taxes but face no cost-sharing (so no funds flow directly from enrollees to providers); the federal government (Financial Intermediary 1) transfers funds to the provincial governments (Financial Intermediary 2), which then fully fund physician services.
- Scheme (iv) represents funding for hospital services in provinces that have regionalized systems of governance. It is similar to (iii) except that a new financial intermediary has been added—regional health authorities—who directly fund hospitals using funds transferred from the provincial government.

The different arrays of participants in such schemes partly reflect different financing arrangements and political considerations, and they partly reflect economic considerations. Different participants have differential access to information, differing abilities to bear risk, and access to different sets of instruments with which to monitor and enforce funding arrangements. Other things equal, funding decisions should reside with those who have the most relevant information, who are best able to bear the necessary risks, and who are well positioned to monitor and enforce the funding regulations. The choice of participants and the relationships among them must incorporate these and other factors (see Box 12.2 for a discussion of economic rationales for regional funding authorities).

FIGURE 12.1
Payment Schemes
This figure depicts the participants and money flows in common funding schemes.

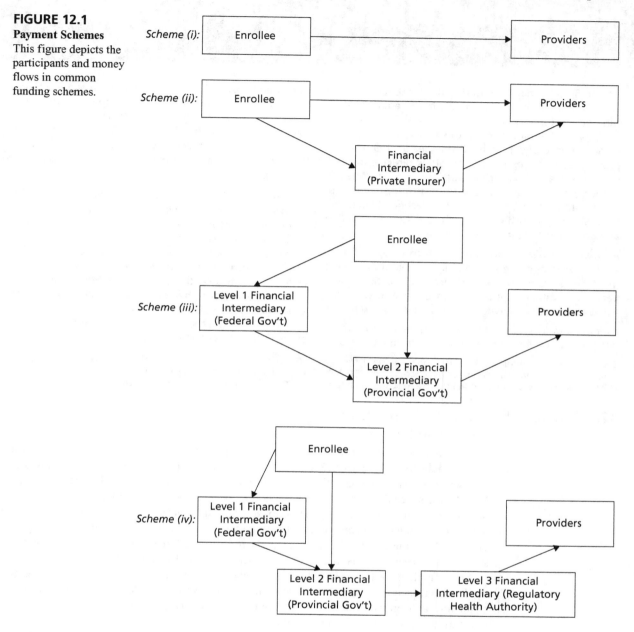

12.3   FUNDING MECHANISMS

funding mechanism
The method by which funds are transferred among participants in a funding system.

Funding mechanisms refer to the methods by which funds are transferred among participants in the funding system. Chapter 1 introduced some funding mechanisms such as fee-for-service and capitation. Here we review more comprehensively a relatively small set of funding mechanisms that dominate in health care. No single mechanism is used for the whole of a health care system. Rather, different types of mechanisms are used for different services and settings.

As discussed in Chapter 1, during the 1990s a number of Canadian provinces created a new intermediary in their funding system—regional health authorities—which were part of a larger move toward devolved systems of governance and funding (Hurley et al. 1994). These provinces no longer funded hospitals directly. Instead, the provinces allocated monies to regional health authorities that funded specific institutions and programs within their borders. From an economic perspective, why might such a regionalized system of funding and governance improve performance?

Population health: Allocating funds to regional health authorities responsible for meeting the health care needs of all residents in the region encourages a population perspective rather than a focus on those who seek care (which can arise when care providers are funded directly).

Funding equity: Such a funding system facilitates a geographic funding equity that reflects differences in population needs. That is, the province can allocate funds to the regions using needs-adjusted capitation payment (Birch et al. 1993). This again contrasts with provider-based methods, which transfer funds directly to providers, with the result that regions with few providers (but potentially large needs, such as rural and remote regions) get few resources.

Efficiency: Regional level decision-makers are closer to local information regarding the health care needs of residents and how best to respond to those needs, potentially increasing both the technical and allocative efficiency of service provision (Hurley et al. 1994). Funding a broader basket of services (e.g., hospital, home care, long-term care) through a single budget allocated by a single regional health authority also encourages a broader system perspective when making allocation decisions, reducing the incentive for individual programs or institutions to engage in cost shifting.

Sources: Based on: Hurley, J., J. Lomas, and V. Bhatia. 1994. "When Tinkering is Not Enough: Provincial Reform to Manage Health Care Resources." *Canadian Public Administration.* Vol. 37(3):490–514; Birch S., J. Eyles, J. Hurley, B. Hutchison, and S. Chambers. 1993. "A needs-based approach to resource allocation in health care." *Canadian Public Policy.* Vol. 19(1):68–85.

12.3.1 Types of Payment Mechanisms

Fee-for-Service

Under fee-for-service payment, the funder pays a provider each time the provider delivers a reimbursable health care service (e.g., office visit, surgical procedure). The set of reimbursable services and the fee associated with each covered service are listed in a fee schedule. Modern fee schedules normally include thousands of items, reflecting the large number of health care services that may be offered to patients. The fees can be set in a variety of ways: individual providers can sometimes set their own fees, fees may be negotiated between providers and the funder, or fees may be set unilaterally by the funder. Fee-for-service is used in some form in nearly all health care systems, especially for physician services.

Many funders are trying to reduce their reliance on fee-for-service funding because of the financial incentives it creates. Recall that funders want providers to produce services efficiently and provide enrollees with (only) needed services. Fee-for-service creates a range of incentives inconsistent with this.

Fee-for-service does create incentive for providers to produce their own services in the least-cost way consistent with funding regulations (since the difference between the fee and their costs determines their income/profit). However, because the fee is usually paid only when the provider (rather than, for example, a qualified assistant) delivers the service, fee-for-service payment often limits the ability to produce a service with the least-cost combination of inputs.

And because a provider is paid every time a reimbursable service is provided, regardless of whether the service is needed or effective, it creates incentive to over-provide services (recall the randomized controlled trial of fee-for-service and salary (Hickson et al. 1987) discussed in Chapter 8 in reference to supplier-induced demand). In particular, it biases providers toward inefficient over-provision of reimbursable services and under-provision of services not listed in the fee schedule. This latter feature makes it poorly suited for contexts for which good care requires a customized set of activities and services not easily listed in a fee schedule, such as the management of complex chronic diseases.

Finally, fee-for-service is also troublesome for funders. It is very difficult to set a true budget at the beginning of a funding period because total expenditures depend on the amount and type of services ultimately provided.

Case-Based Funding

case-based funding
Providers receive a fixed, specified payment for each case they treat.

skimping
Providing less than the appropriate level of care, particularly in response to financial incentives.

gaming
In the economic context, to use the policies, rules, and procedures of a system to increase one's financial gain in a manner contrary to the intended purpose of those policies, regulations, and procedures.

up-coding
Gaming a funding system by claiming reimbursement for a service that pays more than the service that was actually provided.

Under **case-based funding** (sometimes called "diagnosis-based" funding) providers receive a fixed, specified payment for each "case" they treat. Case-based funding is used primarily for funding hospital care, where a case is defined as a hospital admission and the payment varies according to the diagnosis (e.g., pneumonia, myocardial infarction, Caesarean section, etc.) of the individual admitted (see Box 12.1). The payment is set in advance and is designed to equal the expected costs of treating individuals with that diagnosis; it does not vary with the actual services provided to treat an individual. As a result, for each case treated, the provider organization bears some risks associated with treatment costs. If the costs of the services provided to a patient exceed the diagnosis-based payment, the organization must absorb the excess costs; if actual costs are below the diagnosis-based payment, the organization retains the difference.

This creates provider incentive to produce services in the least-cost manner and to provide only necessary services, so as to minimize the total cost of treating the case. Unfortunately, it also creates incentive to under-treat patients (**skimp on care**), to cream-skim by selecting only the less severe cases within a diagnostic category, and when patients have multiple diagnoses, to strategically assign patients to reimbursement categories to maximize payments associated with the patients treated, a form of **gaming** also known as **up-coding**.

Capitation

Under capitation funding, a health care provider receives a fixed, specified payment per time period (e.g. month, year) for each individual for whom it accepts responsibility to meet defined health care needs (e.g., primary care, primary and secondary care). The payment received per person is fixed in advance and does not vary with the actual services provided to the individual. In most settings, the capitation payment is risk-adjusted to reflect the differing needs of individuals.

Because the payment is fixed ahead of time, the provider bears financial risk associated with meeting the health needs. Indeed, the provider effectively becomes an integrated health care insurer and delivery organization. For this reason, capitation payment can be used only when the size of the population for which the provider is responsible is large enough to pool the financial risks effectively. Because the provider absorbs treatment costs in excess of the capitation payment and retains the difference when actual costs are less than the capitation payment, the provider has incentive to produce care in the least-cost manner and to provide only necessary, effective health care services. Capitation payment also creates incentive to under-provide care (skimp) and to cream-skim by attracting relatively low-risk, healthy individuals within each risk class.

enrolled population
A group of individuals who have registered to obtain care from a particular provider (or provider organization).

Capitation payment is used widely to fund both enrolled populations and geographically defined populations. An **enrolled population** is one in which individuals sign up to receive care from a particular provider, which then receives the capitation payment. Capitation funding for enrolled populations, for example, dominates for primary care in the United Kingdom's National Health System, is used for a full spectrum of primary and secondary care in the U.S., and is increasingly used within primary care in Canada.

geographically defined population
Residents of a defined jurisdiction that is funded to meet specified health care needs of the population.

Capitation funding for **geographically defined populations**—usually those associated with regional health authorities—is used to fund a broad basket of services in many countries, including regional health authorities in Canadian provinces with a regionalized system of governance. (Geographically defined populations include residents who live within a defined jurisdiction.)

Global Budget

global budget
Providers receive a total budget for a defined period of time.

A **global budget** is a payment mechanism whereby a provider receives a total budget for a defined period of time. The size of the total budget can be based on a number of factors: historical costs, the number of services provided last period, the number of cases treated last period, the size of the population served, and so forth.

case-mix adjustment
The process of adjusting the raw number of cases treated by a provider to account for the severity of the conditions of those treated (e.g., heart surgery versus uncomplicated pneumonia).

A global budget, for instance, can be based on the sum of **case-mix adjusted** number of individuals treated in the last period, or on the sum of capitation payments for patients for whom the organization accepts responsibility. When the budget is fixed ahead of time, global budgets can be effective in containing health care costs while providing the funded organization considerable discretion for use of funds. This discretion is lost when the global budget is made up of a pre-determined amount allocated to particular categories of spending, or "line items." Such a line-item budget restricts the organization's ability to allocate resources among inputs or programs as it deems appropriate.

Global budgets are used widely in many countries to fund various aspects of health care. Global budgets have historically been used in Canada to fund hospitals.

Bonus or Incentive Payments

bonus payment
A special payment received for meeting specified performance targets.

Funders increasingly use bonus, or incentive, payments to fund health care providers. The details vary by context, but most systems involve setting a target or benchmark pertaining to some aspect of service provision, then calibrating a scheme in which providers that meet or exceed the target receive the **bonus payment**.

The heart of any such scheme is the activity for which the bonus payments are paid. Managed care organizations in the U.S. often use bonus payments to encourage lower-cost utilization patterns among affiliated providers: physicians whose utilization rates fall below a target receive a bonus.

performance-based payment
Providers whose care patterns conform to known standards of quality receive bonuses (or avoid penalties). Also known as "pay for performance."

More recently, bonus payments have been advocated as part of **performance-based payment** schemes to improve quality of care (Cutler 2004). In this context, providers whose care patterns conform to known standards of quality receive bonuses. It is well established, for example, that people who have suffered a heart attack benefit greatly from drugs called beta blockers, which can cut the risk of recurrent heart attack by up to 25 percent. Yet many patients who could benefit do not. A bonus scheme might, therefore, pay a provider a bonus based on the proportion of post-heart-attack patients in their care who are regularly prescribed beta blockers. Box 12.3 highlights a range of issues that arise when using such incentive schemes.

prospective payment
Payment for a service is fixed in advance of the actual provision of the service.

Table 12.1 summarizes key incentives and policy challenges associated with the different funding mechanisms.

12.3.2 Retrospective Payment, Prospective Payment, Risk, and Efficiency

retrospective payment
Payment for a service is determined only after the provision of the service.

A funding scheme is **prospective** when the total amount of funding a provider organization receives in return for meeting the health care needs of its enrollees is set before the services are provided. A funding scheme is **retrospective** when the total amount of funding that the provider organization receives is determined only after all services have been provided. The extent of prospectiveness or retrospectiveness depends on the mix of funding mechanisms used in the funding scheme and determines who bears the financial risk associated

TABLE 12.1
Common Funding Mechanisms
For each of the common funding mechanisms listed, this table documents the unit of payment, some of the major incentives created by the funding mechanism, and the policy challenges associated with using the funding mechanism.

Funding Mechanism	Unit of Payment	Incentives	Major Policy Challenges
Fee-for-Service	Fixed payment per individual health care service as defined in fee schedule (e.g., initial visit, tonsillectomy)	• Increase the number of services • Decrease resources used per service	• Over-provision of care: too many services per patient or episode of illness • "Turnstile" medicine: visits that are too brief • Can encourage procedural orientation (i.e., tests and procedures) over cognitive orientation (e.g., good history-taking) • Determining fee levels
Case-Based Funding	Fixed payment per episode of illness, normally defined by in-patient admission	• Increase number of cases • Decrease resources per case	• Cream-skimming less severe cases within diagnostic category • Cream-skimming most-profitable diagnoses • Up-coding: strategically classifying cases to maximize reimbursement • Under-providing care: too few services provided per case • Determining expected cost per case per diagnosis
Capitation	Fixed payment per person enrolled in practice per month	• Increase number of enrollees • Decrease resources per enrollee	• Cream-skimming relatively healthy individuals (within each risk class) • Under-providing care: too few services provided per enrollee • Risk-adjusting capitation rates
Global Budget	Payment for all activities associated with a health care program or institution per year	• Increase activities used as basis for justifying budget	• Shirking on activities not used to justify budget • Avoiding cost overruns and associated appeals for additional funding
Bonus Payments and Performance-Based Payments	Payment based in part on extent to which provider organization meets pre-defined performance targets	• Provide the minimum level of services to reach target	• Setting performance targets • Measuring performance • Gaming to meet targets • Diverting resources from unmeasured aspects of performance

Which works best to motivate others and alter behaviour using financial incentives: carrots (i.e., positive "bonus" payments to those who perform as desired) or sticks (i.e., negative sanctions to those who perform in ways not desired)? This is a long-standing question in economics and psychology. There is no clear-cut answer. In many formal economic models of behaviour, the two are symmetrical—just flip sides of the same coin—and it does not make a difference (i.e., forgoing a potential $100 gain is equivalent in principle to paying $100). But in real-world funding and payment systems, the two can generate quite different effects.

Changing behaviour is not easy. Much behaviour is driven by habits and norms worn into our routines over many years. Bonus schemes offer the possibility of making a person better off if the person changes; but relative to the status quo, they are no worse off if they don't bother changing. If they are reasonably satisfied before the bonus scheme, the costs (psychological and material) of change may weigh more heavily than the possibility of being even better off.

In contrast, penalty-based schemes imply that, in order for a person to maintain their current level of well-being, they will have to change. Failure to change means a reduction in well-being.

These subtle differences appear to play an important role—shown, for example, in the differential responses by British Columbia pharmacists to two incentive-based schemes that encouraged them to dispense generic medications (Grootendorst et al. 1996). In 1990, the province of British Columbia instituted the Prescription Incentive Plan (PIP). Every time a pharmacist dispensed a generic drug, they received a bonus payment equal to 20 percent of the difference between the price of the generic medication dispensed and the price of the equivalent brand-name drug. What happened? Very little. Over a 3-year period, PIP increased generic prescribing from about 55 percent to 60 percent of prescribing in situations where both generic and brand name drugs were available. Indeed, the plan was not even self-funding: the increase in generic prescribing was not large enough to offset the 20 percent bonus paid to pharmacists.

In 1994, B.C. changed to the Low Cost Alternative Plan, whereby a pharmacist was paid only the average price of low-cost generic alternatives regardless of what drug was dispensed. Pharmacists could still dispense the brand-name drug, but they would have to absorb the difference in cost between the brand-name and generic drug. Rather than receiving a bonus to dispense a generic drug, they now faced a penalty for dispensing a brand-name drug.

The response was immediate and clear—within three months, generic prescribing increased from about 60 percent at the end of PIP to over 90 percent. As might

be expected, pharmacists were much less happy under the penalty-based scheme (as is often the case when sticks are used rather than carrots), but the latter policy was much more effective.

The two types of policies also have very different financial implications for the funder. Bonus payment schemes require positive payments to those who conform; sanctions, in contrast, require no outlay of monies (and where there is a positive financial penalty, may even raise monies). These differences become particularly important when considering the cost per marginal change in behaviour. Most bonus schemes pay the bonus to all those individuals or organizations whose performance meets the standard or criterion. Many of the providers, however, met the target before the bonus scheme was instituted—among British Columbian pharmacists, for example, before PIP, over 50 percent of pharmacists already substituted generic drugs for brand-name drugs. For such individuals, the bonus scheme is a pure windfall: it had no impact on their behaviour yet they reaped the rewards. The funder had to pay the bonus to all such individuals just to influence the behaviour of that subset who were under-performing.

Similarly, a recent analysis of performance-based pay found that, while it did result in a small improvement in average quality, the cost per unit change was very high because a large proportion of payments went to those who already provided high-quality care even in the absence of the bonus scheme (Rosenthal et al. 2005).

These and related issues are part of the larger set of challenges associated with using financial incentives as a tool to guide behaviour. All funding and payment mechanisms create both "good" and "bad" financial incentives.

A funder ignores this basic fact at its peril. There is a subtle though important difference between ensuring that financial incentives do not inhibit people from performing in the desired ways and using financial incentives as an active policy tool to guide behaviour. Using financial incentives as an active policy tool risks creating perverse side effect; the policy landscape is littered with incentive schemes that went awry because of unanticipated perverse responses. This is particularly the case when many of the desired outcomes are difficult to observe and measure, as is the case with many health care settings.

A central lesson from the principal–agent literature is that tying rewards to only a subset of all performance dimensions can systematically divert attention from important but difficult-to-observe or unmeasured aspects of performance. Financial rewards must also be placed in the context of a mutually reinforcing system of financial and non-financial rewards, each used where it has most advantage.

with meeting the health care needs of individuals, and consequently a provider's incentive to produce and use health care services efficiently to improve health.

Figure 12.2 shows the prospective and retrospective components of the funding mechanisms discussed in the previous section. The figure breaks the total health care expenditures incurred in a population into components. These expenditures depend on the intensity of service provision for an episode of illness, the health risks of those in the population, and the number of individuals in the relevant population. In the figure, the solid line associated with each funding mechanism represents that portion of total funding that is determined prospectively.

- When the funding is fee-for-service, only the revenue per service is fixed prospectively.[2] Funding varies after the fact (retrospectively) with changes in all other factors that determine total expenditures. The provider receives more funding if it increases intensity of servicing per episode of illness, takes on patients with lower health status (higher risk), or provides services to more people. Therefore, the only financial risk borne by the provider is that associated with the cost per service: as long as the provider keeps the actual cost per service below the fee received for a service, the provider makes money.

- When the funding is case-based, the prospective component extends to include those elements associated with an entire episode of care. The provider organization is at risk for expenditures associated with both the costs of each service and the number of services used to treat an episode of care.

- Under capitation payment, most of the funding to a provider organization is fixed ahead of time; it does not change with the actual quantity of services provided. Funding varies only with the number of enrollees associated with the provider organization

FIGURE 12.2
Prospective and Retrospective Elements of Alternative Payment Mechanisms
This figure identifies the degree of prospectiveness of each of the common funding mechanisms. For each funding mechanism, the solid line represents those components of total expenditure that are determined prospectively.

Source: Hurley and Giacomini (1998)

Total Expenditures =

$$\underbrace{\frac{\text{Cost}}{\text{Service}} \times \frac{\text{\# Services}}{\text{Episode}}}_{(Service\ Intensity)} \times \underbrace{\frac{\text{\# Episodes}}{\text{Illness}} \times \frac{\text{\# Illnesses}}{\text{Enrollee}}}_{(Population\ Health\ Risk)} \times \underbrace{\text{\# Enrollees}}_{(Population\ Size)}$$

Fee-for-service[1]

Case-Based Funding

Capitation[2]

Prospective Global Budget[3]

Key: ▬▬ Prospective Component
▬ ▬ Retrospective Component

[1] Assumes fixed fees. If providers can set and adjust fees unilaterally, then not even fees are prospective.
[2] Capitation can be unadjusted or risk-adjusted, both of which are prospective. Unadjusted capitation rates are equal for all enrollees regardless of risk status. Risk-adjusted capitation payments vary according to an enrollee's health risks, thereby reducing the scope for cream-skimming by the funded organization.
[3] Global budgets are increasingly (but not universally) prospective.

[2] This is the situation in many settings that currently use fee-for-service (e.g., Medicare in Canada and the U.S.).

(and, if the capitation is risk adjusted, the risk status of those individuals). The provider organization is at risk for expenditures associated with the cost per service, the services per episode, and the number and types of illnesses experienced by its enrollees.

- Finally, with a truly fixed global budget, the provider organization bears financial risk for all components that determine actual expenditure.

From a funder's perspective, increasing prospectiveness is advantageous because it encourages efficiency in the production and use of all covered health care services, and it increases the predictability of the funding levels. Prospectiveness, however, also transfers financial risk to the funded organization, increasing the organization's incentive to under-treat enrollees and to engage in risk selection. Funders face an efficiency–selection trade-off (Newhouse 1996). A fully retrospective system of payment (such as certain forms of fee-for-service) encourages inefficient over-provision of services but provides little incentive to engage in risk selection and care skimping; a fully prospective system of payment (such as pure capitation) discourages inefficient over-provision of services but provides incentive for risk selection and skimping.

blended funding
A provider's funding comprises a mixture of payment mechanisms.

In the face of this trade-off, **blended funding** approaches may be optimal. Under blended funding, a provider's total funding comprises a mixture of payment mechanisms to optimally balance the contrasting incentives. Myriad blends are possible, and health care systems across the world exhibit considerable variety. A blended funding model may, for instance, provide a base amount through capitation funding but pay fee-for-service for a portion of the cost of actual services provided (optimally, the fee-for-service proportion depends on the marginal cost of service provision), or for some specific services that are thought to be under-provided. It is also common to lessen the financial risks associated with prospective payment by funding the care of "outliers" (i.e., unexpectedly costly cases) retro-spectively. Box 12.4 describes a blended funding scheme used in Ontario for primary care.

12.4 DESIGNING FUNDING SCHEMES

A well-designed funding scheme must encourage efficiency in the production and use of health services by targeting the right participants with good incentives. It must also be administratively efficient in that it is not overly costly to administer and generates an equitable allocation of resources for both members of society and providers.

12.4.1 Administrative Feasibility and Efficiency

Administering funding schemes can create large demands on information technologies, knowledge development, and organizational management. The funding agency must have the capacity to meet these demands.

- A funding scheme based on fee-for-service, for instance, must be able to develop and maintain a fee schedule, including processes to modify fees as well as to add and delete items from the schedule. It must also have the information technology to pay millions of individual claims submitted by providers.

- A capitation system must have the mechanisms to calculate risk-adjusted capitation rates and maintain accurate rosters of the individuals associated with each practice.

- A performance-based payment system must include explicit measures of performance that can be linked to payment and an ability to measure performance.

Such requirements can pose tremendous challenges for funders. Even where feasible, the costs of administering complex funding schemes can exceed the benefits of ever-more-refined attempts to guide behaviour through financial incentives.

Ontario's Family Health Networks (FHNs) are primary care practices that are paid through a blended funding scheme that includes capitation, fee-for-service, programmatic funding, and bonus payments. The payment scheme distinguishes payments to go to the Family Health Network itself (to be divided among network providers according a remuneration scheme agreed to by the participating members) and payments that are made directly from the Ministry to the physicians.

Payments made to the FHN itself include:

Base capitation rate: An age–sex risk-adjusted monthly payment paid for each enrollee in the FHN.

FFS blend: For services included in the base capitation rate, the FHN receives 10 percent of the listed fee when a service is provided to an enrollee.

Payment for enrollees in long-term care institutions: The FHN receives a fixed annual amount ($941.16 in 2008) for each enrollee who resides in a long-term care facility plus 10 percent of the fee for services provided to such enrollees.

Bonus payment for meeting the needs of enrollees: The FHN is eligible for a special payment equal to $48,500 less the value of claims paid by the Ministry of Health to primary care providers outside the FHN. This payment encourages the FHN to meet the needs of its enrollees, so that they do not seek primary care outside the FHN in which they are enrolled.

Excessive enrollment penalty: When the average number of enrollees per FHN physician exceeds 2400, the average base capitation rate will be reduced by 50 percent for the number of enrollees in excess of the 2400 target multiplied by the number of FHN physicians.

Service enhancement codes: A service enhancement fee of $6.86 is payable to a FHN physician for each enrollee the physician contacts for the purpose of scheduling an appointment for one of the following preventive care management services: pap smear, mammogram for women aged 50 to 70, flu vaccine for those 65 or older, and immunization for children under 2 years of age.

Cumulative preventive care management service enhancement code: The FHN is eligible to receive bonus payments based on the performance of the physicians in the FHN. For each physician in the FHN, the FHN receives the following bonus payments if the proportion of a physician's enrollees who have received the following services exceeds the thresholds listed below.

Percentage of Enrollees	Pap Smear	Flu Vaccine > 65 years	Mammogram Fem, 50-70	Immunization < 2 years	Colorectal Screening Age 50–74
15					$ 220
20					$ 440
40					$1100
50					$2200
55			$ 220		
60	$ 220	$ 220	$ 440		
65	$ 440	$ 440	$ 770		
70	$ 660	$ 770	$1320		
75	$1320	$1100	$2200		
80	$2200	$2200			
85				$ 440	
90				$1100	
95				$2200	

(Continued)

Some of the payments made directly to a FHN physician include:

Targeted medical education service enhancement codes: $100 per hour annually for time spent in approved continuing medical education activities

Special payments: An FHN physician who provides a defined minimum amount of the following categories of service receives the special payment listed.

obstetrical deliveries: $3200
hospital-based care: $5000
palliative care: $2000
office procedures: $2000
prenatal care: $2000
home visits: $2000

Source: Government of Ontario (2006). *General Blended Payment Template.* Toronto: Ontario Ministry of Health.

Finally, every system of funding requires an administratively effective system of monitoring to detect gaming, fraud, and related activities.

12.4.2 Distributing Risk

A funder must ensure that participants in the funding scheme can pool the risk they bear. As emphasized above, the greater the extent of prospectiveness in the funding scheme, the greater the amount of risk transferred from the funder to the funded organizations. The efficiency, equity, and sustainability of a funding scheme depend on the ability of funded organizations to bear the risk transferred to them.

The amount of risk transferred by the funder to the provider organization depends on the basket of services being funded. The financial risk associated with a basket that includes only primary care services is relatively small; in contrast, risk associated with a basket of services that includes primary and secondary care can be quite large, because secondary care is less predictable and more costly.

stop-loss mechanism
A provision within a prospective payment system that specifies a threshold for very costly cases, such that additional expenditures on the individual are either partially or fully paid by the funder (rather than forcing the provider to absorb them).

The ability of an organization to pool risk effectively depends on the size of its care population (see Chapter 9 on risk pooling). Under a system of capitation, a single physician practice may be able to pool risk effectively for a basket of primary care services alone, but it would not be able to pool risk effectively for both primary and specialty secondary care (specialty services and hospital care). If a funder wants to use capitation for a full range of primary and secondary services, the funded organizations would have to enrol a sufficiently large number of individuals; and even then, it should have a mechanism in place to deal with undue risk. Blended arrangements or well-designed **stop-loss mechanisms** can increase the range of settings in which capitation can be used, because such measures reduce the amount of risk transferred to the provider organization. The critical point is to match the transfer of risk to the ability to pool risk.

12.4.3 Minimizing the Scope for Self-Interested Strategic Responses by Funded Organizations

Self-interested strategic responses are inefficient because the funded organizations expend effort to increase revenues (and profits) in ways that allow them to capture a larger share of the funding without being more productive. Such responses can include the following:

- provision of unnecessary services under retrospective payment systems
- risk selection

- strategic up-coding to garner more payment than is appropriate (for example, in fee-for-service billing, an intermediate assessment rather than a minor assessment; in case-based funding, choosing the diagnostic category that will maximize reimbursement)

- strategic referral patterns to off-load costs, such as when a capitation-funded primary care physician more frequently refers patients to a specialist, shifting the costs to a separate funding stream

A number of design principles can be used to reduce opportunities for self-interested strategic responses:

- Minimizing the extent to which payment (including risk adjustment) is determined by factors under the control of the funded organization. This reduces the scope for gaming.

- Eliminating "budget boundaries." Budget boundaries created by different funding methods for subsets of services, or for different subsets of patients, tend to create opportunities for cost shifting and strategic selection, thereby reducing the incentive for a funded organization to realize efficiencies and coordinate care across service areas.

- Developing effective monitoring mechanisms that dissuade funded organizations from responding to those incentives (because it is impossible to remove all incentive for strategic responses).

12.4.4 Matching the Payment Mechanism to the Context

There is no universally best way to fund care. The optimal method depends on the system's objectives, and the nature and demands associated with the activities being funded. Fee-for-service, for instance, is reasonable when core activities can be well represented in a fee schedule, where there is concern about under-provision, and when utilization can be easily monitored. Fee-for-service, however, is unlikely to be optimal where complex case management is required, because such care cannot easily be represented in a fee schedule.

Chapter Summary

This chapter has examined a range of issues associated with the funding of health care. The key points are as follows:

- Funding health care represents one example of a larger economic phenomenon called the principal–agent problem, which has been used to analyze a wide variety of financial incentive schemes.

- The nature of the funding scheme plays a crucial role in determining who has incentive to provide what services to which individuals in alternative settings.

- Three basic elements of any health care funding scheme include the participants, the activities and services funded, and the funding mechanism.

- Participants include funders, provider organizations, financial intermediaries, and enrollees.

- Sets of funded services range from narrow subsets of health care services to broad baskets of services including primary care, specialized care, long-term care, and public health.

- The predominant funding mechanisms include fee-for-service, case-based funding, capitation funding, global budgets, and bonus or incentive payments.

- In order to address the trade-off between efficiency and risk selection, many funding schemes employ blended funding arrangements that balance the retrospective and prospective elements of funding.
- Key principles for the design of funding schemes include the following:
  - ensuring administrative feasibility and efficiency
  - distributing risk appropriately between funders and funded organizations
  - guarding against self-interested strategic behaviour and ensuring that a funding approach cannot easily be manipulated by the funded organizations
  - ensuring that the choice of funding mechanisms matches the context

Key Terms

blended funding, *316*
bonus payments, *312*
case-based funding, *311*
case-mix adjustment, *312*
enrolled population, *311*
funding mechanism, *309*
gaming, *311*

geographically defined
   population, *312*
global budget, *312*
performance-based
   payment, *312*
principal–agent
   problem, *304*

prospective payment, *312*
retrospective payment, *312*
skimping, *311*
stop-loss mechanism, *318*
up-coding, *311*

End-of-Chapter Questions

For each of the statements below, indicate whether the statement is true or false and explain why it is true or false.

1. Designing a funding system necessitates a trade-off between encouraging productive efficiency and discouraging strategic selection.
2. Using a scheme that pays physicians through a blend of capitation and fee-for-service rather than through pure capitation may help reduce risk selection.
3. Changing from fee-for-service payment to capitation payment transfers risk from the funder to the funded provider.
4. Fee-for-service payment is more likely to be efficient in settings for which the funder wants to encourage a specific set of services that are thought to be under-utilized.
5. All payment systems promote self-interested strategic or manipulative responses by those funded.
6. Fee-for-service provides no incentive to be efficient.
7. Because participation is mandatory for all residents within a universal, public insurance system, risk selection is not a concern when providers in such a system are funded using capitation payment.
8. Diagnosis-based payment transfers more risk from the funder to a provider than does fee-for-service payment.
9. Variables used to risk-adjust capitation payments should be under the control of providers.
10. The size of a provider organization (e.g., a physician practice or clinic) influences its ability to bear risk.

References

Australia Department of Health and Aging. 2005. *Home medicines review answers*. Canberra: Australia Department of Health and Aging. Available online at http://www.health.gov.au/internet/main/publishing.nsf/Content/ppsac-hmr.

Birch, S., J. Eyles, J. Hurley, B. Hutchison, and S. Chambers. 1993. A needs-based approach to resource allocation in health care. *Canadian Public Policy* 19(1):68–85.

Canadian Institute for Health Information. 2007. *Hospital report 2007: Acute care*. Ottawa: Canadian Institute for Health Information, in Collaboration with the Ontario Ministry of Health and Long-term Care and the Ontario Hospital Association.

Cutler, D. M. 2004. *Your money or your life*. Cambridge, MA: MIT Press.

Economist. 2005. Searching for a miracle solution. *The Economist* 43–4

Government of Ontario. 2006. *General blended payment template*. Toronto: Government of Ontario, December 13.

Grootendorst, P., L. Goldsmith, J. Hurley, B. O'Brien, and L. Dolovish. 1996. *Financial incentives to dispense low-cost drugs: A case study of British Columbia Pharmacare*. Hamilton, ON.: McMaster University Centre for Health Economics and Policy Analysis, Working Paper 96-08.

Hickson, G. B., W. A. Altemeier, and J. M. Perrin. 1987. Physician reimbursement by salary or fee-for-service: Effect on physician practice behaviour in a randomized prospective study. *Pediatrics* 80(3):344–50.

Hurley, J., S. Birch, and J. Eyles. 1995. Geographically-decentralized planning and management in health care: Some information issues and their implications for efficiency. *Social Science and Medicine* 41(1):3–11.

Hurley, J., and M. Giacomini. 1998. Funding and remuneration in health care. In *Introduction to the concepts and analytical tools of health sector reform and sustainable financing*. Washington, D.C.: Economic Development Institute of the World Bank. 7:129–46.

Hurley, J., J. Lomas, and V. Bhatia. 1994. When tinkering is not enough: Provincial reform to manage health care resources. *Canadian Public Administration* 37(3):490–514.

Newhouse, J. P. 1996. Reimbursing health plans and health providers: Efficiency in production versus selection. *Journal of Economic Literature* 34(3):1236–63.

Petersen, T. 1994. The principal–agent relationship in organizations. In *Economic approaches to organizations and institutions*, P. Foss (ed.). Aldershot, U.K.: Dartmouth Publishing Company. 9:187–212.

Propper, C., S. Burgess, and K. Green. 2004. Does competition between hospitals improve the quality of care? Hospital death rates and the NHS internal market. *Journal of Public Economics* 88(7/8):1247–72.

Ranade, W. E. 1998. *Markets and health care*. New York: Longman.

Rosenthal, M., R. Frank, Z. Li, and A. Epstein. 2005. Early experience with pay for performance: From concept to practice. *JAMA* 294(14):1788–93.

Saltman. R. B., and C. E. von Otter. 1995. *Implementing planned markets in health care: Balancing social and economics responsibility*. Buckingham: Open University Press.

Sappington, D. E. M. 1991. Incentives in principal–agent relationships. *Journal of Economic Perspectives* 5(2):45–66.

Appendix 12

Chapter 12: Health Care Funding

12.1 THE PRINCIPAL–AGENT FRAMEWORK AND FUNDING SYSTEMS

The principal–agent literature is huge, highly technical, and encompasses innumerable special cases that depend on the particular set of assumptions in a model. A common reference point is the canonical model, for which the optimal contract between the principal and the agent is fully prospective so that the agent bears all the risk. Sappington (1991) presents the optimality of this solution in the context of a one-period model, with a single principal and a single agent, in which the principal desires to maximize surplus.

The optimal payment scheme is one in which the agent pays a fixed "franchise" fee to the principal in return for the right to the value of the surplus (i.e., profits). Incentives are aligned because, at the margin, the agents are able to capture all the rewards for their efforts.

Shliefer (1985), in contrast, considers a setting in which a regulator faces a number of firms operating in different markets and must set an output price for each regulated firm. The first-best solution is one that induces each firm to produce the output efficiently and that induces the right level of output (price = marginal cost). The regulator, however, does not know the production function and so cannot administratively set price to accomplish this objective. The solution is to use a pricing strategy that induces firms to compete with each other to lower costs, a type of competition called yardstick competition.

This closely parallels the problem faced by a funder: a funder, for example, must reimburse hospitals but does not know the hospitals' true cost function. Retrospectively paying each hospital's incurred costs induces inefficient production. The funder wants to induce each hospital to produce care efficiently.

Following Shleifer, consider the problem more formally in a simplified setting and then consider the implications of relaxing some of the assumptions. Assume a one-period model.

- N identical, risk-neutral firms operating in a setting with no uncertainty
- each firm faces a downward-sloping demand curve, $q(p)$
- each firm has an initial marginal cost of c_0
- each firm can reduce its marginal cost to c by spending $R(c)$—that is, by investing in cost reduction, it can increase efficiency
- in addition to setting the price, p, the regulator may make lump-sum transfers to the firm, T
- a firm's profits are given by: $V = (p-c)q(p) + T - R(c)$

The regulator must choose c, p, and T so as to maximize the sum of consumers' and producers' surplus subject to each firm breaking even, so

$$\text{Max}\left[\left(\int_p^\infty q(x)dx\right) + (p - c)q(p) - R(c)\right] \text{s.t. } V \geq 0 \qquad \textbf{(12A.1)}$$

where the first term is consumers' surplus (the area under the demand curve above the price) and the second term is the producers' surplus.

The three conditions for optimum are as follows:

1. set the price equal to the marginal cost of production: $p^* = c^*$
2. minimize the total cost of producing output q: $-R'(c^*) = q(p^*)$[3]
3. provide a transfer so that the firm breaks even; since $p^* = c^*$, to break even, set $T^* = R(c^*)$

The problem is that the regulator does not know the production function, and therefore $R(c)$, so it does not know how to attain c^*. How can the regulator use price and the lump-sum transfer to induce a profit-motivated producer to choose c^*?

---

[3] This condition is not intuitive. Observe that $R'(c)$ is the marginal cost of cost reduction. Lowering unit costs by Δc requires investment expenditure of $-R'(c)\Delta c$; this reduces costs of production by $q(p)\Delta c$. The optimum requires that these be equal, which leads directly to the condition as listed above.

The solution is to eliminate any dependence between the price a firm receives and the firm's chosen cost level. One such price is the average cost incurred by all other firms operating in the sector. Let $\bar{c}_{-i}$ be the mean marginal cost of production for all firms other than i, and $\bar{R}_{-i}$ be the mean investment in cost reduction by all firms other than i. The optimal price and transfer for firm i is this:

$$p_i = \bar{c}_{-i} \text{ and } T_i = \bar{R}_{-i} \qquad\qquad \textbf{(12A.2)}$$

Because firm i's revenue is independent of its own costs and depends only on the costs incurred by other firms, this pricing strategy induces a kind of competition: If firm i can produce at lower cost than the other firms, it keeps the surplus. If it produces at a higher cost than the other firms, it incurs a loss. This is what is meant by yardstick competition: the performance of the other firms is used as a yardstick by which to gauge the performance of firm i. Shleifer (1985) shows that this pricing strategy leads to an equilibrium at the social optimum.

This solution corresponds almost exactly with the case-based funding used in health care in which the price per case that a hospital receives is equal to the average cost of treating such a case among all hospitals (if a single hospital's contribution to the calculation of average cost is small, this approximates the solution above). It also corresponds to capitation payment in which the rate received is equal to the average cost of meeting the health care needs of an enrollee. In the first case, the payment per case is fully prospective; in the second, the payment per enrollee is prospective. The model of yardstick competition provides a theoretical foundation for such a reimbursement policy.

Yet, it is clear that the above model makes a number of assumptions that do not hold in the health care sector. Focusing on hospital funding alone, for example, reveals that not all hospitals are identical. Hospitals do not produce a single, homogeneous good. Hospitals are more likely risk-averse than risk-neutral. Modifying these assumptions alters the optimal payment structure. Paying a fixed rate per patient for patients that differ in unobservable (to the funder) ways that correlate with the cost of treatment leads to inefficient risk selection by hospitals.

The solution is to introduce a component of retrospective payment: a blended formula with a fixed component independent of costs and a component that depends on the hospital's own costs. This reduces the incentive for risk selection. It also reduces the chance that a hospital will go insolvent, but it is possible that an unlucky draw of very expensive cases could bankrupt a hospital. If the hospital (and the regulator) is risk averse, welfare may be improved by avoiding this.

The solution to this latter problem is special payments for extremely high-cost outlier patients. In the U.S. Medicare system, for instance, payment for patients for whom the cost of care exceeds a pre-specified outlier threshold is based on the hospital's actual incurred costs for services to treat the patient. For a patient whose costs approach the outlier threshold value, however, the hospital has incentive to game the system and boost costs to reach the threshold (and obtain the cost-based rather than the fixed payment). This is a form of moral hazard associated with the outlier payment scheme. Companion literature (e.g., Bovberg 1992; van Barneveld and colleagues 1996; 1997; 1998; and van de Ven and Ellis 2000) analyzes alternative risk-pooling mechanisms for high-cost outlier patients in order to determine which types of schemes pool the risks effectively among providers while reducing moral hazard. Newhouse (1996) provides a general discussion of the application of yardstick models to health care reimbursement.

References

Bovbjerg, R. R. 1992. Reform of financing for health coverage: What can reinsurance accomplish? *Inquiry* (29):158–75.

Newhouse, J. P. 1996. Reimbursing health plans and health providers: Efficiency in production versus selection. *Journal of Economic Literature* 34(3):1236–63.

Sappington, D. E. M. 1991. Incentives in principal–agent relationships. *Journal of Economic Perspectives* 5(2):45–66.

Shleifer, A. 1985. A theory of yardstick competition. *Rand Journal of Economics* 16(3):319–27.

van Barneveld, E. M., L. M. Lamers, R. C. van Vliet, and W. P. van de Ven. 1998. Mandatory pooling as a supplement to risk-adjusted capitation payments in a competitive health insurance market. *Social Science and Medicine* 47(2):223–32.

van Barneveld, E. M., R. C. J. A. van Vliet, and W. P. M. M. van de Ven. 1996. Mandatory high-risk pooling: An approach to reducing incentives for cream skimming. *Inquiry* 33(2):133–43.

van Barneveld, E., R. van Vliet, and W. van de Ven. 1997. Risk-adjusted capitation payments for catastrophic risks based on multi-year prior costs. *Health Policy* 39(2):123–35.

van de Ven, W., and R. Ellis. 2000. Risk adjustment in competitive health plan markets. In *Handbook of Health Economics*, A. J. Culyer, and J. P. Newhouse (eds.). Amsterdam: Elsevier Science B.V. 755–846.

The Supply Side of Health Care Provision

In Chapters 13, 14, and 15, we turn our attention to the supply side of the health care sector. The analysis focuses on the individuals and organizations that deliver health care services or produce health care goods such as drugs and medical devices. The analysis focuses in particular on physicians, who constitute the most influential provider group within health care; hospitals, which constitute the dominant delivery institution; and drugs, which constitute the most common type of health care good used to treat individuals. Each is important in and of itself for understanding the supply side of health care, but each also represents distinct types of supply-side actors.

Some of the most interesting challenges for economic analysis arise from unusual features found among health care organizations—features that differ from a standard firm (as described by microeconomic theory) that supplies a good or service to a market. A standard firm is assumed to pursue a single objective—profit maximization—and to operate in a perfectly competitive market. The disciplining forces of a competitive market leave the firm no real choice except to determine how much of a good to produce. The firm has no control over the price it can charge (the market determines price) and it must produce in the least-cost manner (otherwise competitors would drive it out of business).

In health care, however, most markets are far from perfectly competitive. Physicians retain considerable market power because of informational problems and the regulatory policies designed to mitigate the effects of such problems. Hospitals outside of large cities often constitute local monopolies. And the pharmaceutical sector is a highly concentrated, profitable industry, with a small number of multinational producers. Market power gives each of these types of suppliers considerable discretion over what to produce, how to produce it, and what objectives to pursue.

Following Evans (1984), we distinguish three types of supply-side organizations in health care. The first are *not-for-profit* organizations. The distinguishing feature of a not-for-profit organization is a legal prohibition against distributing any financial surplus to the organization's principals. Nothing prohibits a not-for-profit organization from earning a surplus (i.e., profit). The legal status as a non-profit simply limits what can be done with any such surplus.

Many health care delivery institutions, and most hospitals in Canada and other countries, are not-for-profit religious, community-based, or public institutions. A principal challenge in analyzing such organizations is to identify their key objectives—what goal are they pursuing if, unlike the standard economic firm, they do not pursue profit to be distributed to the owners? The analysis of hospital behaviour and performance draws on a growing branch of economics devoted to the economic analysis of non-profit organizations.

The second type of organization is a *not-only-for-profit* organization. Such an organization includes among its objectives earning a profit that can be retained by its owner, but earning a profit is not its only objective. Most health care professional practices, including those of physicians, constitute such not-only-for-profit organizations. A physician's income derives from the practice, but a physician is presumed to pursue professional objectives besides income maximization.

As has been emphasized, a physician's medical training strives to inculcate an agency relationship in which a physician pursues patient interests rather than financial self-interest. Such agency is never perfect, but it creates a set of expectations and obligations quite different from a standard profit-maximizing firm. Physician practices in Canada are almost exclusively owned by physicians, so physicians do not have any fiduciary financial obligations to arms-length third parties such as equity shareholders. The economic analysis of physician practices incorporates objectives beyond income that physicians are assumed to pursue.

Finally, the health care sector includes *for-profit* firms, including large equity-financed corporations. Such organizations have a fiduciary responsibility to maximize profits for equity shareholders. For-profit organizations dominate the drug, medical device, and health care goods sectors more generally. One of the most important products of such research-intensive organizations is knowledge—knowledge that is ultimately embodied in a pill, diagnostic test, or medical advance. This raises special economic challenges because knowledge is a public good: many people can simultaneously "consume" the same knowledge and it can be difficult to exclude others from consuming it.

Free private markets systematically under-produce public goods, including knowledge, because an innovator cannot reap a financial reward once the knowledge innovation enters the public domain where others can freely transmit and use it. To encourage greater research and investment to generate knowledge, the government either finances research directly or protects innovators through patent legislation and the related regulation of intellectual property. Economic analysis of the pharmaceutical industry, therefore, draws heavily on the economics of research and development.

The supply side of health care is evolving through technological and organizational innovation. Solo physician practices are no longer the dominant physician practice model in many areas. New organizational forms and relationships are emerging as physician practices integrate increasingly sophisticated equipment into community-based settings, and as services move from in-patient hospital settings to free-standing diagnostic and day-surgery clinics.

Novel network relationships are emerging among providers, between providers and funders, and between providers and patients. These new relationships sometimes develop organically, as providers respond to the changing economics of practice. For example, the growth of privately financed "lifestyle" health care services is injecting a new entrepreneurial element into many aspects of medicine. Other times, these new relationships emerge in response to deliberate policies, such as those embodied in primary care reform. Still others arise in response to the growing importance of other provider services, such as home care for an aging population.

Economic analysis of the supply side of health care must evolve as well, to support the development of sound policy. These chapters are intended to provide some key concepts that can be used in such analysis.

Reference   Evans, R. G. 1984. *Strained mercy: The economics of Canadian health care.* Toronto: Buttersworth.

Physicians, Their Practices, and the Market for Physician Services

Learning Objectives

After studying this chapter, you will understand

LO1 Principal institutional features of the physician services sector

LO2 Common elements of economic models of physicians and their practices

LO3 Salient features of the market for physician services and the policy implications of these features

---

Economic analysis must distinguish three distinct elements of the physician sector: physicians themselves, physician practices, and the market for physician services. The market for physician services sets the economic context—including both constraints and opportunities—within which individual physicians contribute their labour and expertise to a physician practice. The practice combines these physician inputs with other inputs to produce physician services.

We begin this chapter, therefore, with a brief account of institutional features of the market for physician services, focusing on Canada. We then examine models of physician practices and physician behaviour, which are often modelled jointly. Finally, we turn to a specific context where economic analysis can play an important role in guiding policy—physician human resource planning.

Supplier-induced demand, a topic central to many analyses of the physician sector, is not covered extensively in this chapter; however, the chapter does draw on the concept of supplier-induced demand and assumes familiarity with it. To review this material, see Chapter 8 on the demand for health care.

13.1 THE PHYSICIAN SERVICES SECTOR

Expenditure on physician services constituted 13.2 percent of all Canadian health care expenditures in 2006 (Canadian Institute for Health Information 2008a). This proportion remained relatively constant for many years at between 14 and 16 percent, but began falling slowly in the early 1990s (Figure 13.1). This modest proportion of expenditure, however, understates the importance of physicians in the health care system because it is

FIGURE 13.1   **Physician Expenditures as a Percentage of Total Health Care Expenditures, Canada, 1975–2005**

Source: Canadian Institute for Health Information (2008a, Table A.3.1.2). Canadian Institute for Health Information 2008b. Physicians in Canada: The Status of Alternate Payment Programs, 2005–06. Ottawa: Canadian Institute for Health Information.

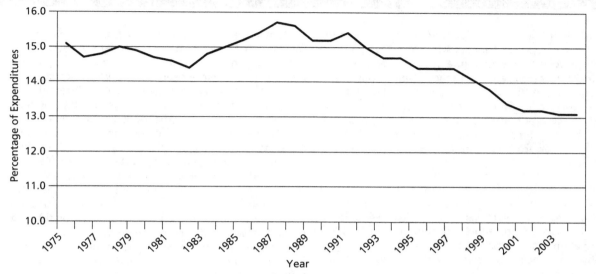

physician treatment decisions that allocate the majority of health care resources. Physician recommendations influence expenditures on hospital-based services, drugs, home care, and many other services. Consequently, understanding physician behaviour is essential to achieving an efficient and equitable allocation of health care resources.

As was noted in Chapter 1, in recent years access to physician services has been a policy concern in Canada. During the 1990s, an increasing number of Canadians had difficulty securing access to a regular family physician and certain types of specialist care (Chan 2002). Although most policy attention focused on changes in the number of physicians as the primary culprit, analyses suggest a more complex set of factors at work.

Between 1982 and 2003, for instance, general/family practitioners reduced their average hours of direct patient care from just over 45 hours per week to approximately 38 hours per week (Crossley et al. 2009). This reflects three factors:

1. Female physicians, who tend to work fewer hours than male physicians, account for a growing proportion of the physician supply: in 1978, female physicians constituted 11 percent of all physicians; by 2008, their proportion had grown to over 35 percent (Canadian Institute for Health Information 2009), and they now make up more than half of new physicians.

2. The physician workforce, along with the rest of the population, is aging. The average age of physicians increased from 45.3 years in 1978 to 49.8 years in 2008 (Canadian Institute for Health Information 2009).

3. The average hours of direct patient care by male physicians fell, but the causes of this phenomenon are not well understood.

Physician practices are also changing (see, for example, Box 13.1). Between 1986 and 2007, for example, the proportion of Canadian family physicians working in a solo practice fell while the proportion of those working in multi-provider practices increased to 74.2 percent in 2007, including 23.5 percent working in inter-professional settings (National Physician Survey 2009). Among those in group practice, there was a trend toward working in larger groups. This partially reflects primary care reform, which has sought to increase the proportion of physicians working in group settings, especially with non-physician providers.

Family physicians are the foundation of the primary health care system in Canada, which provides the first point of access to the full range of health care services. But the practice patterns of Canadian family physicians are changing. Although the proportion of family physicians working in office-based settings has remained relatively constant, the activities of family physicians are changing. Tepper (2004) documents the increasing trend toward specialization by Canada's family physicians.

- The proportion of family physicians providing a full range of services, including basic surgical services, anaesthesiology services, surgical assists, basic and advanced procedures, obstetrics, and hospital in-patient care is falling as the majority of family physicians focus on a core of office-based visits and consultations.
- The only exception to this pattern is mental health services, which family physicians are increasingly providing.

Rather than having all family physicians provide a full range of services, the pool of family physicians is segmenting into subsets that emphasize specific practice areas. This may partly explain the pattern documented by Barer et al. (2004) that the number of different general practitioners seen by the average British Columbian increased notably over the period 1985–1996, while the number of visits to each general practitioner fell. These trends partially reflect responses to ongoing system challenges (e.g., the shortage of psychiatrists, which shifts more care onto family physicians), economic forces (e.g., malpractice premium increases for those who provide obstetric care), changing attitudes (e.g., desire for more predictable hours of work), and other less well-understood forces. They raise a number of issues regarding system performance, including its effects on quality and continuity of care, access to services, and the relationship between general practitioners and specialists. Health analysts are studying these and other effects of the evolving role of family physicians in health care.

Specialists in Canada, like their U.S. counterparts, are generally not employed by hospitals, but rather have independent practices with the right to admit patients to hospital. This differs from many European countries in which specialists are salaried employees of hospitals.

Although fee-for-service remains the dominant mechanism to fund both primary care and specialist services in Canada, alternative forms of payment—including salary, capitation, blended formulae, and other methods—are growing (see Chapter 12 on funding). Between 2000 and 2005 in Canada, for instance, the proportion of clinical income derived from non-fee-for-service sources rose from 13.0 percent to 21.3 percent (Canadian Institute for Health Information 2008b). Responses to the National Physician Survey in 2007 indicated that less than half of all Canadian physicians earned more than 90 percent of their income from fee-for-service sources, and approximately one-third were paid through blended systems that combine multiple types of payments.

The use of alternative payments varies substantially across provinces, with the Maritime provinces in general having a higher proportion of physicians paid at least partly through non-fee-for-service methods (often salary or sessional payments), while Ontario has made the greatest (albeit still limited) use of capitation, especially in primary care.

Physician incomes have consistently been well above the earnings of average Canadians since the 1940s (when the income data begin), though they have fluctuated considerably in recent decades under Medicare. Grant (2005) identifies five distinct trends since the 1950s:

1. The period from 1950 to 1970 was one of steady growth in average physician incomes: physician average annual earnings grew in absolute terms from about $54,000 to $146,000

(measured in constant 2003 dollars) and in relative terms from about 2.5 times to more than 4 times the average earnings of all Canadian workers.

2. The introduction of Medicare brought retrenchment as governments began their never-ending struggle to limit growth of health care costs. Between 1972 and 1975, real incomes fell from $146,000 to $130,000, while average physician earnings fell from 4.4 times to only 3.5 times those of all other workers.

3. The third period, 1979–1991, saw steady recovery of physician incomes, with average physician earnings rising from $130,000 to $160,000, or approximately 4.5 times the earnings of all other workers.

4. The first half of the 1990s once again saw retrenchment as governments squeezed health care, imposing global expenditure caps in the physician sector, causing physician earnings to decline both in absolute and relative terms.

5. Finally, fueled by the removal of global expenditure caps, steady economic growth more generally, and fee increases as provinces compete for physicians, average annual physician incomes since 1996 have grown steadily so that physicians once again earn more than 4 times the average Canadian worker.

In summary, many dimensions of physician practices have evolved in recent decades in response to changing technologies, changing physician attitudes, and deliberate policy reform within the health care system. This evolution will likely continue or even accelerate in coming years as governments push for primary care reform, as the supply of new types of allied health providers such as nurse practitioners and physician assistants expands, as the supply of physicians expands, and as physicians choose from an expanded set of work settings in which to practise.

13.1.1 Regulation of Physicians and Their Practices

Rationale for Physician Regulation

Physicians and their practices are highly regulated. As we have seen, the regulation is motivated primarily by asymmetry of information between physicians and patients, which gives physicians considerable market power and potentially exposes patients to risks from poor-quality care. In an unregulated physician sector, poorly informed patients would have trouble distinguishing "quacks" from those who offer valuable, high-quality services.

Much regulation aims to ensure a minimum level of quality and to limit competitive pressures that would force physicians to put their own economic interests before patients' interests. Physician regulation must balance two counter-acting welfare effects: (1) increasing social welfare by raising quality and facilitating the physician–patient agency relationship, and (2) reducing social welfare by inhibiting competition and thereby engendering inefficiency in the physician sector.

Physician Self-Regulation In regulating physicians, policy-makers themselves face informational asymmetry directly analogous to that faced by patients seeking treatment (Tuohy and Wolfson 1978). Policy-makers often do not have the requisite knowledge to judge physician competency, to assess quality of care, and more generally to "police" physicians. Policy-makers, therefore, delegate regulation to physicians themselves—physicians are a self-regulating profession.

In Canada, government has delegated regulation of physicians to the Royal College of Physicians and Surgeons, the Royal College of Family Physicians, and the provincial counterparts that act as regulatory agents on behalf of government. The Colleges are responsible for accrediting physicians, monitoring quality and practice behaviour, adjudicating patient complaints regarding physician performance, and disciplining physicians who violate professional regulations.

Regulation of Entry Entry into the profession is tightly controlled in all developed countries. Canada has seventeen accredited medical schools, and the number of training slots for both undergraduate and graduate medical training is tightly controlled. Foreign-trained physicians can enter medical practice in Canada only after passing the relevant licensing exams and, in many cases, undergoing further postgraduate training in Canada. Only individuals with a valid license from the relevant College of Physicians and Surgeons or College of Family Physicians can practise medicine.

Regulation of Medical Acts Health-profession regulations tightly control who is allowed to perform defined medical acts. Such regulation stipulates, for example, that (with minor exceptions) only physicians are allowed to write prescriptions for prescription drugs.[1] Similarly, with the exception of dental surgery that can be performed by dental surgeons, only physicians can perform surgery. Physicians, therefore, have a monopoly with respect to the production and delivery of many medical services.

Regulation of Physician Advertising Although physician advertising is no longer legally prohibited, it remains severely limited, is discouraged by many of the physician regulatory bodies, and almost never emphasizes price competition.

Regulation of Physician Payment Physician payment is tightly regulated. In most countries, payment rates, especially in the public health care systems, are set administratively through negotiation between funders and physicians. Fees for services provided through the public insurance plan in Canada, for instance, are set provincially through periodic negotiation between the provincial government and the provincial medical association. Physicians in Canada are not allowed to charge a fee higher than the negotiated fee. Charging a fee above the public reimbursement (a practice called **extra billing** in Canada and "balance billing" in Europe, the U.S., and Australia) violates the 1984 Canada Health Act.[2]

extra billing
The practice by a physician of charging a fee greater than the public reimbursement, requiring the patient to pay the difference between the two.

As described in Chapter 1, a physician's ability and incentive to provide privately financed services in Canada is also highly regulated. Physicians paid by the public plan can, of course, provide privately financed non-medically-necessary services that fall outside the Canada Health Act and set their own fees for such services. But for publicly insured physician services, most provinces require that a physician either fully opt into the provincial plan or fully opt out; in such provinces, a physician cannot choose to charge privately for some patients but publicly for others.[3]

In addition, many provinces also regulate the fees that can be charged by physicians who opt out of the public plan (Flood and Archibald 2001). Manitoba, Ontario, and Nova Scotia prohibit opted-out physicians from charging private fees greater than the fees paid by the public plan. Other provinces permit opted-out physicians to charge fees higher than

---

[1] Dentists and nurse practitioners can also write prescriptions in some jurisdictions, and there is a trend in many jurisdictions to extend limited prescribing privileges to other health professions such as physician assistants, pharmacists, dental hygienists, and others.

[2] It is permitted but discouraged in most other countries.

[3] Since September 2004, physicians in Ontario have been prohibited from opting out of the public plan and receiving payment from a private third party, although physicians who had opted out prior to September 2004 were grandfathered in the legislation. Four provinces—Alberta, Saskatchewan, New Brunswick, and Prince Edward Island—allow physicians to opt out for specific patients and bill the patients directly rather than bill the provincial plan. Regulations vary across the provinces as to whether a physician can charge a fee for the service in excess of the public fee and as to whether patients can seek reimbursement from the provincial insurance plan (Boychuk 2006). In 2009, Quebec began allowing some specialist physicians to provide care in both publicly funded clinics and private clinics.

those in the public plan; however, all but Newfoundland and Prince Edward Island prohibit such patients from receiving any public subsidy.

Newfoundland is the only province that currently allows private health insurance coverage for publicly insured physician and hospital services, allows opted-out physicians to charge more than the public fee, and allows patients to receive public coverage for a service even when the fees charged are higher than those of the public plan. In such cases, the physician must bill the patient directly and the patient must subsequently obtain reimbursement from the province as is applicable.

Consequently, few physicians opt out of the public plan: the estimates as of March 31, 2008, are that no physicians are opted out in 7 of the 10 provinces—Alberta, Saskatchewan, Manitoba, New Brunswick, Nova Scotia, Prince Edward Island, and Newfoundland—while 5 are opted out in British Columbia, and 40 in Ontario (Health Canada 2008).[4]

13.1.2 The Market for Physician Services

The market for physician services determines the economic environment in which physicians practise medicine. It also shapes the organization of practices, the economic relationship among physicians and between physicians and other providers, as well as the options patients face when seeking medical care. In turn, the market evolves in response to changing technologies, changing consumer preferences and expectations, and changing demands of funders of care.

Markets for physician services are not perfectly competitive. Physicians derive their market power both from informational asymmetry between themselves and patients and from the deliberate regulation of their practices to limit entry, inhibit advertising, and more generally reduce competitive pressure.

The organization of markets for physician services varies markedly across health care systems. Further, it is a misnomer to speak of "the market" for physician services: the physician sector comprises many related markets for the services of different types of physicians, and the operation of these sub-markets can differ considerably.

The market for primary care physician services, for example, operates differently from the market for specialist services. Most primary care markets are local and include a number of family physicians "competing" directly for patients among the general public. In contrast, specialists concentrate in larger towns and cities, often draw patients from large catchment areas, and either depend on referrals from family physicians or are based in hospitals where they are salaried members of the physician staff.

Competition among physicians emphasizes the non-price dimensions of care, both because insurance insulates individuals from price and because many systems set physician fees administratively. Hence, to the extent that competition occurs, it is over style of practice, the range of services offered, perceived quality, hours of operation, and so forth.

Physicians practise in an environment populated with an increasing number of alternative providers (e.g., chiropractors, optometrists, midwives)[5] and a broadening array of services (many of them privately financed, non-medically necessary services) that increase economic opportunities for expanding their market. The evolution of the physician services market is having a corresponding impact on how physicians organize their practices, the nature of the settings in which they work, and the nature of the services provided.

[4] The figure is unavailable for Quebec.

[5] How this "competition" is viewed depends on the relative supply of physicians. In areas with a physician shortage, such alternative providers may be viewed by overburdened physicians not as competition but as relief.

13.2 MODELLING THE PHYSICIAN PRACTICE AND PHYSICIAN BEHAVIOUR

Developing policies to promote the efficient delivery of and equitable access to needed physician services requires models to analyze physician behaviour, the supply of physician services, and performance in the physician sector. Such models allow analysts to predict the effects of reform in the physician sector and, more generally, of changes in economic aspects of medical practice. The models can also guide empirical investigation into physician performance and provide insight into observed behaviours.

Policy-makers, for instance, are keenly interested in the feasibility of using explicit financial incentives to achieve more appropriate patterns of delivery for physician services. Assessing such a policy requires a model of how physicians will respond to differential fees across services in a fee schedule. Analogously, assessing the impact of permitting parallel private finance for publicly insured physician services depends on analyzing how physicians will respond to new market opportunities for their services (see Chapter 11). This section examines some of the ways economists have modelled physicians and their practices to analyze these and other policy questions in the physician sector.

Historically, most physician practices, and especially solo practices, have been structured much like many owner-operated small businesses, such as a farm or a corner grocery store. The physician plays two roles in the practice: (1) the physician supplies labour to the practice; and (2) the physician is the owner of the practice with a right to the net income of the practice. The practice combines physician labour with other labour inputs (e.g., nurses) and capital (e.g., examining rooms, stethoscopes, laboratory equipment) to produce physician services for patients. Even though most formal models give scant attention to the institutional details of a practice—in most cases, the practice amounts to little more than a production function that transforms inputs into outputs—the distinction between the physician and the practice remains crucial for economic analysis and related policy development in the physician sector.

Although the physician and the practice are distinct, they are not economically independent. In a standard economic setting, a firm purchases labour (and other) inputs from a competitive input market at a fixed price, produces a good, and then sells the good in the market to make a profit (its sole objective). In physician practices, physicians supply labour to practices (which they own) and draw income from practice earnings. The **implicit wage** a physician earns is the net income of the practice divided by the number of hours the physician works.

implicit wage
The imputed wage earned by a physician equal to the earnings from the physician's practice divided by the number of hours of labour supplied to the practice.

Most physician models are developed within the household production framework (see Box 5.1 in Chapter 5). Physicians have objectives and use their own time plus inputs purchased on the market to produce physician services in the practice. These services are sold to generate the income the physicians use to purchase consumer goods. Such models have three key elements: the physician objective function, the production function (practice), and the constraints.

Depending on the focus of the model, one element may be emphasized over others. Models that investigate the implications of alternative specifications of physician objectives, for instance, may simplify assumptions regarding the production of services to allow for a richer specification of the objective function. Analogously, models developed to explore the implications of differing assumptions regarding production may specify a simpler objective function. Nonetheless, any model of physician practice and behaviour makes implicit or explicit assumptions about each of these elements.

Physician Preferences

Physicians are generally assumed to maximize utility subject to the constraints imposed by production technology, time, and market conditions. As we will see below, the exact specification of physician preferences varies from model to model, but a general formulation of the utility function is as follows:

$$U = U(C, L, E) \tag{13.1}$$

where C = consumption, L = leisure, and E = ethics.

Consumption reflects a physician's desire to purchase consumer goods with the income earned from the practice.[6] Higher levels of consumption increase utility. Leisure is simply time spent not working. If A is hours of work, then $L = 24 - A$.[7] Utility is assumed to be positively related to leisure, and leisure is assumed to be a normal good (other things equal, the higher a physician's income, the greater is the demand for leisure). "Ethics" refers to a physician's professional ethics; it represents the idea that physicians are socialized through their training to provide appropriate, good-quality care and to abide by certain professional ethics (e.g., *primum non nocere*—"first, do no harm"); and ethics have been modelled in various ways. Most commonly, utility is assumed (other things equal) to be maximized by providing the level of care a physician judges to be appropriate given the patient's clinical condition. The physician's utility falls as the amount of care provided deviates from the appropriate level.

The Production Function for Medical Services (The Practice)

The practice, which combines physician labour with other inputs to produce medical services, is represented by a production function:

$$M = M(A, I) \tag{13.2}$$

where M is the quantity of medical care provided, A is physician labour (measured in hours), and I is other inputs to the practice. For simplicity, most models assume that production exhibits constant returns to scale (so that if all inputs double, output doubles), as well as some substitutability between physician labour and other inputs.

Constraints

The budget constraint requires that the total expenditures by the physician do not exceed the total amount of money available to the physician:

$$O + F_M M - P_I I - P_C C = 0 \tag{13.3}$$

where O is non-practice income (e.g., a spouse's earnings, investment income), F_M is the fee received for providing a unit of medical care, P_I is the price of a unit of non-physician input, and P_C is the price of a unit of consumption. Equation 13.3 simply says that the sum of expenses a physician incurs purchasing other inputs ($P_I I$) and consumption goods ($P_C C$) cannot exceed total monies available to the physician from the revenue of the practice ($F_M M$) and other non-practice sources (O).

Most models assume that P_C and P_I are beyond the control of physicians, set in competitive markets. F_M is also commonly assumed to be outside the control of a physician, not because fees are set in a competitive market but because fees are set by funders, either unilaterally or in negotiation with medical associations. So physicians are "price takers"—they accept as given the price for their services.[8]

---

[6] In some models, income (not consumption) enters directly as an argument in the utility function. Either way, the purpose is to represent the desire of a physician to have the financial resources to purchase goods and services for consumption.

[7] Some models specify a composite commodity "leisure" that the household produces using time plus consumer goods. So, for instance, time plus a book produces an hour of "reading."

[8] This assumption is realistic in most public systems of financing; it accords less well with reality for privately financed services in many settings.

Finally, there is a time constraint:

$$L + A = 24 \qquad\qquad \textbf{(13.4)}$$

Total hours each day (working and not working) must equal 24.

Choice Problem

The physician must choose the level of consumption, leisure, other inputs, and medical care so as to maximize utility. The model allows us to explore the effects of changes in physician preferences, the fees paid (or more generally, changes in the way physicians' practices are funded), and the price of non-physician inputs. We can also use the model to look at the effects of non-practice income on the amount of medical care produced, the physician work effort, and the combination of inputs used to produce physician services.

13.2.1 Alternative Assumptions Regarding Physician Objectives

The above framework can be modified to accommodate a wide variety of assumptions regarding physician objectives. Some economists, for example, argue that physicians are essentially income maximizers, who behave no differently in their professional lives than standard economic firms. An income-maximizing model corresponds to a utility function with only consumption (income) in the physician's utility function; i.e., $U = U(C)$. This is the physician as *Homo economicus*—economic man. Many early critiques of physician-induced demand implicitly or explicitly assumed such a model.

At the other extreme, some writers assume that physicians are totally uninfluenced by financial interests and simply respond to objectively given patient needs. This is the physician as *Homo clinicus*—clinical man. This corresponds to a utility function with ethics as the only argument (supplemented with a further assumption that need is objectively defined outside the control of physicians): $U = U(E)$.

Neither of these polar cases is realistic, though they still retain hold over certain groups of economists and physicians. More common are models of physician practices as not-only-for-profit organizations motivated by both income (consumption) and ethics as in equation 13.1.

Ethical Physicians and Financial Incentives: The Woodward and Warren-Bolton Model

Woodward and Warren-Bolton (1984) present a model of an "ethical" physician who cares about both income and providing the appropriate level of care. They use the model to explore the impact of different payment mechanisms on the level of care provided by such a physician. The physician's utility function incorporates ethics in the following way:

$$U = U(C,[M_{act} - M_{app}]) \qquad\qquad \textbf{(13.5)}$$

where C is a composite consumption commodity produced using own leisure time and purchased consumer goods, M_{act} is the number of services actually provided per patient, and M_{app} is the appropriate number of services based on the physician's best clinical judgment. The physician is ethical in the sense that the utility derived from providing medical care is highest when the physician provides the level of care he or she judges to be most appropriate, and decreases with both under- and over-provision of care.

This model shows that even an ethical physician will tend to under-provide care when paid by salary, and may over-provide care when paid by fee-for-service.

Service Provision When Paid by Salary   To see why a physician paid by salary will provide less than the appropriate amount of care, imagine a physician paid by salary who provides exactly the appropriate level of care. Suppose the physician makes a one-unit reduction in work effort. This causes service provision to fall below the appropriate level, decreasing utility. At the same time, the additional free time increases the amount of the composite leisure good (C) available for consumption, increasing the physician's utility.

When paid by salary, the only way a physician can increase such consumption is by working less (since additional work does not generate any additional income). As long as the marginal utility of such consumption is positive, the utility maximizing amount of service provision is below the appropriate level. Exactly how far below depends on the physician's preferences: if even small deviations from the appropriate level of care cause large decreases in utility, then service provision will be very close to the appropriate level. But if such deviations cause only small drops in utility and the marginal utility of leisure consumption is large, the deviation from appropriate levels will be greater.

Service Provision Under Fee-for-Service   The situation changes when the physician is paid by fee-for-service because now physicians earn additional income by working more and providing more services. If a physician uses that additional income to purchase more market goods, the physician may be able to simultaneously increase both the production of medical care and the consumption commodity (although leisure time will decrease).

If such a physician currently provides exactly the appropriate level of care, increasing service provision will decrease utility from service provision, but the additional income may more than compensate by allowing for increased consumption. If so, the physician will maximize utility by providing more than the appropriate level of care. The model can further be used to identify conditions under which under- and over-provision are most likely to arise.

The important message of the model is that even ethical physicians who care about providing the appropriate level of care may systematically deviate from that level in response to the financial incentives they face.

Ethical Physicians and Financial Incentives: The McGuire–Pauly Model

McGuire and Pauly (1991) present a model that is useful for investigating how physicians respond to changes in fees. They specify the physician utility function as follows:

$$U = U(Y, L, E) \tag{13.6}$$

where Y is income from the practice, L is leisure, and E represents ethical considerations such that inducing the provision of medical care away from the appropriate level reduces the physician's utility. They assume a very simple production process: one unit of physician labour is required to produce one unit of medical care.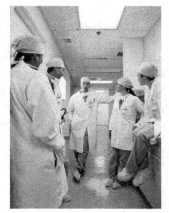

To understand the predictions of this and other models we will discuss below, it is useful to quickly review labour supply curves (Chapter 3). Figure 13.2 depicts a labour supply curve, which shows the number of hours a person would work at each wage level.

The labour supply curve reflects two counter-acting effects: substitution and income effects. When a wage increases, work becomes more financially remunerative;

FIGURE 13.2   **Labour Supply Curve**

A labour supply curve, which depicts the number of hours a person would work at each wage level, reflects counter-acting effects. A change in wages creates both substitution and income effects. When a wage increases, working becomes more financially attractive, so substitution effects say "work more and take less leisure." The wage increase raises the opportunity cost of not working—leisure time—so we want less of it. But the wage increase also raises our income. Leisure is a normal good—something we want more of as our income rises. So the income effect says "take more leisure and work less." At low and middle wages, the substitution effect is larger, so wage increases lead us to work more. But if the wage gets high enough (W* in the figure), the income effect begins to dominate the substitution effect: further increases in wages actually cause us to work less. We now have lots of income; what we desire is more leisure—time to enjoy that income. The portion of the labour supply curve above W* is called the "backward-bending" portion of the supply curve.

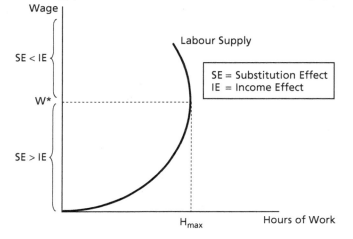

so the substitution effect says "work more and take less leisure." That is, the wage increase raises the opportunity cost of not working, so a person wants less leisure.

On the other hand, the wage increase also raises our income. And leisure is a normal good—something we want more of as income rises. So the income effect caused by the wage increase says "take more leisure and work fewer hours."

At low and middle wages, the substitution effect is larger, so wage increases make us work more. Hence, the lower portion of the supply curve is positively sloped. But if the wage gets high enough (W* in the figure), the income effect begins to dominate the substitution effect: a further increase in wages actually causes us to work less.

At high wages, we have lots of income; what we desire is more leisure—time to enjoy that income. The portion of the labour supply curve above W* is called the **backward-bending labour supply curve**.

Using their model, McGuire and Pauly demonstrate that for a utility-maximizing physician who cares about more than just income, the impact of a change in fees on the level of service provision cannot be determined from theory alone, because the fee change creates counteracting effects. Imagine first that the fees for all services change by the same percentage amount, so there is no change in the relative fees among services. A change in fees creates two sets of counteracting effects:

backward-bending labour supply curve
A labour supply curve that, at high wages, bends backward, changing from a positive to a negative slope as the income effect associated with a wage increase dominates the substitution effect.

1. The first set relates to labour supply. A fee increase, for example, raises the physician's implicit wage. The change in the wage creates income and substitution effects in labour supply.

2. The second set of effects relates to the disutility of inducing demand. Although the fee increase creates incentive to provide more services, if increasing service delivery requires inducement above the appropriate level, this causes disutility.

In the end, the effect of a fee change depends on the relative strength of these effects.

McGuire and Pauly were particularly interested in the effects of changes in relative fees across services. To simplify matters, imagine that a physician provides only two services. They could be two different services funded by the same insurer, such as two services within a single fee schedule, or they could be the same service provided to patients of two different insurers whose fees differ.

This situation is more complicated than that considered above. As before, a change in the fee for a service creates income and substitution effects between work and leisure and potential utility effects from inducement; but in addition, it can generate substitution effects across services (or payers). The ultimate impact of a change in the fee for a service depends on how large a share of physician activity is accounted for by that service: the larger the share of activity accounted for by the service, the larger are the income effects associated with a fee change for that service.

target-income model

A model of physician behaviour theorizing that physicians have a target income and adjust their service activities to achieve that target income.

The Target-Income Model   A special case of the McGuire and Pauly model is known as the target-income model of physician behaviour, which has been highly controversial in health economics. The **target-income model** posits that physicians have a target income and, as economic aspects of the physician sector change, they adjust their service activity to achieve that target income.

The target-income model was first proposed by R. Evans (1974) to explain observed patterns of physician services utilization under fee-for-service. He observed that when fees fell, utilization increased, and when fees increased, utilization fell. It was as if the physicians had a "target income" to which they aspired and adjusted their practice activities to reach that target.

The model was heavily criticized by many neoclassical economists, in part because it implied that physicians had full economic power to reach their desired incomes, in part because it provided no insight into how physicians set their target income, and in part because it implied non-maximizing behaviour: if physicians had such power, why would they not maximize their income at all times? Within Evans's formulation, such behaviour was inhibited by the disutility of providing unnecessary care that violates the physician-agency patient relationship.

The target-income model can be derived as a special case of physician preferences within the McGuire–Pauly model: below the target income level, the marginal utility of income is very high (an increase in income raises utility a lot); and above the target income, the marginal utility of income is very low (an increase in income has little effect on utility). Assuming a physician is already at the target level, the target-income model predicts that an increase (decrease) in fees will definitely lead a physician to decrease (increase) service delivery.

Although controversial, the target-income model fits within a long-standing stream of reasoning in economics that argues that people's behaviour is driven by their relative position rather than their absolute position (Rizzo and Blumenthal 1996); that is, a person's well-being is determined not by the absolute dollar amount of income or consumption, but by their income compared to some reference standard. The standard could be determined externally (e.g., what my neighbour or colleague earns) or internally (what I expected when I decided to pursue a certain profession).

Using data with information on both a physician's actual earnings and the income the physician considers to be "adequate," Rizzo and Blumenthal (1996) find support for the target-income model. Although the target income is rejected in its strongest form—that which implies physicians have unlimited economic power to reach a target income and always react to counter changes in the economic environment of practice—the model seems to capture certain stylized facts about the physician sector and, therefore, retains a place among models of physician behaviour.

The above models generally assume a simple, fixed production process whereby each unit of service requires a fixed amount of physician time, and physicians are the sole input into production. Even in these simple models, predicting physician responses to payment changes (and financial incentives more generally) is more complicated than is true for simple profit-maximizing models of a firm.

A fuller development of the production side of a physician practice provides even further insight into the variety of ways physicians can respond to their economic environment.

13.2.2 Physician Labour Supply and the Production of Physician Services

Society generally seeks to ensure access to needed medical services. Physicians are a major input into the production of medical services, but they are not the only input. A physician, for instance, may supervise the provision of a service by another health professional. Physicians may also use differing amounts and types of equipment to produce a medical service.

Models of physicians and their practices that more fully develop the production component generally specify a simpler utility function with only consumption (C) and leisure (L) as arguments. A physician again earns income through the practice by producing and selling medical services.

Medical services (M) are produced using physician labour (A) and other inputs (I), as in equation 13.2. Within limits, physician and non-physician inputs can be substituted for each other (e.g., a nurse takes part of the patient history). A physician faces the usual time constraint (leisure plus work time equals 24 hours a day) and the usual financial constraint (total spending on consumption is less than or equal to the sum of net earnings from practice and non-practice sources):

$$P_C C = O + Y \qquad\qquad \textbf{(13.7)}$$

where P_C is the price of a unit of the consumption good, O is non-practice income such as a spouse's earnings or investment earnings, and Y is net practice earnings.

$$Y = F_M M - P_I I \qquad\qquad \textbf{(13.8)}$$

where F_M is the fee the physician receives for a unit of medical service provided, and P_I is the price a physician must pay for a unit of non-physician input.

The physician must choose the levels of consumption, leisure, and other inputs to the practice so as to maximize utility. Solving this problem identifies the optimal levels of consumption, hours of work, and use of other inputs, and by implication (given the production function), the optimal number of medical services to provide.

Within this framework, the optimal level of labour supply, input demand, and service supply depends on four features of the practice environment: the general level of consumer prices (P_C), the price of medical services (F_M), the price of non-physician inputs (P_I), and non-practice income (O).

The model allows us to explore how changes in these aspects of practice influence the amount of time physicians work, how physicians combine their effort with other inputs to produce services, and the number of services physicians provide. The ultimate effect of a change in any of these on the supply of medical services (which is often the underlying policy concern) works through its impact on physician labour supply, its impact on the desired mix of physician and non-physician inputs into production, or both. The optimal mix of non-physician and physician inputs depends solely on the relative price of the two inputs: (P_I/F_M), where F_M determines the implicit wage a physician earns from working and producing additional services.[9] Let's consider a change in each of these aspects of the practice environment, working from the simplest to the most complicated cases.

Change in Non-Practice Income   A change in non-practice income (O) generates only one type of effect on service supply: an income effect that works through physician labour supply. If leisure is a normal good, an increase in non-practice income will reduce physician labour supply and a decrease in non-practice income will increase physician labour supply. Because a change in non-practice income does not alter any relative input prices, it does not change the relative mix of physician and non-physician inputs.[10] Consequently, physician labour supply and medical service supply move in tandem: an increase in non-practice income causes a reduction in both physician labour supply and medical service supply; a decrease in non-practice income causes an increase in both physician labour supply and medical service supply.

Change in Consumer Prices   A change in general consumer prices, P_C, affects medical service supply solely through its impact on physician labour supply; but now there are two effects to consider. First, a change in consumer prices (holding F_M constant) changes a physician's real wage for working. Second, it reduces the real value of non-practice income. An increase in P_C reduces the real wage, creating both a substitution effect (the price of leisure has now fallen) and an income effect (real income has fallen) that work in opposite directions: the substitution effect says "work less" and the income effect says "work more" because leisure is a normal good.

In contrast, an increase in general prices creates only an income effect for non-practice income (it reduces real, non-practice income). An increase in consumer prices reduces real non-practice income which, as we saw before, increases labour supply. The net impact of these substitution and income effects on labour supply depends on their relative sizes, so we cannot say (based on theory alone) whether a change in general prices will increase or decrease physician labour supply and, concomitantly, medical service supply.

Changes in Fees or the Price of Inputs   The effects of changes in both the fee paid for medical services (F_M) and price of other inputs (P_I) are more complicated because they affect both physician labour supply and the optimal mix of physician and non-physician inputs. It is useful to distinguish two cases: one in which the physician labour supply is assumed to be positively sloped, so that increases in the real wage increase labour supply, and another in which the labour supply curve is backward bending, so that increases in the real wage cause physicians to reduce labour supply.

- *Positively Sloped Labour Supply Curve.* An increase in fees will increase a physician's implicit wage for working, causing the physician to work more. Increasing physician

[9] The physician does not have any preferences regarding the organization of the practice. The practice is valued purely instrumentally as a way to generate income.

[10] Maintaining a constant relative mix of non-physician and physician inputs implies that any changes in the absolute level of physician labour supply will cause corresponding changes in the demand for non-physician inputs.

wages while holding the price of non-physician inputs constant also increases the desired ratio of non-physician to physician inputs, thereby increasing the demand for non-physician inputs (e.g., both physicians and nurses work more hours). An increase in both inputs will lead to an increase in medical service supply.

An increase in the price of non-physician inputs (P_I), holding other prices constant, reduces a physician's real wage (because the physician's fee has not changed but the cost of producing the service has increased). This decrease in the real wage causes a physician to reduce labour supply. An increase in the price of non-physician inputs causes a physician to reduce the ratio of non-physician to physician inputs. A decrease in both physician labour supply and non-physician inputs reduces medical service supply.

- *Backward-Bending Labour Supply Curve.* In contrast, when the physician labour supply curve is backward bending, the impact of a change in the physician fee (F_M) on the demand for other inputs and on medical service supply is indeterminate. The fee increase has three effects:

  1. It reduces physician labour supply.
  2. It increases the desired ratio of non-physician to physician inputs.
  3. It encourages the substitution of non-physician inputs for physician labour.

Whether the demand for other inputs increases or decreases depends on the relative magnitudes of these effects. The easier it is to substitute non-physician for physician inputs, the more likely it is that an increase in fees will both increase demand for non-physician inputs and increase medical service supply even though it reduces physician labour supply.

Similar reasoning applied for an increase in P_I. An increase in P_I reduces real wage, which causes physician labour supply to increase and lowers the optimal ratio of non-physician to physician inputs. The ultimate impact on demand for non-physician inputs and on medical service supply depends on the relative magnitudes of the labour supply response and the ability to substitute the two inputs in production.

Table 13.1 summarizes key conclusions from the above analysis. The analysis is admittedly rather complex and perhaps even unsatisfying because a number of the predictions depend on the specific values of certain parameters. But this complexity is an important message. Even within the relatively simplified context of a model, it is very hard to predict how physicians and medical service supply will be affected by changes in the practice environment. It cautions against the overly simplistic predictions so prevalent in many policy discussions.

Empirical Evidence on Labour and Service Supply

Analyses of physician labour supply and services supply confirm many of these types of effects. Feldstein (1970), Brown and Lapan (1979), Hu and Yang (1988), and Brown (1989) all found evidence of a backward-bending physician labour supply curve. More recent studies are mixed. Thornton (1998) and Rizzo and Blumenthal (1994) found a positive relationship between fees and physician labour supply, with wage-elasticity of labour supply substantially higher for female physicians than for male physicians.

Thornton and Eakin (1997) found evidence of a backward-bending labour supply curve; but because fee increases caused physicians to employ more medical supplies and auxiliary services while working fewer hours, the supply of services actually increased overall. Both Rizzo and Blumenthal (1994) and Thorton and Eakin (1997) found evidence that nonpractice earnings have a substantial negative effect on labour supply for both male and female physicians.

TABLE 13.1 Effects of Changes in the Economic Environment on Physician Labour Supply, Demand for Non-Physician Inputs, and Physician Service Supply

		Physician Labour Supply (A)	Demand for Non-Physician Inputs (I)	Medical Service Supply (M)
Increase in Non-Practice Income (Y)		−	−	−
Increase in General Consumer Prices (P_C)	If income effects are greater than substitution effect	+	+	+
	If income effects are less than substitution effect	−	−	−
Increase in Fee Paid for a Medical Service (F_M)	If physician labour supply curve is positively sloped	+	+	+
	If the physician labour supply curve is backward bending	−	+ or − depending on the relative sizes of the elasticity of labour supply and the scope for substitution between physician and non-physician inputs in production	+ or − depending on the relative sizes of the elasticity of labour supply and the scope for substitution between physician and non-physician inputs in production
Increase in Price of Non-Physician Inputs (P_I)	If physician labour supply curve positively sloped	−	−	−
	If backward-bending physician labour supply curve	+	+ or − depending on the relative sizes of the elasticity of labour supply and the scope for substitution between physician and non-physician inputs in production	+ or − depending on the relative sizes of the elasticity of labour supply and the scope for substitution between physician and non-physician inputs in production

13.3 PLANNING PHYSICIAN SUPPLY: AN ECONOMIC PERSPECTIVE

Because entry into the medical profession is highly regulated, health planners must forecast the supply of physicians required to ensure reasonable access to medical services. In Canada, it seems that nearly every decade witnesses a major effort to project physician requirements and recommend related health human resource policies. Canada is not alone. In the United States, the Graduate Medical Education National Advisory Committee conducted ongoing assessments of physician requirements through the 1980s and 1990s, and the Council of Graduate Medical Education recently re-assessed physician resource requirements (Cooper 2004).

Such planning efforts face a number of challenges. The long training time needed to become a physician means that the planning models must predict decades into the future.

Planning physician supply has been a near-constant activity in Canada since the first Hall Commission Report in 1964 calling for the establishment of Medicare. Policy concern in this early period focused on the potential for substantial shortages of physicians as insurance coverage in the population expanded (Judek 1964). In response, Canada opened new medical schools and expanded enrolment in existing schools.

Concerns about the rapid growth of physician supply emerged in the mid-1970s as governments struggled to control expenditures. The concept of supplier-induced demand and its implications for health care policy, especially with respect to human resource policies, was first emerging. The growing understanding of the link between physician supply and expenditures prompted a federal study under the auspices of the National Committee on Physician Manpower (Canada 1975). Although the analysis did not call for major policy changes, it led to the first efforts to control physician supply, in the form of restrictions on the immigration of foreign-trained physicians.

The second Hall report (Hall 1980) issued the first explicit, public statement that a chief policy problem facing the health care system was an oversupply of physicians. In its wake, a series of provincial reports called for modest cuts to medical school enrolment, though, for the most part, no policy action followed.

By the late 1980s, concern regarding a physician surplus, rooted in the pressures a growing physician supply exerted on provincial health budgets, prompted the Conference of Federal-Provincial-Territorial Deputy Ministers of Health to commission the Barer–Stoddart Report (Barer and Stoddart 1991). Unlike many previous reports that attempted to forecast future requirements for physicians, the Barer–Stoddart report attempted a more comprehensive analysis of a full range of the factors that should inform human resource planning in health services. The report supported the then-common assessment that there was a surplus of physicians and it made a wide-ranging and, in the authors' view, linked set of recommendations with respect to physician and non-physician health human resource policies. Governments, however, acted almost exclusively on the recommendation to reduce medical school enrolments, cutting them by 10 percent.

By the late 1990s, the concerns regarding a physician shortage emerged. This prompted yet another round of provincial and national analyses, perhaps best exemplified by the Physician Human Resource Strategy for Canada, a joint effort of a wide-ranging set of health professional organizations and government ministries that aims to take a broad, more coordinated approach to physician human resource planning. The policy response has again focused primarily on medical school enrolment, which provincial governments have increased by over 50 percent since 2000. At the same time, they have expanded training for "physician substitutes" such as nurse practitioners, physician assistants, and midwives. In another decade, expect to hear concerns of a physician surplus . . .

The continuing evolution of the physician services market and medical technology create even greater uncertainty with respect to both the need for medical services and the configuration of resources best suited to meet that need.

The experience of Canada highlights these challenges (Box 13.2). In the late 1990s, Canada began to experience a perceived shortage of physicians, especially family physicians, less than a decade after having a perceived surplus.

Surprisingly, physician resource planning models have not relied heavily on an economic analysis of physicians, their practices, the production of medical services, and the market for health care. Planning models have historically tended to lack behavioural, economic foundations. The models, for instance, have often assumed that a physician represents a fixed amount of labour (sometimes with adjustment for the fact that females work fewer hours on average) and that physician labour is a fixed input into the production of health care.

Within such models, the main planning task is to project the future demand or need for health care services, and then work backward to derive the number of physicians required to provide the needed quantity of services. Economics-based analysis, however, emphasizes that physicians are not fixed entities in a fixed production process.

Rather, they respond to their economic environment by altering their professional behaviour, including both how much they work and what they do while they work. Incorporating a stronger economic and behavioural perspective expands the range of factors that might impinge on access and physician requirements in addition to expanding the range of policy levers available to ensure access to needed medical services.

Changes in Hours of Patient Care by Canadian Physicians

Such an economic perspective can provide insight into recent problems of access to physician services in Canada. As noted above, during the period in which the shortage and access problems became acute, the supply of physicians per person in Canada did not change appreciably. Physician work patterns, however, did change. The average amount of time a Canadian family physician spent in direct patient care fell substantially between 1982 and 2002 (Buske 2004; Crossley et al. 2009). The same supply of physicians provided fewer hours of access than if work patterns had not changed.

Some of this decline was due to the increasing proportion of female family physicians and to the aging of the physician population during this period. But these well-documented determinants of work patterns explain only part of the overall decline. The decrease in hours worked by the existing supply of physicians had a larger impact on access to services than did the changes in medical school enrolment and other commonly cited "causes" of the physician shortage.

We do not have a definitive answer at present regarding what was responsible for the decline, but an analysis by Crossley and colleagues rules out certain hypotheses (Crossley et al. 2009):

- The decline among physicians is not simply part of a larger trend among professionals in society. Among eleven professional groups for which the census measures hours of work, only physicians and veterinarians reduced average hours of work per week between 1981 and 2001 (a number of other professionals actually increased average hours over the period).
- Nor does it represent a reallocation of time within the work week: total hours of work fell in the same way as did hours of direct patient care.
- The decline was not driven primarily by changes among younger cohorts of physicians. Younger physicians today face different family and income constraints than previous cohorts of physicians faced, and these would be expected to affect physician labour supply (e.g., younger physicians are much more likely to be married to another professional than were earlier cohorts of physicians). If these factors were driving the reduced work time, we would expect to observe clear cohort effects in which younger cohorts behave differently today than did earlier cohorts at the same age, while older physicians would behave similarly to earlier generations. Crossley et al. (2009), however, fail to find such cohort effects; rather they find that the labour supply of all male physicians up to age 55 fell over this period.

Analogous studies of physician service supply (Watson et al. 2003; Watson et al. 2006) find similar cohort-related patterns with respect to the total volume of services provided per physician. It does not appear that physicians were simply substituting non-physician inputs for their own time. Combined, these findings suggest something more general was affecting physician labour supply over this period.

Policy Responses

Policies to increase access to needed services should consider both increasing the supply of physicians and modifying the practice environment in ways that elicit more services from the existing stock of physicians. Policy response has thus far emphasized the former through the expansion of medical school enrolment. (Association of Faculties of Medicine of Canada 2008).

But policies to elicit greater labour and service supply from the existing stock of physicians have the potential to resolve access more quickly and to be quantitatively more important because they affect the whole stock of current physicians. Analyses focused on the economic environment of practice also allow for the incorporation of alternative providers and of the effects (positive and negative) on service supply of policies pursued for wholly different reasons. The following factors in the physician sector, for example, likely will have both intended and unintended impacts on physician service supply:

- *Fee increases.* Some argue that it is necessary to increase fees in order to increase service provision and access to services. While this is possible, economic models of physicians and their practices allow that fee increases could have the opposite effect. If physicians are on the backward-bending portion of their labour supply curve and there is limited ability to substitute other inputs, physician fee increases could actually decrease service provision and access to medical services.

- *Increasing role for non-fee-for-service payment.* Models of physician behaviour and empirical evidence indicate that physicians paid under fee-for-service provide more services than those paid by other methods (Devlin and Sarma 2008). Increasing reliance on alternative payment methods will create two counter-acting effects: incentive for physicians to reduce their own work effort (and service intensity in particular), and incentive and greater flexibility to substitute non-physician inputs for physician inputs. (Alternative payment methods are an important condition for encouraging substitution of non-physician for physician personnel in the production of medical services.) The net effect on access to medical services depends on which dominates.

- *Multi-disciplinary primary care reform.* A number of primary care reform initiatives emphasize multi-disciplinary, group organizations. Such models may create two effects: (1) to increase the productivity of physicians by allowing them to work with a greater amount of non-physician inputs, and (2) to allow some services to be provided wholly by non-physician providers. Both reflect greater substitution of non-physician inputs for physician inputs, potentially increasing access to primary care even as physician inputs fall.

- *Growth of privately financed, non-medically-necessary care.* One of the fastest growing components of health care is privately financed non-medically-necessary health services (e.g., liposuction, botox treatments). Such services must be provided by a health professional and are appropriately privately financed. Such services, however, draw physician effort from the core public system. It will be increasingly important for health human resource planning to model all sources of demand, even if the public policy goal is to ensure access to publicly financed, medically necessary services.

- *Debt relief.* Debt relief for medical students may have a complex set of effects. Debt relief policies may increase the proportion of medical students who choose family practice rather than specialization, may reduce the incentive for physicians to provide financially more remunerative private-sector services (re-allocating time to publicly financed services), and may reduce labour supply overall (since debt relief acts like an increase in unearned income).

These examples illustrate some principles that should inform health human resource planning: the objective is to ensure access to needed health care services, not necessarily the services of a specific provider; the models must reflect the ability of system actors to respond to changes in their economic environment; and, as a corollary, planning models must be comprehensive, encompassing all sectors that have the potential to influence service provision.

Chapter Summary

This chapter has examined a range of issues associated with the physician sector. Some of the major points include the following:

- When analyzing the physician sector, it is essential to distinguish physicians, physician practices, and the physician services market.
- The physician services market is not perfectly competitive for two reasons: physicians derive market power from the asymmetry of information between patients and physicians, and the regulations designed to address informational asymmetry reduce the competitive pressures on physicians.
- Because of informational problems, medicine is a self-regulating profession: the state generally delegates regulation of the medical profession to physicians.
- Economic models of physicians and their practices generally include three elements: the objective function that physicians are pursuing, a production function that describes how physician and non-physician inputs can be combined to produce health care services, and a series of constraints.
- The objective of a physician is normally posited to include income, leisure, and practising in a manner consistent with professional ethics.
- Models of physicians and their practices highlight the complex nature of physician responses to changes in their economic environment. Many responses of policy interest, such as physician responses to changes in the fees they are paid, cannot be known based on theory alone. Such models, however, can provide important insight into the analysis of many health care policy issues. The chapter illustrated such insights by considering how such economic models, and economic reasoning more generally, can inform health human resource planning.

Key Terms

backward-bending labour supply curve, *338*

extra billing, *332*

implicit wage, *334*

target-income model, *339*

End-of-Chapter Questions

For each of the statements below, indicate whether the statement is true or false and explain why it is true or false.

1. There is no substitute for a physician in producing health care services.
2. Within a target-income model of physician behaviour, income effects associated with fee increases can never be small.
3. Changing physician funding from fee-for-service to capitation would be expected to have no effect on the required supply of physicians in Ontario.
4. The impact of an increase in the fee for a service would depend on the share of income derived from the service.
5. Changes in physician fees can cause physician service supply to change in either the same or opposite direction as physician labour supply.
6. Increased physician fees may worsen the physician-service shortage by causing physicians to work fewer hours.
7. Because it reduces the extent of competition in the health care market, *ceteris paribus*, a limitation on advertising by physicians reduces social welfare.
8. Demand inducement is inconsistent with standard income and substitution effects in response to fee changes.

9. The expected net effect of an increase in spousal earnings on labour supply of physicians depends on the size of the substitution effect and income effect if leisure is a normal good.

10. Strong ethics training can reduce but not eliminate the possibility that physicians will provide a quantity of care that is different from what they judge to be in the best interest of a patient.

References

Association of Faculties of Medicine of Canada. 2008. *Canadian medical education statistics, 2008*. Ottawa: Association of Faculties of Medicine of Canada.

Barer, M., and G. L. Stoddart. 1991. *Toward integrated medical human resource policy for Canada*. Ottawa: Report submitted to the Federal-Provincial-Territorial Conference of Deputy Ministers of Health.

Barer, M. L., R. G. Evans, K. McGrail, B. Green, C. Hertzman, and S. Sheps. 2004. Beneath the calm surface: The changing face of physician-service use in British Columbia, 1985/86 versus 1996/97. *CMAJ* 170(5):803–7.

Boychuk, G. 2006. Provincial approaches to funding health services in the post-Chaoulli era. Unpublished document.

Brown, D. M., and H. E. Lapan. 1979. The supply of physicians' services. *Economic Inquiry* 17:269–79.

Brown, M. C. 1989. Empirical determinants of physician incomes: Evidence from Canada. *Empirical Economics* 14(4):273–89.

Buske, L. 2004. Younger physicians providing less direct patient care. *CMAJ* 170(8):1217.

Canada. 1975. *Report of the Requirements Committee on Physician Manpower to the National Committee on Physician Manpower*. Ottawa: Department of National Health and Welfare.

———. 2009. *Supply, distribution and migration of Canadian physicians, 2008*. Ottawa: Canadian Institute for Health Information.

———. 2008a. *National health expenditure trends, 1975–2008*. Ottawa: Canadian Institute for Health Information.

———. 2008b. *Physicians in Canada: The status of alternate payment programs, 2005–06*. Ottawa: Canadian Institute for Health Information.

Cooper, R. 2004. Weighing the evidence for expanding physician supply. *Annals of Internal Medicine* 141(9):1–10.

Crossley, T., J. Hurley, and S.-H. Jeon. 2009. Physician labour supply in Canada: A cohort analysis. *Health Economics* 18 (4):437–56.

Devlin, R. A., and S. Sarma. 2008. Do physician remuneration schemes matter? The case of Canadian family physicians. *Journal of Health Economics* 25(7):1168–81.

Evans, R. G. 1974. Supplier-induced demand: Some empirical evidence and implications. In *The economics of health and medical care*, M. Perlman (ed.). New York: John Wiley. 162–73.

Feldstein, M. 1970. The rising price of physicians' services. *Review of Economics and Statistics* 52(2):215–27.

Flood, C., and T. Archibald. 2001. The illegality of private health care in Canada. *Canadian Medical Association Journal* 164(6):825–30.

Grant, H. 2005. The earnings of Canadian physicians. Winnipeg, MN: University of Winnipeg Department of Economics, unpublished document.

Hall, E. M. 1980. *Canada's National–Provincial Health Program for the 1980s*. Ottawa: Department of National Health and Welfare.

Health Canada. 2008. *Canada Health Act— Annual report for 2007–2008*. Ottawa: Health Canada.

Hu, T. W., and B. M. Yang. 1988. The demand for and supply of physician services in the U.S.: A disequilibrium analysis. *Applied Economics* 20:995–1006.

Judek, S. 1964. *Medical manpower in Canada*. Ottawa: Queen's Printer.

McGuire, A., and M. V. Pauly. 1991. Physician response to fee changes with multiple payers. *Journal of Health Economics* 10(4):385–420.

National Physician Survey. 2009. *2007 national physician survey results.* Available at: http://www. nationalphysiciansurvey.ca/nps/home-e.asp.

Rizzo, J., and D. Blumenthal. 1996. Is the target income hypothesis an economic heresy? *Medical Care Research and Review* 53(3):243–66.

———. 1994. Physician labor supply: Do income effects matter? *Journal of Health Economics* 13(4):433–53.

Tepper, J. 2004. *The evolving role of Canada's family physicians, 1992–2001.* Ottawa: Canadian Institute for Health Information.

Thornton, J. 1998. The labour supply behaviour of self-employed solo practice physicians. *Applied Economics* 30(1):85–94.

Thornton, J., and B. K. Eakin. 1997. The utility-maximizing self-employed physician. *The Journal of Human Resources* 32(1):98–128.

Tuohy, C., and A. Wolfson. 1978. Self-regulation: Who qualifies? In *The professions and public policy*, P. Slayton, and M. Trebilcock (eds.). Toronto: University of Toronto Press. 111–22.

Watson, D., B. Bogdanovic, P. Heppner, A. Katz, R. Reid, and N. Roos. 2003. *Supply, availability and use of family physicians in Winnipeg.* Winnipeg: Manitoba Centre for Health Policy.

Watson, D., S. Slade, L. Buske, and J. Tepper. 2006. Intergenerational differences in workloads among primary care physicians: A ten-year, populations-based study. *Health Affairs* 25(6):1620–28.

Woodward, R. S., and F. Warren-Boulton. 1984. Considering the effects of financial incentives and professional ethics on 'appropriate' medical care. *Journal of Health Economics* 3(3):223–37.

Appendix 13

Chapter 13: Physicians, Their Practices, and the Market for Physician Services

13.2.1 Alternative Assumptions Regarding Physician Objectives

Let's examine in more detail the two models discussed in the chapter.

Woodward and Warren-Boulton (1984)

This model uses the household production framework with preferences, production, and constraints.

Preferences A physician cares about two things: a composite commodity called leisure and the provision of the appropriate level of medical care. Utility is specified as

$$U = U(C,(M/N) - (MA)) \tag{13A.1}$$

where U = utility, C = the composite commodity (leisure), M/N = medical care per patient, and MA = appropriate level of medical care per patient.

Utility increases in C and decreases in the deviation between the actual level of care per patient and the appropriate level of care per patient. The physician determines the

FIGURE 13A.1
Physician
Indifference Curves

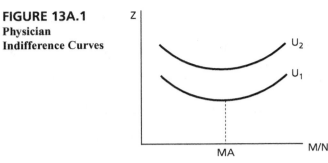

appropriate level of medical care using criteria the physician judges most relevant (i.e., it is not externally determined).

These preferences lead to unusual-looking indifference curves. Assume a physician currently provides MA services. If the physician were to deviate from this (in either direction), the utility from providing medical care would go down, so that the amount of C would have to increase to maintain the physician's level of utility. This leads to U-shaped indifference curves as in Figure 13A.1

Production The production of leisure is specified as $C = C(t_C, x_C)$ where t_z = leisure time and x_z = market goods used to produce leisure. Production of C is increasing in both inputs and subject to diminishing returns.

Medical Care is specified as $M = M(t_M, x_M, N)$, where t_M = time spent, producing medical care; x_M = purchased inputs used to produce medical care; and N = number of patients. Production of M is increasing in t_M and x_M and subject to diminishing returns.

Constraints The time is $T = t_C + t_M$, where T is total time available. Income constraint is $Y = x_C + x_M$ where Y = income from practice and $Px_C = Px_M = 1$.

Physician Problem The physician maximizes utility subject to the production, time, and income constraints. Income depends on how the physician is paid. Consider two methods: salary and fee-for-service.

Salary: $Y = Y_s$ where income over the time period is fixed at the level of the salary and does not depend on how many services are provided.

Fee-for-service: $Y = F \cdot M$, where F is the fee per unit of service provided. F is set exogenously and is beyond the control of the physician.

Question of Interest How will the physician's optimal number of services per patient (M/N) compare to the appropriate number of services per patient under the different payment methods?

To answer this question, we simply need to know the shape of the production possibilities frontier for C and M/N. Given the U-shape of the indifference curve, if the PPF is negatively sloped, a utility-maximizing physician will provide less than the appropriate quantity of services; if it is positively sloped, the physician will provide more than the appropriate quantity of services; if it is flat, the physician will provide exactly the appropriate quantity (Figure 13A.2).

Salary The PPF is formally derived by maximizing M/N for a given level of C, (i.e., maximize M/N such that $C = \bar{C}$).

We can also think through this intuitively. Imagine the physician is on the PPF at a particular combination of C and M/N. If the physician wants to increase M/N, the only way to

FIGURE 13A.2
The Slope of the PPF and the Utility-Maximizing Level of Service Provision

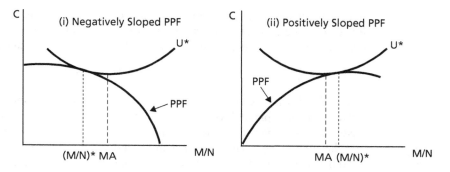

do this is to reallocate time, goods, or both from the production of leisure. Consider first the reallocation of time. This will reduce the amount of C that can be produced unless there is a compensating increase in x_C.

But spending more time producing medical care does not increase income, so the only way to increase x_C is to decrease x_M. This will in turn reduce M/N, counteracting the effect of allocating more time to M. As long as the marginal products of time and market inputs are positive in producing health care, there is a trade-off between the production of the two goods and the PPF will be downward sloping. The optimal level of medical care for a physician (M/N)* is, therefore, less than the appropriate level of care (MA).

Fee-for-Service Under fee-for-service, the PPF may be positively or negatively sloped. To understand why, consider the following: hold t_M and t_C constant, but shift a unit of x from production of leisure to production of medical care. The amount of medical care will increase as long as the marginal product of x is positive.

This increase in medical care increases income. If the increase in income is greater than 1, the additional income can be used to purchase more than one unit of x. This x can then be used to increase production of C (we only took one unit of x away initially). So it is possible for both C and M to increase simultaneously, giving the PPF a positive slope. If the increase in income is less than 1, the PPF has a negative slope. The exact outcome depends on the relative magnitudes of the marginal products. So under fee-for-service, the optimal level of medical care could be less than or greater than the appropriate level. In this model, fee-for-service is a necessary but not sufficient condition for supplier-induced over-utilization of care.

McGuire and Pauly (1991)

McGuire and Pauly developed a general model to investigate the effect of fee changes on service supply. The model is general in the sense that it includes two special cases:

1. a profit-maximizing physician for which income effects are absent, so that the service supply curve is unequivocally positively sloped
2. the literal target-income model in which income effects are large, fee changes are exactly offset by changes in service provision, and the service supply curve is negatively sloped

Single Payer or Service

Consider first a situation with a single service, or equivalently, a single payer who increases all fees proportionately.

Preferences The physician cares about net revenue from the practice (income), Y; leisure, L; and inducement, I. Utility is increasing in Y and L subject to diminishing returns. Utility is decreasing in I and is subject to increasing returns (i.e., the disutility of inducement increases at the margin). Utility in Y, L, and I are separable in the sense that the marginal utility of Y does not depend on the level of L or I, and so forth.

$$U = U(Y, L, I) \tag{13A.2}$$

where $Y = mX(I)$. X is the quantity of services provided, which depends on whether inducement takes place. X is increasing in inducement ($X_I > 0$) at a constant rate ($X_{II} = 0$). Given the increasing marginal disutility of inducement, this implies that a finite amount of inducement is optimal. In this equation, m is the profit margin per service. If the fee is f and the cost of producing a service is c, then $m = f - c$. A change in the fee changes the margin.

Production Production is particularly simple. A physician service is produced using a constant amount of non-physician inputs and a constant amount of physician time, t. No substitution is possible between the non-physician input and physician time. This implies that the number of services supplied (X) is directly proportional to the amount of time a physician devotes to producing medical care.

Constraint No goods are purchased in the market, so the only relevant constraint is the time constraint:

$$L + tX(I) = 24 \tag{13A.3}$$

Physician Choice Problem The physician has to choose how many services to supply (i.e., the level of I) so as to maximize utility.

$$\text{Max } U = U(Y, L, I) \text{ subject to } L = 24 - tX(I)$$

Solution The first-order condition for utility maximization is

$$U_Y X' m + U_I + U_L(-X')t = 0 \tag{13A.4}$$

We are interested in how a change in the fee affects service supply. A change in the fee is equivalent to a change in the margin (m). This can be found by solving for how a change in the margin affects the level of inducement, I. To do this, take the derivative of equation 13A.4 with respect to m and solve for I_m, the impact of a change in m on inducement. Doing so results in

$$I_m = \frac{-U_{YY}X(X'm) - U_Y X'}{U_{YY}(X'm)^2 + U_{II} + U_{LL}(-X't)^2} \tag{13A.5}$$

In general, the sign of this is indeterminate (the denominator is negative, but the numerator can be positive or negative). So we cannot predict *a priori* how a change in fees will affect the supply of physician services. But we can do so in two special cases, the target-income model and the income-maximizing model.

Target-Income Model Assume that a physician has achieved a specified target income. The literal target-income model says that the marginal utility of income below the target is very high (i.e., the physician gets a very large amount of utility by raising income from below the target to equal the target), and that the marginal utility of income is very small (even zero) above the target (i.e., the physician gets little or no utility from additional income above the target). This implies that the change in the marginal utility of income is very large right at the target income level, after which the marginal utility of income decreases very fast: $U_{YY} \rightarrow -\infty$. If this is the case, then only terms involving U_{YY} matter and equation 13A.5 simplifies to

$$I_m = \frac{-X}{X'm} \qquad (13A.6)$$

This has a negative sign, so the fee increases led to a reduction in the number of physician services supplied. In fact, using the definition of elasticity, the elasticity of the supply of X with respect to m is

$$\varepsilon = \frac{m}{X}(I_m X') \qquad (13A.7)$$

Substituting equation 13A.6 into this, we get $\varepsilon = -1$. Under the literal target-income model, a physician reacts to a fee change by perfectly offsetting the change in the margin so as to maintain the target income. Note that because the margin is only a fraction of the total price, this offsetting response increases total expenditure for the payer (i.e., if the price is \$20, and the margin is \$4, then a fee decrease of 5 percent (\$1) represents a 25 percent decrease in the margin. Utilization increases by 25 percent, which is more than the fee decrease of 5 percent, causing total expenditures to increase).

No Income Effects   Now assume that a physician is an income maximizer in the sense that the marginal utility of income is constant ($U_{YY} = 0$ so that income is not subject to diminishing marginal utility). In this case, equation 13A.5 reduces to

$$I_m = \frac{-U_Y X'}{U_{II} + U_{LL}(-X't)^2} \qquad (13A.8)$$

The denominator is negative as before but now the numerator is definitely negative, so that $I_m > 0$. An increase in the fee causes service supply to increase, and a decrease causes it to decrease: we have the usual positively sloped supply curve.

What determines the slope of the supply curve?   These polar cases highlight that whether the slope of the service supply curve is positively or negatively sloped depends on the size of the income effect. If the income effect is sufficiently large, the supply curve will have a negative slope.

Multiple Payers or Services

McGuire and Pauly extend the analysis to consider the case of multiple payers (e.g., a public and a private payer) or multiple services (e.g., two services within the fee schedule of a public payer).

The setup is exactly as before, only now there are two services:

$$U = U(Y, L, I_1, I_2) \qquad (13A.9)$$

Where $Y = X_1(I_1)m_1 + X_2(I_2)m_2$ and $L = 24 - t_1 X_1(I_1) - t_2 X_2(I_2)$.

Question of Interest   How does the change in the fee for one service affect the supply of both the service itself and the other service? The analysis proceeds largely as above, but the expressions are more complicated because the effects depend on many more parameters. A physician now has many more possible ways to respond to a change in fees. In the end, McGuire and Pauly use numerical simulations to investigate the various effects. Insight can be gained by considering the various factors that affect how a physician will respond. These factors are the following:

- *differences in the ease and psychic costs of inducement across services.* Other things equal, physicians will induce more of those services that are easier to provide, causing the physician less disutility.
- *the share of income derived from a service.* A fee change for a service that constitutes 80 percent of revenue will affect income much more than a fee change for a service that constitutes only 5 percent of revenue.
- *the relative margins of the services.* Other things equal, a physician would induce demand for the service with the larger margin.
- *time cost of producing the service.* Other things equal, a physician would induce demand for services that are less time intensive to produce.

References

McGuire, A., and M. V. Pauly. 1991. Physician response to fee changes with multiple payers. *Journal of Health Economics* 10(4):385–420.

Woodward, R. S., and F. Warren-Boulton. 1984. Considering the effects of financial incentives and professional ethics on 'appropriate' medical care. *Journal of Health Economics* 3(3):223–37.

Health Care Institutions: Hospitals

Learning Objectives

After studying this chapter, you will understand

LO1 Predominant institutional features of the hospital sector

LO2 Central ideas in theories of non-profit organizations and the economic modelling of hospital behaviour

LO3 Core approaches to the economic assessment of hospital efficiency and major findings from such studies

LO4 Empirical evidence on the relative performance of for-profit and not-for-profit health care institutions

---

A hospital is the archetypal health care institution. It is where we go when we are injured or acutely ill to get the most sophisticated care possible. It is the setting of health care's life-and-death dramas. But the place and role of a hospital in modern health care is changing. In simpler times, people obtained care in three basic settings: home, an in-patient hospital, and "the old folks home." But economic pressures and changes in medical technology have altered the nature and scope of many hospital-based activities and populated the health care landscape with a variety of health care provider organizations.

- Today, the majority of hospital-based procedures are done on an out-patient basis; a large number of procedures, such as cataract operations, that once required long hospital stays, can be done in free-standing clinics unconnected with a hospital.

- Hospital pressure to discharge patients quickly has both created more sophisticated non-hospital settings, such as skilled nursing facilities, and migrated increasingly complex care into patients' homes where it is delivered through home care programs or "hospitals without walls." Hospitals are left with only the most acutely ill patients during the most acute phases of their illnesses.

- "Old folks homes" have transformed into a long-term care sector that includes everything from accommodations that rival four-star hotels to institutions with continuing care for those with profound disabilities.

- The traditional, clear distinctions between a hospital and a community-based clinic are blurring, both in a physical sense and in an economic sense, as these various care settings sometimes compete for the same pool of patients.

The institutional sector of health care is now characterized by a multi-dimensional continuum of facilities that offer overlapping sets of services to patients.

Institutions, however, continue to be the settings where most health care resources are expended. The hospital sector constitutes the largest component of the health care system—but represents a shrinking proportion of overall health care expenditures. In Canada, for instance, although hospital spending per capita has increased over time (with the exception of the short-lived dip in the mid-1990s), the growth in hospital spending has been smaller than that in other sectors such as drugs, long-term care, and home care (Figure 14.1). So while in 1975 the hospital sector accounted for 45 percent of all health care expenditures, in 2006 it accounted for only 28 percent of all health expenditures. During this period, spending on other institutions increased slightly as a proportion of overall health care spending from 9.2 percent to 10.0 percent (Canadian Institute for Health Information 2008).[1]

As documented in Chapter 1, Canada had about 740 hospitals in 2004, the vast majority of which were general hospitals that treated acute illness. Nearly all hospitals in Canada are not-for-profit institutions, either privately owned with community or religious boards, or public institutions. Most hospitals are relatively small (fewer than 100 beds); but care is concentrated in larger, urban hospitals with hundreds of beds. Recent years have witnessed both a falling number of hospital facilities (mostly as small rural hospitals close) and, quantitatively more important, a falling number of in-patient beds within existing facilities.

Technological advances, however, have allowed hospitals to increase the number of cases treated while decreasing the number of beds and in-patient admissions. Between 1995 and 2004, age-adjusted in-patient discharges in Canada fell by 24 percent (Canadian Institute for Health Information 2005); but between 1995 and 2002, same-day surgeries in hospitals increased by 57 percent (Canadian Institute for Health Information 2004). Canada also makes greater use of its bed capacity than nearly any other OECD country, with hospital

---

[1] The data on other institutions refer only to residential care facilities such as nursing homes and facilities for persons with physical, mental, or emotional disabilities.

FIGURE 14.1

Hospital Spending, Canada, 1975–2006

Although hospital spending per capita has been increasing in Canada with the exception of a dip in the mid-1990s, hospital spending has gradually decreased as a share of all health spending since 1975.

Source: Canadian Institute for Health Information, 2008. National Health Expenditure Trends, 1975–2008. Ottawa: Canadian Institute for Health Information. ISBN: 978-1-55465-359-1 Table A.3.1.2—Part 1 (p. 106) and Table A.3.3.3—Part 1, (p. 120).

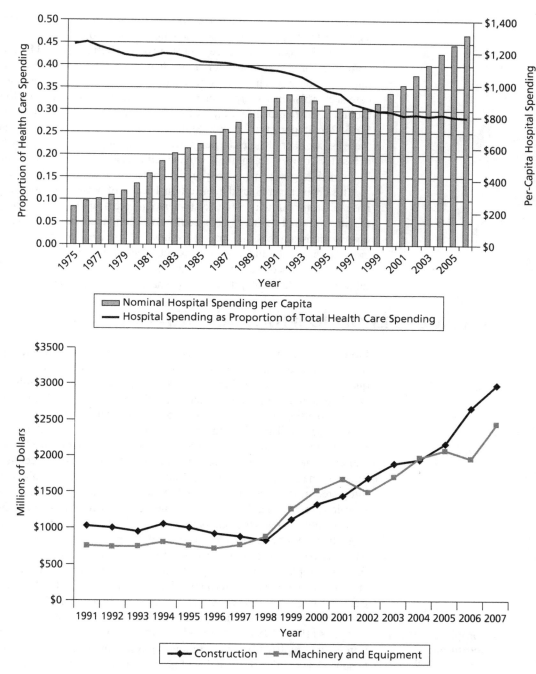

FIGURE 14.2

Real Capital Investment in Canadian Hospitals, 1991–2007

After being flat during the 1990s, capital investments in both hospital construction and machinery and equipment for hospitals have been increasing since 1998.

Source: CANSIM Table 29-0019. Capital and Repair Expenditures, Industry Sector 62, Health Care and Social Assistance: Capital and Repair Expenditures, Actual, Preliminary Actual and Intentions.

Note: Construction and machinery and equipment exclude expenditures for repair.

occupancy rates that regularly exceed 85 percent (in contrast, in the U.S., rates of 65 percent are common). Recent years have witnessed substantial capital reinvestment in hospitals, many of which were built during the expansion of the 1950s and 1960s (Figure 14.2).

The long-term care sector is characterized by greater heterogeneity than the hospital sector. Statistics Canada recognizes seven levels of care among residential care facilities, ranging from those that offer only room and board to those with highly skilled nursing care.

Of the 4313 residential care facilities in Canada in 2007, 1615 provided a level of care associated with a nursing home (Statistics Canada 2008).

Unlike hospitals, which are over 90 percent publicly funded by global budgets, nursing homes are funded primarily on a per-diem basis through a mix of public funding, private out-of-pocket payment, and a nascent long-term care insurance industry. The long-term care sector also has a larger for-profit component, varying from a low of 15 percent of all facilities in Manitoba to a high of over 60 percent of all facilities in Ontario (Berta et al. 2005; McGregor et al. 2006). And even within the for-profit and not-for-profit sectors, there is substantial heterogeneity, with some large chains owning hundreds of facilities across the country, stand-alone single facilities, and various types of public facilities owned by municipal governments, regional authorities, provinces, and the federal government.

This chapter examines the institutional sector of health care, focusing on hospitals and the hospital sector but with reference (where data are available) to the long-term care sector and nursing homes. It begins by considering how economists have modelled hospitals as economic organizations, turns to the market for hospital services, and examines evidence for the efficiency of hospitals, and to a lesser extent, long-term care facilities. It closes with a discussion of one of the most debated issues in the institutional sector: the rationale for not-for-profit institutions and evidence of differences in behaviour of not-for-profit and for-profit institutions.

14.1 MODELS OF HOSPITALS AS ORGANIZATIONS

From an economic perspective, hospitals display two distinctive features compared to standard firms. The first is a dominance of not-for-profit ownership. Not-for-profit status raises questions regarding the objectives hospitals pursue. And the highly regulated environment within which hospitals operate shields individual hospitals from normal competitive pressures, providing freedom to pursue objectives other than simple economic survival.

The second distinctive feature is an unusual organizational structure. A standard business organization (at least in theory) has a clear hierarchical chain of accountability, authority, and decision-making that runs from the Board of Directors to the CEO and other senior managers to lower-level employees. Accountability and decision-making are fully integrated among the units and individuals who make up a single, unified organization. Hospitals in Canada, the U.S., and some European countries[2] don't fit this model.

Most physicians who treat patients in a hospital are not formally employed by the hospital. Instead, physicians are affiliated with the hospital through "admitting privileges," which allow them to admit patients to the hospital even though the physicians are not formally employees of the hospital. This is puzzling from an economic perspective; affiliated physicians largely determine what patients a hospital will treat, the services used to treat them, and how those services are produced—in short, how a hospital's resources are allocated—yet the physicians are not employed by the organization.

incomplete vertical integration
An organizational form typical of North American hospitals in which physicians have a long-term relationship with a hospital but are neither employed by nor fully independent of the hospital.

Evans (1981; 1984) has termed this **incomplete vertical integration**. The integration is "incomplete" because, although physicians have a long-term relationship with the hospital, they are neither employed nor fully independent of the hospital.

These features raise two questions central to any effort to model hospital behaviour: (1) who runs a hospital (board, management, or medical staff)?; and (2) what objectives do they pursue?

Early economic models of hospitals tended to downplay or ignore the incomplete vertical integration, positing that a hospital functioned as a unified organization with a single

[2] Particularly those whose health care systems were not historically organized as national health services in which hospitals are owned by the public sector.

decision-maker. This assumption was usually justified by the argument that the interests of the board of directors, the managers, and the medical staff were sufficiently aligned that a hospital could be treated as a unified decision-making organization.

The various models made somewhat different assumptions about a hospital's objectives, but in most cases hospitals were assumed to care about two dimensions of output: quantity and quality. Quantity was usually measured by the number of patients treated. Quality was usually conceptualized as intensity of servicing (i.e., more services or more higher-tech service per patient indicated higher quality). Sometimes quality entered the objective function as a goal to be pursued; other times it entered as a constraint in the hospital maximization problem (e.g., maximize quantity subject to a minimum quality level).

14.1.1 Newhouse's Model of Quantity–Quality Trade-off

Newhouse (1970) is representative of this approach. Newhouse sets up his model in a way that reflects the institutional features of the environment in which he was working (the U.S. in the late 1960s), but a number of the insights generalize beyond the specifics of his model.

Hospital Preferences Over Quality and Quantity   A hospital is assumed to care about the quality and quantity of care it provides, neither of which is necessarily easy to measure. Measuring quantity is complicated by the multi-product nature of the output, but Newhouse represents it as the number of patient-days of treatment. Quality could be indicated by a number of characteristics, but the basic assumption is that higher quality required more resources and that each level of quality is associated with a level of costs. Consequently, costs can serve as an indicator of quality.[3] For each level of quality, there is an associated demand curve, which shifts out as quality increases (the model assumes patients are paying at least part of the cost of care, a point we will return to shortly). These cost and demand relationships can be represented as in Figure 14.3.

The Quality–Quantity Trade-Off Frontier   For a given level of quality, a hospital will choose the highest quantity of output at which it will at least break even: for the base case in Figure 14.3, this occurs at output level q_0. Now suppose it increases quality: this will both increase costs and shift demand outward. At this new level of quality, the optimal quantity is q_1 (it could be higher or lower than q_0). This analysis can be done for all possible quality levels, thereby identifying all possible optimal combinations of quality and quantity. These combinations can be graphed to represent the quality–quantity trade-off frontier as in Figure 14.4.

[3] In this sense, like other models from this period, it falsely equates quality with intensity of servicing (much like poorly informed patients often do).

FIGURE 14.3
Optimal Quantity Given Chosen Level of Quality in the Newhouse Model
For a baseline level quality, let AC_0 represent the average cost of producing a patient-day as the number of days varies (AC first falls as economies of scale arise, but after a point rises again as coordination problems occur in a large institution), and D_0 represent patient demand. The maximum quantity of patient-days the hospital can produce at this level of quality and still break even is q_0. If quality is increased, the costs increase (AC_1) and demand shifts out (D_1), so that the maximum quantity of patient-days changes to q_1. By doing this for all quality levels, one can trace out the quality–quantity frontier.

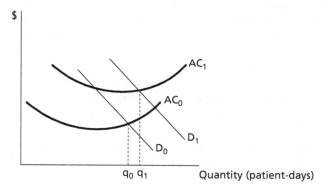

FIGURE 14.4

The Optimal Combination of Quality and Quantity for a Hospital

The optimal combination of quality and quantity of care for a hospital is the point at which the hospital's preferences over quality and quantity are tangent to the quality–quantity production frontier.

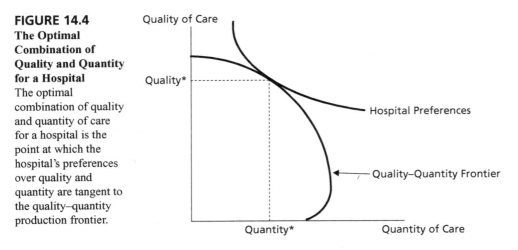

The precise shape and position of this frontier—and the implied trade-offs between quantity of care and quality of care—depend on production technology and the cost structure of a hospital. If quality is subject to diminishing utility for patients and its production is subject to diminishing returns, then the frontier will have a negative slope over at least a portion of its range as further increases in quality generate relatively small increases in demand but large increases in costs. In a public system, such as Canada's, that funds hospitals by fixed global budgets, the frontier would be negatively sloped because a hospital can increase quality only by decreasing quantity.

Optimal Quality–Quantity Combination   The hospital's preferences determine the rate at which it is willing to trade off quantity and quality (e.g., how much it is willing to reduce the number of patient-days of care to increase the quality of care to each patient). Given the frontier and the relative weight the hospital gives to quantity and quality of care, a hospital chooses the point that maximizes its utility—the intersection of (Quality*, Quantity*) in Figure 14.4.

The Efficiency of this Optimal Combination   In this framework, even though the hospital is not-for-profit, it has incentive to produce services in the least-cost, efficient manner. If it did not do so, by adopting efficient production techniques it could shift the frontier outward, increasing its utility. This represents a specific instance of a more general point: as long as a not-for-profit institution is a maximizer (the objective function may contain many valued outcomes), it has incentive to produce services in a least-cost manner. Indeed, just like a for-profit firm, the hospital has an incentive to produce efficiently.

Newhouse argues, however, that the output combination chosen by the hospital will be allocatively inefficient: the hospital will produce an inefficiently high level of quality. The allocative inefficiency arises because of the hospital's own preference for quality. This conclusion is a consequence of Newhouse's assumption that the demand curve represents the fully informed preferences of individuals. If this is true, the optimal level of quality should depend only on the patients' preferences. Instead, the hospital's optimal quality depends on both patients' valuation of quality as embodied in the demand curve and the hospital's intrinsic valuation of quality.[4] This quality bias, he argued, was a possible source

---

[4] To make an analogy, it is as if the hospital is an imperfect agent for patients in which the quality–quantity combination reflects both hospital and patient preferences instead of just patient preferences.

of the duplication of underutilized high-technology equipment observed in U.S. hospitals at that time.

This conclusion may not hold, however, once one admits the possibility of poorly informed patients who under-demand care, or other possible factors that might cause patient demand to be less than the socially optimal level. It also points to the limitations of models that do not include physicians acting as agents for patients.

Still, the notion that hospitals care about both the quantity and the quality of care they provide is an important legacy of this class of models.

14.1.2 Hospitals as Doctors' Workshops

A second approach to modelling hospitals as unified organizations, exemplified by Pauly and Redisch (1973), posits that the medical staff—physicians—are effectively in charge and that the medical staff acts so as to maximize the net income per physician derived from hospital-based care. The medical staff functions as a cooperative directing the hospital's activity; the hospital is a non-profit firm that produces hospital services using three inputs: physician labour, non-physician labour, and capital. Hospitals and physicians bill separately for their components of the cost of production, and hospitals charge the break-even price for the non-physician component of care.

The hospital is effectively a free workshop enabling staff physicians to produce services that generate income for them. As the group in control of the hospital, physicians make decisions regarding the size of the hospital, capital investments, and other aspects of the hospital's operations so as to maximize their incomes. Because physicians don't pay the cost of non-physician inputs, they over-invest in these complementary inputs, especially when hospital costs are reimbursed on a cost basis by insurers (as was prevalent at the time). Pauly and Redisch argue that their model is able to explain both over-investment in hospital inputs, especially high-technology equipment, and other observations such as hospitals being smaller than optimal hospital size (smaller hospitals make it easier to coordinate the medical staff and retain control by the staff).

Although Pauly and Redisch assume that physicians control the hospital, they explicitly recognize the formal separation between physicians and the hospital, and offer a first tentative explanation for this incomplete vertical integration. There are two predominant ways the production of hospital care might be organized. One is a fully decentralized approach in which the hospital organizes the production of non-physician hospital services and then sells them to physicians in a market. A second is full integration in which the physician becomes an employee of the hospital, which then combines physician and non-physician inputs to produce needed services.

In both of these cases, the physician loses control over the use of capital and non-physician labour inputs to produce the hospital component of the service, potentially reducing the incomes of physicians. But incomplete vertical integration, Pauly and Redisch argue, allows physicians to retain control of the production of care and retain access to the hospital as a workshop to maximize their income, without assuming all the responsibility of owning the hospital.

14.1.3 The Transactions Costs Model of Hospitals

Harris (1977) views the incomplete vertical integration as the fundamental feature of hospitals that needs to be understood and modelled, offering an alternative explanation to Pauly and Redisch. Though Harris does not present a formal model, he offers a detailed economic analysis of a hospital that draws on insights gained as both a practising physician and an economist.

transactions costs model

A model that posits that hospitals are two "firms" within a single organization, each with its own objectives. One is led by the medical staff and the other is led by the hospital management.

His analysis typifies an approach that is variously termed an "exchange" or **transactions costs model**, which drops the assumption of unitary control and emphasizes the split organization of a hospital. A hospital, he argued, does not have a single objective or a single group in control. Rather, a hospital actually comprises two organizations: one controlled by the medical staff and another controlled by hospital managers. Physicians are demanders of non-physician inputs in the production of care for their patients; hospitals are suppliers of non-physician inputs. Each pursues its own objectives and Harris's analysis focuses on the process of internal resource allocation and conflict resolution.

Why Incomplete Vertical Integration?

For Harris, the reason hospitals have chosen incomplete vertical integration rather than either full vertical integration or complete separation lies in the nature of the hospital care patients require and the nature of the physician–patient relationship.

Hospitals must be organized to produce highly complex, customized care on very short notice. Patients in cardiac arrest not only need care quickly, they need care that specifically matches their clinical and physiological characteristics (co-morbidities, blood type, etc.). In such a situation, the argument against full separation of physicians and hospitals, as independent, arms-length transactors interacting only through market exchange, is clear. The transactions costs and coordination problems of negotiating for the necessary hospital services through a market exchange would delay care unreasonably; further, the hospital could charge exorbitant prices which, in a serious health crisis, physicians and their patients would be willing to pay to get quick access to the required medical inputs.

Harder to understand is why physicians and hospitals don't fully integrate, as this would be a way to ensure necessary access to inputs. Harris's answer is physician agency. As agent for the patient, the physician's obligation is to do everything potentially beneficial for the patient. If the physician were an employee of the hospital, this agency relationship with the patient would be compromised because the physician would also have a fiduciary relationship as agent for the hospital.

The solution is incomplete vertical integration. The long-run, non-employment-based relationship between the physician and the hospital gives the physician ready access to a hospital's wide range of expensive, highly sophisticated technology. But the non-employment relationship and separate payment process maintains a clear distinction between the physician (and their obligations) and the hospital.

Resolving the Internal Conflict

This arrangement, however, creates a new problem: resolving conflicts between the medical staff and management over resource allocation. Physicians care most about assured, immediate access to necessary services for their patients. For them, idle capacity and continuous investment in new equipment is a good thing. The managers, in contrast, have responsibility to ensure the financial soundness of the hospital; idle capacity is costly and new equipment must be justified on financial grounds.

To be viable, a hospital must resolve this conflict. In the very short run (with fixed inputs), it is resolved by an array of non-price mechanisms, including rules of thumb, bargaining, standards of practice, and professional custom. But in the longer run, during the era of retrospective reimbursement at the time of Harris's initial analysis, the answer was to grow bigger. As long as the hospital was reimbursed for the actual costs of services provided, administrators bowed to the demands of physicians. In other words, Harris offers an alternative explanation to excess capacity, duplication, and unnecessary acquisition of expensive technologies.

retrospective funding was critical to the long-run resolution of internal con-
duction of prospective payment in the U.S. in 1983 and the end of automatic

funding of budget deficits in Canada in the 1990s, however, precluded such a resolution. One of the most profound effects of these funding reforms was to change the balance of power in North American hospitals. Hospitals are still split organizations, and tension still exists; but these initiatives have strengthened the power of hospital managers relative to the physician staff. More and more, financial imperatives drive internal resource allocation in hospitals.

Since the early 1980s, the imperative in health economics to build "the economic model" of hospitals has waned. This partly reflects difficulty in formally modelling institutional details of the organization of hospitals, partly recognizes the heterogeneity of hospital types so that it perhaps does not make sense to speak of "the hospital," and partly acknowledges the realization that the returns in building a general model are not as large as those of less-general models that provide insight into the specific economic and policy challenges associated with reimbursement, capital regulation, quality regulation, and technological change. Economic modelling of hospitals has, therefore, yielded to more narrowly focused efforts better targeted at particular economic and policy phenomena of concern.

14.2 HOSPITAL MARKETS AND HOSPITAL COMPETITION

Hospitals compete with other hospitals and, increasingly, other types of provider organizations. But the nature of these markets and of hospital competition differs importantly from standard competitive markets (described in Chapter 3). These differences derive from a number of factors including the nature of hospital services, the regulatory and funding environment in which hospitals operate, and the ways in which hospitals gain access to their "customers," the patients.

Hospital Markets are Local

local monopoly
A single organization enjoys monopoly power in a specific region even though it is one of many such organizations provincially or nationally.

Markets for most hospital services are highly local. This is certainly true for emergency services; it is also true for many routine elective services. For everything but highly specialized care, few people travel outside their region to obtain hospital care. Consequently, many hospitals enjoy **local monopoly** power in their respective geographic localities; even medium-sized cities seldom have more than two or three hospitals, and only the largest cities sustain five or more hospitals.

Only for a small set of highly specialized services does the relevant market extend across cities, provinces, or even countries.[5] Consequently, even when policy tries to foster competition among hospitals, for most of its services a hospital would compete with only a small number of other institutions in the region. Technological advances that allow some traditionally hospital-based services to be provided in free-standing clinics and other non-hospital settings have eroded local hospital market power, forcing hospitals to compete with these other provider organizations in these service markets. But for the bulk of services, competition in such markets is best characterized as oligopolistic, with strategic interaction among a small number of organizations (Chapter 3).

market concentration
An indicator of the extent of competition in a market based on the share of sales held by a given number of firms (e.g., 5, 10, 25) in the market.

Competition in hospital markets is usually measured in terms of **market concentration**[6], which represents the extent to which a small number of hospitals account for a large share of hospital activity in a region.

[5] There is also a growing market in "health care tourism"—travel to places such as India to obtain an operation at much lower cost than in a high-income country. But such care still constitutes a tiny proportion of health care.

[6] A commonly used measure, for instance, is the Herfindahl-Hirshman Index, defined as the sum of the squares of the market shares of up to the 50 largest firms in an industry.

Hospitals Often Don't Compete Directly for Patients

Historically, hospitals have not competed directly for patients. Rather they have competed over intermediaries that provide access to patients. Traditionally, the intermediaries were physicians: hospitals competed for physicians because physicians were the portal to patients. Hospitals competed to grant admitting privileges to the "best" local doctors, a competition that usually involved buying the latest technology desired by those doctors (much like in the Harris model discussed above) and granting other perks to physicians. As we might expect, hospitals placed greater priority on satisfying the preferences of physicians than the preferences of patients.

But in many settings, the locus of competition in recent years has changed: the competition is now for payers of care. Within a number of public systems, the intermediary is a regional health authority that is responsible for providing care to residents. Through negotiations or bidding, hospitals seek to be identified as a provider to residents of a region. In the U.S., the paying intermediaries are large private health care plans that provide insurance through employers. Hospitals negotiate (and in some cases bid) to be a care provider to the enrollees of a health plan.

Regulation and Competition in the Hospital Sector

Although some type of "competition" among hospitals exists in all health care systems, the scope for competition and the nature of competition depends on the public regulatory schemes, both in the health sector and in a country's broader competition policy, which sets the context for competition among hospitals. A crucial part of this is the funding method used by major payers.

In a country such as Canada, which funds hospitals through global budgets and provides care free to patients, no price even exists so there can be no price competition. Internationally, it is useful to distinguish among three fundamental regulatory designs that drive the nature and extent of hospital competition—non-market, public market, and private market—which are found in the health care systems in Canada, the U.K., and the U.S. respectively.

The Non-Market Approach   Canada's regulatory framework exemplifies a non-market approach that explicitly rejects competition among hospitals as a tool to achieve system efficiency and equity goals, and deliberately inhibits market competition among hospitals (see Chapter 1 for a fuller description).

Instead, Canada adopts a systems-based, "rational planner" regulatory approach to achieve the efficient organization of the hospital sector, exploiting fiscal pressure through its budgetary allocations to wring operational efficiencies out of individual institutions. In some Canadian provinces, all hospitals within a region are owned and operated by the local regional health authorities; even where this is not the case, regionally based planning exerts considerable influence on the organization of the hospital sector.

As a consequence, highly specialized services (e.g., advanced cardiovascular care, respiratory care, nephrology, cancer care) are regionalized in particular facilities (usually the large teaching hospitals). Such regionalization reduces inefficient duplication of expensive technology across hospitals in a region, achieves economies of scale, and increases quality of care by concentrating expertise and service provision in designated sites.[7] Hospitals are not free to purchase expensive new technologies independently. Instead, such purchases must be approved to ensure that they fit within the broader service plan for a region. In short, hospitals, overseen by a higher-level coordinating body (a regional health authority or

---

[7] In areas like surgery, although practice does not make perfect, considerable evidence indicates that rates of complications and other adverse side effects decrease substantially the more often a surgeon (and the associated surgical team) perform a procedure (Birkmeyer et al. 2002).

provincial ministry) are expected to work in a coordinated, cooperative way with other local institutions. The fundamental dynamic is system-based planning.

Such a regulatory approach does not stamp out all competition—independent hospitals often still see other institutions as rivals—but such competition manifests as attempts to garner new programs, new technology, expanded mandates, or a larger budget from the ministry or regional health authority. Although some of this can be efficiency-enhancing, as a hospital attempts to demonstrate that it merits such investments because of superior performance, it can also take the form of inefficient political rent-seeking among system stakeholders.

The Public Competition Approach   The view that a purely non-market approach leaves substantial inefficiencies in hospital performance led to the development of regulatory approaches that seek to harness market forces within a publicly financed health care system. During the 1990s, a number of European countries implemented versions of public competition in an attempt to enhance system efficiency.

The reforms to the United Kingdom's National Health Service are one example. Prior to 1991, the NHS employed a non-market regulatory approach. Hospitals were owned and operated by the NHS and managed by regional health authorities. Beginning in 1991, however, the NHS undertook a reform to create an **internal market**. The reform sought to create a public market for hospital services by creating a **purchaser–provider split** between the health authorities and the hospitals. To do this, hospitals were converted into autonomous independent trusts: they became providers of services. The regional health authorities continued to receive budget allocations from the central NHS to meet the health care needs of residents: they became purchasers.

A regional authority was to use its budget allocation from the central NHS to purchase needed hospital services from hospital trusts, and it could purchase such services from any hospital trust—those in its own region or even another region altogether. To purchase such services, the regional health authority issued tenders for services to which hospital trusts could respond. The competition for such contracts was predicted to increase efficiency in the production of hospital services. The goal was to exploit market competition among suppliers of hospital services to further health system goals while maintaining full public financing and free care for the public.

Although there is evidence that the internal market had some positive effects on prices and costs (Propper 1996; Propper et al. 1998), by the late 1990s the internal market was largely judged to have failed (Cookson and Dawson 2006). A recent study of the effect of competition on quality and wait-times in hospitals during the period of the internal market concluded that competition was associated with reduced wait-times but increased mortality (Propper et al. 2008). The authors surmise that the hospital diverted resources to improve performance on a measure of output (wait-times) that was closely monitored, at the cost of reduced performance on unmeasured aspects of quality.

Although some reasons for this result undoubtedly lay with how the internal market was implemented in the NHS, the failure points to more fundamental problems associated with fostering such supply-side competition within public health care systems:

- As noted, in many regions, especially rural areas, the scope for competition is very limited because there are only one or two potential suppliers.
- It can be difficult to maintain competition over time even where there are multiple suppliers. A hospital cannot easily shut down and ramp up production as it wins and loses contracts in complex medical areas such as cardiac care, neurosurgery, and the like. A decision not to award a specific contract for such care to a hospital trust may preclude the hospital from competing for future contracts if the clinical centre closes as a consequence of losing the contract.

internal market
A deliberately constructed market within a publicly financed health care system in which there is a purchaser–provider split.

purchaser–provider split
Providers must bid to win contracts to provide services to individuals covered by purchasers such as regional health authorities.

- It is not possible to write contracts that anticipate all the issues that will arise over the life of the contract. In such settings long-run relational contracts, in which the purchaser and provider regularly discuss and negotiate as contingencies arise, are often more efficient. But such arrangements inhibit competition.

- Inevitably, political interference—such as ensuring that a local facility remains open and resisting sending patients to another region—seeps into the process.

The U.K. experience, and similar experiences in other jurisdictions, does not imply that contractual approaches that attempt to exploit competitive forces can never work in health care. They can, but their scope is more limited than is often claimed. Contracting approaches will only increase efficiency under certain circumstances (Globerman and Vining 1996).[8]

The Private Market Approach   A third approach—using regulation in an attempt to create well-functioning private markets—predominates in the U.S. In addition to health-sector-specific regulations designed to support competition among market players, the anti-trust section of the U.S. Justice Department actively pursues anti-trust enforcement in health care, attempting to prevent collusion among market participants and challenging (with mixed success) hospital mergers that it believes will concentrate market power and unduly inhibit competition in a particular area.[9]

Although there is tremendous heterogeneity across markets in the U.S., broadly speaking hospitals must compete for patients from a variety of sources. They compete in part for people with health insurance who have a choice of hospital, such as those aged 65 or over who are covered by the public Medicare plan and are permitted to go to the hospital of their choice. Hospitals also compete for contracts to be among the providers for large health plans with hundreds of thousands of enrollees and that, from a hospital perspective, control access to patients.

Evidence of the effects of competition in the U.S. is mixed. Hospital competition for contracts with large insurance plans under managed care contributed to reductions in prices, costs, and excess capacity in the 1990s (Cookson and Dawson 2006); but evidence about the impact of competition on quality is more limited, contradictory, and sensitive to the time period and broader context. Gaynor (2004) divides studies into those that focus on the impact of market structure in sectors with fixed prices (e.g., U.S. Medicare patients) and those that focused on sectors with price competition as well. Theory suggests that quality improvements are more likely in the former setting.

One of the most widely cited studies of competition under fixed prices is that of Kessler and McLellan (2000), whose study of cardiac care concluded that competition harmed quality prior to 1991 but increased quality after 1991, as measured by one-year mortality rates and re-admissions for acute myocardial infarction. A second study of Medicare patients with heart attacks found that the impact of quality varied by patient severity: competition was associated with less intensive treatment of people who were less severely ill, but with more intensive treatment that led to better health outcomes among those who were more severely ill (Kessler and Geppert 2005).

A study of cardiac care and pneumonia that included both Medicare patients and non-Medicare patients concluded that the impact of competition depended on the method of payment (Gowrisankaran and Town 2003). Competition was associated with reduced

---

[8] Beginning in 2002, the U.K. government shifted focus from supply-side competition between trusts and health authorities to an approach based on demand-side patient-based competition through greater patient choice within the public system. No evidence is yet available as to the effects of this approach.

[9] As an interesting case in point, the U.S. Justice Department indicated that collusion among hospitals to hold *down* the rate of growth in prices to help curb costs as part of President Obama's health care plans is just as illegal as collusion to increase prices to raise profits. Any such collusive behaviour to hold down prices would be challenged under anti-trust regulations.

quality among Medicare patients, for whom hospitals are paid by fixed price contracts (a finding at odds with the previous two studies cited), but was associated with increased quality when contracts for care were negotiated (competition for HMO patients).

Finally, a study from California that included all hospital discharges from short-term general hospital stays concluded that competition was associated with lower mortality rates following discharge for three to five of the six medical conditions studied depending on how competition was measured (Rogowski et al. 2006).

This is an area for which research has exploded in recent years due to innovative new methods and the availability of much better data. As the literature develops, a stronger consensus may emerge on the effects of competition on different aspects of performance, but at this time the mixture of findings precludes strong conclusions.

14.3 ASSESSING HOSPITAL EFFICIENCY

Two aspects of hospital efficiency have received considerable study. The first is allocative efficiency in using health care to produce health. As has been noted in other chapters, evidence points to substantial inefficiencies due to the provision of unnecessary and inappropriate procedures that offer little prospect of health gain for patients (e.g., Siu et al. 1986; Wright et al. 2002). Such care may constitute the single largest source of inefficiency in the health care sector.

The second is economic analyses of the cost structure and the operational efficiency of health care institutions. Although such analyses have been applied to a variety of care settings, including hospitals, nursing homes, physician practices, and district health authorities, the vast majority have been applied to hospitals and nursing homes (Hollingsworth et al. 2003; Worthington 2004).

Early studies analyzed the relationship between costs (e.g., cost per day, cost per admission) and characteristics of an institution (e.g., size, teaching status, ownership status) to investigate what is termed the **behavioural cost function** (Evans 1984). Such analyses do not identify inefficiency *per se*, but the average relationship between costs (which may embody considerable inefficiencies) and certain observable characteristics of institutions.

Recent work has pursued the more ambitious goal of assessing the efficiency (technical or cost-effective efficiency) of institutions by estimating the structural production or cost function (costs solely as a function of inputs and prices) using frontier estimation techniques (Box 14.1). In many cases, a second-stage analysis investigates the relationship between efficiency scores and characteristics of the institutions.

To illustrate the different types of cost/efficiency analyses, Figure 14.5 presents a simplified production example that assumes hospitals produce a single output using a single input, in this case the number of beds (which represents size or amount of capital inputs).[10] The figure includes a hypothetical scatterplot of bed/output combinations for a set of hospitals.

- The behavioural approach would estimate the relationship between output and hospital characteristics (in this case, hospital size) using regression methods that fit a line passing through the centre of the scatterplot, showing the average relationship between hospital size and expected output. The line does not represent efficiency: it passes through the centre of the scatterplot (with deviations assumed to be random noise). Highly inefficient observations (well below the line) influence the estimated relationship just as much as observations above the line.

behavioural cost function
The relationship between hospital costs and hospital characteristics such as size, teaching status, ownership status, and location.

[10] The figure presents the analysis in terms of a production function, which shows the maximum output for a given set of inputs. A perfectly analogous presentation could be done using the cost function, which depicts the lowest-cost way to produce a given output.

The results can potentially be used to inform an array of policy decisions.

Hospital Amalgamation and Mergers

Public authorities regularly confront questions about whether to allow or, in cases such as the Ontario Hospital Restructuring Commission, even force hospitals to amalgamate. A critical aspect of such decisions is the anticipated effect on efficiency. Efficiency analysis can identify how costs and efficiency vary with the size of a hospital; that is, whether or not hospitals exhibit increasing or decreasing returns to scale in production can inform decisions about hospital amalgamation and mergers.

Scope of Services

Technology allows more and more services to be provided in specialized facilities rather than full-service hospitals. Many argue that such clinics can provide services more efficiently because they don't require as much capital as is present in a full-service hospital. Implicitly they argue that there are diseconomies of scope in the provision of health care: average costs rise as the range of services provided expands. Efficiency analysis can address whether economies of scope exist.

Funding Adjustment

In Chapter 13, we discussed the need for risk (or need) adjustment when calculating capitation payments to health care providers. An analogous problem arises when funding institutions. If the costs of an efficiently operating teaching hospital are higher than a non-teaching hospital, then, other things equal, the payment should be correspondingly higher. Efficiency analysis has the potential to identify characteristics of hospitals associated with differential cost structures that constitute a legitimate basis for funding adjustments. A second potential funding application is to base funding levels only on the costs of efficiently operating facilities, thereby penalizing those facilities that operate inefficiently and providing incentive to improve performance.

Testing Theories of Organizational Performance

Many argue that for-profit institutions are more efficient than private not-for-profit or public institutions; they advocate for greater use of for-profit provision. Efficiency analyses enable us to test such propositions, allowing policy-makers to make better-informed decisions about the relative role of different types of institutions within the system.

---

frontier cost estimation
Techniques for empirically identifying the frontier of lowest-cost (highest productivity) hospitals in order to assess efficiency.

- In contrast, **frontier cost estimation** methods seek to identify the production (cost) frontier. A hospital's efficiency is measured by the difference between its production and the production frontier, in this case denoted by the curved line on the upper edge of the points.

Although health economists have been estimating frontier models to assess efficiency since the mid-1980s, they are still viewed with mixed success. Some of the specific challenges include the following issues:

- The complexity of hospitals and the outputs they produce. Hospitals produce many outputs, including many types of in-patient care, emergency care, day procedures, and diagnostic tests, each used to differing extents to treat hundreds of different diagnoses. What

FIGURE 14.5

Methods of Cost and Efficiency Analysis
Behavioural cost analyses assess the average relationship between hospital characteristics (in this case, hospital size) and hospital productivity. Frontier approaches attempt to identify the production frontier– those hospitals that are producing care efficiently.

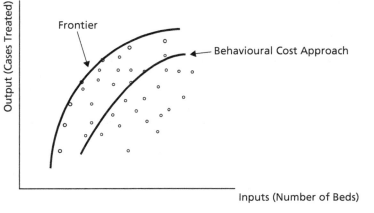

looks like inefficiency may simply be a failure to measure output properly (including adjustment for quality).

• Similarly, the costs for efficient hospitals vary with the health status of patients, yet data upon which analyses are based never have complete information on the average severity of a hospital's patient population. Again, what looks like inefficiency may be a failure to adjust fully for patient severity.

Such challenges have led some to argue that these methods are not adequate for making institution-specific assessments (e.g., using them as a basis for rewarding and penalizing specific institutions as part of funding or performance reviews) (Newhouse 1994). Rather, at best, they can support assessments of groups of hospitals classified by relevant characteristics (e.g., size, profit status).

14.4 NOT-FOR-PROFIT VERSUS FOR-PROFIT: DOES OWNERSHIP MATTER?

The economic analyses of for-profit versus not-for-profit ownership emphasize two questions:

1. Analytically, what economic rationales might explain the preponderance of not-for-profit organizations in sectors of the economy such as health care?

2. Empirically, what differences in behaviour and performance do we observe between not-for-profit and for-profit organizations?

Legally, for-profit organizations and not-for-profit organizations differ in these important ways:

non-distribution constraint
The legal restriction that prohibits not-for-profit organizations from distributing any financial surplus to the officers of the organization.

• While a for-profit organization is permitted (indeed expected) to distribute profits to its owners, a not-for-profit organization is prohibited from distributing profits to its owners/managers. This **non-distribution constraint** does not prohibit a not-for-profit from making a profit; it simply limits how profits can legally be used. A not-for-profit organization is expected to invest profits in the organization itself and the services it provides.

• A not-for-profit organization must explicitly declare a "public purpose" (the range of acceptable "public purposes" appears quite broad) and is expected to pursue this public purpose through its activities. It cannot exist just to make profit or pursue other purely private goals, even if it abides by the non-distribution constraint.

• Not-for-profit organizations enjoy a number of important legal and tax advantages, including exemption from corporate income taxes, exemption from property taxes, and the ability to attract donations that are tax deductible. These tax advantages are, in principle, justified by a not-for-profit's pursuit of an approved public purpose.

The preferred tax treatment of not-for-profits stirs considerable debate, especially in sectors where for-profit and not-for-profit organizations operate side by side (Schlesinger and Gray 2006). Supporters of non-profit organizations cite the public-purpose requirement as evidence that not-for-profit organizations pursue different objectives than for-profit organizations. Skeptics reply that although (by definition) the stated goals differ, the underlying behavioural differences are often minor; not-for-profit status is sometimes chosen simply to take advantage of the legal advantages it offers, and the social benefits produced by not-for-profit organizations do not justify preferential tax treatment. The resolution of this debate rests on the extent to which they do pursue different objectives that lead to socially desirable differences in behaviour.

An Economic Theory of Non-Profit Organizations

Economists have developed many theories to explain why not-for-profit organizations dominate certain sectors of the economy, such as health care, and to predict differences in behaviour between not-for-profit and for-profit organizations operating in the same sector (Sloan 2000 provides a brief review of these theories).

To explain the dominance of not-for-profits in certain sectors, some argue that not-for-profit organizations are a response to a type of market failure, such as public goods (Weisbrod 1988) or contracting problems due, for instance, to informational asymmetries (Hansmann 1980). This latter idea was earlier raised by Arrow (1963), who conjectured that not-for-profit organizations dominate in health care because of informational problems faced by health care consumers. Because consumers often cannot judge what health care services they require and the quality of services provided, a profit-maximizing delivery organization could exploit this informational asymmetry to increase profits by providing unnecessary services and by skimping on quality. Such an outcome is inefficient.

In contrast, a not-for-profit organization that intrinsically values quality and responding to patient needs will not opportunistically exploit its informational advantage over health care consumers. Not-for-profit organizations, Arrow argues, are a social institution designed to overcome market failure associated with information problems: provision of care by not-for-profit organizations potentially produces more socially efficient outcomes than provision by for-profit organizations.

This theory predicts that we should observe systematically different behaviours from not-for-profits and for-profits operating in the same sector. Some specific predictions are that a not-for-profit organization is more likely than a for-profit organization to

- invest in quality beyond the profit-maximizing level
- invest in aspects of quality that are hard for consumers to observe and that consumers don't readily perceive as linked to quality; for-profits, in contrast, will over-invest in observable aspects of quality and those aspects of care that consumers associate with quality even though they may have little true bearing on quality
- provide a full range of services, including both profitable services and services that are unprofitable but needed

It is often claimed that, because not-for-profit managers have no claim to profits, not-for-profit organizations will be less efficient than for-profit organizations. But as noted, the critical issue for productive efficiency is less what an organization maximizes than whether it is a maximizer. As long as an organization seeks to maximize a defined set of organizational objectives, it has incentive to produce its services in the least-cost manner. The fact that it maximizes an objective other than profits is irrelevant for productive efficiency.

The Behaviour of Not-for-Profits and For-Profits: Empirical Evidence from Health Care

Most studies comparing not-for-profit and for-profit health care organizations are U.S.-based, and some of the findings depend on the institutional environment in which organizations operate. Consequently, one must be cautious about generalizing from U.S.-based studies to other settings. Still, the studies provide insight into a number of the predicted differences between the two types of organizations.[11]

---

[11] The literature sometimes finds differences between public and private non-profit organizations. Most of this discussion focuses on non-profit (often including both private and public) versus for-profit organizations.

Perhaps the most salient finding is that the behaviour and performance of not-for-profit and for-profit health care organizations are more alike than different (Horwitz 2005a; Schlesinger and Gray 2006). This should not be surprising: they operate in many of the same markets, they produce many of the same services using the same basic inputs subject to many of the same regulatory controls, and they are paid according to the same reimbursement schemes.

There is also considerable heterogeneity of behaviour within each organizational type: not all not-for-profits behave one way and all for-profits another.

However, we do find important differences in performance. Schlesinger and Gray (2006) argue in particular that many policy discussions inappropriately lump studies from different sectors, obscuring patterns of real differences between the two forms in some settings. Below we consider evidence with respect to differences in quality of care, efficiency, service mix, and responsiveness to financial incentives.

Quality   Theory predicts both higher quality overall in not-for-profit institutions and differential patterns of investment in quality. Although quality varies substantially among organizations within each ownership type, the evidence generally indicates higher quality in not-for-profit institutions: the differences identified more often favour quality in not-for-profit settings.

The two most common quality indicators investigated for hospitals are mortality rates and re-admission rates. Some of the recent findings are as follows:

- In a review of studies up to the late 1990s, Sloan (2000) concludes that there is essentially no difference in quality across ownership status.

meta-analysis
A statistical technique for formally combining results from separate studies in order to derive an estimate of the overall, collective effect across all the studies.

- A **meta-analysis** of 15 U.S. studies comparing mortality rates across private for-profit and private not-for-profit institutions found that private for-profit hospitals were associated with a 2 percent increased risk of death compared to not-for-profit hospitals (Devereaux et al. 2002).

- A review of studies through 2005 found that, where quality differences exist between the two, in the majority of cases the difference favoured not-for-profit hospitals (Schlesinger and Gray 2006).

- A study of admissions for acute myocardial infarction (heart attack) in all general, acute-care hospitals in the U.S. between 1985 and 1994 found that for-profit hospitals had a higher rate of adverse events, including mortality and complications, than did private not-for-profit hospitals and public hospitals (Shen 2002). During this period, some hospitals changed their ownership status. The study found that the incidence of adverse outcomes increased after hospitals converted from not-for-profit to for-profit status, but not the converse.

- A study of admissions for acute myocardial infarction (Sloan et al. 2003) that, the authors argue, controls better for patient health status than did Shen (2002), found no difference in in-patient, 30-day or 1-year mortality rates across not-for-profit and for-profit hospitals. This study did find, however, that those discharged from a not-for-profit hospital were more likely to take aspirin and ACE-inhibitors on discharge (appropriate care for cardiac patients).

- A third study of cardiovascular admission, this time in Taiwan—which has national health insurance and, therefore, fewer patient selection problems than U.S.-based studies—found that not-for-profit hospitals had lower 1-month and 12-month mortality rates following stroke and cardiac treatment than did for-profit hospitals (Lien et al. 2008).

- Evidence consistently documents higher quality in not-for-profit nursing homes. A systematic review of studies concluded that quality was higher in not-for-profit homes as indicated by structural measures (e.g., staffing levels), process measures (use of patient restraints), and outcome measures (e.g., incidence of pressure ulcers among patients) (Hillmer et al. 2005). A second review also found that both measures of adverse events and process measures indicate higher quality in not-for-profit homes (Schlesinger and Gray 2006).

Fewer studies examine differential patterns of quality investment with respect to their observability and to patients' understanding of quality. In general, the findings are consistent with such differential investment behaviour: for example, for-profit nursing homes have been found to make greater use of sedatives and restraints, and they also employ fewer staff (Hillmer et al. 2005; Weisbrod 1998). In an interesting study of the nursing home sector, Chou (2002) found that quality was, in general, higher in not-for-profit homes, but that the difference was particularly large for patients who had no visits from spouses or children in the month following admissions (i.e., no one to hold the facility accountable).

Service Mix   The evidence indicates that, as expected, for-profit institutions concentrate on a more profitable mix of services. Horwitz (2005a; 2005b) examined approximately 30 types of services offered by private for-profit, private not-for-profit, and government hospitals in the U.S. She divided the services into those that are consistently profitable (e.g., cardiac procedures), consistently not profitable (e.g., emergency psychiatric care), and of variable profitability (e.g., home care and other post-acute-care services); and she examined the probability that a hospital of each type would offer the service.

Horwitz found that for-profit hospitals were most likely to offer the highly profitable services; government hospitals were most likely to offer unprofitable but high-need services; and private not-for-profit hospitals fell in between, offering a mix of profitable and unprofitable but needed services.[12] Sloan et al.'s (2003) analysis of cardiac care found that for-profit hospitals were more likely to use expensive high-tech care such as percutaneous transluminal angioplasty (PCTA) and coronary artery bypass surgery (CABG), an effect the authors argue derives from the greater likelihood that for-profit institutions locate in areas with high demand for such care.

Costs and Efficiency   Three recent reviews all conclude that there are no meaningful differences in costs between for-profit and not-for-profit hospitals (Shen et al. 2005; Sloan 2000; Worthington 2004). Studies of technical efficiency in the production of hospital services find mixed results, with no clear patterns of findings (Schlesinger and Gray 2006). In contrast, studies of technical efficiency consistently find evidence of greater efficiency in for-profit nursing homes, but the parallel consistent finding of lower quality in for-profit nursing homes raises the question of whether an adjustment for quality would erase this advantage.

Responsiveness to Incentives and Market Effects   A variety of types of evidence document that for-profit organizations are more responsive to financial incentives than are not-for-profit organizations. This manifests itself in a number of ways. For-profit organizations are more likely to locate in markets with higher profit potential than not-for-profits, and they more readily enter and exit markets in response to changes in economic conditions (Horwitz 2003). For-profits increased provision most rapidly when the services were profitable and ended provision most rapidly after changes in reimbursement policy

---

[12] The analysis also classified the procedures as costly and capital intensive versus not, and compared the provision of each type of service by ownership type. For–profits were more likely to provide some expensive services and private not-for-profit more likely to provide others (government hospitals were less likely to provide all such services), a pattern not consistent with capital cost as an important driver of behaviour with respect to services provided.

made them less profitable. Private not-for-profit hospitals were less responsive to economic changes, and government hospitals were the least responsive.

For-profit hospitals also appear to engage more readily in practice to maximize payments for care provided. A review of U.S. Medicare admissions for pneumonia and respiratory infection (Silverman and Skinner 2004) found evidence of more up-coding from respiratory infection to pneumonia (which paid about $2000 more per case) among for-profit hospitals than not-for-profit hospitals: the proportion of cases in the most expensive category increased by 10 percent in stable not-for-profit hospitals, 23 percent in stable for-profit hospitals, and 37 percent in hospitals that had changed from not-for-profit to for-profit.

Convergence of Behaviour   The evidence indicates that the behaviour of the two types of organizations can depend on the relative market shares of for-profit and not-for-profit institutions. In particular, behaviour sometimes converges, especially in markets in which for-profits constitute a sizeable proportion of hospitals and when both face severe financial pressures (Horwitz and Nichols 2009).

On the negative side, not-for-profits sometimes more closely mimic the behaviour of their for-profit competitors. Duggan (2002), for example, found that in response to a large increase in the payment rate for beneficiaries of the California Medicaid program (public insurance for low-income individuals) both for-profit and not-for-profit hospitals cream-skimmed newly profitable indigent patients from the public hospital system. Among for-profit hospitals, this practice was not related to the composition of the hospital market in the local area, while not-for-profit hospitals located in areas with a high for-profit presence engaged more aggressively in this practice than did not-for-profit hospitals located areas with few for-profit competitors.

Horwitz (2005a; 2005b) found that *all* hospitals were more likely to offer a highly profitable service such as cardiac surgery in markets with high for-profit penetration. Horwitz and Nichols (2009) found that not-for-profits operating in markets with high concentrations of for-profits are more likely to offer relatively profitable services and are less likely to provide relatively unprofitable services than are not-for-profits that operate in markets with low concentrations of for-profits. And Silverman and Skinner (2004) found that not-for-profit hospitals operating in heavily for-profit markets were as likely to up-code as were the for-profit hospitals.

On the positive side, Grabowski and Hirth (2003) found evidence that the presence of not-for-profit nursing homes in a community increased quality in the for-profit homes.

For-Profit Versus Not-for-Profit: Summing Up

The literature comparing for-profit and not-for-profit health care organizations contains a sufficiently mixed set of findings (and suffers from a sufficient number of limitations) that advocates on each side can find evidence to support their claims. Although it may not be possible to make general statements about the two types of organizations, evidence does indicate important differences in behaviour in the hospital and nursing home sectors, differences that on balance suggest better performance by not-for-profits.

An important message from this literature, however, is that an exclusive focus on ownership status makes for bad policy. The variation in performance within each of the not-for-profit and for-profit sectors is large. Both financial performance and quality of care vary substantially with other characteristics of institutions and the broader regulatory and payment context in which they operate. Good policy must focus on these aspects of health care institutions and markets to elicit good performance from any health care organization, regardless of ownership status.

Chapter Summary

Health care institutions, the relationships among them, and the relationships between institutions and providers are all changing, growing more complex due to technological change and economic pressure in the health care sector.

- Hospitals remain the dominant health care institutions, though hospitals' share of all health care activity is falling.
- The analysis of hospitals presents substantial conceptual and empirical challenges.
  - A dominance of not-for-profit ownership and incomplete vertical integration make application of standard models of the firm invalid.
  - The production of multiple outputs using a complex array of inputs, the relative infancy of quality measurement, and the substantial heterogeneity of patients treated complicate the empirical assessment of hospital performance.
  - Often it is hard to distinguish inefficiency from higher quality or a less-healthy case load.
- The performance of hospitals and other health care institutions is shaped by the overall context of their operation, including ownership status, the ownership status of competitors, the nature of the funding model, the nature and extent of competition in the market area, and the regulatory scheme under which they operate.
- For these reasons, policy approaches to the institutional sector must aim for a coherent, complementary set of policies related to payment, ownership, competition, and regulation.

Key Terms

behavioural cost function, *367*
frontier cost estimation, *368*
incomplete vertical
  integration, *358*

internal market, *365*
local monopoly, *363*
market concentration, *363*
meta-analysis, *371*

non-distribution
  constraint, *369*
purchaser–provider split, *365*
transactions costs model, *362*

Study Questions

For each of the statements below, indicate whether the statement is true or false and explain why it is true or false.

1. The shift of many traditionally hospital-based in-patient procedures to day surgery has weakened hospital market power.
2. Incomplete vertical integration of hospitals can be explained in part by the highly complex care required when using sophisticated health technologies.
3. Informational asymmetry is one possible rationale for the dominance of not-for-profit organizations in health care.
4. Failure to adjust for differences in case mix may compromise empirical comparisons of for-profit and not-for-profit institutions.
5. Not-for-profit organizations have little incentive to operate efficiently.
6. A transactions costs model of hospitals would explain the separate billing for physician and hospital services received while a hospital in-patient as a result of physician self-regulation.
7. The fact that many hospitals enjoy local monopolies enhances the effectiveness of contracting approaches to service provision by reducing the complexity of the contracting process.
8. One might expect that not-for-profit hospitals will provide higher quality on difficult-to-measure dimensions of quality than would for-profit hospitals.

9. Demand-side, patient-based competition can only be effective if there is excess capacity on the supply side.

10. Compared to retrospective reimbursement, prospective reimbursement would be expected to weaken the ability of hospital managers to exercise managerial control over the medical staff.

References

Arrow, K. J. 1963. Uncertainty and the welfare economics of medical care. *American Economic Review* 53(5):941–73.

Berta, W., A. LaPorte, and V. Valdmanis. 2005. Observations on institutional long-term care in Ontario: 1996–2002. *Canadian Journal on Aging* 24(1):71–84.

Birkmeyer, J. D., A. Siewers, E. Finlayson, T. Stukel, F. L. Lucas, I. Batistia, H. G. Welch, and D. Wennberg. 2002. Hospital volume and surgical mortality in the United States. *New England Journal of Medicine* 346(15):1128–37.

Canadian Institute for Health Information. 2004. *Inpatient hospitalizations continue to decline, same-day surgery visits on the rise, reports CIHI.* Ottawa: Canadian Institute for Health Information.

———. 2005. *Inpatient hospitalizations and average length of stay trends in Canada, 2003–2004 and 2004–2005.* Ottawa: Canadian Institute for Health Information.

———. 2008. *National health expenditure trends, 1975–2008.* Ottawa: Canadian Institute for Health Information.

Chou, S. Y. 2002. Asymmetric information, ownership and quality of care: An empirical analysis of nursing homes. *Journal of Health Economics* 21(2):293–311.

Cookson, R., and D. Dawson. 2006. Hospital competition and patient choice in publicly funded health care. In *The Elgar companion to health economics*, A. Jones (ed.). Cheltenham, U.K.: Edward Elgar. 221–32.

Devereaux, P., P. Choi, C. Lacchetti, B. Weaver, H. Schunemann, T. Haines, J. Lavis, B. Grant, D. Haslam, M. Bahandari, T. Sullivan, D. Cook, M. Meade, H. Khan, N. Bhatnagar, and G. Guyatt. 2002. A systematic review and meta-analysis of studies comparing mortality rates of private for-profit and private not-for-profit hospitals. *CMAJ* 166(11): 1399–1406.

Duggan, M. 2002. Hospital market structure and the behaviour of not-for-profit hospitals. *RAND Journal of Economics* 33(3):433–46.

Evans, R. G. 1981. Incomplete vertical integration: The distinctive structure of the health-care industry. In *Health, economics, and health economics*, J. van der Gaag, and M. Perlman (eds.). New York: North-Holland Publishing Company, 229–354.

———. 1984. *Strained mercy: The economics of Canadian health care.* Toronto: Buttersworth.

Gaynor, M. 2004. Competition and quality in hospital markets: What do we know? What don't we know? *Economie Publique* 15(2):3–40.

Globerman, S., and A. Vining. 1996. A framework for evaluating the government contracting-out decision with an application to information technology. *Public Administration Review* 56(6):577–86.

Gowrisankaran, G., and R. Town. 2003. Competition, payers and hospital quality. *Health Services Research* 38(6):1403–21.

Grabowski, D. C, and R. A. Hirth. 2003. Competitive spillovers across non-profit and for-profit nursing homes. *Journal of Health Economics* 22(1):1–22.

Hansmann, B. 1980. The role of nonprofit enterprise. *Yale Law Journal* 89:835–901.

Harris, J. E. 1977. The internal organization of hospitals: Some economic implications. *The Bell Journal of Economics* 8:467–82.

Hillmer, M. P., W. P. Wodchis, S. S. Gill, G. M. Anderson, and P. A. Rochon. 2005. Nursing home profit status and quality of care: Is there any evidence of an association? *Medical Care Research and Review* 62(2):139–66.

Hollingsworth, B., P. Dawson, and N. Maniadakis. 2003. Efficiency measurement of health care: A review of non-parametric methods and applications. *Health Care Management Science* 2(3):161–72.

Horwitz, J. 2003. Why we need the independent sector: The behaviour, law, and ethics of not-for-profit hospitals. *UCLA Law Review* 50(6):1345–411.

———. 2005a. *Does corporate ownership matter: Service provision in the hospital industry.* Cambridge, MA: NBER Working Paper 11376.

———. 2005b. Making profits and providing care: Comparing nonprofit, for-profit, and government hospitals. *Health Affairs* 24(3):790–801.

Horwitz, J., and A. Nichols. 2009. Hospital ownership and medical services: Market mix, spillover effects, and nonprofit objectives. *Journal of Health Economics* 28(5):924–37.

Kessler, D., and J. Geppert. 2005. The effects of competition on variation in the quality and cost of medical care. *Journal of Economics and Management Strateg.* 14(3):575–89.

Kessler, D., and M. McClellan. 2000. Is hospital competition socially wasteful? *Quarterly Journal of Economics* 115(2):577–615.

Lien, H. M., S. Y. Chou, and J. T. Liu. 2008. Hospital ownership and performance: Evidence from stroke and cardiac treatment in Taiwan. *Journal of Health Economics* 27(5):1208–23.

McGregor, M., R. Tate, K. McGrail, L. Ronald, A.-M. Broemeling, and M. Cohen. 2006. Care outcomes in long-term care facilities in British Columbia, Canada: Does ownership matter? *Medical Care* 44(10):929–35.

Newhouse, J. 1970. Toward a theory of non-profit institutions: An economic model of a hospital. *American Economic Review* 60(1):64–74.

———. 1994. Frontier estimation: How useful a tool for health economics. *Journal of Health Economics* 13:317–22.

Pauly, M. V., and M. Redisch. 1973. The not-for-profit hospital as a physicians' cooperative. *The American Economic Review* 63(1):87–99.

Propper, C. 1996. Market structure and prices: The responses of hospitals in the U.K. National Health Service to competition. *Journal of Public Economics* 61:307–35.

Propper, C., S. Burgess, and D. Gossage. 2008. Competition and quality: Evidence from the NHS internal market 1991–9. *Economic Journal* 118(525):138–70.

Propper, C., D. Wilson, and N. Soderland. 1998. The effects of regulation and competition in the NHS internal market: The case of general practice fundholders. *Journal of Health Economics* 17(6):645–73.

Rogowski, J., A. Jain, and J. Escarce. 2006. Hospital competition, managed care, and mortality after hospitalization for medical conditions in California. *Health Services Research* 42(2):682–705.

Schlesinger, M., and B. H. Gray. 2006. How nonprofits matter in American medicine, and what to do about it. *Health Affairs Web Exclusive* 25(June 20):w287–w303.

Shen, Y.-C., K. Eggleston, J. Lau, and C. Schmid. 2005. *Hospital ownership and financial performance: A quantitative research review.* Cambridge, MA: NBER Working Paper 11662.

Shen, Y. 2002. The effect of hospital ownership choice on patient outcomes after treatment for acute myocardial infarction. *Journal of Health Economics.* 21(5):9901–22.

Silverman, E., and J. Skinner. 2004. Medicare upcoding and hospital ownership. *Journal of Health Economics* 23(2):369–89.

Siu, S., F. Sonneberg, W. Manning, G. Goldberg, E. Bloomfield, J. Newhouse, and R. Brook. 1986. Inappropriate use of hospitals in a randomized trial of health insurance plans. *New England Journal of Medicine* 315(20):1259–66.

Sloan, F. 2000. Not-for-profit ownership and hospital behaviour. In *Handbook of health economics,* A. J. Culyer, and J. P. Newhouse (eds.). Amsterdam: Elsevier Science B.V. 1142–74.

Sloan, F, J. Trogdon, L. Curtis, and K. Schulman. 2003. Does the ownership of the admitting hospital make a difference? *Medical Care* 41(10):1193–205.

Statistics Canada. 2008. *Residential care facilities*. Ottawa: Statistics Canada, Report 83-237-X.

Weisbrod, B. 1988. *The non-profit economy*. Cambridge, MA: Harvard University Press.

———. 1998. Institutional form and organizational behaviour. In *Private action and the public good*, W. Powell, and E. Clemens (eds.). New Haven: Yale University Press. 69–83.

Worthington, A. 2004. Frontier efficiency measurement in health care: A review of empirical techniques and selected applications. *Medical Care Research and Review* 61(2):135–70.

Wright, C., G. K. Chambers, and Y. Robens-Paradise. 2002. Evaluation of indications for and outcomes of elective surgery. *Canadian Medical Association Journal* 167(5):461–66.

Appendix 14

Chapter 14: Health Care Institutions: Hospitals

14.2 HOSPITAL MARKETS AND HOSPITAL COMPETITION

The Public Competition Approach Internal market and purchaser-provider-split arrangements are premised on the efficacy of contracting: rather than producing a good or service "in-house," the government contracts with a non-governmental organization to produce it. Governments have for many years used contracting in areas such as road construction, garbage collection, and building maintenance. Similarly, health care institutions regularly contract for non-medical inputs such as laundry, housekeeping, and food service. But the idea of using contracts for health care services within public systems to foster competition is fairly recent.

The goal of contracting is to improve efficiency by reducing the social costs of providing a good or service. The social costs include both the costs of production and the transactions costs associated with writing and enforcing a contract. Social costs also include more than just the costs that fall on a public budget; they also include costs that fall on private individuals and organizations. Even if the private sector can produce the good or service at lower cost, in some instances the sum of the production and transactions costs can exceed the cost of in-house production. How can we know when contracting might be advantageous?

S. Globerman and A. Vining (Globerman and Vining 1996; Vining and Globerman 1999) present a framework to help answer this question. The framework draws heavily on ideas from the principal–agent literature that was discussed in Chapter 12. In addition to production costs, they identify two types of transactions costs that are particularly relevant: bargaining costs and the costs of opportunism.

- Bargaining costs refer to the costs of negotiating a contract in the first place, the costs of negotiating contract changes when unforeseen events arise, the costs of monitoring performance, and the costs of dispute resolution. Bargaining costs arise when each side acts self-interestedly but in good faith.

- Opportunism, in contrast, arises when one side acts self-interestedly but in bad faith, trying to change the agreed terms of the contract in its own favour. Opportunism involves taking advantage of an opportunity to breach the contract when there is a chance of success. Opportunism costs are the costs of such behaviour.

The size of these respective costs varies systematically with the contracting environment. Three aspects of the environment are particularly important (for the discussion below, assume the contractor is the government and the contractee is a non-governmental organization):

1. *Task Complexity:* Task complexity refers to the difficulty a contractor faces in specifying and monitoring performance. Task complexity is low, for example, when contracting for the provision of routine out-patient laboratory services and for the processing of such laboratory tests. Task complexity is higher for the provision of primary care services and substantially higher for the provision of complex secondary and tertiary hospital care. In these cases, provision requires specialized knowledge and includes considerable uncertainty in outcomes even with good quality care. Because task complexity is often associated with informational asymmetry, it affects bargaining and opportunism costs.

2. *Contestability:* Contestability is the extent of real or potential competition in a market. The idea of potential competition is critical: even if there are currently few producers, if new producers can easily enter a market in response to profit opportunities, the market is highly contestable. Low contestability increases the risks of opportunism because the government has few options if contractees perform poorly. Contestability is high for lab provision and primary care providers where there are currently many suppliers or where it is relatively easy for new providers to enter the market. In contrast, the market for organizations that can provide a full spectrum of secondary and tertiary services has considerably lower contestability.

3. *Asset Specificity:* Asset specificity refers to the value, in their next best use, of assets (physical and human) used in the production of the good or service. It is easier to contract for services for which production requires assets with low specificity because there is less risk to a contractee in making the necessary investments. In particular, low specificity reduces the investor's vulnerability to a type of opportunism called the hold-up problem. If, to fulfill a contract, the contractee invests in expensive assets with high specificity, the government knows that the contractee has few options if the government breaches the contract. This makes the contractee more willing to renegotiate the contract *ex post,* accepting a lower price rather than abandoning the assets and losing the investment. The assets required to establish an out-patient lab and a primary care office are of low specificity: if necessary, a facility could be closed and readily converted to other uses. In contrast, high-tech equipment required to process hundreds of thousands of lab tests has more specificity, and a tertiary-care hospital has high specificity.

The combination of these characteristics determines the nature and severity of the contracting problems likely to be encountered and the nature of potential solutions. Table 14A.1 summarizes this for the service examples noted in the discussion above. An under-appreciated aspect of contracting is that even if government gets out of the business of producing a good or service, it must make a corresponding investment in the expertise required to negotiate and monitor contracts.

TABLE 14A.1 **Examples of Contracting Environments**

Service	Task Complexity	Asset Specificity	Contestability	Problems/Solutions
Out-patient Laboratory	Low	Low	High	No serious problems; the best context for contracting.
Large-Scale Lab Test Processing	Low	High	High	Problem: opportunism by contractor–hold-up problem. Risky for contractee to invest resources in asset. Solution: • Can be mitigated if contractee can contract with multiple contractors so it can drop a contract if the contractor attempts a hold-up. • Contractor (government) can own assets and contract only for the management of the process.
Primary Care Services	High	Low	High	Problem: asymmetry of information; disputes about quality/performance. Solution: • If possible, establish explicit performance standards (e.g., clinical practice guidelines). • Establish low-cost dispute resolution process that involves independent adjudicator with requisite knowledge (may come from outside jurisdiction).
Tertiary Level Care	High	High	Low	Problems: many problems; poor context for contracting. Solution: • Again, contractor owns the asset. • Contracting may require long-term relational contracting in which contractor and contractee negotiate solutions on an on-going basis.

References

Globerman, S., and A. Vining. 1996. A framework for evaluating the government contracting-out decision with an application to information technology. *Public Administration Review* 56(6):577–86.

Vining, A., and S. Globerman. 1999. Contracting out health care services: A conceptual framework. *Health Policy* 46:77–96.

Pharmaceuticals

Learning Objectives

After studying this chapter, you will understand

LO1   Salient institutional features of the pharmaceutical sector

LO2   The economic analysis of
   • research and innovation in the drug sector, including patent legislation
   • safety and efficacy regulations
   • competition in the drug sector
   • critical aspects of the design of drug benefit programs

Pharmaceuticals constitute an increasingly important component of health care. Therapeutically, prescription drugs are becoming an ever-more-important weapon in the arsenal available to health care providers. Drugs are used to treat a growing array of conditions for which no treatment was previously available (e.g., Alzheimer's disease, AIDS) or that previously required major surgery (e.g., ulcers). Drugs are also now used prophylactically by millions of at-risk individuals for an array of preventable health conditions (e.g., statins drugs to lower cholesterol). Modern medicines extend and improve the quality of life for a large proportion of the population.

Partly because of their increased use, pharmaceuticals constitute an increasing share of health care expenditures in Canada, as in nearly all industrialized countries. In 1985, prescription drug expenditures accounted for 9.5 percent of all health care spending in Canada; in 2008, they accounted for an estimated 17.4 percent, nearly doubling their share of spending on the way to becoming the second largest component of health care expenditures (Figure 15.1). On a per-capita basis, annual spending on prescription drugs in Canada rose from just under $100 in 1985 to over $750 in 2008, with private spending rising slightly faster than public spending over this period. Canada's drug spending as a share of total spending places it in the lower half among comparator OECD countries (Canadian Institute for Health Information 2009).

The pharmaceutical sector presents public policy-makers with unique challenges. Developing new drugs is a research-intensive endeavour undertaken predominately by large, multinational, for-profit companies. The pharmaceutical sector is one of the most research-intensive sectors of the economy, undertaking nearly 10 percent of all industrial research and development spending in Canada (Statistics Canada 2008). Public policy must recognize

   • the special nature of research as an economic activity and acknowledge it as an economic commodity

FIGURE 15.1

Prescription Drug Expenditures Per Capita, and Prescription Drug Expenditures as a Proportion of Total Health Care Expenditures, Canada, 1985–2008

Both public and private drug expenditures per capita have been rising over time both in absolute terms and as a proportion of total health care expenditures.

Source: Canadian Institute for Health Information, 2009. Drug Expenditure in Canada, 1985–2008. Ottawa: Canadian Institute for Health Information. Table A, pp. 60–63. ISBN: 978-1-55465-510-6 (PDF).

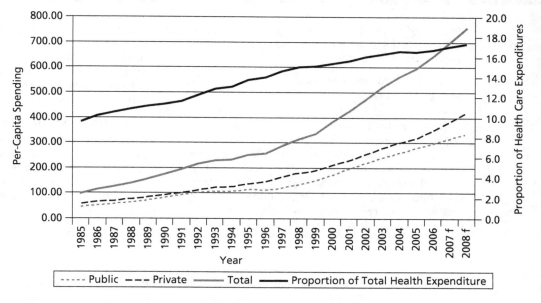

- the strategic challenges in regulating an industry that moves investments across borders with ease
- the increasing calls for policy coordination among countries, most notably the pressure for international harmonization of patent policies through international trade agreements

Pharmaceuticals are not just of interest to ministries of health; in many countries, they are also of interest for industry policy, especially in the economies of industrialized countries seeking to develop high-tech industries as part of a knowledge-based economy. This dual interest creates tensions up through the highest levels of government: while the ministry of industry seeks to create a "drug-friendly" environment hoping to attract pharmaceutical-related investment, the ministry of health seeks to purchase drugs as inexpensively as is possible, which usually means hard bargaining over prices and resisting company threats to pull out its investment if it does not get its price.

This chapter is organized around these two facets of the pharmaceutical sector. The first part focuses on the economics of the pharmaceutical industry as a producer and supplier of drugs, with particular emphasis on important characteristics of the industry, economic aspects of drug development, testing and marketing, and the associated regulatory issues. The second part of the chapter focuses on the demand side of the sector: the design of pharmaceutical insurance programs, and in particular purchasing policies, formulary policy and coverage decision-making, reimbursement methods, and related matters. In the real world, these two elements of the sector are connected—pricing and regulatory policies implemented by a ministry of health affect production and pricing decisions by the drug firms. Consequently, a full analysis of many policy questions cannot be treated in isolation. But as a first approximation, this division is useful for a high-level economic analysis of the pharmaceutical sector.

15.1 THE PHARMACEUTICAL INDUSTRY

The pharmaceutical industry is consistently one of the most profitable among all industries. From 1955 to 2002, it was the most profitable industry ranked by return on sales, return on assets, and return on equity. The industry has not performed quite as strongly in

The set of all pharmaceutical drugs can be divided two different ways that are useful for understanding the economics of the sector.

Over-the-Counter Versus Prescription Drugs

One distinction is between drugs that a person can purchase without a prescription and drugs for which a physician prescription is required. Drugs that a person can purchase in the drugstore without a prescription (e.g., aspirin (ASA), antihistamines) are called "over-the-counter" drugs. Drugs that require a physician's prescription are called "prescription drugs." A drug can change status. For example, when ibuprofen was first introduced, it could only be purchased by prescription. After a number of years, during which evidence accumulated that it could be used safely by consumers without explicit advice from a physician, it became available without a prescription. This chapter concentrates on prescription drugs, which are the focus of most policy attention.

Brand-Name Versus Generic Drugs

A second distinction is between brand-name drugs and generic drugs. Brand-name drugs are produced and sold by brand-name pharmaceutical companies who develop and patent new drugs. Generic drugs are produced and sold by generic drug companies that copy a brand-name drug once the brand-name drug's patent has expired.

recent years—in 2008, it was ranked third in return on sales and return on assets, and fifth for return on shareholder equity—but its average return remains many times that of an average industry (*Fortune* 2009).

The industry includes two distinct types of drug manufacturers (Box 15.1). **Brand-name drug manufacturers** undertake research to develop new drugs. **Generic drug manufacturers** produce and sell drug products that have already been developed, normally either under license from a brand-name manufacturer or after the brand-name manufacturer's patent has expired.

Brand-Name Drug Manufacturers

brand-name drug manufacturers
Pharmaceutical companies that undertake research to develop new drugs.

generic drug manufacturers
Pharmaceutical companies that produce and sell drug products that have already been developed, either under license from a brand-name manufacturer or after the brand-name manufacturer's patent has expired.

Brand-name manufacturers include those names most familiar to the general public, such as Bayer, Glaxo-Smith-Kline, and Merck-Frosst. The brand-name sector is dominated by a small number of large multinational companies. The sector has experienced two contrasting trends in recent years. At the top end, the brand-name sector has become more concentrated through mergers between the large traditional firms in the industry. In 2004, the top ten companies accounted for just over 50 percent of global pharmaceutical sales. The period between 1999 and 2004 witnessed over 20 mergers among large international brand-name drug companies (Class 2004; Demirbag et al. 2007). The companies argue that consolidation is necessary to take advantage of the economies of scale in drug development.

But in the shadow of these huge, multinational companies, a proliferation of small, biotech start-ups have sprouted that focus on a single drug or a narrow set of products linked to a particular discovery (Dewan 2009). This trend has been driven in part by technological developments that have altered the ways new drug compounds can be developed, lowering the costs and making it possible for small players to carve out niche markets in the industry. Regardless of the size of the company, all brand-name manufacturers undertake research to develop new medicines that can be patented to provide the exclusive right to manufacture and sell the product.

Generic Drug Manufacturers

Generic manufacturers, in contrast, do not develop new drugs. Rather, they produce generic versions of brand-name drugs after their patents have expired; or, if the patent is still valid, they produce a generic version under license from the brand-name manufacturer. A generic drug is certified as bio-equivalent to the brand-name version, which means that the active ingredients (the compounds that create the desired effect) are identical to the brand-name drug and the drug has been certified to produce the same clinical effects as the brand-name drug. The difference is in the non-active ingredients (the compounds that bind the ingredients together, the colouring added, etc.). Hence, a generic drug should be just as effective as the original brand-name drug.

Generic drugs are usually much less expensive than the brand-name version, and generics compete for market share with the brand-name version. Historically, generic manufacturers tend be national rather than international in scope, but an increasing number of generic companies from other countries market drugs in Canada.

15.2 GOVERNMENT REGULATION OF THE PHARMACEUTICAL INDUSTRY

Government regulation of the pharmaceutical industry takes four important forms: regulation of intellectual property through patent policy, regulation of drug safety, regulation of drug prices, and regulation of drug advertising and promotion. The first two are relatively standardized internationally; the latter two are more country-specific and can best be appreciated through an examination of the nature of competition in the drug sector.

15.2.1 Patent Regulation

Knowledge as Public Good Subject to Market Failure

Research is a central activity of the brand-name drug manufacturers. The goal of research is to produce new knowledge (and for a drug company, new knowledge that can be embodied in a product). But once produced and in the public domain, in the absence of regulation, knowledge can be freely used by many people simultaneously; indeed, it is difficult to exclude others from using the knowledge gained. Knowledge is a classic economic **public good**. Market allocation fails for such public goods: markets produce too little of a public good.

public good
A good that can be simultaneously consumed by many individuals and which it is very costly to exclude others from consuming.

The market fails because producing knowledge through research is costly, and the person or organization that incurs the cost of discovering new knowledge will not be able to recoup those costs in a free market: once the knowledge is produced, others can acquire the knowledge and use it at little or no cost. Pharmaceuticals, which are characterized by high, fixed research and development costs that must be incurred regardless of how many units of a drug are eventually sold, and low marginal costs of production once a drug has been developed, exemplify this problem. In a free market, a drug company that incurred all the costs of discovering a new drug would soon go out of business as other companies entered the market to manufacture and sell the drug for the marginal costs of production. Consequently, if left purely to market forces, society would under-invest in research and knowledge creation. In the drug sector, this would translate into less innovation in the development of new drugs.

The policy response to this market failure takes two basic forms: (1) direct public investment in research and (2) patent protection.

Direct Public Investment in Research   Direct public investment in research tries to partially fill the void left by a lack of private investment in research and focuses particularly on basic scientific research. The government of Canada, for instance, funds basic scientific research through its research granting councils (the National Science and Engineering Research Council, the Social Sciences and Humanities Research Council, and the Canadian Institutes of Health Research), through research infrastructure programs such as the Canadian Foundation for Innovation, and through hundreds of other funding programs that support research in specific areas. Similar public research programs exist in nearly all OECD countries (e.g., U.S. National Institutes of Health).

Patent Protection   The second response is regulation to create incentive for private-sector investment in research. The centrepiece of such regulation is patent legislation. A **patent** gives the developer exclusive rights to produce and sell the patented product for a defined period of time. In effect, it grants a legal monopoly to the developer of the good or process covered by the patent. This exclusive right to sell the patented good offers the developer an opportunity to earn back the cost of development plus a profit. (A patent does not guarantee a profit: the product has to be something that people want to buy.)

Patent policy must balance two counteracting effects on social welfare:

- By increasing the chances of earning a profit on a new product, patents spur the development of important new knowledge and products, improving social welfare.
- By granting monopoly power to the developer for a period of time, the price for the product is, at least temporarily, set above the socially optimal level, reducing access to this welfare-enhancing product.

Patent policy seeks to balance these competing welfare effects so as to maximize social welfare over time. The pivotal element in the design of patent policy for striking this balance is the length of time for which a patent grants the holder exclusive market access.

The impact of a country's patent protection on innovation depends on the size of the country's market relative to the international market. Because drug sales in Canada constitute a small proportion of international sales,[1] Canada's patent policy exerts negligible influence on a multinational company's incentive to develop a drug, so Canada's policy has little impact on the pace of innovation in the international drug market. Consequently, Canada could provide lesser patent protection and capture more of the social gain associated with new drugs without negatively affecting the rate of innovation internationally (this would constitute a form of free riding).

For many years, Canada took this approach to its patent policy for pharmaceuticals (Table 15.1). Beginning in 1923, Canada's Patent Act allowed compulsory licensing for pharmaceutical products. A **compulsory license** grants a generic manufacturer permission to manufacture and sell a patented drug product before the patent has expired. Under the license, the generic manufacturer was required to pay a royalty to the patent-holding firm. But the policy had little impact on fostering generic manufacturing in Canada because the compulsory license required that the generic manufacturer produce the active ingredient in Canada, and the Canadian market was not big enough to achieve economies of scale in production of such ingredients.

To encourage greater generic production, the Canadian government amended the Patent Act in 1969 to permit compulsory licenses to be issued when the generic manufacturer

patent
An exclusive right, granted by government, to produce and sell a patented product for a defined period of time. It grants a legal monopoly to the developer of the good or process covered by the patent.

compulsory license
A license that grants a generic manufacturer permission to manufacture and sell a patented drug product before the patent has expired and that requires that the generic manufacturer pay a royalty to the patent holder.

---

[1] In 2007, pharmaceutical sales in Canada constituted 2.3 percent of global pharmaceutical sales. Sales in the U.S. constituted 36 percent of global sales; combined sales in the top 5 European Union countries (France, Germany, Italy, Spain, and the U.K.) constituted 21 percent of global sales, and sales in Japan constituted over 10 percent of global sales (IMS Canada 2009).

TABLE 15.1 **Key Dates in Canadian Patent Legislation for Pharmaceutical Products**

1923	The Patent Act is amended to allow a compulsory license to be issued if the active ingredients for the drug product are manufactured in Canada. Such licenses can be granted without the permission of the patent holder; the licensee is required to pay a royalty to the patent holder.
1969	The Patent Act is amended to permit compulsory licenses to be issued even when the ingredients are imported into Canada (where the generic manufacturer simply processes them to create the drug). Generic manufacturers are required to pay a royalty of 4 percent of the net selling price of the drug.
1983	Ministry of Consumer and Corporate Affairs calls for a re-examination of the compulsory licensing policy in order to encourage growth in the pharmaceutical industry in Canada. Shortly thereafter, the Commission of Inquiry on the Pharmaceutical Industry is created.
1987	Bill C-22 amends the Patent Act • guaranteeing brand-name drug manufacturers 10 years of protection against compulsory licenses for generic manufacturers seeking to import active ingredients and 7 years of protection against generic manufacturers who would manufacture active ingredients in Canada • ensuring that compulsory licenses to import would not be issued for drugs invented and developed in Canada • changing the term of a patent from 17 years following the date of issue of the patent to 20 years from the date the patent application is filed
1991	The federal government introduces Bill C-91, legislation to amend the Patent Act to bring it into conformity with the intellectual property provisions of both the North American Free Trade Agreement and the Trade-Related Aspects of Intellectual Property Rights (TRIPS) of the General Agreement on Tariffs and Trade. The legislation is passed in 1993 • eliminating compulsory licensing for pharmaceutical products (compulsory licenses already issued are grandfathered) • effectively providing brand-name manufacturers the ability to delay the introduction of generic drugs by up to 24 months following patent expiry. Once a generic manufacturer satisfies the conditions to receive a Notice of Compliance from Health Canada (allowing it to market a drug coming off patent), the generic manufacturer must notify the patent holder that it will not infringe on any active patents. The patent holder can apply to have the Notice of Compliance blocked, which automatically blocks the issuance of the Notice of Compliance until whichever of the following occurs first: 24 months pass, a court hearing resolves the issue, or the patent expires.

imported the active ingredients for processing a drug into Canada. This had a dramatic impact on the generic industry. It gave birth to the Canadian industry that now includes firms with sales well over a billion dollars per year. Perhaps it was too successful. By the early 1980s, arguments arose that the patent legislation needed to be rebalanced to encourage greater investment in Canada by the brand-name pharmaceutical industry. The response in 1987 was Bill C-22, which

• weakened compulsory licensing regulations and extended patent protection in return for a commitment by the brand-name drug manufacturers to increase research and development spending in Canada

• created the Patented Medicines Prices Review Board (PMPRB), a quasi-judicial body mandated to regulate the pricing of patented brand-name drugs in Canada

In the early 1990s, Canada was required to further strengthen patent protection for brand-name manufacturers and align its policies with provisions of the North American Free Trade Agreement and broader world trade agreements to which it was party, which sought to harmonize pharmaceutical patent legislation internationally. Bill C-91, passed in 1993,

- eliminated compulsory licensing altogether
- included provisions that enable brand-name manufacturers to delay the introduction of generic drugs following patent expiry
- introduced a requirement that a generic manufacturer notify the brand-name manufacturer that it intends to market a generic drug
- provides the brand-name manufacturer the opportunity to legally challenge the generic company's claim that it does not infringe on any of the brand-name company's patents, delaying the introduction of a generic by up to 24 months and forcing the generic firm to incur legal costs to fight the challenge

This legislation, plus additional regulations issued in 2006, gives the brand-name manufacturer exclusive access to the information on which its drug approval was based for eight years from the date of approval for sale. This means that the patent protection for brand-name drugs is now stronger in Canada than at any time in its history, and it is equal to that provided by all other industrialized countries.

15.2.2 Drug Safety and the Drug Approval Process

In all industrialized countries, before a newly developed drug can be sold to the public, the drug must be certified as safe and efficacious by the relevant government agency: in Canada, the Therapeutic Products Branch of Health Canada; in the U.S., the Food and Drug Administration (FDA); and in the European Union, the European Medicinal Products Evaluation Agency (EMEA). The modern era of safety and efficacy regulation began in the early 1960s following a series of instances in the late 1950s and early 1960s in which drugs marketed to the public were found to cause severe harmful side effects. The most famous of these was thalidomide, which had been marketed to pregnant woman and was subsequently found to cause severe birth defects in children.

Welfare Effects of Drug Safety Regulation

From an economic perspective, safety regulation must balance counteracting welfare effects. To the extent that the safety regulation prevents harmful drug products from reaching the market, the regulations improve social welfare. But undertaking the research required to document safety and efficacy is time-consuming, delaying the time until a product reaches market so that people can benefit from it. This process is also costly, which may prevent some drugs from ever being produced and marketed. In this respect, the regulations impose a welfare cost on society.

This trade-off is illustrated in Figure 15.2. The figure depicts three demand curves for a particular prescription drug assumed to sell at a fixed price, P*. Let D_{NT} represent demand for the drug based on consumers' and physicians' best estimates of the effects of the drug in the absence of any formal testing of its safety and efficacy. Individuals consume X_{NT} units of the drug. Now imagine that safety regulations are imposed that require testing of a drug's safety and efficacy before it can be sold. To assess the welfare effects of the regulation, we need to compare welfare during two periods:

1. the period of time between the development of the drug and approval following testing: in the absence of safety regulations, the drug would be available during this time; but under the regulation, the drug's availability is delayed
2. the period after the drug has been evaluated, during which it is available under both situations

Now consider three cases that may arise under regulations that require formal testing and evaluation of new drugs.

FIGURE 15.2
Welfare Consequences of Safety and Efficacy Regulations
This figure illustrates the welfare effects of drug safety regulations. Assume that consumption would be X_{NT} in the absence of any testing. If testing reveals that the drug is less effective or has more severe side effects than anticipated, demand shifts inward to D_{T1} and consumption is X_1. During the delay in availability caused by testing, consumers lost benefit equal to the sum of the areas CDP* (positive benefit) and DEH (negative benefit), because they would have consumed at level X_{NT} with no testing. Following the test, they consume at X_1 avoiding the welfare loss DEH that would have arisen in the absence of evidence. An analogous analysis can be done if the testing reveals better-than-expected effectiveness and shifts demand out to D_{T2}.

Source: Adapted from Scherer (2000), Figure 2, p. 1312.

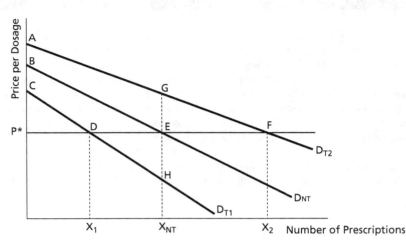

Case 1: Testing Reveals Adverse Side Effects or Less-than-Expected Efficacy   Let the demand curve D_{T1} represent the full-information demand curve in a world of regulatory testing for safety and efficacy that reveals adverse side effects of the drug or less-than-expected efficacy. The information revealed by testing causes the demand curve to shift inward, so that it lies to the left of D_{NT}. Individuals would consume only X_1.

Period of delay: During the period of delay, in the absence of regulation, individuals would have consumed X_{NT}, which would have generated social benefits equal to the triangle CDP* (consumption for which benefits exceed costs) and social costs equal to the triangle DEH (consumption for which the costs exceed the benefits). As drawn, these nearly offset each other.

Period after introduction: During the period after the drug's introduction, by reducing consumption, the regulation avoids a welfare loss of DEH. In this case, the total welfare loss avoided over the life of the drug (or until consumers would be able to identify the adverse effects) likely exceeds any potential temporary loss of welfare caused by the delayed introduction due to testing.

Case 2: Testing Reveals Unanticipated Benefits   Now consider a situation in which testing reveals substantially higher benefits than consumers would expect without testing. The full information demand curve is D_{T2}.

Period of delay: Consumption without regulation would again have been at X_{NT}. During the period of testing, individuals obtain benefit equal to AGEP*.

Period after introduction: Once the drug is introduced, full-information demand is X_2 generating a welfare gain equal to AFP*. This is greater (by the amount GFE) than it would have been had the regulations not established the larger-than-expected benefits.

Once again, over the lifetime of the drug, the extra benefits after introduction likely exceed the lost benefits from the delay in its availability.

Case 3: The Cost of Testing Prevents the Drug from Reaching Market   Suppose that the additional costs of testing prevent a drug company from developing and marketing a drug. Then consumers lose the benefit the drug would have provided over the life of the drug (e.g., for case 2 above, AGEP* for all periods).

The challenge for the regulatory authorities is to impose testing that is sufficiently rigorous to identify the true effects of a drug and then apply decision criteria that balance the losses and gains from its decisions, while not imposing such large costs as to unduly inhibit drug development.

Developing a new drug is costly and time consuming. The average time from the synthesis of a new drug molecule (time of patent) to regulatory approval for sale was 12.8 years in the 1990s, up from 7.9 years in the 1960s (Dickson and Gagnon 2004). Much of this increase is due to longer periods of clinical testing. Estimates of the cost of developing a drug are hugely variable and not well validated, ranging from $500 million to up to $1.8 billion.

The industry has focused particular attention on the length of the approval process itself. It typically takes a little over a year from the time of submission for a Notice of Compliance from the Therapeutics Products Directorate of Health Canada to a final decision. In 2007, the median length for all new drug submissions was 392 days. The length of the process for Canada is comparable to that for the U.S.: for 16 products submitted to both countries, the average length of time for approval was 489 days in Canada and 484 days in the U.S. Compared to the European Union, Canada was a bit slower: 382 days versus 318 days (Canada's Research-Based Pharmaceutical Companies (Rx&D) 2007).

The regulatory processes are similar across industrialized countries and generally proceed in the following five stages:

1. A drug company synthesizes a promising new drug compound.
2. The drug company conducts testing in animals to establish the basic properties and effects of a drug.
3. If promising, the drug company conducts clinical testing in humans:
   - Phase 1 Clinical Studies involve 20–100 healthy volunteers, largely to establish safe dosage levels and other information required for safe testing in larger populations.
   - Phase 2 Clinical Studies involve 50–300 patients with the target disease.
   - Phase 3 Clinical Studies involve 1000–5000 patients with the target disease.
4. The drug company seeking approval to sell the drug submits the results of testing to a regulatory agency.
5. The agency makes a decision: approve for sale, do not approve for sale, or request additional information before making a final decision.

Industry has argued for years that the approval process is too onerous and costly and that it causes unwarranted delay in the introduction of new, beneficial drugs (Box 15.2). Because a drug company obtains patent approval before documenting safety and efficacy, every extra month of delay in approval is one month less that it will be able to sell the drug under patent. Because of concerns about unwarranted delay, regulatory agencies in Canada, the U.S., and Europe have established fast-tracking procedures for promising drugs and have at times undertaken controversial changes to the approval processes to reduce processing times.

post-marketing surveillance
The systematic collection of data about users of a newly marketed drug to identify any potential side effects that occur too rarely to have been revealed by the pre-approval clinical trial research.

A series of recent drug warnings and recalls following severe adverse side effects associated with newly approved drugs (most famously Vioxx) created two effects. They have reinforced concerns raised by those who oppose relaxing approval requirements; and they have strengthened the case for more formalized and adequately funded **post-marketing surveillance**, a process that systematically collects data on users of newly marketed drugs to identify any potential side effects that occur too rarely to have been revealed by the pre-approval clinical trial research. As a consequence, regulatory agencies are enhancing their capacity to undertake post-marketing surveillance.

15.2.3 Competition in the Pharmaceutical Industry

Market competition can be intense in the pharmaceutical industry, but once again there are important differences when it is compared with competition in standard markets. Unlike a standard market with a set of undifferentiated producers selling to a set of undifferentiated

Nearly all industrialized countries regulate the prices of patented, brand-name drugs. In Canada, these prices are regulated by the Patented Medicines Prices Review Board (PMPRB). The PMPRB regulates only the prices of brand-name drugs while they are on patent; it does not regulate the prices of brand-name drugs after their patents have expired, or the prices of generic drugs. The PMPRB regulates the price at which the brand-name manufacturer sells a patented drug to wholesalers, hospitals, and pharmacies, using a form of direct price control designed to ensure that the prices of such medicines in Canada are not "excessive." To determine if a price is excessive, the PMPRB applies four basic principles as set out in the Patent Act:

1. The price of a new patented drug should be in the range of the cost of therapy for existing drugs sold in Canada used to treat the same disease.

2. The price of a new, breakthrough drug cannot exceed the median price for the same drug in seven other industrialized countries as specified in the Patent Act: France, Germany, Italy, Sweden, Switzerland, the U.K., and the U.S.

3. The rate of increase in the prices of existing patented drugs cannot exceed the Consumer Price Index.

4. The Canadian prices of patented medicines can never be the highest in the world.

Basing price regulation on international comparisons is also common among European Union countries (Mossialos et al. 2004). It can lead to strange circularity as country A regulates its prices in reference to countries B, C, and D; country B regulates its prices in reference to countries A, C, and D, and so on. Strategically, drug companies seek to introduce drugs and establish high initial drug prices in the few countries that do not practise direct price regulation, such as Germany, the U.K., and the U.S. Rather than regulate prices directly, Germany and the U.K. regulate the overall rate of return, or profitability, allowed by brand-name drug manufacturers in their countries. The U.S. has no form of price regulation.

Over time there has been a trend toward greater convergence in prices internationally. The U.S. consistently has the highest average prices for patented medicines, well above prices in other industrialized countries. Average Canadian prices for patented drugs have fluctuated relative to its set of reference countries, but they are typically above average; in 2007, they were second only to U.S. prices. Among industrialized countries, New Zealand, which uses a competitive tendering process to acquire drugs and which has deliberately eschewed price concessions made by many countries in an effort to attract drug industry investment, has the lowest prices.

Source: Canada's Research-Based Pharmaceutical Companies (Rx&D). 2007. Rx&D 2007 NOC Survey: Results and Key Messages. Downloaded from www.canadapharma.org, June 4, 2009.

(except in willingness to pay) buyers, the pharmaceutical market has at least six distinct types of actors on the supply and demand sides: brand-name manufacturers, generic manufacturers, pharmacies, insurers, doctors, and patients.[2] The overall pharmaceutical market is made up of sub-markets in which players compete on different terms and conditions: competition among the brand-name manufacturers, competition between brand-name and generic manufacturers, and competition among generic manufacturers.

Brand-Name Competition

Competition among brand-name manufacturers is about securing and extending monopoly power. A firm wants to be first to market a new type of drug and then wants to extend the market power gained from this first patent through the strategic use of secondary patents and alternative formulations of the original **breakthrough drug**.

Competition among brand-name manufacturers (and even, as we will see later, between brand-name manufacturers and generic manufacturers) is seldom about price. When a drug is under patent, the patentee has a monopoly and faces no direct competition. Prices are regulated in nearly all industrialized countries except the U.S. (See Box 15.3 regarding

breakthrough drug
The first drug to treat effectively a particular illness or which provides substantial improvement over existing drugs.

[2] Some might add to this list the pharmacists (as distinct from the pharmacies in which they work) and wholesale distributors, who often act as intermediaries between drug manufacturers and pharmacies. Both of these can be important to understanding market dynamics in certain situations.

Canadian regulations.) Competition occurs among a small number of firms internationally, so it tends to focus on highly strategic decisions relating to research and development, patent issues, product launches, and how aggressively to enter certain markets.

Being first into a market with a genuinely innovative, breakthrough drug confers enormous market advantage. The innovating company's primary objective is to exploit this initial advantage to extract as much profit as is possible for as long as possible. It does this by pursuing two complementary strategies: building brand loyalty and extending patent protection.

Building Brand Loyalty   Drug companies strive to build brand loyalty among doctors, historically the only professionals who could legally prescribe drugs and who, therefore, controlled access to the ultimate users, patients. Such brand loyalty can protect the innovator's market share from encroachment once a patent expires.

detailing
A promotional practice by drug companies in which a company drug representative visits a doctor to promote the company's drugs.

Consequently, brand-name companies have historically targeted most of their marketing and promotional efforts at physicians through a process known as **detailing**: a company drug representative visits a doctor to promote the company's drugs and provide free samples. In addition, drug companies lavish free "continuing education" sessions and other perks on physicians (held at golf resorts, on Caribbean cruises, and at similar venues), all paid for by the drug company.[3]

direct-to-consumer advertising
Advertising by drug companies targeted directly at consumers rather than physicians or pharmacies.

In recent years, due in part to changed regulations in the U.S., drug companies increasingly target consumers directly through print and television advertising. **Direct-to-consumer advertising** remains illegal in Canada and all other countries except New Zealand. In Canada, a series of cases are now before the courts arguing for the removal of the prohibition (Box 15.4).

me-too drug
A minor variant of an existing drug that offers little improvement over existing drugs.

Extending Patent Protection   The second strategy is the strategic use of patents to extend the effective length of patent protection. One such tactic is the introduction of low-cost, **me-too** versions that slightly alter the original formulation of a drug in a way that earns new patents. This can be done, for instance, by developing a slow-release version of the drug or by developing a capsule formulation rather than a tablet (Box 15.5).

This can inhibit entry after the original patent expires, both by other brand-name manufacturers who may introduce their own me-too versions of blockbuster drugs with annual sales worth billions of dollars and by generic drug makers who must demonstrate that their generic version does not violate any existing patents.

Hollis (2008) provides an interesting example of this practice. The cholesterol-lowering drug Lipitor is one of the best-selling drugs in history. Pfizer, which developed the drug, filed its first patent for the drug in 1990 and gained approval to sell the drug in Canada in 1997. The original patent will expire in 2010, at which point one might expect generic firms to enter the market with a generic version. But in the intervening years, Pfizer has filed 16 additional patents related to Lipitor, the latest of which was filed in 2002. This potentially extends Lipitor's patent protection until 2022. A generic firm could try to enter the market before then, but in doing so it would incur the legal costs to challenge the validity of these later patents. It would be a gamble with large potential costs if the generic firm lost the challenge.

authorized generic
A drug manufactured by a brand-name drug company (or under license from the brand-name company) that is identical to its brand-name version, is introduced at the time of patent expiry under a different name, and sells at a lower price to compete with generic drugs.

A variation on this strategy, targeted specifically at potential generic competition after a patent expires, is for the brand-name manufacturer to introduce an **authorized generic** just prior to the end of patent protection. An authorized generic is identical to the brand-name version. It is produced either by the brand-name company itself or under license from the brand-name company, but sold under a different name. The objective is to capture a portion of the generic market before generic manufacturers are able to introduce their generic versions.

[3] Such activities are coming under increasing scrutiny and regulation.

Few practices generate as much controversy as direct-to-consumer advertising (DTCA). DTCA can take three basic forms: (a) disease-focused advertising that does not promote a particular product; (b) advertising that mentions the name of a particular product to raise brand awareness but does not make any health claims; and (c) full product-specific advertising that contains health claims, and efficacy and safety information. A certain amount of the first two types has always taken place in print media, but DTCA has exploded in the U.S. since 1997 when the U.S. Food and Drug Administration first allowed DCTA via radio and television and relaxed its regulations regarding the information that must be presented in ads. Only one country besides the U.S.—New Zealand—allows full DTCA; Canada allows only the first two types, though up to 30 percent of English-speaking Canada is exposed to U.S.-based advertising through U.S. satellite and cable channels (Law et al. 2008).

Why all the controversy? Advertising is a way to disseminate information and, to the extent that it is targeted at fully rational people with well-defined preferences, economic theory suggests that it will improve welfare (Morgan et al. 2003). This is the basic argument made by advocates of DTCA: it provides information that raises awareness both of health conditions and effective treatments for those conditions, reducing unmet need and promoting more appropriate treatment. Opponents emphasize that many people are not fully rational, do not have well-formed preferences over treatments and illness, and are susceptible to undue influence by DTCA. Such advertising, they argue, will lead to inappropriate drug use that can decrease welfare. Many physicians fear getting caught between their judgment regarding a patient's need for a drug and a patient's advertising-induced request for a specific drug. Economic theory also predicts that when people are not fully rational, advertising will be biased, emphasizing benefits and downplaying risks. Furthermore, it will be concentrated on those products for which it offers the greatest potential profit, not necessarily the greatest improvement in welfare.

What does the evidence say? As predicted, such advertising is biased: one in four ads violates the FDA's basic guidelines, with minimization and omission of drug risks the most frequent violation (Gilbody et al. 2005; Mintzes

et al. 2009). Curiously, drug benefits are commonly presented at a 6th grade language level while risks are presented at a 9th grade level, allowing a larger proportion of the population to understand benefits than risks (Gellad and Lyles 2007).

Advertising is highly concentrated among a small number of drugs: those under patent and used for chronic conditions, and lifestyle drugs. Advertising appears to affect behaviour (Gilbody et al. 2005): it increases the number of new diagnoses of the disease for which a drug is advertised; and, of those treated, the proportion of patients who get the drug advertised. Some evidence, however, suggests that such effects may be only temporary (Law et al. 2008).

DTCA increases the requests for a specific drug and the likelihood of being prescribed the requested drug (Mintzes et al. 2002; Mintzes et al. 2003). A randomized trial using simulated patients uncovered a number of interesting effects (Kravitz et al. 2005). In the study, simulated patients (individuals trained to simulate suffering from differing degrees of depression and/or adjustment disorder) presented to physicians and made either no request, a general request, or a brand-specific request for a prescription medicine. For major depression, rates of antidepressant prescribing were 76 percent, 53 percent, and 31 percent respectively among those who made a general request, brand-specific request, and no request. For those presenting with adjustment disorder, the rates were 55 percent, 39 percent, and 10 percent respectively. Patient requests clearly had a large impact on prescribing. Such requests improved minimally acceptable treatment for major depression, though general requests were more effective than brand-name requests. For adjustment disorder, for which an anti-depressant is of questionable appropriateness, brand-specific requests had the largest impact.

So the effects of DTCA are complicated. It can have the beneficial effects, advocates claim; unfortunately, it also brings unwanted negative effects emphasized by its detractors, and the balance likely varies by condition and drug. As governments face increasing pressure to allow such advertising, a pivotal question is whether regulations can be designed to selectively achieve the beneficial effects while avoiding the negative, or whether, on balance, given our current abilities, an overall ban remains the wisest policy.

Such an authorized generic can deter entry by generics (Grootendorst 2006) and allow a brand-name manufacturer to price discriminate, charging a high price to those loyal to the brand-name version even after generics are available, while capturing part of the market among those who are price sensitive. Hollis (2008) notes that the market split between the brand-name version and generic versions of a drug does not depend on the number of generic versions in the market. So any market share captured by the brand-name company's

How innovative is the brand-name drug industry?

One indicator is the proportion of patents that are for a truly innovative, "breakthrough" drug—the first drug to treat effectively a particular illness or a drug that provides a substantial improvement over existing drug products—compared to the me-too drugs that are minor variants of established drugs and that often offer no substantial improvement over existing drug products. Of the 1147 new patented drugs reviewed by the Patented Medicine Prices Review Board between 1990 and 2003, just over 5 percent (68 drugs) met the criteria for being a breakthrough drug; the remaining drugs were me-too drugs (Morgan et al. 2005).

Why the preponderance of me-too drugs? The economics of drug development make them an attractive option for drug companies. Developing a truly innovative breakthrough drug is risky and expensive. Industry cost estimates vary widely—anywhere from $500 million to $1.8 billion—and are poorly documented; but no one disputes that development is costly, and that only a small portion of new discoveries will ever make it to market. In contrast, tweaking an existing molecule is a low-cost sure bet that can extend patent protection for years into the future or allow a company to enter an existing lucrative market. And me-too drugs are often priced substantially higher than the existing therapies.

authorized generic reduces the market share available to a generic manufacturer's version. In the specific case of Lipitor, Pfizer has decided to license the generic firm Ranbaxy to sell an authorized generic of Lipitor beginning in 2011 or 2012. This suggests that Pfizer perceives that some of its later patents on Lipitor could be vulnerable to a challenge by generic manufacturers after 2010.

Competition Among Generic Manufacturers

Competition among generic manufacturers is quite different from the competition among brand-name manufacturers. The major strategic decision for generic manufacturers is whether or not to enter the market for a brand-name drug once the patent expires, and in particular, whether to be the first generic into the market. The decision depends on a number of factors such as the size of the market, potential responses by the brand-name manufacturer (e.g., will it market an authorized generic?), what other generic manufacturers are expected to enter the market, and the costs of developing the bio-equivalent generic drug.

One critical factor is the regulatory requirement that a generic manufacturer notify the brand-name manufacturer when it intends to market a generic, providing the brand-name manufacturer the opportunity to legally challenge the generic company's claim that the generic company's drug does not infringe on any of the brand-name company's patents. The legal costs and financial risks associated with this are borne exclusively by the first generic to enter the market. Once the court rules that the first generic does not violate patents, the brand-name company is unlikely to challenge subsequent filings by other generic manufacturers.

The best strategy for a generic firm, therefore, is to sit on the sidelines while a competitor incurs the costs of fighting the legal battle, and then enter the market immediately upon a successful court ruling—to free-ride on the efforts of the first entrant. The effect of this strategic game, as one would predict, is too little entry by generics as they all wait on the sidelines.

Once multiple generics have entered a market, competition is primarily on price—but not the price consumers pay. For generic manufacturers, the key customer is neither doctors nor patients: it is pharmacies. Because stocking multiple versions of the same drug is costly, pharmacies generally carry one or two brands, at most. The generic companies compete aggressively to be one of those brands.

For a variety of reasons, and in part because of provincial price regulations, this competition has not resulted in lower listed generic drug prices that get passed on to the insurers and patients who pay for drugs (Box 15.6). Instead, competition has taken the form of secret rebates, discounts negotiated between the pharmacies and the generic manufacturers. Such rebates have typically been equal to about 40 percent of the list price—in some cases as high as 80 percent. Because insurers reimburse a pharmacy based on a drug's list price, this difference (or, as it is sometimes called, the **price spread**) between the list price and the much lower real cost to the pharmacy is captured by the pharmacy. A number of provinces have either reformed their regulations for generic drug pricing or are considering such reforms, in order to counteract these practices and to foster greater price competition that gets passed on to patients.

price spread
The difference between the listed price of a drug purchased by a pharmacy for resale and the effective price after the hidden manufacturer discounts are applied.

15.3 DESIGN OF PHARMACEUTICAL BENEFITS PROGRAMS

The predominant payers for drugs are drug insurers, and the predominant drug insurers in most industrialized countries are the public drug insurance programs. As large payers, drug insurers have two major goals: to purchase the lowest-cost version of available drugs that will effectively achieve the desired health effect, and to ensure that only necessary, effective medications are purchased.

Confronted with budget pressures in the face of rising prices, expanding types of drugs, and increasing indications for the use of existing drugs, drug insurers have devised numerous policies aimed at containing costs and improving the appropriateness of drug prescribing and drug consumption.

Drug expenditures are simply the product of the prices paid for drugs and the quantity of the drugs purchased (i.e., Expenditure $= P \times Q$). It is analytically useful, therefore, to distinguish policies aimed at affecting consumption (Q) from policies aimed at the price paid (P).

15.3.1 Targeting the Type and Quantity of Drugs Consumed

formulary
A list of all the drugs eligible for reimbursement by a drug insurance plan.

A drug **formulary**, which is simply a list of all the drugs eligible for reimbursement by a drug insurance plan,[4] is perhaps the most fundamental policy instrument used by a drug insurer to ensure that it purchases only effective, high-value medicines. Each of the provincial public drug plans in Canada has a drug formulary; each formulary includes only a subset of all the drugs approved for sale in Canada.

Because public drug plans account for about 45 percent of all prescription drug purchases in Canada (Canadian Institute for Health Information 2009), getting a drug listed on the public drug formularies is essential for gaining market share. The criteria for listing drugs are growing more stringent over time. Perhaps the most important new criterion is economic efficiency: to be listed on a provincial formulary and be eligible for public funding, in addition to demonstrating a drug's safety and efficacy, a drug company must now provide evidence that a drug is cost-effective, as demonstrated by a health technology assessment that calculates the cost of an additional unit of health gain (e.g. quality-adjusted life-year) achieved by a drug (see Chapter 4 and Box 15.7). In many cases, efficiency is judged relative to currently available drugs on the market (rather than relative to a placebo,

---

[4] Such a list of covered drugs is called a "positive formulary." Some countries, such as the U.K., list only the drugs that are not covered. Such a formulary is called a "negative formulary."

Canadians pay some of the highest prices in the world for generic drugs. The Patented Medicines Prices Review Board found that, on average, prices for generic drugs in 2005 were higher in Canada than in 11 comparator countries (PMPRB 2006).

The key policy question is why. At least part of the reason is regulatory policies adopted by provincial governments, which have either inhibited competition or have fostered competition that does not advance the broader public interest. Two provincial regulations are particularly cited.

Price Regulation in Ontario

Prior to 2006, Ontario set the maximum price it would pay for the first generic drug to enter a market at 70 percent of the brand-name price, and the maximum price of subsequent entrants at 90 percent of that (i.e., 63 percent of the brand-name price). Perhaps not surprisingly, generic drug prices soon converged on these price levels. What was meant as a price ceiling effectively also became a price floor. And because Ontario is the dominant market, Ontario prices established the trend across Canada.

"Most-Favoured Nation" Clauses

"Most-favoured nation" clauses, such as those in Quebec and Newfoundland, stipulate that the maximum a province will pay is the lowest price offered in any other province. This inhibits competition because a drug manufacturer hesitates to lower a price in one province if it automatically results in a lower price in other provinces.

The regulation creates a type of negative financial externality to lowering prices in specific markets where competition may be more intense.

In addition to reducing competition, these policies have also changed the locus of competition away from official, listed prices—the prices paid by drug plans and consumers—to discounts and secret rebates provided to pharmacies. Such competition has been intense, but does not benefit the broader public.

In 2006, Ontario made two important changes to its regulations: the price of a generic drug now cannot exceed 50 percent of the brand-name drug, and the province prohibits discounts and rebates to pharmacies. Although this has notably lowered the prices paid by the Ontario Drug Benefit program for generic drugs (and by Quebec, given its most-favoured nation clause), it has also raised the prices paid by private payers and other provinces, creating a two-tiered pricing structure in Canada. The regulation also does not advance price competition in the generic sector. To generate such competition, a number of provinces are experimenting with competitive tendering processes whereby the province invites generic manufacturers to submit bids to be the exclusive supplier of a generic drug to beneficiaries of the public plan (Competition Bureau of Canada 2007). In some cases, such efforts are even inducing competition between the off-patent brand-name drugs and generic drugs. It is too early to see what effects these and other initiatives will have, but the generic drug sector in Canada is undergoing fundamental change.

FIGURE B15.6

Average Ratio of Foreign Generic Drug Prices to Canadian Generic Drug Prices

Source: "Non-Patented Prescription Drug Prices Reporting, Canadian and Foreign Price Trends," Patented Medicine Prices Review Board, June 2006, ISSN: 1911-0014, Chart 2, Page 2, "Average Foreign-to-Canadian Price Ratio at Market Exchange Rates, Patented, Generic, and Non-Patented Branded Prescription Drug Market Segments, by Bilateral Comparator."

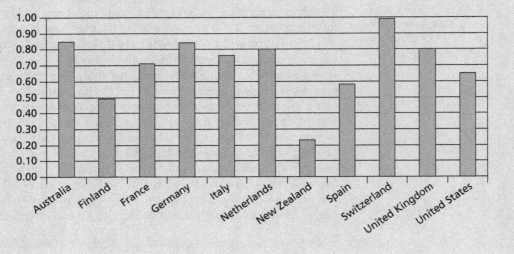

Governments increasingly demand evidence of value for money before agreeing to list a drug on the formulary of its public drug insurance program. Australia, which has a national pharmacare program, was the first country to require such evidence in the late 1990s. Governments in the U.K. and New Zealand also formally require such evidence.

In Canada, because drug insurance programs are provincially administered, each province has its own formulary. In 2003, the provinces launched a coordinated national approach to evaluating evidence of economic efficiency for drugs seeking listing on provincial drug formularies. The process, called the Common Drug Review, is administered by the Canadian Agency for Drugs and Technologies in Health (CADTH).

Drug companies submit to CADTH the required clinical and economic evaluation evidence on a drug's cost-effectiveness. This evidence is reviewed by a team of expert clinicians, pharmaco-epidemiologists, and economists who prepare a report that summarizes a drug's effectiveness, safety, and cost-effectiveness. This report is then forwarded to the Canadian Expert Drug Advisory Committee (which comprises both scientific experts and two members of the general public), and the committee makes a recommendation regarding formulary listing.

This recommendation is not binding on the provincial drug plans: each provincial drug plan makes its own decision about whether or not to list a drug, based on the recommendations of the Advisory Committee, the province's own health priorities, budget, and previous formulary decisions. The provinces follow the Committee's recommendations about 90 percent of the time.

as is the case for evidence of efficacy). Such regulations are aimed particularly at new me-too drugs, which often confer very little clinical benefit over existing medications but come with much higher price tags.

Coverage decisions regarding inclusion of drugs on the formulary are a relatively crude policy instrument that can be applied only to newly developed drugs. A greater source of inefficiency and actual harm is clinically inappropriate use of existing covered medicines. Insurers attempt to combat such inappropriate use through a variety of mechanisms, including the following:

academic detailing

A public policy in which government representatives visit doctors to provide unbiased evidence on the effectiveness of drugs and the appropriate conditions for their use (designed to counter the influence of drug industry drug detailers).

- conditional coverage decisions, which explicitly limit reimbursement for a drug to patients with identified clinical conditions
- **academic detailing**, which provides physicians with unbiased evidence on the effectiveness of drugs and the appropriate conditions for their use (meant to counter the influence of drug industry drug detailers)
- providing greater scope for pharmacists to be involved in the process of drug selection
- auditing and feedback to clinicians to improve their prescribing

Of particular concern is poly-pharmacy, a situation in which an individual simultaneously takes multiple medications (e.g., individuals with multiple chronic conditions). Sometimes these combinations can cause severe adverse side effects. Evidence suggests that up to 20 percent of emergency room visits are linked to adverse drug reactions; similarly, up to 20 percent of elderly patients admitted to hospital may suffer from an adverse drug reaction (Canadian Institute for Health Information 2007; Mannesse et al. 1997).

15.3.2 Policies that Attempt to Ensure that the Lowest-Cost Product is Purchased

Reimbursement at the Price of the Lowest-Cost Bio-Equivalent Drug In addition to price regulation, public insurers design regulations to ensure that, conditional on a drug being prescribed, the lowest-cost version of the drug is dispensed to the patient. The most common such regulation applies when one or more generic versions of a drug are available. The regulation stipulates that the insurance plan will reimburse the pharmacy only for the lowest-cost bio-equivalent version of the drug, regardless of what the pharmacy actually dispenses.[5] This provides the pharmacy strong incentive to dispense the cheapest version of the drug, saving insurers tens of millions of dollars annually.

This type of regulation exerts little downward pressure on prices themselves. A company knows that if it lowers price in an attempt to capture market share, other producers will match the price decrease. While such behaviour would be expected in a perfectly competitive market for which market forces would inexorably push price down, in oligopolistic markets such as these, such competitive pressures on price do not work automatically.

reference-based pricing
A policy of reimbursing only the price of the lowest-cost drug intended to treat the condition in question, including drugs that are not bio-equivalent.

Reference-Based Pricing   A broader version of this approach is called **reference-based pricing**. Many medical conditions have multiple types of effective drugs that differ substantially in cost. These drugs are not bio-equivalent; they are distinct types of drugs that work via different mechanisms. Reference-based pricing stipulates that the drug plan will only reimburse the price of the lowest-cost drug intended to treat the condition in question.

Hypertension provides a good example. Hypertension is one of the most common diseases in the industrialized world,[6] and uncomplicated hypertension can be treated effectively with a number of different medicines: thiazide diuretics, which have been available for decades, or ACE inhibitors, Beta-blockers, and calcium channel blockers (CCB), all newer, more expensive drugs.

A systematic review of the clinical evidence (Tran et al. 2007) concluded that treatment with thiazide diuretics reduced all cardiovascular and cerebrovascular events in subjects with uncomplicated essential hypertension as compared to placebo or no treatment; that thiazide diuretics were just as effective as ACE inhibitors, Beta-blockers, and calcium channel blockers in reducing total cardiovascular and cerebrovascular morbidity and mortality. The review also found that thiazide diuretics were actually better in reducing stroke events relative to ACE inhibitors, and in reducing heart failure events relative to calcium channel blockers.

The cost of treatment with thiazide diuretics, however, is typically an eighth to a third as much as the alternative newer drugs. The drugs are not bio-equivalent, and so would not be substitutable under generic substitution regulations; but because they are all used to treat hypertension, they are classified in the same therapeutic category for first-line treatment of uncomplicated hypertension, and under a reference-based pricing scheme, reimbursement would be limited to the lowest cost option: thiazide diuretics.

Reference-based pricing was pioneered in Germany. In Canada, the only province to use it is British Columbia, where reference-based pricing for ACE inhibitors alone prescribed to seniors has been estimated to save approximately $6 million per year (accounting for administrative costs), savings equal to 6 percent of all cardiovascular drug expenditures among seniors (Schneeweiss et al. 2004).

---

[5] Subject to documented exceptions, such as a physician's "no substitution" order or a clinical reason why the lowest-cost alternative is not appropriate for the patient in question (e.g., they cannot tolerate one of the inactive ingredients).

[6] In Canada in 2008, for instance, it accounted for more office-based physician visits than any other condition. Close to 60 percent of such visits result in a drug recommendation (new prescription or renewal).

Chapter Summary

Some of the main themes from this chapter included the following:

- The pharmaceutical sector is of growing importance in health care as the range of application of drugs expands and expenditures increase.
- The pharmaceutical industry is characterized by features that create substantial regulatory challenges.
- The industry is research intensive and the production of a drug is characterized by large fixed costs and low marginal costs. Fostering the socially optimal amount of innovation requires a public role both in basic research and in encouraging private research and development through patent protection.
- The monopoly power associated with such patent protection has led many countries to regulate the price of brand-name pharmaceuticals.
- Countries have also, with varying degrees of success, tried to foster generic drug competition once the patent for a brand-name drug patent has expired.
- In addition to regulating policy regarding the industry, governments have also pursued policies to purchase drugs through their public insurance programs at low prices and to improve the appropriateness with which drugs are used to achieve therapeutic goals.
  - Such policies include stricter formulary policies for deciding which drugs will be eligible for reimbursement, reimbursement policies that pay for only the lowest-cost drug available, and a variety of initiatives to improve prescribing patterns of physicians.

Key Terms

academic detailing, *395*
authorized generic, *390*
brand-name drug
 manufacturers, *382*
breakthrough drug, *389*
compulsory license, *384*
detailing, *390*

direct-to-consumer
 advertising, *390*
formulary, *393*
generic drug
 manufacturers, *382*
me-too drug, *390*
patent, *384*

post-marketing
 surveillance, *388*
price spread, *393*
public good, *383*
reference-based
 pricing, *396*

End-of-Chapter Questions

For each of the statements below, indicate whether the statement is true or false and explain why it is true or false.

1. From an economic perspective, patent protection is most important when fixed costs of production are low and marginal costs of production are high.
2. Compulsory licensing requires that a brand-name drug manufacturer allow a drug under patent to be produced by a generic drug manufacturer in return for royalties.
3. The above-average profits of drug companies are necessary given the high risks associated with drug development and the number of drugs that never even make it to market.
4. It is unlikely that the extension of patent protection in Canada has had a notable impact on the rate of drug innovation worldwide.
5. Drug safety regulation unambiguously improves social welfare.
6. Competitive tendering would shift the locus of generic competition from pharmacies to payers.
7. With all of the information provided by advertising these days, it is no longer necessary to regulate drug safety and efficacy.
8. "Most-favoured nation" regulations, which require that one's jurisdiction pay a price no higher than the lowest price among a defined set of other jurisdictions, is one of the most effective ways to foster lower prices through competition.

9. Authorized generic drugs reduce competition in the drug sector.

10. Differences in the demand for generic drugs could not be a factor contributing to the higher prices of generic drugs in Canada compared to the United States.

References

Canada's Research-Based Pharmaceutical Companies (Rx&D). 2007. *Rx&D 2007 NOC survey: Results and key messages.* Available from www.canadapharma.org, June 4, 2009.

Canadian Institute for Health Information. 2007. *Drug claims by seniors: An analysis focusing on potentially inappropriate use of medications, 2000–2006.* Ottawa: Canadian Institute for Health Information.

———. 2009. *Drug expenditure in Canada, 1985–2008.* Ottawa: Canadian Institute for Health Information.

Class, S. 2004. Health care in focus: The pharmaceutical industry is seeking a new prescription for success as it faces pricing pressures, challenges from generics, and consumer disenchantment. *Chemical & Engineering News* 82(49):18–29.

Competition Bureau of Canada. 2007. *Canadian generic drug sector study.* Ottawa: Government of Canada.

Demirbag, M., C.-K. Ng, and E. Tatoglu. 2007. Performance of mergers and acquisitions in the pharmaceutical industry: A comparative perspective. *Multinational Business Review* 15(2): 61.

Dewan, S. 2009. Despite odds, cities race to bet on biotech. *New York Times.* Accessed at http://www.nytimes.com/2009/06/11/us/11biotech.html?_r=1&emc=eta1.

Dickson, M., and J. P. Gagnon. 2004. The cost of new drug discovery and development. *Discovery Medicine* 4(22):172–79.

Fortune. 2009. Top industries: Most profitable. *Fortune Magazine* at http://money.cnn.com/magazines/fortune/fortune500/2009/performers/industries/profits/equity.html, accessed June 11, 2009.

Gellad, Z. F, and K. W. Lyles. 2007. Direct-to-consumer advertising of pharmaceuticals. *American Journal of Medicine* 120(6):475–80.

Gilbody S., P. Wilson, and I. Watt. 2005. Benefits and harms of direct to consumer advertising: A systematic review. *Qual Saf Health Care* 14(4):246–50.

Grootendorst, P. 2006. Effects of "authorized generics" on Canadian drug prices. Hamilton, ON: McMaster University, Social and Economic Dimensions of an Aging Population, Research Paper 201.

Hollis, A. 2008. Generic drug pricing and procurement: A policy for Alberta. Calgary, AB: University of Calgary, School of Policy Studies, Research Paper 2(1).

IMS Canada. 2009. http://www.imshealthcanada.com/web/home/0,3153,77303623_63872702,00.html, accessed June 3, 2009.

Kravitz, R. L., R. M. Epstein, M. D. Feldman, C. E. Fanz, R. Azari, M. S. Wilkes, L. Hinton, and P. Franks. 2005. Influence of patients' requests for direct-to-consumer advertised antidepressants: A randomized control trial. *Journal of the American Medical Association* 293(16):1995–2002.

Law, M., S. Majumdar, and S. Soumerai. 2008. Effect of illicit direct-to-consumer advertising on use of Etanercept, Mometasone, and Tegaserod in Canada: Controlled longitudinal study. *BMJ* 337:a1055: doi:10.1136/bmj.a1055.

Mannesse, C. K., F. Derkx, and M. de Ridder. 1997. Adverse drug reactions in elderly patients as a contributing factor for hospital admissions: A cross-sectional study. *BMJ* 315(7115):1057–58.

Mintzes, B., M. Barer, R. Kravitz, K. Bassett, J. Lexchin, A. Kazanjian, R. Evans, R. Pan, and S. Marion. 2003. How does direct-to-consumer advertising affect prescribing? A survey of primary care environments with and without legal DCTA. *CMAJ* 169(5):405–12.

Mintzes, B., M. Barer, R. Kravitz, A. Kazanjian, K. Bassett, J. Lexchin, R. Evans, and S. Marion. 2002. The influence of direct-to-consumer pharmaceutical advertising and patients' requests on prescribing decisions: Two-site cross-sectional survey. *BMJ* 324(7332):278–79.

Mintzes, B., S. Morgan, and J. Wright. 2009. Twelve years' experience with direct-to-consumer advertising of prescription drugs in Canada: A cautionary tale. *PLoS ONE* 4(5):e5699-doi:10.1371/journal.pone.0005699.

Morgan, S., K. Bassett, J. Wright, R. Evans, M. Barer, P. Caetano, and C. Black. 2005. "Breakthrough" drugs and growth in expenditure on prescription drugs in Canada. *BMJ* 331(7520):815–16.

Morgan, S., B. Mintzes, and M. Barer. 2003. The economics of direct-to-consumer advertising of prescription-only drugs: Prescribed to improve consumer welfare? *Journal of Health Services Research and Policy* 8(4):237–44.

Mossialos, E., M. Mrazek, and T. Walley (eds.). 2004. *Regulating pharmaceuticals in Europe: Striving for efficiency, equity and quality*. Berkshire, UK: Open University Press.

Patented Medicine Prices Review Board. 2006. *Non-patented prescription drug prices reporting: Canadian and foreign price trends*. Ottawa: Patented Prices Medicine Review Board.

Scherer, F. M. 2000. The pharmaceutical industry. In *Handbook of health economics*, A. J. Culyer, and J. P. Newhouse (eds.). Amsterdam: Elsevier Science B.V. 1297–1335.

Schneeweiss, S., C. Dormuth, P. Grootendorst, S. B. Soumerai, and M. McClure. 2004. Net health plan savings for reference pricing for angiotension converting enzyme inhibitors in elderly British Columbia residents. *Medical Care* 42(7):653–60.

Statistics Canada. 2008. Industrial research and development, 2004 to 2008. *Science Statistics* 32(5):Catalogue No 88-001-X.

Tran, L., C. Ho, H. Noorani, A. Hodgson, D. Coyle, K. Coyle, M. Myers, and J. Wright. 2007. *Thiazide diuretics as first-line treatment for hypertension: Meta-analysis and economic evaluation*. Ottawa: Canadian Agency for Drugs and Technology in Health Care, Technology Report 95.

Appendix **15**

Chapter 15: Pharmaceuticals

15.2.1　Patent Regulation

Intellectual property such as information and knowledge raises a number of difficult economic issues. The basic economic analysis of patent policy, the predominant instrument used to address these issues, can be illustrated as follows (overviews can be found in Kaufer (1989) and Lévêque and Ménière (2004)).

Let the initial situation be the equilibrium in a perfectly competitive industry with demand curve D and constant-returns-to-scale production with marginal cost c_0 (Figure 15A.1). Price is p_0, consumption is q_0, producer profits are zero and consumers' surplus is area A.

Suppose one firm in the industry invents and patents a production process that lowers production costs to c_1. The firm can reduce price to just below p_0, capture all sales, and earn profits just less than the rectangle B. Alternatively, it could license the technology to all other firms, obtain a royalty per unit sold equal to $(c_0 - c_1)$, and earn profit equal to the rectangle B.

Assume that while the patent is in effect the firm licenses the innovation to other firms. In the post-patent situation, while the patent is in effect, price and output are exactly as before, consumers' surplus is unchanged, but the firm obtains profit equal to area B. Social

FIGURE 15A.1

The Static Welfare Effects of Patent Protection

There are three periods to consider. Before the introduction of the new cost-lowering production technology, costs are c_0 and the market is in equilibrium with price p_0, consumption q_0, zero profits, and consumers' surplus equal to the triangle A. After a firm develops the new technology, patents it, and licenses it to its competitors, the competitors must pay a per-unit royalty to the firm equal to $(c_0 - c_1)$, the equilibrium remains (p_0, q_0), but now total welfare is A + B: A is consumers' surplus and B is profit for the firm. After the patent expires so that the technology is freely available, price falls to p_1, the new equilibrium is (p_1, q_1), and social welfare is A + B + C. Triangle C is the welfare loss (relative to the maximum potential gain) each period while the patent is active.

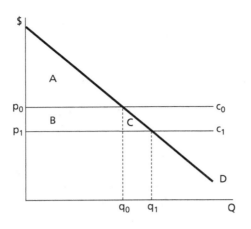

welfare has increased (from A to A + B), and the firm captures the increase in welfare. But this holds true only for the period of the patent. Once the patent expires, the technology can be used freely by all firms, driving price to p_1 and output to q_1, and increasing social welfare to A + B + C.

In the absence of patent protection, the firm would not have expended any resources creating innovation because it could never recoup its investment. Consequently, although the patent reduces the potential welfare gain from the innovation by the area C during the life of the patent (this is sometimes called the "static loss"), the patent increases dynamic efficiency by increasing the incentive for firms to invest in research and development (R&D). This gain takes two forms: first, it provides the financial incentive to increase innovation; and second, a patent requires that the patentee make public the details of the good or process it has patented. This ensures that the new information is in the public domain where it can be used by other inventors to create related processes or spur developments that build on the insights contained in the patent.

One of the fundamental questions this analysis raises is the optimal length of the patent. For any given innovation, the optimal patent length equals that amount of time which allows the innovator to recoup R&D costs. So the optimal patent length depends on the costs of development as well as on market conditions that determine the profit that can be earned each period. In reality, it is not possible to have different lengths of patents for different innovations. If the chosen patent length is too short, it will not provide incentive for inventions that are R&D intensive; if it is too long, it will reward low-cost inventions longer than is necessary to induce the innovation. The optimal patent length, therefore, balances these welfare effects.

This model depicts the effects of an idealized patent system. In recent years, patent policy has come under considerable criticism by analysts, many of whom argue that it may actually inhibit important types of innovation (Baker 2007; Boldrin and Levine 2008; Heller and Eisenberg 1998). The criticism has been particularly sharp with respect to pharmaceutical innovation. There are several lines of criticism (see Grootendorst (2009a; 2009b)).

The patent incentive derives from the ability of a patent-holder to charge a high price. This induces a number of effects that can reduce the desirability and effectiveness of patents:

- *Welfare Loss*: There is evidence that the welfare loss from high prices is substantial, particularly in the pharmaceutical sector, where it has been estimated to be up to 60 percent of sales revenue (Guell and Fischbaum 1997).
- *Counterfeiting*: High profit margins encourage counterfeiting, which is becoming a substantial problem for drugs even in developed country markets. This reduces the returns to patenting, making patents less effective.

- *Parallel Trade*: High but unequal prices across countries encourage purchase in low-price countries for resale in high-price countries, which wastes resources and also makes patents less effective.
- *Excessive Patent Litigation*: The current system generates substantial litigation over the validity of patents, patent infringement, and related issues. This both consumes valuable resources and increases uncertainty regarding the return to a patent.
- *Patent Extension and Gaming*: As noted in the text, the effective life of a patent can be extended by filing patents for minor variations on a basic drug, extending the period of market exclusivity.

In addition, patents are sometimes associated with other deleterious effects:

- *Patent Races*: When more than one firm is competing to develop a technology, the patent creates a "winner-take-all" system that can lead to over-investment in R&D. Across all the competing firms, total R&D exceeds the socially optimal amount. Such effects have been documented, for instance, in laboratory experiments investigating R&D decision-making (Davis et al. 1995; Isaac and Reynolds 1986).
- *The "Hold-Up" Problem*: Much research and innovation is cumulative: individuals build on earlier innovation. These later developers must obtain a license to use the earlier patented process or good upon which their work is based. If the subsequent discovery is highly profitable, the holder of the initial patent can hold out for a large share of the profits (since the later item cannot go to market without permission); i.e., the initial patent holder can "hold-up" the subsequent innovator. This can inhibit innovation.
- *High Administrative Costs*: Administering the current patent system is very expensive for the government, patentees, and patent holders (who must defend their patents).

If the current patent system is not achieving the desired social objectives, what are the alternatives? The options are generally of two types: public subsidy of research and development (sometimes called "push" methods); incentives for innovations that operate on different principles than the current patent system (sometimes called "pull" methods). Push mechanisms range from full public funding of biomedical research to public subsidy at various phases of the research process from basic science, through early clinical research and phase 3 clinical trials (Baker 2008; Jayadev and Stiglitz 2009). Some of the most widely discussed pull mechanisms make payments to an innovator:

- The payment could be from an auction of the rights to an innovation, which should elicit bids equal to the expected present value of the future stream of profits (e.g., Kremer (1998)).
- Payments to the innovator based on the health gain produced by a drug (e.g., Hollis and Pogge (2008)). The goal is to induce innovations with high value.
- Prizes of various types for desired innovations (e.g., drug to treat malaria).

The money for these payments would come from private or public sources depending on the proposal.

Each of these proposals has its own potential drawbacks, but widespread judgment that we can do better than the current patent policy is spurring much creative thinking about how to encourage socially valuable innovation while minimizing the associated social costs.

References

Baker, D. 2007. *Stagnation in the drug development process: Are patents the problem?* Washington, D.C.: Centre for Economic and Policy Research.

———. 2008. The benefits and savings from publicly funded clinical trials. *International Journal of Health Services* 38(4):731–50.

Boldrin, M., and D. Levine. 2008. *Against intellectual monopoly.* Cambridge: Cambridge University Press.

Davis, J. S., H. C. Quirmbach, and C. W. Swenson. 1995. Income tax subsidies and research and development spending in a competitive economy: An experimental study. *Journal of the American Taxation Association* 17(Supplement):1–26.

Grootendorst, P. 2009a. How should we support pharmaceutical innovation? *Expert Review of Pharmacoeconomics and Outcomes Research* 9(4):313–20.

———. 2009b. *Patents, public–private partnerships or prizes: How should we support pharamceutical innovation?* Hamilton, ON: McMaster University, Social and Economics Dimensions of an Aging Population, Research Paper 250.

Guell, R., and M. Fischbaum. 1997. Estimating allocative efficiency in the prescription drug ondustry. *Applied Economic Letters* 4(7):419–23.

Heller, M. A, R. S. Eisenberg. 1998. Can patents deter innovation? The anticommons in biomedical research. *Science* 280:698–701.

Hollis, A., and T. Pogge. 2008. *The health impact fund: Making new medicines accessible to all.* Incentives for Global Health, available at http://www.yale.edu/macmillan/igh/hif_book.pdf.

Isaac, R. M., and S. Reynolds. 1986. Innovation and property rights in information: An experimental approach to testing hypotheses about private R&D behaviour. In *Advances in the study of entrepreneurship, innovation and economic growth*, G. Libecap (ed.). Greenwich, CN: JAI Press. 1:129–56.

Jayadev, A., and J. Stiglitz. 2009. Two ideas to increase innovation and reduce pharmaceutical costs and prices. *Health Affairs* 28(1):w165–w168.

Kaufer, E. 1989. *The economics of the patent system.* London: Harwood Academic Publishers.

Kremer, M. 1998. Patent buy-outs: A mechanism for encouraging innovation. *Quarterly Journal of Economics* 113:1137–67.

Lévêque, F., and Y. Ménière. 2004. *The economics of patents and copyright.* Berkeley: The Berkeley Electronic Press.

Looking Ahead: Aging, Technology, and the Health Care System

In each of the last few chapters, we analyzed a specific component or function of a health care system. This closing chapter changes tack to examine two phenomena—population aging and technological innovation in health care—that are widely argued to threaten the sustainability of Canada's publicly financed health care system.

Both are characterized in many policy debates as unavoidable and beyond the control of policy; their consequences are portrayed as inescapable. Both phenomena are unavoidable: the population will unquestionably age over the coming decades and health technology will unquestionably advance. But their impacts on the health care system are not beyond the influence of policy. Analysis of each suggests that the problem is not aging and technology themselves but rather the way the system responds to them. Carefully crafted financing, funding, and delivery policies have the potential to address some of the most serious challenges they pose.

These issues are all the more pressing in light of the economic downturn of 2008–2009, the end of which is not completely in sight at the time of writing. The downturn ended one of the longest periods of virtually uninterrupted economic growth in recent history. During this period, governments across Canada transformed their fiscal predicaments from persistent deficits and accumulating debt to balanced budgets, budget surpluses, and falling debt accompanied by a reduced tax burden on Canadians. This was accomplished in the mid-1990s through difficult, painful retrenchment across many types of government services. But in more recent years, it was financed by a buoyant economy (Chapter 16 in Mankiw and Scarth (2010) provides a succinct analysis of these issues).

The health sector has enjoyed the dividends of this growth disproportionately. During the 10-year period from 1997 to 2007, for example, health care spending in Canada more than doubled from $78.8 billion to $161.6 billion; even in real terms, spending increased by more than 60 percent (Canadian Institute for Health Information 2008). Health spending grew faster than the economy and faster than just about any other component of government spending.

Current estimates put the total amount of government deficits in Canada for 2009 at approximately $100 billion dollars. However necessary such deficits may be in the short term given the economic crisis faced by society, they will have a long-lasting legacy. Reducing these deficits over the coming decade will strain federal and provincial government budgets. Governments will sustain a continuation of health care's decade-long rate of spending growth into the future.

Reference
Mankiw, G., and W. Scarth. 2010. *Macroeconomics*. New York: Worth Publishers.

Aging and Technology: Do They Threaten the Sustainability of the Health Care System?

Learning Objectives

After studying this chapter, you will understand

LO1 Economic challenges to the health care system from population aging and potential policy responses to address these challenges

LO2 Economic drivers of technological innovation in health care, challenges for the Canadian health care system posed by technological innovation, and potential policy responses to address these challenges

---

16.1 HEALTH CARE AND THE AGING OF THE CANADIAN POPULATION

The aging of the population is one of the most commented-upon social, demographic, and economic phenomena of recent years. The basic facts of it are quite simple: in 2011, the baby boom generation born in the years just following World War II begins to turn 65 (the unofficial age at which one becomes "elderly"). Table 16.1 presents Statistics Canada projections for the age-structure of the Canadian population from now until 2031, at which point the youngest of the baby boom generation will begin to retire. Over the next 20 years, the proportion of the population aged 50 or younger will fall, while that aged over 50 will grow; and growth will be highest among the oldest age groups.

The precise implications of this demographic trend for the economy and for society will depend on a variety of factors, including future immigration, fertility, labour-force participation, and savings. Yet it is clear that it will have particular impact on the health care sector. Two implications of the aging of the population are of particular interest for health care: fiscal implications and the impact on the patterns of disease in the population (with the associated demands for the delivery of care).

TABLE 16.1 **Projected Share of Population Age Group, Canada, 2006–2031**

The Canadian population of elderly will grow larger over the next 20 years as the baby boom generation turns 65. The percentage of the population aged 65–79 is projected to grow from 9.7 percent to 17.1 percent, and the percentage aged 80 or over is projected to grow from 3.6 percent to 6.3 percent.

Source: Adapted from Statistics Canada publication Population Projections for Canada, Provinces and Territories—2005 to 2031. Catalogue 91-520-XWE, table 10-1, 149, http://www.statcan.gc.ca/bsolc/olc-cel/olc-cel?catno=91-520-X&lang=eng.

	2006	2011	2016	2021	2026	2031
0–19	0.239	0.224	0.211	0.206	0.202	0.199
20–39	0.278	0.274	0.272	0.263	0.251	0.241
40–64	0.350	0.358	0.352	0.344	0.334	0.326
65–79	0.097	0.105	0.123	0.143	0.162	0.171
80+	0.036	0.039	0.041	0.044	0.051	0.063
	1.000	1.000	1.000	1.000	1.000	1.000

16.1.1 Fiscal Implications of an Aging Population

The elderly use substantially more health care than the young (Barer et al. 1995; Barer et al. 1987; Denton et al. 2002; Lubitz et al. 2001). The exact age–use relationship varies by service and sex; but overall use starts at a high point in infancy, falls in adolescence, and then rises through life until very old age, at which point use declines. Figure 16.1, which displays age–use curves for different types of physician services, illustrates these patterns.

Overall use of physician services for males follows the pattern described above, with 75-year-old males using nearly five times the value of services as a 25- to 30-year-old male. Life-cycle patterns differ for females, largely because of differences during the reproductive years when females use more services. Overall use starts high during infancy, declines until adolescence, and then begins rising until about age 30, after which it dips a bit before rising again from about age 40 until the mid-to-late 80s, at which point use again declines.

General practitioner services are distinctive in that they are the only type of service for which the old-age decline does not occur. Two specialties, obstetrics/gynecology and urology, exhibit the expected large difference between males and females at different points in the life cycle, and psychiatry exhibits a sharp peak in mid-life then declines into old age.

But amid these variations, the obvious implication of the overall age–use pattern is that the health care use of the aging baby boomers will place considerable demands on the health care system as they move through their elderly years. Such age-related increases in utilization, it is argued, threaten the sustainability of the health care system.

The Impact of Aging on Health Care Expenditures

Given the age–use curves noted above, the aging of the population will unquestionably increase demands on the health care system. The relevant policy question, however, is not the direction but the speed and magnitude of this effect. Both of these considerations suggest that the impact of aging itself will be manageable. The effects of aging are gradual and predictable; there will be no "shock" to the system in any particular year or short period of time. The effects are not destabilizing. Also, careful analysis demonstrates that the impact of the aging of the population alone on health care expenditures will be modest, in the neighbourhood of 1 percent per year (Denton et al. 2002; Denton and Spencer 1975; Evans et al. 2001).

To put this in perspective, annual growth in Canadian GDP per capita in recent decades has been 2–3 percent; if growth were to continue at this rate (or even somewhat more

FIGURE 16.1

Age–Utilization Profiles, Physician Services, by Sex, Ontario, 1995

Source: Denton, Gafni, and Spencer (2001).

Note: Five-year age categories are shown on the horizontal axis; dollar value of services per capita is on the vertical axis.

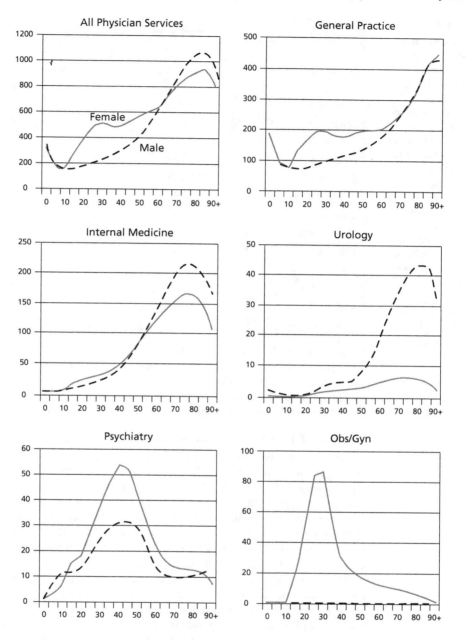

slowly), aging itself would not require any increase in the share of national income devoted to health care.

Hence, although the aging of the population will exert some upward pressure on costs, the pure effects of aging are manageable under plausible economic scenarios. Evidence for this can be found in the experience of other countries. A number of other countries' current population age profiles already correspond to the age profile that Canada will not experience for years (Table 16.2). The proportion of Canada's population over age 65 currently ranks 13 out of the 16 OECD countries included in the table. The proportion of the population over age 65 in countries such as Germany and Japan exceeds 20 percent, a

TABLE 16.2
Percentage of the Population by Age Group, Selected OECD Countries, 2007
Canada has a relatively young population relative to a number of other OECD countries. Its proportion of the population aged 65 or over ranks 13th out of 16 in this set of comparator OECD countries; its proportion of the population under age 14 ranks 8th out of 16.

Source: OECD (2009), OECD Health Data 2009: Statistics and Indicators for 30 countries, www.oecd.org/health/healthdata.

	Age 0–14	Age 15–64	Age ≥ 65
Japan	13.5	65.0	21.5
Germany	13.4	66.3	20.2
Sweden	16.9	65.7	17.4
Belgium	16.9	66.0	17.1
Austria	15.5	67.5	17.0
Finland	17.0	66.5	16.5
France	18.4	65.2	16.4
Switzerland	15.6	68.1	16.3
United Kingdom	17.6	66.4	16.0
Denmark	18.5	66.0	15.5
Netherlands	18.0	67.4	14.6
Norway	19.3	66.1	14.6
Canada	17.0	69.6	13.4
Australia	19.4	67.5	13.1
United States	20.2	67.3	12.6
New Zealand	21.0	66.5	12.5

proportion Canada is not expected to reach until around 2025. Yet these countries' health care systems meet their population's needs while devoting a similar share of GDP to health care as Canada currently does.

The aging of the population *per se*—which, given Canada's current population structure, is inevitable and unavoidable—will not bankrupt the health care system.

The Real Challenge: Increased Use by the Elderly

Although aging itself does not present insurmountable policy problems, the increasingly service-intensive way the health care system responds to the elderly does pose some difficult policy challenges. In recent decades, rates of health care use by the elderly have been growing faster than rates for the population as a whole: the age–use curves have been rising and rotating counter-clockwise, steepening the age–use gradient (Barer et al. 1995; Barer et al. 1987; Hertzman et al. 1990; Lubitz et al. 2001). The elderly, like all age groups, now use more services than in the past; but in addition, the difference in usage between the elderly and younger age groups has grown.

This increased relative rate of use by the elderly could be caused by three distinct factors: (1) the elderly today are sicker than they were previously; (2) technological progress has expanded the range of conditions for which the elderly are treated; and (3) the system responds differently to aging and its manifestations than it did previously, due to a combination of changed individual attitudes and provider responses (Barer et al. 1987).

The limited evidence available does not suggest that the elderly today are sicker than previously. Analyses of health survey data over the last 20–30 years do not reveal any obvious trends in health status. Technological innovation has expanded the set of treatments available, but it is not obvious that this expansion has been notably greater for conditions that affect the elderly than for those that affect the non-elderly. Detailed analyses of British Columbian data further document that much of the increased use of hospital services in recent decades occurred for conditions for which there has been no notable technological change (Evans et al. 2001; Hertzman et al. 1990). This leaves the rather non-specific explanation of "system response" as the most likely culprit.

Although "system response" is ill-defined and non-specific, this category has two valuable attributes with respect to the implications of aging for health system sustainability. First, although poorly understood at present, more detailed analysis—epidemiological, clinical, and economic—can identify some of the important underlying causes of the increased rates of utilization. The cause need not stay ill-defined and non-specific. Second, "system response" is amenable to policy intervention: with an understanding of the causes, policies can be developed to address them (an issue we will return to later).

Aging and Systems of Finance

The financial consequences of aging and the associated increase in health care use depend in part on how health care is financed. Tax-financed systems such as Canada's are likely more robust with regard to the effects of aging than are social insurance systems or private insurance systems. Both social insurance systems and private insurance systems tend to rely heavily on contributions from the subset of the population that is employed. In the case of social insurance, as we saw previously, contributions are generally mandatory among the employed and administered as a payroll contribution. In the case of private insurance, access to insurance is often linked to employment, as in the U.S.

dependency ratio
The ratio of the proportion of the population aged 65 or over to the proportion aged 15–64.

As the population ages, the working-age employed constitute a smaller and smaller share of the population: the proportion of the population contributing to support the system shrinks relative to the proportion that draws on the system. (This phenomenon is captured in part by the **dependency ratio**: the ratio of the proportion of the population aged 65 or over to the proportion aged 15–64.) The increased burden of financing that falls on employed contributors has important efficiency effects; for example, the need to raise contribution rates by both workers and firms affects labour supply and related outcomes. In fact, the costs of meeting the health care obligations to retired workers (who no longer contribute to finance health benefits) was an important factor in the bankruptcy of General Motors and Chrysler.[1]

In contrast, the revenue base for tax-financed systems is less vulnerable to such changes in labour force participation. Income taxes apply to both earned and unearned (investment) income. And consumption taxes do not depend in any way on the source of the income used to purchase goods and services. Even though out of the labour force, the retired still pay income and consumption taxes. Consequently, tax financing such as that used in Canada is more robust to the effects of aging than are social insurance or private insurance. For precisely this reason, France has been trying in recent years to shift from a social insurance system based on employment-related contributions to a stronger base of tax finance (Sandier et al. 2004).

Having said this, one component of Canada's system of finance will be particularly affected by the aging of the population: drugs. A number of provincial drug programs use age-based criteria to define eligibility for public financing, with the most generous coverage for those aged 65 or over (Canadian Institute for Health Information 2009). As an increasing proportion of the population reaches age 65, drug costs will shift from private budgets to public budgets.[2] Provinces may, therefore, seek to change from age-based coverage policies to income-based policies, much like the province of British Columbia's change in 2001 (Hanley et al. 2007).

---

[1] The magnitude of General Motors' health care obligations to current and retired employees once led an American health economist to quip that General Motors was really a health insurer that sold cars to raise revenue!

[2] A similar logic explains why some of the dire predictions of the effects of aging on public-sector finances based on U.S. analysis do not apply to Canada. The largest public health care program in the U.S. (Medicare) covers primarily those aged 65 or over, so population aging in the U.S. will cause a much larger share of health care expenditures to shift from the private to the public sector.

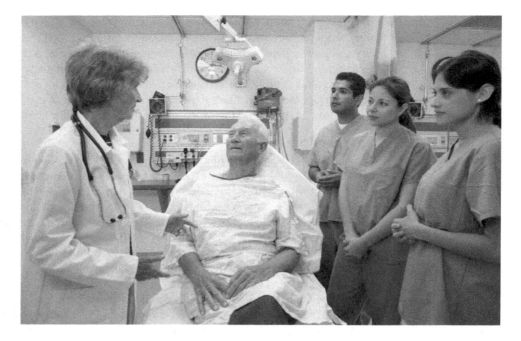

16.1.2 Aging and Chronic Disease

A second consequence of the aging population will be a change in the pattern of disease in Canada. Specifically, the prevalence of chronic conditions will increase substantially. Although there is no widely accepted definition of a chronic condition, common attributes are that it lasts for an extended period (e.g., over one year) and has no cure, though often the course of the disease can be altered and managed through effective treatment.

Many chronic conditions result at least in part from aging, as the effects of poor health-related behaviours accumulate and our bodies naturally wear out. Figure 16.2 presents the age-related prevalence for some common chronic diseases in Canada. There is a strong age-related gradient to the number of chronic conditions, and especially with respect to those who suffer from multiple chronic conditions.

Presently, our health care system is poorly equipped to meet the needs of those with chronic diseases. Our physician- and hospital-centric system is fundamentally designed to treat acute episodes: an illness or injury that requires a discrete, often intensive intervention using specialized knowledge and equipment. As a consequence, even though approximately 95 percent of those with a chronic condition have a regular physician, the quality of care they receive is below that which is possible. Analyses of diabetes care by the Health Council of Canada, for instance, found that fewer than half of Canadians with diabetes get all the recommended lab tests and procedures to monitor diabetes-related health problems, that many of them have poor control of risk factors for complications of diabetes, and that most do not have regular access to providers other than physicians (Health Council of Canada 2007b).

Yet, there is convincing evidence that approaches to care based on **chronic disease management** are effective. (Chronic disease management emphasizes helping individuals to maintain independence and health as much as possible through prevention, early detection, and management of chronic conditions.) This approach requires a team effort that involves multiple providers (physicians, nurses, nutritionists, pharmacists) in order to improve care and reduce health care costs by preventing serious complications (Dorland et al. 2007).

chronic disease management
An approach to health care that emphasizes helping individuals maintain independence and health through prevention, early detection, and management of chronic conditions.

FIGURE 16.2

Prevalence of Selected Chronic Conditions by Age, Canada, 2005

Source: Health Council of Canada, "Population Patterns of Chronic Health Conditions in Canada: A Data Supplement To: Why Health Care Renewal Matters: Learning from Canadians with Chronic Health Conditions," Figure 3, "Chronic Health Conditions are more common among Canadians and among women" from: http://www. healthcouncilcanada.ca/docs/rpts/2007/outcomes2/PopFig3.jpg.

Note: Selected chronic conditions include arthritis, cancer, chronic obstructive pulmonary disease, diabetes, heart disease, high blood pressure, and mood disorders.

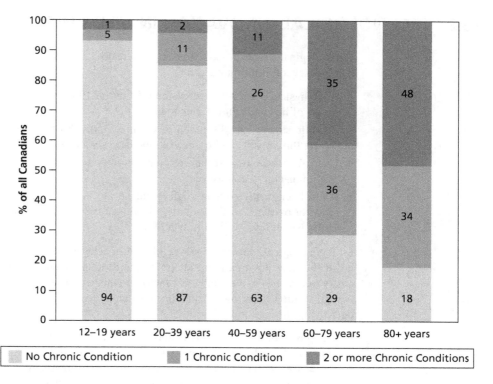

In economic terms, chronic disease management calls for producing a different type of output. This requires a different way of organizing the production of care, which in turn requires different payment modalities and different delivery arrangements.

Funding Fee-for-service is poorly suited for chronic disease management. Fee-for-service reimburses particular professionals for specific actions that can easily be described in a fee schedule. In contrast, managing a chronic condition requires many non-medical or non-clinical activities in coordinating care, providing information, and monitoring symptoms and behaviours. The specific tasks are varied and many do not need to be provided by a physician. Hence, capitation, salary, or programmatic funding—or blends of these—are better suited for such an approach to care.

Scope of Practice A team (or network) approach to managing chronic conditions may provide scope for a greater role for non-physician professionals, and for reducing barriers to substituting among different professionals as is consistent with a high quality of care. This may call for reviewing scope-of-practice regulations that limit the actions and services that can be performed by different professionals.

Organization of Practices The traditional solo general practitioner will become even more anachronistic as care demands call for practices that make a fuller range of skills easily available and that integrate multiple providers. Many of the directions currently being pursued through primary care reform are consistent with the emerging needs of those with chronic conditions. A model based on primary care may be particularly important given the rising proportion of elderly with multiple chronic conditions (disease-based approaches to care are poorly suited for those with multiple health problems).

16.2 TECHNOLOGICAL INNOVATION IN MEDICINE

Technological advances have transformed health care since World War II. This transformation has several important aspects:

- It is physical—a health professional from the 1940s would hardly recognize many elements of hospitals and clinics today.
- It is life-saving—as discussed in Chapter 6, much of the extension of life expectancy during this period can be traced to medical advances.
- It is life-enhancing—technology has improved quality of life among many who suffer from non-fatal conditions.
- It has been costly—technological innovation in health care is estimated to be responsible for over half of the growth in health care expenditures since the 1940s (Newhouse 1992; Newhouse 1993; Smith et al. 2009).

Technological innovation is not inherently cost-increasing—advances such as vaccines avoid the need for treatment altogether, and others substitute lower-cost approaches for costly treatment—but a number of factors in the health sector have historically biased technological innovation toward quality-enhancing, cost-increasing advances rather than cost-decreasing innovation:

- The spread of insurance and technological innovation are mutually reinforcing: the development of costly new technologies that offer effective treatment increases the demand for insurance; the spread of insurance fuels investments in health-related R&D because insurance increases people's ability to pay for such treatments (Weisbrod 1991).
- Insurance insulates consumers from the costs of care and allows physicians to provide expensive care with the knowledge that the individual does not have to bear the cost.
- Insurers for many years funded care through retrospective, cost-based reimbursement schemes that automatically paid for any increased costs associated with innovation. This led to a bias toward quality-enhancing rather than cost-reducing innovation.
- Greater use of prospective funding, particularly of hospital care, has moderated some of these forces and encouraged the development of lower-cost approaches to care (e.g., a shift from in-patient to out-patient or day surgeries); but this has had only a limited effect on expenditures for these reasons:
  - When an innovation reduces either the cost per treatment or the non-monetary costs of care (such as with day surgery), changes in the threshold for recommending care can cause utilization to increase, resulting in an increase in costs overall.
  - Insurance does not cover a fixed set of technologies; rather, it offers a more open-ended contract that expands the set of covered services in line with technological innovation. Innovation has dramatically expanded the set of conditions that can be treated effectively.
- Improvements in health status and longevity due to medical innovation can raise total costs; annual costs may fall, but we incur those costs over more years.

The effect of all these factors is that, on balance, technological innovation has increased total health care costs (and, it is important to note, the health benefits achieved).

Technological development is driven largely by the expected returns on investments in research and development. The policies of a small country such as Canada with respect to insurance, funding, and R&D have little or no effect on the rate or nature of technological innovation in health care. Rather, the rate and nature of innovation are determined by policies set in large markets such as the U.S., which is both the largest producer and the largest consumer of medical technology internationally. Consequently, Canada must take technological innovation as exogenously determined, beyond its control.

Further, the forces of aging and technological innovation will interact: the elderly will comprise the largest market for health care goods and services, so technological innovation will increasingly be targeted at the types of conditions they experience. This fact does not change the above analysis in any fundamental way, but it suggests that the overall pressures will exceed the independent effects of each.

Even if Canadian policy cannot influence the pace and direction of technological innovation in health care, it can influence the nature of the new technologies adopted by the health care system and the extent of their diffusion within the system. Perhaps most importantly, the rates and contexts of the use of technology are not beyond the control of health policy. The primary instruments available to health policy-makers for exerting such control are funding and regulatory policies.

Capital Budgeting

Canada has traditionally exercised control over the adoption and diffusion of expensive, big-ticket items through the control of capital budgets. Capital investment for health care institutions has always been funded separately from annual operating expenditures. Historically, hospitals have been required to apply to the health ministry for approval and funding to obtain expensive equipment such as CAT scanners and MRI machines. This control has weakened somewhat in recent years as the role of hospital foundations and community fundraising in financing such items has expanded; but the ministry still exercises considerable control over the diffusion of such items through the combination of capital approval, operating budgets (fundraising only finances the purchase of the equipment; institutions still require operating funds to run them), and other planning regulations.

However effective such policies are, highly visible, big-ticket items represent only a small part of the challenge. More important and more challenging are the adoption and diffusion of hundreds of less costly (on a per-unit basis) devices, tests, goods, and services throughout the system. For this, governments must rely on three basic sets of policies.

Decisions About Coverage

With the exception of drugs, few services have historically been explicitly evaluated and approved for use through a formal process. New techniques (e.g., laparoscopic surgery), new goods (e.g., contrast die media, lenses for cataract surgery), and new devices (e.g., artificial hips) are simply adopted through hundreds of local decisions by medical staff, clinic managers, and hospital administrators. Innovation is forcing this to change in two ways:

1. A broader array of health care goods and services are subject to formal evaluation and decisions regarding coverage.
2. Such evaluations increasingly demand evidence of economic efficiency using the methods described in Chapter 4.

Even if fully developed and effectively implemented, such efforts are at best a partial solution, for two principal reasons:

1. Most goods and services are effective for some conditions and, therefore, deserve a place in the set of goods and services offered through the system. The challenge is to limit their use to the contexts for which they are demonstrably effective. This requires

a policy of conditional coverage: the service will only be covered under certain conditions. Such rules are notably complex to develop, administer, and enforce.

2. Cost-effectiveness analysis and related evaluation technologies are not designed for expenditure control. They are designed to identify goods and services that are efficient, that offer good value for money. If a costly new intervention produces commensurate health benefits, it is efficient to adopt it. It is critical to distinguish efficiency—which considers costs and benefits—from expenditure control.

Prospective Funding

As emphasized in Chapter 12, funding methods exert substantial influence on the way that care is produced and delivered. Retrospective funding policies effectively insulate providers from the cost consequences of their decisions. Prospective funding policies force providers to consider the opportunity costs of how services are produced and how they are used. It encourages the adoption of cost-lowering technologies. Such funding leaves the decisions in the hands of clinicians, but it tries to better align incentives for the use of available technologies.

Practice Guidelines and Related Mechanisms

Financial incentives are only one instrument for changing behaviour. One alternative approach is to provide greater direction regarding the use of certain services through the development of practice guidelines for clinicians. A practice guideline is a short statement of what the best current evidence indicates regarding the effectiveness of a good or service and the clinical indications for its use. Practice guidelines are widely used in cancer care, for instance, where continual innovation with new (often very expensive) chemotherapy agents, and new combinations of old and new agents, demand a systematic approach to treatment at different stages of the progression of cancer.

Although many policy discussions argue that the only solution to cost pressures exerted by technological innovation is to increase reliance on private finance, such an approach does not address the underlying problem. It simply shifts the cost from the public to the private purse, leaving the underlying problem unaddressed, while reducing the efficiency and equity of the health care system. An effective policy approach must address the underlying problem. No single policy—incentives, regulations, punishments—provides the answer. Only a systematic, coordinated approach using a number of policy instruments can be effective.

16.3 PROJECTIONS AND POLICY

Figure 16.3 compares two trends, both beginning in 1969. The first is a projection of the expected number of acute hospital days per thousand residents in British Columbia based on hospitalization rates in British Columbia in 1969. It shows a gradual increase due to the aging of the population.[3] The second trend is the actual number of acute hospital days per thousand residents in B.C.—hospitalization rates have steadily decreased over time. The divergence between the projection at the start of the period and actual experience is remarkable.

Two important things happened to cause the divergence between the projected and actual experience. First, there was general agreement in 1969 that rates of hospitalization in B.C. (and in Canada more generally) were too high. At the time, these rates were among

---

[3] This serves as a reminder that population aging is not a new phenomenon. It has been happening in Canada since fertility rates began dropping in the mid-1960s.

FIGURE 16.3
Projected and Actual Hospital Utilization, British Columbia
Based on age-specific rates of in-patient hospitalization in 1969, the aging of the population would have been predicted to increase the overall rate of hospital utilization into the future. But both a conscious policy decision to reduce hospitalization rates and the development of new technologies such as day surgery caused the overall rate to decline between 1970 and 2000.

Source: Evans et al. (2001), Figure 2, p. 168.

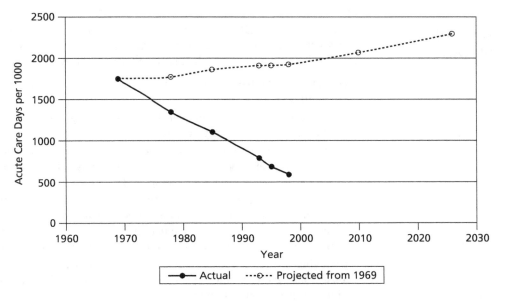

the highest internationally, and there was a conscious policy decision to reduce the rates. Second—and unanticipated—was the development of technologies that allowed the care of many conditions to be shifted out of hospital. It serves as a useful reminder of three things about projections:

1. Pushed far enough, almost any projection creates hair-raising concerns.
2. The future is very difficult to predict.
3. If policy is effective, a projection will certainly be wrong.

This last point is particularly important. One critical purpose of a projection is to mobilize a response to ensure that the imagined scenario does not come to pass: the projection prompts action. It is vital, however, that it prompt the right action.

The aging of the population and the continued development of medical technology pose serious challenges for the health care sector and call for difficult policy action in the coming years. The above analysis suggests that the crucial policy reforms necessary to address these challenges fall in the domains of funding and the organization of the delivery of care. Funding reforms can create incentives that support both the reorganization of care to better meet changing needs and the adoption of innovations that enhance system performance. Reforms to the organization of care include new regulations and the introduction of non-financial instruments to support the delivery of effective, high-quality care that can reduce the complications associated with chronic conditions.

Aging and technology will put pressure on public health care budgets, creating two new tasks related to financing. The first is to develop more comprehensive, more effective processes and mechanisms for deciding which of the new health care services will be integrated into public coverage and how they will be integrated into the system. The second is to manage the interaction of the public and private sectors as an increasing number of services are not publicly covered, either because they do not address a health concern or they are not judged to represent good value for money.

Chapter Summary

This chapter has briefly examined two policy challenges that the Canadian health care system will confront in the coming years: population aging and technical innovation in health care. Some of the important points raised by the analysis include the following:

- The aging of the baby boom generation will exert an upward pressure on health care expenditures.
  - The impact of aging itself will be predictable, gradual, and under most scenarios, manageable within the parameters of the current system.
  - Of greater concern is the trend for services provided to the elderly to grow over time, both absolutely and relative to the non-elderly. This trend is quantitatively more important than the impact of aging itself.
  - A publicly financed system that raises revenue from a broad base of individuals and organizations, and that uses a mix of tax instruments, is better able to accommodate the demands of an aging population than are social insurance systems or private insurance systems where contributions are more strongly related to employment.
- The aging of the population will also change the pattern of disease in the population, substantially increasing the prevalence of chronic conditions (and especially individuals with multiple chronic conditions).
  - Responding effectively to the increased prevalence of chronic conditions will call for changes in the funding and delivery of care.
- Technical innovation in health care has historically tended to be quality-enhancing and cost-increasing.
- The rate and direction of technical innovation in health care is beyond the control of Canadian policy; it is driven by policies set in large markets such as the U.S.
- Canada must develop a set of financing, funding, and regulatory policies that shape the types of technologies that are integrated into the health care system as well as the rates and settings in which they are used.
- The cost pressures posed by the aging of the population and the continued development of medical technology, combined with the compromised fiscal situation of the federal and provincial governments, will continue to fuel debate about the roles of public and private finance in Canada.

Key Terms

chronic disease
    management, *410*

dependency ratio, *409*

End-of-Chapter Questions

For each of the statements below, indicate whether the statement is true or false and explain why it is true or false.

1. Prospective reimbursement systems slow the rate of technological innovation.
2. The best economic projections always come true.
3. The aging of the population inexorably increases public expenditures.
4. Technological innovation in health care is by its very nature cost-increasing.
5. Because social insurance systems raise revenue from workers rather than the general population, they are better suited to financing health care for an aged population with a large proportion of retired individuals.

References

Barer, M., R. G. Evans, and C. Hertzman. 1995. Avalanche or glacier?: Health care and the demographic rhetoric. *Canadian Journal on Aging* 14(2):193–224.

Barer, M., R. Evans, C. Hertzman, and J. Lomas. 1987. Aging and health care utilization: New evidence on old fallacies. *Social Science and Medicine* 24(10):851–62.

Canadian Institute for Health Information. 2008. *National health expenditure trends, 1975–2008*. Ottawa: Canadian Institute for Health Information.

———. 2009. *Drug expenditure in Canada, 1985–2008*. Ottawa: Canadian Institute for Health Information.

Denton, F., A. Gafni, and B. Spencer. 2001. Exploring the effects of population change on the costs of physician services. Hamilton, ON: McMaster University Research Institute for Quantitative Studies in Economics (QSEP), Research Report 358.

———. 2002. Exploring the effects of population change on the costs of physician services. *Journal of Health Economics* 21(5):781–803.

Denton, F., and B. G. Spencer. 1975. Health care costs when the population changes. *Canadian Journal of Economics* 7(1):34–48.

Dorland, J., and M. McColl (eds.) 2007. *Emerging approaches to chronic disease management in primary health care*. Montreal/Kingston: McGill-Queens University Press and School of Policy Studies, Queen's University.

Evans, R. G., K. McGrail, S. Morgan, M. Barer, and C. Hertzman. 2001. Apocalypse no: Population aging and the future of health care systems. *Canadian Journal on Aging* 20(Supplement):160–91.

Hanley, G., S. Morgan, J. Hurley, and E. Van Doorslaer. 2007. Distributional consequences of the transition from age-based to income-based prescription drug coverage in British Columbia, Canada. *Health Economics* 17(12):1379–92.

Health Council of Canada. 2007a. *Population patterns of chronic health conditions in Canada: A data supplement to why health care renewal matters: Learning from Canadians with chronic health conditions*. Toronto: Health Council of Canada.

———. 2007b. *Why health renewal matters: Lessons from diabetes*. Toronto: Health Council of Canada.

Hertzman, C., I. Pulcins, M. Barer, R. Evans, G. Anderson, and J. Lomas. 1990. Flat on your back or back to your flat? Sources of increased hospital services utilization among the elderly in British Columbia. *Social Science and Medicine* 30(7):819–28.

Lubitz, J., L. G. Greenberg, Y. Gorina, L. Wartzman, and D. Gibson. 2001. Three decades of health care use by the elderly, 1965–1998. *Health Affairs* 20(2):19–32.

Newhouse, J. P. 1992. Medical care costs: How much welfare loss? *Journal of Economic Perspectives* 6(3):3–21.

———. 1993. An iconoclastic view of cost containment. *Health Affairs* 12(Supplement):152–71.

OECD. 2009. *OECD health data 2009.* Paris: OECD.

Sandier, S., V. Paris, and D. Polton. 2004. *Health care systems in transition: France*. Copenhagen: WHO Regional Office or Europe on behalf of the European Observatory on Health Systems and Policies.

Smith, S., J. Newhouse, and M. Freeland. 2009. Income, insurance and technology: Why does health spending outpace economic growth? *Health Affairs* 28(5):1276–84.

Statistics Canada. 2005. *Population projections for Canada, provinces and territories*. Ottawa: Government of Canada, Statistics Canada Catalogue No. 91-520-XIE.

Weisbrod, B. A. 1991. The health care quadrilemma: An essay on technological change, insurance, quality of care, and cost containment. *Journal of Economic Literature* 29(2):523–52.

Glossary

Ability-to-pay principle: The amount individuals contribute should depend on their ability to pay, not their need or their ability to benefit from the goods financed.

Academic detailing: A public policy in which government representatives visit doctors to provide unbiased evidence on the effectiveness of drugs and the appropriate conditions for their use (designed to counter the influence of drug industry drug detailers).

Access motive: The benefit of insurance that enables an individual to obtain extremely high-cost care to which they would otherwise not have access.

Actuarially fair premium: An insurance premium that is equal to the expected value of the insured loss.

Adverse risk selection: When an insurance pool systematically attracts individuals of above-average risk status within a risk class.

Allocative Efficiency: Using limited resources to produce and distribute goods and services in accord with the value individuals place on those goods and services.

Appropriateness: A health research approach that investigates the appropriateness of health care utilization by examining the clinical records of those who have received care, and assessing that care against established criteria for the appropriate delivery of a service.

Asymmetry of information: A situation in which participants on one side of a market (e.g., sellers) have more information relevant to a transaction than do those on the other side (e.g., purchasers). Depending on the situation, either sellers or purchasers may have an informational advantage.

Authorized generic: A drug manufactured by a brand-name drug company (or under license from the brand-name company) that is identical to its brand-name version, is introduced at the time of patent expiry under a different name, and sells at a lower price to compete with generic drugs.

Backward-bending labour supply curve: A labour supply curve that, at high wages, bends backward, changing from a positive to a negative slope as the income effect associated with a wage increase dominates the substitution effect.

Behavioural cost function: The relationship between hospital costs and hospital characteristics such as size, teaching status, ownership status, and location.

Benefit principle: The amount individuals contribute should be proportional to the benefit they receive from the goods financed.

Blended funding: A provider's funding comprises a mixture of payment mechanisms.

Body Mass Index: A person's weight in kilograms divided by the square of their height in metres (BMI = kg/m^2).

Bonus payment: A special payment received for meeting specified performance targets.

Brand-name drug manufacturers: Pharmaceutical companies that undertake research to develop new drugs.

Breakthrough drug: The first drug to treat effectively a particular illness or which provides substantial improvement over existing drugs.

Capacity constraint approach: Supply-side model to control moral hazard and expenditure growth; relies primarily on aggregate, system-level capacity constraints rather than micro-management of individual decisions of clinicians.

Capitation: A method of paying physicians in which a physician (or the practice of which the physician is a part) receives a specified amount of money each period (month or year) for each person enrolled in the physician's practice, in return for a commitment by the physician to meet defined health care needs of the individuals.

Caring externality: A health-related externality that arises when one person cares about the health status of others and, consequently, their consumption of needed health care.

Case-based funding: Providers receive a fixed, specified payment for each case they treat.

Case-mix adjustment: The process of adjusting the raw number of cases treated by a provider to account for the severity of the conditions of those treated (e.g., heart surgery versus uncomplicated pneumonia).

Causal relationship: A situation in which one variable determines (in whole or in part) the value of a second variable. Causation is one possible source of a correlation between two variables.

Cherry picking: See **favourable risk selection**.

Chronic disease management: An approach to health care that emphasizes helping individuals maintain independence and health through prevention, early detection, and management of chronic conditions.

Co-insurance: A form of **cost-sharing** that requires an individual to pay a specified proportion of the cost of any health care services received.

Commitment devices: Strategies that people with time-inconsistent preferences develop to help ensure that they honour commitments they make to themselves regarding aspects of their behaviour, such as quitting smoking or losing weight.

Community-rated premium: Insurance premiums for which there is no risk adjustment; the premium is the same for everyone.

Complementary good: Two goods that are normally consumed together, so that an increase in the price of one causes a decrease in the demand for the other, and a decrease in the price of one causes an increase in the demand for the other (e.g., hamburgers and hamburger buns). See also **substitute good.**

Complementary private finance: Private financing (often through insurance) of services not covered by the public insurance plan.

Compulsory license: A license that grants a generic manufacturer permission to manufacture and sell a patented drug product before the patent has expired and that requires that the generic manufacturer pay a royalty to the patent holder.

Consumer sovereignty: The assumption that consumers are the best judges of their own welfare, and that their decisions should determine the amount and distribution of goods in society.

Consumers' surplus: The difference between the maximum amount a person is willing to pay for a good minus the amount they actually have to pay. For a well-functioning market in equilibrium, the area above the equilibrium price line and below the demand curve.

Consumption demand for health: An individual's demand for health capital that derives from the non-monetary, direct utility benefits associated with improved health.

Contingent valuation: A hypothetical scenario in which individuals assess a health risk and their willingness to pay to mitigate that risk.

Co-payment: A form of **cost-sharing** that requires an individual to pay a specified, fixed dollar amount of the cost of a health care service received.

Correlation: A measure of the strength of the (linear) relationship between two variables. The correlation can be positive when two variables increase or decrease together (e.g., rain and use of umbrellas) or negative when two variables move in opposite directions (e.g., amount of sunshine and use of umbrellas).

Cost-benefit analysis: An analysis which values health outcomes in monetary terms.

Cost-effectiveness analysis: An analysis which measures consequences in the natural units in which they occur (e.g., life-years gained, cases prevented); it does not assign a social value to the consequences as part of the evaluation. See also **cost-utility analysis** and **cost-benefit analysis.**

Cost-effectiveness efficiency: Producing a good using the least-cost method of production from among all technically efficient methods.

Cost-sharing: An insurance provision that requires an individual to pay part of the cost of an insured health care service. Also called a **user charge.**

Cost-utility analysis: An analysis which values health outcomes in terms of quality-adjusted life-years.

Counterfactual problem: The difficulty in knowing what the outcome would have been had an alternative course of action (the counterfactual) been pursued.

Coverage limit: Some insurance contracts specify that once the dollar amount of benefits paid to an individual by the insurer reaches a certain amount, no further coverage is provided.

Cream-skimming: Favourable risk selection; when an insurance pool systematically attracts individuals of below-average risk status within a risk class.

Cross-sectional design: Research studies that use variation across units (people, jurisdictions, etc.) at a single point in time to investigate the phenomenon under study.

Deductible: A form of **cost-sharing** that requires an individual to pay the full cost of any services received until the individual's spending has reached a specified limit (the deductible).

Demand curve: A graph depicting the relationship between the price of a good and the quantity of the good demanded, holding all other determinants of demand (e.g., income, price of other goods) constant.

Dependency ratio: The ratio of the proportion of the population aged 65 or over to the proportion aged 15–64.

Depreciation rate of health capital: The amount by which health diminishes each period if an individual does not invest in maintaining health.

Derived demand for health care: The demand for health care derives from the demand for health.

Detailing: A promotional practice by drug companies in which a company drug-representative visits a doctor to promote the company's drugs.

Diminishing marginal returns: Successive incremental additions of one production input, holding the amounts of all other inputs constant, are associated with successively smaller increases in total output.

Diminishing marginal utility: Consuming more of a good increases utility, but at a diminishing rate.

Direct-to-consumer advertising: Advertising by drug companies targeted directly at consumers rather than physicians or pharmacies.

Discounting: The process of converting a multi-year stream of costs or consequences into its present-discounted value.

Discount rate: The rate of discount applied to convert a multi-year stream of costs or benefits to its present value.

Distributional equity: The distribution of a good (e.g., income, health care) or a burden (e.g., tax payments) among members of society is judged to be fair.

Distributional weights: A set of weights used when adding up the costs and consequences of a program, policy, or service. The weights differ depending on the characteristics of the person or organization to whom the costs and benefits accrue.

Economic evaluation: A systematic, comparative analysis of two (or more) courses of action in terms of both their costs and their consequences.

Economies of scale: A situation in which the average cost of production falls as output rises over most of the relevant range of production in the industry.

Efficiency: Getting as much as is possible from scarce resources. Economists distinguish among three types of efficiency: technical efficiency, cost-effectiveness efficiency, and allocative efficiency.

Elastic demand: An **elasticity** of greater than 1.0, indicating that one variable is relatively responsive to changes in another variable of interest. See also **unitary elasticity** and **inelastic demand**.

Elasticity: A measure of the responsiveness of one variable to a change in the value of another variable; defined as the ratio of the percentage change in the former to the percentage change in the latter. See also **own-price elasticity of demand, income-elasticity of demand,** and **price-elasticity of supply.**

Enrolled population: A group of individuals who have registered to obtain care from a particular provider (or provider organization).

Equity: A concern for fairness.

Ex ante **moral hazard:** Insurance-induced changes in behaviour that alter the probability that an insured event occurs.

Expected utility: In a risky situation, the sum over all possible outcomes of the product of the utility associated with each outcome and the probability that the outcome will occur.

Ex post **moral hazard:** Insurance-induced changes in behaviour that alter the insured loss after the insured event occurs.

Externality: Costs imposed or benefits gained by individuals other than the individual or organization that undertakes an action, and which are not captured by a relevant market.

Extra billing: The practice by a physician of charging a fee greater than the public reimbursement, requiring the patient to pay the difference between the two.

Favourable risk selection: When an insurance pool systematically attracts individuals of below-average risk status within a risk class. Also called **cream-skimming** or **cherry picking**.

Fee-for-service: Method of physician payment in which physicians receive a fee each time they provide a reimbursable service. See also **salary** and **capitation**.

Financing health care: The activity of raising the revenue required to support the provision of health care.

Formulary: A list of all the drugs eligible for reimbursement by a drug insurance plan.

Free riding: When producers or consumers obtain benefit from a good, service, or activity without contributing toward the cost of producing it.

Frontier cost estimation: Techniques for empirically identifying the frontier of lowest-cost (highest productivity) hospitals in order to assess efficiency.

Funding: The allocation of revenue, raised through financing, to alternative activities within the health care sector—normally the health care programs and providers delivering health care services.

Funding mechanism: The method by which funds are transferred among participants in a funding system.

Gaming: In the economic context, using the policies, regulations, and procedures of a system to increase one's financial gain in a manner contrary to the intended purpose of those policies, regulations, and procedures.

Gatekeeper model: A delivery model in which the primary care provider (normally a family physician) regulates access to specialist and diagnostic services, which patients are not permitted to access directly.

Generic drug manufacturers: Pharmaceutical companies that produce and sell drug products that have already been developed, either under license from a brand-name manufacturer or after the brand-name manufacturer's patent has expired.

Geographically defined population: Residents of a defined jurisdiction that is funded to meet specified health care needs of the population.

Global budget: Providers receive a total budget for a defined period of time.

Gradient: An increase (decrease) in one variable is associated with an increase (decrease) in another variable throughout the relevant range of the variables.

Gross Domestic Product (GDP): The total value of all goods and services produced within a country.

Health capital model: An economic model of the individual-level demand for and production of health over a person's lifetime, based on the assumption that health can be analyzed as a durable capital good.

Horizontal equity: A type of distributional equity whereby those who are equal with respect to an equity-relevant characteristic (e.g., income, need) are treated equally.

Human capital approach: A method that values a health gain in terms of the accompanying increase in a person's market productivity, as measured by the person's wage rate.

Identification of costs and consequences: The enumeration (as part of an **economic evaluation**) of all the resources used, and all the effects generated, by each alternative being compared. See also **measurement** and **valuation of costs and consequences**.

Imperfectly (or quasi) rational addiction model: Economic model of the consumption of addictive substances that assumes people strive to be rational but suffer from biases in decision-making.

Implicit wage: The imputed wage earned by a physician equal to the earnings from the physician's practice divided by the number of hours of labour supplied to the practice.

Incidence: The ultimate distribution of the burden of a tax or the benefits of a good.

Incidence rate: Measures the number of new cases of a given condition that arise in a given population during a given time period.

Income effect: The change in the demand for a good caused by the change in real (price-adjusted) income.

Income-elasticity of demand: A measure of the responsiveness of the demand for a good to changes in income, defined as (% change in demand for a good)/ (% change in income).

Incomplete vertical integration: An organizational form typical of North American hospitals in which physicians have a long-term relationship with a hospital but are neither employed by nor fully independent of the hospital.

Incremental cost-effectiveness ratio: A way of expressing the results of a **cost-effectiveness analysis** equal to the ratio of the difference in costs between two alternatives to the difference in the effects between the two alternatives.

Inelastic demand: An **elasticity** of less than 1.0, indicating that one variable is relatively unresponsive to changes in another variable of interest. See also **elastic demand** and **unitary elasticity.**

Inferior good: A good for which the quantity demanded decreases as income rises; a good with a negative **income-elasticity of demand.** See also **normal good.**

Internal market: A deliberately constructed market within a publicly financed health care system in which there is a **purchaser–provider split;** providers must bid to win contracts to provide services to individuals covered by purchasers such as regional health authorities.

Investment demand for health: An individual's demand for health capital that derives from the monetary benefits (due to increased time available for work) associated with improved health.

Job lock: Impediment to labour mobility that arises when health care insurance is obtained as a benefit of employment.

Licensure: A regulatory policy that requires an individual to pass a qualifying exam before being legally permitted to perform specified medical acts.

Loading costs: The administration costs associated with providing insurance.

Local monopoly: A single organization enjoys monopoly power in a specific region even though it is one of many such organizations provincially or nationally.

Loss aversion: A tendency to prefer to avoid losses over accruing gains, when making decisions under uncertainty.

Managed care: A delivery model that monitors and controls the provision of care in an effort to reduce moral hazard and increase quality by regulating the choices of providers and patients.

Marginal analysis: A method of analysis that focuses on the effects of doing just a little bit more or a little less than the baseline level of an activity.

Marginal cost: The increase in total cost associated with producing one more unit of a good.

Marginal private benefit (MPB): The marginal benefit obtained by the individual who consumes a good.

Marginal private cost (MPC): The marginal cost incurred by the organization that produces a good.

Marginal product: The increase in total output associated with a one unit increase in an input.

Marginal revenue: The increase in total revenue associated with a one-unit increase in sales of a good.

Marginal social benefit (MSB): The marginal benefit obtained by both the individual who consumes a good and others in society who obtain external benefits.

Marginal social cost (MSC): The marginal costs incurred by both the organization that produces a good and others in society who are affected by external costs.

Marginal utility: The increase in total utility associated with consuming one more unit of a good.

Market concentration: An indicator of the extent of competition in a market based on the share of sales held by a given number of firms (e.g., 5, 10, 25) in the market.

Market equilibrium: The price–quantity combination in a market at which there is no tendency for price or output to change unless one of the determinants of demand or supply changes.

Market failure: A situation in which an unregulated market generates an inefficient allocation of resources.

Market-led regulatory approach: An approach to health sector **regulation** that attempts to harness competitive markets to achieve social objectives in the health care sector. See also **non-market-led regulatory approach.**

Market power: An ability to influence the market price.

Maximum expenditure limit: A specified dollar limit such that, once an individual's out-of-pocket expenditures reach this limit, services become fully insured with no **cost-sharing** required.

Measurement of costs and consequences: The process of quantifying (as part of an **economic evaluation**) the amount of each resource used and each effect generated by each alternative being compared. See also **identification** and **valuation of costs and consequences.**

Meta-analysis: A statistical technique for formally combining results from separate studies in order to derive an estimate of the overall, collective effect across all the studies.

Me-too drug: A minor variant of an existing drug that offers little improvement over existing drugs.

Monetary equivalent of the loss: The amount of money that can be paid to an individual to exactly balance the negative effects of an event. The result is that the person is just as well off as they would have been if the event had not occurred.

Monopolistic competition: A market with imperfect competition characterized by many producers selling slightly differentiated products, where this product differentiation gives each producer a small amount of market power.

Monopoly: A market with only one producer (seller) of a good or service.

Monopsony: A market with a single purchaser of a good or service.

Moral hazard: A tendency for the expected loss associated with an adverse event to change in the presence of insurance. The expected loss can change because insurance changes the probability that the event will occur (a person takes less care to avoid the loss) or because, conditional on the event happening, the loss is larger (those affected seek more expensive care than if the loss was not insured).

Natural or quasi-experiment: Research that exploits a discrete, measurable change in an environment, often the result of policy reform, that can be used to identify the effect of the change on an outcome of interest.

Need: A good is judged to be needed if it meets two conditions: (1) the good is effective in achieving a stated objective, and (2) the objective has been judged as a legitimate reason for drawing on others' resources to attain the objective.

Net benefit: The total social benefit associated with the consumption of a good minus the total social cost of its production.

Net incidence: The distribution of the difference between tax benefits and burdens.

Non-distribution constraint: The legal restriction that prohibits not-for-profit organizations from distributing any financial surplus to the officers of the organization.

Non-market-led regulatory approach: An approach to health sector **regulation** that de-emphasizes the role of competitive market forces by tightly controlling markets or supplanting markets to achieve social objectives in the health care sector. See also **market-led regulatory approach.**

Normal good: A good for which the quantity demanded increases as income rises; a good with a positive **income-elasticity of demand.** See also **inferior good.**

Normative economics: Economic analysis that attempts to identify what policies, actions, or outcomes are desirable from an economic perspective. It attempts to discern what society *should* do.

Oligopolistic competition: A market with imperfect competition characterized by a small number of producers each of which constitutes a large share of the market.

Opportunity cost: The cost of using a resource for one purpose is the benefits forgone from the highest-valued alternative use.

Out-of-pocket spending: Direct spending by an individual from their own resources for the receipt of a health care service. See also **cost-sharing.**

Own-price elasticity of demand: A measure of the responsiveness of the demand for a good to a change in its price, defined as (percentage change in the quantity of a good demanded)/(percentage change in its price).

Panel design: Research that follows a number of units (people, jurisdictions) over time, and that can exploit both cross-sectional variation at each point in time and time-series variation over a number of periods to investigate the phenomenon under study.

Pareto Criterion: A criterion that defines an allocation of resources to be allocatively efficient if it is impossible to reallocate the resources so as to make at least one person better off without making someone else worse off. See also **potential Pareto Criterion.**

Patent: An exclusive right, granted by government, to produce and sell a patented product for a defined period of time. It grants a legal monopoly to the developer of the good or process covered by the patent.

Performance-based payment: Providers whose patterns of care conform to known standards of quality receive bonuses (or avoid penalties). Also known as "pay for performance."

Physical (selfish) externality: A health-related externality in which even a purely selfish person cares about others' consumption of health care because such care reduces their risk of ill health (for example, the chance that a communicable disease will spread).

Physician agency: A principle that holds that in making treatment decisions a physician is to act in the interest of patients rather than out of self-interest, providing those services that patients would want if they had the same medical knowledge as the physician.

Positive economics: Economic analysis that attempts to accurately describe and predict economic phenomenon. It attempts to describe *what is,* or *what will be.*

Post-marketing surveillance: The systematic collection data about users of a newly marketed drug to identify any potential side effects that occur too rarely to have been revealed by the pre-approval clinical trial research.

Potential Pareto Criterion: Defines a reallocation of resources as allocatively efficient if the gains to the winners are sufficiently large that the winners could compensate the losers and still be better off. The criterion does not require that the winners actually compensate the losers; for this reason, it is sometimes called the hypothetical compensation criterion.

Present discounted value: The value, in today's dollars, of a future, multi-year stream of costs or benefits.

Prevalence rate: Measures the proportion of people in a population who have a given condition at a given point in time.

Price-elasticity of supply: Measure of the responsiveness of the supply of a good to a change in its price, defined as (percentage change in the quantity of a good supplied)/ (percentage change in its price).

Price spread: The difference between the listed price of a drug purchased by a pharmacy for resale and the effective price after the hidden manufacturer discounts are applied.

Primary care physicians: Physicians, especially general practitioners and family physicians, who are the first point of contact with the health care system. Primary care physicians are one type of provider within the primary care system. See also **specialist physicians.**

Principal–agent problem: One individual or organization (the principal) wants to accomplish some task or objective but must contract with another individual or organization (the agent) to undertake the work necessary to achieve the desired objective.

Procedural equity: A situation in which the process whereby a good (e.g., income, health care) or a burden (e.g., tax payments) is distributed among members of society is judged to be fair.

Producers' surplus: The difference between the amount a firm actually receives for selling a unit of a good less the minimum amount a firm would accept to sell it. For a well-functioning market in equilibrium, the area above the supply curve and below the equilibrium price line.

Production: The process whereby an individual or organization transforms inputs into outputs.

Production function: The relationship that describes the maximum amount of output that can be produced from a given set of inputs using currently available technologies.

Production possibilities frontier: A graph that represents the maximum combinations of two goods that society can produce given its available resources and production technologies.

Profits: Total revenue minus total costs.

Progressive financing: The proportion of income that a person pays (for example, in taxes) increases as income increases.

Proportional financing: The proportion of income that a person pays is constant as income increases.

Prospective payment: Payment for a service is fixed in advance of the actual provision of the service.

Public good: A good that can be simultaneously consumed by many individuals and which it is very costly to exclude others from consuming.

Purchaser–provider split: Providers must bid to win contracts to provide services to individuals covered by purchasers such as regional health authorities. See **internal market**.

Quality-adjusted life-year (QALY): A measure that incorporates the effect of a health intervention on both the quantity (length of life) and quality of life (as indicated by people's subjective rating of the health state).

Rate of time preference: A measure of the extent to which individuals value benefits and costs that arise in the future differently (usually less) than if they arise today.

Rational addiction model: An economic model of the consumption of addictive substances that assumes people make fully rational choices.

Reference-based pricing: A policy of reimbursing only the price of the lowest-cost drug intended to treat the condition in question, including drugs that are not bio-equivalent.

Regressive financing: The proportion of income that a person pays falls as income increases.

Regulation: The use of authority to guide or direct the behaviour of individuals, providers, and organizations.

Remuneration: Compensation to individuals employed in the health care sector.

Resources: *Raw materials* such as minerals, wood, oil, and other natural resources; *physical capital* such as machines; *human labour;* and *intellectual capital* in the form of knowledge.

Retrospective payment: Payment for a service is determined only after the provision of the service.

Risk: Risk is present when it is not certain whether an event will occur. The amount of risk depends on the size of the potential gains or losses associated with the event, and the probability that the event will occur.

Risk adjustment: The process by which insurers adjust premiums to reflect observable characteristics of an individual that are associated with expected health care costs.

Risk attitude: The extent to which a person likes or dislikes risk. A person who likes to take risks is **risk loving**; a person who does not like to take risks is **risk averse**; a person who is indifferent is **risk neutral**.

Risk averse: A person who prefers a certain (perfectly predictable) level of wealth over a risky alternative that has the same expected value.

Risk class: Individuals classified by an insurance agency as having the same risk (based on observable characteristics) and who are, therefore, each charged the same premium.

Risk loving: A person who prefers a risky alternative with a given expected value over a certain (perfectly predictable) level of wealth equal to the expected value of the gamble.

Risk neutral: A person who is indifferent between a certain (perfectly predictable) level of wealth and a risky alternative that has the same expected value.

Risk pooling: When each member of a large group contributes a small amount to the "pool" in return for the promise that, if a specified risky event happens to one of the members, money from the pool will be used to compensate the individual for the loss experienced.

Risk premium: The amount of money above the actuarially fair premium that a person is willing to pay for insurance.

Risk selection: The phenomenon whereby an insurer's risk pool systematically attracts individuals of either below-average or above-average risk status given the premiums charged.

Roemer's Law: "A bed built is a bed filled." In the presence of full insurance, capacity often defines the level of facility utilization.

Salary: A method of paying physicians in which a physician receives a specified annual amount of income, independent of the number of patients seen or services provided.

Second-best: A situation in which it is not possible to correct all sources of market failure and in which correcting a single source may make matters worse.

Self-regulation: When the government delegates regulatory authority with respect to members of a profession to the profession itself. See also **regulation.**

Shadow price: The imputed value of a resource assigned by an analyst when a market price does not exist or does not reflect the true social cost of the resource.

Skimping: Providing less than the appropriate level of care, particularly in response to financial incentives.

Small-area variation: A health research approach that investigates patterns of variation in health care utilization across small geographic areas.

Social gradient in health: A pattern of population health, observed in many countries, in which average health status is directly related to social rank or social status throughout the range of social ranks.

Social health insurance: A system of insurance through social insurance organizations (normally quasi-public, non-profit sickness funds) in which contribution rates, membership, benefit packages, and other aspects are heavily regulated by government.

Social welfare function: A function that depicts how the overall welfare in society depends on the amount and distribution of welfare among individual members of society.

Specialist physicians: Physicians who specialize in a particular area of medicine and whose practice is often made up mainly of patients referred by primary care physicians.

Spurious correlation: Two variables are correlated, but neither is causally related to the other. Ice cream consumption and swimming are positively correlated, but they do not cause each other. Both are caused by hot weather.

Stop-loss mechanism: A provision within a prospective payment system that specifies a threshold for very costly cases, such that additional expenditures on the individual are either partially or fully paid by the funder (rather than forcing the provider to absorb them).

Substitute goods: Two goods that can satisfy a similar want so that an increase in the price of one causes an increase in the demand for the other, and a decrease in the price of one causes a decrease in the demand for the other (e.g., hamburgers and pizza). See also **complementary good.**

Substitution (or pure-price) effect: The effect on the demand for a good caused by a change in the relative price of the good, holding real income constant.

Substitutive private finance: When an individual is permitted to opt out of the public plan altogether (making no contributions) and finance health care privately.

Supplementary (or parallel) private finance: When a service included within the public health plan can also be obtained (and paid for) privately if desired.

Supplier-induced demand: At its most general, an individual's demand for care that arises at least in part from the influence of the individual's care provider.

Target-income model: A model of physician behaviour theorizing that physicians have a target income and adjust their service activity to achieve that target income.

Technical efficiency: Producing the maximum possible amount of output from the inputs used, given the chosen production method.

Time-consistent preferences: Rates of time preference in which judgments of what will be optimal at a future time remain optimal when the time arrives, assuming no other change but the passage of time. Such preferences can be characterized by a single, constant rate of discount.

Time-inconsistent preferences: Rates of time preference in which judgments of what will be optimal at a future time are no longer judged to be optimal when the time arrives, even though nothing has changed but the passage of time. Such preferences can be characterized by rates of discount which are not constant but which decrease the further is an event in the future.

Time preference: See **rate of time preference.**

Time-series design: Research that uses variation within the units under study (people, jurisdictions) over time to investigate a phenomenon.

Transactions costs model: A model that posits that hospitals are two "firms" within a single organization, each with its own objectives. One is led by the medical staff and the second is led by the hospital management.

Unitary elasticity: An **elasticity** of 1.0, indicating that a percentage change in one variable will cause an equal percentage change in a second variable. See also **elastic demand** and **inelastic demand.**

Up-coding: Gaming a funding system by claiming reimbursement for a service that pays more than the service that was actually provided.

User charge: An insurance provision that requires an individual to pay part of the cost of an insured health care service. Also called **cost-sharing.**

Utility: The subjective satisfaction an individual derives from consuming a good or undertaking an activity.

Utilization: The amount of health care that is consumed.

Valuation of costs and consequences: The process of assigning (as part of an economic evaluation) the social value of the resources used and the effects generated by each alternative being compared. See also **identification** and **measurement of costs and consequences.**

Vertical equity: A type of distributional equity whereby those who are unequal with respect to an equity-relevant characteristic (e.g., income, need) are treated in an appropriately equal manner.

Viewpoint: The perspective adopted for an economic evaluation, which determines the set of people and organizations whose costs and benefits are included in the evaluation.

Welfare loss (deadweight loss): The reduction in welfare (compared to the welfare level attained in a well-functioning market) due to either **market failure** or a distortion introduced into a market by policy (e.g., taxes in certain circumstances).

Willingness to pay: In general, the maximum amount a person is willing to pay to obtain a unit of a good or service. In the context of an economic evaluation of health programs or services, it refers to a method that values a health gain in terms of the amount a person is willing to pay to obtain the health gain.

Photo Credits

Chapter 1:
Page 24: Royalty-Free/CORBIS

Chapter 2:
Page 34: Ryan McVay/Getty Images

Chapter 3:
Page 64: Royalty-Free/CORBIS

Chapter 4:
Page 109: © Comstock Images/PictureQuest

Chapter 5:
Page 148: © Brand X Pictures/JupiterImages

Chapter 6:
Page 169: D. Falconer/PhotoLink/Getty Images

Chapter 7:
Page 185: Comstock Images/JupiterImages

Chapter 8:
Page 209: CORBIS

Chapter 9:
Page 236: © Pixtal/SuperStock

Chapter 10:
Page 259: Jack Star/PhotoLink/Getty Images

Chapter 11:
Page 283: BananaStock/PictureQuest

Chapter 12:
Page 315: © Image Club

Chapter 13:
Page 337: © Digital Vision/PunchStock

Chapter 14:
Page 356: © Jupiter Images/Dynamic Graphics

Chapter 15:
Page 383: Siede Preis/Getty Images

Chapter 16:
Page 410: © Masterfile

Index

A

ability-to pay principle, 282
aboriginal life expectancy, 2
academic detailing, 395
access motive, 241
accessibility criterion of Canada
    Health Act, 8
actuarially fair premium, 238
administrative costs in health care
    financing, 277, 278–279
adverse risk selection, 258–262
    definition, 257–258
    illustration, 258–259
    informational asymmetry and,
        268–271
    market failure and, 259–260
    policies to address, 261–262
    private insurance market and, 261
    Rothschild-Stiglitz equilibrium,
        268–271
aging population, 405–411
    fiscal implications, 406–409
    patterns in disease, 410–411
Akerlof, G., 259
Allin, S., 292
allocation. See also allocative
    efficiency
    efficiency-equity tradeoff, 45–46
    equity in, 41–46
    graphical illustration of, 53–56
    and marginal analysis, 39–40
    opportunity cost and, 33
    Pareto Criterion, 38–39, 55–56
    preferences and, 36–37, 40–41,
        53–54
    of resources, 29–30, 33
    utility in, 37–38, 53–56
allocative efficiency
    comparison of methods, 39
    definition, 36
    graphical illustration of, 53–56
    and health care financing, 277
    illustration, 37–38
    and Pareto Criterion, 38–39, 55–56
    prices and, 91, 94–95
    taxes and, 90–91, 123–124
    utility and, 37
appropriateness, 188
Arrow, K. J., 248, 370
Arrow-Pratt Measure of Risk
    (Absolute) Aversion, 244
asymmetry of information, 65. See
    also informational asymmetry in
    health care
Auld, C., 150
Auster, R. D., 230
Australia, 261

authorized generic, 390
Avian flu, 190

B

backward-bending labour supply
    curve, 338
balanced billing, 332
behavioural cost function, 367
benefit principle, 282
"beyond-the-skin" definitions of
    health, 128–129
blended funding, 316, 317–318
Blue Cross, 12
Blumenthal, D., 339, 342
Body Mass Index (BMI), 146
bonus payment, 312, 313
brand-name drug manufacturers, 382
    brand loyalty, 390
    competition, 389–390
    patent protection, 390–392
    prices, 389
breakthrough drug, 389
Brown, D. M., 342
Brown, M. C., 342
budget boundaries, 319

C

Campbell, T., 278–279
Canada
    annual death rates, 168
    drug formulary, 393, 395
    enrolled population, 311
    financing of health care, 9–14,
        278–279
    generic drug prices, 394
    geographically defined population,
        312
    global budget, 312
    health care spending versus
        utilization, 33
    health care system governance,
        6–9
    hospital beds per 1000 population,
        20
    infant mortality rate, 2–3
    insurance-based financing, 15
    life expectancy at birth, 2–3, 166
    non-market approach to hospital
        market, 364–365
    physician response to fee changes,
        220–221
    physicians per 100,000
        population, 19

prescription drug use, 381
    public health care system, 6
    regulatory approach, 22–23
    socio-economics and health, 2, 174
    wait-times and delivery of health
        care, 19–22
    wait-times for surgery, 22
Canada Health Act, 7–9, 189
Canada Health Transfer, 7
capacity constraint approach, 257
capitation
    definition, 16
    as health care funding, 311–312,
        313
    physician services and, 16–18
    prospective payment and, 315–316
caring externality, 190–191, 192
case-based funding, 311, 313, 315
case-mix adjustment, 312
causal relationship, 127
Chaoulli, J, 290
Chaoulli vs. Quebec, 290
cherry picking, 258
Chou, S. Y., 372
chronic disease management, 410
co-insurance, 13, 14
College of Family Physicians, 16
College of Physicians and Surgeons,
    16
commitment devices, 152
community-level determinants
    of health, 4–5, 127. See also
    population health
community-rated premiums, 241
compensating variation, 121
competition
    and hospital organization,
        364–367, 377–379
    in pharmaceutical sector, 388–393
complementary good, 71
complementary private finance,
    292–293
complementary service and demand,
    212–213
comprehensiveness criterion, 8
compulsory license, 384
concentration index, 57–59
constraints, 155–157, 133–134,
    335–336
consumer sovereignty, 84
consumer surplus, 85–87
consumption demand for health
    aging effect, 139, 141
    education effect, 140, 141
    efficiency of derived demand,
        187–188
    predictions, 141
    rate of time preference, 139

smoking predictions, 151
    wage rate effect, 139–140, 141
contingent valuation, 107, 108
Contoyannis, P., 228–229
co-payment, 13, 14
correlation, 127
cost control of health care
    system, 7
cost-benefit analysis method of
    economic evaluation, 108–112,
        120–121
    application in health sector,
        110–111
    contingent valuation, 107, 108
    definition, 108
    efficiency of, 109–110
    human capital approach, 108
    monetary valuation of gain,
        111–112
    origins of method, 110, 121–122
    willingness to pay, 107, 108,
        120–121
cost-effectiveness analysis method
    of economic evaluation, 104–106,
        109–112
    application in health sector,
        110–111
    definition, 104
    efficiency of, 109–110
    incremental cost-effectiveness
        ratio, 105
    monetary valuation of gains,
        111–112
    origins of method, 110, 121–122
    outcomes possibilities, 105, 106
cost-effectiveness efficiency, 34, 35,
    39, 50, 122
cost-sharing
    definition, 12, 241
    and health care financing, 12–14
    and insurance contracts, 241
    and moral hazard, 253–254
    RAND Health Insurance
        Experiment, 249–250, 252
    welfare effects of, 255
cost-utility analysis (CUA), 105–112,
    121–122
    application in health sector,
        110–111
    case study, 107–109
    definition, 105
    efficiency of, 109–110
    monetary valuation of gains,
        111–112
    origins of method, 110, 121–122
    outcomes possibilities, 105–106
    quality-adjusted life-years
        (QALY), 105–106

counterfactual problem, 193
Cournot model, 96
coverage limit, 241
cream-skimming, 258, 262–263
Cromwell, J., 218
cross-sectional design, 218–219
crude mortality rate, 130
CUA. *See* cost-utility analysis (CUA)
Cuba, 172
Cutler, D., 149, 169, 170, 261, 264

D

deadweight loss. *See* welfare
    (deadweight) loss
decentralization of governance, 9
deductible, 13
delivery of health care, 16–22
    hospitals, 18–19, 355–373
    overview, 16
    physician services, 16–18,
        328–333
    privately financed, 23
    wait times, 19–22
demand curve
    analysis, 71–73
    definition, 71
    deriving, 94–95
    for health care, 210–211, 228–229
    and optimal level of health capital,
        135
demand for health
    consumption demand, 139–140,
        141
    demand curve for, 135
    evidence for education-health
        relationship in, 142–146
    the health capital model, 132–142,
        155–157
    investment demand, 135–139, 141
    supply curve for, 136
demand for health care. *See* health
    care demand
demand for insurance, 234–246
    actuarially fair premium, 238
    benefits of, 238–239
    expectation, 235
    expected utility, 235–236
    framing effect, 240
    limitations of standard insurance
        model, 239–241
    loading costs, 238
    loss aversion, 239, 241
    monetary equivalent of the loss,
        235
    risk aversion, 236–238, 244
    risk pooling, 244
    risk premium, 238
    welfare gain through, 233, 237,
        238–239, 244–246
demand side of market, 67–75
    complementary good, 71
    demand curve, 71–73, 94–95
    elasticity of demand, 73–75,
        210–214

factors affecting, 68
    income effect, 69–71, 94–95
    power of, 65
    substitution (pure-price) effect,
        69–71, 94–95
    and supply, 80–81
    total market demand, 74–75, 81
    utility, 68–71, 187
demographics and health, 2
Denmark, 10. *See also* OECD
    countries
dependency ratio, 409
depreciation rate of health capital,
    134
derived demand for health. *See also*
    individual-level demand for and
    production of health
    definition, 133
    Grossman health capital model,
        133, 141
    need for health care as, 201–202
    utility and, 187
detailing, 390
determinants of health, 126–127. *See
    also* population health
    community-level, 4–5, 127
    health production function and,
        127–128
    individual-level, 4, 5, 127,
        146–153
    overview, 3–4
determinants of health care demand,
    208–214. *See also* health care
    demand
    health status, 210
    income, 213–214
    preferences, 209, 210
    price of health care, 210–212,
        228–230
    price of substitutes and
        complements, 212–213
    risk attitude, 210
diminishing marginal returns, 76
diminishing marginal utility, 68–69
direct-to-consumer advertising, 390
discount rate, 115, 122–124
discounting, 113–116, 122–124
distributional equity, 42–43, 57–59,
    282–284
distributional weight, 116
doctors' workshop hospital
    organizational model, 361
double-counting costs or benefits, 113
"dream equation," 127
drug companies, as for-profit firms,
    326
Duggan, M., 373

E

Eakin, B. K., 342
economic evaluation of policy
    options, 98–124
    analytical challenges of
        conducting, 112–116, 122–124

comparison of methods, 109–110,
    121–122
cost-benefit analysis method,
    108–112, 120–121
cost-effectiveness analysis method,
    104–106, 109–112
cost-utility analysis (CUA) as,
    105–112, 121–122
definition and terms, 100–101
government market intervention,
    98
informational asymmetry in health
    care demand, 195–196
judgment in analyses, 111–112
schematic representation of,
    101–102
stages of, 102–104
technology assessment, 98–100
viewpoint and, 102
economics and allocation of
    resources, 29–30, 33
economics of health
    definitions of health, 128–129
    determinants of health, 126–127.
        See also determinants of
        health
    health production function,
        127–128. *See also* health
        production function
    individual-level demand for and
        production of health, 125–127,
        132–153
    measurement of health, 128–130
    population health, 164–178
    socio-economics and health,
        173–178
    value of health, 125
economies of scale, 263
Edgeworth Box, 50, 52
education-health relationship in
    demand for health, 142–146
    and consumption demand for
        health, 140, 141
    education impact, 144–145
    efficiency of health production
        impact, 145
    gradient and, 142–143
    health impact, 144
    income effect, 144–145
    investment demand for health and,
        137, 139, 141
    policy implications of, 143,
        145–146
    preferences and, 145, 182
    spurious correlation, sources of in,
        143–144
efficiency, 34–41. *See also* economic
    evaluation of policy options
    in allocation, 36–41. *See also*
        allocative efficiency
    cost-effectiveness, 34, 35, 39,
        50, 122
    definition, 34
    of discounting, 113
    of economic analysis methods,
        109–110

in economy as health care
    financing effect, 280–281
education effect on health
    production, 145
and equity relationship, 45–46,
    59–61
ethical principles of, 40–41
funding and regional health
    authorities, 310
graphical illustration of, 49–56,
    59–61
of health care consumption,
    187–188
in health care financing, 286, 287
in health care financing system,
    277
in health production function,
    187–188, 192–193
of health system, 24–25
of hospitals, 367–369
marginal analysis, 39–40
in market for health care services,
    278–280
moral hazard effect, 247–248
and opportunity cost, 34
Pareto Criterion, 38–39, 45,
    55–56, 95
in production, 34–36
production possibilities frontier,
    35–36, 37, 50–53
resources, use of, 34–39
social welfare function, 45, 59–61
taxes and, 90–91, 123–124
technical, 34–35, 49–50
utility and allocation, 37–38,
    53–54
utilization of health care services,
    278–279
elastic, 74
elasticity, 73
elasticity of demand, 73–75,
    210–214
endogenous price of health care, 228
enrolled population, 311
enrollee, in funding scheme, 308,
    309
equilibrium of market, 81
equity
    in allocation, 41–46
    concentration index, 57–59
    definition, 41–42
    distributional, 42–43, 57–59,
        282–284
    and efficiency relationship, 45–46,
        59–61
    funding and regional health
        authorities, 310
    government market intervention,
        66–67
    graphical illustration of, 57–61
    in health care financing, 282–284,
        287, 297–302
    of health system, 24–25
    horizontal, 42–43
    procedural, 42, 43–44
    social welfare function, 45, 59–61

of utilization as effect of health care financing, 284
vertical, 43
equivalent variation, 121
Escarce, J. J., 220
ethical principles of efficiency, 40–41
evaluation of health system, 24–25
Evans, R. G., 177–178, 279, 325, 339, 358
ex ante moral hazard, 248
ex post moral hazard, 248
expectation and risk, 235
expected utility, 235
externalities
caring, 192
definition, 66
in demand for health care, 190–191, 202–203
health care as an economic commodity, 202–203
physical (selfish), 190
welfare effects of, 88
and welfare loss from moral hazard, 250, 252
extra billing, 332

F

fair process. *See* distributional equity; procedural equity
favourable risk selection, 258, 262–263
fee-for-service, 310–311, 313
and capitation, 16
chronic disease management and, 411
definition, 16
and financial incentives, 16
prospective payment and, 315
Feldstein, M., 342
financial incentives
and capitation, 17–18
and fee-for-service, 16, 310–311
and insurance-based financing, 15
in principle–agent problem, 307
schemes for, 314
financial intermediary, in funding scheme, 308, 309
financing health care. *See* health care financing
firm behaviour and supply of goods and services. *See* supply of goods and services
Fogel, Robert, 167
formulary, 393
for-profit firms, 326
behaviour and performance, 370–373
versus not-for-profit, 369–373
framing effect, 240
France. *See also* OECD countries
administrative costs in health care financing, 278–279
health spending and GDP, 5

life expectancy, 2
private insurance, 12
public financing of health care, 10
social health insurance, 11
social insurance health care financing, 300–302
free riding, 280
frontier cost estimation, 367, 368
Fuchs, V. R., 218
funding, 273. *See also* health care funding
funding mechanism, 309. *See also* mechanisms of health care funding

G

gaming, 311
gatekeeper model, 256
general equilibrium analysis, 95
generic drug manufacturers, 382–383
geographically defined population, 312
Germany. *See also* OECD countries
administrative costs in health care financing, 278–279
health spending and GDP, 5
private insurance, 12
public financing of health care, 10
social health insurance, 11
social insurance financing, 300–302
substitutive private finance, 290, 292
Gini coefficient, 299
Glied, S., 293
global budget, 312, 313, 316
Globerman, S., 377
Goodman, A., 158
governance of health care system, 7–9
government market intervention, 66–67, 383–393
Grabowski, D. C., 373
gradient, 142
grand utility possibilities frontier (GUPF), 38, 55–56
Gray, B. H., 371
gross domestic product (GDP)
definition, 5
and health care spending, 5, 7
and population health, 169–170
Grossman, M., 132, 133–142, 158
Grossman health capital model. *See* health capital model
GUPF. *See* grand utility possibilities frontier (GUPF)

H

H1N1, 190
Hanley, G., 284
Harris, J. E., 361–363
health, definitions of, 128–129

health, measurement of, 128–130
health capital model, 132–142, 155–163
alternative model, 158–163
assessment of, 140–142
benefits of health, 133, 134
constraints, 133–134
consumption demand for health, 139–140, 141
definition, 132–133
demand curve for optimal level, 135
demand for health, 141–142, 155–157
depreciation rate of health capital, 134
derived demand, 133
education-health relationship, 142–146
formal structure of, 155–157
health-related behaviours, 146–153
household production model, 134, 156
investment demand for health, 135–139, 141
optimal level of health, 134–135
and preferences, 133
and utility, 133, 140, 155–156
health care as an economic commodity, 184–199
defining health care, 185–186
derived demand characteristic, 187–189, 201–202
externalities characteristic, 190–191, 202–203
informational asymmetry characteristic, 191–196, 203
overview, 183
second-best, 197
versus standard commodities, 184–185, 197–198
uncertainty characteristic, 196
vulnerability characteristic, 196–197
health care demand, 206–231
appropriateness, 188
demand curve for, 210–211, 228–229
as derived demand, 187–189, 201–202
health status and, 210
income and, 213–214
informational asymmetry and. *See* supplier-induced demand
need (for health care), 188–189
need/demand/utilization relationship, 207–208
need/utilization relationship, 227
preferences and, 209, 210
price of health care, 210–212, 228–230
price of substitutes and complements, 212–213
risk attitude, 210
small-area variation, 188

standard economic analysis of, 208–214
supplier-induced demand, 214–223, 230–231
health care financing, 9–15, 275–302. *See also* private financing of health care; public financing of health care; health care funding
aging population effect, 409
and broader economy, efficiency in, 280–281
in Canada, 9–14, 278–279
caveats of public and private systems, 275–276
criteria for determining arrangements, 294
efficiency summary, 286, 287
equity, 282–284, 286, 287, 297–302
and financing system, efficiency in, 277
funding of health care, 273
insurance based, market effect of, 14–15
and market for services, efficiency in, 278–280
mixed systems, 286–294
net incidence, 284–286
out-of-pocket spending, 12–14, 276
overview, 9–10, 275
sources of, 276
spillover effect from private to public, 293
taxes, 10–11, 276
health care funding, 303–319
administrative issues, 316
definition, 273
and effect on health care, 305
elements of, 303
mechanisms of, 309–316
participants in schemes, 308–309
policy challenges, 313, 314
principle–agent framework, 304–308, 321–323
principles of fund design, 316, 318–319
prospective, 414
significance of, 303
health care scorecard, 307
health care system, 5–25. *See also* health system
and aging population, 405–411
Canada Health Act, 7–9
capacity constraint approach, 257
cost control, 7
definition, 5
delivery of, 16–22
efficiency of, 24–25
equity of, 24–25
financing, 9–15
gatekeeper model, 256
and GDP, 7
governance, 6–9

health care system—*Cont.*
  increased use by elderly, 408–409
  managed care, 256–257
  monopsony, 65
  privately financed delivery in
    Canada, 23
  projections, 414–415
  versus public health system, 6
  regulation of, 22–23
  services market efficiency,
    278–280
  spending and GDP, 5
  spending versus utilization, 33
  and technological innovation in
    medicine, 412–414
health determinants. *See*
    determinants of health
health measurement, 2–3
health policy
  to address informational
    asymmetry in health care
    demand, 194
  economic evaluation of, 98–124
  economic issues of, 30
  education-health relationship
    implications, 143, 145–146
  funding policy challenges, 313,
    314
  and insurance-based financing, 14
  mixed systems of health care
    financing debate, 293
  need (for health care), 188–189,
    201–202
  pharmaceuticals challenges,
    380–381
  and physician practice modelling,
    334
  planning physician supply,
    343–346
  population health determinants,
    implications, 170–173
  primary care reform, 18
  projections, 414–415
  relationship of demand, need, and
    utilization, 207–208
  and smoking, economics of, 152
  social forces and, 178
  supply of physicians, 18
health production function
  causal relationship, 127
  community-level determinants,
    4–5. *See also* population
    health
  definition, 34
  efficiency in, 145, 187–188,
    192–193
  individual-level determinants, 4,
    5, 146–153
health system. *See also* health care
    system
  definition, 1–2
  determinants of health. *See*
    determinants of health
  efficiency of, 24–25
  equity of, 24–25
  measurement of health, 2–3

health-related behaviours, economics
  of, 146–153
  obesity, 146–150
  smoking, 150–153
  stress, 176
Hickson, G. B., 219
Himmelstein, D., 278–279
Hirth, R. A., 373
Hollis, A., 390, 391
horizontal equity, 42–43
Horowitz, J., 372, 373
hospitals, 355–373
  competition, 364, 377379
  doctors' workshop organizational
    model, 361
  efficiency, 367–369
  market, 363–367, 377–379
  non-market approach, 364–365
  as not-for-profit, 326
  not-for-profit versus for-profit,
    369–373
  organizational structure, 358–359
  overview, 355–358
  private market approach,
    366–367
  public competition approach,
    365–366, 377–379
  quantity-quality trade-off
    organizational model, 359–361
  spending trends, 356–358
  transactions cost organizational
    model, 361–363
hospitals and delivery of health care,
    18–19
household production model, 134,
    156, 334. *See also* health capital
    model
Hu, T. W., 342
human capital approach, 108
Hurley, J., 292
Hutchison, B., 43

I

identification of costs and
    consequences, 102–104
imperfect competition in market, 87,
    96, 250, 251, 252
imperfectly (quasi) rational addiction
    model, 152
implicit wage, 334
incidence, 283, 297–298
incidence rate, 129
income and health care demand,
    213–214
income constraint, 134, 157
income effect, 69–71, 94–95
  definition, 69
  on health through education,
    144–145
  and welfare loss from moral
    hazard, 251
income-elasticity of demand, 73, 75
incomplete vertical integration,
    358, 362

incremental cost-effectiveness ratio,
    105
indifference curve, 53, 59–61
individual response and health, 178
individual-level demand for and
    production of health, 132–153
  and economic analysis of health,
    125–127
  education-health relationship as
    evidence, 142–146
  health capital model, 132–142
  health-related behaviour, 146–153,
    178
  measurement of health, 129–130
individual-level determinants of
    health
  and community-level determinants,
    5, 127
  in the health production function,
    127
  obesity, 146–150
  smoking, 150–153
  types of, 4
individual-level measurement of
    health, 128–129, 130
inelastic, 74
inequalities in population health,
    173–178
  determinants of, 176–178
  social gradient and, 173–176
infant mortality rate, 2–3, 130
inferior good, 74
information condition of market
    functioning, 65, 89, 91, 192–193
informational asymmetry in health
    care, 191–196
  adverse risk selection and,
    268–271
  barriers to informed patients,
    193–194
  counterfactual problem, 193
  definition, 65
  and demand. *See* supplier-induced
    demand
  and economic analysis, 195–196
  licensure, 194
  and market power, 194
  and physician agency, 194, 203
  policies to address, 194
  principle–agent problem, 304, 306
  requirements for efficiency,
    192–193
  and risk selection, 257, 260
  Rothschild-Stiglitz equilibrium,
    268–271
  significance of, 191–192
  and supplier-induced demand,
    214–223
  and welfare loss from moral
    hazard, 251–252, 254
insurance, 232–246. *See also* private
    financing of health care; public
    financing of health care
  access motive, 241
  benefits of, 238–239
  contracts, 241

demand model, 234–238, 244–246
  effects of insurance-based
    financing, 14
  limitations of standard model,
    239–241
  loss aversion, 239, 241
  moral hazard, 234
  risk, 232
  risk aversion, 244
  risk pooling, 233–234, 244
  welfare gain through, 233, 237,
    238–239, 244–246
insurance-based financing
  effect on markets, 14–15
  effect of supplier-induced demand,
    222
  RAND Health Insurance
    Experiment, 211–212
internal market, 365
investment demand for health,
    135–139
  aging effect, 136–138, 141
  definition, 135
  demand curve for health capital,
    135
  education effect, 137, 139, 141
  predictions, 141
  supply curve for health capital,
    136
  wage rate effect, 137–139, 141
"invisible hand," 95
isoquant, 49–51

J

Japan, 2, 3
job lock, 280

K

Kahneman, D., 46, 239
Kakwani index, 298–302
Kaufer, E., 399
Kessler, D., 366
knowledge
  and free private markets, 326
  as product, 326
  as public good, 383

L

Labelle, R., 215, 219–220
labour supply curve, 338
Lapan, H. E., 342
Lévêque, F., 399
Lewicki, A. M., 40–41
licensure, 194
life expectancy
  at birth, 2–3, 130
  Cuban success, 172, 173
  and GDP, 169–170
  USSR reversal, 171–172

lifestyle health care services, 327
loading costs, 238
local monopoly, 363
long-term facilities, 357–358
Lorenz curve, 298–302
loss aversion, 239

M

managed care, 256–257
marginal analysis, 39–40
marginal cost, 76–77
marginal private benefit (MPB), 84
marginal private cost (MPC), 84
marginal product, 76
marginal revenue, 77
marginal social benefit (MSB), 84
marginal social cost (MSC), 84
marginal utility, 69
market concentration, 363
market equilibrium, 81
market failure
    adverse risk selection, 259–260
    conditions for, 87–89, 91
    definition, 66
    favourable risk selection, 262–263
    government intervention, 66–67
    private insurance, 247–264
    public good, 383
    welfare effects, 87–89, 91
market power, 63–65
market-led regulatory approach, 22
markets, 62–91
    consumer sovereignty, 84
    consumer surplus, 85–87
    definition, 30
    demand side, 67–75, 80–81, 94–95
    equilibrium, 81, 86
    failure of. *See* market failure
    government intervention, 66–67
    hospitals, 363–367, 377–379
    imperfect competition in, 87, 96
    net benefit, 84–85
    normative economic analysis of,
        84–85, 95–97
    positive economic analysis of,
        81–84
    prices in, 86–87
    producer surplus, 85–87
    public policy impact on, 82–84
    supply of goods and services,
        76–81
    welfare effects and failure, 87–89,
        91
    welfare loss, 88
    well-functioning, 62, 63–67
Marmot, M., 126
maximum expenditure limit, 13, 14
McGrail, K., 283
McGuire, A., 337, 338, 339
McKeown, Thomas, 166–168
McLellan, M., 366
measurement of costs and
    consequences, 102–104

measurement of health, 2–3, 128–130
mechanisms of health care funding,
    309–316. *See also* health care
    financing
    blended funding, 316, 317–318
    bonus payment, 312, 313
    capitation, 311–312, 313, 315–316
    case-based funding, 311, 313, 315
    definition, 309
    fee-for-service, 16, 310–311,
        313, 315
    financing incentive schemes, 314
    global budget, 312, 313, 316
    policy challenges, 313, 314
    prospective payment, 312,
        315–316
    retrospective payment, 312,
        315–316
    risk distribution in, 318
Ménière, Y., 399
meta-analysis, 371
me-too drug, 390
Miller, G., 169
Mitchell, J. B., 218
mixed systems of health care
    financing, 286–294
    complementary public and private,
        288, 292–293
    joint public and private, 287, 288
    public and private as alternatives,
        287, 289–292
monetary equivalent of the loss, 235
money price of health care and
    demand, 210–212
monopolistic competition, 87, 96
monopoly, 64, 96
monopsony, 65
moral hazard, 247–257
    critique of standard analysis,
        250–256
    definition, 234
    effects of cost-sharing, 253–254
    ex ante, 248
    ex post, 248
    and informational asymmetry,
        251–252, 254
    managed care, 256–257
    measurement of social value,
        254–256
    as a source inefficiency, 247–248
    standard analysis, 248–250
    supply-side approach against,
        256–257
    welfare effects of market power,
        248–252, 267–268
morbidity-based measure of health,
    129–130
mortality rates
    Canadian, historical, 2–3
    as a measure of health, 129–130
    and population health
        improvement, 166–168
    social gradient in health, 164,
        173–176
mortality-based measure of health,
    129–130

multi-player systems. *See* private
    financing of health care
Mustard, C., 285

N

natural or quasi-experiment, 219–220
need (for health care)
    and caring externalities, 190–191
    versus demand and utilization,
        207–208
    versus demand for health care, 227
    derived demand and, 188–189
net benefit, 84–85
net incidence, 284–286
Netherlands, 23, 300–302. *See also*
    OECD countries
Newhauser, D., 40–41
Newhouse, J. P., 323, 359–361
Nichols, A., 373
non-distribution constraint, 369–373
non-market-led regulatory
    approach, 23
non-money price of health care and
    demand, 212
non-patient revenue and health care
    financing, 276
normal good, 74
normative economics
    analysis of markets, 84–85, 95–97
    definition, 30
    and informational asymmetry in
        health care demand, 196
    and supplier-induced demand, 214,
        216, 222
Norway, 2, 10. *See also* OECD
    countries
not-for-profit organizations
    behaviour and performance,
        370–373
    distinguishing feature, 325
    economic theory of, 370
    versus for-profit, 369–373
not-only-for-profit organizations,
    326
nursing homes, 358, 372
Nyman, J., 241

O

Oaxaca, R. L., 230
obesity, economics of, 146–150
    causes, 147–150
    price impact, 150
    rates of, 147
    rise in, 146–147
O'Brien, B., 107–108
OECD countries
    cost-related access problems, 14
    health care spending as share of
        GDP, 6
    health care spending versus
        utilization, 33

hospital beds per 1000 population,
    20
infant mortality rate, 3
life expectancy at birth, 2
measurement of health, 130
obesity rates, 147, 148
physicians per 1000 population, 19
population age-group percentages,
    408
primary care practices, 18
public health care spending as
    percentage of total, 10
supplementary (or parallel) private
    finance, 290
wait-times for surgery, 22
oligopolistic competition, 87
oligopoly, 96
Ontario Family Health Network
    (FHN), 318–319
opportunity cost
    and allocation, 33
    definition, 33
    and discount rate, 122–123, 124
    and efficiency, 34
    illustration of, 36, 37
    and PPF, 36
    and valuation, 104
optimal level of health, 134–135,
    158–162
Organization of Economic
    Cooperation
    and Development (OECD),
    countries of. *See* OECD countries
out-of-pocket spending and health
    care financing, 12–14, 276
own-price elasticity, 73, 75

P

panel design, 219
parallel private finance, 289–292
Pareto Criterion, 38–39, 45, 55–56,
    95
partial equilibrium analysis, 95
patent, 384, 390–392
Patent Act, 384
patent regulation, 383–386, 399–401
Pauly, M., 248–250, 337, 338, 339,
    361
performance-based payment, 312,
    313
Pfizer, 390, 392
pharmaceuticals, 380–396
    advertising, 391
    and aging population, 409
    background, 380–381
    competition, 388–393
    design of benefits programs,
        393–396
    development, 388
    drug approval process, 388
    generic drug manufacturers,
        392–393
    history of patent legislation,
        385–386

pharmaceuticals—*Cont.*
  industry overview, 381–383
  innovation, 392
  Patent Act, 384
  patent regulation, 383–386,
    399–401
  policy challenges, 380–381
  price regulation, 389
  welfare effects of drug safety
    regulation, 386–388
physical (selfish) externality, 190
physician agency, 194, 203. *See also*
  supplier-induced demand
physician labour supply and service
  production, 340–343
physician practice modelling,
  334–343
  choice problem, 336
  constraints, 335–336
  impact of fee changes model,
    337–339
  impact of payment mechanisms
    model, 336–337
  labour supply and production of
    services, 340–343
  physician objectives, 336–340
  planning supply, 343–346
  preferences, 334–335
  production function for, 335
  target-income model, 339–340
physician services sector, 328–333
  chronic disease management, 411
  and delivery of health care, 16–18
  impact of population aging,
    406–408
  labour supply and service
    production, 340–343
  market for physician services, 333
  as not-only-for-profit
    organizations, 326
  overview and changes, 328–331
  planning supply, 343–346
  practice patterns, 330
  regulation, 331–333
policy. *See* health policy
population health, 164–178
  aging population, 405–411
  community-level determinants,
    4–5
  determinants of inequalities,
    176–178
  economic growth determinant,
    166–168
  and economics of health, 125–128
  individual-level determinants, 4,
    5, 146–153
  inequalities in, 173–178
  measurement of, 128–129, 130
  modern medicine determinant,
    170
  overview of determinants,
    165–166
  policy implications of
    determinants, 170–173
  public health determinant,
    168–170

and regional health authorities,
    310
  social gradient in health, 164–165,
    173–176
  Thomas McKeown and, 166–168
  world variations in, 170–173
portability criterion of Canada
  Health Act, 8
positive economics
  analysis of markets, 81–84
  definition, 30
  and informational asymmetry in
    health care demand, 195–196
  and supplier-induced demand, 214,
    221–222
post-marketing surveillance, 388
potential life–years lost, 130
potential Pareto Criterion, 39, 45,
    59–60
Powell, L., 150
power condition of market
  functioning, 63–65, 88–89
PPF. *See* production possibilities
  frontier (PPF)
preferences. *See also* utility
  allocation and, 36–37, 40–41,
    53–54
  cost-effectiveness efficiency and,
    110, 122
  demand, 68, 209, 210
  education, 145, 182
  health capital model, 133
  physician practice, 334–335
  PPF, 160
  social discount rate, 124
  social welfare function, 45, 59–61
  time, 146, 147, 151–152
  treatment decisions, 195
  utility, 53–54, 68, 155–156
  wants versus needs, 188–189
premiums, 276, 263–264
present discounted value, 113
Preston, S., 169–170
Preston curve, 169
prevalence rate, 129
price elasticity of supply, 80
price of health care and demand,
    210–212
price spread, 393
prices and allocative efficiency, 91,
    94–95
primary care physicians, 16, 330
primary care reform, 18
principle–agent problem, 304–308,
    321–323
private benefit, 66
private financing of health care. *See
  also* private insurance market
  in Canada, 23
  caveats of, 275–276
  effects of insurance-based
    financing, 14–15
  efficiency in market for services,
    278–280
  efficiency in system, 277, 287
  equity in, 287

incidence, 283
  mixed systems, 286–294
  out-of-pocket spending, 12–14
  private insurance, 11–12
  sources of, 276
  spillover effect to public
    financing, 293
  substitutive private finance, 289
  supplementary (or parallel) private
    finance, 289
private insurance market, 247–272.
  See also private financing of
  health care
  adverse risk selection, 261
  capacity constraint approach, 257
  economies of scale, 263
  gatekeeper model, 256
  incidence in, 283–284
  managed care, 256–257
  moral hazard in, 247–257
  overview, 11–12
  premium increases, 263–264
  risk selection, 257–263
  sources of market failure, 247
private market approach to hospital
  markets, 366–367
procedural equity, 42, 43–44
producer surplus, 86–87
producers and supply of goods and
  services. *See* supply of goods and
  services
production, 34
production constraints, 134
production function, 34, 335. *See
  also* health production function
production possibilities frontier (PPF)
  definition, 35–36
  Edgeworth Box, 50, 52
  example, 37
  graphical illustration of, 50–53
  and utility, 37–38
profits, 76
progressive financing, 282–283,
    298–302
proportional financing, 282–283
prospective payment, 312, 315–316
provider, 306, 308, 309
public administration criterion of
  Canada Health Act, 8
public competition approach to
  hospital market, 365–366
public financing of health care
  and aging population, 409
  in Canada, 10–11, 278–279
  caveats of, 275–276
  efficiency in market for services,
    278–280
  efficiency in system, 277, 287
  equity in, 282–284, 287, 297–302
  mixed systems, 286–294
  risk selection, 263
  social insurance, 10–11, 276,
    300–302
  sources of, 276
  spillover effect from private, 293
  tax, 10–11, 276, 277

public good, 383
public health system, 6, 168–170
purchaser-provider split, 365
pure-price effect. *See* substitution
  (pure-price) effect

Q

QALY. *See* quality-adjusted life-year
  (QALY)
quality-adjusted life-year (QALY),
    105–106, 107–108, 111
quantity-quality trade-off hospital
  organizational model, 359–361

R

Rabin, M., 240
Ramsey, F., 123
Ramsey, J. B., 230
RAND Health Insurance Experiment,
    211–212, 222, 249–250, 252
rate of time preference, 113, 139
rational addiction model, 150–152
Reber, S. J., 261
Redisch, M., 361
reference-based pricing, 396
regional health authorities, 310
regressive financing, 282–283,
    300–302
regulation, of health care, 22–23
Reinhardt, U., 255
remuneration, 273
resources. *See also* allocation;
  allocative efficiency
  allocation of, 29–30, 33
  definition, 32
  efficiency in use of, 34–39
  efficiency-equity tradeoff, 45–46
  equity in use of, 41–46
  market externalities condition, 66
  versus money, 32–33, 212
retrospective payment, 312, 315–316
Rice, T. H., 219–220
risk
  aversion to, 236–238, 244
  benefits of insurance, 238–239
  definition, 232
  distribution in funding schemes,
    318
  expectation, 235
  framing effect, 240
  insurance demand model, 234–238
  limitations of standard insurance
    model, 239–241
  minimization of, 233–234, 244
  risk attitude, 210
risk adjustment, 241
risk attitude, 210
risk averse, 236, 244
risk class, 257
risk loving, 236
risk neutral, 236

risk pooling, 233–234, 244
risk premium, 238
risk selection, 257–263
    adverse selection, 258–262,
        268–271
    definition, 257
    favourable risk selection, 258,
        262–263
    and public financing of health
        care, 263
    and public insurance, 263
Rizzo, J., 339, 342
Roemer's Law, 216
Rothschild-Stiglitz equilibrium,
    268–271

S

salary, 16–18
Sappington, D. E. M., 322
SARS, 190
Schlesinger, M., 371
second-best, 197
self-regulation, 16
Severe Acute Respiratory Syndrome
    (SARS), 190
shadow price, 112–113, 122–124
Sheifer, A., 322, 323
Silverman, E., 373
single-player systems. *See* public
    financing of health care
skimp on care, 311
skimping, 311
Skinner, J., 373
Sloan, F., 372
small-area variation, 188
smoking, economics of, 150–153
    commitment devices, 152
    consumption predictions, 151
    imperfectly (quasi) rational
        addiction model, 152
    as irrational behaviour, 150
    policy implications, 152
    rational addiction model, 150–152
    time-consistent preferences, 151
    time-inconsistent preferences, 152
social benefit, 66
social discount rate. *See* discount rate
social environment and health,
    176–178
social forces, 178, 126
social gradient in health, 164–165,
    173–176
social health insurance, 11. *See* also
    public financing of health care
social indifference curve, 53, 59–61
social policy, and health, 126
social value of health care,
    measurement, 254–256
social welfare function, 45, 59–61.
    See also welfare effects
socio-economics and health
    in Canada, 2
    determinants of health
        inequalities, 126, 176–178

education effect, 145
    social gradient, 164–165, 173–176
specialist physicians, 16, 330
Spence, M., 259
spurious correlation, 143–144
Stabile, M., 213, 292
Stakelberg model, 97
standardized mortality rate, 130
Stano, M., 158
Stiglitz, J., 259
Stoddart, G. L., 177–178
stop-loss mechanism, 318
substitute good, 71
substitute service and demand,
    212–213
substitution (pure-price) effect,
    69–71, 94–95
substitutive private finance, 289,
    290, 292
supplementary (or parallel) private
    finance, 289–292
supplier-induced demand, 214–223.
    See also informational asymmetry
    in health care
    cross-sectional design, 218–219
    definition, 214
    effect of fee changes, 220–221
    framework for analysis, 215
    implications of, 221–222
    and informational asymmetry,
        223
    measurement and testing of,
        216–221
    measurement of, 230–231
    natural or quasi-experiment,
        219–220
    nature of, 214–215
    panel design, 219
    and physician agency in health
        care, 194, 203
    and RAND health insurance
        experiment, 222
    Roemer's Law, 216
    time-series design, 219
    utilization and inducement, 16
supply curve, 76–81, 136
supply of goods and services, 76–81
    diminishing marginal returns, 76
    marginal cost curve, 77
    price elasticity of supply, 80
    profits, 76
    supply curve, 76–81
    total market supply curve, 80
supply of physicians, 18, 19
supply side of health care, 325–327
supply-side power, 64–65
Sweden, 2. *See* also OECD countries
Switzerland, 5, 300–302. *See* also
    OECD countries
system response, 408–409

T

Tamblyn, R., 253
target-income model, 339–340

taxes
    aging and systems of finance, 409
    and allocative efficiency, 90–91,
        123–124
    as health care financing, 10–11,
        276, 277
    incidence analysis, 297–302
    and net incidence, 284–286
    welfare cost of, 281
technical efficiency, 34–35, 39,
    49–50
technological innovation in medicine,
    412–414
technology assessment as economic
    evaluation of policy options,
    98–100
Thaler, R. H., 240
Thornton, J., 342
Tilford, J., 158
time constraint, 133, 156
time inconsistency, 147
time-consistent preferences, 151
time-inconsistent preferences, 152
time-series design, 219
transactions cost model, 361–363
Tuohy, C., 293
Two Fundamental Theorems of
    Welfare Economics, 95

U

unitary elasticity, 74
United Kingdom. *See* also OECD
    countries
    administrative costs in health care
        financing, 278–279
    capitation, 311
    cost-sharing, 14
    primary care practices, 18
    private insurance in, 12
    progressive financing, 301–302
    public competition approach to
        hospital market, 365–366
    public financing, 10
    supplementary (or parallel) private
        finance, 289
United States. *See* also OECD
    countries
    administrative costs in health care
        financing, 278–279
    aging population effect, 409n
    bonus payment, 312
    health care spending versus
        utilization, 33
    health spending and GDP, 5
    job lock, 280
    managed care, 256–257
    market-led regulatory approach,
        22
    and over-insurance, 249–250
    physician response to fee changes,
        220
    private market approach, 366–367
    public financing, 10
    regressive financing, 301–302

universality criterion of Canada
    Health Act, 8
up-coding, 311
UPF. *See* utility possibilities frontier
    (UPF)
user charges, 241
USSR, reversal of population health,
    171–172
utility
    in allocation, 37–38, 53–56
    cost-utility analysis, 105–108,
        121–122
    demand for health care, 68–71,
        187, 202–203
    demand for insurance, 234–238,
        244–246
    diminishing marginal utility,
        68–69
    health capital model, 133, 140,
        155–156
    household production model, 134
    income effect, 69–71
    marginal utility, 69
    maximization of, 53–54
    Pareto Criterion, 38–39
    PPF, 37–38
    preferences, 53–54, 68, 155–156
    rational addiction model, 151–152
    substitution effect, 69–71
utility possibilities frontier (UPF),
    38, 55–56
utilization
    definition, 207
    versus demand for health care, 227
    efficiency in health care services,
        278–279
    equity in health care, 284
    versus health care spending, 32–33
    versus need for health care, 227
    net incidence, 284–286

V

valuation of costs and consequences,
    102–104
valuation of gains in economic
    evaluation, 111–116
van Doorslaer, E., 284
Varey, C., 46
vertical equity, 43
viewpoint, 102
Vining, A., 377
Viramontes, J. L., 107–108

W

wait-times and delivery of health
    care, 19–22
    Chaoulli vs. Quebec, 290
    parallel private finance, 291–292
    public systems, 280
    supplementary (or parallel) private
        finance, 289

Warren-Bolton, F., 336
Wasow, B., 230
wealth and health care demand, 213–214
welfare (deadweight) loss, 88, 90–91
welfare, level of, 37. *See also* welfare effects
Welfare Economics, Two Fundamental Theorems of, 95
welfare effects. *See also* social welfare function
    cost-sharing, 255
    drug safety regulation, 386–388
    externalities in market, 88
    informational problems in markets, 89, 91

market power in market failure, 88–89
market power in private insurance, 267
moral hazard in health care market, 248–250, 252
physician regulation, 331
risk pooling, 233
taxes, 281
welfare gain
    and moral hazard, 248–250, 267–268
    through insurance, 233, 237, 238–239, 244–246
welfare loss, 88, 248–252, 267–268

well-functioning market conditions
    demand-side power, 65
    externalities, 66
    government intervention, 66–67
    information, 65
    market power, 63–65
    supply-side power, 64–65
willingness to pay
    approach, 107
    and cost-benefit analysis, 120–121
    definition, 108
    as measure of social value, 254–256
"within-the-skin" definitions of health, 128–129
Woodward, R. S., 336

Woolhandler, S., 278–279
World Health Organization, 128

Y

Yang, B. M., 342
Yip, W., 220

Z

Zeckhauser, R., 264
Zeliotis, G., 290